Milligan's Correlated Criminal Code

& Selected Federal Statutes

Butterworths

Printed and Bound in Canada

CANADA:	BUTTERWORTH & CO. (CANADA) LTD. TORONTO: 2265 Midland Avenue, Scarborough, M1P 4S1
UNITED KINGDOM:	BUTTERWORTH & CO. (PUBLISHERS) LTD. LONDON: 88 Kingsway, WC2B 6AB
AUSTRALIA:	BUTTERWORTH PTY. LTD. SYDNEY: 586 Pacific Highway, Chatswood, NSW 2067 MELBOURNE: 343 Little Collins Street, 3000 BRISBANE: 240 Queen Street, 4000
NEW ZEALAND:	BUTTERWORTHS OF NEW ZEALAND LTD. WELLINGTON: 77-85 Custom House Quay, 1
SOUTH AFRICA:	BUTTERWORTH & CO. (SOUTH AFRICA) (PTY.) LTD. DURBAN: 152/154 Gale Street

Canadian Cataloguing in Publication Data

Canada. Laws, statutes, etc.
[Criminal code]
Milligan's correlated criminal code and selected federal statutes

Includes index.
ISBN 0-409-84980-4

1. Criminal law—Canada. I. Milligan, Bruce C.
II. Title.

KE8804.C2 1980   345'.71'02632   C79-094801-X

Preface

For my many years as a police officer, a law instructor and a member of the criminal justice system of Canada, I have lamented the lack of a system which would lead to a better and easier understanding of criminal law and procedure in Canada. Finally, after teaching the system and method for a number of years, I decided to do something about it and this work is the result.

You will notice that I have not included any reported cases or explanations or interpretations of the law, as I believe these should be the subject of a separate work. My work deals only with setting out the statutory law in an orderly fashion, with a classification system of offences and a few explanatory notes which indicate what offences certain section numbers refer to. Many provisions have been repeated in convenient places, with extensive cross-references, to provide a better understanding of the laws and procedures. I am also responsible for the format of the work which was laid out with the rule that there would be no hyphens joining broken words and the reader would only very rarely have to turn the page to continue reading a section. All other contents of this work are copied from the Statutes of Canada and the Regulations of Canada or current gazettes.

In any work of this nature there are thanks to be extended for assistance in its preparation and I wish to offer the following:

Niagara College of Applied Arts and Technology, Welland, Ontario; Jacqueline Robarts, President; for the time and considerations offered to me which allowed me to complete the work:

Brock University, St. Catharines, Ontario, for the use of their facilities which provided considerable assistance to me:

Mr. E. W.(Ted) Morgan, Niagara College AA&T, English instructor and now retired, for giving me the name for my work, a "Correlated" Criminal Code.

This work is dedicated to the Criminal Justice System of Canada, with the sincere wish that it will provide a valuable service to its members, the entire population of Canada.

TABLE OF CONTENTS

INTRODUCTION

This work is termed a "correlated" Criminal Code. Many of its features will be apparent to the reader, but some require explanation.

INTERPRETATION OR DEFINITION OF TERMS

When a term used in a section is defined elsewhere, the term is underlined and a reference appears in the right-hand margin indicating where to find the definition.

> Example
>
> Refer to section 189. Note that in paragraph *(g)* the term "three-card monte" is underlined. The marginal reference indicates that the term is defined in subsection (2), below. For definitions of "public place" and "place" in paragraph *(h)*, the reader is directed to subsection 179(1).

Where both the term in the section and the marginal reference are underlined, the definition is reproduced in smaller type nearby, usually beneath the section.

> Example
>
> In subsection 189(5), the definition for the term "property" is reproduced at the bottom of the page.

Occasionally the definition is reproduced not on the same page but a few pages away; the reader is then guided by an additional marginal reference in square brackets.

> Example
>
> The term "valuable security" is paragraph 189 (1) *(e)* carries an underlined marginal reference to section 2, followed by "[195.1]". The relevant provision of section 2 is reproduced under section 195.1.

Some marginal notes refer to definitions contained in the Interpretation Act. The text of the definition is usually reproduced nearby.

> Example
>
> See paragraph 190(1)*(b)* where it is noted in the margin that the term, "province" is defined in a provision of section 28 of the Interpretation Act which has been reproduced under section 195.1.

Marginal references do not appear for absolutely every term defined in the Criminal Code or the Interpretation Act. Some terms, such as "province" are used so frequently and defined so inconsequentially that continual notation would be redundant. Also, most terms are underlined only where they first appear on a page; the same interpretation or definition applies for any further use of the same term.

PROCEDURAL PROVISIONS

Sometimes the marginal reference is to a procedural provision.

> Example
>
> Refer to subsection 189(4) and note the reference to subsection 722(1) which gives the general penalty for a summary conviction offence.

RELATED PROVISIONS

Notations in the left margin identify offences as belonging to a particular class of offence which allow for application of certain unique provisions of the Criminal Code.

	Example
IPA offence 178.1	The notation to the left indicates that this offence is one of those mentioned in section 178.1, which may authorize an invasion of privacy under Part IV.1.
SPI offence 687	This notation indicates that the offence is mentioned in section 687 as a serious personal injury offence, for which a convicted person may be declared a dangerous offender under Part XXI.

STATUTE MARGINAL NOTES

In the left margin, next to each subsection, brief explanatory notes have been reproduced from the statutes. These provide a quick reference to the contents. By section 13 of the Interpretation Act, these notes are not part of the enactment but are for convenience of reference only.

SYSTEM OF CLASSIFICATION OF CRIMINAL OFFENCES

TYPE 'A'	SUMMARY CONVICTION OFFENCES
TYPE 'B' (C) (D) (E)	DUAL PROCEDURE OFFENCES
TYPE 'C'	ABSOLUTE JURISDICTION OF MAGISTRATE OFFENCES MENTIONED IN SECTION 483
TYPE 'D'	INDICTABLE OFFENCES NOT MENTIONED IN SECTION 483 OR 427 WITH PUNISHMENT UP TO FIVE YEARS
TYPE 'E'	INDICTABLE OFFENCES NOT MENTIONED IN SECTION 483 OR 427 WITH MAXIMUM PUNISHMENT MORE THAN FIVE YEARS
TYPE 'F'	INDICTABLE OFFENCES MENTIONED IN SECTION 429.1
TYPE 'G'	OFFENCES MENTIONED IN SECTION 427 SUPREME COURT EXCLUSIVE

This legend sets out the seven major classifications of criminal offences and briefly describes the type of offence which is included in each classification.

Canadian criminal procedure is divided into the two main categories of summary conviction offences and indictable offences. The latter classification is further divided into six sub-categories, each having its own characteristics, procedures and provisions. In order to provide a better understanding of these classifications, each will be described and their unique provisions set out. When these classifications and provisions are understood, a quick check of the classification as noted in the margin beside the particular offence in the statute will give an immediate indication of the procedures and conditions which generally apply to that particular offence or grouping of offences.

Type 'A' classification includes all summary conviction offences. All other types are indictable offences. There are six separate groupings of indictable offences, each with its own distinctive characteristics, and procedures.

Before we deal with the seven specific types of offences we should become more familiar with the method of determining whether an offence is a summary conviction or Type 'A' offence, or an indictable or Type 'B' to 'G' offence. Section 27 of the Interpretation Act sets out an authority for this determination:

> 27. (1) Where an enactment creates an offence,
>
> *(a)* the offence shall be deemed to be an indictable offence if the enactment provides that the offender may be prosecuted for the offence by indictment;
>
> *(b)* the offence shall be deemed to be one for which the offender is punishable on summary conviction if there is nothing in the context to indicate that the offence is an indictable offence; and
>
> *(c)* if the offence is one for which the offender may be prosecuted by indictment or for which he is punishable on summary conviction, no person shall be considered to have been convicted of an indictable offence by reason only of having been convicted of the offence on summary conviction.
>
> (2) All the provisions of the *Criminal Code* relating to indictable offences apply to indictable offences created by an enactment, and all the provisions of the *Criminal Code* relating to summary conviction offences apply to all other offences created by an enactment, except to the extent that the enactment otherwise provides.

Subsection 27(2) states that all offences against federal statutes are to be dealt with using the procedural provisions of the Criminal Code unless the particular statute provides otherwise. Examples of specific provisions are the unique trial procedure for the offence of "Possession of a narcotic for the purposes of trafficking" under the Narcotic Control Act or the fact that all proceedings under the Juvenile Delinquents Act are to be by way of summary conviction, regardless of the offence charged or whether or not it is an indictable offence.

Subsection 27(1) answers the question of how one is to know whether a particular offence is a summary conviction offence or an indictable offence. If the section that creates the offence or provides the punishment states that the offence is an indictable offence or that the person is liable to punishment upon indictment, then it is an indictable offence. If the provision does not mention anything about the offence being an indictable offence or that the person should be tried on indictment, the offence is deemed to be a summary conviction offence.

With regard to that type of offence known as a dual procedure or hybrid offence, paragraph 27(1)*(a)* provides that an offence shall be deemed to be an indictable offence, ". . if . . the offender may be prosecuted ... by indictment". Until such time as the prosecutor elects or is deemed to have elected to proceed by way of summary conviction the offender may be prosecuted by indictment and these offences are therefore, up until the time of the prosecutor's election, deemed to be indictable offences.

TYPE 'A' OFFENCES

SUMMARY CONVICTION OFFENCES

All offences in federal statutes that have nothing in the text to indicate that the offence is an indictable offence are summary conviction offences and Part 24 of the Criminal Code sets out the manner in which these offences will be proceeded with and the specific conditions applicable.

Unless specifically set out otherwise, there is a six-month time limit to commence proceedings; the trial may be conducted *ex parte* or in the absence of the accused; the accused may be represented by counsel or by an agent; either a magistrate or a justice of the peace may preside at the trial; the general penalty is $500 and/or six months imprisonment; and there are two methods of appeal, stated case and trial *de novo.* These are but a few of the procedural provisions of Part 24 of the Criminal Code; reference should be made to those particular sections or to a text on court procedure for further information on summary conviction procedure.

TYPE 'B' OFFENCES

DUAL PROCEDURE OFFENCES — HYBRID OFFENCES

Any offence which states that the accused may be prosecuted either by way of summary conviction or by way of indictment is this type of offence.

All offences with this dual character are considered to be indictable offences until the accused is arraigned and the prosecutor indicates which method of proceedings will be followed. Accordingly, all pre-trial procedures relating to indictable offences such as powers of arrest, bail applications, the Identification of Criminals Act, etc., apply to these offences. However, once the accused has been arraigned and the prosecutor indicates that the trial procedure will be by way of summary conviction, only summary conviction procedures apply and the accused, if convicted, will be convicted of a summary conviction offence. Paragraph 27(1)*(c)* of the Interpretation Act makes this provision.

If the prosecutor chooses to proceed by way of indictment, the trial procedure and conditions that apply will be those set out for Type 'C', 'D' or 'E' offences, depending upon the maximum penalty provided for the offence or if it is mentioned in section 483. For this reason, after each designation of a Type 'B' offence will be a further designation of either (C), (D) or (E), whichever is applicable for that particular offence.

Because these offences are primarily indictable offences, there is no time limit to commence proceedings. However, if the proceedings are not commenced within six months, the prosecutor has no option but to proceed by way of indictment.

TYPE 'C' OFFENCES

ABSOLUTE JURISDICTION OF MAGISTRATE
OFFENCES MENTIONED IN SECTION 483

All offences that are designated as this type are set out in section 483 of the Criminal Code. They are all indictable offences but the accused is not allowed to elect how he wishes to be tried; he must be tried by a magistrate.

Section 426 states, "Every superior court of criminal jurisdiction has jurisdiction to try any indictable offence." Accordingly, the provisions of section 483 are not always followed if a superior court so directs.

TYPE 'D' OFFENCES MAXIMUM PENALTY FIVE YEARS OR LESS

TYPE 'E' OFFENCES MAXIMUM PENALTY MORE THAN FIVE YEARS

These two types of offences include all the indictable offences that are not mentioned in sections 483 or 427 as being assigned exclusively to either Magistrates or the Supreme Court, nor in section 429.1 with its unique election options. In these types of offences, the accused is given an election as set out in section 464 and 484. These offences differ in a number of ways and these differences are set out below with authorities.

TYPE "D" OFFENCES PUNISHABLE UP TO FIVE YEARS	TYPE "E" OFFENCES PUNISHABLE OVER FIVE YEARS
-Accused may be fined in lieu of sentence of imprisonment 646(1)	-Accused may be fined in addition to imprisonment, but penalty must include imprisonment 646(2)
-Accused's election of trial by magistrate not subject to approval of prosecutor 498	-Prosecutor may require accused to be tried by judge and jury 498
-Officer in charge shall release on promise to appear unless reason to detain in custody 453	-Officer in charge may release or may detain person in custody to appear before justice 454(1.1)
-Justice issuing warrant to apprehend may authorize release of accused by officer in charge 456.3(6)	-No such authority
-No invasion of privacy authorization unless specific offence named in section 178.1	-Invasion of privacy authorization for any offence if it is a part of organized crime 178.1
-Accused entitled to four peremptory challenges of jurors 562(3)	-Accused allowed twelve peremptory challenges of jurors 526(2)
	-Public office vacated if sentence of more than five years imposed 682(1)

TYPE 'F' OFFENCES

OFFENCES MENTIONED IN SECTION 429.1

These offences are true indictable offences, similar to type 'E' offences. The accused is given a choice as to whether he wishes to be tried by a County or District Court Judge and jury or by a Supreme Court Judge and jury. With Type 'D' and 'E' offences the accused was given only a three-way choice as to manner of trial, magistrate, judge or judge and jury; he was not given a choice as to type of judge and jury.

In provinces where county courts do not sit with a jury, this provision does not apply.

TYPE 'G' OFFENCES

SUPREME COURT EXCLUSIVE

These offences are mentioned in section 427 of the Criminal Code and must be tried by a Supreme Court Judge and jury. They are the most serious offences known to our law system and, accordingly, must be tried by the highest form of court. Section 430 provides an exception whereby in the province of Alberta a person accused of an indictable offence may, if he wishes, be tried by a Supreme Court Judge without a jury.

Provisions and amendments applicable only to certain provinces

The following is an excerpt from a bill which did not pass through Parliament and, accordingly, did not become law:

169. (1) Subject to subsections (2) and (3), this Act shall come into force on a day to be fixed by proclamation.

(2) Sections 27 and 32 shall come into force in any province or territory of Canada on a day to be fixed by proclamation with respect to that province or territory.

(3) Section 143 shall come into force in any province or territory of Canada on a day to be fixed by proclamation with respect to that province or territory issued after consultation with the government of that province or territory.

As can be seen from this excerpt, which is an example only, new laws do not always become effective in a neat and orderly fashion across Canada. Sometimes laws come into effect only in certain provinces and then only with the approval of the province effected. There are a few instances of such partial application of the law contained in this present work and with one exception they are noted as they appear.

However, as it was found that no one system worked satisfactorily for all of these instances, a summary of those provisions which apply only to certain provinces or are waiting to be proclaimed in force should be provided.

Subsections 234(2) and 236(2) have been proclaimed in force only in the Province of Alberta and the Northwest Territories.

Section 234.1 has been proclaimed in force in all provinces and territories except British Columbia and Quebec.

Part XIV.1 has been proclaimed in force only in the Province of New Brunswick and the Yukon and Northwest Territories. Paragraph 567(1)*(f)*, an amendment consequential to Part XIV.1 is also only proclaimed in force in the Province of New Brunswick and the Yukon and Northwest Territories.

Clause 237(1)*(f)*(iii)(A), "approved container" in subsection 237(6) and paragraph 104(2)*(c)* are examples of other provisions which have been passed but have not been proclaimed in force.

A final note in this regard, Part II, sections 15 to 19, of the Narcotic Control Act was passed in 1961 and has not yet been proclaimed in force. It has not been included in this work.

CHAPTER C-34

An Act respecting the Criminal Law

SHORT TITLE

Short title

1. This Act may be cited as the *Criminal Code.* 1953-54, c. 51, s. 1.

INTERPRETATION

Definitions

2. In this Act

"Act"

"Act" includes

(a) an Act of the Parliament of Canada,

(b) an Act of the legislature of the former Province of Canada,

(c) an Act of the legislature of a province, and 28 Interp

(d) an Act or ordinance of the legislature of a province, territory or place in force at the time that province, territory or place became a province of Canada;

Interpretation Act

28. In every enactment

"province" means a province of Canada, and includes the Yukon Territory and the Northwest Territories;

"Attorney General"

"Attorney General" means the Attorney General or Solicitor General of a province in which proceedings to which this Act applies are taken and, with respect to

(a) the Northwest Territories and the Yukon Territory, and

(b) proceedings instituted at the instance of the Government of Canada and conducted by or on behalf of that Government in respect of a violation of or conspiracy to violate any Act of the Parliament of Canada or a regulation made thereunder other than this Act,

means the Attorney General of Canada and, except for the purposes of subsections 505(4) and 507(3), includes the lawful deputy of the said Attorney General, Solicitor General and Attorney General of Canada;

"bank-note"

"bank-note" includes any negotiable instrument

(a) issued by or on behalf of a person carrying on the business of banking in or out of Canada,

(b) issued under the authority of the Parliament of Canada or under lawful authority of the government of a state other than Canada,

intended to be used as money or as the equivalent of money, immediately upon issue or at some time subsequent thereto, and includes bank bills and bank post bills;

"Canadian Forces"

"Canadian Forces" means the armed forces of Her Majesty raised by Canada;

"cattle

"cattle" means neat cattle or an animal of the bovine species by whatever technical or familiar name it is known, and includes a horse, mule, ass, pig, sheep or goat;

"clerk of the court"

"clerk of the court" includes a person, by whatever name or title he may be designated, who from time to time performs the duties of a clerk of the court;

"counsel"

"counsel" means a barrister or solicitor, in respect of the matters or things that barristers and solicitors, respectively, are authorized by the law of the province to do or perform in relation to legal proceedings;

"count"

"count" means a charge in an information or indictment;

"court of appeal"

"court of appeal" means

(a) in the Province of Ontario, the Court of Appeal,

(b) in the Province of Quebec, the Court of Appeal,

(c) in the Province of Nova Scotia, the Appeal Division of the Supreme Court,

(d) in the Province of New Brunswick, the Court of Appeal,

(e) in the Province of British Columbia, the Court of Appeal,

(f) in the Province of Prince Edward Island, the Supreme Court,

(g) in the Province of Manitoba, the Court of Appeal,

(h) in the Province of Saskatchewan, the Court of Appeal,

(i) in the Province of Alberta, the Court of Appeal,

(j) in the Province of Newfoundland, the Court of Appeal,

(k) in the Yukon Territory, the Court of Appeal, and

(l) in the Northwest Territories, the Court of Appeal;
1978-79, c. 11, s. 10, I. 6(1),(2).

"court of criminal jurisdiction"

"court of criminal jurisdiction" means

(a) a court of general or quarter sessions of the peace, when presided over by a superior court judge or a county or district court judge, or in the cities of Montreal and Quebec, by a municipal judge of the city, as the case may be, or a judge of the sessions of the peace, and

(b) a magistrate or judge acting under Part XVI;
1978-79, c. 11, s. 10, I. 6(3).

"day"

"day" means the period between six o'clock in the forenoon and nine o'clock in the afternoon of the same day;

"document of title to goods"

"document of title to goods" includes a bought and sold note, bill of lading, warrant, certificate or order for the delivery or transfer of goods or any other valuable thing, and any other document used in the ordinary course of business as evidence of the possession or control of goods, authorizing or purporting to authorize, by endorsement or by delivery, the person in possession of the document to transfer or receive any goods thereby represented or therein mentioned or referred to;

"document of title to lands"

"document of title to lands" includes any writing that is or contains evidence of 2
the title, or any part of the title to real property, or to any interest in real property, and any notarial or registrar's copy thereof, and any duplicate instrument, memorial, certificate or document authorized or required by any law in force in any part of Canada with respect to registration of titles, that relates to title to real property or to an interest in real property;

"dwelling-house"

"dwelling-house" means the whole or any part of a building or structure that is kept or occupied as a permanent or temporary residence and includes

(a) a building within the curtilage of a dwelling-house that is connected to it by a doorway or by a covered and enclosed passageway, and

(b) a unit that is designed to be mobile and to be used as a permanent or temporary residence and that is being used as such a residence;

"every one" "person" "owner"

"every one", "person", "owner", and similar expressions include Her Majesty and public bodies, bodies corporate, societies, companies and inhabitants of counties, parishes, municipalities or other districts in relation to the acts and things that they are capable of doing and owning respectively;

"explosive substance"

"explosive substance" includes

(a) anything intended to be used to make an explosive substance, and

(b) anything, or any part thereof, used or intended to be used, or adapted to cause, or to aid in causing an explosion in or with an explosive substance;

"feeble-minded person"

"febble-minded person" means a person in whom there exists and has existed from birth or from an early age, mental defectiveness not amounting to imbecility, but so pronounced that he requires care, supervision and control for his protection or for the protection of others;

"Her Majesty's Forces"

"Her Majesty's Forces" means the naval, army and air forces of Her Majesty wherever raised, and includes the Canadian Forces;

"highway"

"highway" means a road to which the public has the right of access, and includes bridges over which or tunnels through which a road passes;

"indictment"

"indictment" includes

(a) information, presentment and a count therein,

(b) a plea, replication or other pleading, and

(c) any record;

"internationally" protected person"

"internationally protected person" means

(a) a head of state, including any member of a collegial body performing the functions of a head of state under the constitution of the state concerned, a head of a government or a minister of foreign affairs, whenever such person is in a state other than the state in which he holds such position or office,

(b) a member of the family of a person described in paragraph *(a)* who accompanies that person in a state other than the state in which that person holds such position or office,

(c) a representative or official of a state or an official or agent of an international organization of an intergovernmental character who, at the time when and at the place where an offence referred to in subsection 6(1.2) is committed against his person or any property referred to in section 387.1 that is used by him, is entitled, pursuant to international law, to special protection from any attack on his person, freedom or dignity, or

(d) a member of the family of a representative, official or agent described in paragraph *(c)* who forms part of his household, if such representative, official or agent, at the time when and at the place where any offence referred to in subsection 6(1.2) is committed against the member of his family or any property referred to in section 387.1 that is used by that member, is entitled, pursuant to international law, to special protection from any attack on his person, freedom or dignity;

6. (8) If in any proceedings under this Act a question arises as to whether any person is a person who is entitled, pursuant to international law, to special protection from any attack on his person, freedom or dignity, a certificate purporting to have been issued by or under the authority of the Secretary of State for External Affairs containing any statement of fact relevant to that question is admissible in evidence in such proceedings and in the absence of evidence to the contrary is proof of the statements contained in the certificate.

"justice"

"justice" means a justice of the peace or a magistrate, and includes two or more justices where two or more justices are, by law, required to act or, by law, act or have jurisdiction;

"magistrate"

"magistrate" means a magistrate, a police magistrate, a stipendiary magistrate, a district magistrate, a provincial magistrate, a judge of the sessions of the peace, a recorder, or any person having the power and authority of two or more justices of the peace, and includes

(a) with respect to the Provinces of Ontario, Quebec, New Brunswick and British Columbia, a judge of the provincial court,

(a.1) with respect to the Provinces of Alberta, Manitoba and Prince Edward Island, a provincial judge,

(a.2) with respect to the Province of Nova Scotia, a judge of the Provincial Magistrate's Court,

(b) with respect to the Province of Saskatchewan, a judge of the Magistrates' Courts, and

(c) with respect to the Yukon Territory and the Northwest Territories, a judge of the Supreme Court,

and the lawful deputy of each of them;

"military" "military" shall be construed as relating to all or any of the Canadian Forces; 2

"military law" "military law" includes all laws, regulations or orders relating to the Canadian Forces; 2

"motor vehicle" "motor vehicle" means a vehicle that is drawn, propelled or driven by any means other than by muscular power, but does not include a vehicle of a railway that operates on rails;

"municipality" "municipality" includes the corporation of a city, town, village, county, township, parish or other territorial or local division of a province, the inhabitants of which are incorporated or are entitled to hold property collectively for a public purpose;

"newly-born child" "newly-born child" means a person under the age of one year; 2

3. (1) For the purposes of this Act a person shall be deemed to have been of a given age when the anniversary of his birthday, the number of which corresponds to that age, is fully completed, and until then to have been under that age. 3(1)

"night" "night" means the period between nine o'clock in the afternoon and six o'clock in the forenoon of the following day;

"offensive weapon" "weapon" "offensive weapon" or "weapon" means

(a) anything that is designed to be used as a weapon, or

(b) anything that a person uses or intends to use as a weapon, whether or not it is designed to be used as a weapon,

and, without restricting the generality of the foregoing, includes any firearm as defined in section 82.

82. (1) For the purposes of this Part,

"firearm" means any barrelled weapon from which any shot, bullet or other missile can be discharged and that is capable of causing serious bodily injury or death to a person, and includes any frame or receiver of such a barrelled weapon and anything that can be adapted for use as a firearm;

"peace officer" "peace officer" includes

(a) a mayor, warden, reeve, sheriff, deputy sheriff, sheriff's officer and justice of the peace,

(b) a warden, deputy warden, instructor, keeper, gaoler, guard and any other officer or permanent employee of a prison, 2

(c) a police officer, police constable, bailiff, constable, or other person employed for the preservation and maintenance of the public peace or for the service or execution of civil process,

(d) an officer or person having the powers of a customs or excise officer when performing any duty in the administration of the *Customs Act* or the *Excise Act*,

(d.1) a person appointed or designated as a fishery officer under the *Fisheries Act* when performing any of his duties or functions pursuant to that Act,

(e) the pilot in command of an aircraft

(i) registered in Canada under regulations made under the *Aeronautics Act*, or

(ii) leased without crew and operated by a person who is qualified under regulations made under the *Aeronautics Act* to be registered as owner of an aircraft registered in Canada under those regulations,

while the aircraft is in flight, and 6(6)

(f) officers and men of the Canadian Forces who are 2

(i) appointed for the purposes of section 134 of the *National Defence Act*, or

(ii) employed on duties that the Governor in Council, in regulations made under the *National Defence Act* for the purposes of this paragraph, has prescribed to be of such a kind as to necessitate that the officers and men performing them have the powers of peace officers;

6. (6) For the purposes of this section, of the definition "peace officer" in section 2 and of section 76.1 and 76.2, "flight" means the act of flying or moving through the air and an aircraft shall be deemed to be in flight from the time when all external doors are closed following embarkation until the later of

(a) the time at which any such door is opened for the purpose of disembarkation; and

(b) where the aircraft makes a forced landing in circumstances in which the owner or operator thereof or a person acting on behalf of either of them is not in control of the aircraft, the time at which control of the aircraft is restored to the owner or operator thereof or a person acting on behalf of either of them.

"prison" "prison" includes a penitentiary, common gaol, public or reformatory prison, lock-up, guard-room or other place in which persons who are charged with or convicted of offences are usually kept in custody;

"property" "property" includes

(*a*) real and personal property of every description and deeds and instruments relating to or evidencing the title or right to property, or giving a right to recover or receive money or goods,

(*b*) property originally in the possession or under the control of any person, and any property into or for which it has been converted or exchanged and anything acquired at any time by such conversion or exchange, and

(*c*) any postal card, postage stamp or other stamp issued or prepared for issue under the authority of the Parliament of Canada or of the legislature of a province for the payment to the Crown or a corporate body of any fee, rate or duty, whether or not it is in the possession of the Crown or of any person; 3(2)

3. (2) For the purposes of this Act a postal card or stamp referred to in paragraph (*c*) of the definition "property" in section 2 shall be deemed to be a chattel, and to be equal in value to the amount of the postage, rate or duty expressed on its face.

"prosecutor" "prosecutor" means the Attorney General or, where the Attorney General 2
does not intervene, means the person who institutes proceedings to which
this Act applies, and includes counsel acting on behalf of either of them; 2

"public department" "public department" means a department of the Government of Canada or a branch thereof or a board, commission, corporation or other body that is an agent of Her Majesty in right of Canada;

"public officer" "public officer" includes

(*a*) an officer of customs or excise,

(*b*) an officer of the Canadian Forces,

(*c*) an officer of the Royal Canadian Mounted Police, and

(*d*) any officer while he is engaged in enforcing the laws of Canada relating to revenue, customs, excise, trade or navigation;

"public stores" "public stores" includes any movable property that is under the care, supervision, administration or control of a public department or of any person in the service of a public department;

"steal" "steal" means to commit theft;

"superior court of criminal jurisdiction" "superior court of criminal jurisdiction" means

(*a*) in the Province of Ontario, the Supreme Court,

(*b*) in the Province of Quebec, the Superior Court,

(*c*) in the Provinces of Nova Scotia, Prince Edward Island and Newfoundland respectively, the Supreme Court, 1978-79, c. 11, s. 10, I. 6(4).

(*d*) in the Province of British Columbia, the Supreme Court or the Court of Appeal,

(*e*) in the Provinces of Manitoba, Saskatchewan, Alberta and New Brunswick respectively, the Court of Appeal or the Court of Queen's Bench, 1978-79, c. 11, s. 10, I. 6(5).

(*f*) in the Yukon Territory, the Supreme Court, and

(*g*) in the Northwest Territories, the Supreme Court;

"territorial division"

"territorial division" includes any province, county, union of counties, township, city, town, parish or other judicial division or place to which the context applies; 28 Interp

"testamentary instrument"

"testamentary instrument" includes any will, codicil or other testamentary writing or appointment, as well during the life of the testator whose testamentary disposition it purports to be as after his death, whether it relates to real or personal property, or to both; 2

"trustee"

"trustee" means a person who is declared by any Act to be a trustee or is, by the law of the province, a trustee, and without restricting the generality of the foregoing, includes a trustee on an express trust created by deed, will or instrument in writing, or by parol; 28 Interp

"valuable security"

"valuable security" includes 3(3)

(a) an order, exchequer acquittance or other security that entitles or evidences the title of any person

(i) to a share or interest in a public stock or fund or in any fund of a body corporate, company or society, or

(ii) to a deposit in a savings bank or other bank, 28 Interp

(b) a debenture, deed, bond, bill, note, warrant, order or other security for money or for payment of money,

(c) a document of title to lands or goods wherever situated, 2

(d) a stamp or writing that secures or evidences title to or an interest in a chattel personal, or that evidences delivery of a chattel personal, and 2

(e) a release, receipt, discharge or other instrument evidencing payment of money;

3. (3) For the purposes of this Act, the following rules apply for the purpose of determining the value of a valuable security where value is material, namely,

(a) where the valuable security is one mentioned in paragraph *(a)* or *(b)* of the definition "valuable security" in section 2, the value is the value of the share, interest, deposit or unpaid money, as the case may be, that is secured by the valuable security;

(b) where the valuable security is one mentioned in paragraph *(c)* or *(d)* of the definition "valuable security" in section 2, the value is the value of the lands, goods, chattel personal or interest in the chattel personal, as the case may be; and

(c) where the valuable security is one mentioned in paragraph *(e)* of the definition "valuable security" in section 2, the value is the amount of money that has been paid.

"wreck"

"wreck" includes the cargo, stores and tackle of a vessel and all parts of a vessel separated from the vessel, and the property of persons who belong to, are on board or have quitted a vessel that is wrecked, stranded or in distress at any place in Canada;

"writing"

"writing" includes a document of any kind and any mode in which, and any material on which, words or figures, whether at length or abridged, are written, printed or otherwise expressed, or a map or plan is inscribed. R.S., c. C-34, s. 2; 1972, c. 13, s. 2; 1972, c. 17, s. 2; 1974-75, c. 19, s. 1,2; 1974-75, c. 48, s. 25(1); 1974-75-76, c. 93, s. 2; 1976-77, c. 35, s. 21; 1978-79, c. 11, s. 10.

Descriptive cross reference

2.1 Where, in any provision of this Act, a reference to another provision of this Act or a provision of any other Act is followed by words in parenthesis that are or purport to be descriptive of the subject-matter of the provision referred to, the words in parenthesis form no part of the provision in which they occur but shall be deemed to have been inserted for convenience of reference only. 1976-77, c. 53, s. 2.

PART I

General

Determination of age

3. (1) For the purposes of this Act a person shall be deemed to have been of a given age when the anniversary of his birthday, the number of which corresponds to that age, is fully completed, and until then to have been under that age.

585. (1) In any proceedings to which this Act applies an entry or record of an incorporated society or its officers who have had the control or care of a child or young person at or about the time the child or young person was brought to Canada is evidence of the age of the child or young person if the entry or record was made before the time when the offence is alleged to have been committed.

(2) In the absence of other evidence, or by way of corroboration of other evidence, a jury, judge, justice or magistrate, as the case may be, may infer the age of a child or young person from his appearance.

Postcard a chattel, value

(2) For the purposes of this Act a postal card or stamp referred to in paragraph *(c)* of the definition "property" in section 2 shall be deemed to be a chattel, and to be equal in value to the amount of the postage, rate or duty expressed on its face.

Value of valuable security

(3) For the purposes of this Act, the following rules apply for the purpose of determining the value of a valuable security where value is material, namely,

(a) where the valuable security is one mentioned in paragraph *(a)* or *(b)* of the definition "valuable security" in section 2, the value is the value of the share, interest, deposit or unpaid money, as the case may be, that is secured by the valuable security;

(b) where the valuable security is one mentioned in paragraph *(c)* or *(d)* of the definition "valuable security" in section 2, the value is the value of the lands, goods, chattel personal or interest in the chattel personal, as the case may be; and

(c) where the valuable security is one mentioned in paragraph *(e)* of the definition "valuable security" in section 2, the value is the amount of money that has been paid.

Possession

(4) For the purposes of this Act,

(a) a person has anything in possession when he has it in his personal possession or knowingly

(i) has it in the actual possession or custody of another person, or

(ii) has it in any place, whether or not that place belongs to or is occupied by him, for the use or benefit of himself or of another person; and

(b) where one of two or more persons, with the knowledge and consent of the rest, has anything in his custody or possession, it shall be deemed to be in the custody and possession of each and all of them.

Expressions taken from other Acts

(5) Where an offence that is dealt with in this Act relates to a subject that is dealt with in another Act, the words and expressions used in this Act with respect to that offence have, subject to this Act, the meaning assigned to them in that other Act.

Sexual intercourse

(6) For the purposes of this Act, sexual intercourse is complete upon penetration to even the slightest degree, notwithstanding that seed is not emitted.

Service of process

(7) Where, pursuant to this Act, any summons, notice or other process is required to be or may be served upon a corporation, and no other method of service is provided, such service may be effected by delivering the process 20 Interp

(a) in the case of a municipal corporation, to the mayor, warden, reeve, or other chief officer of the corporation, or to the secretary, treasurer or clerk of the corporation, and

(b) in the case of any other corporation, to the manager, secretary or other executive officer of the corporation or of a branch thereof. 1953-54, c. 51, s. 3; 1960-61, c. 43, s. 2.

NOTE: See section 455.5 for further information regarding summons, required contents, service on accused and methods of proving service.

Canadian Forces not affected

4. Nothing in this Act affects any law relating to the government of the Canadian Forces. 1953-54, c. 51, s. 4. 2

2. In this Act

"Canadian Forces" means the armed forces of Her Majesty raised by Canada;

Punishment

5. (1) Where an enactment creates an offence and authorizes a punishment to be imposed in respect thereof,

(a) a person shall be deemed not to be guilty of that offence until he is convicted thereof; and

(b) a person who is convicted of that offence is not liable to any punishment in respect thereof other than the punishment prescribed by this Act or by the enactment that creates the offence.

Offences outside of Canada

(2) Subject to this Act or any other Act of the Parliament of Canada, no person shall be convicted in Canada for an offence committed outside of Canada. 1953-54, c. 51, s. 5.

Offences committed on aircraft

6. (1) Notwithstanding anything in this Act or any other Act, every one who

(a) on or in respect of an aircraft

(i) registered in Canada under regulations made under the *Aeronautics Act*, or

(ii) leased without crew and operated by a person who is qualified under regulations made under the *Aeronautics Act* to be registered as owner of an aircraft registered in Canada under those regulations,

while the aircraft is in flight, or ss (6)

(b) on any aircraft, while the aircraft is in flight if the flight terminated in Canada,

commits an act or omission in or outside Canada that if committed in Canada would be an offence punishable by indictment shall be deemed to have committed that act or omission in Canada.

Idem

(1.1) Notwithstanding this Act or any other Act, every one who

(a) on an aircraft, while the aircraft is in flight, commits an act or omission outside Canada that if committed in Canada or on an aircraft registered in Canada under regulations made under the *Aeronautics Act* would be an offence against section 76.1 or paragraph 76.2*(a)*, ss (6)

(b) in relation to an aircraft in service, commits an act or omission outside Canada that if committed in Canada would be an offence against any of paragraphs 76.2*(b)*, *(c)* or *(e)*, or ss (7)

(c) in relation to an air navigation facility used in international air navigation, commits an act or omission outside Canada that if committed in Canada would be an offence against paragraph 76.2*(d)*

shall, if he is found anywhere in Canada, be deemed to have committed that act or omission in Canada.

Offences against internationally protected person

(1.2) Notwithstanding anything in this Act or any other Act, every one who, outside Canada, commits an act or omission against the person of an internationally protected person or against any property referred to in section 387.1 used by him that if committed in Canada would be an offence against section 218, 219, 245, 246, 247, 381.1 or 387.1 shall be deemed to commit that act or omission in Canada if 2

(a) the act or omission is committed on a ship registered pursuant to any Act of Parliament;

(b) the act or omission is committed on an aircraft

(i) registered in Canada under regulations made under the *Aeronautics Act*, or

(ii) leased without crew and operated by a person who is qualified under regulations made under the *Aeronautics Act* to be registered as owner of an aircraft in Canada under such regulations;

(c) the person who commits the act or omission is a Canadian citizen or is present in Canada; or

(d) the act or omission is against

(i) a person who enjoys his status as an internationally protected person by virtue of the functions he exercises on behalf of Canada, or

(ii) a member of the family of a person described in subparagraph (i) who qualifies under paragraph *(b)* or *(d)* of the definition "internationally protected person" in section 2. 1974-75-76, c. 93, s. 3(1).

387.1 Every one who commits an attack upon the official premises, private accommodation or means of transport of an internationally protected person that is likely to endanger the life or liberty of such person is guilty of an indictable offence.

218 (murder), 219 (manslaughter), 245 (common assault, assault causing bodily harm), 246 (assault with intent), 247 (kidnapping and forcible confinement), 381.1 (threat to commit offences against internationally protected person) or 387.1 (attack on premises, residence or transport of internationally protected person)

Offences by Public Service employees

(2) Every one who, while employed as an employee within the meaning of the *Public Service Employment Act* in a place outside Canada, commits an act or omission in that place that is an offence under the laws of that place and that, if committed in Canada, would be an offence punishable by indictment, shall be deemed to have committed that act or omission in Canada.

Jurisdiction

(3) Where a person has committed an act or omission that is an offence by virtue of subsection (1), (1.1), (1.2) or (2), the offence is within the competence of and may be tried and punished by the court having jurisdiction in respect of similar offences in the territorial division where he is found in the same manner as if the offence had been committed in that territorial divison. 2

Where previously tried outside Canada

(4) Where, as a result of committing an act or omission that is an offence by virtue of subsection (1), (1.1), (1.2) or (2), a person has been tried and convicted or acquitted outside Canada, he shall be deemed to have been tried and convicted or acquitted, as the case may be, in Canada. 1974-75-76, c. 93, s. 3(2)

Consent

(5) No proceedings shall be instituted under this section without the consent of the Attorney General of Canada if the accused is not a Canadian citizen. 2

"Flight" and "in flight"

(6) For the purposes of this section, of the definition "peace officer" in section 2 and of sections 76.1 and 76.2, "flight" means the act of flying or moving through the air and an aircraft shall be deemed to be in flight from the time when all external doors are closed following embarkation until the later of

(a) the time at which any such door is opened for the purpose of disembarkation; and

(b) where the aircraft makes a forced landing in circumstances in which the owner or operator thereof or a person acting on behalf of either of them is not in control of the aircraft, the time at which control of the aircraft is restored to the owner or operator thereof or a person acting on behalf of either of them.

"In service"

(7) For the purposes of this section and section 76.2, an aircraft shall be deemed to be in service from the time when pre-flight preparation of the aircraft by ground personnel or the crew thereof begins for a specific flight until

(a) the flight is cancelled before the aircraft is in flight, ss (6)

(b) twenty-four hours after the aircraft, having commenced the flight, lands, or

(c) the aircraft, having commenced the flight, ceases to be in flight,

whichever is the latest. R.S., c. C-34, s. 6; 1972, c. 13, s. 3(3).

Evidence

(8) If in any proceedings under this Act a question arises as to whether any person is a person who is entitled, pursuant to international law, to special protection from any attack on his person, freedom or dignity, a certificate purporting to have been issued by or under the authority of the Secretary of State for External Affairs containing any statement of fact relevant to that question is admissible in evidence in such proceedings and in the absence of evidence to the contrary is proof of the statements contained in the certificate. 1974-75-76, c. 93, s. 3(3).

Application to territories

7. (1) The provisions of this Act apply throughout Canada except

(a) in the Northwest Territories, in so far as they are inconsistent with the *Northwest Territories Act*, and

(b) in the Yukon Territory, in so far as they are inconsistent with the *Yukon Act.*

Application of criminal law of England

(2) The criminal law of England that was in force in a province immediately before the 1st day of April 1955 continues in force in the province except as altered, varied, modified or affected by this Act or any other Act of the Parliament of Canada. 28 Interp

Common law principles continued

(3) Every rule and principle of the common law that renders any circumstance a justification or excuse for an act or a defence to a charge continues in force and applies in respect of proceedings for an offence under this Act or any other Act of the Parliament of Canada, except in so far as they are altered by or are inconsistent with this Act or any other Act of the Parliament of Canada. 1953-54, c. 51, ss. 6, 7.

Interpretation Act

28. In every enactment

"province" means a province of Canada, and includes the Yukon Territory and the Northwest Territories;

Criminal offences to be under law of Canada

8. Notwithstanding anything in this Act or any other Act no person shall be convicted

(a) of an offence at common law,

(b) of an offence under an Act of the Parliament of England, or of Great Britain, or of the United Kingdom of Great Britain and Ireland, or

(c) of an offence under an Act or ordinance in force in any province, territory or place before that province, territory or place became a province of Canada,

but nothing in this section affects the power, jurisdiction or authority that a court, judge, justice or magistrate had, immediately before the 1st day of April 1955, to impose punishment for contempt of court. 1953-54, c. 51, s. 8. 2

Appeal

9. (1) Where a court, judge, justice or magistrate summarily convicts a person for a contempt of court committed in the face of the court and imposes punishment in respect thereof, that person may appeal

(a) from the conviction, or

(b) against the punishment imposed.

Idem

(2) Where a court or judge summarily convicts a person for a contempt of court not committed in the face of the court and punishment is imposed in respect thereof, that person may appeal

(a) from the conviction, or

(b) against the punishment imposed.

Part XVIII applies

(3) An appeal under this section lies to the court of appeal of the province in which the proceedings take place, and, for the purposes of this section, the provisions of Part XVIII apply, *mutatis mutandis.* R.S., c. C-34, s. 9; 1972, c. 13, s. 4. 2

mutatis mutandis — after the necessary changes in detail so that the text applies

Civil remedy not suspended

10. No civil remedy for an act or omission is suspended or affected by reason that the act or omission is a criminal offence. 1953-54, c. 51, s.10.

Offence punishable under more than one Act

11. Where an act or omission is an offence under more than one Act of the Parliament of Canada, whether punishable by indictment or on summary conviction, a person who does the act or makes the omission is, unless a contrary intention appears, subject to proceedings under any of those Acts, but is not liable to be punished more than once for the same offence. 1953-54, c.51,s.11.

Child under seven

12. No person shall be convicted of an offence in respect of an act or omission on his part while he was under the age of seven years. 1953-54, c. 51, s. 12. 3(1)

3. (1) For the purposes of this Act a person shall be deemed to have been of a given age when the anniversary of his birthday, the number of which corresponds to that age, is fully completed, and until then to have been under that age.

585. (1) In any proceedings to which this Act applies an entry or record of an incorporated society or its officers who have had the control or care of a child or young person at or about the time the child or young person was brought to Canada is evidence of the age of the child or young person if the entry or record was made before the time when the offence is alleged to have been committed.

(2) In the absence of other evidence, or by way of corroboration of other evidence, a jury, judge, justice or magistrate, as the case may be, may infer the age of a child or young person from his appearance.

Person between seven and fourteen

13. No person shall be convicted of an offence in respect of an act or omission on his part while he was seven years of age or more, but under the age of fourteen years, unless he was competent to know the nature and consequences of his conduct and to appreciate that it was wrong. 1953-54, c. 51, s. 13. 3(1)

Consent to death

14. No person is entitled to consent to have death inflicted upon him, and such consent does not affect the criminal responsibility of any person by whom death may be inflicted upon the person by whom consent is given. 1953-54, c. 51, s. 14.

Obedience to *de facto* law

15. No person shall be convicted of an offence in respect of an act or omission in obedience to the laws for the time being made and enforced by persons in *de facto* possession of the sovereign power in and over the place where the act or omission occurs. 1953-54, c. 51, s. 15.

de facto— The actual state of affairs or circumstances without regard to the right or wrong of it, or title to it.

Insanity

16. (1) No person shall be convicted of an offence in respect of an act or omission on his part while he was insane.

When insane

(2) For the purposes of this section a person is insane when he is in a state of natural imbecility or has disease of the mind to an extent that renders him incapable of appreciating the nature and quality of an act or omission or of knowing that an act or omission is wrong.

Delusions

(3) A person who has specific delusions, but is in other respects sane, shall not be acquitted on the ground of insanity unless the delusions caused him to believe in the existence of a state of things that, if it existed, would have justified or excused his act or omission.

Presumption of sanity

(4) Every one shall, until the contrary is proved, be presumed to be and to have been sane. 1953-54, c. 51, s. 16.

See sections 542 to 547 for Defence of Insanity, Insanity of accused when offence committed and Insanity at time of trial.

Compulsion by threats

17. A person who commits an offence under compulsion by threats of immediate death or grievous bodily harm from a person who is present when the offence is committed is excused for committing the offence if he believes that the threats will be carried out and if he is not a party to a conspiracy or association whereby he is subject to compulsion, but this section does not apply where the offence that is committed is high treason or treason, murder, piracy, attempted murder, assisting in rape, forcible abduction, robbery, causing bodily harm or arson. 1953-54, c. 51, s. 17; 1974-75-76, c. 105, s. 29.

Compulsion of wife

18. No presumption arises that a married woman who commits an offence does so under compulsion by reason only that she commits it in the presence of her husband. 1953-54, c. 51, s. 18.

Ignorance of the law

19. Ignorance of the law by a person who commits an offence is not an excuse for committing that offence. 1953-54, c. 51, s. 19.

Certain acts on holidays valid

20. A warrant or summons that is authorized by this Act or an appearance notice, promise to appear, undertaking or recognizance issued, given or entered into in accordance with Part XIV, XVIII or XXIV may be issued, executed, given or entered into, as the case may be, on a holiday. R.S., c. C-34, s. 20; 28 Interp
R.S., c. 2(2nd Supp.), s. 2.

Interpretation Act

28. In every enactment

"holiday" means any of the following days, namely, Sunday; New Year's Day; Good Friday; Easter Monday; Christmas Day; the birthday or the day fixed by proclamation for the celebration of the birthday of the reigning Sovereign; Victoria Day; Dominion Day; the first Monday in September, designated Labour Day; Remembrance Day; any day appointed by proclamation to be observed as a day of general prayer or mourning or day of public rejoicing or thanksgiving; and any of the following additional days, namely:

(a) in any province, any day appointed by proclamation of the lieutenant governor of the province to be observed as a public holiday or as a day of general prayer or mourning or day of public rejoicing or thanksgiving within the province, and any day that is a non-juridical day by virture of an Act of the legislature of the province, and

(b) in any city, town, municipality or other organized district, any day appointed as a civic holiday by resolution of the council or other authority charged with the administration of the civic or municipal affairs of the city, town, municipality or district;

SOR/57-55 Queen's Birthday, first Monday preceding twenty-fifth day of May . . . .

SOR/57-56 Thanksgiving Day, second Monday in October . . . .

Parties to Offences

Parties to offence

21. (1) Every one is a party to an offence who

(a) actually commits it,

(b) does or omits to do anything for the purpose of aiding any person to commit it, or

(c) abets any person in committing it.

Common intention

(2) Where two or more persons form an intention in common to carry out an unlawful purpose and to assist each other therein and any one of them, in carrying out the common purpose, commits an offence, each of them who knew or ought to have known that the commission of the offence would be a probable consequence of carrying out the common purpose is a party to that offence. 1953-54, c. 51, s. 21.

Person counselling offence

22. (1) Where a person counsels or procures another person to be a party to an offence and that other person is afterwards a party to that offence, the person who counselled or procured is a party to that offence, notwithstanding that the offence was committed in a way different from that which was counselled or procured.

Idem

(2) Every one who counsels or procures another person to be a party to an offence is a party to every offence that the other commits in consequence of the counselling or procuring that the person who counselled or procured knew or ought to have known was likely to be committed in consequence of the counselling or procuring. 1953-54, c. 51, s. 22.

422. Except where otherwise expressly provided by law, the following provisions apply in respect of persons who counsel, procure or incite other persons to commit offences, namely,

(a) every one who counsels, procures or incites another person to commit an indictable offence is, if the offence is not committed, guilty of an indictable offence and is liable to the same punishment to which a person who attempts to commit that offence is liable; and

(b) every one who counsels, procures or incites another person to commit an offence punishable on summary conviction is, if the offence is not committed, guilty of an offence punishable on summary conviction.

Accessory after the fact

23. (1) An accessory after the fact to an offence is one who, knowing that a person has been a party to the offence, receives, comforts or assists him for the purpose of enabling him to escape.

Husband or wife, when not accessory

(2) No married person whose spouse has been a party to an offence is an accessory after the fact to that offence by receiving, comforting or assisting the spouse for the purpose of enabling the spouse to escape.

(3) Repealed. 1974-75-76, c. 66, s. 7.

Attempts

24. (1) Every one who, having an intent to commit an offence, does or omits to do anything for the purpose of carrying out his intention is guilty of an attempt to commit the offence whether or not it was possible under the circumstances to commit the offence.

Question of law

(2) The question whether an act or omission by a person who has an intent to commit an offence is or is not mere preparation to commit the offence, and too remote to constitute an attempt to commit the offence, is a question of law. 1953-54, c. 51, s. 24.

421. Except where otherwise expressly provided by law, the following provisions apply in respect of persons who attempt to commit or are accessories after the fact to the commission of offences, namely,

(a) every one who attempts to commit or is an accessory after the fact to the commission of an indictable offence for which, upon conviction, an accused is liable to be sentenced to death or to imprisonment for life, is guilty of an indictable offence and is liable to imprisonment for fourteen years;

(b) every one who attempts to commit or is an accessory after the fact to the commission of an indictable offence for which, upon conviction, an accused is liable to imprisonment for fourteen years or less, is guilty of an indictable offence and is liable to imprisonment for a term that is one-half of the longest term to which a person who is guilty of that offence is liable; and

(c) every one who attempts to commit or is an accessory after the fact to the commission of an offence punishable on summary conviction is guilty of an offence punishable on summary conviction.

521. Any one who is charged with being an accessory after the fact to any offence may be indicted, whether or not the principal or any other party to the offence has been indicted or convicted or is or is not amenable to justice.

587. Where the complete commission of an offence charged is not proved but the evidence establishes an attempt to commit the offence, the accused may be convicted of the attempt.

588. (1) Where an attempt to commit an offence is charged but the evidence establishes the commission of the complete offence, the accused is not entitled to be acquitted, but the jury may convict him of the attempt unless the judge presiding at the trial, in his discretion, discharges the jury from giving a verdict and directs that the accused be indicted for the complete offence.

(2) An accused who is convicted under this section is not liable to be tried again for the offence that he was charged with attempting to commit.

589. (1) A count in an indictment is divisible and where the commission of the offence charged, as described in the enactment creating it or as charged in the count, includes the commission of another offence, whether punishable by indictment or on summary conviction, the accused may be convicted

(a) of an offence so included that is proved, notwithstanding that the whole offence that is charged is not proved, or

(b) of an attempt to commit an offence so included.

Protection of Persons Administering and Enforcing the Law

Protection of persons acting under authority

25. (1) Every one who is required or authorized by law to do anything in the administration or enforcement of the law

(*a*) as a private person,

(*b*) as a peace officer or public officer, 2

(*c*) in aid of a peace officer or public officer, or

(*d*) by virtue of his office,

is, if he acts on reasonable and probable grounds, justified in doing what he is required or authorized to do and in using as much force as is necessary for that purpose.

Idem

(2) Where a person is required or authorized by law to execute a process or to carry out a sentence, he or any person who assists him is, if he acts in good faith, justified in executing the process or in carrying out the sentence notwithstanding that the process or sentence is defective or that it was issued or imposed without jurisdiction or in excess of jurisdiction.

When not protected

(3) Subject to subsection (4), a person is not justified for the purposes of subsection (1) in using force that is intended or is likely to cause death or grievous bodily harm unless he believes on reasonable and probable grounds that it is necessary for the purpose of preserving himself or any one under his protection from death or grievous bodily harm.

When protected

(4) A peace officer who is proceeding lawfully to arrest, with or without warrant, any person for an offence for which that person may be arrested without warrant, and every one lawfully assisting the peace officer, is justified, if the person to be arrested takes flight to avoid arrest, in using as much force as is necessary to prevent the escape by flight, unless the escape can be prevented by reasonable means in a less violent manner. 1953-54, c. 51, s. 25.

Excessive force

26. Every one who is authorized by law to use force is criminally responsible for any excess thereof according to the nature and quality of the act that constitutes the excess. 1953-54, c. 51, s. 26.

Use of force to prevent commission of offence

27. Every one is justified in using as much force as is reasonably necessary

(*a*) to prevent the commission of an offence

(i) for which, if it were committed, the person who committed it might be arrested without warrant, and

(ii) that would be likely to cause immediate and serious injury to the person or property of anyone; or

(*b*) to prevent anything being done that, on reasonable and probable grounds he believes would, if it were done, be an offence mentioned in paragraph (*a*). 1953-54, c. 51, s. 27.

Arrest of wrong person

28. (1) Where a person who is authorized to execute a warrant to arrest believes, in good faith and on reasonable and probable grounds, that the person whom he arrests is the person named in the warrant, he is protected from criminal responsibility in respect thereof to the same extent as if that person were the person named in the warrant.

Person assisting

(2) Where a person is authorized to execute a warrant to arrest,

(a) every one who, being called upon to assist him, believes that the person in whose arrest he is called upon to assist is the person named in the warrant, and

(b) every keeper of a prison who is required to receive and detain a person who he believes has been arrested under the warrant, 2 [33]

is protected from criminal responsibility in respect thereof to the same extent as if that person were the person named in the warrant. 1953-54, c. 51, s. 28.

Duty of person arresting

29. (1) It is the duty of every one who executes a process or warrant to have it with him, where it is feasible to do so, and to produce it when requested to do so.

Notice

(2) It is the duty of every one who arrests a person, whether with or without warrant, to give notice to that person, where it is feasible to do so, of

(a) the process or warrant under which he makes the arrest, or

(b) the reason for the arrest.

Failure to comply

(3) Failure to comply with subsection (1) or (2) does not of itself deprive a person who executes a process or warrant, or a person who makes an arrest, or those who assist them, of protection from criminal responsibility. 1953-54. c. 51, s. 29.

Preventing breach of peace

30. Every one who witnesses a breach of the peace is justified in interfering to prevent the continuance or renewal thereof and may detain any person who commits or is about to join in or to renew the breach of the peace, for the purpose of giving him into the custody of a peace officer, if he uses no more force than is reasonably necessary to prevent the continuance or renewal of the breach of the peace or than is reasonably proportioned to the danger to be apprehended from the continuance or renewal of the breach of the peace. 1953-54, c. 51, s. 30.

Arrest for breach of peace

31. (1) Every peace officer who witnesses a breach of the peace and every 2 [33]
one who lawfully assists him is justified in arresting any person whom he finds committing the breach of the peace or who, on reasonable and probable grounds, he believes is about to join in or renew the breach of the peace.

Giving person in charge

(2) Every peace officer is justified in receiving into custody any person who is given into his charge as having been a party to a breach of the peace by one who has, or who on reasonable and probable grounds he believes has, witnessed the breach of the peace. 1953-54, c. 51, s. 31.

Suppression of Riots

Use of force to suppress riot

32. (1) Every peace officer is justified in using or in ordering the use of as much force as he believes, in good faith and on reasonable and probable grounds, 2

(*a*) is necessary to suppress a riot, and 65

(*b*) is not excessive, having regard to the danger to be apprehended from the continuance of the riot.

70. A peace officer who receives notice that there is a riot within his jurisdiction and, without reasonable excuse, fails to take all reasonable steps to suppress the riot is guilty of an indictable offence and is liable to imprisonment for two years.

118. Every one who

(*a*) resists or wilfully obstructs a public officer or peace officer in the execution of his duty or any person lawfully acting in aid of such an officer,

(*b*) omits, without reasonable excuse, to assist a public officer or peace officer in the execution of his duty in arresting a person or in preserving the peace, after having reasonable notice that he is required to do so, or

(*c*) resists or wilfully obstructs any person in the lawful execution of a process against lands or goods or in making a lawful distress or seizure,

is guilty of

(*d*) an indictable offence and is liable to imprisonment for two years, or

(*e*) an offence punishable on summary conviction.

Person bound by military law

(2) Every one who is bound by military law to obey the command of his superior officer is justified in obeying any command given by his superior officer for the suppression of a riot unless the order is manifestly unlawful.

Obeying order of peace officer

(3) Every one is justified in obeying an order of a peace officer to use force to suppress a riot if

(*a*) he acts in good faith, and

(*b*) the order is not manifestly unlawful.

Apprehension of serious mischief

(4) Every one who, in good faith and on reasonable and probable grounds, believes that serious mischief will result from a riot before it is possible to secure 387
the attendance of a peace officer is justified in using as much force as he believes in good faith and on reasonable grounds,

(*a*) is necessary to suppress the riot, and

(*b*) is not excessive, having regard to the danger to be apprehended from the continuance of the riot.

Question of law

(5) For the purposes of this section the question whether an order is manifestly unlawful or not is a question of law. 1953-54, c. 51, s. 32.

65. A riot is an unlawful assembly that has begun to disturb the peace tumultuously.

64. (1) An unlawful assembly is an assembly of three or more persons who, with intent to carry out any common purpose, assemble in such a manner or so conduct themselves when they are assembled as to cause persons in the neighbourhood of the assembly to fear, on reasonable grounds, that they

(*a*) will disturb the peace tumultuously, or

(*b*) will by that assembly needlessly and without reasonable cause provoke other persons to disturb the peace tumultuously.

387. (1) Every one commits mischief who wilfully

(a) destroys or damages property,

(b) renders property dangerous, useless, inoperative or ineffective,

(c) obstructs, interrupts or intereferes with the lawful use, enjoyment or operation of property, or

(d) obstructs, interrupts or interferes with any person in the lawful use, enjoyment or operation of property.

Duty of officers if rioters do not disperse

33. (1) Where the proclamation referred to in section 68 has been made or an offence against paragraph 69*(a)* or *(b)* has been committed, it is the duty of a peace officer and of a person who is lawfully required by him to assist, to disperse or to arrest persons who do not comply with the proclamation.

Protection of officers

(2) No civil or criminal proceedings lie against a peace officer or a person who is lawfully required by a peace officer to assist him in respect of any death or injury that by reason of resistance is caused as a result of the performance by the peace officer or that person of a duty that is imposed by subsection (1).

Section not restrictive

(3) Nothing in this section limits or affects any powers, duties or functions that are conferred or imposed by this Act with respect to the suppression of riots. 1953-54, c. 51, s. 33.

2. In this Act

"peace officer" includes

(a) a mayor, warden, reeve, sheriff, deputy sheriff, sheriff's officer and justice of the peace,

(b) a warden, deputy warden, instructor, keeper, gaoler, guard and any other officer or permanent employee of a prison,

(c) a police officer, police constable, bailiff, constable, or other person employed for the preservation and maintenance of the public peace or for the service or execution of civil process,

(d) an officer or person having the powers of a customs or excise officer when performing any duty in the administration of the *Customs Act* or the *Excise Act*,

(d.1) a person appointed or designated as a fishery officer under the *Fisheries Act* when performing any of his duties or functions pursuant to that Act,

(e) the pilot in command of an aircraft

(i) registered in Canada under regulations made under the *Aeronautics Act*, or

(ii) leased without crew and operated by a person who is qualified under regulations made under the *Aeronautics Act* to be registered as owner of an aircraft registered in Canada under those regulations,

while the aircraft is in flight, and

(f) officers and men of the Canadian Forces who are

(i) appointed for the purposes of section 134 of the *National Defence Act*, or

(ii) employed on duties that the Governor in Council, in regulations made under the *National Defence Act* for the purposes of this paragraph, has prescribed to be of such a kind as to necessitate that the officers and men performing them have the powers of peace officers;

"prison" includes a penitentiary, common gaol, public or reformatory prison, lock-up, guard-room or other place in which persons who are charged with or convicted of offences are usually kept in custody;

Defence of Person

Self defence against unprovoked assault

34. (1) Every one who is unlawfully assaulted without having provoked the 36
assault is justified in repelling force by force if the force he uses is not intended to cause death or grievous bodily harm and is no more than is necessary to enable him to defend himself.

Extent of justification

(2) Every one who is unlawfully assaulted and who causes death or grievous bodily harm in repelling the assault is justified if

(a) he causes it under reasonable apprehension of death or grievous bodily harm from the violence with which the assault was originally made or with which the assailant pursues his purposes, and

(b) he believes, on reasonable and probable grounds, that he cannot otherwise preserve himself from death or grievous bodily harm. 1953-54, c. 51, s. 34.

Self defence in case of aggression

35. Every one who has without justification assaulted another but did not commence the assault with intent to cause death or grievous bodily harm, or has
without justification provoked an assault upon himself by another, may justify 36
the use of force subsequent to the assault if

(a) he uses the force

(i) under reasonable apprehension of death or grievous bodily harm from the violence of the person whom he has assaulted or provoked, and

(ii) in the belief, on reasonable and probable grounds, that it is necessary in order to preserve himself from death or grievous bodily harm;

(b) he did not, at any time before the necessity of preserving himself from death or grievous bodily harm arose, endeavour to cause death or grievous bodily harm; and

(c) he declined further conflict and quitted or retreated from it as far as it was feasible to do so before the necessity of preserving himself from death or grievous bodily harm arose. 1953-54, c. 51, s. 35.

Provocation

36. Provocation includes, for the purposes of section 34 and 35, provocation by blows, words or gestures. 1953-54, c. 51, s. 36.

Preventing assault

37. (1) Every one is justified in using force to defend himself or any one under his protection from assault, if he uses no more force than is necessary to prevent the assault or the repetition of it.

Extent of justification

(2) Nothing in this section shall be deemed to justify the wilful infliction of
any hurt or mischief that is excessive, having regard to the nature of the assault 387
that the force used was intended to prevent. 1953-54, c. 51, s. 37.

Defence of Property

Defence of movable property

38. (1) Every one who is in peaceable possession of movable property, and every one lawfully assisting him, is justified

(a) in preventing a trespasser from taking it, or

(b) in taking it from a trespasser who has taken it,

if he does not strike or cause bodily harm to the trespasser.

Assault by trespasser

(2) Where a person who is in peaceable possession of movable property lays hands upon it, a trespasser who persists in attempting to keep it or take it from him or from any one lawfully assisting him shall be deemed to commit an assault without justification or provocation. 1953-54, c. 51, s. 38. 245(1)

245. (1) Every one who commits a common assault is guilty of an offence punishable on summary conviction.

Defence with claim of right

39. (1) Every one who is in peaceable possession of movable property under a claim of right, and every one acting under his authority is protected from criminal responsibility for defending that possession, even against a person entitled by law to possession of it, if he uses no more force than is necessary.

Defence without claim of right

(2) Every one who is in peaceable possession of movable property, but does not claim it as of right or does not act under the authority of a person who claims it as of right, is not justified or protected from criminal responsibility for defending his possession against a person who is entitled by law to possession of it. 1953-54, c. 51, s. 39.

Defence of dwelling

40. Every one who is in peaceable possession of a dwelling-house, and every one lawfully assisting him or acting under his authority, is justified in using as much force as is necessary to prevent any person from forcibly breaking into or forcibly entering the dwelling-house without lawful authority. 1953-54,c.51,s.40. 2

2. In this Act

"dwelling-house" means the whole or any part of a building or structure that is kept or occupied as a permanent or temporary residence and includes

(a) a building within the curtilage of a dwelling-house that is connected to it by a doorway or by a covered and enclosed passageway, and

(b) a unit that is designed to be mobile and to be used as a permanent or temporary residence and that is being used as such a residence;

Defence of house or real property

41. (1) Every one who is in peaceable possession of a dwelling-house or real property and every one lawfully assisting him or acting under his authority is justified in using force to prevent any person from trespassing on the dwelling-house or real property, or to remove a trespasser therefrom, if he uses no more force than is necessary.

Assault by trespasser

(2) A trespasser who resists an attempt by a person who is in peaceable possession of a dwelling-house or real property or a person lawfully assisting him or acting under his authority to prevent his entry or to remove him, shall be deemed to commit an assault without justification or provocation. 1953-54, c. 51, s. 41. 245(1)

Assertion of right to house or real property

42. (1) Every one is justified in peaceably entering a dwelling-house or real property by day to take possession of it if he, or some person under whose authority he acts, is lawfully entitled to possession of it. 2

Assault in case of lawful entry

(2) Where a person

(a) not having peaceable possession of a dwelling-house or real property under a claim of right, or

(b) not acting under the authority of a person who has peaceable possession of a dwelling-house or real property under a claim of right,

assaults a person who is lawfully entitled to possession of it and who is entering it peaceably by day to take possession of it, for the purpose of preventing him from entering, the assault shall be deemed to be without justification or provocation.

Trespasser provoking assault

(3) Where a person

(a) having peaceable possession of a dwelling-house or real property under a 2
claim of right, or

(b) acting under the authority of a person who has peaceable possession of a dwelling-house or real property under a claim of right,

assaults any person who is lawfully entitled to possession of it and who is entering
it peaceably by day to take possession of it, for the purpose of preventing him 2
from entering, the assault shall be deemed to be provoked by the person who is entering. 1953-54, c. 51, s. 42.

2. In this Act

"day" means the period between six o'clock in the forenoon and nine o'clock in the afternoon of the same day;

Protection of Persons in Authority

Correction of child by force

43. Every schoolteacher, parent or person standing in the place of a parent is justified in using force by way of correction toward a pupil or child, as the case may be, who is under his care, if the force does not exceed what is reasonable under the circumstances. 1953-54, c. 51, s. 43.

Master of ship maintaining discipline

44. The master or officer in command of a vessel on a voyage is justified in using as much force as he believes, on reasonable and probable grounds, is necessary for the purpose of maintaining good order and discipline on the vessel. 1953-54, c. 51., s.44.

26. Every one who is authorized by law to use force is criminally responsible for any excess thereof according to the nature and quality of the act that constitutes the excess.

Surgical operations

45. Every one is protected from criminal responsibility for performing a surgical operation upon any person for the benefit of that person if

(a) the operation is performed with reasonable care and skill, and

(b) it is reasonable to perform the operation, having regard to the state of health of the person at the time the operation is performed and to all the circumstances of the case. 1953-54, c. 51. s. 45.

198. Every one who undertakes to administer surgical or medical treatment to another person or to do any other lawful acts that may endanger the life of another person is, except in cases of necessity, under a legal duty to have and to use reasonable knowledge, skill and care in so doing.

PART II

OFFENCES AGAINST PUBLIC ORDER

Treason and other Offences against the Queen's Authority and Person

High treason

46. (1) Every one commits high treason who, in Canada,

(a) kills or attempts to kill Her Majesty, or does her any bodily harm tending to death or destruction, maims or wounds her, or imprisons or restrains her; 24

(b) levies war against Canada or does any act preparatory thereto; or

(c) assists an enemy at war with Canada, or any armed forces against whom Canadian Forces are engaged in hostilities whether or not a state of war exists between Canada and the country whose forces they are. 2

Treason

(2) Every one commits treason who, in Canada,

(a) uses force or violence for the purpose of overthrowing the government of Canada or a province; 28 Interp

(b) without lawful authority, communicates or makes available to an agent of a state other than Canada, military or scientific information or any sketch, plan, model, article, note or document of a military or scientific character that he knows or ought to know may be used by that state for a purpose prejudicial to the safety or defence of Canada;

(c) conspires with any person to commit high treason or to do anything mentioned in paragraph *(a)*;

(d) forms an intention to do anything that is high treason or that is mentioned in paragraph *(a)* and manifests that intention by an overt act; or

(e) conspires with any person to do anything mentioned in paragraph *(b)* or forms an intention to do anything mentioned in paragraph *(b)* and manifests that intention by an overt act.

Canadian citizen

(3) Notwithstanding subsection (1) or (2), a Canadian citizen or a person who owes allegiance to Her Majesty in right of Canada,

(a) commits high treason if, while in or out of Canada, he does anything mentioned in subsection (1); or 26(6) Interp

(b) commits treason if, while in or out of Canada, he does anything mentioned in subsection (2).

Overt act

(4) Where it is treason to conspire with any person, the act of conspiring is an overt act of treason. 1953-54, c. 51, s. 46; 1974-75-76, c. 105, s. 2.

2. In this Act
"Canadian Forces" means the armed forces of Her Majesty raised by Canada;

24. (1) Every one who, having an intent to commit an offence, does or omits to do anything for the purpose of carrying out his intention is guilty of an attempt to commit the offence whether or not it was possible under the circumstances to commit the offence.

(2) The question whether an act or omission by a person who has an intent to commit an offence is or is not mere preparation to commit the offence, and too remote to constitute an attempt to commit the offence, is a question of law.

Interpretation Act

26. (6) Words importing male persons include female persons and corporations.

28. In every enactment
"province" means a province of Canada, and includes the Yukon Territory and the Northwest Territories;

Punishment for high treason
Type 'G' Offence 427(b), (d) and (e)
IPA offence 178.1

47. (1) Every one who commits high treason is guilty of an indictable offence and shall be sentenced to imprisonment for life. 669

669. The sentence to be pronounced against a person who is to be sentenced to imprisonment for life shall be,

(a) in respect of a person who has been convicted of high treason or first degree murder, that he be sentenced to imprisonment for life without eligibility for parole until he has served twenty-five years of his sentence;

(b) in respect of a person who has been convicted of second degree murder,. . . . .

(c) in respect of a person who has been convicted of any other offence, that he be sentenced to imprisonment for life with normal eligibility for parole. Parole Act Reg's section 6

Punishment for treason

(2) Every one who commits treason is guilty of an indictable offence and is liable

Type 'G' Offence 427(b), (d) and (e)
IPA offence 178.1

(a) to be sentenced to imprisonment for life if he is guilty of an offence under paragraph 46(2)(a), (c) or (d); 669

(b) to be sentenced to imprisonment for life if he is guilty of an offence under paragraph 46(2)(b) or (e) committed while a state of war exists between Canada and another country; or

(c) to be sentenced to imprisonment for fourteen years if he is guilty of an offence under paragraph 46(2)(b) or (e) committed while no state of war exists between Canada and another country.

Corroboration

(3) No person shall be convicted of high treason or treason upon the evidence of only one witness, unless the evidence of that witness is corroborated in a material particular by evidence that implicates the accused.

Minimum punishment

(4) For the purposes of Part XX, the sentence of imprisonment for life prescribed by subsection (1) is a minimum punishment. 1953-54, c. 51, s. 47; 1974-75-76, c. 105, s. 2.

510. (4) Where an accused is charged with an offence under section 47 or sections 49 to 53, every overt act that is to be relied upon shall be stated in the indictment.

511. No person shall be convicted for the offence of high treason or first degree murder unless in the indictment charging the offence he is specifically charged with that offence.

529. (9) The authority of a court to amend indictments does not authorize the court to add to the overt acts stated in an indictment for high treason or treason or for an offence against any provision in sections 49, 50, 51 and 53.

532. (1) An accused who is indicted for high treason or treason or for being an accessory after the fact to high treason or treason is entitled to receive, after the indictment has been found and at least ten days before his arraignment,

(a) a copy of the indictment,

(b) a list of the witnesses to be produced on the trial to prove the indictment, and

(c) a copy of the panel of jurors who are to try him, returned by the sheriff.

(2) The list of the witnesses and the copy of the panel of the jurors referred to in subsection (1) shall mention the names, occupations and places of abode of the witnesses and jurors respectively.

(3) The writings referred to in subsection (1) shall be given to the accused at the same time and in the presence of at least two witnesses.

(4) This section does not apply to the offence of high treason by killing Her Majesty, or to the offence of high treason where the overt act alleged in an attempt to injure the person of Her Majesty in any manner or to the offence of being an accessory after the fact in such a case of high treason.

Limitation

48. (1) No proceedings for an offence of treason as defined by paragraph 46(2)(*a*) shall be commenced more than three years after the time when the offence is alleged to have been committed.

Information for treasonable words

(2) No proceedings shall be commenced under section 47 in respect of an overt act of treason expressed or declared by open and considered speech unless

(*a*) an information setting out the overt act and the words by which it was expressed or declared is laid under oath before a justice within six days after the time when the words are alleged to have been spoken, and

(*b*) a warrant for the arrest of the accused is issued within ten days after the time when the information is laid. 1953-54, c. 51, s. 48; 1974-75-76, c. 105, s. 29. 25(3) Interp

Interpretation Act

25. (3) Where there is a reference to a number of days, not expressed to be clear days, between two events, in calculating the number of days there shall be excluded the day on which the first event happens and there shall be included the day on which the second event happens.

Prohibited Acts

Acts intended to alarm Her Majesty or break public peace

Type 'G' Offence 427(d) and (e)

49. Every one who wilfully, in the presence of Her Majesty, 510(4)

(*a*) does an act with intent to alarm Her Majesty or to break the public peace, or 529(9)

55

(*b*) does an act that is intended or is likely to cause bodily harm to Her Majesty,

is guilty of an indictable offence and is liable to imprisonment for fourteen years. 1953-54, c. 51, s. 49.

Assisting alien enemy to leave Canada, or omitting to prevent treason

50. (1) Every one commits an offence who

(*a*) incites or wilfully assists a subject of

(i) a state that is at war with Canada, or

(ii) a state against whose forces Canadian Forces are engaged in hostilities, whether or not a state of war exists between Canada and the state whose forces they are, 2

to leave Canada without the consent of the Crown, unless the accused establishes that assistance to the state referred to in subparagraph (i) or the forces of the state referred to in subparagraph (ii), as the case may be, was not intended thereby; or

(*b*) knowing that a person is about to commit high treason or treason does not, with all reasonable dispatch, inform a justice of the peace or other peace officer thereof or make other reasonable efforts to prevent that person from committing high treason or treason. 2

Punishment

Type 'E' Offence

(2) Every one who commits an offence under subsection (1) is guilty of an indictable offence and is liable to imprisonment for fourteen years. 1953-54, c. 51, s. 50; 1974-75-76, c. 105, s. 29. 510(4)

529(9)

55

Intimidating Parliament or legislature

Type 'G' Offence 427(d) (e) IPA offence 178.1

51. Every one who does an act of violence in order to intimidate the Parliament of Canada or the legislature of a province is guilty of an indictable offence and is liable to imprisonment for fourteen years. 1953-54, c. 51, s. 51.

Section 381 for general intimidation

Sabotage

Type 'E' Offence

IPA offence 178.1

52. (1) Every one who does a prohibited act for a purpose prejudicial to ss (2)

(*a*) the safety, security or defence of Canada, or 510(4)

(*b*) the safety or security of the naval, army or air forces of any state other than Canada that are lawfully present in Canada, 529(9)

is guilty of an indictable offence and is liable to imprisonment for ten years. 55

"Prohibited act"

(2) In this section, "prohibited act" means an act or omission that

(*a*) impairs the efficiency or impedes the working of any vessel, vehicle, aircraft, machinery, apparatus or other thing, or

(*b*) causes property, by whomsoever it may be owned, to be lost, damaged or destroyed.

Saving

(3) No person does a prohibited act within the meaning of this section by reason only that

(*a*) he stops work as a result of the failure of his employer and himself to agree upon any matter relating to his employment,

(*b*) he stops work as a result of the failure of his employer and a bargaining agent acting on his behalf to agree upon any matter relating to his employment, or

(*c*) he stops work as a result of his taking part in a combination of workmen or employees for their own reasonable protection as workmen or employees.

Idem

(4) No person does a prohibited act within the meaning of this section by reason only that he attends at or near or approaches a dwelling-house or place for the purpose only of obtaining or communicating information. 1953-54, c. 51, s. 52. 2

Inciting to mutiny

Type 'G' Offence 427(d) (e)

53. Every one who

(*a*) attempts, for a traitorous or mutinous purpose, to seduce a member of the Canadian Forces from his duty and allegiance to Her Majesty, or 24[46] 2[46]

(*b*) attempts to incite or to induce a member of the Canadian Forces to commit a traitorous or mutinous act, 510(4)

is guilty of an indictable offence and is liable to imprisonment for fourteen years. 1953-54, c. 51, s. 53. 529(9) 55

Assisting deserter

Type 'A' Offence with consent

54. Every one who aids, assists, harbours or conceals a person who he knows is a deserter or absentee without leave from the Canadian Forces is guilty of an offence punishable on summary conviction, but no proceedings shall be instituted under this section without the consent of the Attorney General of Canada. 1953-54, c. 51, s. 54. 722(1) 2

Evidence of overt acts

55. In proceedings for an offence against any provision in section 47 or sections 49 to 53, no evidence is admissible of an overt act unless that overt act is set out in the indictment or unless the evidence is otherwise relevant as tending to prove an overt act that is set out therein. 1953-54, c. 51, s. 55.

56. Repealed. 1972, c. 13, s. 5.

Offences in relation to members of R.C.M.P.

Type 'A' Offence

57. Every one who wilfully

(a) procures, persuades or counsels a member of the Royal Canadian Mounted Police to desert or absent himself without leave,

(b) aids, assists, harbours or conceals a member of the Royal Canadian Mounted Police who he knows is a deserter or absentee without leave, or

(c) aids or assists a member of the Royal Canadian Mounted Police to desert or absent himself without leave, knowing that the member is about to desert or absent himself without leave,

is guilty of an offence punishable on summary conviction. 1953-54, c. 51, s. 57. 722(1)

722. (1) Except where otherwise expressly provided by law, every one who is convicted of an offence punishable on summary conviction is liable to a fine of not more than five hundred dollars or to imprisonment for six months or to both.

Passports

Forgery of or uttering forged passport

Type 'E' Offence

IPA offence 178.1

58. (1) Every one who, while in or out of Canada,

(a) forges a passport, or ss (5)

(b) knowing that a passport is forged

(i) uses, deals with or acts upon it, or

(ii) causes or attempts to cause any person to use, deal with, or act upon it, as if the passport were genuine,

is guilty of an indictable offence and is liable to imprisonment for fourteen years.

False statement to procure passport

Type 'D' Offence

IPA offence 178.1

(2) Every one who, while in or out of Canada, for the purposes of procuring a passport for himself or any other person, makes a written or oral statement that he knows is false or misleading is guilty of an indictable offence and is liable to imprisonment for two years.

Possession of forged, etc., passport

Type 'D' Offence

IPA offence 178.1

(3) Every one who without lawful excuse, the proof of which lies upon him, has in his possession a forged passport or a passport in respect of which an offence under subsection (2) has been committed is guilty of an indictable offence and is liable to imprisonment for five years.

Special provisions applicable

(4) For the purposes of proceedings under this section

(a) the place where a passport was forged is not material; and

(b) the definition "false document" in section 282, section 324 and subsection 325(2) are applicable *mutatis mutandis.*

"Passport"

(5) In this section "passport" means a document issued by or under the authority of the Secretary of State for External Affairs for the purpose of identifying the holder thereof. 1968-69, c. 38, s. 4.

mutatis mutandis — after the necessary changes in detail so that the text applies

282. In this Part

"false document" means a document

(a) the whole or some material part of which purports to be made by or on behalf of a person

(i) who did not make it or authorize it to be made, or

(ii) who did not in fact exist;

(b) that is made by or on behalf of the person who purports to make it but is false in some material particular;

(c) that is made in the name of an existing person, by him or under his authority, with a fraudulent intention that it should pass as being made by some person, real or fictitious, other than the person who makes it or under whose authority it is made;

324. (1) Every one commits forgery who makes a false document, knowing it to be false, with intent

(a) that it should in any way be used or acted upon as genuine, to the prejudice of any one whether within Canada or not, or

(b) that some person should be induced, by the belief that it is genuine, to do or to refrain from doing anything, whether within Canada or not.

(2) Making a false document includes

(a) altering a genuine document in any material part,

(b) making a material addition to a genuine document or adding to it a false date, attestation, seal or other thing that is material, or

(c) making a material alteration in a genuine document by erasure, obliteration, removal or in any other way.

(3) Forgery is complete as soon as a document is made with the knowledge and intent referred to in subsection (1), notwithstanding that the person who makes it does not intend that any particular person should use or act upon it as genuine or be induced, by the belief that it is genuine, to do or refrain from doing anything.

(4) Forgery is complete notwithstanding that the false document is incomplete or does not purport to be a document that is binding in law, if it is such as to indicate that it was intended to be acted upon as genuine.

325. (2) No person shall be convicted of an offence under this section upon the evidence of only one witness unless the evidence of that witness is corroborated in a material particular by evidence that implicates the accused.

514. No count that charges

(a) perjury,

(b) the making of a false oath or a false statement,

(c) fabricating evidence, or

(d) procuring the commission of an offence mentioned in paragraph (a), (b) or (c),

is insufficient by reason only that it does not state the nature of the authority of the tribunal before which the oath or statement was taken or made, or the subject of the inquiry, or the words used or the evidence fabricated, or that it does not expressly negative the truth of the words used.

Fraudulent use of certificate of citizenship

Type 'D' Offence

59. (1) Every one who, while in or out of Canada,

(a) uses a certificate of citizenship or a certificate of naturalization for a fraudulent purpose, or ss (2)

(b) being a person to whom a certificate of citizenship or a certificate of naturalization has been granted, knowingly parts with the possession of that certificate with intent that it should be used for a fraudulent purpose,

is guilty of an indictable offence and is liable to imprisonment for two years.

"Certificate of citizenship" "certificate of naturalization"

(2) In this section, "certificate of citizenship" and "certificate of naturalization", respectively, mean a certificate of citizenship and a certificate of naturalization as defined by the *Canadian Citizenship Act.* 1953-54, c. 51, s. 59; 1968-69, c. 38, s. 5.

Citizenship Act

2. (1) In this Act

"certificate of citizenship" means a certificate of citizenship issued or granted under this Act or the former Act;

"certificate of naturalization" means a certificate of naturalization granted under any Act that was in force in Canada at any time before the 1st day January, 1947;

"former Act" means the *Canadian Citizenship Act;*

Sedition

Seditious words

60. (1) Seditious words are words that express a seditious intention.

Seditious libel

(2) A seditious libel is a libel that expresses a seditious intention.

Seditious conspiracy

(3) A seditious conspiracy is an agreement between two or more persons to carry out a seditious intention.

Seditious intention

(4) Without limiting the generality of the meaning of the expression "seditious intention", every one shall be presumed to have a seditious intention who

(a) teaches or advocates, or

(b) publishes or circulates any writing that advocates,

the use, without the authority of law, of force as a means of accomplishing a governmental change within Canada. 1953-54, c. 51, s. 60.

Exception

61. Notwithstanding subsection 60(4), no person shall be deemed to have a seditious intention by reason only that he intends, in good faith,

(a) to show that Her Majesty has been misled or mistaken in her measures;

(b) to point out errors or defects in

(i) the government or constitution of Canada or a province, 28 Interp

(ii) the Parliament of Canada or the legislature of a province, or

(iii) the administration of justice in Canada;

(c) to procure, by lawful means, the alteration of any matter of government in Canada; or

(d) to point out, for the purpose of removal, matters that produce or tend to produce feelings of hostility and ill-will between different classes of persons in Canada. 1953-54, c. 51, s. 61.

Punishment of seditious offences

Type 'G' Offence 427(d) (e)
IPA offence 178.1

62. Every one who

(a) speaks seditious words, 60(1)

(b) publishes a seditious libel, or 60(2)

(c) is a party to a seditious conspiracy, 60(3)

is guilty of an indictable offence and is liable to imprisonment for fourteen years. 1953-54, c. 51, s. 62.

513. (1) No count for publishing a blasphemous, seditious or defamatory libel, or for selling or exhibiting an obscene book, pamphlet, newspaper or other written matter, is insufficient by reason only that it does not set out the words that are alleged to be libellous or the writing that is alleged to be obscene.

Offences in relation to military forces

Type 'D' Offence

63. (1) Every one who wilfully

(a) interferes with, impairs or influences the loyalty or discipline of a member of a force,

(b) publishes, edits, issues, circulates or distributes a writing that advises, counsels or urges insubordination, disloyalty, mutiny or refusal of duty by a member of a force, or ss (2)

(c) advises, counsels, urges or in any manner causes insubordination, disloyalty, mutiny or refusal of duty by a member of a force,

is guilty of an indictable offence and is liable to imprisonment for five years.

"Member of a force"

(2) In this section, "member of a force" means a member of

(a) the Canadian Forces, or 2

(b) the naval, army or air forces of a state other than Canada that are lawfully present in Canada. 1953-54, c. 51, s. 63.

Unlawful Assemblies and Riots

Unlawful assembly

64. (1) An unlawful assembly is an assembly of three or more persons who, with intent to carry out any common purpose, assemble in such a manner or so conduct themselves when they are assembled as to cause persons in the neighbourhood of the assembly to fear, on reasonable grounds, that they

(a) will disturb the peace tumultuously, or

(b) will by that assembly needlessly and without reasonable cause provoke other persons to disturb the peace tumultuously.

Lawful assembly becoming unlawful

(2) Persons who are lawfully assembled may become an unlawful assembly if they conduct themselves with a common purpose in a manner that would have made the assembly unlawful if they had assembled in that manner for that purpose.

Exception

(3) Persons are not unlawfully assembled by reason only that they are assembled to protect the dwelling-house of any one of them against persons who are threatening to break and enter it for the purpose of committing an indictable offence therein. 1953-54, c. 51, s. 64.

Riot

65. A riot is an unlawful assembly that has begun to disturb the peace tumultuously. 1953-54, c. 51, s. 65. 64

Punishment of rioter

Type 'D' Offence

66. Every one who takes part in a riot is guilty of an indictable offence and is liable to imprisonment for two years. 1953-54, c. 51, s. 66. 65

Punishment for unlawful assembly

Type 'A' Offence

67. Every one who is a member of an unlawful assembly is guilty of an offence punishable on summary conviction. 1953-54, c. 51, s. 67. 64 722(1)

Reading proclamation

68. A justice, mayor or sheriff or the lawful deputy of a mayor or sheriff who receives notice that, at any place within his jurisdiction, twelve or more persons are unlawfully and riotously assembled together, shall go to that place and, after approaching as near as safely he may do, if he is satisfied that a riot is in progress, shall command silence and thereupon make or cause to be made in a loud voice a proclamation in the following words or to the like effect: 2

Her Majesty the Queen charges and commands all persons being assembled immediately to disperse and peaceably to depart to their habitations or to their lawful business upon the pain of being guilty of an offence for which, upon conviction, they may be sentenced to imprisonment for life. GOD SAVE THE QUEEN.

1953-54, c. 51, s. 68.

Offences related to proclamation

Type 'E' Offence

69. Every one is guilty of an indictable offence and is liable to imprisonment for life who 669

(a) opposes, hinders or assaults, wilfully and with force, a person who begins to make or is about to begin to make or is making the proclamation referred to in section 68 so that it is not made,

(b) does not peaceably disperse and depart from a place where the proclamation referred to in section 68 is made within thirty minutes after it is made, or

(c) does not depart from a place within thirty minutes when he has reasonable ground to believe that the proclamation referred to in section 68 would have been made in that place if some person had not opposed, hindered or assaulted, wilfully and with force, a person who would have made it. 1953-54,c.51,s.69.

Neglect by peace officer

Type 'D' Offence

70. A peace officer who receives notice that there is a riot within his jurisdiction and, without reasonable excuse, fails to take all reasonable steps to suppress the riot is guilty of an indictable offence and is liable to imprisonment for two years. 1953-54, c. 51, s. 70. 2

2. In this Act

"peace officer" includes

(a) a mayor, warden, reeve, sheriff, deputy sheriff, sheriff's officer and justice of the peace,

(b) a warden, deputy warden, instructor, keeper, gaoler, guard and any other officer or permanent employee of a prison,

(c) a police officer, police constable, bailiff, constable, or other person employed for the preservation and maintenance of the public peace or for the service or execution of civil process,

(d) an officer or person having the powers of a customs or excise officer when performing any duty in the administration of the *Customs Act* or the *Excise Act*,

(d.1) a person appointed or designated as a fishery officer under the *Fisheries Act* when performing any of his duties or functions pursuant to that Act,

(e) the pilot in command of an aircraft

(i) registered in Canada under regulations made under the *Aeronautics Act*, or

(ii) leased without crew and operated by a person who is qualified under regulations made under the *Aeronautics Act* to be registered as owner of an aircraft registered in Canada under those regulations,

while the aircraft is in flight, and

(f) officers and men of the Canadian Forces who are

(i) appointed for the purposes of section 134 of the *National Defence Act*, or

(ii) employed on duties that the Governor in Council, in regulations made under the *National Defence Act* for the purposes of this paragraph, has prescribed to be of such a kind as to necessitate that the officers and men performing them have the powers of peace officers;

32. (1) Every peace officer is justified in using or in ordering the use of as much force as he believes, in good faith and on reasonable and probable grounds,

(a) is necessary to suppress a riot, and

(b) is not excessive, having regard to the danger to be apprehended from the continuance of the riot.

(2) Every one who is bound by military law to obey the command of his superior officer is justified in obeying any command given by his superior officer for the suppression of a riot unless the order is manifestly unlawful.

(3) Every one is justified in obeying an order of a peace officer to use force to suppress a riot if

(a) he acts in good faith, and

(b) the order is not manifestly unlawful.

(4) Every one who, in good faith and on reasonable and probable grounds, believes that serious mischief will result from a riot before it is possible to secure the attendance of a peace officer is justified in using as much force as he believes in good faith and on reasonable grounds,

(a) is necessary to suppress the riot, and

(b) is not excessive, having regard to the danger to be apprehended from the continuance of the riot.

(5) For the purposes of this section the question whether an order is manifestly unlawful or not is a question of law.

33. (1) Where the proclamation referred to in section 68 has been made or an offence against paragraph 69*(a)* or *(b)* has been committed, it is the duty of a peace officer and of a person who is lawfully required by him to assist, to disperse or to arrest persons who do not comply with the proclamation.

(2) No civil or criminal proceedings lie against a peace officer or a person who is lawfully required by a peace officer to assist him in respect of any death or injury that by reason of resistance is caused as a result of the performance by the peace officer or that person of a duty that is imposed by subsection (1).

(3) Nothing in this section limits or affects any powers, duties or functions that are conferred or imposed by this Act with respect to the suppression of riots.

Unlawful Drilling

Orders by Governor in Council

71. (1) The Governor in Council may from time to time by proclamation make orders 28 Interp

(a) to prohibit assemblies, without lawful authority, of persons for the purpose

(i) of training or drilling themselves,

(ii) of being trained or drilled to the use of arms, or

(iii) of practising military exercises; or

(b) to prohibit persons when assembled for any purpose from training or drilling themselves or from being trained or drilled.

General or special order

(2) An order that is made under subsection (1) may be general or may be made applicable to particular places, districts or assemblies to be specified in the order.

Punishment

(3) Every one who contravenes an order made under this section is guilty of an indictable offence and is liable to imprisonment for five years. 1953-54, c. 51, s. 71.

No orders have been proclaimed under these provisions.

Duels

Duelling

Type 'D' Offence

72. Every one who

(a) challenges or attempts by any means to provoke another person to fight a duel,

(b) attempts to provoke a person to challenge another person to fight a duel, or

(c) accepts a challenge to fight a duel,

is guilty of an indictable offence and is liable to imprisonment for two years. 1953-54, c. 51, s. 72.

Forcible Entry and Detainer

Forcible entry

73. (1) A person commits forcible entry when he enters real property that is in actual and peaceable possession of another in a manner that is likely to cause a breach of the peace or reasonable apprehension of a breach of the peace, whether or not he is entitled to enter.

Section 306 for Breaking and entering with intent

Forcible detainer

(2) A person commits forcible detainer when, being in actual possession of real property without colour of right, he detains it in a manner that is likely to cause a breach of the peace or reasonable apprehension of a breach of the peace, against a person who is entitled by law to possession of it.

Questions of law

(3) The questions whether a person is in actual and peaceable possession or is in actual possession without colour of right are questions of law. 1953-54, c. 51, s. 73.

Punishment

Type 'D' Offence

74. Every one who commits forcible entry or forcible detainer is guilty of an indictable offence and is liable to imprisonment for two years. 1953-54, c. 51, s. 74. 73

Piracy

Piracy by law of nations

75. (1) Every one commits piracy who does any act that, by the law of nations, is piracy.

Punishment
Type 'G' Offence 427(d) (e)

(2) Every one who commits piracy while in or out of Canada is guilty of an indictable offence and is liable to imprisonment for life. 1974-75-76, c. 105, s. 3. 669

Piratical acts
Type 'G' Offence 427(d) (e)

76. Every one who, while in or out of Canada,

(a) steals a Canadian ship, 2

(b) steals or without lawful authority throws overboard, damages or destroys anything that is part of the cargo, supplies or fittings in a Canadian ship,

(c) does or attempts to do a mutinous act on a Canadian ship, or

(d) counsels or procures a person to do anything mentioned in paragraph *(a)*, *(b)* or *(c)*,

is guilty of an indictable offence and is liable to imprisonment for fourteen years. 1953-54, c. 51, s. 76.

Offences Relating to Aircraft

Hijacking
Type 'E' Offence IPA offence 178.1

76.1 Every one who, unlawfully, by force or threat thereof, or by any other form of intimidation, seizes or exercises control of an aircraft with intent

(a) to cause any person on board the aircraft to be confined or imprisoned against his will,

(b) to cause any person on board the aircraft to be transported against his will to any place other than the next scheduled place of landing of the aircraft,

(c) to hold any person on board the aircraft for ransom or to service against his will, or

(d) to cause the aircraft to deviate in a material respect from its flight plan,

is guilty of an indictable offence and is liable to imprisonment for life. 1972, c. 13, s. 6. 669

247. (1) Every one who kidnaps a person with intent

(a) to cause him to be confined or imprisoned against his will,

(b) to cause him to be unlawfully sent or transported out of Canada against his will, or

(c) to hold him for ransom or to service against his will,

is guilty of an indictable offence and is liable to imprisonment for life.

(2) Every one who, without lawful authority, confines, imprisons or forcibly seizes another person is guilty of an indictable offence and is liable to imprisonment for five years.

Endangering safety of aircraft in flight and rendering aircraft incapable of flight
Type 'E' Offence IPA offence 178.1

76.2 Every one who,

(a) on board an aircraft in flight, commits an assault that is likely to endanger the safety of the aircraft, 6(6) 244

(b) causes damage to an aircraft in service that renders the aircraft incapable of flight or that is likely to endanger the safety of the aircraft in flight, 6(7)

(c) places or causes to be placed on board an aircraft in service anything that is likely to cause damage to the aircraft that will render it incapable of flight or that is likely to endanger the safety of the aircraft in flight,

(d) causes damages to or interferes with the operation of any air navigation facility where the damage or interference is likely to endanger the safety of an aircraft in flight, or

(e) endangers the safety of an aircraft in flight by communicating to any other person any information that he knows to be false,

is guilty of an indictable offence and is liable to imprisonment for life. 1972, c. 13, s. 6.

232. Every one who, with intent to endanger the safety of any person, places anything upon or does anything to any property that is used for or in connection with the transportation of persons or goods by land, water or air that is likely to cause death or bodily harm to persons is guilty of an indictable offence and is liable to imprisonment for life.

Offensive weapons and explosive substances

Type 'E' Offence IPA offence 178.1

76.3 (1) Every one, other than a peace officer engaged in the execution of his duty, who takes on board a civil aircraft an offensive weapon or any explosive substance 2 ss. (2) 2

(a) without the consent of the owner or operator of the aircraft or of a person duly authorized by either of them to consent thereto, or

(b) with the consent referred to in paragraph (a) but without complying with all terms and conditions on which the consent was given,

is guilty of an indictable offence and is liable to imprisonment for fourteen years.

Definition of "civil aircraft"

(2) For the purposes of this section, "civil aircraft" means all aircraft other than aircraft operated by the Canadian Forces, a police force in Canada or 2
persons engaged in the administration or enforcement of the *Customs Act* or the *Excise Act*. 1972, c. 13, s. 6.

2. In this Act

"explosive substance" includes

(a) anything intended to be used to make an explosive substance, and

(b) anything, or any part thereof, used or intended to be used, or adapted to cause, or to aid in causing an explosion in or with an explosive substance;

"offensive weapon" or "weapon" means

(a) anything that is designed to be used as a weapon, or

(b) anything that a person uses or intends to use as a weapon, whether or not it is designed to be used as a weapon,

and, without restricting the generality of the foregoing, includes any firearm as defined in section 82;

82. (1) For the purposes of this Part,

"firearm" means any barrelled weapon from which any shot, bullet or other missile can be discharged and that is capable of causing serious bodily injury or death to a person, and includes any frame or receiver of such a barrelled weapon and anything that can be adapted for use as a firearm;

244. A person commits an assault when

(a) without the consent of another person or with consent, where it is obtained by fraud, he applies force intentionally to the person of the other, directly or indirectly;

(b) he attempts or threatens, by an act or gesture, to apply force to the person of the other, if he has or causes the other to believe upon reasonable grounds that he has present ability to effect his purpose; or

(c) while openly wearing or carrying a weapon or an imitation thereof, he accosts or impedes another and begs.

6. (1) Notwithstanding anything in this Act or any other Act, every one who

(a) on or in respect of an aircraft

(i) registered in Canada under regulations made under the *Aeronautics Act*, or

(ii) leased without crew and operated by a person who is qualified under regulations made under the *Aeronautics Act* to be registered as owner of an aircraft registered in Canada under those regulations,

while the aircraft is in flight, or

(b) on any aircraft, while the aircraft is in flight if the flight terminated in Canada,

commits an act or omission in or outside Canada that if committed in Canada would be an offence punishable by indictment shall be deemed to have committed that act or omission in Canada.

(1.1) Notwithstanding this Act or any other Act, every one who

(a) on an aircraft, while the aircraft is in flight, commits an act or omission outside Canada that if committed in Canada or on an aircraft registered in Canada under regulations made under the *Aeronautics Act* would be an offence against section 76.1 or paragraph 76.2*(a)*,

(b) in relation to an aircraft in service, commits an act or omission outside Canada that if committed in Canada would be an offence against any of paragraphs 76.2*(b)*, *(c)* or *(e)*, or

(c) in relation to an air navigation facility used in international air navigation, commits an act or omission outside Canada that if committed in Canada would be an offence against paragraph 76.2*(d)*

shall, if he is found anywhere in Canada, be deemed to have committed that act or omission in Canada.

(3) Where a person has committed an act or omission that is an offence by virtue of subsection (1), (1.1), (1.2) or (2), the offence is within the competence of and may be tried and punished by the court having jurisdiction in respect of similar offences in the territorial division where he is found in the same manner as if the offence had been committed in that territorial division.

(4) Where, as a result of committing an act or omission that is an offence by virtue of subsection (1), (1.1), (1.2) or (2), a person has been tried and convicted or acquitted outside Canada, he shall be deemed to have been tried and convicted or acquitted, as the case may be, in Canada.

(5) No proceedings shall be instituted under this section without the consent of the Attorney General of Canada if the accused is not a Canadian citizen.

(6) For the purposes of this section, of the definition "peace officer" in section 2 and of sections 76.1 and 76.2, "flight" means the act of flying or moving through the air and an aircraft shall be deemed to be in flight from the time when all external doors are closed following embarkation until the later of

(a) the time at which any such door is opened for the purpose of disembarkation; and

(b) where the aircraft makes a forced landing in circumstances in which the owner or operator thereof or a person acting on behalf of either of them is not in control of the aircraft, the time at which control of the aircraft is restored to the owner or operator thereof or a person acting on behalf of either of them.

(7) For the purposes of this section and section 76.2, an aircraft shall be deemed to be in service from the time when pre-flight preparation of the aircraft by ground personnel or the crew thereof begins for a specific flight until

(a) the flight is cancelled before the aircraft is in flight,

(b) twenty-four hours after the aircraft, having commenced the flight, lands, or

(c) the aircraft, having commenced the flight, ceases to be in flight,

whichever is the latest.

2. In this Act

"peace officer" includes

(a) a mayor, warden, reeve, sheriff, deputy sheriff, sheriff's officer and justice of the peace,

(b) a warden, deputy warden, instructor, keeper, gaoler, guard and any other officer or permanent employee of a prison,

(c) a police officer, police constable, bailiff, constable, or other person employed for the preservation and maintenance of the public peace or for the service or execution of civil process,

(d) an officer or person having the powers of a customs or excise officer when performing any duty in the administration of the *Customs Act* or the *Excise Act*,

(d.1) a person appointed or designated as a fishery officer under the *Fisheries Act* when performing any of his duties or functions pursuant to that Act,

(e) the pilot in command of an aircraft

(i) registered in Canada under regulations made under the *Aeronautics Act*, or

(ii) leased without crew and operated by a person who is qualified under regulations made under the *Aeronautics Act* to be registered as owner of an aircraft registered in Canada under those regulations,

while the aircraft is in flight, and

(f) officers and men of the Canadian Forces who are

(i) appointed for the purposes of section 134 of the *National Defence Act*, or

(ii) employed on duties that the Governor in Council, in regulations made under the *National Defence Act* for the purposes of this paragraph, has prescribed to be of such a kind as to necessitate that the officers and men performing them have the powers of peace officers;

6. (6) For the purposes of this section, of the definition "peace officer" in section 2 and of section 76.1 and 76.2, "flight" means the act of flying or moving through the air and an aircraft shall be deemed to be in flight from the time when all external doors are closed following embarkation until the later of

(a) the time at which any such door is opened for the purpose of disembarkation; and

(b) where the aircraft makes a forced landing in circumstances in which the owner or operator thereof or a person acting on behalf of either of them is not in control of the aircraft, the time at which control of the aircraft is restored to the owner or operator thereof or a person acting on behalf of either of them.

Dangerous Substances

Duty of care re explosive

77. Every one who has an explosive substance in his possession or under his care or control is under a legal duty to use reasonable care to prevent bodily harm or death to persons or damage to property by that explosive substance. 1953-54, c. 51, s. 77. 2 3(4)

2. In this Act

"explosive substance" includes

(a) anything intended to be used to make an explosive substance, and

(b) anything, or any part thereof, used or intended to be used, or adapted to cause, or to aid in causing an explosion in or with an explosive substance;

3. (4) For the purposes of this Act,

(a) a person has anything in possession when he has it in his personal possession or knowingly

(i) has it in the actual possession or custody of another person, or

(ii) has it in any place, whether or not that place belongs to or is occupied by him, for the use or benefit of himself or of another person; and

(b) where one of two or more persons, with the knowledge and consent of the rest, has anything in his custody or possession, it shall be deemed to be in the custody and possession of each and all of them.

Breach of duty

Type 'E' Offence

IPA offence 178.1

78. Every one who, being under a legal duty within the meaning of section 77, fails without lawful excuse to perform that duty, is guilty of an indictable offence and if as a result an explosion of an explosive substance occurs that

(a) causes death or is likely to cause death to any person, is liable to imprisonment for life, or 669

(b) causes bodily harm or damage to property or is likely to cause bodily harm or damage to property, is liable to imprisonment for fourteen years. 1953-54, c. 51, s. 78.

Causing injury with intent

79. (1) Every one commits an offence who

(a) does anything with intent to cause an explosion of an explosive substance that is likely to cause serious bodily harm or death to persons or is likely to cause serious damage to property, 2

(b) with intent to do bodily harm to any person

(i) causes an explosive substance to explode,

(ii) sends or delivers to a person or causes a person to take or receive an explosive substance or any other dangerous substance or thing,

(iii) places or throws anywhere or at or upon a person a corrosive fluid, explosive substance or any other dangerous substance or thing,

(c) with intent to destroy or damage property without lawful excuse, places or throws an explosive substance anywhere, or

(d) makes or has in his possession or has under his care or control any explosive substance with intent thereby

(i) to endanger life or to cause serious damage to property, or

(ii) to enable another person to endanger life or to cause serious damage to property.

Type 'E' Offence
IPA offence 178.1

(2) Every one who commits an offence under subsection (1) is guilty of an indictable offence and is liable

(*a*) for an offence under paragraph (*a*) or (*b*), to imprisonment for life, or 669

(*b*) for an offence under paragraph (*c*) or (*d*), to imprisonment for fourteen years. 1953-54, c. 51, s. 79.

Possessing explosive without lawful excuse
Type 'D' Offence
IPA offence 178.1

80. Every one who without lawful excuse, the proof of which lies upon him,

(*a*) makes or has in his possession or under his care or control an explosive substance that he does not make or does not have in his possession or under his care or control for a lawful purpose, or 2

(*b*) has in his possession a bomb, grenade or other explosive weapon,

is guilty of an indictable offence and is liable to imprisonment for five years. 1953-54, c. 51, s. 80.

447. (1) Every person who executes a warrant issued under section 443 may seize any explosive substance that he suspects is intended to be used for an unlawful purpose, and shall, as soon as possible, remove to a place of safety anything that he seizes by virtue of this section and detain it until he is ordered by a judge of a superior court to deliver it to some other person or an order is made purusant to subsection (2).

(2) Where an accused is convicted of an offence in respect of anything seized by virtue of subsection (1), it is forfeited and shall be dealt with as the court that makes the conviction may direct.

(3) Where anything to which this section applies is sold, the proceeds of the sale shall be paid to the Attorney General.

Prize Fights

Engaging in prize fight
Type 'A' Offence

81. (1) Every one who

(*a*) engages as a principal in a prize fight, ss (2)

(*b*) advises, encourages or promotes a prize fight, or

(*c*) is present at a prize fight as an aid, second, surgeon, umpire, backer or reporter,

is guilty of an offence punishable on summary conviction. 722(1)

"Prize fight"

(2) In this section, "prize fight" means an encounter or fight with fists or hands between two persons who have met for that purpose by previous arrangement made by or for them, but a boxing contest between amateur sportsmen, where the contestants wear boxing gloves of not less than five ounces each in weight, or any boxing contest held with the permission or under the authority of an athletic board or commission or similar body established by or under the authority of the legislature of a province for the control of sport within the province, shall be deemed not to be a prize fight. 1953-54, c. 51, s. 81.

722. (1) Except where otherwise expressly provided by law, every one who is convicted of an offence punishable on summary conviction is liable to a fine of not more than five hundred dollars or to imprisonment for six months or to both.

2. In this Act

"property" includes

(a) real and personal property of every description and deeds and instruments relating to or evidencing the title or right to property, or giving a right to recover or receive money or goods,

(b) property originally in the possession or under the control of any person, and any property into or for which it has been converted or exchanged and anything acquired at any time by such conversion or exchange, and

(c) any postal card, postage stamp or other stamp issued or prepared for issue under the authority of the Parliament of Canada or of the legislature of a province for the payment to the Crown or a corporate body of any fee, rate or duty, whether or not it is in the possession of the Crown or of any person;

3. (2) For the purposes of this Act a postal card or stamp referred to in paragraph *(c)* of the definition "property" in section 2 shall be deemed to be a chattel, and to be equal in value to the amount of the postage, rate or duty expressed on its face.

669. The sentence to be pronounced against a person who is to be sentenced to imprisonment for life shall be

(a) in respect of a person who has been convicted of high treason or first degree murder, that he be sentenced to imprisonment for life without eligibility for parole until he has served twenty-five years of his sentence;

(b) in respect of a person who has been convicted of second degree murder, that he be sentenced to imprisonment for life without eligibility for parole until he has served at least ten years of his sentence or such greater number of years, not being more than twenty-five years, as has been substituted therefor pursuant to section 671; and

(c) in respect of a person who has been convicted of any other offence, that he be sentenced to imprisonment for life with normal eligibility for parole.

PART II.1

FIREARMS AND OTHER OFFENSIVE WEAPONS

Interpretation

Definitions

82. (1) For the purposes of the Part,

"antique firearm" — "antique firearm" means any firearm manufactured before 1898 that was not designed to use rimfire or centre-fire ammunition and that has not been redesigned to use such ammunition or, if so designed or redesigned, is capable only of using rimfire or centre-fire ammunition that is no longer commercially manufactured;

"chief provincial firearms officer" — "chief provincial firearms officer" means a person who has been designated in writing by the Attorney General of a province as the chief provincial firearms officer for that province; 2

"Commissioner" — "Commissioner" means the Commissioner of the Royal Canadian Mounted Police;

"firearm" — "firearm" means any barrelled weapon from which any shot, bullet or other missile can be discharged and that is capable of causing serious bodily injury or death to a person, and includes any frame or receiver of such a barrelled weapon and anything that can be adapted for use as a firearm;

"firearms acquisition certificate" — "firearms acquisition certificate" means a firearms acquisition certificate issued by a firearms officer under section 104 or a hunting licence, certificate, permit or other document issued under the authority of a law of a province that, by virtue of an order issued under section 105, is deemed to be a firearms acquisition certificate; 28 Interp

"firearms officer" — "firearms officer" means any person who has been designated in writing as a firearms officer by the Commissioner or the Attorney General of a province or who is a member of a class of persons that has been so designated;

"local registrar of firearms" — "local registrar of firearms" means any person who has been designated in writing as a local registrar of firearms by the Commissioner or the Attorney General of a province or who is a member of a class of police officers or police constables that has been so designated;

"permit" — "permit" means a permit issued under section 106.2;

"prohibited weapon" — "prohibited weapon" means

(*a*) any device or contrivance designed or intended to muffle or stop the sound or report of a firearm,

(*b*) any knife that has a blade that opens automatically by gravity or centrifugal force or by hand pressure applied to a button, spring or other device in or attached to the handle of the knife,

(*c*) any firearm, not being a restricted weapon described in paragraph (*c*) of the definition of that expression in this section, that is capable of firing bullets in rapid succession during one pressure of the trigger,

(*d*) any firearm adapted from a rifle or shotgun, whether by sawing, cutting or other alteration or modification, that, as so adapted, has a barrel that is less than eighteen inches in length or that is less than twenty-six inches in overall length, or

(*e*) a weapon of any kind, not being an antique firearm or a firearm of a kind commonly used in Canada for hunting or sporting purposes, that is declared by order of the Governor in Council to be a prohibited weapon; 28 Interp

"registration certificate" — "registration certificate" means a restricted weapon registration certificate issued under section 106.1;

"regulations" — "regulations" means regulations made by the Governor in Council pursuant to section 106.8

"restricted weapon"

"restricted weapon" means

(a) any firearm, not being a prohibited weapon, designed, altered or intended to be aimed and fired by the action of one hand,

(b) any firearm that

(i) is not a prohibited weapon, has a barrel that is less than eighteen and one-half inches in length and is capable of discharging centre-fire ammunition in a semi-automatic manner, or

(ii) is designed or adapted to be fired when reduced to a length of less than twenty-six inches by folding, telescoping or otherwise, or

(c) any firearm that is designed, altered or intended to fire bullets in rapid succession during one pressure of the trigger and that, on the day on which this paragraph comes into force, was registered as a restricted weapon and formed part of a gun collection in Canada of a *bona fide* gun collector, or Jan. 1, 1978 SI/78-131

(d) a weapon of any kind, not being a prohibited weapon or a shotgun or rifle of a kind that, in the opinion of the Governor in Council, is reasonable for use in Canada for hunting or sporting purposes, that is declared by order of the Governor in Council to be a restricted weapon. 28 Interp

Bona fide — In or with good faith, there is no pretence, it is actually so.

2. In this Act

"Attorney General" means the Attorney General or Solicitor General of a province in which proceedings to which this Act applies are taken and, with respect to

(a) the Northwest Territories and the Yukon Territory, and

(b) proceedings instituted at the instance of the Government of Canada and conducted by or on behalf of that Government in respect of a violation of or conspiracy to violate any Act of the Parliament of Canada or a regulation made thereunder other than this Act,

means the Attorney General of Canada, and except for the purposes of subsections 505(4) and 507(3), includes the lawful deputy of the said Attorney General, Solicitor General and Attorney General of Canada;

Interpretation Act

28. In every enactment

"Governor in Council", or "Governor General in Council" means the Governor General of Canada, or person administering the Government of Canada for the time being, acting by and with the advice of, or by and with the advice and consent of, or in conjunction with the Queen's Privy Council for Canada;

"province" means a province of Canada, and includes the Yukon Territory and the Northwest Territories;

Certain weapons deemed not to be firearms

(2) Notwithstanding the definition "firearm" in subsection (1), for the purposes of the definitions "prohibited weapon" and "restricted weapon" in that subsection and for the purpose of section 91, subsections 95(1) and (3) and sections 100, 102, 103 and 106.8, the following weapons shall be deemed not to be firearms, namely,

(a) an antique firearm unless,

(i) but for this subsection, it would be a restricted weapon, and

(ii) the person in possession thereof intends to discharge it;

(b) any device designed, and intended by the person in possession thereof, for use exclusively for

(i) signalling, notifying of distress or firing stud cartridges, explosive-driven rivets or similar industrial ammunition, or

(ii) firing blank cartridges; and

(c) any shooting device designed, and intended by the person in possession thereof, for use exclusively for

(i) slaughtering of domestic animals,

(ii) tranquilizing animals, or

(iii) discharging projectiles with lines attached thereto; and

(d) any other barrelled weapon where it is proved that such weapon is not designed or adapted to discharge a shot, bullet or other missile at a muzzle velocity exceeding five hundred feet per second or to discharge a shot, bullet or other missile that is designed or adapted to attain a velocity exceeding five hundred feet per second.

Designated officer or constable

(3) A police officer or police constable designated in writing by the Commissioner or the Attorney General of a province for the purposes of this subsection or who is a member of a class of police officers or police constables that has been so designated may perform such functions and duties of a local registrar of firearms under subsections 106.1(1) to (6) and subsections 106.2(3) and (4) as are specified in the designation. 1976-77, c. 53, s. 3.

Offences related to the Use of Firearms and other Offensive Weapons

Use of firearm during commission of offence, etc.

Type 'E' Offence

83. (1) Every one who uses a firearm

(a) while committing or attempting to commit an indictable offence, or

(b) during his flight after committing or attempting to commit an indictable offence,

whether or not he causes or means to cause bodily harm to any person as a result thereof, is guilty of an indictable offence and is liable to imprisonment

(c) in the case of a first offence under this subsection, except as provided in paragraph (d), for not more than fourteen years and not less than one year; and

(d) in the case of a second or subsequent offence under this subsection, or in the case of a first such offence committed by a person who, prior to the coming into force of this subsection, was convicted of an indictable offence or an attempt to commit an indictable offence, in the course of which or during his flight after the commission or attempted commission of which he used a firearm, for not more than fourteen years and not less than three years. 591-592[84] Jan. 1 1978 SI/78-131

Sentences to be served consecutively

(2) A sentence imposed on a person for an offence under subsection (1) shall be served consecutively to any other punishment imposed on him for an offence arising out of the same event or series of events and to any other sentence to which he is subject at the time the sentence is imposed on him for an offence under subsection (1). 1976-77, c. 53, s. 3. 28 Interp

98. (1) Where a person is convicted of an indictable offence in the commission of which violence against a person is used, threatened or attempted and for which the offender may be sentenced to imprisonment for ten years or more or of an offence under section 83, the court shall, in addition to any other punishment that may be imposed for that offence, make an order prohibiting him from having in his possession any firearm or any ammunition or explosive substance for any period of time specified in the order that commences on the day the order is made and expires not earlier than

(a) in the case of a first conviction for such an offence, five years, and

(b) in any other case, ten years,

after the time of his release from imprisonment after conviction for the offence.

Interpretation Act

28. In every enactment

"shall" is to be construed as imperative;

Pointing a firearm

Type 'B' (D) Offence

84. (1) Every one who, without lawful excuse, points a firearm at another person, whether the firearm is loaded or unloaded,

(a) is guilty of an indictable offence and is liable to imprisonment for five years; or

(b) is guilty of an offence punishable on summary conviction. 722(1)

Careless use, etc. of firearm

Type 'B' (D) Offence

(2) Every one who, without lawful excuse, uses, carries, handles, ships or stores any firearm or ammunition in a careless manner or without reasonable precautions for the safety of other persons

(a) is guilty of an indictable offence and is liable to imprisonment

(i) in the case of a first offence, for two years, and

(ii) in the case of a second or subsequent offence, for five years; or 591 592

(b) is guilty of an offence punishable on summary conviction. 722(1)
1976-77, c. 53, s. 3.

591. No indictment in respect of an offence for which, by reason of previous convictions, a greater punishment may be imposed shall contain any reference to previous convictions.

592. (1) Where an accused is convicted of an offence for which a greater punishment may be imposed by reason of previous convictions, no greater punishment shall be imposed upon him by reason thereof unless the prosecutor satisfies the court that the accused, before making his plea, was notified that a greater punishment would be sought by reason thereof.

(2) Where an accused is convicted of an offence for which a greater punishment may be imposed by reason of previous convictions, the court shall, upon application by the prosecutor and upon being satisfied that the accused was notified in accordance with subsection (1), ask the accused whether he was previously convicted and, if he does not admit that he was previously convicted, evidence of previous convictions may be adduced.

(3) Where, pursuant to section 551, the court proceeds with the trial of an accused corporation that has not appeared and pleaded to an indictment, the court may, if the accused is convicted, make inquiries with respect to previous convictions whether or not the accused was notified that a greater punishment would be sought by reason thereof.

Offences Related to Possession of Firearms and other Offensive Weapons

Possession of weapon or imitation

Type 'E' Offence

85. Every one who carries or has in his possession a weapon or imitation thereof, for a purpose dangerous to the public peace or for the purpose of committing an offence, is guilty of an indictable offence and is liable to imprisonment for ten years. 1976-77, c. 53, s. 3. 2

While attending public meeting

Type 'A' Offence

86. Every one who, without lawful excuse, has a weapon in his possession while he is attending or is on his way to attend a public meeting is guilty of an offence punishable on summary conviction. 1976-77, c. 53, s. 3. 3(4) 722(1)

2. In this Act

"offensive weapon" or "weapon" means

(a) anything that is designed to be used as a weapon, or

(b) anything that a person uses or intends to use as a weapon, whether or not it is designed to be used as a weapon,

and, without restricting the generality of the foregoing, includes any firearm as defined in section 82;

3. (4) For the purposes of this Act,

(a) a person has anything in possession when he has it in his personal possession or knowingly

(i) has it in the actual possession or custody of another person, or

(ii) has it in any place, whether or not that place belongs to or is occupied by him, for the use or benefit of himself or of another person; and

(b) where one of two or more persons, with the knowledge and consent of the rest, has anything in his custody or possession, it shall be deemed to be in the custody and possession of each and all of them.

Carrying concealed weapon

Type 'B' (D) Offence

87. Every one who carries a weapon concealed, unless he is the holder of a permit under which he may lawfully so carry it,

(a) is guilty of an indictable offence and is liable to imprisonment for five years; or

(b) is guilty of an offence punishable on summary conviction. 1976-77, c. 53, s. 3.

Possession of prohibited weapon

Type 'B' (D) Offence

IPA offence 178.1

88. (1) Every one who has in his possession a prohibited weapon

(a) is guilty of an indictable offence and is liable to imprisonment for five years; or

(b) is guilty of an offence punishable on summary conviction.

Prohibited weapon in motor vehicle

Type 'B' (D) Offence

IPA offence 178.1

(2) Every one who is an occupant of a motor vehicle in which he knows there is a prohibited weapon 2

(a) is guilty of an indictable offence and is liable to imprisonment for five years; or

(b) is guilty of an offence punishable on summary conviction.

Saving provision

(3) Subsection (1) does not apply to a person who comes into possession of a prohibited weapon by operation of law and thereafter, with reasonable despatch, lawfully disposes thereof.

Idem

(4) Subsection (2) does not apply to an occupant of a motor vehicle in which there is a prohibited weapon where, by virtue of subsection (3) or section 90, subsection (1) does not apply to the person who is in possession of that weapon. 1976-77, c. 53, s. 3.

Possession of unregistered restricted weapon

Type 'B' (D) Offence

89. (1) Every one who has in his possession a restricted weapon for which he does not have a registration certificate 3(4) [84]

(a) is guilty of an indictable offence and is liable to imprisonment for five years; or

(b) is guilty of an offence punishable on summary conviction.

Possession elsewhere than at place authorized

Type 'B' (D) Offence

(2) Every one who has in his possession a restricted weapon elsewhere than at the place at which he is entitled to possess it, as indicated on the registration certificate issued therefor, is, unless he is the holder of a permit under which he may lawfully so possess it,

(a) guilty of an indictable offence and is liable to imprisonment for five years; or

(b) guilty of an offence punishable on summary conviction.

Restricted weapon in motor vehicle

Type 'B' (D) Offence

(3) Every one who is an occupant of a motor vehicle in which he knows there is a restricted weapon is, unless some occupant of the motor vehicle is the holder of a permit under which he may lawfully have that weapon in his possession in such vehicle, or he establishes that he had reason to believe that some occupant of the motor vehicle was the holder of such permit, 2

(a) guilty of an indictable offence and is liable to imprisonment for five years; or

(b) guilty of an offence punishable on summary conviction.

Saving provision

(4) Subsection (1) does not apply to a person

(a) to whom a permit relating to a restricted weapon has been issued under subsection 106.2(3) or (4) and who has such weapon in his possession for the purpose for which that permit was issued;

(b) who has a restricted weapon in his possession while he is under the immediate supervision of a person who may lawfully possess the weapon for the purpose of using the weapon in a manner in which the supervising person may lawfully use it; or

(c) who comes into possession of a restricted weapon by operation of law and thereafter, with reasonable despatch, lawfully disposes thereof or obtains a registration certificate or permit under which he may lawfully possess it.

Idem

(5) Subsection (3) does not apply to an occupant of a motor vehicle in which there is a restricted weapon where, by virtue of subsection (4) or section 90, subsections (1) and (2) do not apply to the person who is in possession of that weapon.

Idem

(6) Subject to sections 98 and 101, subsection 103(4) and to a condition of a probation order referred to in paragraph 663(2)*(d)*, nothing in this Act makes it unlawful for a person to be in possession of a restricted weapon in the ordinary course of a business described in subsection 103(1) or subparagraph 103(2)*(b)*(ii).

2. In this Act

"motor vehicle" means a vehicle that is drawn, propelled or driven by any means other than by muscular power, but does not include a vehicle of a railway that operates on rails;

Members of forces, peace officers, etc.

90. (1) Notwithstanding anything in this Act,

(a) a member of the Canadian Forces or of the armed forces of a state other than Canada that are lawfully present in Canada,

(b) a peace officer or public officer of a class from time to time prescribed by the regulations for the purposes of this Part,

(c) an officer under the *Immigration Act*, the *Customs Act* or the *Excise Act;* or

(d) a person who, under the authority of the Canadian Armed Forces or a police force that includes peace officers or public officers of a class referred to in paragraph *(b)*, imports, manufactures, repairs, alters, modifies or sells weapons for or on behalf of the Canadian Armed Forces or such a police force,

is not guilty of an offence under this Act by reason only that, in the case of a person described in any of paragraphs *(a)* to *(c)*, he has in his possession a restricted or prohibited weapon for the purpose of his duties or employment and, in the case of a person described in paragraph *(d)*, he has in his possession a restricted or prohibited weapon in the course of his business on behalf of the Canadian Armed Forces or a police force referred to in that paragraph.

Museums

(2) Notwithstanding anything in this Act, no operator of or person employed in a museum approved for the purposes of this Part by the Commissioner or the Attorney General of the province in which it is situated is guilty of an offence under this Act by reason only that he has in his possession a restricted or prohibited weapon for the purpose of exhibiting that weapon or of storing, repairing, restoring, maintaining or transporting that weapon for the purpose of exhibiting it. 1976-77, c. 53, s. 3. 2

Offences Related to Sale, Delivery or Acquisition of Firearms and other Offensive Weapons

Transfer of firearm to person under 16

Type 'B' (D) Offence

91. (1) Every one who gives, lends, transfers or delivers any firearm to a person under the age of sixteen years who is not the holder of a permit under which he may lawfully possess the firearm 3(1) 585

(a) is guilty of an indictable offence and is liable to imprisonment for two years; or

(b) is guilty of an offence punishable on summary conviction.

Saving provision

(2) Subsection (1) does not apply to a person lawfully in possession of a firearm who permits a person under the age of sixteen years to use the firearm under his immediate supervision in the same manner in which he may lawfully use it. 1976-77, c. 10, s. 3.

3. (1) For the purposes of this Act a person shall be deemed to have been of a given age when the anniversary of his birthday, the number of which corresponds to that age, is fully completed, and until then to have been under that age.

585. (1) In any proceedings to which this Act applies an entry or record of an incorporated society or its officers who have had the control or care of a child or young person at or about the time the child or young person was brought to Canada is evidence of the age of the child or young person if the entry or record was made before the time when the offence is alleged to have been committed.

(2) In the absence of other evidence, or by way of corroboration of other evidence, a jury, judge, justice or magistrate, as the case may be, may infer the age of a child or young person from his appearance.

Wrongful delivery of firearms, etc.

Type 'B' (D) Offence

92. Every one who sells, barters, gives, lends, transfers or delivers any firearm or other offensive weapon or any ammunition or explosive substance to a person who he knows or has good reason to believe is of unsound mind, is impaired by alcohol or drugs, or is a person who is prohibited by an order made pursuant to section 98 or 101 or by a condition of a probation order referred to in paragraph 663(2)(*d*) from possessing the firearm or other offensive weapon, ammunition or explosive substance so sold, bartered, given, loaned, transferred or delivered, 2

(a) is guilty of an indictable offence and is liable to imprisonment for five years; or

(b) is guilty of an offence punishable on summary conviction.

2. In this Act

"explosive substance" includes

(a) anything intended to be used to make an explosive substance, and

(b) anything, or any part thereof, used or intended to be used, or adapted to cause, or to aid in causing an explosion in or with an explosive substance;

Importing or delivering prohibited weapon

Type 'B' (D) Offence

93. Every one who imports, buys, sells, barters, gives, lends, transfers or delivers a prohibited weapon or any component or part designed exclusively for use in the manufacture or assembly of a prohibited weapon

(a) is guilty of an indictable offence and is liable to imprisonment for five years; or

(b) is guilty of an offence punishable on summary conviction.

Delivery of restricted weapon to person without permit

Type 'B' (D) Offence

94. (1) Every one who sells, barters, gives, lends, transfers or delivers any restricted weapon to a person who is not the holder of a permit authorizing him to possess that weapon,

(a) is guilty of an indictable offence and is liable to imprisonment for five years; or

(b) is guilty of an offence punishable on summary conviction.

Saving provision

(2) Subsection (1) does not apply to a person lawfully in possession of a restricted weapon who permits a person who is not the holder of a permit authorizing him to possess that weapon to use the weapon under his immediate supervision in the same manner in which he may lawfully use it.

Importation

Type 'B' (D) Offence

(3) Every one who imports any restricted weapon when he is not the holder of a permit authorizing him to possess that weapon

(a) is guilty of an indictable offence and is liable to imprisonment for five years; or

(b) is guilty of an offence punishable on summary conviction.
1976-77, c. 10, s. 3.

Delivery of firearm to person without firearms acquisition certificate

Type 'B' (D) Offence

95. (1) Every one who sells, barters, gives, lends, transfers or delivers any firearm to a person who does not, at the time of such sale, barter, giving, lending, 82 transfer or delivery or, in the case of a mail-order sale, within a reasonable time prior thereto, produce a firearms acquisition certificate for inspection by the 82 person selling, bartering, giving, lending, transferring or delivering the firearm, that that person has no reason to believe is invalid or was issued to a person other than the person so producing it,

(a) is guilty of an indictable offence and is liable to imprisonment for two years; or

(b) is guilty of an offence punishable on summary conviction.

Saving provision

(2) Subsection (1) does not apply to a person

(a) lawfully in possession of a firearm who lends the firearm

(i) to a person for use by that person in his company and under his guidance or supervision in the same manner in which he may lawfully use it, or

(ii) to a person who requires the firearm to hunt or trap in order to sustain himself or his family,

(iii) to a person who is the holder of a permit under which he may lawfully 82 possess the firearm;

(b) who returns a firearm to a person who lent it to him in circumstances described in paragraph *(a)*; or

(c) who comes into possession of a firearm in the ordinary course of a business described in subsection 103(1) and who returns that firearm to the person from whom he received it. 1978, c. 10, s. 1.

Acquisition of firearm without firearms acquisition certificate

Type 'B' (D) Offence

(3) Every one who imports or otherwise acquires possession in any manner 3(4)[84] whatever of a firearm while he is not the holder of a firearms acquisition certificate

(a) is guilty of an indictable offence and is liable to imprisonment for two years, or

(b) is guilty of an offence punishable on summary conviction.

Saving provision

(4) Subsection (3) does not apply to a person who

(a) acquires a firearm in circumstances such that, by virtue of subsection (2), subsection (1) does not apply to the person from whom he acquires the firearm;

(b) reacquires a firearm from a person to whom he lent the firearm;

(c) imports a firearm at a time when he is not a resident of Canada;

(d) comes into possession of a firearm by operation of law and thereafter, with reasonable despatch, lawfully disposes thereof or obtains a firearms acquisition certificate under which he could have lawfully acquired the firearm; or

(e) comes into possession of a firearm in the ordinary course of a business described in subsection 103(1) or (2). 1976-77, c. 53, s. 3.

Members of forces, peace officers, etc.

96. (1) Notwithstanding sections 93 to 95,

(a) a member of the Canadian Forces or of the armed forces of a state other than Canada that are lawfully present in Canada, 2

(b) a peace officer or public officer of a class from time to time prescribed by the regulations for the purposes of this Part, or

(c) an operator of or a person employed in a museum approved for the purposes of this Part by the Commissioner or the Attorney General of the province in which it is situated, 2

is not guilty of an offence under this Act by reason only that he imports or otherwise acquires possession in any manner whatever of any weapon or component or part of a weapon in the course of his duties or employment.

Importation, etc., on behalf of armed forces and police forces

(2) Notwithstanding sections 93 to 95, a person who, under the authority of the Canadian Armed Forces or a police force that includes peace officers or public officers of a class referred to in paragraph (1)(*b*), imports, manufactures, repairs, alters, modifies or sells weapons for or on behalf of the Canadian Armed Forces or such a police force, is not guilty of an offence under this Act by reason only that he so imports or manufactures weapons or that he sells, barters, gives, lends, transfers or delivers weapons to the Canadian Armed Forces or such a police force.

Importation etc., on behalf of museums

(3) Notwithstanding sections 93 to 95, a person who, under the supervision of an operator of or a person employed in a museum approved for the purposes of this Part by the Commissioner or the Attorney General of the province in which it is situated, imports, buys, repairs, restores or maintains weapons for or on behalf of the museum is not guilty of an offence under this Act by reason only that he so imports, repairs, restores or maintains weapons or that he sells, barters, gives, lends, transfers or delivers weapons to the museum. 1976-77, c. 10, s. 3.

Exception

97. Notwithstanding sections 94 and 95, a person is not guilty of an offence under this Act by reason only that he transfers or delivers

(a) any restricted weapon to a person who carries on a business described in subparagraph 103(2)(*b*)(ii), or

(b) any firearm, other than a restricted weapon, to a person who carries on a business described in subsection 103(1) or subparagraph 103(2)(*b*)(ii)

for use in the course of such a business. 1976-77, c. 10, s. 3.

Prohibition Orders, Seizure and Forfeiture

Mandatory order prohibiting possession

98. (1) Where a person is convicted of an indictable offence in the commission of which violence against a person is used, threatened or attempted and for which the offender may be sentenced to imprisonment for ten years or more or of an offence under section 83, the court shall, in addition to any other punishment that may be imposed for that offence, make an order prohibiting him from having in his possession any firearm or any ammunition or explosive substance for any period of time specified in the order that commences on the day the order is made and expires not earlier than 28 Interp

(a) in the case of a first conviction for such an offence, five years, and

(b) in any other case, ten years,

after the time of his release from imprisonment after conviction for the offence. ss. (3)

Interpretation Act

28. In every enactment

"shall" is to be construed as imperative;

Order of prohibition after conviction

(2) Where a person is convicted of an offence involving the use, carriage, possession, handling, shipping or storage of any firearm or ammunition or an 82
offence, other than an offence referred to in subsection (1), in the commission of which violence against a person was used, threatened or attempted, the court, judge, justice or magistrate, as the case may be, may, in addition to any other 28 Interp
punishment that may be imposed for that offence, make an order prohibiting him from having in his possession any firearm or any ammunition or explosive substance for any period of time specified in the order that commences on the day the order is made and expires not later than five years after the time of his release from imprisonment after conviction for the offence or, if he is not then ss. (3)
imprisoned or subject to imprisonment, after the time of his conviction for that offence.

Definition of "release from imprisonment"

(3) For the purposes of subsections (1) and (2), "release from imprisonment" means release from confinement by reason of expiration of sentence, commencement of mandatory supervision or grant of parole other than day parole.

Application for order of prohibition

(4) Where a peace officer has reasonable grounds to believe that it is not desirable in the interests of the safety of any person that a particular person should possess any firearm or any ammunition or explosive substance, he may apply to a magistrate for an order prohibiting that particular person from having in his possession any firearm or any ammunition or explosive substance.

Fixing date for hearing and notice

(5) On receipt of an application made pursuant to subsection (4) or on a reference by a firearms officer, pursuant to subsection 104(6), of his opinion that it is not desirable in the interests of the safety of an applicant for a firearms acquisition certificate or of any other person that the applicant for a firearms 82
acquisition certificate acquire a firearm, the magistrate to whom the application or reference is made shall fix a date for the hearing of the application or reference and direct that notice of the hearing be given to the person against whom the order of prohibition is sought or the applicant for the firearms acquisition certificate and the firearms officer, as the case may be, in such manner as the magistrate may specify.

Hearing of application nd disposition

(6) At the hearing of an application made pursuant to subsection (4) the magistrate shall hear all relevant evidence presented by or on behalf of the ss. (11)
applicant and the person against whom the order of prohibition is sought and where, at the conclusion of the hearing, the magistrate is satisfied that there are reasonable grounds to believe that it is not desirable in the interests of the safety of the person against whom the order of prohibition is sought or of any other person that the person against whom the order is sought should possess any firearm or any ammunition or explosive substance, the magistrate shall make an order prohibiting him from having in his possession any firearm or any ammunition or explosive substance for any period of time, not exceeding five years, specified in the order and computed from the day the order is made.

Hearing of reference and disposition

(7) At the hearing of a reference referred to in subsection (5), the magistrate shall hear all relevant evidence presented by or on behalf of the firearms officer and the applicant for a firearms acquisition certificate and where, at the conclusion of the hearing, the firearms officer has satisfied the magistrate that his opinion that it is not desirable in the interests of the safety of the applicant for a firearms acquisition certificate or of any other person that the applicant for a firearms acquisition certificate acquire a firearm is justified, the magistrate shall, by order, confirm that opinion and prohibit the applicant for a firearms acquisition certificate from having in his possession any firearm, ammunition or explosive substance for any period of time, not exceeding five years, specified in the order and computed from the day the order is made.

Idem

(8) Where, at the conclusion of a hearing referred to in subsection (7), the firearms officer has not satisfied the magistrate that his opinion that it is not desirable in the interests of the safety of the applicant for a firearms acquisition certificate or of any other person that the applicant for a firearms acquisition certificate acquire a firearm is justified, the magistrate shall, by order, direct the firearms officer to issue to that person a firearms acquisition certificate and, on payment of the fee, if any, fixed for such a certificate, the firearms officer shall forthwith comply with the direction. 82

When hearing may proceed *ex parte*

(9) A magistrate may proceed *ex parte* to hear and determine an application made pursuant to subsection (4) or a reference referred to in subsection (5) in the absence of the person against whom the order of prohibition is sought or the applicant for a firearms acquisition certificate, as the case may be, in circumstances in which a summary conviction court may, pursuant to Part XXIV, proceed with a trial in the absence of the defendant as fully and effectually as if the defendant had appeared. ss. (11)

ex parte — in the absence of one side or party.

Appeal to appeal court in certain cases

(10) Where a magistrate

(a) makes an order pursuant to subsection (6) or (7), the prohibited person,

(b) refuses to make an order pursuant to subsection (6), the person who made the application pursuant to subsection (4), or

(c) makes an order pursuant to subsection (8), the firearms officer by whom the application for a firearms acquisition certificate that is the subject of the order was referred to the magistrate,

may appeal to the appeal court against the order or refusal to make an order, as the case may be, and the provisions of Part XXIV except sections 752 to 752.3 and sections 761 to 770 apply, *mutatis mutandis,* in respect of such an appeal.

mutatis mutandis — after the necessary changes in detail so that the text applies.

Definitions

(11) In this section,

"appeal court"

"appeal court" means

(a) in the Province of Prince Edward Island, the Supreme Court,

(b) in the Provinces of Nova Scotia, Ontario, Manitoba, British Columbia and Newfoundland, the district or county court of the district or county where the adjudication was made,

(c) in the Province of Quebec, the Superior Court,

(d) in the Provinces of New Brunswick, Alberta and Saskatchewan, the Court of Queen's Bench, and

(e) Repealed. 1978-79, c. 11, s. 10, I. 6(6)

(f) in the Yukon Territory and Northwest Territories, the Supreme Court;

"magistrate"

"magistrate" means a magistrate having jurisdiction in the territorial division where the person against whom the relevant application for an order of prohibition was brought or in respect of whom the reference was made, as the case may be, resides. 2

Possession of firearm, ammunition, etc., while prohibited by order

Type 'B' (D) Offence

(12) Every one who has in his possession any firearm or any ammunition or explosive substance while he is prohibited from doing so by any order made pursuant to this section 3(4)/2

(a) is guilty of an indictable offence and is liable to imprisonment for five years; or

(b) is guilty of an offence punishable on summary conviction.

Defence

(13) An order made pursuant to subsection (1), (2), (6) or (7) shall specify therein a reasonable period of time within which the person against whom the order is made may surrender to a police officer or firearms officer or otherwise 82
lawfully dispose of any firearm or any ammunition or explosive substance 82
lawfully possessed by him prior to the making of the order, and subsection (12) does not apply to him during such period of time. 1976-77, c. 10, s. 3.

2. In this Act

"explosive substance" includes

(a) anything intended to be used to make an explosive substance, and

(b) anything, or any part thereof, used or intended to be used, or adapted to cause, or to aid in causing an explosion in or with an explosive substance;

"magistrate" means a magistrate, a police magistrate, a stipendiary magistrate, a district magistrate, a provincial magistrate, a judge of the sessions of the peace, a recorder, or any person having the power and authority of two or more justices of the peace, and includes

(a) with respect to the Provinces of Ontario, Quebec, New Brunswick and British Columbia, a judge of the provincial court,

(a.1) with respect to the Provinces of Alberta, Manitoba and Prince Edward Island, a provincial judge,

(a.2) with respect to the Province of Nova Scotia, a judge of the Provincial Magistrate's Court,

(b) with respect to the Province of Saskatchewan, a judge of the Magistrates' Courts, and;

(c) with respect to the Yukon Territory and the Northwest Territories, a judge of the Supreme Court,

and the lawful deputy of each of them;

"offensive weapon" or "weapon" means

(a) anything that is designed to be used as a weapon, or

(b) anything that a person uses or intends to use as a weapon, whether or not it is designed to be used as a weapon,

and, without restricting the generality of the foregoing, includes any firearm as defined in section 82;

82. (1) For the purposes of this Part,

"firearm" means any barrelled weapon from which any shot, bullet or other missle can be discharged and that is capable of causing serious bodily injury or death to a person, and includes any frame or receiver of such a barrelled weapon and anything that can be adapted for use as a firearm;

3. (4) For the purposes of this Act,

(a) a person has anything in possession when he has it in his personal possession or knowingly

(i) has it in the actual possession or custody of another person, or

(ii) has it in any place, whether or not that place belongs to or is occupied by him, for the use or benefit of himself or of another person; and

(b) where one of two or more persons, with the knowledge and consent of the rest, has anything in his custody or possession, it shall be deemed to be in the custody and possession of each and all of them.

Search and seizure

99. (1) Whenever a peace officer believes on reasonable grounds that an offence is being committed or has been committed against any of the provisions of this Act relating to prohibited weapons, restricted weapons, firearms or ammunition, he may search, without warrant, a person or vehicle, or place or premises other than a dwelling-house, and may seize anything by means of or in relation to which he reasonably believes the offence is being committed or has been committed. 2 82 ss (3)

Disposition

(2) Anything seized pursuant to subsection (1) shall be dealt with in accordance with sections 446 and 446.1.

"Dwelling-house" defined

(3) For the purposes of this section, "dwelling-house" does not include a unit that is designed to be mobile other than such a unit that is being used as a permanent residence. 1976-77, c. 10, s. 3.

2. In this Act

"dwelling-house" means the whole or any part of a building or structure that is kept or occupied as a permanent or temporary residence and includes

(a) a building within the curtilage of a dwelling-house that is connected to it by a doorway or by a covered and enclosed passageway, and

(b) a unit that is designed to be mobile and to be used as a permanent or temporary residence and that is being used as such a residence;

446. (1) Where anything that has been seized under section 445 or under a warrant issued pursuant to section 443 is brought before a justice, he shall, unless the prosecutor otherwise agrees, detain it or order that it be detained, taking reasonable care to ensure that it is preserved until the conclusion of any investigation or until it is required to be produced for the purposes of a preliminary inquiry or trial, but nothing shall be detained under the authority of this section for a period of more than three months after the time of seizure unless, before the expiration of that period,

(a) a justice is satisfied on application that, having regard to the nature of the investigation, its further detention for a specified period is warranted and he so orders; or

(b) proceedings are instituted in which the thing detained may be required.

(2) When an accused has been committed for trial the justice shall forward anything to which subsection (1) applies to the clerk of the court to which the accused has been committed for trial to be detained by him and disposed of as the court directs.

(3) Where a justice is satisfied that anything that has been seized under section 445 or under a warrant issued pursuant to section 443 will not be required for any purpose mentioned in subsection (1) or (2), he may,

(a) if possession of it by the person from whom it was seized is lawful, order it to be returned to that person, or

(b) if possession of it by the person from whom it was seized is unlawful,

(i) order it to be returned to the lawful owner or to the person who is entitled to possession of it, or

(ii) order it to be forfeited or otherwise dealt with in accordance with law, where the lawful owner or the person who is entitled to possession of it is not known.

(4) Nothing shall be disposed of under subsection (3) pending any proceeding in which the right of seizure is questioned, or within thirty days after an order is made under that subsection.

(5) Where anything is detained under subsection (1), a judge of a superior court of criminal jurisdiction or of a court of criminal jurisdiction may, on summary application on behalf of a person who has an interest in what is detained, after three clear days notice to the Attorney General, order that the person by or on whose behalf the application is made be permitted to examine anything so detained.

(6) An order that is made under subsection (5) shall be made on such terms as appear to the judge to be necessary or desirable to ensure that anything in respect of which the order is made is safeguarded and preserved for any purpose for which it may subsequently be required.

(7) A person who considers himself aggrieved by an order made under subsection (3) may appeal from the order to the appeal court, as defined in section 747, and for the purposes of the appeal the provisions of sections 749 to 760 apply, *mutatis mutandis.*

446.1 (1) Where it is determined by a court that a weapon was used in the commission of an offence and that weapon has been seized and detained, the weapon is, subject to subsection (2), forfeited and may be dealt with as the court that makes the determination directs.

(2) If the court by which a determination referred to in subsection (1) is made is satisfied that the lawful owner of a weapon that, but for this subsection, would be forfeited by virtue of the determination, was not a party to the offence and had no reason to believe that the weapon would or might be used in the commission of an offence, the court shall order the weapon returned to the lawful owner thereof or the proceeds of any sale thereof to be paid to him.

(3) Where any weapon to which this section applies is sold, the proceeds of the sale shall be paid to the Attorney General or, where an order is made under subsection (2), to the person who was, immediately prior to the sale, the lawful owner of the weapon.

Seizure

100. (1) Notwithstanding section 99, a peace officer who finds 2

(a) a person in possession of any restricted weapon who fails then and there 3(4)
to produce, for inspection by the peace officer, a registration certificate or permit under which he may lawfully possess the weapon,

(b) a person under the age of sixteen years in possession of any firearm who 3(1)
fails then and there to produce, for inspection by the peace officer, a permit 106.2(7)
under which he may lawfully possess the firearm, or

(c) any person in possession of a prohibited weapon,

may, unless in a case described in paragraph *(a)* or *(b)* possession of the restricted 82
weapon or firearm by the person in the circumstances in which it is so found is 82
authorized by any provision of this Part, seize such restricted weapon or firearm or such prohibited weapon.

Return

(2) Where a person from whom any restricted weapon or firearm was seized pursuant to subsection (1), within fourteen days thereafter, claims the weapon or firearm and produces to the peace officer by whom the weapon or firearm was seized, or any other peace officer having custody thereof, for inspection by him, a registration certificate or permit under which the person from whom the seizure was made is lawfully entitled to possess the weapon or firearm, the weapon or firearm shall forthwith be returned to him.

Forfeiture

(3) Where any restricted weapon, firearm or prohibited weapon that was seized pursuant to subsection (1) is not returned as and when provided by
subsection (2), a peace officer shall forthwith take it before a magistrate who 2
may, after affording the person from whom it was seized or the owner thereof, if known, an opportunity to establish that he is lawfully entitled to the possession thereof, declare it to be forfeited to Her Majesty, whereupon it shall be disposed of as the Attorney General directs. 1976-77, c. 10, s. 3.

Application for warrant to seize

101. (1) Where, on application to a magistrate made by or on behalf of the ss (9)
Attorney General with respect to any person, the magistrate is satisfied that 2
there are reasonable grounds for believing that it is not desirable in the interests
of the safety of that person, or of any other person, that that person should have
in his possession, custody or control any firearm or other offensive weapon or 2
any ammunition or explosive substance, the magistrate may issue a warrant 2
authorizing the search for and seizure of any firearm or other offensive weapon 82
or any ammunition or explosive substance in the possession, custody or control
of that person.

Seizure without warrant

(2) Where, with respect to any person, a peace officer is satisfied that there are reasonable grounds for believing that it is not desirable in the interests of the safety of that person, or of any other person, that that person should have in his possession, custody or control any firearm or other offensive weapon or any ammunition or explosive substance and that the danger to the safety of that person or other persons is such that to proceed by way of an application under subsection (1) would be impracticable, the peace officer may without warrant search for and seize any firearm or other offensive weapon or any ammunition or explosive substance in the possession, custody or control of that person.

Return to magistrate

(3) On execution of a warrant referred to in subsection (1) or following a search without warrant under subsection (2), the Attorney General shall forthwith make a return to the magistrate by whom the warrant was issued or, if no warrant was issued, to a magistrate by whom a warrant might have issued showing,

(a) in the case of an execution of a warrant referred to in subsection (1), the articles, if any, seized and the date of execution of the warrant; and

(b) in the case of a search without warrant under subsection (2), the grounds on which it was concluded that the peace officer who conducted the search without warrant was entitled to do so and the articles, if any, seized.

Application for disposition

(4) Where any articles have been seized pursuant to subsection (1) or (2), the magistrate by whom a warrant was issued or, if no warrant was issued, a magistrate by whom a warrant might have issued shall, on application to him for an order for the disposition of the articles so seized made by or on behalf of the Attorney General within thirty days from the date of execution of the warrant or of the seizure without warrant, as the case may be, fix a date for the hearing of the application and direct that notice of the hearing be given to such persons or in such manner as the magistrate may specify.

Hearing of application

(5) At the hearing of an application described in subsection (4), the magistrate shall hear any relevant evidence, including evidence as to the value of the articles in respect of which the application was made.

Finding and order of court

(6) If, following the hearing of an application described in subsection (4) made with respect to any person, the magistrate finds that it is not desirable, in the interests of the safety of that person or of any other person, that that person should have in his possession, custody or control any firearm or other offensive weapon or any ammunition or explosive substance, the magistrate may

(a) order that any or all of the articles seized be disposed of on such terms as the magistrate deems fair and reasonable, and give such directions concerning the payment or application of the proceeds, if any, of the disposition as the magistrate sees fit; and

(b) where the magistrate is satisfied that the circumstances warrant such action, order that the possession by that person of any firearm or other offensive weapon or any ammunition or explosive substance specified in the order, or of all such articles be prohibited during any period of time, not exceeding five years, specified in the order and computed from the day the order is made. ss (9) 3(4)

Where no finding or application

(7) Any articles seized under subsection (1) or (2) in respect of which,

(a) no application under subsection (4) is made within thirty days from the date of execution of the warrant or of the seizure without warrant, as the case may be, or 25(3) Interp

(b) where an application under subsection (4) is made within the period referred to in paragraph *(a)*, the magistrate does not make a finding as described in subsection (6),

shall be returned to the person from whom they were seized.

Appeal

(8) Where a magistrate

(a) makes an order under subsection (6) with respect to any person, that person, or

(b) does not make a finding as described in subsection (6) following the hearing of an application under subsection (4), or makes such a finding but does not make an order to the effect described in paragraph (6)*(a)* and to the effect described in paragraph (6)*(b)*, the Attorney General or counsel instructed by him for that purpose 2

may appeal to the appeal court against the making of the order, or against the failure to make such a finding or to make an order to the effects so described, as the case may be, and the provisions of Part XXIV except sections 752 to 752.3 and sections 761 to 770 apply, *mutatis mutandis*, in respect of such an appeal. ss (9)

Definitions

(9) In this section,

"magistrate"

"magistrate" means a magistrate having jurisdiction in the territorial division where the person with respect to whom an application is made under subsection (1) or the person with respect to whom a search without warrant is made under subsection (2) resides; 2

"appeal court"

"appeal court" has the meaning given that expression in subsection 98(11).

Possession of firearm or ammunition while prohibited by order

Type 'B' (D) Offence

(10) Every one who has in his possession any firearm or other offensive weapon or any ammunition or explosive substance while he is prohibited from doing so by any order made pusuant to paragraph (6)*(b)* 3(4)

(a) is guilty of an indictable offence and is liable to imprisonment for five years; or

(b) is guilty of an offence punishable on summary conviction.

3\. (4) For the purposes of this Act,

(a) a person has anything in possession when he has it in his personal possession or knowingly

(i) has it in the actual possession or custody of another person, or

(ii) has it in any place, whether or not that place belongs to or is occupied by him, for the use or benefit of himself or of another person; and

(b) where one of two or more persons, with the knowledge and consent of the rest, has anything in his custody or possession, it shall be deemed to be in the custody and possession of each and all of them.

Interpretation Act

25\. (3) Where there is a reference to a number of days, not expressed to be clear days, between two events, in calculating the number of days there shall be excluded the day on which the first event happens and there shall be included the day on which the second event happens.

Found, Lost, Mislaid, Stolen and Defaced Firearms and other Weapons

Finding weapon
Type 'B' (D) Offence ss (5)

102. (1) Every one commits an offence who, on finding a prohibited weapon 82
or restricted weapon or firearm that he has reasonable grounds to believe has 82
been lost or abandoned, does not with reasonable despatch

(*a*) deliver it to a peace officer, a local registrar of firearms or a firearms 82
officer; or

(*b*) report to a peace officer, a local registrar of firearms or a firearms officer 2
that he has found it.

Lost weapon, etc.
Type 'B' (D) Offence ss (5)

(2) Every one commits an offence who, having lost or mislaid a restricted
weapon for which he has a registration certificate or permit or having had such a 82
restricted weapon stolen from his possession, does not with reasonable despatch report to a peace officer, or a local registrar of firearms that he has lost or mislaid such weapon or that such weapon has been stolen from him.

Tampering with serial number
Type 'B' (D) Offence ss (5)

(3) Every one commits an offence who, without lawful excuse, the proof of which lies on him

(*a*) alters, defaces or removes a serial number on a firearm; or

(*b*) has in his possession a firearm knowing that the serial number thereon has been altered, defaced or removed.

Evidence

(4) In proceedings under subsection (3), evidence that a person has in his possession a firearm the serial number of which has been wholly or partially obliterated is, in the absence of any evidence to the contrary, proof that such person has the firearm in his possession knowing that the serial number thereon has been altered, defaced or removed.

Punishment
Type 'B' (D) Offence

(5) Every one who contravenes this section

(*a*) is guilty of an indictable offence and is liable to imprisonment for five years; or

(*b*) is guilty of an offence punishable on summary conviction.

Firearms and other Businesses

Record of transaction in firearms, etc.
Type 'B' (D) Offence ss (8)

103. (1) Every person who carries on a business that includes the manufacturing, buying or selling at wholesale or retail, importing, repairing, altering or modifying or taking in pawn of restricted weapons or firearms shall

(*a*) keep records of transactions entered into by him with respect to such weapons or firearms in a form prescribed by the Commissioner and containing such information as is prescribed by the Commissioner;

(*b*) keep an inventory of all such weapons and firearms from time to time on hand at his place of business;

(*c*) produce the record and inventory for inspection at the request of any police officer or police constable or any other person authorized by regulations made pursuant to paragraph 106.8(*a*) to enter any place where a business referred to in that paragraph is carried on; and

(*d*) mail a copy of the record and inventory relating to restricted weapons to the Commissioner or to any person authorized by subsection 106.2(5) to issue a permit to carry on the business in accordance with any request in writing made by the Commissioner or any such person.

Report of loss, destruction or theft

Type 'B' (D) Offence ss (8)

(2) A person who carries on

(a) a business described in subsection (1), or

(b) a business that includes

(i) the manufacturing, buying or selling at wholesale or retail or importing of ammunition, or

(ii) the transportation or shipping of restricted weapons, firearms or ammunition

shall report to a local registrar of firearms or a peace officer any loss or destruction of any restricted weapon or firearm or any theft of any such weapon, firearm or ammunition that occurs in the course of the business.

Form of report

(3) A report made pursuant to subsection (2) shall be in a form prescribed by the Commissioner and shall be made forthwith after the loss, destruction or theft occurs or is discovered.

Permit to carry on business

Type 'B' (D) Offence ss (8)

(4) No person shall carry on a business described in subsection (1) or subparagraph (2)*(b)*(i) unless he is the holder of a permit to carry on such business.

Each location a separate business

(5) Where a person carries on a business described in subsection (1) or subparagraph (2)*(b)*(i) at more than one location, each such location shall be deemed for the purposes of this section and regulations made pursuant to paragraphs 106.8*(a)* to *(c)* to be a separate business.

Handling secure storage, etc.

Type 'B' (D) Offence ss (8)

(6) No person shall, in the course of a business described in subsection (1) or subparagraph (2)*(b)*(i),

(a) handle, store, display or advertise any restricted weapon, firearm or ammunition in a manner that contravenes any regulation made by the Governor in Council pursuant to paragraph 106.8*(a)*; or

(b) sell by mail-order any restricted weapon, firearm or ammunition in a manner that contravenes any regulation made by the Governor in Council pursuant to paragraph 106.8*(c)*.

Handling and transportation

Type 'B' (D) Offence ss (8)

(7) No person shall, in the course of a business described in subsection (1) or (2), knowingly handle, ship, store or transport any firearm or ammunition in a manner that contravenes any regulation relating to the secure handling, shipping, storage and transportation of firearms and ammunition made pursuant to paragraph 106.8*(d)*.

Punishment

Type 'B' (D) Offence

(8) Every one who contravenes subsection (1), (2), (4), (6) or (7)

(a) is guilty of an indictable offence and is liable to imprisonment for five years; or

(b) is guilty of an offence punishable on summary conviction.

Firearms Acquisition Certificates

Consideration of application and issuance of firearms acquisition certificate

104. (1) Where a firearms officer to whom an application for a firearms 82
acquisition certificate is made, after considering the information contained in 82
the application, any further information that is submitted to him pursuant to a requirement made under subsection (8) and such other information as may reasonably be regarded as relevant to the application, does not have notice of any matter that may render it desirable in the interests of the safety of the applicant or any other person that the applicant should not acquire a firearm, he shall, subject to subsection (2) and on receipt by him of the appropriate fee, if any, issue a firearms acquisition certificate to the applicant.

Where no certificate may be issued

(2) No firearms acquisition certificate may be issued to a person who

(a) is under the age of sixteen years; 3(1)

(b) is prohibited by an order made pursuant to section 98 or 101 or by a condition of a probation order referred to in paragraph 663(2)*(d)* from having a firearm in his possession; or

(c)

1976-77, chapter 53,
47. (3) Paragraph 104(2)*(c)* of the *Criminal Code*, as enacted by section 3 of this Act, shall come into force in any province only on a day fixed in a proclamation declaring that paragraph of the *Criminal Code* to be in force in that province.

Deemed notice

(3) A firearms officer shall be deemed to have notice of a matter that may render it desirable in the interests of the safety of an applicant for a firearms acquisition certificate or of any other person that the applicant should not
acquire a firearm and a magistrate, on a reference pursuant to subsection (6), 2
is entitled to confirm the opinion of a firearms officer that it is not desirable in the interests of the safety of such applicant or of any other person that such applicant should acquire a firearm, where it is made to appear to him that the applicant

(a) has been convicted within five years immediately preceding the date of his application, in proceedings on indictment, of

(i) an offence in the commission of which violence against another person was used, threatened or attempted, or

(ii) an offence under this Part;

(b) within five years immediately preceding the date of his application, has been treated for a mental disorder, whether in a hospital, mental institute or psychiatric clinic or otherwise and whether or not he was, during that period, confined to such a hospital, institute or clinic, where the disorder for which he was so treated was associated with violence or threatened or attempted violence on the part of the applicant against himself or any other person; or

(c) has a history of behaviour occurring within five years immediately preceding the date of his application, that included violence or threatened or attempted violence on the part of the applicant against himself or any other person.

Notice to be given

(4) Where a firearms officer to whom an application for a firearms acquisition certificate is made has notice of any matter that may render it desirable in the interests of the safety of the applicant or of any other person that the applicant should not acquire a firearm, he shall notify the applicant in writing that in his opinion it is not desirable in the interests of the safety of the applicant or of any other person or description of persons specified in the notice that the applicant acquire a firearm, and of his reasons therefor, and that, unless within thirty days from the day on which the notice is received by the applicant or within such further time as is, before or after the expiration of that period, allowed by a magistrate, the applicant, in writing, requests the firearms officer to refer his opinion to a magistrate for confirmation or variation thereof, the application for the firearms acquisition certificate will be refused by him.

Material to accompany notice under ss. (4)

(5) A notice given by a firearms officer under this section shall be accompanied by a copy or an extract of the provisions of this section and of subsections 98(5) to (13).

Reference to magistrate

(6) On receipt by a firearms officer within the time provided in subsection (4) of a request in writing to refer his opinion referred to in that subsection to a magistrate for confirmation or variation thereof, the firearms officer shall forthwith comply with that request.

Application for firearms acquisition certificate

(7) An application for a firearms acquisition certificate shall be in a form prescribed by the Commissioner and shall be made to a firearms officer. 82

Further information

(8) A firearms officer to whom an application for a firearms acquisition certificate is made may require the applicant to submit such further information in addition to that included in the application as may reasonably be regarded as relevant for the purpose of determining whether there is any matter that might render it dangerous for the safety of the applicant or of any other person if the applicant acquired a firearm.

Limitation

(9) No local registrar of firearms, firearms officer or other person shall 82
require as information, to be submitted by an applicant for a firearms acquisition certificate or permit, details concerning the makes or serial numbers of shotguns or rifles of a type, kind or design commonly used in Canada for hunting or sporting purposes.

Term for which certificate valid and fee

(10) A firearms acquisition certificate is valid for five years from the day on which it is issued, and the fee payable for the issue thereof is ten dollars.

Exception

(11) Notwithstanding subsection (10), no fee is payable in respect of a firearms acquisition certificate that is issued to a person who requires a firearm to hunt or trap in order to sustain himself or his family.

Validity of certificate

(12) A firearms acquisition certificate is valid throughout Canada. 1976-77, C. 10, s. 3.

Alternative firearms acquisition certificate

105. The Governor in Council may, on application by the Attorney General of a province, by order, declare any hunting licence, certificate, permit, or other document described in the order that is issued under the authority of a law of a province to be a valid firearms acquisition certificate where, in the opinion of the Governor in Council, such a licence, certificate, permit or other document may only be issued to persons to whom and in circumstances in which a firearms acquisition certificate could validly be issued if an application were made for such a certificate; and where an order is made under this section, a licence, certificate, permit or other document to which the order relates shall, on and after a day specified in the order, be deemed for all purposes of this Part to be a firearms acquisition certificate, whether or not the licence, certificate, permit or other document was issued before, on or after the day specified in the order. 28 Interp

Agreements with provinces

106. The Solicitor General, with the approval of the Governor in Council, may enter into agreements with the governments of the provinces for the coordination, to the maximum extent possible, of the administration of sections 104, 106.1 and 106.2 with the administration by provinces of provincial laws and programs relating to game hunting, firearms competency testing and firearms safety training. 1976-77, c. 10, s. 3.

Restricted Weapon Registration Certificates

Application for registration certificate

106.1 (1) An application for a registration certificate in respect of a restricted 82
weapon shall be in a form prescribed by the Commissioner and shall be made to 82
a local registrar of firearms. 82

Permit to convey

(2) On receiving an application for a registration certificate, a local registrar of firearms may issue a permit under subsection 106.2(4) authorizing the applicant to convey the weapon to him for examination.

Limitation

(3) A registration certificate may be issued only where a local registrar of firearms indicates on the copy of the application for the certificate that is sent to the Commissioner pursuant to subsection (5) that

(a) the applicant for the certificate is the holder of a firearms acquisition certificate and is eighteen or more years of age, and

(b) the restricted weapon to which the application relates bears a serial number sufficient to distinguish it from other restricted weapons or, in the case of an antique firearm that does not bear such a serial number, it is accurately described in the application,

and further that the restricted weapon to which the application relates

(c) is required by the applicant

(i) to protect life,

(ii) for use in connection with his lawful profession or occupation,

(iii) for use in target practice under the auspices of a shooting club approved for the purposes of this section by the Attorney General of the province in 2
which the premises of the shooting club are located, or

(iv) for use in target practice in accordance with conditions proposed to be attached to the permit to be issued in respect of the restricted weapon under subsection 106.2(1),

(d) will form part of a gun collection of the applicant who is a *bona fide* gun collector, or

(e) is or is deemed pursuant to paragraph 106.8 *(f)* to be a relic for the purposes of this Part.

Idem

(4) A registration certificate may only be issued in respect of a restricted weapon described in paragraph *(c)* of the definition "restricted weapon" in subsection 82(1) where a local registrar of firearms, in addition to the matters referred to in subsection (3), indicates on the copy of the application that is sent to the Commissioner pursuant to subsection (5) that the restricted weapon will form part of a gun collection of the applicant who is a *bona fide* gun collector whose collection includes one or more restricted weapons described in that paragraph.

bona fide — in or with good faith, there is no pretence, it is actually so

82. (1) For the purposes of this Part

"restricted weapon" means

(c) any firearm that is designed, altered or intended to fire bullets in rapid succession during one pressure of the trigger and that, on the day on which this paragraph comes into force, was registered as a restricted weapon and formed part of a gun collection in Canada of a *bona fide* gun collector, or

Jan. 1, 1978

Distribution of copies of application

(5) The local registrar of firearms by whom an application for a registration certificate is received shall

(a) send one copy thereof to the Commissioner;

(b) deliver one copy thereof to the applicant; and

(c) retain one copy thereof.

Matters to be reported to Commissioner

(6) Where a local registrar of firearms to whom an application for a registration certificate is made has notice of any matter that may render it desirable in the interests of the safety of the applicant or any other person that the applicant should not possess a restricted weapon, he shall report that matter to the Commissioner and he may, if the restricted weapon is conveyed to him for examination, hold the weapon pending the final disposition of the application for a registration certificate in respect thereof.

Registration certificate

(7) On receiving an endorsed copy of an application for a registration certificate, the Commissioner shall, subject to subsections (3) and (4) and section 106.4, register the restricted weapon described in the application and issue a restricted weapon registration certificate therefor to the applicant, in such form as the Commissioner may prescribe, indicating thereon the place at which the holder of the certificate is thereby entitled to possess the restricted weapon.

Limitation

(8) No place other than the usual dwelling house of the applicant for a registration certificate or his ordinary place of business may be indicated on the registration certificate as the place at which the holder of the certificate is thereby entitled to possess the restricted weapon to which the certificate relates. 1976-77, c. 10, s. 3.

1976-77, chapter 53,

48. (1) A permit issued under section 97 of the *Criminal Code* remains in force until the expiration of the period for which it is expressed to be issued unless the permit is sooner revoked in the manner provided by section 106.4 of the *Criminal Code,* as enacted by section 3 of this Act, which, by virtue of this subsection, applies to such permits as if they had been issued under section 106.2 of the *Criminal Code,* as enacted by section 3 of this Act.

(2) A registration certificate issued under section 98 of the *Criminal Code* remains in force as if it had been issued under section 106.1 of the *Criminal Code,* as enacted by section 3 of this Act and section 106.4 of the *Criminal Code* as so enacted applies thereto as if the registration certificate had been issued under the said section 106.1.

Carriage Permits, Business Permits and Minors Permits

Permit to carry restricted weapon

106.2 (1) A permit authorizing a person to have in his possession a restricted weapon elsewhere than at the place at which he is otherwise entitled to possess it, as indicated on the registration certificate issued in respect thereof, may be issued by the Commissioner, the Attorney General of a province, a chief provincial firearms officer or a member of a class of persons that has been designated in writing for that purpose by the Commissioner or the Attorney General of a province and shall remain in force until the expiration of the period for which it is expressed to be issued, unless it is sooner revoked. 82

Limitation

(2) A permit described in subsection (1) may be issued only where the person authorized to issue it is satisfied that the applicant therefor requires the restricted weapon to which the application relates

(a) to protect life;

(b) for use in connection with his lawful profession or occupation;

(c) for use in target practice under the auspices of a shooting club approved for the purposes of this section by the Attorney General of the province in which the premises of the shooting club are located; or

(d) for use in target practice in accordance with the conditions attached to the permit.

Permit to transport restricted weapon

(3) A permit to transport a restricted weapon from one place to another place specified therein may be issued by a local registrar of firearms to any person who is required to transport that weapon by reason of a change of residence or for any other *bona fide* reason, and shall remain in force until the expiration of the period for which it is expressed to be issued, unless it is sooner revoked.

Permit to convey restricted weapon

(4) A permit authorizing an applicant for a registration certificate to convey the weapon to which the application relates to a local registrar of firearms may be issued by a local registrar of firearms and shall remain in force until the expiration of the period for which it is expressed to be issued, unless it is sooner revoked.

Permit to carry on business

(5) A permit to carry on a business described in subsection 103(1) or subparagraph 103(2)*(b)*(i) may be issued by the Commissioner, the Attorney General or chief provincial firearms officer of the province where the business is or is to be carried on or by any person whom the Attorney General or the Commissioner designates in writing for that purpose and shall remain in force until the expiration of the period, not exceeding one year, for which it is expressed to be issued, unless it is sooner revoked.

Permits for persons hunting as a way of life

(6) A permit to possess a firearm, other than a restricted weapon, may be issued by a firearms officer to a person under the age of sixteen years who hunts or traps as a way of life if the firearms officer is satisfied that the person needs to hunt or trap in order to sustain himself or his family and the application for the permit includes a consent to the issuance of the permit signed by a parent of the applicant or, if a consent by a parent cannot be obtained because of the death of both parents or for any other reason it is not practicable or desirable in the opinion of the firearms officer to whom the application is made to obtain a parent's consent, a person having custody or control of the applicant.

Permit to person between 12 and 16 years of age

(7) A permit authorizing a person who is twelve or more years of age but under the age of sixteen years to possess a firearm, other than a restricted weapon, may be issued by a firearms officer if he is satisfied that the applicant therefor requires such a permit in order to enable him to possess a firearm for the purpose of target practice, game hunting or instruction in the use of firearms in accordance with conditions for supervision attached to the permit and the application for the permit includes a consent to the issuance of the permit signed by a parent of the applicant or, if a consent by a parent cannot be obtained because of the death of both parents or for any other reason it is not practicable or desirable in the opinion of the firearms officer to whom the application is made to obtain a parent's consent, a person having custody or control of the applicant.

Idem

(8) A permit mentioned in subsection (6) or (7) shall remain in force until

(a) the expiration of the period for which it is expressed to be issued, or

(b) the person to whom it is issued attains the age of sixteen years, 3(1)

whichever first occurs, unless it is sooner revoked.

3. (1) For the purposes of this Act a person shall be deemed to have been of a given age when the anniversary of his birthday, the number of which corresponds to that age, is fully completed, and until then to have been under that age.

Where no fee payable and fee for business permits

(9) Permits mentioned in subsections (1), (3), (4), (6) and (7) shall be issued without payment of a fee but no permit mentioned in subsection (5) may be issued unless the application therefor is accompanied by the prescribed fee.

Validity of permit

(10) No permit, other than

(a) a permit for the possession of a restricted weapon for use as described in paragraph (2)*(c)*,

(b) a permit to transport a restricted weapon from one place to another place specified therein as mentioned in subsection (3), or

(c) a permit authorizing an applicant for a registration certificate to convey the weapon to which the application relates to a local registrar of firearms as mentioned in subsection (4),

is valid outside the province in which it is issued unless it is issued by the Commissioner or a person designated in writing by him and authorized in writing by him to issue permits valid outside the province and is endorsed for the purposes of this subsection by the person who issued it as being valid within the provinces indicated therein.

Form and conditions of permit

(11) Every permit shall be in a form prescribed by the Commissioner, but any person who is authorized to issue a permit relating to any restricted weapon, firearm or ammunition may attach to the permit any reasonable condition relating to the use, carriage, possession, handling or storage of weapons or ammunition that he deems desirable in the particular circumstances and in the interests of the safety of the applicant or any other person. 1976-77, c. 10, s. 3.

Agreements with provinces

106.3 The Solicitor General, with the approval of the Governor in Council, may enter into agreements with the governments of the provinces providing for payments by Canada to the provinces in respect of costs actually incurred by the provinces in the administration of sections 103, 104 and subsection 106.2(5). 1976-77, c. 53, s. 3.

Refusal to Issue and Revocation of Registration Certificates and Permits and Appeals

Revocation of certificate

106.4 (1) A Registration certificate may be revoked by the Commissioner.

Revocation of permit

(2) A permit may be revoked by any person who is authorized to issue such a permit.

Refusal to issue a certificate

(3) The Commissioner may refuse to issue a registration certificate where he has notice of any matter that may render it desirable in the interests of the safety of the applicant or any other person that the applicant should not possess a restricted weapon.

Refusal to issue a permit

(4) Any person who is authorized to issue a permit under any of subsections 106.2(3) to (7) may refuse to issue such a permit where he has notice of any matter that may render it desirable in the interests of the safety of the applicant or any other person that such a permit should not be issued to the applicant.

Notice to be given

(5) Where a registration certificate or permit is revoked or the issue of any registration certificate or permit is refused under this section, the person by whom it is revoked or by whom its issue is refused shall notify the holder of the registration certficate or permit or the applicant, as the case may be, in writing of such revocation or refusal and of his reasons therefor and shall include in such notification a copy or an extract of the provisions of this section.

Disposal of restricted weapons, etc.

(6) A notice under subsection (5) shall specify therein a reasonable period of time within which the person affected by the revocation or refusal may surrender to a police officer or otherwise lawfully dispose of any restricted weapon, firearm or ammunition lawfully possessed by him prior to the revocation or refusal the possession of which by him has thereby become unlawful, and such person is not liable to prosecution by reason only of his having any such restricted weapon, firearm or ammunition in his possession during such period of time.

Idem

(7) Where an appeal is taken under subsection (8), the period of time referred to in subsection (6) does not commence until that appeal is finally disposed of.

Appeal

(8) A person who feels himself aggrieved by

(a) any action or decision taken under this section, or

(b) the failure of a local registrar of firearms to indicate on the copy of an application for a registration certificate that is sent by him to the Commissioner pursuant to subsection 106.1(5), any of the matters referred to in subsections 106.1(3) and (4) that is applicable in respect of the application,

may, within thirty days from the day on which he was notifed of the action or decision or became aware of the failure, unless before or after the expiration of that period further time is allowed by a magistrate, appeal to a magistrate from the action, decision or failure by filing with the magistrate a notice of appeal, setting out with reasonable certainty the action, decision or failure complained of and the grounds of appeal, together with such further material as the magistrate may require.

Service of notice of appeal

(9) A copy of any notice of appeal filed with a magistrate under subsection (8) and of any further material required to be filed therewith shall be served within fourteen days of the filing of the notice, unless before or after the expiration of that period further time is allowed by a magistrate, on the person who took the action or decision or who was responsible for the failure being appealed from or on such other person as the magistrate may direct.

Appellant as witness

(10) For the purposes of an appeal under subsection (8), the appellant is a competent and compellable witness.

Disposition of appeal

(11) On the hearing of an appeal under subsection (8), the magistrate may

(a) dismiss the appeal; or

(b) allow the appeal and

(i) cancel the revocation of the registration certificate or permit or direct that a registration certificate or permit be issued to the applicant, as the case may be, or

(ii) direct that a registration certificate be issued notwithstanding the failure referred to in paragraph (8)*(b)*.

Burden on applicant

(12) A magistrate shall dispose of an appeal under subsection (8) heard by him by dismissing it unless the applicant establishes to the satisfaction of the magistrate that a disposition referred to in paragraph (11)*(b)* is warranted.

Appeal to appeal court

(13) Where the magistrate

(a) dismisses an appeal under subsection (11), the appellant, or

(b) allows an appeal under subsection (11),

(i) the Attorney General of Canada or counsel instructed by him for the purpose, if the person who took the action or decision or who was responsible for the failure referred to in paragraph (8)*(b)* that was appealed from to the magistrate was the Commissioner or a local registrar of firearms appointed by him, or

(ii) the Attorney General or counsel instructed by him for the purpose, in any other case,

may appeal to the appeal court against the dismissal or against the allowing of the appeal, as the case may be, and the provisions of Part XXIV except sections 752 to 752.3 and sections 761 to 770 apply, *mutatis mutandis*, in respect of such an appeal.

mutatis mutandis — after the necessary changes in detail so that the text applies.

Definitions

(14) In this section,

"magistrate"

"magistrate" means a magistrate having jurisdiction in the territorial division where the person who feels himself aggrieved as described in subsection (8) resides;

"appeal court"

"appeal court" has the meaning given that expression in subsection 98(11). 1976-77, c. 53, s. 3.

98. (11) In this section,

"appeal court" means

(a) in the Province of Prince Edward Island, the Supreme Court,

(b) in the Provinces of Nova Scotia, Ontario, Manitoba, British Columbia and Newfoundland, the district or county court of the district or county where the adjudication was made,

(c) in the Province of Quebec, the Superior Court,

(d) in the Provinces of New Brunswick, Alberta and Saskatchewan, the Court of Queen's Bench, and

(e) Repealed. 1978-79, c. 11, s. 10, I. 6(6)

(f) in the Yukon Territory and the Northwest Territories, the Supreme Court;

Offences Relating to Certificate and Permits

False statements to procure firearms acquisition certificate, etc.
Type 'B' (D) Offence

106.5 (1) Every one who, for the purpose of procuring a firearms acquisition 82
certificate, registration certificate or permit for himself or any other person, 82
knowingly makes a statement orally or in writing that is false or misleading or knowingly fails to disclose any information that is relevant to the application for the firearms acquisition certificate, registration certificate or permit

(a) is guilty of an indictable offence and is liable to imprisonment for two years; or

(b) is guilty of an offence punishable on summary conviction. 722(1)

Tampering with firearms acquisition certificate, registration certificate or permit
Type 'B' (D) Offence

(2) Every one who, without lawful excuse the proof of which lies on him, alters, defaces or falsifies a firearms acquisition certificate, registration certificate or permit

(a) is guilty of an indictable offence and is liable to imprisonment for two years; or

(b) is guilty of an offence punishable on summary conviction. 722(1)

Failure to comply with conditions of permit
Type 'B' (D) Offence

(3) Every one who, without lawful excuse, fails to comply with any condition of a permit held by him

(a) is guilty of an indictable offence and is liable to imprisonment for two years; or

(b) is guilty of an offence punishable on summary conviction. 722(1)

Failure to deliver up firearms acquisition certificate, etc.
Type 'A' Offence

(4) Every one who,

(a) being a holder of a registration certificate or permit that is revoked in accordance with this Part, or

(b) being a person against whom an order prohibiting possession of any firearm or ammunition is made under section 98 or paragraph 101(6)*(b)*, or being prohibited by a condition of a probation order referred to in paragraph 663(2)*(d)* from having a firearm in his possession,

fails to deliver up the registration certificate or permit or, in a case described in paragraph *(b)*, any firearms acquisition certificate, registration certificate
or permit held by him, to a peace officer, to a local registrar of firearms or to a 82
firearms officer forthwith after such suspension or revocation or the making of 82
such order or probation order, is guilty of an offence punishable on summary conviction. 1976-77, c. 53, s. 3. 722(1)

722. (1) Except where otherwise expressly provided by law, every one who is convicted of an offence punishable on summary conviction is liable to a fine of not more than five hundred dollars or to imprisonment for six months or to both.

Registry

Registry to be maintained

106.6 (1) The Commissioner shall cause a registry to be maintained in which shall be kept a record of

(a) every registration certificate that is issued under section 106.1;

(b) every registration certificate that is revoked under subsection 106.4(1);

(c) every application for a registration certificate that is refused under subsection 106.4(3);

(d) every permit issued under subsection 106.2(5) that is revoked under subsection 106.4(2);

(e) every application for a permit under subsection 106.2(5) that is refused under subsection 106.4(4);

(f) every application for a firearms acquisition certificate that is refused;

(g) every prohibition order made under section 98 or paragraph 101(6)(*b*); and

(h) every probation order to which a condition referred to in paragraph 663(2)(*d*) is attached.

Information to be submitted to Commissioner

(2) Each person by whom

(a) a firearms acquisition certificate or permit is issued,

(b) a permit is revoked, or

(c) an application for a permit is refused,

shall submit such information in relation thereto at such time and in such form as is prescribed by the regulations for the purpose of enabling the Commissioner to compile the reports referred to in section 106.9.

Idem

(3) Every firearms officer by whom an application for a firearms acquisition certificate is refused, every person by whom an application for a permit under subsection 106.2(5) is refused or by whom a permit issued under that subsection is revoked, every court, judge, justice or magistrate that makes a prohibition order under section 98 or paragraph 101(6)(*b*) and every court that prescribes as a condition of a probation order a condition referred to in paragraph 663(2)(*d*) shall forthwith cause the Commissioner to be notified thereof.
1976-77, c. 53, s. 3.

General

Onus on the accused

106.7 (1) Where, in any proceedings under any of sections 83 to 106.5, any question arises as to whether a person is or was the holder of a firearms acquisition certificate, registration certificate or permit, the onus is on the accused to prove that that person is or was the holder of such firearms acquisition certificate, registration certificate or permit.

Firearms acquisition certificate, etc., as evidence

(2) In any proceedings under any of sections 83 to 106.5, a document purporting to be a firearms acquisition certificate, registration certificate or permit is evidence of the statements contained therein.

Regulations

106.8 The Governor in Council may make regulations

(a) regulating the handling, secure storage, display and advertising of restricted weapons, firearms and ammunition by persons carrying on businesses described in subsection 103(1) or subparagraph 103(2)*(b)*(i) and providing authority for police officers and police constables and members of any other class of persons designated for the purposes of a province by the Attorney General of that province to enter any place where any such business is carried on, at any time during ordinary business hours, for the purpose of inspecting the secure storage facilities therein and the manner in which restricted weapons, firearms and ammunition are handled and displayed in the course of the business;

(b) regulating the handling, secure storage and display of weapons by operators of and persons employed in museums approved for the purposes of this Part by the Commissioner or the Attorney General of the province in which they are situated;

(c) regulating the mail-order sale of restricted weapons, firearms and ammunition by persons carrying on businesses described in subsection 103(1) or subparagraph 103(2)*(b)*(i);

(d) providing for the secure handling, shipping, storing and transportation of firearms and ammunition by persons engaged in businesses that include the transportation of goods;

(e) prescribing the fees to be paid to Her Majesty in right of Canada on filing applications for permits mentioned in subsection 106.2(5);

(f) prescribing classes of firearms that shall be deemed to be relics for the purposes of this Part;

(g) prescribing conditions relating to the storage, display, handling and transportation of restricted weapons that form part of gun collections of *bona fide* gun collectors;

(h) authorizing the destruction, at such times as are specified in the regulations, of such records and inventories that are required by the provisions of this Part to be maintained as are designated in the regulations; and

(i) prescribing anything that is, by any provision of this Part, required to be prescribed by the regulations. 1976-77, c. 53, s. 3.

bona fide — in or with good faith, there is not pretence, it is actually so

Report to Parliament

106.9 The Commissioner shall, within three months after the end of each year and at such other times as the Solicitor General of Canada may, in writing, request, submit to the Solicitor General a report, in such form and setting forth such information as the Solicitor General may direct, with regard to the administration of the provisions of this Part respecting firearms acquisition certificates, registration certificates and permits and the information contained in the registry maintained pursuant to section 106.6, and the Solicitor General shall cause each such report to be laid before Parliament within fifteen days after the receipt thereof by him, or, if Parliament is not then sitting, on any of the first fifteen days next thereafter that Parliament is sitting. 1976-77, c. 53, s. 3. 19 Interp

Interpretation Act

19. Where an Act requires a report or other document to be laid before Parliament and, in compliance with the Act, a particular report or document has been laid before Parliament at a session thereof, nothing in the Act shall be construed as requiring the same report or document to be laid before Parliament at any subsequent session thereof.

Restricted Weapons Orders — Chapters 442-443-444

ORDER DECLARING CERTAIN WEAPONS TO BE RESTRICTED WEAPONS

Short Title

1. This Order may be cited as the *Restricted Weapons Order.*

Declaration

2. The following weapons are hereby declared to be restricted weapons:

(a) the semi-automatic carbine known as the "Commando Mark III";

(b) the auto-loading twelve gauge shotgun known as the "High Standard Model 10, Series "A"" or "High Standard Model 10, Series "B"";

(c) the semi-automatic action rifle known as the "Commando Mark V";

(d) the semi-automatic action rifle known as the "Thompson Model 27A-1"; and

(e) the semi-automatic action rifle known as the "Colt Model AR-15".

SOR/78-42

Prohibited Weapons Order, No. 1 — Chapter 433

ORDER DECLARING CERTAIN DEVICES TO BE PROHIBITED WEAPONS

Short Title

1. This Order may be cited as the *Prohibited Weapons Order*, No. 1.

Declaration

2. Any device designed to be used for the purpose of injuring, immobilizing or otherwise incapacitating any person by the discharge therefrom of

(a) tear gas, Mace or other gas, or

(b) any liquid, spray, powder or other substance that is capable of injuring, immobilizing or otherwise incapacitating any person,

is hereby declared to be a prohibited weapon.

Prohibited Weapons Order, No. 2 — Chapter 434

ORDER DECLARING CERTAIN WEAPONS TO BE PROHIBITED WEAPONS

Short Title

1. This Order may be cited as the *Prohibited Weapons Order, No. 2.*

Declaration

2. The following devices are hereby declared to be prohibited weapons:

(a) any instrument or device commonly known as "*nunchaku*", being two hard non-flexible sticks, clubs, pipes or rods connected by a rope, cord, wire or chain;

(b) any instrument or device commonly known as "*shuriken*", being a hard non-flexible plate having three or more radiating points with one or more sharp edges in the shape of a polygon, trefoil, cross, star, diamond or other geometric shape;

(c) any instrument or device commonly known as "*manrikigusari*" or "*kusari*", being a length of rope, cord, wire or chain fastened at each end of a hexagonal or other geometrically shaped hard weight or hand-grip; and

(d) any finger ring that has one or more blades or sharp objects that are capable of being projected from the surface of the ring. SOR/78-277

Prohibited Weapons Order, No. 3 — Chapter 435

ORDER DECLARING CERTAIN WEAPONS TO BE PROHIBITED WEAPONS

Short Title

1. This Order may be cited as the *Prohibited Weapons Order, No. 3.*

Declaration

2. The following devices are hereby declared to be prohibited weapons:

(a) the device known as "Taser Public Defender", being a gun or a device similar to a gun capable of injuring, immobilizing or otherwise incapacitating a person by the discharge therefrom of darts or any other object carrying an electric current or substance; and

(b) any other device similar to the device referred to in paragraph *(a)*. SOR/78-278

Prohibited Weapons Order, No. 4 — Chapter 436

ORDER DECLARING CERTAIN WEAPONS TO BE PROHIBITED WEAPONS

Short Title

1. This Order may be cited as the *Prohibited Weapons Order, No. 4.*

Declaration

2. The following devices are hereby declared to be prohibited weapons:

(a) the device known as the "Constant Companion", being a belt containing a blade capable of being withdrawn from the belt, with the buckle of the belt forming a handle for the blade;

(b) any other device similar to the device described in paragraph *(a)*. SOR/78-279

Prohibited Weapons Order, No. 5 — Chapter 437

ORDER DECLARING CERTAIN WEAPONS TO BE PROHIBITED WEAPONS

Short Title

1. This Order may be cited as the *Prohibited Weapons Order, No. 5.*

Declaration

2. The following devices are hereby declared to be prohibited weapons:

(a) the device commonly known as a "Spiked Wristband", being a wristband to which a spike or blade is affixed; and

(b) any other device similar to the device described in paragraph *(a)*. SOR/78-280

Prohibited Weapons Order, No. 6 — Chapter 438

ORDER DECLARING CERTAIN WEAPONS TO BE PROHIBITED WEAPONS

Short Title

1. This Order may be cited as the *Prohibited Weapons Order, No. 6.*

Declaration

2. The following devices are hereby declared to be prohibited weapons:

(a) the device commonly known as "Yaqua Blowgun", being a tube or pipe designed for the purpose of shooting arrows or darts by the breath; and

(b) any other device similar to the device referred to in paragraph *(a)*. SOR/78-281

Prohibited Weapons Order, No. 7 — Chapter 439

ORDER DECLARING CERTAIN DEVICES TO BE PROHIBITED WEAPONS

Short Title

1. This Order may be cited as the *Prohibited Weapons Order, No. 7.*

Declaration

2. The following devices are hereby declared to be prohibited weapons

(a) the device commonly known as a "Kiyoga Baton" or "Steel Cobra" and any similar device consisting of a manually-triggerred telescoping spring-loaded steel whip terminated in a heavy calibre striking tip; and

(b) the device commonly known as a "Morning Star" and any similar device consisting of a ball of metal or other heavy material, studded with spikes and connected to a handle by a length of chain, rope or other flexible material.

Prohibited Weapons Order, No. 8 — SOR/79-583

ORDER DECLARING CERTAIN WEAPONS TO BE PROHIBITED WEAPONS

Short Title

1. This Order may be cited as the *Prohibited Weapons Order, No. 8.*

Declaration

2. The following devices are hereby declared to be prohibited weapons:

(a) the device known as the "SSS-1 Stinger" and any similar device consisting of a single shot .22 calibre weapon designed or of a size to fit in the palm of the hand or in a cigarette package; and

(b) the device known as "Brass Knuckles" and any similar device consisting of a band of metal with finger holes designed to fit over the root knuckles of the hand.

NOTE: Prohibited Weapons Order, No. 8 is effective November 1, 1979.

REGULATIONS RESPECTING THE CONTROL OF RESTRICTED WEAPONS AND FIREARMS

Short Title

1. These Regulations may be cited as the *Restricted Weapons and Firearms Control Regulations.*

Interpretation

2. In these Regulations,

"Act" means the *Criminal Code,*

"business" means a business described in subsection 103(1) or subparagraph 103(2)*(b)*(i) of the Act;

"premises" means the premises used in the course of carrying on a business.

Interpretation Act

15. Where an enactment confers power to make regulations, expressions used in the regulations have the same respective meaning as in the enactment conferring the power.

3. Every person who is the holder of a permit to carry on a business shall ensure that, during the course of the business,

(a) every firearm, other than a restricted weapon, that is included in the inventory of the business and on display

(i) is secured by a chain or metal cable, which is passed through the trigger guard, one end of which is attached to a wall or permanent fixture on the premises and the other end of which is attached by a lock to such wall or permanent fixture, to prevent the removal of the firearm by a person other than the holder of the permit or a person employed by the holder of the permit,

(ii) is secured by a metal bar, one end of which is attached to a wall or permanent fixture on the premises and the other end of which is attached by a lock to such wall or permanent fixture, to prevent the removal of the firearm by a person other than the holder of the permit or a person employed by the holder of the permit,

(iii) is placed in a locked display case or cabinet,

(iv) is displayed at a location on the premises readily accessible only to the holder of the permit or a person employed by the holder of the permit, or

(v) is secured by a method that is equal or superior to the methods described in subparagraphs (i) to (iv) and approved in writing by the person authorized by subsection 106.2(5) of the Act to issue the permit;

(b) every restricted weapon that is included in the inventory of the business and on display

(i) is placed in a locked display case or cabinet, and

(ii) is not displayed in a store window;

(c) every restricted weapon or firearm that is included in the inventory of the business and is on the premises but not displayed is placed

(i) in a securely locked cabinet, vault or safe,

(ii) in a securely locked location,

(iii) at a location that is readily accessible only to the holder of the permit or to a person employed by the holder of the permit, or

(iv) in a location the security of which is

(A) equal or superior to the methods described in subparagraphs (i) to (iii), and

(B) approved in writing by the person authorized by subsection 106.2(5) of the Act to issue the permit;

(d) no person handles a loaded restricted weapon or firearm on the premises unless

(i) it is received for the purpose of altering, modifying or repairing the weapon or firearm, or

(ii) in accordance with the conditions set out in the permit; and

(e) no restricted weapon or firearm is handled on the premises except

(i) by him,

(ii) under his supervision,

(iii) by a person employed by him, or

(iv) under the supervision of a person employed by him.

Security of Premises

4. Where the inventory of a business includes restricted weapons that are on the premises, the person who is the holder of the permit to carry on the business shall cause to be installed on the premises a burglar alarm system.

5. Every person who is the holder of a permit to carry on a business shall ensure that every window of the premises that may be opened and every exterior door of the premises is capable of being securely locked.

Advertising

6. No person who is the holder of a permit to carry on a business shall, in an advertisement of any restricted weapon or firearm, depict or extol violence against another person.

Inspection of Secure Storage Facilities

7. Police officers, police constables and firearms officers designated for the purposes of a province by the Attorney General of the province may enter any premises in that province, at any time during ordinary business hours, for the purpose of inspecting the secure storage facilities therein and the manner in which restricted weapons, firearms and ammunition are handled and displayed in the course of the business.

Museums

8. Every person who is the operator of a museum approved by the Commissioner or the Attorney General of the province in which the museum is situated shall ensure that

(a) every restricted weapon or firearm included in the inventory of the museum is unloaded;

(b) every restricted weapon or firearm that is on display in the museum is displayed in a manner and at a location that will prevent its removal by a person other than the operator of or a person employed in the museum;

(c) every restricted weapon or firearm included in the inventory of the museum that is not on display in the museum is placed

(i) in a securely locked cabinet, vault or safe,

(ii) in a securely locked location, or

(iii) at a location readily accessible only to the operator of or a person employed in the museum.

9. Where the inventory of a museum includes restricted weapons or weapons capable of firing bullets in rapid succession during one pressure of the trigger, the operator of the museum shall cause to be installed in the museum a burglar alarm system.

10. Where the inventory of a museum includes restricted weapons or firearms, the operator of the museum shall ensure that every window of the museum that may be opened and every exterior door of the museum is capable of being securely locked.

Mail Order Sales

11. (1) Every person who is the holder of a permit to carry on a business may, by mail order, mail, ship or deliver to any person

(a) a firearm that is a rifle or shot gun if the holder of the permit has in his possession a current firearms acquisition certificate issued to that person; or

(b) a restricted weapon if the holder of the permit has in his possession

(i) a permit issued to that person pursuant to subsection 106.2(4) of the Act, and

(ii) a valid firearms acquisition certificate issued to that person.

(2) Subject to subsection (3), where a restricted weapon or firearm is mailed, shipped or delivered, pursuant to subsection (1), in a container to a consignee in Canada, the markings, if any, on the exterior of the container shall not indicate that a restricted weapon or firearm is contained therein.

(3) Subsection (2) does not apply where the only markings on the exterior of the container indicating that a restricted weapon or firearm is contained therein is the consignee's address.

Transportation of Firearms

12. (1) Any person engaged in a commercial enterprise that includes the transportation of goods may handle and transport any restricted weapon or firearm if

(a) subject to subsection (2), the restricted weapon or firearm is in a container of cardboard, wood or other solid material of such strength, construction and character that it cannot be readily broken or accidentally opened while being conveyed;

(b) subject to subsections (2) and (3), the markings, if any, on the exterior of the container referred to in paragraph *(a)* do not indicate that a restricted weapon or firearm is contained therein;

(c) the restricted weapon or firearm is unloaded; and

(d) except in the case of a carrier that is an aircraft, that part of the carrier conveying the restricted weapon or firearm is securely locked or sealed when left unattended.

(2) Paragraphs (1)*(a)* and *(b)* do not apply where the restricted weapon or firearm is carried and kept on board the carrier by the person who owns or has the use of the restricted weapon or firearm.

(3) Paragraph (1)*(b)* does not apply where

(a) the only markings on the exterior of the container indicating that a restricted weapon or firearm is contained therein is the consignee's address;

(b) the container and its contents are to be delivered to a consignee in a country other than Canada; or

(c) the container and its contents have been imported into Canada.

Destruction of Records and Inventories

13. The records and inventories that are required to be maintained pursuant to section 103 of the Act may be destroyed after they have been kept for a period of five years.

Storage, Display and Transportation of Gun Collections

14. (1) Restricted weapons that form part of a gun collection of a *bona fide* gun collector

(a) shall be stored, unloaded,

(i) in a securely locked display case, cabinet, safe, vault or other secure receptacle, or

(ii) in a securely locked location; and

(b) shall, during any display, be unloaded and where the display is a public display, be under supervision.

(2) A restricted weapon referred to in subsection (1) that is being transported shall be unloaded and where transported

(a) in a motor vehicle equipped with a trunk that may be securely locked, the weapon shall, during any period the vehicle is unattended, to kept in the trunk and the trunk shall be locked; or

(b) in a motor vehicle not equipped with a trunk, the weapon shall, during any period the vehicle is unattended, be kept at a place in the vehicle where it is not readily visible to the general public and the vehicle shall be locked.

Relics

15. For the purposes of Part II.1 of the Act, the following classes of firearms are deemed to be relics:

(a) any firearm that is of value as a curiosity or rarity; and

(b) any firearm that is valued as a memento, remembrance or souvenir.

Permit Fees

16. (1) Subject to subsections (2) to (6), the annual fee to be paid on filing an application for a permit to carry on a business set out in column I of an item of the schedule shall be the fee set out in column II of that item.

(2) Subject to subsection (3), where a person applies for a permit to carry on more than one business set out in column I of an item of the schedule at a location, the annual fee payable by that person for a permit in respect of all the businesses for which he has filed an application referred to in subsection (1) at that location shall be a single fee and that fee shall be the fee payable by him, pursuant to subsection (1), in respect of that business set out in column I of an item of the schedule for which he has filed an application whose fee set out in column II of that item is the greatest.

(3) Subject to subsections (4) to (6), where a permit to carry on a business set out in column I of an item of the schedule has been issued to a person for a period of less than twelve months, the fee payable for that permit for the period shall be that proportion of the amount of the annual fee set out in column II of that item of the schedule that the number of months for which the permit is issued is of twelve months.

(4) Subject to subsections (5) and (6), for the purpose of item 4 of the schedule, the number of restricted weapons or firearms sold by a retailer are deemed to be the number sold by the retailer during the twelve month period immediately prior to the date of any application for a permit authorizing him to carry on or to continue to carry on a business of selling restricted weapons or firearms at retail.

(5) Where a person has not carried on a business of selling restricted weapons or firearms at retail immediately prior to applying for a permit referred to in subsection (4), the first annual fee payable by that person for a permit to carry on such a business shall be twenty-five dollars.

(6) Where a person has carried on a business of selling restricted weapons or firearms at retail for a period of less than twelve months, the first annual fee payable for a permit to continue to carry on the business shall be determined in accordance with item 4 of the schedule based on the number of restricted weapons or firearms sold at retail during that period or twenty-five dollars, whichever is the greater.

Prescribed Classes

17. The following classes of peace officers and public officers are hereby prescribed for the purposes of paragraphs 90(1)*(b)* and 96(1)*(b)* of the Act:

(a) wardens, deputy wardens, instructors, keepers, gaolers, guards and any other officers or permanent employees of a prison;

(b) police officers, police constables, constables and sheriffs; and

(c) employees of federal and provincial departments engaged in the enforcement of federal and provincial game and fisheries laws.

SCHEDULE

FEES FOR A PERMIT TO CARRY ON A BUSINESS

Item	Column I Business	Column II Fee
	Ammunition	
1.	Manufacturer of ammunition	$ 250
2.	Selling ammunition at wholesale	225
3.	Selling ammunition at retail	10
	Restricted Weapons or Firearms	
4.	Selling restricted weapons or firearms at retail	
	(a) for the sale of 15 or less restricted weapons or firearms	25
	(b) for the sale of more than 15 but less than 51 restricted weapons or firearms	75
	(c) for the sale of more than 50 but less than 101 restricted weapons or firearms	125
	(d) for the sale of more than 100 restricted weapons or firearms	175
5.	Selling restricted weapons or firearms at wholesale	225
6.	Manufacturing restricted weapons or firearms	250
7.	Repairing, altering or modifying restricted weapons or firearms	25
8.	Taking in pawn of restricted weapons or firearms	50

SOR/78-670

PART III

OFFENCES AGAINST THE ADMINISTRATION OF LAW AND JUSTICE

Interpretation

Definitions **107.** In this Part

"evidence" "evidence" means an assertion of fact, opinion, belief or knowledge whether material or not and whether admissible or not;

"government" "government" means

(*a*) the Government of Canada,

(*b*) the government of a province, or 28 Interp

(*c*) Her Majesty in right of Canada or in right of a province;

"judicial proceeding" "judicial proceeding" means a proceeding

(*a*) in or under the authority of a court of justice or before a grand jury,

(*b*) before the Senate or House of Commons of Canada or a committee of the Senate or House of Commons, or before a legislative council, legislative 28 Interp
assembly or house of assembly or a committee thereof that is authorized by law to administer an oath, 28 Interp

(*c*) before a court, judge, justice, magistrate or coroner, 2

(*d*) before an arbitrator or umpire, or a person or body of persons authorized by law to make an inquiry and take evidence therein under oath, or 107

(*e*) before a tribunal by which a legal right or legal liability may be established,

whether or not the proceeding is invalid for want of jurisdiction or for any other reason;

"office" "office" includes

(*a*) an office or appointment under the government,

(*b*) a civil or military commission, and

(*c*) a position or employment in a public department;

"official" "official" means a person who

(*a*) holds an office, or 107

(*b*) is appointed to discharge a public duty;

"witness" "witness" means a person who gives evidence orally under oath or by affidavit in 107
a judicial proceeding, whether or not he is competent to be a witness, and 107
includes a child of tender years who gives evidence but does not give it under 16(1) CEA
oath, because, in the opinion of the person presiding, the child does not understand the nature of an oath. 1953-54, c. 51, s. 99.

Interpretation Act

28. In every enactment

"legislature", "legislative council" or "legislative assembly" includes the Lieutenant Governor in Council and the Legislative Assembly of the Northwest Territories, as constituted before the 1st day of September 1905, the Commissioner in Council of the Yukon Territory, and the Commissioner in Council of the Northwest Territories;

"oath" includes a solemn affirmation or declaration, whenever the context applies to any person by whom and case in which a solemn affirmation or declaration may be made instead of an oath; and in like cases the expression "sworn" includes the expression "affirmed" or "declared";

"province" means a province of Canada, and includes the Yukon Territory and the Northwest Territories;

Corruption and Disobedience

Bribery of holder of judicial office

Type 'G' Offence with consent ss. (2)

Bribery of member of Parliament or legislature

Type 'E' Offence

IPA offence 178.1

108. (1) Every one who

(a) being the holder of a judicial office, or being a member of the Parliament of Canada or of a legislature, corruptly 28 Interp

(i) accepts or obtains,

(ii) agrees to accept, or

(iii) attempts to obtain, 24

any money, valuable consideration, office, place or employment for himself or another person in respect of anything done or omitted or to be done or omitted by him in his official capacity, or 107

(b) gives or offers corruptly to a person who holds a judicial office, or is a member of the Parliament of Canada or of a legislature, any money, valuable consideration, office, place or employment in respect of anything done or omitted or to be done or omitted by him in his official capacity for himself or another person,

is guilty of an indictable offence and is liable to imprisonment for fourteen years.

Consent of Attorney General

(2) No proceedings against a person who holds a judicial office shall be instituted under this section without the consent in writing of the Attorney General of Canada. 1953-54, c. 51, s. 100. 2

Bribery of officers

Type 'F' Offence

IPA offence 178.1

109. Every one who

(a) being a justice, police commissioner, peace officer, public officer, or officer of a juvenile court, or being employed in the administration of criminal law, corruptly 2

(i) accepts or obtains,

(ii) agrees to accept, or

(iii) attempts to obtain, 24

for himself or any other person any money, valuable consideration, office, place or employment with intent

(iv) to interfere with the administration of justice,

(v) to procure or facilitate the commission of an offence, or

(vi) to protect from detection or punishment a person who has committed or who intends to commit an offence, or

(b) gives or offers, corruptly, to a person mentioned in paragraph *(a)* any money, valuable consideration, office, place or employment with intent that the person should do anything mentioned in subparagraph *(a)*(iv), (v) or (vi),

is guilty of an indictable offence and is liable to imprisonment for fourteen years. 1953-54, c. 51, s. 101.

127 Obstructing justice

129 Compounding indictable offence

130 Corruptly taking reward for recovery of goods

127. (1) Every one who wilfully attempts in any manner to obstruct, pervert or defeat the course of justice in a judicial proceeding,

(a) by indemnifying or agreeing to indemnify a surety, in any way and either in whole or in part, or

(b) where he is a surety, by accepting or agreeing to accept a fee or any form of indemnity whether in whole or in part from or in respect of a person who is released or is to be released from custody,

is guilty of

(c) an indictable offence and is liable to imprisonment for two years, or

(d) an offence punishable on summary conviction.

(2) Every one who wilfully attempts in any manner other than a manner described in subsection (1) to obstruct, pervert or defeat the course of justice is guilty of an indictable offence and is liable to imprisonment for ten years.

(3) Without restricting the generality of subsection (2), every one shall be deemed wilfully to attempt to obstruct, pervert or defeat the course of justice who in a judicial proceeding, existing or proposed,

(a) dissuades or attempts to dissuade a person by threats, bribes or other corrupt means from giving evidence;

(b) influences or attempts to influence by threats, bribes or other corrupt means, a person in his conduct as a juror; or

(c) accepts or obtains, agrees to accept or attempts to obtain a bribe or other corrupt consideration to abstain from giving evidence, or to do or to refrain from doing anything as a juror.

129. Every one who asks or obtains or agrees to receive any valuable consideration for himself or any other person by agreeing to compound or conceal an indictable offence is guilty of an indictable offence and is liable to imprisonment for two years.

130. Every one who corruptly accepts any valuable consideration, directly or indirectly, under pretence or upon account of helping any person to recover anything obtained by the commission of an indictable offence is guilty of an indictable offence and is liable to imprisonment for five years.

Frauds upon the government
Type 'D' Offence ss. (3)
IPA offence 178.1

110. (1) Every one commits an offence who

(a) directly or indirectly

(i) gives, offers, or agrees to give or offer to an official or to any member of his family, or to any one for the benefit of an official, or 107

(ii) being an official, demands, accepts or offers or agrees to accept from any person for himself or another person,

a loan, reward, advantage or benefit of any kind as consideration for cooperation, assistance, exercise of influence or an act or omission in connection with

(iii) the transaction of business with or any matter of business relating to the government, or

(iv) a claim against Her Majesty or any benefit that Her Majesty is authorized or is entitled to bestow,

whether or not, in fact, the official is able to cooperate, render assistance, exercise influence or do or omit to do what is proposed, as the case may be;

(b) having dealings of any kind with the government, pays a commission or reward to or confers an advantage or benefit of any kind upon an employee or official of the government with which he deals, or to any member of his family, 107 or to any one for the benefit of the employee or official, with respect to those dealings, unless he has the consent in writing of the head of the branch of government with which he deals, the proof of which lies upon him;

(c) being an official or employee of the government, demands, accepts or offers or agrees to accept from a person who has dealings with the government a commission, reward, advantage or benefit of any kind directly or indirectly, by himself or through a member of his family or through any one for his benefit, unless he has the consent in writing of the head of the branch of government that employs him or of which he is an official, the proof of which lies upon him;

(d) having or pretending to have influence with the government or with a minister of the government or an official, demands, accepts or offers or agrees to accept for himself or another person a reward, advantage or benefit of any kind as consideration for cooperation, assistance, exercise of influence or an act or omission in connection with

(i) anything mentioned in subparagraph *(a)*(iii) or (iv), or

(ii) the appointment of any person, including himself, to an office;

(e) offers, gives or agrees to offer or give to a minister of the government or an official a reward, advantage or benefit of any kind as consideration for cooperation, assistance, exercise of influence or an act or omission in connection with

(i) anything mentioned in subparagraph *(a)*(iii) or (iv), or

(ii) the appointment of any person, including himself, to an office; or

(f) having made a tender to obtain a contract with the government

(i) gives, offers or agrees to give to another person who has made a tender, or to a member of his family, or to another person for the benefit of that person, a reward, advantage or benefit of any kind as consideration for the withdrawal of the tender of that person, or

(ii) demands, accepts or agrees to accept from another person who has made a tender a reward, advantage or benefit of any kind as consideration for the withdrawal of his tender.

Contractor subscribing to election fund
Type 'D' Offence ss. (3)
IPA offence 178.1

(2) Every one commits an offence who, in order to obtain or retain a contract with the government, or as a term of any such contract, whether express or implied, directly or indirectly subscribes, gives, or agrees to subscribe or give, to any person any valuable consideration

(a) for the purpose of promoting the election of a candidate or a class or party of candidates to the Parliament of Canada or a legislature, or 28 Interp

(b) with intent to influence or affect in any way the result of an election conducted for the purpose of electing persons to serve in the Parliament of Canada or a legislature.

Punishment

(3) Every one who commits an offence under this section is guilty of an indictable offence and is liable to imprisonment for five years. 1953-54, c. 51, s. 102.

651. (2) Where

(a) a fine, penalty or forfeiture is imposed

(i) in respect of a violation of a revenue law of Canada,

(ii) in respect of a breach of duty or malfeasance in office by an officer or employee of the Government of Canada, or

(iii) in respect of any proceedings instituted at the instance of the Government of Canada in which that government bears the costs of prosecution; or

(b) a recognizance in connection with proceedings mentioned in paragraph *(a)* is forfeited,

the proceeds of the fine, penalty, forfeiture or recognizance belong to Her Majesty in right of Canada and shall be paid by the person who receives them to the Receiver General.

682. (3) No person who is convicted of an offence under section 110, 113 or 376 has, after that conviction, capacity to contract with Her Majesty or to receive any benefit under a contract between Her Majesty and any other person or to hold office under Her Majesty.

(3.1) A person to whom subsection (3) applies may, at any time before a pardon is granted to him under section 4 of the *Criminal Records Act,* apply to the Governor in Council for the restoration of one or more of the capacities lost by him by virtue of that subsection.

(3.2) Where an application is made under subsection (3.1), the Governor in Council may order that the capacities lost by the applicant by virtue of subsection (3) be restored to him in whole or in part and subject to such conditions as he considers desirable in the public interest.

Breach of trust by public officer
Type 'D' Offence
IPA offence 178.1

111. Every official who, in connection with the duties of his office, commits fraud or a breach of trust is guilty of an indictable offence and is liable to imprisonment for five years, whether or not the fraud or breach of trust would be an offence if it were committed in relation to a private person. 1953-54, c. 51, s. 103. 107

Municipal corruption

Type 'D' Offence

IPA offence 178.1

112. (1) Every one who

(a) gives, offers or agrees to give or offer to a municipal official, or ss. (3)

(b) being a municipal official, demands, accepts or offers or agrees to accept from any person,

a loan, reward, advantage or benefit of any kind as consideration for the official

(c) to abstain from voting at a meeting of the municipal council or a committee thereof,

(d) to vote in favour of or against a measure, motion or resolution,

(e) to aid in procuring or preventing the adoption of a measure, motion or resolution, or

(f) to perform or fail to perform an official act,

is guilty of an indictable offence and is liable to imprisonment for two years.

Influencing municipal official

Type 'D' Offence

IPA offence 178.1

(2) Every one who

(a) by suppression of the truth, in the case of a person who is under a duty to disclose the truth,

(b) by threats or deceit, or

(c) by any unlawful means,

influences or attempts to influence a municipal official to do anything mentioned in paragraphs (1)*(c)* to *(f)* is guilty of an indictable offence and is liable to imprisonment for two years. 24

"Municipal official"

(3) In this section "municipal official" means a member of a municipal council or a person who holds an office under a municipal government. 1953-54, c. 51, s. 104.

Selling or purchasing office

Type 'D' Offence

113. Every one who

(a) purports to sell or agrees to sell an appointment to or resignation from an office, or a consent to any such appointment or resignation, or receives, or agrees to receive a reward or profit from the purported sale thereof, or

(b) purports to purchase or gives a reward or profit for the purported purchase of any such appointment, resignation or consent, or agrees or promises to do so,

is guilty of an indictable offence and is liable to imprisonment for five years. 1953-54, c. 51, s. 105.

682. (3) No person who is convicted of an offence under section 110, 113 or 376 has, after that conviction, capacity to contract with Her Majesty or to receive any benefit under a contract between Her Majesty and any other person or to hold office under Her Majesty.

(3.1) A person to whom subsection (3) applies may, at any time before a pardon is granted to him under section 4 of the *Criminal Records Act,* apply to the Governor in Council for the restoration of one or more of the capacities lost by him by virtue of that subsection.

(3.2) Where an application is made under subsection (3.1), the Governor in Council may order that the capacities lost by the applicant by virtue of subsection (3) be restored to him in whole or in part and subject to such conditions as he considers desirable in the public interest.

Influencing or negotiating appointments or dealing in offices

Type 'D' Offence

114. Every one who

(a) receives, agrees to receive, gives or procures to be given, directly or indirectly, a reward, advantage or benefit of any kind as consideration for cooperation, assistance or exercise of influence to secure the appointment of any person to an office, 107

(b) solicits, recommends or negotiates in any manner with respect to an appointment to or resignation from an office, in expectation of a direct or indirect reward, advantage or benefit, or

(c) keeps without lawful authority, the proof of which lies upon him, a place for transacting or negotiating any business relating to

(i) the filling of vacancies in offices,

(ii) the sale or purchases of offices, or

(iii) appointments to or resignations from offices,

is guilty of an indictable offence and is liable to imprisonment for five years. 1953-54, c. 51, s. 106.

Disobeying a statute

Type 'D' Offence

115. (1) Every one who, without lawful excuse, contravenes an Act of the Parliament of Canada by wilfully doing anything that it forbids or by wilfully omitting to do anything that it requires to be done is, unless some penalty or punishment is expressly provided by law, guilty of an indictable offence and is liable to imprisonment for two years. 1953-54, c. 51, s. 107.

Attorney General of Canada may act

(2) Any proceedings in respect of a contravention of or conspiracy to contravene an Act mentioned in subsection (1), other than this Act, may be instituted at the instance of the Government of Canada and conducted by or on behalf of that Government. 1974-75-76, c. 93, s. 4.

658. Every one who is convicted of an indictable offence for which no punishment is specially provided is liable to imprisonment for five years.

Disobeying order of court

Type 'D' Offence

116. (1) Every one who, without lawful excuse, disobeys a lawful order made by a court of justice or by a person or body of persons authorized by any Act to make or give the order, other than an order for the payment of money is, unless some penalty or punishment or other mode of proceeding is expressly provided by law, guilty of an indictable offence and is liable to imprisonment for two years. 1953-54, c. 51, s. 108. 2

Attorney General of Canada may act

(2) Where the order referred to in subsection (1) was made in proceedings instituted at the instance of the Government of Canada and conducted by or on behalf of that Government, any proceedings in respect of a violation of or conspiracy to violate that order may be instituted and conducted in like manner. 1974-75-76, c. 93, s. 5.

2. In this Act

"Act" includes

(a) an Act of the Parliament of Canada,

(b) an Act of the legislature of the former Province of Canada,

(c) an Act of the legislature of a province, and

(d) an Act or ordinance of the legislature of a province, territory or place in force at the time that province, territory or place became a province of Canada;

Misconduct of officers executing process

Type 'D' Offence

117. Every peace officer or coroner who, being entrusted with the execution of a process, wilfully 2

(a) misconducts himself in the execution of the process, or

(b) makes a false return to the process,

is guilty of an indictable offence and is liable to imprisonment for two years. 1953-54, c. 51, s. 109.

Offences relating to public or peace officer

Type 'B' (D) Offence

118. Every one who

(a) resists or wilfully obstructs a public officer or peace officer in the execution of his duty or any person lawfully acting in aid of such an officer, 2

(b) omits, without reasonable excuse, to assist a public officer or peace officer in the execution of his duty in arresting a person or in preserving the peace, after having reasonable notice that he is required to do so, or

(c) resists or wilfully obstructs any person in the lawful execution of a process against lands or goods or in making a lawful distress or seizure,

is guilty of

(d) an indictable offence and is liable to imprisonment for two years, or

(e) an offence punishable on summary conviction. R.S., c. C-34, s. 118; 1972, c. 13, s. 7. 722(1)

228. Every one who, with intent

(a) to wound, maim or disfigure any person,

(b) to endanger the life of any person, or

(c) to prevent the arrest or detention of any person,

discharges a firearm, air gun or air pistol at or causes bodily harm in any way to any person, whether or not that person is the one mentioned in paragraph *(a)*, *(b)* or *(c)*, is guilty of an indictable offence and is liable to imprisonment for fourteen years.

246. (2) Every one who

(a) assaults a public officer or peace officer engaged in the execution of his duty, or a person acting in aid of such an officer;

(b) assaults a person with intent to resist or prevent the lawful arrest or detention of himself or another person; or

(c) assaults a person

(i) who is engaged in the lawful execution of a process against lands or goods or in making a lawful distress or seizure, or

(ii) with intent to rescue anything taken under a lawful process, distress or seizure,

is guilty of

(d) an indictable offence and is liable to imprisonment for five years, or

(e) an offence punishable on summary conviction.

722. (1) Except where otherwise expressly provided by law, every one who is convicted of an offence punishable on summary conviction is liable to a fine of not more than five hundred dollars or to imprisonment for six months or to both.

Personating peace officer

Type 'A' Offence

119. Every one who

(a) falsely represents himself to be a peace officer or a public officer, or

(b) not being a peace officer or public officer uses a badge or article of uniform or equipment in a manner that is likely to cause persons to believe that he is a peace officer or a public officer, as the case may be,

is guilty of an offence punishable on summary conviction. 1953-54, c. 51, s. 111. 722(1)

2. In this Act

"peace officer" includes

(a) a mayor, warden, reeve, sheriff, deputy sheriff, sheriff's officer and justice of the peace,

(b) a warden, deputy warden, instructor, keeper, gaoler, guard and any other officer or permanent employee of a prison,

(c) a police officer, police constable, bailiff, constable, or other person employed for the preservation and maintenance of the public peace or for the service or execution of civil process,

(d) an officer or person having the powers of a customs or excise officer when performing any duty in the administration of the *Customs Act* or the *Excise Act*,

(d.1) a person appointed or designated as a fishery officer under the *Fisheries Act* when performing any of his duties or functions pursuant to that Act,

(e) the pilot in command of an aircraft

(i) registered in Canada under regulations made under the *Aeronautics Act*, or

(ii) leased without crew and operated by a person who is qualified under regulations made under the *Aeronautics Act* to be registered as owner of an aircraft registered in Canada under those regulations,

while the aircraft is in flight, and

(f) officers and men of the Canadian Forces who are

(i) appointed for the purposes of section 134 of the *National Defence Act*, or

(ii) employed on duties that the Governor in Council, in regulations made under the *National Defence Act* for the purposes of this paragraph, has prescribed to be of such a kind as to necessitate that the officers and men performing them have the powers of peace officers;

"public officer" includes

(a) an officer of customs or excise,

(b) an officer of the Canadian Forces,

(c) an officer of the Royal Canadian Mounted Police, and

(d) any officer while he is engaged in enforcing the laws of Canada relating to revenue, customs, excise, trade or navigation;

Misleading Justice

Perjury

120. Every one commits perjury who, being a witness in a judicial proceeding, with intent to mislead gives false evidence, knowing that the evidence is false. 1953-54, c. 51, s. 112. 107 107

Punishment for perjury

Type 'E' Offence

IPA offence 178.1

121. (1) Every one who commits perjury is guilty of an indictable offence and is liable to imprisonment for fourteen years, but if he commits perjury to procure the conviction of a person for an offence punishable by death, he is liable to imprisonment for life. 669

Corroboration required — section 123

Proof of former trial upon trial of indictment for perjury

(2) Where a person is charged with an offence under section 120 or 124, a certificate specifying with reasonable particularity the proceeding in which that person is alleged to have given the evidence in respect of which the offence is charged, is evidence that it was given in a judicial proceeding, without proof of the signature or official character of the person by whom the certificate purports to be signed if it purports to be signed by the clerk of the court or other official 2
having the custody of the record of that proceeding or by his lawful deputy. 1953-54, c. 51, s. 113; 1968-69, c. 38, s. 92.

False statements in extra-judicial proceedings

Type 'E' Offence

122. Every one who, not being a witness in a judicial proceeding but being permitted, authorized or required by law to make a statement by affidavit, by solemn declaration or orally under oath, makes in such a statement, before a 28
person who is authorized by law to permit it to be made before him, an assertion Interp
with respect to a matter of fact, opinion, belief or knowledge, knowing that the assertion is false, is guilty of an indictable offence and is liable to imprisonment for fourteen years. 1953-54, c. 51, s. 114.

Corroboration required — section 123

514. No count that charges

(a) perjury,

(b) the making of a false oath or a false statement,

(c) fabricating evidence, or

(d) procuring the commission of an offence mentioned in paragraph *(a)*, *(b)* or *(c)*,

is insufficient by reason only that it does not state the nature of the authority of the tribunal before which the oath or statement was taken or made, or the subject of the inquiry, or the words used or the evidence fabricated, or that it does not expressly negative the truth of the words used.

Idem

Type 'A' Offence

122.1 (1) Every one who, not being specially permitted, authorized or required by law to make a statement by affidavit, by solemn declaration or orally under oath, makes in such a statement, before a person who is authorized by law to permit it to be made before him, an assertion with respect to a matter of fact, opinion, belief or knowledge, knowing that the assertion is false, is guilty of an offence punishable on summary conviction. 722(1)

Not applicable

(2) Subsection (1) does not apply to a statement referred to therein that is made in the course of a criminal investigation. 1974-75-76, c. 93, s. 6.

Corroboration

123. No person shall be convicted of an offence under section 121 or 122 upon the evidence of only one witness unless the evidence of that witness is corroborated in a material particular by evidence that implicates the accused. 1953-54, c. 51, s. 115.

Witness giving contradictory evidence
Type 'E' Offence with consent ss. (3)

124. (1) Every one who, being a witness in a judicial proceeding, gives evidence with respect to any matter of fact or knowledge and who subsequently, in a judicial proceeding, gives evidence that is contrary to his previous evidence is guilty of an indictable offence and is liable to imprisonment for fourteen years, whether or not the prior or the later evidence or either is true, but no person shall be convicted under this section unless the court, judge or magistrate, as the case may be, is satisfied beyond a reasonable doubt that the accused, in giving evidence in either of the judicial proceedings, intended to mislead. 514

subsection 121(2) Proof of former trial upon trial of indictment for perjury

"Evidence"

(2) Notwithstanding the definition "evidence" in section 107, "evidence", for the purposes of this section, does not include evidence that is not material.

Consent required

(3) No proceedings shall be instituted under this section without the consent of the Attorney General. 1953-54, c. 51, s. 116.

Fabricating evidence
Type 'E' Offence

125. Every one who, with intent to mislead, fabricates anything with intent that it shall be used as evidence in a judicial proceeding, existing or proposed, by any means other than perjury or incitement to perjury is guilty of an indictable offence and is liable to imprisonment for fourteen years. 1953-54, c. 51, s. 117. 514

Offences relating to affidavits
Type 'D' Offence

126. Every one who

(*a*) signs a writing that purports to be an affidavit or statutory declaration and to have been sworn or declared before him when the writing was not so sworn or declared or when he knows that he has no authority to administer the oath or declaration, 28 Interp

(*b*) uses or offers for use any writing purporting to be an affidavit or statutory declaration that he knows was not sworn or declared, as the case may be, by the affiant or declarant or before a person authorized in that behalf, or 28 Interp

(*c*) signs as affiant or declarant a writing that purports to be an affidavit or statutory declaration and to have been sworn or declared by him, as the case may be, when the writing was not so sworn or declared,

is guilty of an indictable offence and is liable to imprisonment for two years. 1953-54, c. 51, s. 118.

Interpretation Act

18. (1) Where by an enactment or by a rule of the Senate or House of Commons, evidence under oath is authorized or required to be taken, or an oath is authorized or directed to be made, taken or administered, the oath may be administered, and a certificate of its having been made, taken or administered may be given by any one authorized by the enactment or rule to take the evidence, or by a judge of any court, a notary public, a justice of the peace, or a commissioner for taking affidavits, having authority or jurisdiction within the place where the oath is administered.

(2) Where power is conferred upon a justice of the peace to administer an oath or affirmation, or to take an affidavit or declaration, the power may be exercised by a notary public or a commissioner for taking oaths.

28. In every enactment

"oath" includes a solemn affirmation or declaration, whenever the context applies to any person by whom and case in which a solemn affirmation or declaration may be made instead of an oath; and in like cases the expression "sworn" includes the expression "affirmed" or "declared";

"statutory declaration" means a solemn declaration made by virtue of the *Canada Evidence Act;*

Obstructing justice
Type 'B' (D) Offence
IPA offence 178.1

127. (1) Every one who wilfully attempts in any manner to obstruct, pervert or defeat the course of justice in a judicial proceeding, 24 107

(a) by indemnifying or agreeing to indemnify a surety, in any way and either in whole or in part, or

(b) where he is a surety, by accepting or agreeing to accept a fee or any form of indemnity whether in whole or in part from or in respect of a person who is released or is to be released from custody,

is guilty of

(c) an indictable offence and is liable to imprisonment for two years, or

(d) an offence punishable on summary conviction.

Idem
Type 'E' Offence
IPA offence 178.1

(2) Every one who wilfully attempts in any manner other than a manner described in subsection (1) to obstruct, pervert or defeat the course of justice is guilty of an indictable offence and is liable to imprisonment for ten years.

Idem

(3) Without restricting the generality of subsection (2), every one shall be deemed wilfully to attempt to obstruct, pervert or defeat the course of justice who in a judicial proceeding, existing or proposed,

(a) dissuades or attempts to dissuade a person by threats, bribes or other corrupt means from giving evidence;

(b) influences or attempts to influence by threats, bribes or other corrupt means, a person in his conduct as a juror; or

(c) accepts or obtains, agrees to accept or attempts to obtain a bribe or other corrupt consideration to abstain from giving evidence, or to do or to refrain from doing anything as a juror. R.S., c. C-34, s. 127; R.S., c. 2(2nd Supp.), s. 3; 1972, c. 13, s. 8.

24. (1) Every one who, having an intent to commit an offence, does or omits to do anything for the purpose of carrying out his intention is guilty of an attempt to commit the offence whether or not it was possible under the circumstances to commit the offence.

(2) The question whether an act or omission by a person who has an intent to commit an offence is or is not mere preparation to commit the offence, and too remote to constitute an attempt to commit the offence, is a question of law.

109. Every one who

(a) being a justice, police commissioner, peace officer, public officer, or officer of a juvenile court, or being employed in the administration of criminal law, corruptly

(i) accepts or obtains,

(ii) agrees to accept, or

(iii) attempts to obtain,

for himself or any other person any money, valuable consideration, office, place or employment with intent

(iv) to interfere with the administration of justice,

(v) to procure or facilitate the commission of an offence, or

(vi) to protect from detection or punishment a person who has committed or who intends to commit an offence, or

(b) gives or offers, corruptly, to a person mentioned in paragraph *(a)* any money, valuable consideration, office, place or employment with intent that the person should do anything mentioned in subparagraph *(a)*(iv), (v) or (vi),

is guilty of an indictable offence and is liable to imprisonment for fourteen years.

Public Mischief
Type 'B' (D) Offence

128. Every one who, with intent to mislead, causes a peace officer to enter upon an investigation by 2

(*a*) making a false statement that accuses some other person of having committed an offence,

(*b*) doing anything that is intended to cause some other person to be suspected of having committed an offence that he has not committed, or to divert suspicion from himself,

(*c*) reporting that an offence has been committed when it has not been committed, or

(*d*) reporting or in any other way making it known or causing it to be made known that he or some other person has died when he or that other person has not died,

is guilty of

(*e*) an indictable offence and is liable to imprisonment for five years, or

(*f*) an offence punishable on summary conviction. R.C., c. C-34, s. 128; 1972, c. 13, s. 8. 722(1)

329. Every one who, with intent to defraud, causes or procures a telegram, cablegram or radio message to be sent or delivered as being sent by the authority of another person, knowing that it is not sent by his authority and with intent that the message should be acted on as being sent by his authority, is guilty of an indictable offence and is liable to imprisonment for five years.

330. (1) Every one who, with intent to injure or alarm any person, conveys or causes or procures to be conveyed by letter, telegram, telephone, cable, radio, or otherwise, information that he knows is false is guilty of an indictable offence and is liable to imprisonment for two years.

Compounding indictable offence
Type 'D' Offence

129. Every one who asks or obtains or agrees to receive or obtain any valuable consideration for himself or any other person by agreeing to compound or conceal an indictable offence is guilty of an indictable offence and is liable to imprisonment for two years. 1953-54, c. 51, s. 121.

Corruptly taking reward for recovery of goods
Type 'D' Offence

130. Every one who corruptly accepts any valuable consideration, directly or indirectly, under pretence or upon account of helping any person to recover anything obtained by the commission of an indictable offence is guilty of an indictable offence and is liable to imprisonment for five years. 1953-54, c. 51, s. 122.

Advertising reward and immunity
Type 'A' Offence

131. Every one who

(*a*) publicly advertises a reward for the return of anything that has been stolen or lost, and in the advertisement uses words to indicate that no questions will be asked if it is returned,

(*b*) uses words in a public advertisement to indicate that a reward will be given or paid for anything that has been stolen or lost, without interference with or inquiry about the person who produces it,

(*c*) promises or offers in a public advertisement to return to a person who has advanced money by way of loan on, or has bought, anything that has been stolen or lost, the money so advanced or paid, or any other sum of money for the return of that thing, or

(*d*) prints or publishes any advertisement referred to in paragraph (*a*), (*b*) or (*c*),

is guilty of an offence punishable on summary conviction. 1953-54, c. 51, s. 123. 722(1)

Escapes and Rescues

Prison breach
Type 'E' Offence
IPA offence 178.1

132. Every one who

(a) by force or violence breaks a prison with intent to set at liberty himself or any person confined therein, or 2

(b) with intent to escape forcibly breaks out of, or makes any breach in, a cell or other place within a prison in which he is confined,

is guilty of an indictable offence and is liable to imprisonment for ten years. 1976-77, c. 53, s. 5.

2. In this Act

"prison" includes a penitentiary, common gaol, public or reformatory prison, lock-up, guard-room or other place in which persons who are charged with or convicted of offences are usually kept in custody;

Escape and being at large without excuse
Type 'D' Offence
IPA offence 178.1

133. (1) Every one who

(a) escapes from lawful custody, or

(b) is, before the expiration of a term of imprisonment to which he was sentenced, at large within Canada without lawful excuse, the proof of which lies upon him,

is guilty of an indictable offence and is liable to imprisonment for two years.

Failure to attend court when at large on undertaking or recognizance
Type 'B' (D) Offence

(2) Every one who, being at large on his undertaking or recognizance given to or entered into before a justice or a judge, fails, without lawful excuse, the proof of which lies upon him, to attend court in accordance therewith or to surrender himself in accordance with an order of the judge, as the case may be, is guilty of 448

(a) an indictable offence and is liable to imprisonment for two years, or

(b) an offence punishable on summary conviction. 722(1)

Failure to comply with condition of undertaking or recognizance
Type 'B' (D) Offence
ss. (7)

(3) Every one who, being at large on his undertaking or recognizance given to or entered into before a justice or a judge and being bound to comply with a condition of that undertaking or recognizance directed by a justice or a judge, fails, without lawful excuse, the proof of which lies upon him, to comply with that condition, is guilty of 457(4)

(a) an indictable offence and is liable to imprisonment for two years, or

(b) an offence punishable on summary conviction. 722(1)

457. (4) The justice may direct as conditions under subsection (2) that the accused shall do any one or more of the following things as specified in the order, namely:

(a) report at times to be stated in the order to a peace officer or other person designated in the order;

(b) remain within a territorial jurisdiction specified in the order;

(c) notify the peace officer or other person designated under paragraph *(a)* of any change in his address or his employment or occupation;

(d) abstain from communicating with any witness or other person expressly named in the order except in accordance with such conditions specified in the order as the justice deems necessary;

(e) where the accused is the holder of a passport, deposit his passport as specified in the order; and

(f) comply with such other reasonable conditions specified in the order as the justice considers desirable.

Failure to appear or to comply with summons

Type 'B' (D) Offence ss. (7)

(4) Every one who is served with a summons and who fails, without lawful excuse, the proof of which lies upon him, to appear at a time and place stated therein, if any, for the purposes of the *Identification of Criminals Act* or to attend court in accordance therewith, is guilty of

(*a*) an indictable offence and is liable to imprisonment for two years, or

(*b*) an offence punishable on summary conviction. 722(1)

455.5 (1) A summons issued under section 455.3 shall

(*a*) be directed to the accused;

(*b*) set out briefly the offence in respect of which the accused is charged; and

(*c*) require the accused to attend court at a time and place to be stated therein and to attend thereafter as required by the court in order to be dealt with according to law.

(2) A summons shall be served by a peace officer who shall deliver it personally to the person to whom it is directed or, if that person cannot conveniently be found, shall leave it for him at his last or usual place of abode with some inmate thereof who appears to be at least sixteen years of age.

(3) Service of a summons may be proved by the oral evidence, given under oath, of the peace officer who served it or by his affidavit made before a justice or other person authorized to administer oaths or to take affidavits.

(4) A summons shall set out therein the text of subsection 133(4) and section 455.6.

(5) A summons may, where the accused is alleged to have committed an indictable offence, require the accused to appear at a time and place stated therein for the purposes of the *Identification of Criminals Act*, and a person so appearing is deemed, for the purposes only of that Act, to be in lawful custody charged with an indictable offence.

455.6 Where an accused who is required by a summons to appear at a time and place stated therein for the purposes of the *Identification of Criminals Act*, does not appear at that time and place, a justice may issue a warrant for the arrest of the accused for the offence with which he is charged.

738. (3) Where a defendant to whom an appearance notice that has been confirmed by a justice under section 455.4 has been issued or who has been served with a summons does not appear at the time and place appointed for the trial and the issue of the appearance notice or service of the summons within a reasonable time before the appearance was required is proved, or where a defendant does not appear for the resumption of a trial that has been adjourned in accordance with subsection (1), the summary conviction court

(*a*) may proceed *ex parte* to hear and determine the proceedings in the absence of the defendant as fully and effectually as if the defendant had appeared, or

(*b*) may, if it thinks fit, issue a warrant in Form 7 for the arrest of the defendant, and adjourn the trial to await his appearance pursuant thereto.

(3.1) Where, at the trial of a defendant, the summary conviction court proceeds in the manner described in paragraph (3)*(a)*, no proceedings under section 133 arising out of the failure of the defendant to appear at the time and place appointed for the trial or for the resumption of the trial shall be instituted or if instituted shall be proceeded with, except with the consent of the Attorney General.

Failure to appear or to comply with appearance notice or promise to appear

Type 'B' (D) Offence ss. (7)

(5) Every one who is named in an appearance notice or promise to appear, 448
or in a recognizance entered into before an officer in charge, that has been 448
confirmed by a justice under section 455.4 and who fails, without lawful excuse, the proof of which lies upon him, to appear at a time and place stated therein, if any, for the purposes of the *Identification of Criminals Act*, or to attend court in accordance therewith, is guilty of

(*a*) an indictable offence and is liable to imprisonment for two years, or

(*b*) an offence punishable on summary conviction.

453.4 Where an accused who is required by an appearance notice or promise to appear or by a recognizance entered into before an officer in charge to appear at a time and place stated therein for the purposes of the *Identification of Criminals Act* does not appear at that time and place, a justice may, where the appearance notice, promise to appear or recognizance has been confirmed by a justice under section 455.4, issue a warrant for the arrest of the accused for the offence with which he is charged.

Idem

(6) For the purposes of subsection (5), it is not a lawful excuse that an appearance notice, promise to appear or recognizance states defectively the substance of the alleged offence.

No prosecution by indictment unless previous conviction

(7) Notwithstanding anything in this section, where an accused is charged with an offence under subsection (3), (4) or (5), he shall not be prosecuted by indictment unless he has previously been convicted of an offence under this section.

Where person charged with summary conviction offence

(8) For the purposes only of the *Identification of Criminals Act*, a person charged with or convicted of an offence under this section punishable on summary conviction shall be deemed to be charged with or to have been convicted of an indictable offence. R.S., c. C-34, s. 133; R.S., c. 2(2nd Supp.), s. 4.

Proof of certain facts by certificate

(9) In any proceedings under subsection (2), (4) or (5), a certificate of the
clerk of the court or a judge of the court before which the accused is alleged to 2
have failed to attend or of the person in charge of the place at which it is alleged the accused failed to attend for the purposes of the *Identification of Criminals Act* stating that,

(a) in the case of proceedings under subsection (2), the accused gave or entered into an undertaking or recognizance before a justice or a judge and failed to attend court in accordance therewith,

(b) in the case of proceedings under subsection (4), a summons was issued to and served on the accused and the accused failed to attend court in accordance therewith or failed to appear at the time and place stated therein for the purposes of the *Identification of Criminals Act*, as the case may be, and

(c) in the case of proceedings under subsection (5), the accused was named in an appearance notice, a promise to appear or a recognizance entered into before an officer in charge, that was confirmed by a justice under section 455.4, and the accused failed to attend court in accordance therewith or failed to appear at the time and place stated therein for the purposes of the *Identification of Criminals Act*, as the case may be,

is evidence of the statements contained in the certificate without proof of the signature or the official character of the person appearing to have signed the certificate.

Attendance and right to cross-examination

(10) An accused against whom a certificate described in subsection (9) is produced may, with leave of the court, require the attendance of the person making the certificate for the purposes of cross-examination.

Notice of intention to produce

(11) No certificate shall be received in evidence pursuant to subsection (9) unless the party intending to produce it has, before the trial, given to the accused reasonable notice of his intention together with a copy of the certificate. 1974-75-76, c. 93, s. 7(2).

455.3 (7) Where, pursuant to subsection (6), a justice authorizes the release of an accused pursuant to section 453.1, a promise to appear given by the accused or a recognizance entered into by the accused pursuant to that section shall be deemed, for the purposes of subsection 133(5), to have been confirmed by a justice under section 455.4.

Permitting or assisting escape

Type 'D' Offence

134. Every one who

(a) permits a person whom he has in lawful custody to escape, by failing to perform a legal duty,

(b) conveys or causes to be conveyed into a prison, anything, with intent to facilitate the escape of a person imprisoned therein, or 2

(c) directs or procures, under colour of pretended authority, the discharge of a prisoner who is not entitled to be discharged,

is guilty of an indictable offence and is liable to imprisonment for two years. 1953-54, c. 51, s. 126.

Rescue or permitting escape

Type 'D' Offence

135. Every one who

(a) rescues any person from lawful custody or assists any person in escaping or attempting to escape from lawful custody, 24

(b) being a peace officer, wilfully permits a person in his lawful custody to escape, or 2

(c) being an officer of or an employee in a prison, wilfully permits a person to escape from lawful custody therein,

is guilty of an indictable offence and is liable to imprisonment for five years. 1953-54, c. 51, s. 127.

Assisting prisoner of war to escape

Type 'D' Offence

136. Every one who knowingly and wilfully

(a) assists a prisoner of war in Canada to escape from a place where he is detained, or

(b) assists a prisoner of war, who is permitted to be at large on parole in Canada, to escape from the place where he is at large on parole,

is guilty of an indictable offence and is liable to imprisonment for five years. 1953-54, c. 51, s. 128.

Service of term for escape and portion of unserved sentence

137. (1) A person convicted for an escape committed while undergoing imprisonment shall be sentenced to serve the term of imprisonment to which he is sentenced for the escape either concurrently with the portion of the term of imprisonment that he was serving at the time of his escape that he had not served or if the court, judge, justice or magistrate by whom he is sentenced for the escape so orders, consecutively and such imprisonment shall be served ss.(3)

(a) in a penitentiary if the time to be served is two years or more; or

(b) if the time to be served is less than two years,

(i) in a prison, or

(ii) notwithstanding the *Parole Act* and section 659, in a penitentiary if the court, judge, justice or magistrate by whom he is sentenced for the escape so orders.

Determination of unserved portion of sentence

(2) For the purpose of subsection (1), section 14 of the *Parole Act* applies in determining the term of imprisonment that a person who escapes while undergoing imprisonment was serving at the time of his escape. 14 Parole Act

"Escape" defined

(3) For the purposes of subsection (1), "escape" means breaking prison, escaping from lawful custody or, without lawful excuse, being at large before the expiration of a term of imprisonment to which a person has been sentenced. 1976-77, c. 53, s. 6.

Parole Act

14. (1) Where, either before, on or after the 25th day of March 1970,

(a) a person is sentenced to two or more terms of imprisonment, or

(b) an inmate who is in confinement is sentenced to an additional term or terms of imprisonment,

the terms of imprisonment to which he has been sentenced, including in a case described in paragraph *(b)* any term or terms that resulted in his being in confinement, shall, for all purposes of this Act, the *Criminal Code*, the *Penitentiary Act* and the *Prisons and Reformatories Act*, be deemed to constitute one sentence consisting of a term of imprisonment commencing on the earliest day on which any of those sentences of imprisonment commences and ending on the expiration of the last to expire of such terms of imprisonment.

(2) This section does not affect the time at which any sentences that are deemed by subsection (1) to constitute one sentence commence pursuant to subsection 649(1) of the *Criminal Code*.

PART IV

SEXUAL OFFENCES, PUBLIC MORALS AND DISORDERLY CONDUCT

Interpretation

Definitions

138. In this Part

"guardian"

"guardian" includes any person who has in law or in fact the custody or control of another person;

"public place"

"public place" includes any place to which the public have access as of right or by invitation, express or implied;

"theatre"

"theatre" includes any place that is open to the public where entertainments are given, whether or not any charge is made for admission. 1953-54, c. 51, s. 130.

Special Provisions

Corroboration

139. (1) No accused shall be convicted of an offence under section 148, 150, 151, 152, 153, 154 or 166 upon the evidence of only one witness unless the evidence of the witness is corroborated in a material particular by evidence that implicates the accused.

148 (Sexual intercourse with feeble-minded, etc.), 150 (Incest), 151 (Seduction of female between sixteen and eighteen), 152 (Seduction under promise to marry), 153 (Sexual intercourse with step-daughter, etc., or female employee), 154 (Seduction of female passengers on vessels) or 166 (Parent or guardian procuring defilement)

Marriage a defence

(2) No accused shall be convicted of an offence under section 152, paragraph 153*(b)* or section 154 where he proves that, subsequent to the time of the alleged offence, he married the person in respect of whom he is alleged to have committed the offence.

152 (Seduction under promise to marry), 153*(b)* (Sexual intercourse with employee) or 154 (Seduction of female passengers on vessels)

Burden of proof

(3) In proceedings for an offence under subsection 146(2) or section 151, 152 or paragraph 153*(b)* the burden of proving that the female person in respect of whom the offence is alleged to have been committed was not of previously chaste character is upon the accused.

146(2) (Sexual intercourse with female between fourteen and sixteen), 151 (Seduction of female between sixteen and eighteen), 152 (Seduction under promise to marry), 153*(b)* (Sexual intercourse with employee)

Previous sexual intercourse with accused

(4) In proceedings for an offence under subsection 146(2) or under section 151 or paragraph 153*(b)*, evidence that the accused had, prior to the time of the alleged offence, sexual intercourse with the female person in respect of whom the offence is alleged to have been committed shall be deemed not to be evidence that she was not of previously chaste character. 1953-54, c. 51, s. 131.

Consent of child under fourteen no defence

140. Where an accused is charged with an offence under section 146, 149 or 156 in respect of a person under the age of fourteen years, the fact that the person consented to the commission of the offence is not a defence to the charge. 1953-54, c. 51, s. 132. 3(1)

146(1) (Sexual intercourse with female under fourteen years), 149 (Indecent assault on female) or 156 (Indecent assault on male)

3. (1) For the purposes of this Act a person shall be deemed to have been of a given age when the anniversary of his birthday, the number of which corresponds to that age, is fully completed, and until then to have been under that age.

585. (1) In any proceedings to which this Act applies an entry or record of an incorporated society or its officers who have had the control or care of a child or young person at or about the time the child or young person was brought to Canada is evidence of the age of the child or young person if the entry or record was made before the time when the offence is alleged to have been committed.

(2) In the absence of other evidence, or by way of corroboration of other evidence, a jury, judge, justice or magistrate, as the case may be, may infer the age of a child or young person from his appearance.

Limitation

141. No proceedings for an offence under section 151, 152, paragraph 153*(b)*, or under section 166, 167 or 168 shall be commenced more than one year after the time when the offence is alleged to have been committed. 1953-54, c. 51, s. 133.

151 (Seduction of female between sixteen and eighteen). 152 (Seduction under promise to marry), 153*(b)* (Sexual intercourse with employee) 166 (Parent or guardian procuring defilement), 167 (Householder permitting defilement), 168 (Corrupting children)

No question of sexual conduct

142. (1) Where an accused is charged with an offence under section 144 or 145 or subsection 146(1) or 149(1), no question shall be asked by or on behalf of the accused as to the sexual conduct of the complainant with a person other than the accused unless

(a) reasonable notice in writing has been given to the prosecutor by or on behalf of the accused of his intention to ask such question together with particulars of the evidence sought to be adduced by such question and a copy of such notice has been filed with the clerk of the court; and 2

(b) the judge, magistrate or justice, after holding a hearing *in camera* in the absence of the jury, if any, is satisfied that the weight of the evidence is such that to exclude it would prevent the making of a just determination of an issue of fact in the proceedings, including the credibility of the complainant.

144 (Rape), 145 (Attempt rape), 146(1) (Sexual intercourse with female under fourteen) 149(1) (Indecent assault on female)

Publication prohibited

(2) The notice given under paragraph (1)*(a)* and the evidence taken, the information given or the representations made at a hearing referred to in paragraph (1)*(b)* shall not be published in any newspaper or broadcast. ss. (4) 28 Interp

Type 'A' Offence

(3) Every one who, without lawful excuse the proof of which lies upon him, contravenes subsection (2) is guilty of an offence punishable on summary conviction.

"Newspaper" defined

(4) In this section, "newspaper" has the same meaning as it has in section 261.

"Complainant" defined

(5) In this section and in section 442, "complainant" means the person against whom it is alleged that the offence was committed. 1974-75-76, c. 93, s. 8.

Sexual Offences

Rape

143. A male person commits rape when he has sexual intercourse with a female person who is not his wife, 3(6)

(*a*) without her consent, or

(*b*) with her consent if the consent

(i) is extorted by threats or fear of bodily harm,

(ii) is obtained by personating her husband, or

(iii) is obtained by false and fraudulent representations as to the nature and quality of the act. 1953-54, c. 51, s. 135.

3. (6) For the purposes of this Act, sexual intercourse is complete upon penetration to even the slightest degree, notwithstanding that seed is not emitted.

Punishment for rape

Type 'F' Offence

IPA offence 178.1

SPI offence 687

144. Every one who commits rape is guilty of an indictable offence and is 143
liable to imprisonment for life. R.S., c. C-34, s. 144; 1972, c. 13, s. 70. 669

147. No male person shall be deemed to commit an offence under section 144, 145, 146 or 150 while he is under the age of fourteen years.

Canada Evidence Act

4. (2) The wife or husband of a person charged with an offence against section 33 or 34 of the *Juvenile Delinquents Act* or with an offence against any of sections 143 to 146, 148, 150 to 155, 157, 166 to 169, 175, 195, 197, 200, 248 to 250, 255 to 258, 289, paragraph 423(1)(*c*) or an attempt to commit an offence under section 146 or 155 of the *Criminal Code,* is a competent and compellable witness for the prosecution without the consent of the person charged.

Attempt to commit rape

Type 'F' Offence

SPI offence 687

145. Every one who attempts to commit rape is guilty of an indictable offence and is liable to imprisonment for ten years. R.S., c. C-34, s. 145; 1972, c. 13, s. 70. 24

Section 147 applies.

Section 4(2) Canada Evidence Act applies.

24. (1) Every one who, having an intent to commit an offence, does or omits to do anything for the purpose of carrying out his intention is guilty of an attempt to commit the offence whether or not it was possible under the circumstances to commit the offence.

(2) The question whether an act or omission by a person who has an intent to commit an offence is or is not mere preparation to commit the offence, and too remote to constitute an attempt to commit the offence, is a question of law.

261. In sections 262 to 281, "newspaper" means any paper, magazine or periodical containing public news, intelligence or reports of events, or any remarks or observations thereon, printed for sale and published periodically or in parts or numbers, at intervals not exceeding thirty-one days between the publication of any two such papers, parts or numbers, and any paper, magazine or periodical printed in order to be dispersed and made public, weekly or more often, or at intervals not exceeding thirty-one days, that contains advertisements, exclusively or principally.

Interpretation Act

28. In every enactment

"broadcasting" means any radiocommunication in which the transmissions are intended for direct reception by the general public;

"radio" or "radiocommunication" means any transmission, emission or reception of signs, signals, writing, images, sounds or intelligence of any nature by means of electromagnetic waves of frequencies lower than three thousand Gigacycles per second propagated in space without artifical guide;

Sexual intercourse with female under fourteen

Type 'E' Offence

SPI offence 687

146. (1) Every male person who has sexual intercourse with a female person who 3(6)

(*a*) is not his wife, and

(*b*) is under the age of fourteen years, 3(1)

whether or not he believes that she is fourteen years of age or more, is guilty of an indictable offence and is liable to imprisonment for life. 669

3. (1) For the purposes of this Act a person shall be deemed to have been of a given age when the anniversary of his birthday, the number of which corresponds to that age, is fully completed, and until then to have been under that age.

585. (1) In any proceedings to which this Act applies an entry or record of an incorporated society or its officers who have had the control or care of a child or young person at or about the time the child or young person was brought to Canada is evidence of the age of the child or young person if the entry or record was made before the time when the offence is alleged to have been committed.

(2) In the absence of other evidence, or by way of corroboration of other evidence, a jury, judge, justice or magistrate, as the case may be, may infer the age of a child or young person from his appearance.

3. (6) For the purposes of this Act, sexual intercourse is complete upon penetration to even the slightest degree, notwithstanding that seed is not emitted.

140. Where an accused is charged with an offence under section 146, 149 or 156 in respect of a person under the age of fourteen years, the fact that the person consented to the commission of the offence is not a defence to the charge.

Section 142 applies.

147. No male person shall be deemed to commit an offence under section 144, 145, 146 or 150 while he is under the age of fourteen years.

Canada Evidence Act

4. (2) The wife or husband of a person charged with an offence against section 33 or 34 of the *Juvenile Delinquents Act* or with an offence against any of sections 143 to 146, 148, 150 to 155, 157, 166 to 169, 175, 195, 197, 200, 248 to 250, 255 to 258, 289, paragraph 423(1)*(c)* or an attempt to commit an offence under section 146 or 155 of the *Criminal Code*, is a competent and compellable witness for the prosecution without the consent of the person charged.

Sexual intercourse with female between fourteen and sixteen

Type 'D' Offence

SPI offence 687

(2) Every male person who has sexual intercourse with a female person who

(*a*) is not his wife,

(*b*) is of previously chaste character, and

(*c*) is fourteen years of age or more and is under the age of sixteen years,

whether or not he believes that she is sixteen years of age or more, is guilty of an indictable offence and is liable to imprisonment for five years.

Where accused not more to blame

(3) Where an accused is charged with an offence under subsection (2), the court may find the accused not guilty if it is of opinion that the evidence does not show that, as between the accused and the female person, the accused is more to blame than the female person. R.S., c. C-34, s. 146; 1972, c. 13, s. 70.

139. (3) In proceedings for an offence under subsection 146(2) or section 151, 152 or paragraph 153*(b)* the burden of proving that the female person in respect of whom the offence is alleged to have been committed was not of previously chaste character is upon the accused.

139. (4) In proceedings for an offence under subsection 146(2) or under section 151 or paragraph 153*(b)*, evidence that the accused had, prior to the time of the alleged offence, sexual intercourse with the female person in respect of whom the offence is alleged to have been committed shall be deemed not to be evidence that she was not of previously chaste character.

Age

147. No male person shall be deemed to commit an offence under section 144, 145, 146 or 150 while he is under the age of fourteen years. 1953-54, c. 51, s. 139. 3(1)

144 (Rape), 145 (Attempted rape), 146 (Sexual intercourse with female under fourteen and sexual intercourse with female between fourteen and sixteen), 150 (Incest)

Sexual intercourse with feeble-minded, etc.

Type 'D' Offence

148. Every male person who, under circumstances that do not amount to rape, has sexual intercourse with a female person 3(6)

(*a*) who is not his wife, and

(*b*) who is and who he knows or has good reason to believe is feeble-minded, insane, or is an idiot or imbecile, 2

is guilty of an indictable offence and is liable to imprisonment for five years. 1953-54, c. 51, s. 140.

2. In this Act

"feeble-minded person" means a person in whom there exists and has existed from birth or from an early age, mental defectiveness not amounting to imbecility, but so pronounced that he requires care, supervision and control for his protection or for the protection of others.

139. (1) No accused shall be convicted of an offence under section 148, 150, 151, 152, 153, 154 or 166 upon the evidence of only one witness unless the evidence of the witness is corroborated in a material particular by evidence that implicates the accused.

Canada Evidence Act, subsection 4(2) applies.

Indecent assault on female

Type 'D' Offence

149. (1) Every one who indecently assaults a female person is guilty of an indictable offence and is liable to imprisonment for five years.

Consent by false representations

(2) An accused who is charged with an offence under subsection (1) may be convicted if the evidence establishes that the accused did anything to the female person with her consent that, but for her consent, would have been an indecent assault, if her consent was obtained by false and fraudulent representations as to the nature and quality of the act. R.S., c. C-34, s. 149; 1972, c. 13, s. 70.

140. Where an accused is charged with an offence under section 146, 149 or 156 in respect of a person under the age of fourteen years, the fact that the person consented to the commission of the offence is not a defence to the charge.

Section 142 applies.

Incest

150. (1) Every one commits incest who, knowing that another person is by blood relationship his or her parent, child, brother, sister, grandparent or grandchild, as the case may be, has sexual intercourse with that person. ss. (4) 3(6)

Type 'E' Offence

(2) Every one who commits incest is guilty of an indictable offence and is liable to imprisonment for fourteen years.

Compulsion of female

(3) Where a female person is convicted of an offence under this section and the court is satisfied that she committed the offence by reason only that she was under restraint, duress or fear of the person with whom she had the sexual intercourse, the court is not required to impose any punishment upon her.

"Brother" "sister"

(4) In this section, "brother" and "sister", respectively, include half-brother and half-sister. R.S., c. C-34, s. 150; 1972, c. 13, s. 10.

3. (6) For the purposes of this Act, sexual intercourse is complete upon penetration to even the slightest degree, notwithstanding that seed is not emitted.

17. A person who commits an offence under compulsion by threats of immediate death or grievous bodily harm from a person who is present when the offence is committed is excused for committing the offence if he believes that the threats will be carried out and if he is not a party to a conspiracy or association whereby he is subject to compulsion, but this section does not apply where the offence that is committed is high treason or treason, murder, piracy, attempted murder, assisting in rape, forcible abduction, robbery, causing bodily harm or arson.

139. (1) No accused shall be convicted of an offence under section 148, 150, 151, 152, 153, 154 or 166 upon the evidence of only one witness unless the evidence of the witness is corroborated in a material particular by evidence that implicates the accused.

147. No male person shall be deemed to commit an offence under section 144, 145, 146 or 150 while he is under the age of fourteen years.

Canada Evidence Act

4. (2) The wife or husband of a person charged with an offence against section 33 or 34 of the *Juvenile Delinquents Act* or with an offence against any of sections 143 to 146, 148, 150 to 155, 157, 166 to 169, 175, 195, 197, 200, 248 to 250, 255 to 258, 289, paragraph 423(1)(*c*) or an attempt to commit an offence under section 146 or 155 of the *Criminal Code*, is a competent and compellable witness for the prosecution without the consent of the person charged.

Seduction of female between sixteen and eighteen

Type 'D' Offence

151. Every male person who, being eighteen years of age or more, seduces a female person of previously chaste character who is sixteen years or more but less than eighteen years of age is guilty of an indictable offence and is liable to imprisonment for two years. 1953-54, c. 51, s. 143. 3(1)

139. (3) In proceedings for an offence under subsection 146(2) or section 151, 152 or paragraph 153*(b)* the burden of proving that the female person in respect of whom the offence is alleged to have been committed was not of previously chaste character is upon the accused.

139. (4) In proceedings for an offence under subsection 146(2) or under section 151 or paragraph 153*(b)*, evidence that the accused had, prior to the time of the alleged offence, sexual intercourse with the female person in respect of whom the offence is alleged to have been committed shall be deemed not to be evidence that she was not of previously chaste character.

141. No proceedings for an offence under section 151, 152, paragraph 153*(b)*, or under section 166, 167 or 168 shall be commenced more than one year after the time when the offence is alleged to have been committed.

Canada Evidence Act, subsection 4(2) applies.

Seduction under promise of marriage

Type 'D' Offence

152. Every male person, being twenty-one years of age or more, who, under promise of marriage, seduces an unmarried female person of previously chaste character who is less than twenty-one years of age is guilty of an indictable offence and is liable to imprisonment for two years. 1953-54, c. 51, s. 144. 3(1)

139. (1) No accused shall be convicted of an offence under section 148, 150, 151, 152, 153, 154 or 166 upon the evidence of only one witness unless the evidence of the witness is corroborated in a material particular by evidence that implicates the accused.

139. (2) No accused shall be convicted of an offence under section 152, paragraph 153*(b)* or section 154 where he proves that, subsequent to the time of the alleged offence, he married the person in respect of whom he is alleged to have committed the offence.

139. (3) In proceedings for an offence under subsection 146(2) or section 151, 152 or paragraph 153*(b)* the burden of proving that the female person in respect of whom the offence is alleged to have been committed was not of previously chaste character is upon the accused.

141. No proceedings for an offence under section 151, 152, paragraph 153*(b)*, or under section 166, 167 or 168 shall be commenced more than one year after the time when the offence is alleged to have been committed.

Canada Evidence Act, subsection 4(2) applies.

Sexual intercourse with step-daughter, etc., or female employee

Type 'D' Offence

153. (1) Every male person who

(a) has illicit sexual intercourse with his step-daughter, foster daughter or female ward, or 3(6)

(b) has illicit sexual intercourse with a female person of previously chaste character and under the age of twenty-one years who 3(1) [146]

(i) is in his employment,

(ii) is in a common, but not necessarily similar, employment with him and is, in respect of her employment or work, under or in any way subject to his control or direction, or

(iii) receives her wages or salary directly or indirectly from him,

is guilty of an indictable offence and is liable to imprisonment for two years.

Where accused not more to blame

(2) Where an accused is charged with an offence under paragraph (1)*(b)*, the court may find the accused not guilty if it is of opinion that the evidence does not show that, as between the accused and the female person, the accused is more to blame than the female person. 1953-54, c. 51, s. 145; 1959, c. 41, s.10.

Subsections 139 (1), (2) and (3) apply.

139. (4) In proceedings for an offence under subsection 146(2) or under section 151 or paragraph 153*(b)*, evidence that the accused had, prior to the time of the alleged offence, sexual intercourse with the female person in respect of whom the offence is alleged to have been committed shall be deemed not to be evidence that she was not of previously chaste character.

Section 141 applies.

Canada Evidence Act, subsection 4(2) applies.

Seduction of female passengers on vessels

Type 'D' Offence

154. Every male person who, being the owner or master of, or employed on board a vessel, engaged in the carriage of passengers for hire, seduces, or by threats or by the exercise of his authority, has illicit sexual intercourse on board the vessel with a female passenger is guilty of an indictable offence and is liable to imprisonment for two years. 1953-54, c. 51, s. 146.

139. (1) No accused shall be convicted of an offence under section 148, 150, 151, 152, 153, 154 or 166 upon the evidence of only one witness unless the evidence of the witness is corroborated in a material particular by evidence that implicates the accused.

Canada Evidence Act, subsection 4(2) applies.

Buggery or bestiality

Type 'E' Offence

155. Every one who commits buggery or bestiality is guilty of an indictable offence and is liable to imprisonment for fourteen years. 1953-54, c. 51, s. 147.

Section 158 for exception

Canada Evidence Act, subsection 4(2) applies.

Indecent assault on male

Type 'E' Offence

SPI offence 687

156. Every male person who assaults another person with intent to commit buggery or who indecently assaults another male person is guilty of an indictable offence and is liable to imprisonment for ten years. R.S., c. C-34, s. 156; 1972, c. 13, s. 70.

140. Where an accused is charged with an offence under section 146, 149 or 156 in respect of a person under the age of fourteen years, the fact that the person consented to the commission of the offence is not a defence to the charge.

Acts of gross indecency

Type 'D' Offence

SPI offence 687

157. Every one who commits an act of gross indecency with another person is guilty of an indictable offence and is liable to imprisonment for five years. 1953-54, c. 51, s. 149.

Section 158 for exception

Canada Evidence Act, subsection 4(2) applies.

Exception re acts in private between husband and wife or consenting adults

158. (1) Section 155 and 157 do not apply to any act committed in private between

(*a*) a husband and his wife, or

(*b*) any two persons, each of whom is twenty-one years or more of age,

both of whom consent to the commission of the act.

Idem

(2) For the purposes of subsection (1),

(*a*) an act shall be deemed not to have been committed in private if it is committed in a public place, or if more than two persons take part or are present; and

(*b*) a person shall be deemed not to consent to the commission of an act

(i) if the consent is extorted by force, threats or fear of bodily harm or is obtained by false and fraudulent misrepresentations as to the nature and quality of the act, or

(ii) if that person is, and the other party to the commission of the act knows or has good reason to believe that that person is feeble-minded, insane, or an idiot or imbecile. 1968-69, c. 38, s. 7.

138. In this Part

"public place" includes any place to which the public have access as of right or by invitation, express or implied;

Offences Tending to Corrupt Morals

Corrupting morals
Type 'B' (D) Offence 165
IPA offence paragraph (a) only, 178.1

159. (1) Every one commits an offence who

(a) makes, prints, publishes, distributes, circulates, or has in his possession for the purpose of publication, distribution or circulation any obscene written matter, picture, model, phonograph record or other thing whatsoever, or 3(4) ss. (8) 2

(b) makes, prints, publishes, distributes, sells or has in his possession for the purpose of publication, distribution or circulation, a crime comic. ss. (7)

Idem
Type 'B' (D) Offence 165

(2) Every one commits an offence who knowingly, without lawful justification or excuse,

(a) sells, exposes to public view or has in his possession for such a purpose any obscene written matter, picture, model, phonograph record or other thing whatsoever,

(b) publicly exhibits a disgusting object or an indecent show,

(c) offers to sell, advertises, publishes an advertisement of, or has for sale or disposal any means, instructions, medicine, drug or article intended or represented as a method of causing abortion or miscarriage, or

252. Every one who unlawfully supplies or procures a drug or other noxious thing or an instrument or thing, knowing that it is intended to be used or employed to procure the miscarriage of a female person, whether or not she is pregnant, is guilty of an indictable offence and is liable to imprisonment for two years.

(d) advertises or publishes an advertisement of any means, instructions, medicine, drug or article intended or represented as a method for restoring sexual virility or curing venereal diseases or diseases of the generative organs.

Defence of public good

(3) No person shall be convicted of an offence under this section if he establishes that the public good was served by the acts that are alleged to constitute the offence and that the acts alleged did not extend beyond what served the public good.

Question of law and question of fact

(4) For the purposes of this section it is a question of law whether an act served the public good and whether there is evidence that the act alleged went beyond what served the public good, but it is a question of fact whether the acts did or did not extend beyond what served the public good.

Motives irrelevant

(5) For the purposes of this section the motives of an accused are irrelevant.

Ignorance of nature no defence

(6) Where an accused is charged with an offence under subsection (1) the fact that the accused was ignorant of the nature or presence of the matter, picture, model, phonograph record, crime comic or other thing by means of or in relation to which the offence was committed is not a defence to the charge.

"Crime comic"

(7) In this section, "crime comic" means a magazine, periodical or book that exclusively or substantially comprises matter depicting pictorially

(a) the commission of crimes, real or fictitious, or

(b) events connected with the commission of crimes, real or fictitious, whether occurring before or after the commission of the crime.

"Obscene"

(8) For the purposes of this Act, any publication a dominant characteristic of which is the undue exploitation of sex, or of sex and any one or more of the following subjects, namely, crime, horror, cruelty and violence, shall be deemed to be obscene. 1953-54, c. 51, s. 150; 1959, c. 41, s. 11; 1968-69, c. 41, s. 13.

2. In this Act

"writing" includes a document of any kind and any mode in which, and any material on which, words or figures, whether at length or abridged, are written, printed or otherwise expressed, or a map or plan is inscribed.

Warrant of seizure

160. (1) A judge who is satisfied by information upon oath that there are reasonable grounds for believing that any publication, copies of which are kept for sale or distribution in premises within the jurisdiction of the court, is obscene or a crime comic, shall issue a warrant under his hand authorizing seizure of the copies. ss. (8) 159(8) 159(7)

Summons to occupier

(2) Within seven days of the issue of the warrant, the judge shall issue a summons to the occupier of the premises requiring him to appear before the court and show cause why the matter seized should not be forfeited to Her Majesty. ss (8)

Owner and author may appear

(3) The owner and the author of the matter seized and alleged to be obscene or a crime comic may appear and be represented in the proceedings in order to oppose the making of an order for the forfeiture of the said matter.

Order of forfeiture

(4) If the court is satisfied that the publication is obscene or a crime comic, it shall make an order declaring the matter forfeited to Her Majesty in right of the province in which the proceedings take place, for disposal as the Attorney General may direct. 28 Interp 2

Disposal of matter

(5) If the court is not satisfied that the publication is obscene or a crime comic, it shall order that the matter be restored to the person from whom it was seized forthwith after the time for final appeal has expired.

Appeal

(6) An appeal lies from an order made under subsection (4) or (5) by any person who appeared in the proceedings

(a) on any ground of appeal that involves a question of law alone,

(b) on any ground of appeal that involves a question of fact alone, or

(c) on any ground of appeal that involves a question of mixed law and fact,

as if it were an appeal against conviction or against a judgment or verdict of acquittal, as the case may be, on a question of law alone under Part XVIII and sections 601 to 624 apply *mutatis mutandis.*

mutatis mutandis — after the necessary changes in detail so that the text applies

Consent

(7) Where an order has been made under this section by a judge in a province with respect to one or more copies of a publication, no proceedings shall be instituted or continued in that province under section 159 with respect to those or other copies of the same publication without the consent of the Attorney General.

Definitions

(8) In this section

"court"

"court" means

(a) in the Province of Quebec, the provincial court, the court of the sessions of the peace, the municipal court of Montreal and the municipal court of Quebec;

(a.1) in the Provinces of New Brunswick, Alberta and Saskatchewan, the Court of Queen's Bench; 1978-79, c. 11, s. 10, I. 6(7).

(b) in the Province of Prince Edward Island, the Supreme Court; or

(c) in any other province, a county or district court;

"crime comic"

"crime comic" has the same meaning as it has in section 159;

"judge"

"judge" means a judge of a court. 1959, c. 41, s. 12; 1968-69, c. 38, s. 8; 1974-75, c. 48, s. 25(1); 1978-79, c. 11, s. 10, I. 6(7).

Tied sale
Type 'B' (D) Offence 165

161. Every one commits an offence who refuses to sell or supply to any other person copies of any publication for the reason only that such other person refuses to purchase or acquire from him copies of any other publication that such other person is apprehensive may be obscene or a crime comic. 1959, c. 41, s. 12. 159(8)

Restriction on publication of reports of judicial proceedings
Type 'B' (D) Offence 165 with consent ss. (3)

162. (1) A proprietor, editor, master printer or publisher commits an offence who prints or publishes

(a) in relation to any judicial proceedings any indecent matter or indecent medical, surgical or physiological details, being matter or details that, if published, are calculated to injure public morals;

(b) in relation to any judicial proceedings for dissolution of marriage, nullity of marriage, judicial separation or restitution of conjugal rights, any particulars other than

(i) the names, addresses and occupations of the parties and witnesses,

(ii) a concise statement of the charges, defences and countercharges in support of which evidence has been given,

(iii) submissions on a point of law arising in the course of the proceedings, and the decision of the court in connection therewith, and

(iv) the summing up of the judge, the finding of the jury and the judgment of the court and the observations that are made by the judge in giving judgment.

Saving

(2) Nothing in paragraph (1)(*b*) affects the operation of paragraph (1)(*a*).

Consent of Attorney General

(3) No proceedings for an offence under this section shall be commenced without the consent of the Attorney General.

Exceptions

(4) This section does not apply to a person who

(a) prints or publishes any matter for use in connection with any judicial proceedings or communicates it to persons who are concerned in the proceedings;

(b) prints or publishes a notice or report pursuant to directions of a court; or

(c) prints or publishes any matter

(i) in a volume or part of a *bona fide* series of law reports that does not form part of any other publication and consists solely of reports of proceedings in courts of law, or

(ii) in a publication of a technical character that is *bona fide* intended for circulation among members of the legal or medical professions. 1953-54, c. 51, s. 151.

bona fide — In or with good faith, there is no pretence, it is actually so.

Immoral theatrical performance
Type 'B' (D) Offence 165

163. (1) Every one commits an offence who, being the lessee, manager, agent or person in charge of a theatre, presents or gives or allows to be presented or 138
given therein an immoral, indecent or obscene performance, entertainment or 159(8)
representation.

Person taking part
Type 'B' (D) Offence 165

(2) Every one commits an offence who takes part or appears as an actor, performer, or assistant in any capacity, in an immoral, indecent or obscene performance, entertainment or representation in a theatre. 1953-54, c. 51, s. 152.

138. In this Part
"theatre" includes any place that is open to the public where entertainments are given, whether or not any charge is made for admission.

Mailing obscene matter

Type 'B' (D) Offence 165

164. Every one commits an offence who makes use of the mails for the purpose of transmitting or delivering anything that is obscene, indecent, immoral or scurrilous, but this section does not apply to a person who makes use of the mails for the purpose of transmitting or delivering anything mentioned in subsection 162(4). 1953-54, c. 51, s. 153. 159(8)

Punishment

Type 'B' (D) Offences

165. Every one who commits an offence under section 159, 161, 162, 163 or 164 is guilty of

(a) an indictable offence and is liable to imprisonment for two years, or

(b) an offence punishable on summary conviction. 1953-54, c. 51, s. 154; 1959, c. 41, s. 13. 722(1)

Parent or guardian procuring defilement

166. Every one who, being the parent or guardian of a female person, 138

(a) procures her to have illicit sexual intercourse with a person other than the procurer, or

(b) orders, is party to, permits or knowingly receives the avails of, the defilement, seduction or prostitution of the female person,

is guilty of an indictable offence and is liable to

Type 'E' Offence

(c) imprisonment for fourteen years, if the female person is under the age of fourteen years, or 3(1)

Type 'D' Offence

(d) imprisonment for five years, if the female person is fourteen years of age or more. 1953-54, c. 51, s. 155.

3. (1) For the purposes of this Act a person shall be deemed to have been of a given age when the anniversary of his birthday, the number of which corresponds to that age, is fully completed, and until then to have been under that age.

585. (1) In any proceedings to which this Act applies an entry or record of an incorporated society or its officers who have had the control or care of a child or young person at or about the time the child or young person was brought to Canada is evidence of the age of the child or young person if the entry or record was made before the time when the offence is alleged to have been committed.

(2) In the absence of other evidence, or by way of corroboration of other evidence, a jury, judge, justice or magistrate, as the case may be, may infer the age of a child or young person from his appearance.

3. (6) For the purposes of this Act, sexual intercourse is complete upon penetration to even the slightest degree, notwithstanding that seed is not emitted.

138. In this Part

"guardian" includes any person who has in law or in fact the custody or control of another person;

139. (1) No accused shall be convicted of an offence under section 148, 150, 151, 152, 153, 154 or 166 upon the evidence of only one witness unless the evidence of the witness is corroborated in a material particular by evidence that implicates the accused.

141. No proceedings for an offence under section 151, 152, paragraph 153*(b)*, or under section 166, 167 or 168 shall be commenced more than one year after the time when the offence is alleged to have been committed.

Canada Evidence Act

4. (2) The wife or husband of a person charged with an offence against section 33 or 34 of the *Juvenile Delinquents Act* or with an offence against any of sections 143 to 146, 148, 150 to 155, 157, 166 to 169, 175, 195, 197, 200, 248 to 250, 255 to 258, 289, paragraph 423(1)*(c)* or an attempt to commit an offence under section 146 or 155 of the *Criminal Code*, is a competent and compellable witness for the prosecution without the consent of the person charged.

Householder permitting defilement

Type 'D' Offence

167. Every one who

(a) being the owner, occupier or manager of premises, or

(b) having control of premises or assisting in the management or control of premises,

knowingly permits a female person under the age of eighteen years to resort to or to be in or upon the premises for the purpose of having illicit sexual intercourse with a particular male person or with male persons generally is guilty of an indictable offence and is liable to imprisonment for five years. 1953-54, c. 51, s. 156. 3(1)

141. No proceedings for an offence under section 151, 152, paragraph 153*(b)*, or under section 166, 167 or 168 shall be commenced more than one year after the time when the offence is alleged to have been committed.

Canada Evidence Act

4. (2) The wife or husband of a person charged with an offence against section 33 or 34 of the *Juvenile Delinquents Act* or with an offence against any of sections 143 to 146, 148, 150 to 155, 157, 166 to 169, 175, 195, 197, 200, 248 to 250, 255 to 258, 289, paragraph 423(1)(*c*) or an attempt to commit an offence under section 146 or 155 of the *Criminal Code,* is a competent and compellable witness for the prosecution without the consent of the person charged.

Corrupting children

Type 'D' Offence with consent or ss. (4)

168. (1) Every one who, in the home of a child, participates in adultery or sexual immorality or indulges in habitual drunkenness or any other form of vice, and thereby endangers the morals of the child or renders the home an unfit place for the child to be in, is guilty of an indictable offence and is liable to imprisonment for two years. ss. (3)

Limitation

(2) No proceedings for an offence under this section shall be commenced more than one year after the time when the offence was committed.

"Child"

(3) For the purposes of this section, "child" means a person who is or appears to be under the age of eighteen years. 3(1)

Who may institute prosecutions

(4) No proceedings shall be commenced under subsection (1) without the consent of the Attorney General, unless they are instituted by or at the instance of a recognized society for the protection of children or by an officer of a juvenile court. 1953-54, c. 51, s. 157. 2

Canada Evidence Act

4. (2) The wife or husband of a person charged with an offence against section 33 or 34 of the *Juvenile Delinquents Act* or with an offence against any of sections 143 to 146, 148, 150 to 155, 157, 166 to 169, 175, 195, 197, 200, 248 to 250, 255 to 258, 289, paragraph 423(1)(*c*) or an attempt to commit an offence under section 146 or 155 of the *Criminal Code,* is a competent and compellable witness for the prosecution without the consent of the person charged.

Disorderly conduct

Indecent acts
Type 'A' Offence

169. Every one who wilfully does an indecent act

(a) in a public place in the presence of one or more persons, or 138

(b) in any place, with intent thereby to insult or offend any person,

is guilty of an offence punishable on summary conviction. 1953-54, c. 51, s. 158. 722(1)

138. In this Part

"public place" includes any place to which the public have access as of right or by invitation, express or implied;

Canada Evidence Act

4. (2) The wife or husband of a person charged with an offence against section 33 or 34 of the *Juvenile Delinquents Act* or with an offence against any of sections 143 to 146, 148, 150 to 155, 157, 166 to 169, 175, 195, 197, 200, 248 to 250, 255 to 258, 289, paragraph 423(1)(*c*) or an attempt to commit an offence under section 146 or 155 of the *Criminal Code*, is a competent and compellable witness for the prosecution without the consent of the person charged.

Nudity
Type 'A' Offence with consent ss. (3)

170. (1) Every one who, without lawful excuse,

(a) is nude in a public place, or 138

(b) is nude and exposed to public view while on private property, whether or not the property is his own,

is guilty of an offence punishable on summary conviction. 722(1)

Nude

(2) For the purposes of this section a person is nude who is so clad as to offend against public decency or order.

Consent of Attorney General

(3) No proceedings shall be commenced under this section without the consent of the Attorney General. 1953-54, c. 51, s. 159. 2

Causing disturbance, indecent exhibition, loitering, etc.
Type 'A' Offence

171. (1) Every one who

(a) not being in a dwelling-house causes a disturbance in or near a public place, 2 138

(i) by fighting, screaming, shouting, swearing, singing or using insulting or obscene language,

(ii) by being drunk, or

(iii) by impeding or molesting other persons,

(b) openly exposes or exhibits an indecent exhibition in a public place,

(c) loiters in a public place and in any way obstructs persons who are there, or

(d) disturbs the peace and quiet of the occupants of a dwelling-house by discharging firearms or by other disorderly conduct in a public place or who, 82 not being an occupant of a dwelling-house comprised in a particular building or structure, disturbs the peace and quiet of the occupants of a dwelling-house comprised in the building or structure by discharging firearms or by other disorderly conduct in any part of a building or structure to which, at the time of such conduct, the occupants of two or more dwelling-houses comprised in the building or structure have access as of right or by invitation, express or implied,

is guilty of an offence punishable on summary conviction. R.S., c. C-34, s. 171; 1972, c. 13, s. 11.

(2) In the absence of other evidence, or by way of corroboration of other evidence, a summary conviction court may infer from the evidence of a peace 2 officer relating to the conduct of a person or persons, whether ascertained or not, that a disturbance described in paragraph (1)*(a)* or *(d)* was caused or occurred. 1974-75-76, c. 93, s. 9.

2. In this Act

"dwelling-house" means the whole or any part of a building or structure that is kept or occupied as a permanent or temporary residence and includes

(a) a building within the curtilage of a dwelling-house that is connected to it by a doorway or by a covered and enclosed passageway, and

(b) a unit that is designed to be mobile and to be used as a permanent or temporary residence and that is being used as such a residence;

82. (1) For the purposes of this Part,

"firearm" means any barrelled weapon from which any shot, bullet or other missile can be discharged and that is capable of causing serious bodily injury or death to a person, and includes any frame or receiver of such a barrelled weapon and anything that can be adapted for use as a firearm;

84. (2) Every one who, without lawful excuse, uses, carries, handles, ships or stores any firearm or ammunition in a careless manner or without reasonable precautions for the safety of other persons

(a) is guilty of an indictable offence and is liable to imprisonment

(i) in the case of a first offence, for two years, and

(ii) in the case of a second or subsequent offence, for five years; or

(b) is guilty of an offence punishable on summary conviction.

228. Every one who, with intent

(a) to wound, maim or disfigure any person,

(b) to endanger the life of any person, or

(c) to prevent the arrest or detention of any person,

discharges a firearm, air gun or air pistol at or causes bodily harm in any way to any person, whether or not that person is the one mentioned in paragraph *(a)*, *(b)* or *(c)*, is guilty of an indictable offence and is liable to imprisonment for fourteen years.

Obstructing or violence to or arrest of officiating clergyman

Type 'D' Offence

172. (1) Every one who

(a) by threats or force, unlawfully obstructs or prevents or endeavours to obstruct or prevent a clergyman or minister from celebrating divine service or performing any other function in connection with his calling, or

(b) knowing that a clergyman or minister is about to perform, is on his way to perform, or is returning from the performance of any of the duties or functions mentioned in paragraph *(a)*

(i) assaults or offers any violence to him, or 244

(ii) arrests him upon a civil process, or under the pretence of executing a civil process,

is guilty of an indictable offence and is liable to imprisonment for two years.

Disturbing religious worship or certain meetings

Type 'A' Offences

(2) Every one who wilfully disturbs or interrupts an assemblage of persons met for religious worship or for a moral, social or benevolent purpose is guilty of an offence punishable on summary conviction. 722(1)

(3) Every one who, at or near a meeting referred to in subsection (2), wilfully does anything that disturbs the order or solemnity of the meeting is guilty of an offence punishable on summary conviction. 1953-54, c. 51, s. 161. 722(1)

244. A person commits an assault when

(a) without the consent of another person or with consent, where it is obtained by fraud, he applies force intentionally to the person of the other, directly or indirectly;

(b) he attempts or threatens, by an act or gesture, to apply force to the person of the other, if he has or causes the other to believe upon reasonable grounds that he has present ability to effect his purpose; or

(c) while openly wearing or carrying a weapon or an imitation thereof, he accosts or impedes another person and begs.

Trespassing at night
Type 'A' Offence

173. Every one who, without lawful excuse, the proof of which lies upon him, loiters or prowls at night upon the property of another person near a 2
dwelling-house situated on that property is guilty of an offence punishable on 2
summary conviction. 1953-54, c. 51, s. 162. 722(1)

2. In this Act

"dwelling-house" means the whole or any part of a building or structure that is kept or occupied as a permanent or temporary residence and includes

(*a*) a building within the curtilage of a dwelling-house that is connected to it by a doorway or by a covered and enclosed passageway, and

(*b*) a unit that is designed to be mobile and to be used as a permanent or temporary residence and that is being used as such a residence;

"night" means the period between nine o'clock in the afternoon and six o'clock in the forenoon of the following day;

Offensive volatile substance
Type 'A' Offence

174. Every one other than a peace officer engaged in the discharge of his 2
duty who has in his possession in a public place or who deposits, throws or 3(4)
injects or causes to be deposited, thrown or injected in, into or near any place, 138

(*a*) an offensive volatile substance that is likely to alarm, inconvenience, discommode or cause discomfort to any person or to cause damage to property, or

(*b*) a stink or stench bomb or device from which any substance mentioned in paragraph (*a*) is or is capable of being liberated,

is guilty of an offence punishable on summary conviction. 1953-54, c. 51, s. 163. 722(1)

3. (4) For the purposes of this Act,

(*a*) a person has anything in possession when he has it in his personal possession or knowingly

(i) has it in the actual possession or custody of another person, or

(ii) has it in any place, whether or not that place belongs to or is occupied by him, for the use or benefit of himself or of another person; and

(*b*) where one of two or more persons, with the knowledge and consent of the rest, has anything in his custody or possession, it shall be deemed to be in the custody and possession of each and all of them.

138. In this Part

"public place" includes any place to which the public have access as of right or by invitation, express or implied;

722. (1) Except where otherwise expressly provided by law, every one who is convicted of an offence punishable on summary conviction is liable to a fine of not more than five hundred dollars or to imprisonment for six months or to both.

Vagrancy
Type 'A' Offence

175. (1) Every one commits vagrancy who

(a) to *(c)* Repealed, 1972, c. 13, s. 12;

(d) supports himself in whole or in part by gaming or crime and has no lawful profession or calling by which to maintain himself; or

(e) having at any time been convicted of an offence under a provision mentioned in paragraph 689(1)*(a)* or *(b)*, is found loitering or wandering in or near a school ground, playground, public park or bathing area.

Type 'A' Offence

(2) Every one who commits vagrancy is guilty of an offence punishable on summary conviction. R.S., c. C-34, s. 175; 1972, c. 13, s. 12. 722(1)

(3) Repealed, 1972, c. 13, s. 12.

689. (1) Where an accused has been convicted of

(a) an offence under section 144, 146, 149, 155, 156 or 157; or

(b) an attempt to commit an offence under a provision mentioned in paragraph (a),

the court shall, upon application, hear evidence as to whether the accused is a dangerous sexual offender.

(This provision repealed by 1976-77, c. 53, s. 14.)

Interpretation Act

36. Where an enactment (in this section called the "former enactment") is repealed and another enactment (in this section called the "new enactment") is substituted therefor,

(h) any reference in an unrepealed enactment to the former enactment shall, as regards a subsequent transaction, matter or thing, be read and construed as a reference to the provisions of the new enactment relating to the same subject-matter as the former enactment, but where there are no provisions in the new enactment relating to the same subject-matter, the former enactment shall be read as unrepealed in so far as is necessary to maintain or give effect to the unrepealed enactment.

Canada Evidence Act

4. (2) The wife or husband of a person charged with an offence against section 33 or 34 of the *Juvenile Delinquents Act* or with an offence against any of sections 143 to 146, 148, 150 to 155, 157, 166 to 169, 175, 195, 197, 200, 248 to 250, 255 to 258, 289, paragraph 423(1)(*c*) or an attempt to commit an offence under section 146 or 155 of the *Criminal Code,* is a competent and compellable witness for the prosecution without the consent of the person charged.

144 (Rape), 146 (Sexual intercourse with female under fourteen years or with female between fourteen and sixteen years), 149 (Indecent assault on female), 155 (Buggery or beastiality), 156 (Indecent assault on male) or 157 (Acts of gross indecency)

Nuisances

Common nuisance
Type 'D' Offence

176. (1) Every one who commits a common nuisance and thereby

(a) endangers the lives, safety or health of the public, or

(b) causes physical injury to any person,

is guilty of an indictable offence and is liable to imprisonment for two years.

Definition

(2) For the purposes of this section, every one commits a common nuisance who does an unlawful act or fails to discharge a legal duty and thereby

(a) endangers the lives, safety, health, property or comfort of the public, or

(b) obstructs the public in the exercise or enjoyment of any right that is common to all the subjects of Her Majesty in Canada. 1953-54, c. 51, s. 165.

Spreading false news
Type 'D' Offence

177. Every one who wilfully publishes a statement, tale or news that he knows is false and that causes or is likely to cause injury or mischief to a public interest is guilty of an indictable offence and is liable to imprisonment for two years. 1953-54, c. 51, s. 166.

Dead body
Type 'D' Offence

178. Every one who

(a) neglects, without lawful excuse, to perform any duty that is imposed upon him by law or that he undertakes with reference to the burial of a dead human body or human remains, or

(b) improperly or indecently interferes with or offers any indignity to a dead human body or human remains, whether buried or not,

is guilty of an indictable offence and is liable to imprisonment for five years. 1953-54, c. 51, s. 167.

PART IV.1

INVASION OF PRIVACY

Interception of Communications

Definitions **178.1** In this Part

"authorization" "authorization" means an authorization to intercept a private communication given under section 178.13 or subsection 178.15(2);

"electromagnetic, acoustic, mechanical or other device" "electromagnetic, acoustic, mechanical or other device" means any device or apparatus that is used or is capable of being used to intercept a private communication, but does not include a hearing aid used to correct subnormal hearing of the user to not better than normal hearing;

"intercept" "intercept" includes listen to, record or acquire a communication or acquire the substance, meaning or purport thereof;

"offence" "offence" means an offence contrary to, any conspiracy or attempt to commit or being an accessory after the fact in relation to an offence contrary to, or any counselling, procuring or inciting in relation to an offence contrary to section 47 (high treason), 51 (intimidating Parliament or a legislature), 52 (sabotage), 58 (forgery, etc.), 62 (sedition), 76.1 (hijacking), 76.2 (endangering aircraft, etc.), 76.3 (offensive weapons, etc., on aircraft), 78 (breach of duty), 79 (causing injury with intent), 80 (possessing explosive), 88 (possession of prohibited weapon), 108 (bribery, etc.), 109 (bribery, etc.), 110 (fraud upon government), 111 (breach of trust), 112 (municipal corruption), 121 (perjury), 127 (obstructing justice), 132 (prison breach), 144 (rape), 178.11 (unlawful interception), 178.18 (possession of intercepting device), 218 (murder), 247 (kidnapping), 281.1 (advocating genocide), 303 (robbery), 305 (extortion), 306 (breaking and entering), 312 (possession), 314 (theft from mail), 325 (forgery), 326 (uttering forged document), 331 (threatening letters, etc.), 338 (fraud on public, etc.), 339 (using mails to defraud), 340 (fraudulent manipulation of stock exchange transactions), 383 (secret commissions), 389 (arson), 407 (making counterfeit money), 408 (possession of counterfeit money), 410 (uttering, etc., counterfeit money), subsection 133(1) (escape, etc.), 185(1) (keeping gaming or betting house) or 245(2) (assault causing bodily harm), paragraph 159(1)*(a)* (pornographic materials), 186(1)*(e)* (pool-selling, etc.), 195(1)*(a)* (procuring) or 294*(a)* (theft in excess of $200, etc.,), section 4 (trafficking) or 5 (importing or exporting) of the *Narcotic Control Act*, section 34 or 42 (trafficking) of the *Food and Drugs Act*, section 192 (smuggling) of the *Customs Act*, section 158 or 163 (unlawful distillation or selling of spirits) of the *Excise Act*, section 169 (fraudulent bankruptcy) of the *Bankruptcy Act;* or any other offence created by this Act for which an offender may be sentenced to imprisonment for five years or more or that is an offence mentioned in section 3 or 20 of the *Small Loans Act*, that there are reasonable and probable grounds to believe is part of a pattern of criminal activity planned and organized by a number of persons acting in concert;

"private communication" "private communication" means any oral communication or any telecommunication made under circumstances in which it is reasonable for the originator thereof to expect that it will not be intercepted by any person other than the person intended by the originator thereof to receive it; 28 Interp

"sell" "sell" includes offer for sale, expose for sale, have in possession for sale, distribute or advertise for sale; 3(4) [178.18]

"solicitor" "solicitor" means, in the Province of Quebec, an advocate or notary and, in any other province, a barrister or solicitor. 1973-74, c. 50, s. 2; 1976-77, c. 53, s. 7.

Interpretation Act

28. In every enactment

"telecommunication" means any transmission, emission or reception of signs, signals, writing, images or sounds or intelligence of any nature by wire, radio, visual or other electromagnetic system;

Interception
Type 'D' Offence
IPA offence 178.1

178.11 (1) Every one who, by means of an electromagnetic, acoustic, mechanical or other device, wilfully intercepts a private communication is guilty of an indictable offence and liable to imprisonment for five years. 178.1 178.1

Saving provision

(2) Subsection (1) does not apply to

(a) a person who has the consent to intercept, express or implied, of the originator of the private communication or of the person intended by the originator thereof to receive it;

(b) a person who intercepts a private communication in accordance with an authorization or any person who in good faith aids in any way a person 178.1
whom he has reasonable and probable grounds to believe is acting with any such authorization;

(c) a person engaged in providing a telephone, telegraph or other communication service to the public who intercepts a private communication,

(i) if such interception is necessary for the purpose of providing such service,

(ii) in the course of service observing or random monitoring necessary for the purpose of mechanical or service quality control checks, or

(iii) if such interception is necessary to protect the person's rights or property directly related to providing such service; or

(d) an officer or servant of Her Majesty in right of Canada in respect of a private communication intercepted by him in the course of random monitoring that is necessarily incidental to radio frequency spectrum management in Canada.

Consent to interception

(3) Where a private communication is originated by more than one person or is intended by the originator thereof to be received by more than one person, a consent to the interception thereof by any one of such persons is sufficient for the purposes of paragraph (2)*(a)*, subsection 178.16(1) and subsection 178.2(1). 1973-74, c. 50, s. 2.

Application for authorization

178.12 (1) An application for an authorization shall be made *ex parte* and in writing to a judge of a superior court of criminal jurisdiction, or a judge as 2
defined in section 482 and shall be signed by the Attorney General of the 2
province in which the application is made or the Solicitor General of Canada or an agent specially designated in writing for the purposes of this section by

(a) the Solicitor General of Canada personally, if the offence under investigation is one in respect of which proceedings, if any, may be instituted at the instance of the Government of Canada and conducted by or on behalf of the Attorney General of Canada, or

(b) the Attorney General of a province personally, in respect of any other offence in that province, 178.1

and shall be accompanied by an affidavit, which may be sworn on the information and belief of a peace officer or public officer deposing to the following matters, 2
namely:

(c) the facts relied upon to justify the belief that an authorization should be given together with particulars of the offence;

(d) the type of private communication proposed to be intercepted;

(e) the names, addresses and occupations, if known, of all persons, the interception of whose private communications there are reasonable and probable grounds to believe may assist the investigation of the offence, a general description of the nature and location of the place, if known, at which private communications are proposed to be intercepted and a general description of the manner of interception proposed to be used;

(e.1) the number of instances, if any, on which an application has been made under this section in relation to the offence and a person named in the affidavit pursuant to paragraph *(e)* and on which the application was withdrawn or no authorization was given, the date on which each such application was made and the name of the judge to whom each such application was made;

(f) the period for which the authorization is requested; and

(g) whether other investigative procedures have been tried and have failed or why it appears they are unlikely to succeed or that the urgency of the matter is such that it would be impractical to carry out the investigation of the offence using only other investigative procedures. 1973-74, c. 50, s. 2; 1976-77, c. 53, s. 8(1).

Extension of period for notification

(2) An application for an authorization may be accompanied by an application personally signed by the Attorney General of the province in which the application for the authorization is made or the Solicitor General of Canada if the application for the authorization is made by him or on his behalf, to substitute for the period mentioned in subsection 178.23(1) such longer period not exceeding three years as is set forth in the application. 178.23(1) "ninety days"

Where extension to be granted

(3) Where an application for an authorization is accompanied by an application referred to in subsection (2), the judge to whom the applications are made shall first consider the application referred to in subsection (2) and where, on the basis of the affidavit in support of the application for the authorization and any other affidavit evidence submitted in support of the application referred to in subsection (2), the judge is of the opinion that the interests of justice warrant the granting of such application, he shall fix a period, not exceeding three years, in substitution for the period mentioned in subsection 178.23(1).

Where extension not granted

(4) Where the judge to whom an application for an authorization and an application referred to in subsection (2) are made refuses to fix a period in substitution for the period mentioned in subsection 178.23(1) or where the judge fixes a period in substitution therefor that is less than the period set forth in the application referred to in subsection (2), the person appearing before the judge on the application for the authorization may withdraw the application for the authorization and thereupon the judge shall not proceed to consider the application for the authorization or to give the authorization and shall return to the person appearing before him on the application for the authorization both applications and all other material pertaining thereto. 1976-77, c. 53, s. 8(2).

Judge to be satisfied

178.13 (1) An authorization may be given if the judge to whom the application is made is satisfied

(a) that it would be in the best interests of the administration of justice to do so; and

(b) that other investigative procedures have been tried and have failed, other investigative procedures are unlikely to succeed or the urgency of the matter is such that it would be impractical to carry out the investigation of the offence using only other investigative procedures.

Where authorization not to be given

(1.1) No authorization may be given to intercept a private communication at the office or residence of a solicitor, or at any other place ordinarily used by a solicitor and by other solicitors for the purpose of consultation with clients, unless the judge to whom the application is made is satisfied that there are reasonable grounds to believe that the solicitor, any other solicitor practising with him, any person employed by him or any other such solicitor or a member of the solicitor's household has been or is about to become a party to an offence.

Terms and conditions

(1.2) Where an authorization is given in relation to the interception of private communications at a place described in subsection (1.1), the judge by whom the authorization is given shall include therein such terms and conditions as he considers advisable to protect privileged communications between solicitors and clients. 1976-77, c. 53, s. 9(1).

Content and limitation of authorization

(2) An authorization shall

(a) state the offence in respect of which private communications may be intercepted;

(b) state the type of private communication that may be intercepted;

(c) state the identity of the persons, if known, whose private communications are to be intercepted, generally describe the place at which private communications may be intercepted, if a general description of that place can be given, and generally describe the manner of interception that may be used; 1976-77, c. 53, s. 9(2).

(d) contain such terms and conditions as the judge considers advisable in the public interest; and

(e) be valid for the period, not exceeding sixty days, set forth therein. 1976-77, c. 53, s. 9(3).

(2.1) The Solicitor General of Canada or the Attorney General, as the case may be, may designate a person or persons who may intercept private communications under authorizations.

Renewal of authorization

(3) Renewals of an authorization may be given from time to time by a judge of a superior court of criminal jurisdiction or a judge as defined in section 482 upon receipt by him of an *ex parte* application in writing signed by the Attorney General of the province in which the application is made or the Solicitor General of Canada or an agent specially designated in writing for the purposes of section 178.12 by the Solicitor General of Canada or the Attorney General, as the case may be, accompanied by an affidavit of a peace officer or public officer deposing to the following matters, namely:

(a) the reason and period for which the renewal is required,

(b) full particulars, together with times and dates, when interceptions, if any, were made or attempted under the authorization, and any information that has been obtained by any interception, and

(c) the number of instances, if any, on which, to the knowledge and belief of the deponent, an application has been made under this subsection in relation to the same authorization and on which the application was withdrawn or no renewal was given, the date on which each such application was made and the name of the judge to whom each such application was made,

and supported by such other information as the judge may require. 1976-77, c. 53, s. 9(3.1).

Renewal

(4) A renewal of an authorization may be given if the judge to whom the application is made is satisfied that any of the circumstances described in subsection (1) still obtain, but no such renewal shall be for a period exceeding sixty days. 1973-74, c. 50, s. 2; 1976-77, c. 53, s. 9(4).

Manner in which application to be kept secret

178.14 (1) All documents relating to an application made pursuant to section 178.12 or subsection 178.13(3) are confidential and, with the exception of the authorization, shall be placed in a packet and sealed by the judge to whom the application is made immediately upon determination of such application, and such packet shall be kept in the custody of the court in a place to which the public has no access or in such other place as the judge may authorize and shall not be

(a) opened or the contents thereof removed except

(i) for the purpose of dealing with an application for renewal of the authorization, or

(ii) pursuant to an order of a judge of a superior court of criminal jurisdiction or a judge as defined in section 482; and

(b) destroyed except pursuant to an order of a judge referred to in subparagraph *(a)*(ii).

Order of judge

(2) An order under subsection (1) may only be made after the Attorney General or the Solicitor General by whom or on whose authority the application was made for the authorization to which the order relates has been given an opportunity to be heard. 1973-74, c. 50, s. 2.

Applications to specially appointed judges

178.15 (1) Notwithstanding section 178.12, an application for an authorization may be made *ex parte* to a judge of a superior court of criminal jurisdiction, or a judge as defined in section 482, designated from time to time by the Chief Justice, by a peace officer specially designated in writing for the purposes of this section by ss. (4)

(a) the Solicitor General of Canada, if the offence is one in respect of which proceedings, if any, may be instituted by the Government of Canada and conducted by or on behalf of the Attorney General of Canada, or

(b) the Attorney General of a province, in respect of any other offence in the province,

if the urgency of the situation requires interception of private communications to commence before an authorization could, with reasonable diligence, be obtained under section 178.13.

Authorizations in emergency

(2) Where the judge to whom an application is made pursuant to subsection (1) is satisfied that the urgency of the situation requires that interception of private communications commence before an authorization could, with reasonable diligence, be obtained pursuant to section 178.13, he may, on such terms and conditions, if any, as he considers advisable, give an authorization in writing for a period of up to thirty-six hours.

Certain interceptions deemed not lawful

(3) For the purposes of section 178.16 only, an interception of a private communication in accordance with an authorization given pursuant to this section shall be deemed not to have been lawfully made unless the judge who gave the authorization or, if such judge is unable to act, a judge of the same jurisdiction, certifies that if the application for the authorization had been made to him pursuant to section 178.12 he would have given the authorization.

"Chief Justice" defined

(4) In this section, "Chief Justice" means

(a) in the Province of Ontario, the Chief Justice of the Supreme Court;

(b) in the Province of Quebec, the Chief Justice of the Superior Court;

(c) in the Provinces of Nova Scotia, Prince Edward Island and Newfoundland, the Chief Justice of the Supreme Court;

(c.1) in the Provinces of New Brunswick and Alberta, the Chief Justice of the Court of Queen's Bench; 1978-79, c. 11, s. 10, I. 6(8).

(d) in the Province of British Columbia, the Chief Justice of the Supreme Court;

(e) in the Provinces of Manitoba and Saskatchewan, the Chief Justice of the Court of Queen's Bench;

(f) in the Yukon Territory, the judge of the Supreme Court; and

(g) in the Northwest Territories, the judge of the Supreme Court.
1974-75, c. 19, s. 1.

Inadmissibility of evidence

(5) The trial judge may deem inadmissible the evidence obtained by means of an interception of a private communication pursuant to a subsequent authorization given under this section, where he finds that the application for such subsequent authorization was based on the same facts, and involved the interception of the private communications of the same person or persons, or related to the same offence, on which the application for the original authorization was based. 1973-74, c. 50, s. 2;

Intercepted private communication admissibility

178.16 (1) A private communication that has been intercepted is inadmissible as evidence against the originator of the communication or the person intended by the originator to receive it unless

(a) the interception was lawfully made; or

(b) the originator thereof or the person intended by the originator to receive it has expressly consented to the admission thereof;

but evidence obtained directly or indirectly as a result of information acquired by interception of a private communication is not inadmissible by reason only that the private communication is itself inadmissible as evidence.

Idem

(2) Notwithstanding subsection (1), the judge or magistrate presiding at any proceedings may refuse to admit evidence obtained directly or indirectly as a result of information acquired by interception of a private communication that is itself inadmissible as evidence where he is of the opinion that the admission thereof would bring the administration of justice into disrepute.

Idem

(3) Where the judge or magistrate presiding at any proceedings is of the opinion that a private communication that, by virtue of subsection (1), is inadmissible as evidence in the proceedings

(a) is relevant to a matter at issue in the proceedings, and

(b) is inadmissible as evidence therein by reason only of a defect of form or an irregularity in procedure, not being a substantive defect or irregularity, in the application for or the giving of the authorization under which such private communication was intercepted,

he may, notwithstanding subsection (1), admit such private communication as evidence in the proceedings.

Idem

(3.1) A private communication that has been intercepted and that is admissible as evidence may be admitted in any criminal proceeding or in any civil proceeding or other matter whatever respecting which the Parliament of Canada has jurisdiction, whether or not the criminal proceeding or the civil proceeding or other matter relates to the offence specified in the authorization pursuant to which the communication was intercepted. 1976-77, c. 53, s. 10.

Notice of intention to produce evidence

(4) A private communication that has been lawfully intercepted shall not be received in evidence unless the party intending to adduce it has given to the accused reasonable notice of his intention together with

(a) a transcript of the private communication, where it will be adduced in the form of a recording, or a statement setting forth full particulars of the private communication, where evidence of the private communication will be given *viva voce;* and

(b) a statement respecting the time, place and date of the private communication and the parties thereto, if known.

Privileged evidence

(5) Any information obtained by an interception that, but for the interception would have been privileged, remains privileged and inadmissible as evidence without the consent of the person enjoying the privilege. 1973-74, c. 50, s. 2.

Canada Evidence Act

4. (3) No husband is compellable to disclose any communication made to him by his wife during their marriage, and no wife is compellable to disclose any communication made to her by her husband during their marriage.

viva voce — orally

Further particulars

178.17 Where an accused has been given notice pursuant to subsection 178.16(4), any judge of the court in which the trial of the accused is being or is to be held may at any time order that further particulars be given of the private communication that is intended to be adduced in evidence. 1973-74, c. 50, s. 2.

Possession, etc.
Type 'D' Offence
IPA offence 178.1

178.18 (1) Every one who possesses, sells or purchases any electromagnetic, acoustic, mechanical or other device or any compenent thereof knowing that the design thereof renders it primarily useful for surreptitious interception of private communications is guilty of an indictable offence and liable to imprisonment for two years. 3(4)

Exemptions

(2) Subsection (1) does not apply to

(a) a police officer or police constable in possession of a device or component described in subsection (1) in the course of his employment;

(b) a person in possession of such a device or component for the purpose of using it in an interception made or to be made in accordance with an authorization;

(c) an officer or servant of Her Majesty in right of Canada or a member of the Canadian Forces in possession of such a device or component in the course of his duties as such an officer, servant or member, as the case may be; and

(d) any other person in possession of such a device or component under the authority of a licence issued by the Solicitor General of Canada.

Terms and conditions of licence

(3) A licence issued for the purpose of paragraph (2)*(d)* may contain such terms and conditions relating to the possession, sale or purchase of a device or component described in subsection (1) as the Solicitor General of Canada may prescribe. 1973-74, c. 50, s. 2.

3. (4) For the purposes of this Act,

(a) a person has anything in possession when he has it in his personal possession or knowingly

(i) has it in the actual possession or custody of another person, or

(ii) has it in any place, whether or not that place belongs to or is occupied by him, for the use or benefit of himself or of another person; and

(b) where one of two or more persons, with the knowledge and consent of the rest, has anything in his custody or possession, it shall be deemed to be in the custody and possession of each and all of them.

Forfeiture

178.19 (1) Where a person is convicted of an offence under section 178.11 or 178.18, any electromagnetic, acoustic, mechanical or other device by means of which the offence was committed or the possession of which constituted the offence, upon such conviction, in addition to any punishment that is imposed, may be ordered forfeited to Her Majesty whereupon it may be disposed of as the Attorney General directs.

Limitation

(2) No order for forfeiture shall be made under subsection (1) in respect of telephone, telegraph or other communication facilities or equipment owned by a person engaged in providing telephone, telegraph or other communication service to the public or forming part of the telephone, telegraph or other communication service or system of such a person by means of which an offence under section 178.11 has been committed if such person was not a party to the offence. 1973-74, c. 50, s. 2.

Disclosure of information

Type 'D' Offence

178.2 (1) Where a private communication has been intercepted by means of an electromagnetic, acoustic, mechanical or other device without the consent, express or implied, of the originator thereof or of the person intended by the originator thereof to receive it, every one who, without the express consent of the originator thereof or of the person intended by the originator thereof to receive it, wilfully

(a) uses or discloses such private communication or any part thereof or the substance, meaning or purport thereof or of any part thereof, or

(b) discloses the existence thereof,

is guilty of an indictable offence and liable to imprisonment for two years.

Exemptions

(2) Subsection (1) does not apply to a person who discloses a private communication or any part thereof or the substance, meaning or purport thereof or of any part thereof or who discloses the existence of a private communication

(a) in the course of or for the purpose of giving evidence in any civil or criminal proceedings or in any other proceedings in which he may be required to give evidence on oath where the private communication is admissible as evidence under section 178.16 or would be admissible under that section if it applied in respect of the proceedings;

(b) in the course of or for the purpose of any criminal investigation if the private communication was lawfully intercepted;

(c) in giving notice under section 178.16 or furnishing further particulars pursuant to an order under section 178.17;

(d) in the course of the operation of

(i) a telephone, telegraph or other communication service to the public, or

(ii) a department or agency of the Government of Canada,

if the disclosure is necessarily incidental to an interception described in paragraph 178.11(2)*(c)* or *(d)*; or

(e) where disclosure is made to a peace officer and is intended to be in the interests of the administration of justice.

Publishing of prior lawful disclosure

(3) Subsection (1) does not apply to a person who discloses a private communication or any part thereof or the substance, meaning or purport thereof or of any part thereof or who discloses the existence of a private communication where that which is disclosed by him was, prior to such disclosure, lawfully disclosed in the course of or for the purpose of giving evidence in proceedings referred to in paragraph (2)*(a)*. 1973-74, c. 50, s. 2; 1976-77, c. 53, s. 11.

Damages

178.21 (1) Subject to subsection (2), a court that convicts an accused of an offence under section 178.11 or 178.2 may, upon the application of a person aggrieved, at the time sentence is imposed, order the accused to pay to that person an amount not exceeding $5,000 as punitive damages.

No damages where civil proceedings commenced

(2) No amount shall be ordered to be paid under subsection (1) to a person who has commenced an action under Part I.1 of the *Crown Liability Act.*

Judgment may be registered

(3) Where an amount that is ordered to be paid under subsection (1) is not paid forthwith, the applicant may, by filing the order, enter as a judgment, in the superior court of the province in which the trial was held, the amount ordered to be paid, and that judgment is enforceable against the accused in the same manner as if it were a judgment rendered against the accused in that court in civil proceedings. 28 Interp

Moneys in possession of accused may be taken

(4) All or any part of an amount that is ordered to be paid under subsection (1) may be taken out of moneys found in the possession of the accused at the time of his arrest, except where there is a dispute as to ownership of or right of possession to those moneys by claimants other than the accused. 1973-74, c. 50, s. 2.

Annual report

178.22 (1) The Solicitor General of Canada shall, as soon as possible after the end of each year, prepare a report relating to

(a) authorizations for which he and agents to be named in the report who were specially designated in writing by him for the purposes of section 178.12 made application, and

(b) authorizations given under section 178.15 for which peace officers to be named in the report who were specially designated by him for the purposes of that section made application,

and interceptions made thereunder in the immediately preceding year.

Information respecting authorizations

(2) The report referred to in subsection (1) shall, in relation to authorizations and interceptions made thereunder, set forth

(a) the number of applications made for authorizations;

(b) the number of applications made for renewal of authorizations;

(c) the number of applications referred to in paragraphs *(a)* and *(b)* that were granted, the number of such applications that were refused and the number of applications referred to in paragraph *(a)* that were granted subject to terms and conditions;

(d) the number of persons identified in an authorization against whom proceedings were commenced at the instance of the Attorney General of Canada in respect of

(i) an offence specified in the authorization,

(ii) an offence other than an offence specified in the authorization but in respect of which an authorization may be given, and

(iii) an offence in respect of which an authorization may not be given;

(e) the number of persons not identified in an authorization against whom proceedings were commenced at the instance of the Attorney General of Canada in respect of

(i) an offence specified in such an authorization,

(ii) an offence other than an offence specified in such an authorization but in respect of which an authorization may be given, and

(iii) an offence other than an offence specified in such an authorization and for which no such authorization may be given,

and whose commission or alleged commission of the offence became known to a peace officer as a result of an interception of a private communication under an authorization;

(f) the average period for which authorizations were given and for which renewals thereof were granted;

(g) the number of authorizations that, by virtue of one or more renewals thereof, were valid for more than thirty days, for more than sixty days, for more than ninety days and for more than one hundred and eighty days;

(g.1) the number of notifications given pursuant to section 178.23;

(h) the offences in respect of which authorizations were given, specifying the number of authorizations given in respect of each such offence;

(i) a description of all classes of places specified in authorizations and the number of authorizations in which each such class of place was specified;

(j) a general description of the methods of interception involved in each interception under an authorization;

(k) the number of persons arrested whose identity became known to a peace officer as a result of an interception under an authorization;

(l) the number of criminal proceedings commenced at the instance of the Attorney General of Canada in which private communications obtained by interception under an authorization were adduced in evidence and the number of such proceedings that resulted in a conviction; and

(m) the number of criminal investigations in which information obtained as a result of the interception of a private communication under an authorization was used although the private communication was not adduced in evidence in criminal proceedings commenced at the instance of the Attorney General of Canada as a result of the investigations. 1976-77, c. 53, s. 11.1.

Other information

(3) The report referred to in subsection (1) shall, in addition to the information referred to in subsection (2), set forth

(a) the number of prosecutions commenced against officers or servants of Her Majesty in right of Canada or members of the Canadian Forces for offences under section 178.11 or section 178.2; and

(b) a general assessment of the importance of interception of private communications for the investigation, detection, prevention and prosecution of offences in Canada.

Report to be laid before Parliament

(4) The Solicitor General of Canada shall cause a copy of each report prepared by him under subsection (1) to be laid before Parliament forthwith upon completion thereof, or if Parliament is not then sitting, on any of the first fifteen days next thereafter that Parliament is sitting.

Interpretation Act

19. Where an Act requires a report or other document to be laid before Parliament and, in compliance with the Act, a particular report or document has been laid before Parliament at a session thereof, nothing in the Act shall be construed as requiring the same report or document to be laid before Parliament at any subsequent session thereof.

Report by Attorneys General

(5) The Attorney General of each province shall, as soon as possible after the end of each year, prepare and publish or otherwise make available to the public a report relating to

(a) authorizations for which he and agents specially designated in writing by him for the purposes of section 178.12 made application, and

(b) authorizations given under section 178.15 for which peace officers specially designated by him for the purposes of that section made application,

and interceptions made thereunder in the immediately preceding year setting forth, with such modifications as the circumstances require, the information described in subsections (2) and (3). 1973-74, c. 50, s. 2.

Witten notification to be given

178.23 (1) The Attorney General of the province in which an application for an authorization was made or the Solicitor General of Canada if the application was made by him or on his behaf shall, within ninety days next following the period for which the authorization was given or renewed or within such other period as is fixed pursuant to subsection 178.12(3) or subsection (4) of this section, notify in writing the person who was the object of the interception pursuant to the authorization and shall, in a manner prescribed by regulations made by the Governor in Council, certify to the court that issued the authorization that such person has been so notified.

Exception

(2) Subsection (1) does not apply in the case of a warrant issued under subsection 16(2) of the *Official Secrets Act.*

Extension of period for notification

(3) At any time within the ninety day period mentioned in subsection (1) or any other period that is less than three years that was fixed by a judge pursuant to subsection 178.12(3) or substituted pursuant to this subsection in relation to a particular authorization, the Attorney General by or on whose behalf the application for the authorization was made or the Solicitor General of Canada if the application was made by him or on his behalf may apply to a judge of a superior court of criminal jurisdiction or a judge as defined in section 482 to substitute for the ninety day period mentioned in subsection (1) or the other period so fixed or substituted, such longer period not exceeding three years as is set forth in the application.

Where extension to be granted

(4) Where the judge to whom an application referred to in subsection (3) is made, on the basis of an affidavit submitted in support of the application, is satisfied that the investigation of the offence to which the authorization relates is continuing and is of the opinion that the interests of justice warrant the granting of the application, he shall fix a period, not exceeding three years, in substitution for the ninety day period mentioned in subsection (1) or the period fixed pursuant to subsection 178.12(3).

Idem

(5) An application pursuant to subsection (3) shall be accompanied by an affidavit which may be sworn on the information and belief of a peace officer or public officer deposing to

(a) the facts relied on to justify the belief that an extension of the ninety day period mentioned in subsection (1) or any other period fixed or substituted therefor should be granted; and

(b) the number of instances, if any, on which an application has been made under that subsection in relation to the particular authorization and on which the application was withdrawn or the application was not granted, the date on which each such application was made and the name of the judge to whom each such application was made. 1973-74, c. 50, s. 2; 1976-77, c. 53, s. 12.

Protection of Privacy Regulations — Chapter 440

REGULATIONS PRESCRIBING THE MANNER OF CERTIFICATION OF CERTAIN MATTERS RELATING TO THE INTERCEPTION OF PRIVATE COMMUNICATIONS UNDER AUTHORIZATIONS

Short Title

1. These Regulations may be cited as the *Protection of Privacy Regulations.*

General

2. For the purposes of subsection 178.23(1) of the *Criminal Code*, the Attorney General of a province who gave a notice required to be given by that subsection, or the Solicitor General of Canada where the notice was given by him, shall certify to the court that issued the authorization that such notice was given by filing with a judge of the court a certificate signed by the person who gave the notice specifying

(*a*) the name and address of the person who was the object of the interception;

(*b*) the date on which the authorization and any renewal thereof expired;

(*c*) if any delay for the giving of notice was granted under paragraph 178.23(2)(*b*) of the *Criminal Code*, the period of such delay; and

(*d*) the date, place and method of the giving of the notice.

3. For the purposes of subsection 178.23(2) of the *Criminal Code*, the Attorney General of a province by whom or on whose behalf an application for a delay is made in accordance with paragraph (*b*) of that subsection, or the Solicitor General of Canada where the application is made by him or on his behalf, shall certify to the judge who granted the authorization to which the application relates that the investigation thereunder is continuing by filing with the judge a certificate signed by the person making it setting forth

(*a*) that the investigation is continuing;

(*b*) the length of the delay sought; and

(*c*) information on the basis of which the judge may form an opinion as to whether the interests of justice require that a delay of a determinate reasonable length be granted.

4. A certificate filed pursuant to section 2 or 3 shall be treated as a confidential document, shall be placed in a packet, sealed by the judge with whom it is filed and kept with the packet sealed pursuant to section 178.14 of the *Criminal Code* that relates to the authorization to which the certificate relates.

—NOTES—

PART V

DISORDERLY HOUSES, GAMING AND BETTING

Interpretation

Definitions

179. (1) In this Part

"bet"

"bet" means a bet that is placed on any contingency or event that is to take place in or out of Canada, and without restricting the generality of the foregoing, includes a bet that is placed on any contingency relating to a horse-race, fight, match or sporting event that is to take place in or out of Canada;

"common bawdy-house"

"common bawdy-house" means a place that is

(a) kept or occupied, or

(b) resorted to by one or more persons

for the purpose of prostitution or the practice of acts of indecency;

"common betting house"

"common betting house" means a place that is opened, kept or used for the purpose of

(a) enabling, encouraging or assisting persons who resort thereto to bet between themselves or with the keeper, or

(b) enabling any person to receive, record, register, transmit or pay bets or to announce the results of betting;

"common gaming house"

"common gaming house" means a place that is

(a) kept for gain to which persons resort for the purpose of playing games, or

(b) kept or used for the purpose of playing games

(i) in which a bank is kept by one or more but not all of the players,

(ii) in which all or any portion of the bets on or proceeds from a game is paid, directly or indirectly, to the keeper of the place,

(iii) in which, directly or indirectly, a fee is charged to or paid by the players for the privilege of playing or participating in a game or using gaming equipment, or

(iv) in which the chances of winning are not equally favourable to all persons who play the game, including the person, if any, who conducts the game;

"disorderly house"

"disorderly house" means a common bawdy-house, a common betting house or a common gaming house;

"game"

"game" means a game of chance or mixed chance and skill;

"gaming equipment"

"gaming equipment" means anything that is or may be used for the purpose of playing games or for betting;

"keeper"

"keeper" includes a person who

(a) is an owner or occupier of a place,

(b) assists or acts on behalf of an owner or occupier of a place,

(c) appears to be, or to assist or act on behalf of an owner or occupier of a place,

(d) has the care or management of a place, or

(e) uses a place permanently or temporarily, with or without the consent of the owner or occupier;

"place"

"place" includes any place, whether or not

(a) it is covered or enclosed,

(b) it is used permanently or temporarily, or

(c) any person has an exclusive right of user with respect to it;

"public place"

"public place" includes any place to which the public have access as of right or by invitation, express or implied.

Exception

(2) A place is not a common gaming house within the meaning of paragraph *(a)* or subparagraph *(b)*(ii) or (iii) of the definition "common gaming house" in subsection (1) while it is occupied and used by an incorporated *bona fide* social club or branch thereof, if

(a) the whole or any portion of the bets on or proceeds from games played therein is not directly or indirectly paid to the keeper thereof, and

(b) no fee is charged to persons for the right or privilege of participating in the games played therein other than under the authority of and in accordance with the terms of a licence issued by the Attorney General of the province in which the place is situated or by such other person or authority in the province as may be specified by the Attorney General thereof. 28 Interp 2

Onus

(3) The onus of proving that, by virtue of subsection (2), a place is not a common gaming house is on the accused.

Effect when game partly played on premises

(4) A place may be a common gaming house notwithstanding that

(a) it is used for the purpose of playing part of a game and another part of the game is played elsewhere; or

(b) the stake that is played for is in some other place. R.S., c. C-34, s. 179; 1972, c. 13, s. 13.

bona fide — In or with good faith, there is no pretence, it is actually so.

2. In this Act

"Attorney General" means the Attorney General or Solicitor General of a province in which proceedings to which this Act applies are taken and, with respect to

(a) the Northwest Territories and the Yukon Territory, and

(b) proceedings instituted at the instance of the Government of Canada and conducted by or on behalf of that Government in respect of a violation of or conspiracy to violate any Act of the Parliament of Canada or a regulation made thereunder other than this Act,

means the Attorney General of Canada, and except for the purposes of subsections 505(4) and 507(3), includes the lawful deputy of the said Attorney General, Solicitor General and Attorney General of Canada;

Interpretation Act

28. In every enactment

"province" means a province of Canada, and includes the Yukon Territory and the Northwest Territories;

591. No indictment in respect of an offence for which, by reason of previous convictions, a greater punishment may be imposed shall contain any reference to previous convictions.

592. (1) Where an accused is convicted of an offence for which a greater punishment may be imposed by reason of previous convictions, no greater punishment shall be imposed upon him by reason thereof unless the prosecutor satisfies the court that the accused, before making his plea, was notified that a greater punishment would be sought by reason thereof.

(2) Where an accused is convicted of an offence for which a greater punishment may be imposed by reason of previous convictions, the court shall, upon application by the prosecutor and upon being satisfied that the accused was notified in accordance with subsection (1), ask the accused whether he was previously convicted and, if he does not admit that he was previously convicted, evidence of previous convictions may be adduced.

(3) Where, pursuant to section 551, the court proceeds with the trial of an accused corporation that has not appeared and pleaded to an indictment, the court may, if the accused is convicted, make inquiries with respect to previous convictions whether or not the accused was notified that a greater punishment would be sought by reason thereof.

Presumptions

Presumptions

180. (1) In proceedings under this Part,

(a) evidence that a peace officer who was authorized to enter a place was wilfully prevented from entering or was wilfully obstructed or delayed in entering is, in the absence of any evidence to the contrary, proof that the place is a disorderly house; 2 179(1)

(b) evidence that a place was found to be equipped with gaming equipment or any device for concealing, removing or destroying gaming equipment is, in the absence of any evidence to the contrary, proof that the place is a common gaming house or a common betting house, as the case may be; 179(1) 179(1)

(c) evidence that gaming equipment was found in a place entered under a warrant issued pursuant to this Part, or on or about the person of anyone found therein, is, in the absence of any evidence to the contrary, proof that the place is a common gaming house and that the persons found therein were playing games, whether or not any person acting under the warrant observed any persons playing games therein; and 181 179(1)

(d) evidence that a person was convicted of keeping a disorderly house is, for the purpose of proceedings against any one who is alleged to have been an inmate or to have been found in that house at the time the person committed the offence of which he was convicted, in the absence of any evidence to the contrary, proof that the house was, at that time, a disorderly house.

Conclusive presumption from slot machine

(2) For the purpose of proceedings under this Part, a place that is found to be equipped with a slot machine shall be conclusively presumed to be a common gaming house. ss. (3)

"Slot machine" defined

(3) In subsection (2), "slot machine" means any automatic machine or slot machine

(a) that is used or intended to be used for any purpose other than vending merchandise or services; or

(b) that is used or intended to be used for the purpose of vending merchandise or services if

(i) the result of one of any number of operations of the machine is a matter of chance or uncertainty to the operator,

(ii) as a result of a given number of successive operations by the operator the machine produces different results, or

(iii) on any operation of the machine it discharges or emits a slug or token,

but does not include an automatic machine or slot machine that dispenses as prizes only one or more free games on that machine. 1953-54, c. 51, ss. 169, 170; 1968-69, c. 38, s. 92; 1974-75-76, c. 93, s. 10.

Search

Warrant to search

181. (1) A justice who receives from a peace officer a report in writing that 2
he has reasonable ground to believe and does believe that an offence under section 185, 186, 187, 189, 190 or 193 is being committed at any place within the jurisdiction of the justice may issue a warrant under his hand authorizing a peace officer to enter and search the place by day or night and seize anything found therein that may be evidence that an offence under section 185, 186, 187, 189, 190 or 193, as the case may be, is being committed at that place, and to take into custody all persons who are found in or at that place and requiring those persons and things to be brought before him or before another justice having jurisdiction, to be dealt with according to law.

185 (Keeping gaming or betting house), 186 (Betting, pool-selling, book-making, etc.), 187 (Placing bets on behalf of others), 189 (Offence in relation to lotteries and games of chance), 190 (Lotteries) or 193 (Keeping common bawdy-house)

Search without warrant, seizure and arrest

(2) A peace officer may, whether or not he is acting under a warrant issued pursuant to this section, take into custody any person whom he finds keeping a common gaming house and any person whom he finds therein, and may seize anything that may be evidence that such an offence is being committed and shall ss. (6)
bring those persons and things before a justice having jurisdiction, to be dealt with according to law.

Disposal of property seized

(3) Except where otherwise expressly provided by law, a court, judge, justice or magistrate before whom anything that is seized under this section is brought may declare that the thing is forfeited, in which case it shall be disposed of or dealt with as the Attorney General may direct if no person shows sufficient 2
cause why it should not be forfeited.

When declaration or direction may be made

(4) No declaration or direction shall be made pursuant to subsection (3) in respect of anything seized under this section until

(*a*) it is no longer required as evidence in any proceedings that are instituted pursuant to the seizure, or

(*b*) the expiration of thirty days from the time of seizure where it is not required as evidence in any proceedings.

Conversion into money

(5) The Attorney General may, for the purpose of converting anything forfeited under this section into money, deal with it in all respects as if he were the owner thereof.

Telephones exempt from seizure

(6) Nothing in this section or in section 445 authorizes the seizure, forfeiture or destruction of telephone, telegraph or other communication facilities or equipment that may be evidence of or that may have been used in the commission of an offence under section 185, 186, 187, 189, 190 or 193 and that is owned by a person engaged in providing telephone, telegraph or other communication service to the public or forming part of the telephone, telegraph or other communication service or system of such a person.

Exception

(7) Subsection (6) does not apply to prohibit the seizure, for use as evidence, of any facility or equipment described in that subsection that is designed or adapted to record a communication. 1953-54, c. 51, s. 171; 1968-69, c. 37, s. 1; 1968-69, c. 38. s. 10.

Search for woman in bawdy-house

182. (1) A justice who is satisfied by information upon oath that there is reasonable ground to believe that a female person has been enticed to or is concealed in a common bawdy-house may issue a warrant under his hand authorizing a peace officer or other person named therein to enter and search the place, by day or night, and requiring her and the keeper of the place to be brought before him or another justice having jurisdiction to be kept in custody or released as he considers proper. 2 179(1) 2 179(1)

Use of force

(2) A peace officer may, for the purpose of executing a warrant issued under section 181 or this section, use as much force as is necessary to effect entry into the place in respect of which the warrant is issued. 1953-54, c. 51, ss. 172, 173.

Examination of persons arrested in disorderly houses

183. (1) A justice before whom a person is taken pursuant to a warrant issued under section 181 or 182 may require that person to be examined on oath and to give evidence with respect to 28 Interp

(a) the purpose for which the place referred to in the warrant is or has been used, kept or occupied, and

(b) any matter relating to the execution of the warrant.

Person refusing to be examined

(2) A person to whom this section applies who

(a) refuses to be sworn, or

(b) refuses to answer a question,

may be dealt with in the same manner as a witness appearing before a superior court of criminal jurisdiction pursuant to a subpoena. 472

Use of evidence

(3) No evidence that is given by a person under this section may be used or received in evidence in any criminal proceedings against him, except proceedings for perjury in giving that evidence. 1953-54, c. 51, s. 174. 121

472. (1) Where a person, being present at a preliminary inquiry and being required by the justice to give evidence,

(a) refuses to be sworn,

(b) having been sworn, refuses to answer the questions that are put to him,

(c) fails to produce any writings that he is required to produce, or

(d) refuses to sign his deposition,

without offering a reasonable excuse for his failure or refusal, the justice may adjourn the inquiry and may, by warrant in Form 16, commit the person to prison for a period not exceeding eight clear days or for the period during which the inquiry is adjourned, whichever is the lesser period.

(2) Where a person to whom subsection (1) applies is brought before the justice upon the resumption of the adjourned inquiry and again refuses to do what is required of him, the justice may again adjourn the inquiry for a period not exceeding eight clear days and commit him to prison for the period of adjournment or any part thereof, and may adjourn the inquiry and commit the person to prison from time to time until the person consents to do what is required of him.

Interpretation Act

28. In every enactment

"oath" includes a solemn affirmation or declaration, whenever the context applies to any person by whom and case in which a solemn affirmation or declaration may be made instead of an oath; and in like cases the expression "sworn" includes the expression "affirmed" or "declared";

Obstruction

Obstructing execution of warrant
Type 'A' Offence

184. Every one who, for the purpose of preventing, obstructing or delaying a peace officer who is executing a warrant issued under this Part in respect of a disorderly house or who is otherwise authorized to enter a disorderly house, does anything, or being the keeper of the disorderly house, permits anything to be done to give effect to that purpose is guilty of an offence punishable on summary conviction. 1953-54, c. 51, s. 175.

2
179(1)
179(1)
722(1)

Gaming and betting

Keeping gaming or betting house
Type 'C' Offence
IPA offence 178.1

185. (1) Every one who keeps a common gaming house or common betting house is guilty of an indictable offence and is liable to imprisonment for two years. 179(1)

Person found in or owner permitting use
Type 'A' Offence

(2) Every one who

(a) is found, without lawful excuse, in a common gaming house or common betting house, or

(b) as owner, landlord, lessor, tenant, occupier or agent, knowingly permits a place to be let or used for the purposes of a common gaming house or common betting house, 179(1)

is guilty of an offence punishable on summary conviction. 1953-54, c. 51, s. 176. 722(1)

180. (1) In proceedings under this Part,

(d) evidence that a person was convicted of keeping a disorderly house is, for the purpose of proceedings against any one who is alleged to have been an inmate or to have been found in that house at the time the person committed the offence of which he was convicted, in the absence of any evidence to the contrary, proof that the house was, at that time, a disorderly house.

Betting, pool-selling, book-making, etc.
Type 'C' Offence

186. (1) Every one commits an offence who

(a) uses or knowingly allows a place under his control to be used for the purpose of recording or registering bets or selling a pool; 179(1)

(b) imports, makes, buys, sells, rents, leases, hires or keeps, exhibits, employs or knowingly allows to be kept, exhibited or employed in any place under his control a device or apparatus for the purpose of recording or registering bets or selling a pool, or any machine or device for gambling or betting;

(c) has under his control any money or other property relating to a transaction that is an offence under this section;

(d) records or registers bets or sells a pool;

Paragraph (e) only IPA offence 178.1

(e) engages in pool-selling or book-making, or in the business or occupation of betting, or makes any agreement for the purchase or sale of betting or gaming privileges, or for the purchase or sale of information that is intended to assist in book-making, pool-selling or betting;

(f) prints, provides or offers to print or provide information intended for use in connection with book-making, pool-selling or betting upon any horse-race, fight, game or sport whether or not it takes place in or out of Canada or has or has not taken place; 179(1)

(g) imports or brings into Canada any information or writing that is intended or is likely to promote or be of use in gambling, book-making, pool-selling or betting upon a horse-race, fight, game or sport, and where this paragraph applies it is immaterial

(i) whether the information is published before, during or after the race, fight, game or sport, or

(ii) whether the race, fight, game or sport takes place in Canada or elsewhere,

but this paragraph does not apply to a newspaper, magazine or other periodical published in good faith primarily for a purpose other than the publication of such information;

(h) advertises, prints, publishes, exhibits, posts up, or otherwise gives notice of any offer, invitation or inducement to bet on, to guess or to foretell the result of a contest, or a result of or contingency relating to any contest;

(i) wilfully and knowingly sends, transmits, delivers or receives any message by radio, telegraph, telephone, mail or express that conveys any information relating to book-making, pool-selling, betting or wagering, or that is intended to assist in book-making, pool-selling, betting or wagering; or

(j) aids or assists in any manner in anything that is an offence under this section.

Punishment

Type 'C' Offence

(2) Every one who commits an offence under this section is guilty of an indictable offence and is liable

(a) for a first offence, to imprisonment for not more than two years,

(b) for a second offence, to imprisonment for not more than two years and not less than fourteen days, and 591 592 [179]

(c) for each subsequent offence, to imprisonment for not more than two years and not less than three months. 1953-54, c. 51, s. 177; 1959, c. 41, s. 14; 1974-75-76, c. 93, s. 11.

Placing bets on behalf of others

Type 'C' Offence

187. Every one who

(a) places or offers or agrees to place a bet on behalf of another person for a consideration paid or to be paid by or on behalf of that other person,

(b) engages in the business or practice of placing or agreeing to place bets on behalf of other persons, whether for a consideration or otherwise, or

(c) holds himself out or allows himself to be held out as engaging in the business or practice of placing or agreeing to place bets on behalf of other persons, whether for a consideration or otherwise,

is guilty of an indictable offence and is liable

(d) for a first offence, to imprisonment for not more than two years,

(e) for a second offence, to imprisonment for not more than two years and not less than fourteen days, and 591 592 [179]

(f) for each subsequent offence, to imprisonment for not more than two years and not less than three months. 1968-69, c.37, s.1; 1974-75-76, c.93, s.11.

Exemption

188. (1) Sections 185 and 186 do not apply to

(a) any person or association by reason of his or their becoming the custodian or depository of any money, property or valuable thing staked, to be paid to ss. (9)

(i) the winner of a lawful race, sport, game or exercise, 179(1)

(ii) the owner of a horse engaged in a lawful race, or

(iii) the winner of any bets between not more than ten individuals;

(b) a private bet between individuals not engaged in any way in the business of betting;

(c) bets made or records of bets made through the agency of a pari-mutuel system only as hereinafter in this section provided, upon the race course of an association during the actual progress of a race meeting conducted by an association upon running, trotting or pacing horse races being run thereon and if the provisions of this section and any regulations made thereunder are complied with.

Limitation on daily number of races

(2) No pari-mutuel system of betting shall be used during a race meeting conducted upon any race course in respect of more than ten races on any one calendar day, unless the Minister of Agriculture or a person designated by him for that purpose approves of the use of such system in respect of additional races upon that race course on that day and

(a) each such additional race is run to make up for a race that was previously scheduled to be run during that race meeting on that race course and that was cancelled due to inclement weather or other unforeseen circumstances, or

(b) there are two cards of races run upon that race course on that day, each card having a minimum of eight and a maximum of ten races with the second card commencing not sooner than two hours following the completion of the last race on the first card.

Operation of pari-mutuel system

(3) No pari-mutuel system of betting shall be used upon any race course unless the system has been approved by and its operation is carried on under the supervision of an officer appointed by the Minister of Agriculture and the person or association conducting a race meeting shall pay to the Receiver General one-half of one per cent or such greater fraction not exceeding one per cent as may be fixed from time to time by the Governor in Council of the total amount of bets, made through the agency of a pari-mutuel system operated under such supervision, on any race run at such meeting.

Percentage that may be deducted and retained

(4) Where any person or association becomes a custodian or depository of any money, bet or stakes under a pari-mutuel system during the actual progress of a race meeting conducted by and on the race course of an association in accordance with this section, upon races being run thereon, the percentage that may be deducted and retained by the person or association in respect of each individual pool of each race or each individual feature pool from the total amount of money so deposited, or of which the person or association becomes the custodian, shall not exceed

(a) 12%, if the average amount wagered per race at that race course during the calendar year immediately preceding the running of the race (hereinafter in this subsection called the "average amount wagered") did not exceed ten thousand dollars; 28 Interp

(b) 11.5%, if the average amount wagered exceeded ten thousand dollars and did not exceed fifteen thousand dollars;

(c) 11%, if the average amount wagered exceeded fifteen thousand dollars and did not exceed twenty thousand dollars;

(d) 10.5%, if the average amount wagered exceeded twenty thousand dollars and did not exceed twenty-five thousand dollars;

(e) 10%, if the average amount wagered exceeded twenty-five thousand dollars and did not exceed thirty thousand dollars; or

(f) 9.5%, if the average amount wagered exceeded thirty thousand dollars;

plus any odd cents over any multiple of five cents in the amount calculated in accordance with the regulations to be payable in respect of each dollar wagered.

Where no race meeting previously conducted

(5) Where no race meeting was conducted upon a race course in accordance with this section during the calendar year referred to in subsection (4), the average amount that shall be deemed to have been wagered per race at that race course during that year shall be an amount specified by the Minister of Agriculture.

Stopping of betting

(6) Where an officer referred to in subsection (3) is not satisfied that the provisions of this section and any regulations made thereunder are being carried out in good faith by the association conducting the race meeting, he may at any time order the betting to be stopped for any period that he considers proper.

Regulations

(7) The Minister of Agriculture may make regulations respecting

(a) the supervision and operation of pari-mutuel systems related to race meetings, and the fixing of the dates on which and the places at which an association may conduct such meetings;

(b) the calculation for the purposes of subsection (4) of the amount payable in respect of each dollar wagered;

(c) the conduct of race meetings in relation to the supervision and operation of pari-mutuel systems, including photo-finishes, film patrol and urine and saliva testing of horses engaged in racing at such meetings;

(d) the prohibition, restriction or regulation of

(i) the possession of drugs or medicaments or of equipment used in the administering of drugs or medicaments at or near race courses, or

(ii) the administering of drugs or medicaments to horses participating in races run at a race meeting during which a pari-mutuel system of betting is used; and

(e) the provision, equipment and maintenance of accommodation, services or other facilities for the proper supervision and operation of pari-mutuel systems related to race meetings, by associations conducting such meetings.

Violations

Type 'B' (D) Offences

(8) Every person who violates or fails to comply with any of the provisions of this section or of any regulations made thereunder is guilty of

(a) an indictable offence and is liable to imprisonment for two years, or

(b) an offence punishable on summary conviction.

"Association"

(9) For the purposes of this section "association" means an association incorporated by or pursuant to an Act of the Parliament of Canada or of the legislature of a province, having as its purpose or one of its purposes the conduct of horse races. 1955, c. 45, s. 1; 1960-61, c. 21, s. 1; 1968-69, c. 38, s. 11.

Interpretation Act

28. In every enactment

"year" means any period of twelve consecutive months, except that a reference to a "calendar year" means a period of twelve consecutive months commencing on the first day of January and a reference by number to a Dominical year means the period of twelve consecutive months commencing on the first day of January of that year.

Offence in relation to lotteries and games of chance
Type 'C' Offence

189. (1) Every one is guilty of an indictable offence and is liable to imprisonment for two years who

(*a*) makes, prints, advertises or publishes, or causes or procures to be made, printed, advertised or published, any proposal, scheme or plan for advancing, lending, giving, selling or in any way disposing of any property, by lots, cards, tickets, or any mode of chance whatever;

(*b*) sells, barters, exchanges or otherwise disposes of, or causes or procures, or aids or assists in, the sale, barter, exchange or other disposal of, or offers for sale, barter or exchange, any lot, card, ticket or other means or device for advancing, lending, giving, selling or otherwise disposing of any property, by lots, tickets or any mode of chance whatever;

(*c*) knowingly sends, transmits, mails, ships, delivers or allows to be sent, transmitted, mailed, shipped or delivered, or knowingly accepts for carriage or transport or conveys any article that is used or intended for use in carrying out any device, proposal, scheme or plan for advancing, lending, giving, selling or otherwise disposing of any property by any mode of chance whatever;

339. Every one who makes use of the mails for the purpose of transmitting or delivering letters or circulars concerning schemes devised or intended to deceive or defraud the public, or for the purpose of obtaining money under false pretences, is guilty of an indictable offence and is liable to imprisonment for two years.

(*d*) conducts or manages any scheme, contrivance or operation of any kind for the purpose of determining who, or the holders of what lots, tickets, numbers or chances, are the winners of any property so proposed to be advanced, loaned, given, sold or disposed of;

(*e*) conducts, manages or is a party to any scheme, contrivance or operation of any kind by which any person, upon payment of any sum of money, or the giving of any valuable security, or by obligating himself to pay any sum of money or give any valuable security, shall become entitled under the scheme, contrivance or operation, to receive from the person conducting or managing the scheme, contrivance or operation, or any other person, a larger sum of money or amount of valuable security than the sum or amount paid or given, or to be paid or given, by reason of the fact that other persons have paid or given, or obligated themselves to pay or give any sum of money or valuable security under the scheme, contrivance or operation; 2 [195.1]

(*f*) disposes of any goods, wares or merchandise by any game of chance or any game of mixed chance and skill in which the contestant or competitor pays money or other valuable consideration;

(*g*) induces any person to stake or hazard any money or other valuable property or thing on the result of any dice game, three-card monte, punch board, coin table or on the operation of a wheel of fortune; ss. (2)

(*h*) for valuable consideration carries on or plays or offers to carry on or to play, or employs any person to carry on or play in a public place or a place to which the public have access, the game of three-card monte; 179(1)

(*i*) receives bets of any kind on the outcome of a game of three-card monte; or

(*j*) being the owner of a place, permits any person to play the game of three-card monte therein.

"Three-card monte"

(2) In this section "three-card monte" means the game commonly known as three-card monte and includes any other game that is similar to it, whether or not the game is played with cards and notwithstanding the number of cards or other things that are used for the purpose of playing.

Exemption of agricultural fairs

(3) Paragraphs (1)*(f)* and *(g)*, in so far as they do not relate to a dice game, three-card monte, punch board or coin table, do not apply to an agricultural fair or exhibition, or to any operator of a concession leased by an agricultural fair or exhibition board within its own grounds and operated during the period of the annual fair on those grounds.

Type 'A' Offence

(4) Every one who buys, takes or receives a lot, ticket or other device mentioned in subsection (1) is guilty of an offence punishable on summary conviction. 722(1)

Lottery sale void

(5) Every sale, loan, gift, barter or exchange of any property, by any lottery, ticket, card or other mode of chance depending upon or to be determined by chance or lot, is void, and all property so sold, lent, given, bartered or exchanged, is forfeited to Her Majesty. 2

Bona fide purchase

(6) Subsection (5) does not affect any right or title to property acquired by any *bona fide* purchaser for valuable consideration without notice.

bona fide — In or with good faith, there is no pretence, it is actually so.

Foreign lottery included

(7) This section applies to the printing or publishing, or causing to be printed or published, of any advertisement, scheme, proposal or plan of any foreign lottery, and the sale or offer for sale of any ticket, chance or share, in any such lottery, or the advertisement for sale of such ticket, chance or share, and the conducting or managing of any such scheme, contrivance or operation for determining the winners in any such lottery.

Saving

(8) This section does not apply to

(a) the division by lot or chance of any property by joint tenants or tenants in common, or persons having joint interests in any such property;

(b) the distribution by lot of premiums given as rewards to promote thrift by punctuality in making periodical deposits of weekly savings in any chartered savings bank; or

(c) bonds, debentures, debenture stock or other securities recallable by drawing of lots and redeemable with interest and providing for payment of premiums upon redemption or otherwise. 1953-54, c. 51, s. 179; 1968-69, c. 38, s. 12.

2. In this Act

"property" includes

(a) real and personal property of every description and deeds and instruments relating to or evidencing the title or right to property, or giving a right to recover or receive money or goods,

(b) property originally in the possession or under the control of any person, and any property into or for which it has been converted or exchanged and anything acquired at any time by such conversion or exchange, and

(c) any postal card, postage stamp or other stamp issued or prepared for issue under the authority of the Parliament of Canada or of the legislature of a province for the payment to the Crown or a corporate body of any fee, rate or duty, whether or not it is in the possession of the Crown or of any person;

3. (2) For the purposes of this Act a postal card or stamp referred to in paragraph *(c)* of the definition "property" in section 2 shall be deemed to be a chattel, and to be equal in value to the amount of the postage, rate or duty expressed on its face.

Permitted lotteries

190. (1) Notwithstanding any of the provisions of this Part relating to gaming and betting, it is lawful

(*a*) for the Government of Canada to conduct and manage a lottery scheme in accordance with regulations made by the Governor in Council and for that purpose for any person in accordance with such regulations to do any thing described in any of paragraphs 189(1)(*a*) to (*f*) or subsection 189(4); ss. (5) 28 Interp [195.1]

(*b*) for the government of a province, either alone or in conjunction with the government of another province, to conduct and manage a lottery scheme in that province, or in that and such other province, in accordance with any law enacted by the legislature of that province and for that purpose for any person in accordance with such law to do any thing described in any of paragraphs 189(1)(*a*) to (*f*) or subsection 189(4); 28 Interp [195.1]

(*c*) for a charitable or religious organization, under the authority of a licence issued by the Lieutenant Governor in Council of a province or by such other person or authority in the province as may be specified by the Lieutenant Governor in Council thereof, to conduct and manage a lottery scheme in that province and for that purpose for any person under the authority of such licence to do any thing described in any of paragraphs 189(1)(*a*) to (*g*) or subsection 189(4), otherwise than in relation to a dice game, three-card monte, punch board or coin table, if 28 Interp [195.1] 189(2)

(i) the proceeds from the lottery scheme are used for a charitable or religious object or purpose, and

(ii) in the case of a lottery scheme conducted by the charitable or religious organization at a bazaar,

(A) the amount or value of each prize awarded does not exceed one hundred dollars, and

(B) the money or other valuable consideration paid to secure a chance to win a prize does not exceed fifty cents;

(*d*) for an agricultural fair or exhibition or an operator of a concession leased by an agricultural fair or exhibition board, under the authority of a licence issued by the Lieutenant Governor in Council of a province or by such other person or authority in the province as may be specified by the Lieutenant Governor in Council thereof, to conduct and manage a lottery scheme in that province and for that purpose for any person under the authority of such licence to do any thing described in any of paragraphs 189(1)(*a*) to (*f*) or subsection 189(4);

(*e*) for any person, under the authority of a licence issued by the Lieutenant Governor in Council of a province or by such other person or authority in the province as may be specified by the Lieutenant Governor in Council thereof, to conduct and manage a lottery scheme at a public place of amusement in that province and for that purpose for any person under the authority of such licence to do any thing described in any of paragraphs 189(1)(*a*) to (*g*) or subsection 189(4), otherwise than in relation to a dice game, three-card monte, punch board or coin table, if

(i) the amount or value of each prize awarded does not exceed one hundred dollars, and

(ii) the money or other valuable consideration paid to secure a chance to win a prize does not exceed fifty cents; and

(*f*) for the government of a province to agree with the government of another province that lots, cards or tickets in relation to a lottery scheme that is by any of paragraphs (*b*) to (*e*) authorized to be conducted and managed in that other province may be sold in the province and thereafter it is lawful for any person under the authority of such agreement, to do anything described in any of paragraphs 189(1)(*a*) to (*c*) or subsection 189(4) in the province. 1974-75-76, c. 93, s. 12(1).

Idem

(1.1) The Lieutenant Governor in Council of a province or such other person or authority in the province as may be designated by the Lieutenant Governor in Council thereof may issue a licence for the conduct and management in the province of a lottery scheme that is authorized to be conducted and managed in one or more other provinces where the authority by which the lottery scheme was first authorized to be conducted and managed consents thereto and, notwithstanding any of the provisions of this Part, it is lawful for any person under the authority of such licence to do anything described in any of paragraphs (189(1)*(a)* to *(f)* or subsection 189(4) in the province.

Terms and conditions of licence

(2) Subject to this Act, a licence issued by or under the authority of the Lieutenant Governor in Council of a province as described in paragraph (1)*(c)*, *(d)* or *(e)* or subsection (1.1) may contain such terms and conditions relating to the conduct and management of the lottery scheme to which the licence relates as the Lieutenant Governor in Council of that province or the person or authority in the province designated by him may prescribe.

Conducting lottery in province other than province where authorized

Type 'D' Offence

(3) Every one who, in any province other than a province in which

(a) a lottery scheme is by any of paragraphs (1)*(b)* to *(e)* or subsection (1.1) authorized to be conducted and managed, or

(b) lots, cards or tickets in relation to a lottery scheme are by paragraph (1)(f) authorized to be sold,

does anything described in paragraphs (189(1)*(a)* to *(f)* in a case described in paragraph *(a)* or in paragraphs 189(1)*(a)* to *(c)* in a case described in paragraph *(b)* for the purpose of that lottery scheme is guilty of an indictable offence and liable to imprisonment for two years.

Receiving lottery tickets in province other than province where authorized

Type 'A' Offence

(4) Every one who, in any province other than a province in which

(a) a lottery scheme is by any of paragraphs (1)*(b)* to *(e)* or subsection (1.1) authorized to be conducted and managed, or

(b) lots, cards or tickets in relation to a lottery scheme are by paragraph (1)*(f)* authorized to be sold,

does anything described in subsection 189(4) for the purpose of that lottery scheme is guilty of an offence punishable on summary conviction. 722(1)

Printing and shipping of lottery tickets authorized

(4.1) Notwithstanding subsections (3) and (4), it is lawful for any person to make or print anywhere in Canada or to cause or procure to be made or printed anywhere in Canada lots, cards or tickets in relation to a lottery scheme that is by any of paragraphs (1)*(b)* to *(e)* authorized to be conducted and managed in any province or to send, transmit, mail, ship, deliver or allow to be sent, transmitted, mailed, shipped or delivered or accept for carriage or transport or convey any such lots, cards or tickets where the destination thereof is a place where, by virtue of any of paragraphs (1)*(b)* to *(f)* or subsection (1.1) it is lawful to sell such lots, cards or tickets.

"Lottery scheme"

(5) In this section "lottery scheme" includes a game. 179(1)

Exception re pari-mutuel betting

(6) Nothing in this section shall be construed as authorizing the making or recording of bets made through the agency of a pari-mutuel system, other than in accordance with section 188. 1968-69, c. 38, s. 13.

National Lottery Regulations — Chapter 431

REGULATIONS RESPECTING A NATIONAL LOTTERY

Short Title

1. These Regulations may be cited as the *National Lottery Regulations.*

PART I

Interpretation

2. In this Part,

"Account" means the account or accounts, established pursuant to section 11;

"cash" includes a cheque or a postal money order;

"Corporation" means Loto Canada Inc., a corporation incorporated under the *Canada Business Corporations Act;*

"insurance company" means a company that, pursuant to any Act of Parliament or of the legislature of a province, is authorized to engage in and carry on the business of insurance;

"lottery scheme" means a lottery scheme conducted and managed by the Corporation pursuant to section 3;

"lottery ticket" means a ticket under a lottery scheme;

"money prize" means a sum of money payable by the Corporation under a lottery scheme;

"retailer" means any person, group of persons or co-operative credit society or association or public body that sells lottery tickets to the public;

"trust company" means a company that, pursuant to any Act of Parliament or of the legislature of a province, is authorized to engage in and carry on the business of a trust company within the meaning of the *Trust Companies Act;*

"wholesaler" means any person, group of persons or co-operative credit society or association or public body to whom the Corporation sells lottery tickets at a price less than the face value of the tickets.

Lottery Schemes

3. The Corporation, on behalf of the Government of Canada, may conduct and manage one or more lottery schemes including lottery schemes for wholesalers or retailers only.

Lottery Tickets

4. The Corporation may sell lottery tickets to wholesalers or directly to the public or award lottery tickets under a lottery scheme.

5. A wholesaler may sell lottery tickets

(a) to a retailer at a price that is less than the face value of the ticket; or

(b) directly to the public at the face value of the ticket.

6. (1) No person shall sell a lottery ticket at a price exceeding the face value of the ticket.

(2) No person shall sell a lottery ticket at a price that is less than the face value of the ticket, except in accordance with these Regulations. SOR/78-681

7. Each lottery ticket shall indicate thereon the face value of the ticket.

8. Any statement, information, notice or condition that is required by these Regulations to appear on a lottery ticket shall be in both official languages.

9. (1) The Corporation may only sell lottery tickets if payment is made by cash for the tickets at the time of the sale, except that where tickets are sold to chartered banks, trust companies, credit unions, caisses populaires or non-profit corporations or organizations, payment for tickets may be made in such instalments as the Corporation determines.

(2) For the purposes of this section, a corporation or organization is a non-profit corporation or organization if it is so recognized by the Minister of National Revenue. SOR/78-681

SOR/78-681

Drawings

10. Where a drawing under a lottery scheme cannot be held on the date fixed therefor, the Corporation shall fix a date, as soon as possible thereafter, for the holding of the drawing.

Payment of Prizes

11. (1) The Corporation shall cause to be printed on every lottery ticket a notice to the effect that the sale of the ticket is subject to the following conditions:

(a) any claim arising from a drawing for a money prize in respect of that lottery ticket made after twelve months have elapsed from the date of that drawing is void; and

(b) the holder of a lottery ticket who claims a money prize gives to the Corporation the right to publish his name and address without any claim on the Corporation for broadcasting, printing, royalty or other rights.

(2) A claim for a prize other than a money prize in respect to a lottery ticket made after the period provided for on the ticket is void. SOR/78-681

12. The C

12. The Corporation shall establish at least one account with a chartered bank or trust company, in the name of the Corporation, called the "Prize Account" or "Compte des prix".

13. All proceeds to the Corporation from a lottery scheme shall be deposited in the Account unless the amount of money in the Account is equal to the aggregate of

(a) the total amount of money prizes outstanding that may be claimed by persons in respect of any drawing that has been held under a lottery scheme; and

(b) the total amount of money prizes liable to be paid by the Corporation in respect of any drawing to be held under a lottery scheme for which lottery tickets have been sold or awarded.

14. Except for the payment of money prizes, no payment shall be made out of the Account that would have the effect of reducing the amount of money in the Account below the aggregate total amount described in paragraphs 12*(a)* and *(b)*.

15. (1) Where a money prize or a part of a money prize is payable in instalments, the Corporation shall enter into a contract with an insurance company or a trust company whereby the company agrees to pay in instalments to the person to whom the money prize is payable the money prize or part of the money prize to which that person is entitled.

(2) The Corporation shall ensure that any contract entered into pursuant to subsection (1) provides that where the person entitled to the payment of the money prize in instalments dies before all the instalments have been paid, the capitalized value of the remaining instalments shall be paid to that person's estate.

16. A money prize or part of a money prize that is payable in instalments is deemed, for the purpose of section 12, to have been paid when

(a) a contract has been entered into pursuant to section 14; and

(b) the Corporation has assigned all its rights and interests under the contract to the person or to the estate of the person to whom the money prize is payable.

Wholesalers and Retailers

17. (1) The Corporation may enter into a contract with a wholesaler in respect of the distribution and sale of lottery tickets to retailers or to the public within a territory to be defined by the Corporation in the contract. SOR/78-681

(2) Where the Corporation has entered into a contract referred to in subsection (1) with a wholesaler, the Corporation, shall issue to that wholesaler a certificate in both official languages, certifying that the wholesaler is authorized under a contract with the Corporation to distribute and sell lottery tickets to retailers or to the public.

(3) Where a contract referred to in subsection (1) between the Corporation and a wholesaler is terminated, the wholesaler shall forthwith return to the Corporation the certificate issued to him pursuant to subsection (2).

(4) Every wholesaler shall have available the certificate referred to in subsection (2).

18. (1) Every retailer and wholesaler shall have available copies of these Regulations in both official languages at the place where the lottery tickets are sold or offered for sale to the public.

(2) No retailer may purchase a lottery ticket at a price that is less than the face value of the ticket unless it is purchased from a wholesaler who is authorized to sell lottery tickets to that retailer. SOR/78-681

Registry

19. (1) The Corporation shall keep a registry in which shall be listed the name and address of each wholesaler.

(2) Any person may, during normal business hours, examine the registry referred to in subsection (1) by attending at the registered office of the Corporation and requesting that the registry be produced for examination.

Annual Financial Statement

20. (1) Every wholesaler shall furnish the Corporation with an annual audited financial statement of its operations that are related directly or indirectly to the sale of lottery tickets.

(2) The books, accounts and records of a wholesaler in respect of the sale of lottery tickets shall be readily accessible during normal business hours for examination by representatives of the Corporation.

Gambling in public conveyances
Type 'D' Offence

191. (1) Every one who obtains or attempts to obtain anything from any person by playing a game in a vehicle, aircraft or vessel used as a public conveyance for passengers is guilty of an indictable offence and is liable to imprisonment for two years. 179(1)

Arrest without warrant

(2) Every person in charge of a vehicle, aircraft or vessel and any person authorized by him may arrest, without warrant, a person who he has good reason to believe has committed or attempted to commit or is committing or attempting to commit an offence under this section.

Posting up section
Type 'A' Offence

(3) Every person who owns or operates a vehicle, aircraft or vessel to which this section applies shall keep posted up, in some conspicuous part thereof, a copy of this section or a notice to the like effect, and in default thereof is guilty of an offence punishable on summary conviction. 1953-54, c. 51, s. 180. 722(1)

Cheating at play
Type 'C' Offence

192. Every one who, with intent to defraud any person, cheats while playing a game or in holding the stakes for a game or in betting is guilty of an indictable offence and is liable to imprisonment for two years. 1953-54, c. 51, s. 181.

Bawdy-houses

Keeping common bawdy-house
Type 'C' Offence

193. (1) Every one who keeps a common bawdy-house is guilty of an indictable offence and is liable to imprisonment for two years. 179(1)

Landlord, inmate, etc.
Type 'A' Offence

(2) Every one who

(*a*) is an inmate of a common bawdy-house

(*b*) is found, without lawful excuse, in a common bawdy-house, or

(*c*) as owner, landlord, lessor, tenant, occupier, agent or otherwise having charge or control of any place, knowingly permits the place or any part thereof to be let or used for the purposes of a common bawdy-house, 179(1)

is guilty of an offence punishable on summary conviction. 722(1)

180. (1) In proceedings under this Part,

(*d*) evidence that a person was convicted of keeping a disorderly house is, for the purpose of proceedings against any one who is alleged to have been an inmate or to have been found in that house at the time the person committed the offence of which he was convicted, in the absence of any evidence to the contrary, proof that the house was, at that time, a disorderly house.

Notice of conviction to be served on owner

(3) Where a person is convicted of an offence under subsection (1), the court shall cause a notice of the conviction to be served upon the owner, landlord or lessor of the place in respect of which the person is convicted or his agent, and the notice shall contain a statement to the effect that it is being served pursuant to this section.

Duty of landlord on notice

(4) Where a person upon whom a notice is served under subsection (3) fails forthwith to exercise any right he may have to determine the tenancy or right of occupation of the person so convicted, and thereafter any person is convicted of an offence under subsection (1) in respect of the same premises, the person upon whom the notice was served shall be deemed to have committed an offence under subsection (1) unless he proves that he has taken all reasonable steps to prevent the recurrence of the offence. 1953-54, c. 51, s. 182.

Transporting person to bawdy-house
Type 'A' Offence

194. Every one who knowingly takes, transports, directs, or offers to take, transport, or direct any other person to a common bawdy-house is guilty of an offence punishable on summary conviction. 1953-54, c. 51, s. 183. 722(1)

Procuring

Procuring

Type 'E' Offence

Paragraph (a) only IPA offence 178.1

One year limitation ss. (4)

195. (1) Every one who

(a) procures, attempts to procure or solicits a female person to have illicit sexual intercourse with another person, whether in or out of Canada, 24

(b) inveigles or entices a female person who is not a common prostitute or a person of known immoral character to a common bawdy-house or house of assignation for the purpose of illicit sexual intercourse or prostitution, 179(1)

(c) knowingly conceals a female person in a common bawdy-house or house of assignation,

(d) procures or attempts to procure a female person to become, whether in or out of Canada, a common prostitute,

(e) procures or attempts to procure a female person to leave her usual place of abode in Canada, if that place is not a common bawdy-house, with intent that she may become an inmate or frequenter of a common bawdy-house, whether in or out of Canada,

(f) on the arrival of a female person in Canada, directs or causes her to be directed, or takes or causes her to be taken, to a common bawdy-house or house of assignation,

(g) procures a female person to enter or leave Canada, for the purpose of prostitution,

(h) for the purposes of gain, exercises control, direction or influence over the movements of a female person in such manner as to show that he is aiding, abetting or compelling her to engage in or carry on prostitution with any person or generally,

(i) applies or administers to a female person or causes her to take any drug, intoxicating liquor, matter, or thing with intent to stupefy or overpower her in order thereby to enable any person to have illicit sexual intercourse with her, or

(j) lives wholly or in part on the avails of prostitution of another person, ss. (3) 175(1)(d)

(k) Repealed, 1972, c. 13, s. 14,

is guilty of an indictable offence and is liable to imprisonment for ten years.

Presumption

(2) Evidence that a male person lives with or is habitually in the company of prostitutes, or lives in a common bawdy-house or house of assignation is, in the absence of any evidence to the contrary, proof that he lives on the avails of prostitution.

Corroboration

(3) No person shall be convicted of an offence under subsection (1), other than an offence under paragraph *(j)* of that subsection, upon the evidence of only one witness unless the evidence of that witness is corroborated in a material particular by evidence that implicates the accused.

Limitation

(4) No proceedings for an offence under this section shall be commenced more than one year after the time when the offence is alleged to have been committed. R.S., c. C-34, s. 195; 1972, c. 13, s. 14.

Canada Evidence Act

4. (2) The wife or husband of a person charged with an offence against section 33 or 34 of the *Juvenile Delinquents Act* or with an offence against any of sections 143 to 146, 148, 150 to 155, 157, 166 to 169, 175, 195, 197, 200, 248 to 250, 255 to 258, 289, paragraph 423(1)*(c)* or an attempt to commit an offence under section 146 or 155 of the *Criminal Code,* is a competent and compellable witness for the prosecution without the consent of the person charged.

Soliciting

Soliciting

195.1 Every person who solicits any person in a public place for the purpose of prostitution is guilty of an offence punishable on summary conviction. 1972, c. 13, s. 15. 179.1 722(1)

2. In this Act

"valuable security" includes

(a) an order, exchequer acquittance or other security that entitles or evidences the title of any person

(i) to a share or interest in a public stock or fund or in any fund of a body corporate, company or society, or

(ii) to a deposit in a savings bank or other bank,

(b) a debenture, deed, bond, bill, note, warrant, order or other security for money or for payment of money,

(c) a document of title to lands or goods wherever situated,

(d) a stamp or writing that secures or evidences title to or an interest in a chattel personal, or that evidences delivery of a chattel personal, and

(e) a release, receipt, discharge or other instrument evidencing payment of money;

3. (3) For the purposes of this Act, the following rules apply for the purpose of determining the value of a valuable security where value is material, namely,

(a) where the valuable security is one mentioned in paragraph *(a)* or *(b)* of the definition "valuable security" in section 2, the value is the value of the share, interest, deposit or unpaid money, as the case may be, that is secured by the valuable security;

(b) where the valuable security is one mentioned in paragraph *(c)* or *(d)* of the definition "valuable security" in section 2, the value is the value of the lands, goods, chattel personal or interest in the chattel personal, as the case may be; and

(c) where the valuable security is one mentioned in paragraph *(e)* of the definition "valuable security" in section 2, the value is the amount of money that has been paid.

24. (1) Every one who, having an intent to commit an offence, does or omits to do anything for the purpose of carrying out his intention is guilty of an attempt to commit the offence whether or not it was possible under the circumstances to commit the offence.

(2) The question whether an act or omission by a person who has an intent to commit an offence is or is not mere preparation to commit the offence, and too remote to constitute an attempt to commit the offence, is a question of law.

Interpretation Act

28. In every enactment

"Governor in Council", or "Governor General in Council" means the Governor General of Canada, or person administering the Government of Canada for the time being, acting by and with the advice of, or by and with the advice and consent of, or in conjunction with the Queen's Privy Council for Canada;

"lieutenant governor in council" means the lieutenant governor, or person administering the government of the province indicated by the enactment, for the time being, acting by and with the advice of, or by and with the advice and consent of, or in conjuction with the executive council of such province and, in relation to the Yukon Territory or the Northwest Territories, means the Commissioner thereof;

"province" means a province of Canada, and includes the Yukon Territory and the Northwest Territories;

—NOTES—

PART VI

OFFENCES AGAINST THE PERSON AND REPUTATION

Interpretation

Definitons 196. In this Part

"abandon" "abandon" or "expose" includes

(a) a wilful omission to take charge of a child by a person who is under a legal duty to do so, and

(b) dealing with a child in a manner that is likely to leave that child exposed to risk without protection;

"child" "child" includes an adopted child and an illegitimate child;

"form of marriage" "form of marriage" includes a ceremony of marriage that is recognized as valid

(a) by the law of the place where it was celebrated, or

(b) by the law of the place where an accused is tried, notwithstanding that it is not recognized as valid by the law of the place where it was celebrated;

"guardian" "guardian" includes a person who has in law or in fact the custody or control of a child. 1953-54, c. 51, s. 185.

Interpretation Act

26. (6) Words importing male persons include female persons and corporations.

(7) Words in the singular include the plural, and words in the plural include the singular.

(8) Where a word is defined, other parts of speech and grammatical forms of the same word have corresponding meanings.

28. In every enactment

"month" means a calendar month;

Duties Tending to Preservation of Life

Duty of persons to provide necessaries

197. (1) Every one is under a legal duty

(a) as a parent, foster parent, guardian or head of a family, to provide necessaries of life for a child under the age of sixteen years; 196 3(1)

(b) as a married person, to provide necessaries of life to his spouse; and 26(6) Interp

(c) to provide necessaries of life to a person under his charge if that person

(i) is unable, by reason of detention, age, illness, insanity or other cause, to withdraw himself from that charge, and

(ii) is unable to provide himself with necessaries of life. 1974-75-76, c. 66, s. 8(1).

Offence

Type 'B' (D) Offence

(2) Every one commits an offence who, being under a legal duty within the meaning of subsection (1), fails without lawful excuse, the proof of which lies upon him, to perform that duty, if

(a) with respect to a duty imposed by paragraph (1)*(a)* or *(b)*,

(i) the person to whom the duty is owed is in destitute or necessitous circumstances, or

(ii) the failure to perform the duty endangers the life of the person to whom the duty is owed, or causes or is likely to cause the health of that person to be endangered permanently; or

(b) with respect to a duty imposed by paragraph (1)*(c)*, the failure to perform the duty endangers the life of the person to whom the duty is owed or causes or is likely to cause the health of that person to be injured permanently.

Punishment

(3) Every one who commits an offence under subsection (2) is guilty of

(a) an indictable offence and is liable to imprisonment for two years, or

(b) an offence punishable on summary conviction.

Presumptions

(4) For the purpose of proceedings under this section,

(a) evidence that a person has cohabited with a person of the opposite sex or has in any way recognized that person as being his spouse is, in the absence of any evidence to the contrary, proof that they are lawfully married; 26(6) Interp

(b) evidence that a person has in any way recognized a child as being his child is, in the absence of any evidence to the contrary, proof that the child is his child;

(c) evidence that a person has left his spouse and has failed, for a period of any one month subsequent to the time of his so leaving, to make provision for the maintenance of his spouse or for the maintenance of any child of his under the age of sixteen years is, in the absence of any evidence to the contrary, proof that he has failed without lawful excuse to provide necessaries of life for them; and 28 Interp

(d) the fact that a spouse or child is receiving or has received necessaries of life from another person who is not under a legal duty to provide them is not a defence. 1953-54, c. 51, s. 186; 1968-69, c. 38, s. 92; 1974-75-76, c. 66, s. 8(2).

3. (1) For the purposes of this Act a person shall be deemed to have been of a given age when the anniversary of his birthday, the number of which corresponds to that age, is fully completed, and until then to have been under that age.

585. (1) In any proceedings to which this Act applies an entry or record of an incorporated society or its officers who have had the control or care of a child or young person at or about the time the child or young person was brought to Canada is evidence of the age of the child or young person if the entry or record was made before the time when the offence is alleged to have been committed.

(2) In the absence of other evidence, or by way of corroboration of other evidence, a jury, judge, justice or magistrate, as the case may be, may infer the age of a child or young person from his appearance.

Canada Evidence Act

4. (2) The wife or husband of a person charged with an offence against section 33 or 34 of the *Juvenile Delinquents Act* or with an offence against any of sections 143 to 146, 148, 150 to 155, 157, 166 to 169, 175, 195, 197, 200, 248 to 250, 255 to 258, 289, paragraph 423(1)(*c*) or an attempt to commit an offence under section 146 or 155 of the *Criminal Code,* is a competent and compellable witness for the prosecution without the consent of the person charged.

Duty of persons undertaking acts dangerous to life

198. Every one who undertakes to administer surgical or medical treatment to another person or to do any other lawful act that may endanger the life of another person is, except in cases of necessity, under a legal duty to have and to use reasonable knowledge, skill and care in so doing. 1953-54, c. 51, s. 187.

45. Every one is protected from criminal responsibility for performing a surgical operation upon any person for the benefit of that person if

(*a*) the operation is performed with reasonable care and skill, and

(*b*) it is reasonable to perform the operation, having regard to the state of health of the person at the time the operation is performed and to all the circumstances of the case.

Duty of persons undertaking acts

199. Every one who undertakes to do an act is under a legal duty to do it if an omission to do the act is or may be dangerous to life. 1953-54, c. 51, s. 188.

380. (1) Every one who wilfully breaks a contract, knowing or having reasonable cause to believe that the probable consequences of doing so, whether alone or in combination with others, will be

(*a*) to endanger human life,

(*b*) to cause serious bodily injury,

(*c*) to expose valuable property, real or personal, to destruction or serious injury,

(*d*) to deprive the inhabitants of a city or place, or part thereof, wholly or to a great extent, of their supply of light, power, gas or water, or

(*e*) to delay or prevent the running of a locomotive engine, tender, freight or passenger train or car, on a railway that is a common carrier,

is guilty of

(*f*) an indictable offence and is liable to imprisonment for five years, or

(*g*) an offence punishable on summary conviction.

(2) No person wilfully breaks a contract within the meaning of subsection (1) by reason only that

(*a*) being the employee of an employer, he stops work as a result of the failure of his employer and himself to agree upon any matter relating to his employment, or,

(*b*) being a member of an organization of employees formed for the purpose of regulating relations between employers and employees, he stops work as a result of the failure of the employer and a bargaining agent acting on behalf of the organization to agree upon any matter relating to the employment of members of the organization,

if, before the stoppage of work occurs, all steps provided by law with respect to the settlement of industrial disputes are taken and any provision for the final settlement of differences, without stoppage of work, contained in or by law deemed to be contained in a collective agreement is complied with and effect given thereto.

(3) No proceedings shall be instituted under this section without the consent of the Attorney General.

Abandoning child

Type 'D' Offence

200. Every one who unlawfully abandons or exposes a child who is under the age of ten years, so that its life is or is likely to be endangered or its health is or is likely to be permanently injured, is guilty of an indictable offence and is liable to imprisonment for two years. **1953-54, c. 51, s. 189.** 196 3(1)

Canada Evidence Act

4. (2) The wife or husband of a person charged with an offence against section 33 or 34 of the *Juvenile Delinquents Act* or with an offence against any of sections 143 to 146, 148, 150 to 155, 157, 166 to 169, 175, 195, 197, 200, 248 to 250, 255 to 258, 289, paragraph 423(1)(*c*) or an attempt to commit an offence under section 146 or 155 of the *Criminal Code*, is a competent and compellable witness for the prosecution without the consent of the person charged.

Apprentice or servant

Type 'D' Offence

201. Every master who

(*a*) unlawfully does, or causes to be done, bodily harm to his apprentice or servant so that his life is endangered or his health is or is likely to be permanently injured, or

(*b*) omits, without lawful excuse, to provide necessaries of life for an apprentice or servant in accordance with any contract that he has entered into with respect to that apprentice or servant,

is guilty of an indictable offence and is liable to imprisonment for two years. **1953-54, c. 51, s. 190.**

Section 380, Criminal Breach of Contract, noted after section 199.

Criminal Negligence

Criminal negligence

202. (1) Every one is criminally negligent who

(a) in doing anything, or

(b) in omitting to do anything that it is his duty to do, ss. (2)

shows wanton or reckless disregard for the lives or safety of other persons.

"Duty"

(2) For the purposes of this section, "duty" means a duty imposed by law. 1953-54, c. 51, s. 191.

Causing death by criminal ngligence

Type 'F' Offence

203. Every one who by criminal negligence causes death to another person is guilty of an indictable offence and is liable to imprisonment for life. 1953-54, c. 51, s. 192. 669(c)

210. No person commits culpable homicide or the offence of causing the death of a human being by criminal negligence unless the death occurs within one year and one day commencing with the time of the occurrence of the last event by means of which he caused or contributed to the cause of death.

589. (5) Where a count charges an offence under section 203, 204 or 219 arising out of the operation of a motor vehicle or the navigation or operation of a vessel, or an offence under subsection 233(1), and the evidence does not prove such offence but does prove an offence under subsection 233(4) or 240(1), the accused may be convicted of an offence under subsection 233(4) or 240(1), as the case may be.

If a vessel is involved, see subsection 240(7) regarding order of prohibition.

Causing bodily harm by criminal negligence

Type 'E' Offence

204. Every one who by criminal negligence causes bodily harm to another person is guilty of an indictable offence and is liable to imprisonment for ten years. 1953-54, c. 51, s. 193.

233. (1) Every one who is criminally negligent in the operation of a motor vehicle is guilty of

(a) an indictable offence and is liable to imprisonment for five years, or

(b) an offence punishable on summary conviction.

Homicide

Homicide

205. (1) A person commits homicide when, directly or indirectly, by any means, he causes the death of a human being. 206

Kinds of homicide

(2) Homicide is culpable or not culpable.

Non culpable homicide

(3) Homicide that is not culpable is not an offence.

Culpable homicide

(4) Culpable homicide is murder or manslaughter or infanticide.

Idem

(5) A person commits culpable homicide when he causes the death of a human being,

(a) by means of an unlawful act,

(b) by criminal negligence,

(c) by causing that human being, by threats or fear of violence or by deception, to do anything that causes his death, or

(d) by wilfully frightening that human being, in the case of a child or sick person.

Exception

(6) Notwithstanding anything in this section, a person does not commit homicide within the meaning of this Act by reason only that he causes the death of a human being by procuring, by false evidence, the conviction and death of that human being by sentence of law. 1953-54, c. 51, s. 194.

When child becomes human being

206. (1) A child becomes a human being within the meaning of this Act when it has completely proceeded, in a living state, from the body of its mother whether or not

(a) it has breathed,

(b) it has an independent circulation, or

(c) the navel string is severed.

Killing child

(2) A person commits homicide when he causes injury to a child before or during its birth as a result of which the child dies after becoming a human being. 1953-54, c. 51, s. 195; 1968-69, c. 38, s. 14.

Death which might have been prevented

207. Where a person, by an act or omission, does any thing that results in the death of a human being, he causes the death of that human being notwithstanding that death from that cause might have been prevented by resorting to proper means. 1953-54, c. 51, s. 196.

Death from treatment of injury

208. Where a person causes to a human being a bodily injury that is of itself of a dangerous nature and from which death results, he causes the death of that human being notwithstanding that the immediate cause of death is proper or improper treatment that is applied in good faith. 1953-54, c. 51, s. 197.

Acceleration of death

209. Where a person causes bodily injury to a human being that results in death, he causes the death of that human being notwithstanding that the effect of the bodily injury is only to accelerate his death from a disease or disorder arising from some other cause. 1953-54, c. 51, s. 199.

Death within year and a day

210. No person commits culpable homicide or the offence of causing the death of a human being by criminal negligence unless the death occurs within one year and one day commencing with the time of the occurrence of the last event by means of which he caused or contributed to the cause of death. 1953-54, c. 51, s. 198.

Killing by influence on the mind

211. No person commits culpable homicide where he causes the death of a human being

(a) by any influence on the mind alone, or

(b) by any disorder or disease resulting from influence on the mind alone,

but this section does not apply where a person causes the death of a child or sick person by wilfully frightening him. 1953-54, c. 51, s. 200.

Murder, Manslaughter and Infanticide

Murder

212. Culpable homicide is murder

(a) where the person who causes the death of a human being

(i) means to cause his death, or

(ii) means to cause him bodily harm that he knows is likely to cause his death, and is reckless whether death ensues or not;

(b) where a person, meaning to cause death to a human being or meaning to cause him bodily harm that he knows is likely to cause his death, and being reckless whether death ensues or not, by accident or mistake causes death to another human being, notwithstanding that he does not mean to cause death or bodily harm to that human being; or

(c) where a person, for an unlawful object, does anything that he knows or ought to know is likely to cause death, and thereby causes death to a human being, notwithstanding that he desires to effect his object without causing death or bodily harm to any human being. 1953-54, c. 51, s. 201.

Murder in commission of offences

213. Culpable homicide is murder where a person causes the death of a human being while committing or attempting to commit high treason or treason or an offence mentioned in section 52 (sabotage), 76 (piratical acts), 76.1 (hijacking an aircraft), 132 or subsection 133(1) or sections 134 to 136 (escape or rescue from prison or lawful custody), 143 or 145 (rape or attempt to commit rape), 149 or 156 (indecent assault), subsection 246(2) (resisting lawful arrest), 247 (kidnapping and forcible confinement), 302 (robbery), 306 (breaking and entering) or 389 or 390 (arson), whether or not the person means to cause death to any human being and whether or not he knows that death is likely to be caused to any human being, if 2.1

(a) he means to cause bodily harm for the purpose of

(i) facilitating the commission of the offence, or

(ii) facilitating his flight after committing or attempting to commit the offence,

and the death ensues from the bodily harm;

(b) he administers a stupefying or overpowering thing for a purpose mentioned in paragraph *(a)*, and the death ensues therefrom;

(c) he wilfully stops, by any means, the breath of a human being for a purpose mentioned in paragraph *(a)*, and the death ensues therefrom; or

(d) he uses a weapon or has it upon his person 2

(i) during or at the time he commits or attempts to commit the offence, or

(ii) during or at the time of his flight after committing or attempting to commit the offence,

and the death ensues as a consequence. 1953-54, c. 51, s. 202; 1974-75-76, c. 93, s. 13: 1974-75-76, c. 105, s. 29.

2.1 Where, in any provision of this Act, a reference to another provision of this Act or a provision of any other Act is followed by words in parenthesis that are or purport to be descriptive of the subject-matter of the provision referred to, the words in parenthesis form no part of the provision in which they occur but shall be deemed to have been inserted for convenience of reference only.

Classification of murder

214. (1) Murder is first degree murder or second degree murder.

Planned and deliberate murder

(2) Murder is first degree murder when it is planned and deliberate.

Contracted murder

(3) Without limiting the generality of subsection (2), murder is planned and deliberate when it is committed pursuant to an arrangement under which money or anything of value passes or is intended to pass from one person to another, or is promised by one person to another, as consideration for that other's causing
or assisting in causing the death of anyone or counselling or procuring another 22
person to do any act causing or assisting in causing that death.

Murder of peace officer, etc.

(4) Irrespective of whether a murder is planned and deliberate on the part of any person, murder is first degree murder when the victim is

(a) a police officer, police constable, constable, sheriff, deputy sheriff, sheriff's officer or other person employed for the preservation and maintenance of the public peace, acting in the course of his duties;

(b) a warden, deputy warden, instructor, keeper, gaoler, guard or other officer
or a permanent employee of a prison, acting in the course of his duties; or 2

(c) a person working in a prison with the permission of the prison authorities and acting in the course of his work therein.

Hijacking, kidnapping or sexual offence

(5) Irrespective of whether a murder is planned and deliberate on the part of any person, murder is first degree murder in respect of a person when the death is caused by that person

(a) while committing or attempting to commit an offence under section 76.1 (hijacking aircraft) or 247 (kidnapping and forcible confinement); or

(b) while committing an offence under section 144 (rape) or 145 (attempt to commit rape) or while committing or attempting to commit an offence under section 149 (indecent assault on female) or 156 (indecent assault on male).

First degree murder

(6) Murder is first degree murder in respect of a person when the death is caused by that person and that person has been previously convicted of either first degree murder or second degree murder.

Second degree murder

(7) All murder that is not first degree murder is second degree murder. 1974-75-76, c. 105, s. 4.

2. In this Act

"prison" includes a penitentiary, common gaol, public or reformatory prison, lock-up, guard-room or other place in which persons who are charged with or convicted of offences are usually kept in custody;

"offensive weapon" or "weapon" means

(a) anything that is designed to be used as a weapon, or

(b) anything that a person uses or intends to use as a weapon, whether or not it is designed to be used as a weapon,

and, without restricting the generality of the foregoing, includes any firearm as defined in section 82;

82. (1) For the purposes of this Part,

"firearm" means any barrelled weapon from which any shot, bullet or other missile can be discharged and that is capable of causing serious bodily injury or death to a person, and includes any frame or receiver of such a barrelled weapon and anything that can be adapted for use as a firearm;

Murder reduced to manslaughter

215. (1) Culpable homicide that otherwise would be murder may be reduced to manslaughter if the person who committed it did so in the heat of passion caused by sudden provocation.

What is provocation

(2) A wrongful act or insult that is of such a nature as to be sufficient to deprive an ordinary person of the power of self-control is provocation for the purposes of this section if the accused acted upon it on the sudden and before there was time for his passion to cool.

Questions of fact

(3) For the purposes of this section the questions

(*a*) whether a particular wrongful act or insult amounted to provocation, and

(*b*) whether the accused was deprived of the power of self-control by the provocation that he alleges he received,

are questions of fact, but no one shall be deemed to have given provocation to another by doing anything that he had a legal right to do, or by doing anything that the accused incited him to do in order to provide the accused with an excuse for causing death or bodily harm to any human being.

Death during illegal arrest

(4) Culpable homicide that otherwise would be murder is not necessarily manslaughter by reason only that it was committed by a person who was being arrested illegally, but the fact that the illegality of the arrest was known to the accused may be evidence of provocation for the purpose of this section. 1953-54, c. 51, s. 203.

Infanticide

Type 'D' Offence Section 220

216. A female person commits infanticide when by a wilful act or omission she causes the death of her newly-born child, if at the time of the act or omission 2
she is not fully recovered from the effects of giving birth to the child and by reason thereof or of the effect of lactation consequent on the birth of the child her mind is then disturbed. 1953-54, c. 51, s. 204.

2. In this Act

"newly-born child" means a person under the age of one year;

Manslaughter

217. Culpable homicide that is not murder or infanticide is manslaughter. 1953-54, c. 51, s. 205.

Punishment for murder

Type 'G' Offence

IPA offence 178.1

218. (1) Every one who commits first degree murder or second degree murder is guilty of an indictable offence and shall be sentenced to imprisonment for life. 28 Interp 669

Interpretation Act

28. In every enactment

"shall" is to be construed as imperative;

Minimum punishment

(2) For the purposes of Part XX, the sentence of imprisonment for life 669
prescribed by this section is a minimum punishment. 1974-75-76, c. 105, s. 5.

Punishment for manslaughter

Type 'F' Offence

219. Every one who commits manslaughter is guilty of an indictable offence and is liable to imprisonment for life. 1953-54, c. 51, s. 207. 669

If a motor vehicle or vessel is involved, see subsection 589(5), noted after section 203.

If a vessel is involved, see subsection 240(7) regarding order of prohibition.

Punishment for infanticide

Type 'D' Offence

220. Every female person who commits infanticide is guilty of an indictable offence and is liable to imprisonment for five years. 1953-54, c. 51, s. 208. 216

423. (1) Except where otherwise expressly provided by law, the following provisions apply in respect of conspiracy, namely,

(a) every one who conspires with any one to commit murder or to cause another person to be murdered, whether in Canada or not, is guilty of an indictable offence and is liable to imprisonment for fourteen years;

511. No person shall be convicted for the offence of high treason or first degree murder unless in the indictment charging the offence he is specifically charged with that offence.

518. No count that charges an offence other than murder shall be joined in an indictment to a count that charges murder.

538. (1) Where an indictment charges substantially the same offence as that charged in an indictment on which an accused was previously convicted or acquitted, but adds a statement of intention or circumstances of aggravation tending, if proved, to increase the punishment, the previous conviction or acquittal bars the subsequent indictment.

(2) A conviction or acquittal on an indictment for murder bars a subsequent indictment for the same homicide charging it as manslaughter or infanticide, and a conviction or acquittal on an indictment for manslaughter or infanticide bars a subsequent indictment for the same homicide charging it as murder.

(3) A conviction or acquittal on an indictment for first degree murder bars a subsequent indictment for the same homicide charging it as second degree murder, and a conviction or acquittal on an indictment for second degree murder bars a subsequent indictment for the same homicide charging it as first degree murder.

(4) A conviction or acquittal on an indictment for infanticide bars a subsequent indictment for the same homicide charging it as manslaughter, and a conviction or acquittal on an indictment for manslaughter bars a subsequent indictment for the same homicide charging it as infanticide.

589. (1) A count in an indictment is divisible and where the commission of the offence charged, as described in the enactment creating it or as charged in the count, includes the commission of another offence, whether punishable by indictment or on summary conviction, the accused may be convicted

(a) of an offence so included that is proved, notwithstanding that the whole offence that is charged is not proved, or

(b) of an attempt to commit an offence so included.

(2) For greater certainty and without limiting the generality of subsection (1), where a count charges first degree murder and the evidence does not prove first degree murder but proves second degree murder or an attempt to commit second degree murder, the jury may find the accused not guilty of first degree murder but guilty of second degree murder or an attempt to commit second degree murder, as the case may be.

(3) Subject to subsection (4), where a count charges murder and the evidence proves manslaughter or infanticide but does not prove murder, the jury may find the accused not guilty of murder but guilty of manslaughter or infanticide, but shall not on that count find the accused guilty of any other offence.

(4) Where a count charges the murder of a child or infanticide and the evidence proves the commission of an offence under section 227 but does not prove murder or infanticide, the jury may find the accused not guilty of murder or infanticide, as the case may be, but guilty of an offence under section 227.

590. Where a female person is charged with infanticide and the evidence establishes that she caused the death of her child but does not establish that, at the time of the act or omission by which she caused the death of the child,

(a) she was not fully recovered from the effects of giving birth to the child or from the effect of lactation consequent on the birth of the child, and

(b) the balance of her mind was, at the time, disturbed by reason of the effect of giving birth to the child or of the effect of lactation consequent on the birth of the child,

she may be convicted unless the evidence establishes that the act or omission was not wilful.

669. The sentence to be pronounced against a person who is to be sentenced to imprisonment for life shall be,

(a) in respect of a person who has been convicted of high treason or first degree murder, that he be sentenced to imprisonment for life without eligibility for parole until he has served twenty-five years of his sentence;

(b) in respect of a person who has been convicted of second degree murder, that he be sentenced to imprisonment for life without eligibility for parole until he has served at least ten years of his sentence or such greater number of years, not being more than twenty-five years, as has been substituted therefor pursuant to section 671; and

(c) in respect of a person who has been convicted of any other offence, that he be sentenced to imprisonment for life with normal eligibility for parole.

670. Where a jury finds an accused guilty of second degree murder, the judge who presides at the trial shall, before discharging the jury, put to them the following question:

"You have found the accused guilty of second degree murder and the law requires that I now pronounce a sentence of imprisonment for life against him. Do you wish to make any recommendation with respect to the number of years that he must serve before he is eligible for release on parole? You are not required to make any recommendation but if you do, your recommendation will be considered by me when I am determining whether I should substitute for the ten year period, which the law would otherwise require the accused to serve before he is eligible to be considered for release on parole, a number of years that is more than ten but not more than twenty-five."

671. At the time of the sentencing of an accused under section 669 who is convicted of second degree murder, the judge presiding at the trial of the accused or, if that judge is unable to do so, any judge of the same court may, having regard to the character of the accused, the nature of the offence and the circumstances surrounding its commission, and to any recommendation made pursuant to section 670, by order, substitute for ten years a number of years of imprisonment, (being more than ten but not more than twenty-five) without eligibility for parole, as he deems fit in the circumstances.

672. (1) Where a person has served at least fifteen years of his sentence

(a) in the case of a person who has been convicted of high treason or first degree murder, or

(b) in the case of a person convicted of second degree murder who has been sentenced to imprisonment for life without eligibility for parole until he has served more than fifteen years of his sentence, he may apply to the appropriate Chief Justice in the province or territory in which the conviction took place for a reduction in his number of years of imprisonment without eligibility for parole.

(2) Upon receipt of an application under subsection (1), the appropriate Chief Justice shall designate a judge of the superior court of criminal jurisdiction to empanel a jury to hear the application and determine whether the applicant's number of years of imprisonment without eligibility for parole ought to be reduced having regard to the character of the applicant, his conduct while serving his sentence, the nature of the offence for which he was convicted and such other matters as the judge deems relevant in the circumstances and such determination shall be made by no less than two-thirds of such jury.

(3) Where the jury hearing an application under subsection (1) determine that the applicant's number of years of imprisonment without eligibility for parole ought not to be reduced, the jury shall set another time at or after which an application may again be made by the applicant to the appropriate Chief Justice for a reduction in his number of years of imprisonment without eligibility for parole.

(4) Where the jury hearing an application under subsection (1) determine that the applicant's number of years of imprisonment without eligibility for parole ought to be reduced, the jury may, by order,

(a) substitute a lesser number of years of imprisonment without eligibility for parole than that then applicable; or

(b) terminate the ineligibility for parole.

(5) The appropriate Chief Justice in each province or territory may make such rules in respect of applications and hearings under this section as are required for the purposes of this section.

(6) For the purposes of this section the "appropriate Chief Justice" is

(a) in relation to

(i) the Provinces of British Columbia and Prince Edward Island, respectively, the Chief Justice of the Supreme Court,

(ii) the Provinces of Nova Scotia and Newfoundland, respectively, the Chief Justice of the Supreme Court, Trial Division,

(iii) the Provinces of Saskatchewan, Manitoba, Alberta and New Brunswick, respectively, the Chief Justice of the Court of Queen's Bench,

(iv) Repealed.

(v) the Province of Ontario, the Chief Justice of the High Court of Justice, and

(vi) the Province of Quebec, the Chief Justice of the Superior Court;

(b) in relation to the Yukon Territory, the Chief Justice of the Court of Appeal thereof, and

(c) in relation to the Northwest Territories, the Chief Justice of the Court of Appeal thereof.

(7) For the purposes of this section, when the appropriate Chief Justice is designating a judge of the superior court of criminal jurisdiction to empanel a jury to hear an application in respect of a conviction that took place in the Yukon Territory or the Northwest Territories, the appropriate Chief Justice may designate the judge from the Court of Appeal or the Supreme Court of the Yukon Territory or Northwest Territories, as the case may be.

673. In calculating the period of imprisonment served for the purposes of section 669, 671 or 672, there shall be included any time spent in custody between,

(a) in the case of a sentence of imprisonment for life imposed after the commencement of the *Criminal Law Amendment Act (No. 2), 1976*, the day on which that person was arrested and taken into custody in respect of the offence for which he was sentenced to imprisonment for life and the day the sentence was imposed; or

(b) in the case of a sentence of death that has been or is deemed to have been commuted to a sentence of imprisonment for life, the day on which that person was arrested and taken into custody in respect of the offence for which he was sentenced to death and the day the sentence was commuted or deemed to have been commuted to a sentence of imprisonment for life.

674. (1) Unless the Parliament of Canada otherwise provides by an enactment making express reference to this section, no person who has been sentenced to imprisonment for life without eligibility for parole for a specified number of years pursuant to this Act shall be considered for parole or released pursuant to the terms of a grant of parole under the *Parole Act* or any other Act of the Parliament of Canada until the expiration or termination of his specified number of years of imprisonment without eligibility for parole.

(2) Notwithstanding the *Penitentiary Act* and the *Parole Act,* in the case of any person sentenced to imprisonment for life without eligibility for parole for a specified number of years pursuant to this Act, until the expiration of all but three years of his number of years of imprisonment without eligibility for parole, no absence without escort may be authorized under the *Penitentiary Act,* no absence with escort for humanitarian and rehabilitative reasons may be authorized under the *Penitentiary Act* without the approval of the National Parole Board and no day parole may be granted under the *Parole Act.*

Criminal Law Amendment Act (No. 2), 1976 (1974-75-76, c. 105)

25. (1) If, on the day this Act comes into force, any person is under a sentence of death for murder punishable by death that has not been commuted, that sentence thereupon becomes a sentence of imprisonment for life for first degree murder without eligibility for parole until he has served twenty-five years of his sentence.

(2) If, after the coming into force of this Act, an appeal against conviction by a person under sentence of death upon the coming into force of this Act for murder punishable by death is dismissed, that sentence thereupon becomes a sentence of imprisonment for life for first degree murder without eligibility for parole until he has served twenty-five years of his sentence.

(3) If, on the day this Act comes into force, any person is under a sentence of death for treason or piracy that has not been commuted, that sentence is deemed to have been commuted to imprisonment for life with like effect as if the commutation had been granted before the day this Act came into force.

(4) If, after the coming into force of this Act, an appeal against conviction by a person under a sentence of death on the coming into force of this Act for treason or piracy is dismissed, the sentence is deemed to have been commuted to imprisonment for life immediately upon the dismissal with the like effect as if the commutation had been granted before the day this Act came into force.

(5) In calculating the period of imprisonment served for the purposes of subsection (1) or (2), section 673 of the *Criminal Code* applies *mutatis mutandis.*

26. (1) Where, in proceedings commenced before the coming into force of this Act, a person is found guilty after the coming into force of this Act of an offence punishable by death, whether the offence be treason, piracy or murder, he shall be sentenced therefor and all further proceedings in respect thereof shall be continued as if the offence had been committed after the coming into force of this Act.

(2) Where, in proceedings commenced before the coming into force of this Act, a person is found guilty after the coming into force of this Act of murder that is not punishable by death, he shall be sentenced therefor and all further proceedings in respect thereof shall be continued as if this Act had not come into force.

27. (1) Where proceedings in respect of any offence of treason, piracy or murder, whether punishable by death or not, that was committed before the coming into force of this Act are commenced after the coming into force of this Act, the offence shall be dealt with, inquired into, tried and determined, and any punishment in respect of the offence shall be imposed as if the offence had been committed after the coming into force of this Act irrespective of when it was actually committed.

(2) Where proceedings in respect of any offence of treason, piracy or murder, whether punishable by death or not, were commenced before the coming into force of this Act, and a new trial of a person for the offence has been ordered and the new trial is commenced after the coming into force of this Act, the new trial shall be commenced by the preferring of a new indictment before the court before which the accused is to be tried, and thereafter the offence shall be dealt with, inquired into, tried and determined, and any punishment in respect of the offence shall be imposed as if it had been committed after the coming into force of this Act.

28. (1) Subsection 218(5) (except paragraph *(e)* thereof) and subsections 218(6), (7) and (9) of the *Criminal Code*, as they read immediately before the coming into force of this Act, shall be read as unrepealed by this Act in so far as it is necessary to give effect to any term of imprisonment for life imposed before the coming into force of this Act upon a person described in paragraph 218(5)*(a)*, *(b)* or *(c)* of the *Criminal Code* as it read immediately before the coming into force of this Act.

(2) Where

(a) subsection 25(1) or (2) of this Act applies in respect of a person, or

(b) a person described in paragraph 218(5)*(a)*, *(b)* or *(c)* of the *Criminal Code* as it read immediately before the coming into force of this Act had been sentenced to a term of imprisonment for life and a judge that had, under subsection 218(6) of the *Criminal Code* as it read before the coming into force of this Act, by order substituted for the number of years specified in paragraph 218(5)*(d)* of the *Criminal Code* as it then read a number of years that is more than ten but not more than twenty,

that person may, after having served at least fifteen years of his sentence, make an application under section 672 of the *Criminal Code* as enacted by this Act and that section applies *mutatis mutandis* in respect of that person.

Criminal Code (these provisions repealed by 1974-75-76, c. 105, s. 5.)

218. (5) Notwithstanding anything in the Parole Act and unless the Parliament of Canada otherwise directs, no person

(a) upon whom a sentence of imprisonment for life in respect of murder has been imposed after the coming into force of this subsection,

(b) upon whom a sentence of imprisonment for life is deemed by section 8 of the Criminal Law Amendment (Capital Punishment) Act to have been imposed, or

(c) in respect of whom a sentence of death in respect of murder has been commuted after the coming into force of this section to imprisonment for life,

shall be released pursuant to the terms of a grant of parole under the Parole Act unless

(d) at least ten years of that sentence calculated in the manner described in subsection (7) have been served, and

(e) Not applicable. 1974-75-76, c. 105, s. 28(1).

(6) Notwithstanding paragraph (5)(d), the judge presiding at the trial of an accused who is or was convicted of murder or, where such judge is unable to do so, another judge of the same court may

(a) at the time of sentencing of the accused, in a case referred to in paragraph (5)(a), or

(b) at any time on application made to him within a reasonable time after

(i) the coming into force of this section, in a case referred to in paragraph (5)(b), or

(ii) the execution of an instrument or writing mentioned in subsection 684(2) declaring that a sentence of death has been commuted, in a case referred to in paragraph (5)(c),

having regard to the character of the accused, the nature of the offence and the circumstances surrounding its commission, and to any recommendation made pursuant to subsection (8), by order substitute for the number of years specified in paragraph (5)(d) a number of years that is not more than twenty but more than ten.

(7) In calculating the time referred to in paragraph (5)(d) or the time substituted therefor pursuant to subsection (6), there shall be included any time spent in custody between,

(a) in the case of a sentence of imprisonment for life, the day on which the person was arrested and taken into custody in respect of the offence for which he was sentenced to imprisonment for life and the day the sentence was imposed or was deemed by section 8 of the Criminal Law Amendment (Capital Punishment) Act to have been imposed, or

(b) in the case of a sentence of death, the day on which the person was arrested and taken into custody in respect of the offence for which he was sentenced to death and the day the sentence was commuted.

(9) Notwithstanding the Penitentiary Act and the Parole Act, in the case of any person described in paragraph (5)(a), (b) or (c), no absence without escort may be authorized under section 26 of the Penitentiary Act and no day parole may be granted under section 10 of the Parole Act until the expiration of all but three years of the time referred to in paragraph (5)(d) or the time substituted therefor pursuant to subsection (6), as the case may be.

Killing unborn child in act of birth

Type 'E' Offence

221. (1) Every one who causes the death, in the act of birth, of any child that has not become a human being, in such a manner that, if the child were a human being, he would be guilty of murder, is guilty of an indictable offence and is liable to imprisonment for life. 206 669

Saving

(2) This section does not apply to a person who, by means that, in good faith, he considers necessary to preserve the life of the mother of a child, causes the death of such child. 1968-69, c. 38, s. 15.

Attempt to commit murder

Type 'F' Offence

222. Everyone who attempts by any means to commit murder is guilty of an indictable offence and is liable to imprisonment for life. 1953-54, c. 51, s. 210. 24 669

24. (1) Every one who, having an intent to commit an offence, does or omits to do anything for the purpose of carrying out his intention is guilty of an attempt to commit the offence whether or not it was possible under the circumstances to commit the offence.

(2) The question whether an act or omission by a person who has an intent to commit an offence is or is not mere preparation to commit the offence, and too remote to constitute an attempt to commit the offence, is a question of law.

Accessory after fact to murder

Type 'G' Offence

223. Every one who is an accessory after the fact to murder is guilty of an indictable offence and is liable to imprisonment for life. 1953-54, c. 51, s. 211. 23 669

23. (1) An accessory after the fact to an offence is one who, knowing that a person has been a party to the offence, receives, comforts or assists him for the purpose of enabling him to escape.

(2) No married person whose spouse has been a party to an offence is an accessory after the fact to that offence by receiving, comforting or assisting the spouse for the purpose of enabling the spouse to escape.

Suicide

Counselling or aiding suicide

Type 'E' Offence

224. Every one who

(*a*) counsels or procures a person to commit suicide, or

(*b*) aids or abets a person to commit suicide,

whether suicide ensues or not, is guilty of an indictable offence and is liable to imprisonment for fourteen years. 1953-54, c. 51, s. 212.

225. Repealed, 1972, c. 13, s. 16.

Neglect in Childbirth and Concealing Dead Body

Neglect to obtain assistance in childbirth

Type 'D' Offence

226. A female person who, being pregnant and about to be delivered, with intent that the child shall not live or with intent to conceal the birth of the child, fails to make provision for reasonable assistance in respect of her delivery is, if the child is permanently injured as a result thereof or dies immediately before, during or in a short time after birth, as a result thereof, guilty of an indictable offence and is liable to imprisonment for five years. 1953-54, c. 51, s. 214.

Concealing body of child

Type 'D' Offence

227. Every one who in any manner disposes of the dead body of a child, with intent to conceal the fact that its mother has been delivered of it, whether the child died before, during or after birth, is guilty of an indictable offence and is liable to imprisonment for two years. 1953-54, c. 51, s. 215.

Sections 220 and 689(5).

Bodily Harm and Acts and Omissions Causing Danger to the Person

Causing bodily harm with intent

Type 'E' Offence

228. Every one who, with intent

(a) to wound, maim or disfigure any person,

(b) to endanger the life of any person, or

(c) to prevent the arrest or detention of any person,

discharges a firearm, air gun or air pistol at or causes bodily harm in any way to any person, whether or not that person is the one mentioned in paragraph *(a)*, *(b)* or *(c)*, is guilty of an indictable offence and is liable to imprisonment for fourteen years. 1953-54, c. 51, s. 216. 82

82. (1) For the purposes of this Part,

"firearm" means any barrelled weapon from which any shot, bullet or other missile can be discharged and that is capable of causing serious bodily injury or death to a person, and includes any frame or receiver of such a barrelled weapon and anything that can be adapted for use as a firearm;

84. (2) Every one who, without lawful excuse, uses, carries, handles, ships or stores any firearm or ammunition in a careless manner or without reasonable precautions for the safety of other persons

(a) is guilty of an indictable offence and is liable to imprisonment

(i) in the case of a first offence, for two years, and

(ii) in the case of a second or subsequent offence, for five years; or

(b) is guilty of an offence punishable on summary conviction.

171. (1) Every one who

(d) disturbs the peace and quiet of the occupants of a dwelling-house by discharging firearms or by other disorderly conduct in a public place or who, not being an occupant of a dwelling-house comprised in a particular building or structure, disturbs the peace and quiet of the occupants of a dwelling-house comprised in the building or structure by discharging firearms or by other disorderly conduct in any part of a building or structure to which, at the time of such conduct, the occupants of two or more dwelling houses comprised in the building or structure have access as of right or by invitation, express or implied,

is guilty of an offence punishable on summary conviction.

Administering noxious thing

Type 'D' Offence

229. Every one who administers or causes to be administered to any person or causes any person to take poison or any other destructive or noxious thing is guilty of an indictable offence and is liable

(a) to imprisonment for fourteen years, if he intends thereby to endanger the life of or to cause bodily harm to that person; or

(b) to imprisonment for two years, if he intends thereby to aggrieve or annoy that person. 1953-54, c. 51, s. 217.

Overcoming resistance to commission of offence

Type 'E' Offence

230. Every one who, with intent to enable or assist himself or another person to commit an indictable offence,

(a) attempts, by any means, to choke, suffocate or strangle another person, or by any means calculated to choke, suffocate or strangle, attempts to render another person insensible, unconscious or incapable of resistance, or

(b) administers, or causes to be administered to any person, or attempts to administer to any person, or causes or attempts to cause any person to take a stupefying or overpowering drug, matter or thing,

is guilty of an indictable offence and is liable to imprisonment for life. R.S., c. C-34, s. 230; 1972, c. 13, s. 70.

195. (1) Every one who

(i) applies or administers to a female person or causes her to take any drug, intoxicating liquor, matter, or thing with intent to stupefy or overpower her in order thereby to enable any person to have illicit sexual intercourse with her, or

is guilty of an indictable offence and is liable to imprisonment for ten years.

246. (1) Every one who assaults a person with intent to commit an indictable offence is guilty of an indictable offence and is liable to imprisonment for five years.

Traps likely to cause bodily harm

Type 'D' Offence

231. (1) Every one who, with intent to cause death or bodily harm to persons, whether ascertained or not, sets or places or causes to be set or placed a trap, device or other thing whatsoever that is likely to cause death or bodily harm to persons is guilty of an indictable offence and is liable to imprisonment for five years.

(2) A person who, being in occupation or possession of a place where anything mentioned in subsection (1) has been set or placed, knowingly and wilfully permits it to remain there, shall be deemed, for the purposes of that subsection, to have set or placed it with the intent mentioned therein. 1953-54, c. 51, s. 219.

176. (1) Every one who commits a common nuisance and thereby

(a) endangers the lives, safety or health of the public, or

(b) causes physical injury to any person,

is guilty of an indictable offence and is liable to imprisonment for two years.

(2) For the purposes of this section, every one commits a common nuisance who does an unlawful act or fails to discharge a legal duty and thereby

(a) endangers the lives, safety, health, property or comfort of the public, or

(b) obstructs the public in the exercise or enjoyment of any right that is common to all the subjects of Her Majesty in Canada.

Interfering with transportation facilities

Type 'E' Offence

232. Every one who, with intent to endanger the safety of any person, places anything upon or does anything to any property that is used for or in connection with the transportation of persons or goods by land, water or air that is likely to cause death or bodily harm to persons is guilty of an indictable offence and is liable to imprisonment for life. 1953-54, c. 51, s. 220.

Section 76.2 Endangering safety of aircraft in flight and rendering aircraft incapable of flight.

Automobiles, Dangerous Places and Unseaworthy Ships

Criminal negligence in operation of motor vehicle

Type 'B' (D) Offence

233. (1) Every one who is criminally negligent in the operation of a motor vehicle is guilty of 202 2

(a) an indictable offence and is liable to imprisonment for five years, or

(b) an offence punishable on summary conviction. 722(1)

2. In this Act

"motor vehicle" means a vehicle that is drawn, propelled or driven by any means other than muscular power, but does not include a vehicle of a railway that operates on rails;

202. (1) Every one is criminally negligent who

(a) in doing anything, or

(b) in omitting to do anything that it is his duty to do,

shows wanton or reckless disregard for the lives or safety of other persons.

(2) For the purposes of this section, "duty" means a duty imposed by law.

589. (5) Where a count charges an offence under section 203, 204 or 219 arising out of the operation of a motor vehicle or the navigation or operation of a vessel, or an offence under subsection 233(1), and the evidence does not prove such offence but does prove an offence under subsection 233(4) or 240(1), the accused may be convicted of an offence under subsection 233(4) or 240(1), as the case may be.

Failing to stop at scene of accident

Type 'B' (D) Offence

(2) Every one who, having the care, charge or control of a vehicle that is involved in an accident with a person, vehicle or cattle in the charge of a person, with intent to escape civil or criminal liability fails to stop his vehicle, give his name and address and, where any person has been injured, offer assistance, is guilty of 2

(a) an indictable offence and is liable to imprisonment for two years, or

(b) an offence punishable on summary conviction. 722(1)

2. In this Act

"cattle" means neat cattle or an animal of the bovine species by whatever technical or familiar name it is known, and includes a horse, mule, ass, pig, sheep or goat;

Proof in absence of evidence to contrary

(3) In proceedings under subsection (2), evidence that an accused failed to stop his vehicle, offer assistance where any person has been injured and give his name and address is, in the absence of any evidence to the contrary, proof of an intent to escape civil and criminal liability.

Dangerous driving

Type 'B' (D) Offence

(4) Every one who drives a motor vehicle on a street, road, highway or other public place in a manner that is dangerous to the public, having regard to all the circumstances including the nature, condition and use of such place and the amount of traffic that at the time is or might reasonably be expected to be on such place, is guilty of 2

(a) an indictable offence and is liable to imprisonment for two years, or

(b) an offence punishable on summary conviction. 1953-54, c. 51, s. 221; 1960-61, c. 43, s. 3; 1968-69, c. 38, s. 92. 722(1)

2. In this Act

"highway" means a road to which the public has the right of access, and includes bridges over which or tunnels through which a road passes;

Driving while ability to drive is impaired

234. (1) Every one who, while his ability to drive a motor vehicle is impaired by alcohol or a drug, drives a motor vehicle or has the care or control of a motor vehicle, whether it is in motion or not, is guilty of an indictable offence or an offence punishable on summary conviction and is liable 2 724(2) 740

(a) for a first offence, to a fine of not more than two thousand dollars and not less than fifty dollars or to imprisonment for six months or to both;

(b) for a second offence, to imprisonment for not more than one year and not less than fourteen days; and 591 592

(c) for each subsequent offence, to imprisonment for not more than two years and not less than three months. 1968-69, c. 38, s. 16; 1974-75-76, c. 93, s. 14(1).

Conditional and absolute discharge

(2) Notwithstanding subsection 662.1(1), where an accused pleads guilty to or is found guilty of an offence under subsection (1), the court before which he appears may, after hearing medical or other evidence, if it considers that the accused is in need of curative treatment in relation to his consumption of alcohol or drugs and that it would not be contrary to the public interest, instead of convicting the accused, by order direct that the accused be discharged upon conditions prescribed in a probation order, including a condition respecting his attendance for curative treatment in relation to his consumption of alcohol or drugs, and the provisions of subsections 662.1(2) to (4) apply *mutatis mutandis.* 1974-75-76, c. 93, s. 14(2). 663

mutatis mutandis — after the necessary changes in detail so that the text applies

NOTE: Subsection 234(2) has been proclaimed in force only in the Province of Alberta and the Northwest Territories.

Road-side testing

234.1 (1) Where a peace officer reasonably suspects that a person who is driving a motor vehicle or who has the care or control of a motor vehicle, whether it is in motion or not, has alcohol in his body, he may, by demand made to that person, require him to provide forthwith such sample of his breath as in the opinion of the peace officer is necessary to enable a proper analysis of his breath to be made by means of an approved roadside screening device and, where necessary, to accompany the peace officer for the purpose of enabling such a sample of his breath to be taken. 2 ss. (4)

Failure or refusal to provide sample

Type 'B' (D) Offence

(2) Every one who, without reasonable excuse, fails or refuses to comply with a demand made to him by a peace officer under subsection (1) is guilty of a an indictable offence or an offence punishable on summary conviction and is liable 724(2) 740

(a) for a first offence, to a fine of not more than two thousand dollars and not less than fifty dollars or to imprisonment for six months or to both;

(b) for a second offence, to imprisonment for not more than one year and not less than fourteen days; and 591 592

(c) for each subsequent offence, to imprisonment for not more than two years and not less than three months.

Person deemed to have care or control of vehicle

(3) In proceedings under this section, where it is proved that the accused occupied the seat ordinarily occupied by the driver of a motor vehicle, he shall be deemed to have had the care or control of the vehicle unless he establishes that he did not enter or mount the vehicle for the purpose of setting it in motion.

"Approved road-side screening device" defined

(4) In this section, "approved road-side screening device" means a device of a kind that is designed to ascertain the presence of alcohol in the blood of a person and that is approved for the purpose of this section by order of the Attorney General of Canada.

NOTE: Section 234.1 has been proclaimed in force in all provinces except British Columbia and Quebec.

Samples of breath where reasonable belief of commission of offence under s. 234 or 236

235. (1) Where a peace officer on reasonable and probable grounds believes that a person is committing, or at any time within the preceding two hours has committed, an offence under section 234 or 236, he may, by demand made to that person forthwith or as soon as practicable, require him to provide then or as soon thereafter as is practicable such samples of his breath as in the opinion of a qualified technician referred to in subsection 237(6) are necessary to enable a proper analysis to be made in order to determine the proportion, if any, of alcohol in his blood, and to accompany the peace officer for the purpose of enabling such samples to be taken.

Failure or refusal to provide sample

Type 'B' (D) Offence

(2) Every one who, without reasonable excuse, fails or refuses to comply with a demand made to him by a peace officer under subsection (1) is guilty of an indictable offence or an offence punishable on summary conviction and is liable 724(2) 740

(*a*) for a first offence, to a fine of not more than two thousand dollars and not less than fifty dollars or to imprisonment for six months or to both;

(*b*) for a second offence, to imprisonment for not more than one year and not less than fourteen days; and 591 592

(*c*) for each subsequent offence, to imprisonment for not more than two years and not less than three months.

Driving with more than 80 mgs. of alcohol in blood

Type 'B' (D) Offence

236. (1) Every one who drives a motor vehicle or has the care or control of a motor vehicle, whether it is in motion or not, having consumed alcohol in such a quantity that the proportion thereof in his blood exceeds 80 milligrams of alcohol in 100 millilitres of blood, is guilty of an indictable offence or an offence punishable on summary conviction and is liable 724(2) 740

(*a*) for a first offence, to a fine of not more than two thousand dollars and not less than fifty dollars or to imprisonment for six months or to both;

(*b*) for a second offence, to imprisonment for not more than one year and not less than fourteen days; and 591 592

(*c*) for each subsequent offence, to imprisonment for not more than two years and not less than three months.

Conditional and absolute discharge

(2) Notwithstanding subsection 662.1(1), where an accused pleads guilty to or is found guilty of an offence under subsection (1), the court before which he appears may, after hearing medical or other evidence, if it considers that the accused is in need of curative treatment in relation to his consumption of alcohol and that it would not be contrary to the public interest, instead of convicting the accused, by order direct that the accused be discharged upon conditions prescribed in a probation order, including a condition respecting his attendance 663
for curative treatment in relation to his consumption of alcohol, and the provisions of subsections 662.1(2) to (4) apply *mutatis mutandis.* 1959, c. 41, s. 15; 1968-69, c. 38, s. 16; 1974-75-76, c. 93, s. 17.

mutatis mutandis — after the necessary changes in detail so that the text applies

NOTE: Subsection 236(2) has been proclaimed in force only in the province of Alberta and the Northwest Territories.

Idem

236.1 **Where a person who is guilty of an offence under section 234, 234.1, 235 or 236 has previously been convicted of an offence under any of those sections, that conviction or those convictions shall be deemed to be, for the purpose of determining the punishment to which the person is subject under any of those sections, a first or second offence, as the case may be. 1974-75-76, c. 93, s. 17.**

724. (2) No information in respect of an offence for which, by reason of previous convictions, a greater punishment may be imposed shall contain any reference to previous convictions.

740. (1) Where a defendant is convicted of an offence for which a greater punishment may be imposed by reason of previous convictions, no greater punishment shall be imposed upon him by reason thereof unless the prosecutor satisfies the summary conviction court that the defendant, before making his plea, was notified that a greater punishment would be sought by reason thereof.

(2) Where a defendant is convicted of an offence for which a greater punishment may be imposed by reason of previous convictions, the summary conviction court shall, upon application by the prosecutor, and upon being satisfied that the defendant was notified in accordance with subsection (1), ask the defendant whether he was previously convicted, and if he does not admit that he was previously convicted, evidence of previous convictions may be adduced.

(3) A summary conviction court that holds a trial pursuant to subsection 738(3) may, if it convicts the defendant, make inquiries with respect to previous convictions, whether or not the defendant was notified that a greater punishment would be sought by reason thereof.

(4) For the purposes of this section, a previous conviction may be proved in the manner prescribed by section 594.

591. No indictment in respect of an offence for which, by reason of previous convictions, a greater punishment may be imposed shall contain any reference to previous convictions.

592. (1) Where an accused is convicted of an offence for which a greater punishment may be imposed by reason of previous convictions, no greater punishment shall be imposed upon him by reason thereof unless the prosecutor satisfies the court that the accused, before making his plea, was notified that a greater punishment would be sought by reason thereof.

(2) Where an accused is convicted of an offence for which a greater punishment may be imposed by reason of previous convictions, the court shall, upon application by the prosecutor and upon being satisfied that the accused was notified in accordance with subsection (1), ask the accused whether he was previously convicted and, if he does not admit that he was previously convicted, evidence of previous convictions may be adduced.

(3) Where, pursuant to section 551, the court proceeds with the trial of an accused corporation that has not appeared and pleaded to an indictment, the court may, if the accused is convicted, make inquiries with respect to previous convictions whether or not the accused was notified that a greater punishment would be sought by reason thereof.

Approved Instruments Order — Chapter 428

ORDER APPROVING CERTAIN INSTRUMENTS AS SUITABLE FOR THE PURPOSES OF SECTION 237 OF THE CRIMINAL CODE

Short Title

1. This Order may be cited as the *Approved Instruments Order.*

Approved Instruments

2. The following instruments, each being instruments of a kind that is designed to receive and make a chemical analysis of a sample of the breath of a person in order to measure the proportion of alcohol in the blood of that person, are hereby approved as suitable for the purposes of section 237 of the *Criminal Code:*

(a) Intoximeter Mark II;

(a.1) Intoximeter Mark IV; SI/78-23

(b) Borkenstein Breathalyzer, Rex model;

(c) Borkenstein Breathalyzer, RFL model;

(d) Borkenstein Breathalyzer, Model 800;

(e) Borkenstein Breathalyzer, Model 900; and

(f) Borkenstein Breathalyzer, Model 900A.

Approved Roadside Screening Device Order — Chapter 429

ORDER APPROVING THE ALCOHOL LEVEL EVALUATION ROADSIDE TESTER (A.L.E.R.T.) MODEL J2A-1000 AND MODEL J3A

Short Title

1. This Order may be cited as the *Approved Roadside Screening Device Order.*

Approval

2. The following devices, each being a device of a kind that is designed to ascertain the presence of alcohol in the blood of a person, are hereby approved for the purposes of section 234.1 of the *Criminal Code:*

(a) the Alcohol Level Evaluation Roadside Tester (A.L.E.R.T.) Model J2A-1000;

(b) the Alcohol Level Evaluation Roadside Tester (A.L.E.R.T.) Model J3A.

SI/78-49

—NOTES—

594. (1) In any proceedings,

(a) a certificate setting out with reasonable particularity the conviction or the conviction and sentence in Canada of a person for an indictable offence, signed by

(i) the person who made the conviction,

(ii) the clerk of the court in which the conviction was made, or

(iii) a fingerprint examiner,

is, upon proof that the accused is the person referred to in the certificate, evidence that the accused was so convicted or so convicted and sentenced without proof of the signature or the official character of the person appearing to have signed the certificate;

(b) evidence that the fingerprints of the accused are the same as the fingerprints of the person whose fingerprints are reproduced in a certificate issued under subparagraph *(a)*(iii) is, in the absence of any evidence to the contrary, proof that the accused is the person referred to in that certificate;

(c) a certificate of a fingerprint examiner stating that he has compared the fingerprints attached to that certificate with the fingerprints reproduced in a certificate issued under subparagraph *(a)*(iii) and that they are those of the same person is evidence of the statements contained in the certificate without proof of the signature or the official character of the person appearing to have signed the certificate; and

(d) a certificate under subparagraph *(a)*(iii) may be in Form 42, and a certificate under paragraph *(c)* may be in Form 43.

(2) In any proceedings, a copy of the summary conviction in Canada of an accused, signed by the person who made the conviction or by the clerk of the court in which the conviction was made, is, upon proof of the identity of the accused, evidence of the conviction of the accused without proof of the signature or the official character of the person appearing to have signed it.

(3) An accused against whom a certificate issued under subparagraph (1)*(a)*(iii) or paragraph (1)*(c)* is produced may, with leave of the court, require the attendance of the person who signed the certificate for the purposes of cross-examination.

(3.1) No certificate issued under subparagraph (1)*(a)*(iii) or paragraph (1)*(c)* shall be received in evidence unless the party intending to produce it has given to the accused reasonable notice of his intention together with a copy of the certificate.

(4) In this section "fingerprint examiner" means a person designated as such for the purposes of this section by the Solicitor General of Canada.

Proceedings under s. 234 or 236

237. (1) In any proceedings under section 234 or 236,

(a) where it is proved that the accused occupied the seat ordinarily occupied by the driver of a motor vehicle, he shall be deemed to have had the care or 2
control of the vehicle unless he establishes that he did not enter or mount the vehicle for the purpose of setting it in motion;

(b) the result of a chemical analysis of a sample of the breath of the accused (other than a sample taken pursuant to a demand made under subsection 235(1)) or of the blood, urine or other bodily substance of the accused may be admitted in evidence notwithstanding that, before he gave the sample, he was not warned that he need not give the sample or that the result of the analysis of the sample might be used in evidence;

(c) where samples of the breath of the accused have been taken pursuant to a demand made under subsection 235(1), if

(i) *(Not yet proclaimed in force)*

(ii) each sample was taken as soon as practicable after the time when the offence was alleged to have been committed and in any event not later than two hours after that time, with an interval of at least fifteen minutes between the times when the samples were taken,

(iii) each sample was received from the accused directly into an approved container or into an approved instrument operated by a qualified technician, ss. (6)
and

(iv) a chemical analysis of each sample was made by means of an approved instrument operated by a qualified technician,

evidence of the results of the chemical analyses so made is, in the absence of any evidence to the contrary, proof that the proportion of alcohol in the blood of the accused at the time when the offence was alleged to have been committed was, where the results of the analyses are the same, the proportion determined by such analyses and, where the results of the analyses are different, the lowest of the proportions determined by such analyses;

(c.1) where a sample of blood of the accused was taken, if the sample was taken as soon as practicable after the time when the offence was alleged to have been committed and in any event not later than two hours after that time, evidence of the result of a chemical analysis of the sample of blood is, in the absence of any evidence to the contrary, proof of the proportion of alcohol in the blood of the accused at the time when the offence was alleged to have been committed; 1954-65-75, c. 93, s. 18(1).

(d) a certificate of an analyst stating that he has made a chemical analysis of a sample of the blood, urine, breath or other bodily substance of the accused and stating the result of his analysis is evidence of the statements contained in the certificate without proof of the signature or the official character of the person appearing to have signed the certificate;

(e) a certificate of an analyst stating that he has made an analysis of a sample of any substance or solution intended for use in an approved instrument and identified in the certificate and that the sample analyzed by him was found to be suitable for use in an approved instrument, is evidence that the substance or solution so identified is suitable for use in an approved instrument, without proof of the signature or the official character of the person appearing to have signed the certificate; and

(*f*) where samples of the breath of the accused have been taken pursuant to a demand made under subsection 235(1), a certificate of a qualified technician stating ss. (6)

(i) that each chemical analysis of the samples has been made by means of an approved instrument operated by him in which a substance or solution suitable for use in that approved instrument and identified in the certificate was used,

(ii) the results of the chemical analyses so made, and

(iii) if the samples were taken by him,

(A) (Not yet proclaimed in force)

(B) the time when and place where each sample and any specimen described in clause (A) was taken, and

(C) that each sample was received from the accused directly into an approved container or into an approved instrument operated by the technician,

is evidence of the statements contained in the certificate without proof of the signature or the official character of the person appearing to have signed the certificate. 1974-75-76, c. 93, s. 18(2).

No obligation to give sample except as required under ss. 234.1, 235, 240.1

(2) No person is required to give a sample of blood, urine or other bodily substance for chemical analysis for the purposes of this section except breath as required under section 234.1, 235 or 240.1, and evidence that a person failed or refused to give such a sample or that such a sample was not taken is not admissible nor shall such a failure or refusal or the fact that a sample was not taken be the subject of comment by any person in the proceedings.

Evidence of failure to comply with demand where offence under s. 234 charged

(3) In any proceedings under section 234, evidence that the accused, without reasonable excuse, failed or refused to comply with a demand made to him by a peace officer under section 234.1 or subsection 235(1) is admissible and the court may draw an inference therefrom adverse to the accused.

Attendance and right to cross-examine

(4) An accused against whom a certificate described in paragraph (1)*(d)*, *(e)* or *(f)* is produced may, with leave of the court, require the attendance of the analyst or of the qualified technician, as the case may be, for the purposes of cross-examination.

Notice of intention to produce certificate

(5) No certificate shall be received in evidence pursuant to paragraph (1)*(d)*, *(e)* or *(f)* unless the party intending to produce it has, before the trial, given to the accused reasonable notice of his intention together with a copy of the certificate.

Definitions

(6) In this section

"analyst"

"analyst" means a person designated by the Attorney General as an analyst for the purposes of this section;

"approved container" (Not yet proclaimed in force)

"approved instrument"

"approved instrument" means an instrument of a kind that is designed to receive and make a chemical analysis of a sample of the breath of a person in order to measure the proportion of alcohol in the blood of that person and that is approved as suitable for the purposes of this section by order of the Attorney General of Canada;

"qualified technician"

"qualified technician" means a person designated by the Attorney General as being qualified to operate an approved instrument. 1968-69, c. 38, s. 16. 2

238. (1) Repealed, 1974-75-76, c. 93, s. 19(1).

(2) Repealed, 1974-75-76, c. 93, s. 19(1).

Driving while disqualified

Type 'B' (C) Offence

(3) Every one who drives a motor vehicle in Canada while he is disqualified or prohibited from driving a motor vehicle by reason of the legal suspension or cancellation, in any province, of his permit or licence or of his right to secure a permit or licence to drive a motor vehicle in that province is guilty of 2

(*a*) an indictable offence and is liable to imprisonment for two years; or

(*b*) an offence punishable on summary conviction. 1974-75-76, c. 93, s. 19(2). 722(1)

(3.1) Repealed, 1974-75-76, c. 93, s. 19(3).

Evidence

(4) In proceedings under subsection (3), a certificate setting out with reasonable particularity that a person is disqualified or prohibited from driving a motor vehicle in a province by reason of the suspension or cancellation of his permit or licence or of his right to secure a permit or licence, purporting to be signed by the registrar of motor vehicles for that province is evidence of the facts ss. (6) alleged therein without proof of the signature or official character of the person by whom it purports to be signed.

Notice to accused

(5) Subsection (4) does not apply in any proceedings unless at least seven 25 days notice in writing is given to the accused that it is intended to tender the Interp certificate in evidence.

"Registrar of motor vehicles" defined

(6) For the purposes of subsection (4), "registrar of motor vehicles" includes his deputy and any other person, by whatever name or title he may be designated, who from time to time performs the duties of superintending the registration of motor vehicles in the province. 1974-75-76, c. 93, s. 19(4).

2. In this Act

"Attorney General" means the Attorney General or Solicitor General of a province in which proceedings to which this Act applies are taken and, with respect to

(*a*) the Northwest Territories and the Yukon Territory, and

(*b*) proceedings instituted at the instance of the Government of Canada and conducted by or on behalf of that Government in respect of a violation of or conspiracy to violate any Act of the Parliament of Canada or a regulation made thereunder other than this Act,

means the Attorney General of Canada, and except for the purposes of subsections 505(4) and 507(3), includes the lawful deputy of the said Attorney General, Solicitor General and Attorney General of Canada;

"motor vehicle" means a vehicle that is drawn, propelled or driven by any means other than by muscular power, but does not include a vehicle of a railway that operates on rails;

Interpretation Act

25. (2) Where there is a reference to a number of clear days or "at least" a number of days between two events, in calculating the number of days there shall be excluded the days on which the events happen.

Vessel equipped with smoke screen

239. Every one who, without lawful excuse, owns or has the care, charge or control of a motor vehicle or vessel equipped with an apparatus for making a smoke screen is guilty of an offence punishable on summary conviction. 1953-54, c. 51, s. 226. 2 722(1)

722. (1) Except where otherwise expressly provided by law, every one who is convicted of an offence punishable on summary conviction is liable to a fine of not more than five hundred dollars or to imprisonment for six months or to both.

Dangerous operation of vessel, etc.
Type 'B' (D) Offence

240. (1) Every one who navigates or operates a vessel or any water skis, surf board, water sled or other towed object on or over any of the internal waters of Canada or the territorial sea of Canada, in a manner that is dangerous to navigation, life or limb, having regard to all the circumstances including the nature and condition of such waters or sea and the use that at the time is or might reasonably be expected to be made of such waters or sea, is guilty of ss. (10)

(a) an indictable offence and is liable to imprisonment for two years, or

(b) an offence punishable on summary conviction.

Failure to keep watch on person towed
Type 'A' Offence

(2) Every one who navigates or operates a vessel while towing a person on any water skis, surf board, water sled or other object, when there is not on board such vessel another responsible person keeping watch on the person being towed, is guilty of an offence punishable on summary conviction. 722(1)

Towing of person after dark
Type 'A' Offence

(3) Every one who navigates or operates a vessel while towing a person on any water skis, surf board, water sled or other object during the period from one hour after sunset to sunrise is guilty of an offence punishable on summary conviction. 722(1)

Operation of vessel while ability is impaired
Type 'A' Offence

(4) Every one who, while his ability to navigate or operate a vessel is impaired by alcohol or a drug, navigates or operates a vessel is guilty of an offence punishable on summary conviction. 722(1)

Failing to stop at scene of accident
Type 'B' (D) Offence

(5) Every one who, having the care, charge or control of a vessel that is involved in an accident with a person or another vessel in the charge of a person, with intent to escape civil or criminal liability fails to stop his vessel, give his name and address and, where any person has been injured or appears to require assistance, offer assistance, is guilty of

(a) an indictable offence and is liable to imprisonment for two years, or

(b) an offence punishable on summary conviction. 722(1)

Proof in absence of evidence to contrary

(6) In proceedings under subsection (5), evidence that an accused failed to stop his vessel, offer assistance where any person has been injured or appears to require assistance and give his name and address is, in the absence of any evidence to the contrary, proof of an intent to escape civil or criminal liability.

Order prohibiting operation of vessel

(7) Where an accused is convicted of an offence under section 203, 204, 219, subsection (1), (2), (3), (4) or (5) of this section, section 240.1 or 240.2, committed by means of a vessel, the court, judge, justice or magistrate, as the case may be, may, in addition to any other punishment that may be imposed for that offence, make an order prohibiting him from navigating or operating a vessel on or over any of the internal waters of Canada or the territorial sea of Canada at all times or at such times and places as may be specified in the order 28 Interp

(a) during any period that the court, judge, justice or magistrate considers proper, if he is liable to imprisonment for life in respect of that offence, or

(b) during any period not exceeding three years, if he is not liable to imprisonment for life in respect of that offence.

203 (Causing death by criminal negligence), 204 (Causing bodily harm by criminal negligence), 219 (Manslaughter)

Saving provision

(8) No order made under subsection (7) shall operate to prevent any person from acting as master, mate or engineer of a vessel that is required to carry officers holding certificates as master, mate or engineer.

Operating vessel while disqualified

Type 'A' Offence

(9) Every one who navigates or operates a vessel on or over any of the internal waters of Canada or the territorial sea of Canada while he is prohibited from navigating or operating a vessel by reason of an order made pursuant to subsection (7) is guilty of an offence punishable on summary conviction. 722(1)

Interpretation

(10) For the purposes of this section and sections 240.1, 240.2 and 295, "vessel" includes a machine designed to derive support in the atmosphere primarily from reactions against the earth's surface of air expelled from the machine. R.S., c. C-34, s. 240; 1972, c. 13, s. 19.

Sample of breath where reasonable belief of commission of offence under s. 240(4)

240.1 (1) Where a peace officer on reasonable and probable grounds believes that a person is committing, or at any time within the preceding two hours has committed, an offence under subsection 240(4), he may, by demand made to that person forthwith or as soon as practicable, require him to provide then or as soon thereafter as is practicable such samples of his breath as in the opinion of a qualified technician referred to in subsection 237(6) are necessary to enable a proper analysis to be made in order to determine the proportion, if any, of alcohol in his blood, and to accompany the peace officer for the purpose of enabling such a sample to be taken. 1974-75-76, c. 93, s. 20.

Failure or refusal to provide sample

Type 'A' Offence

(2) Every one who, without reasonable excuse, fails or refuses to comply with a demand made to him by a peace officer under subsection (1) is guilty of an offence punishable on summary conviction. 1972, c. 13, s. 20. 722(1)

Navigating or operating a vessel with more than 80 mgs. of alcohol in blood

Type 'A' Offence

240.2 Every one who navigates or operates a vessel having consumed alcohol in such a quantity that the proportion thereof in his blood exceeds 80 milligrams of alcohol in 100 millilitres of blood, is guilty of an offence punishable on summary conviction. 1972, c. 13, s. 20.

Application of section 237

240.3 Those provisions of section 237 that are in force apply *mutatis mutandis* to any proceedings under section 240 or 240.2. 1972, c. 13, s. 20.

mutatis mutandis — after the necessary changes in detail so that the text applies

722. (1) Except where otherwise expressly provided by law, every one who is convicted of an offence punishable on summary conviction is liable to a fine of not more than five hundred dollars or to imprisonment for six months or to both.

Interpretation Act

28. In every enactment

"may" is to be construed as permissive;

Impeding attempt to save life
Type 'E' Offence

241. Every one who

(a) prevents or impedes or attempts to prevent or impede any person who is attempting to save his own life, or 24

(b) without reasonable cause prevents or impedes or attempts to prevent or impede any person who is attempting to save the life of another person,

is guilty of an indictable offence and is liable to imprisonment for ten years. 1953-54, c. 51, s. 227.

24. (1) Every one who, having an intent to commit an offence, does or omits to do anything for the purpose of carrying out his intention is guilty of an attempt to commit the offence whether or not it was possible under the circumstances to commit the offence.

(2) The question whether an act or omission by a person who has an intent to commit an offence is or is not mere preparation to commit the offence, and too remote to constitute an attempt to commit the offence, is a question of law.

Duty to safeguard opening in ice

242. (1) Every one who makes or causes to be made an opening in ice that is open to or frequented by the public is under a legal duty to guard it in a manner that is adequate to prevent persons from falling in by accident and is adequate to warn them that the opening exists.

Excavation on land

(2) Every one who leaves an excavation on land that he owns or of which he has charge or supervision is under a legal duty to guard it in a manner that is adequate to prevent persons from falling in by accident and is adequate to warn them that the excavation exists.

(3) Every one who fails to perform a duty imposed by subsection (1) or (2)

Type 'F' Offence

(a) is guilty of manslaughter, if the death of any person results therefrom;

Type 'D' Offence

(b) is guilty of an offence under subsection 245(2), if bodily harm to any person results therefrom; or

Type 'A' Offence

(c) is guilty of an offence punishable on summary conviction. 1953-54, c. 51, s. 228. 722(1)

219. Every one who commits manslaughter is guilty of an indictable offence and is liable to imprisonment for life.

Sending or taking unseaworthy ship to sea
Type 'D' Offence with consent ss. (3)

243. (1) Every one who sends or attempts to send or being the master knowingly takes a Canadian ship

(a) on a voyage from a place in Canada to any other place, whether that voyage is by sea or by coastal or inland waters, or

(b) on a voyage from a place on the inland waters of the United States to a place in Canada,

in an unseaworthy condition from any cause, and thereby endangers the life of any person, is guilty of an indictable offence and is liable to imprisonment for five years.

Defences

(2) An accused shall not be convicted of an offence under this section where he proves

(a) that he used all reasonable means to ensure that the ship was in a seaworthy state, or

(b) that to send or take the ship in that unseaworthy condition was, under the circumstances, reasonable and justifiable.

Consent of Attorney General

(3) No proceedings shall be instituted under this section without the consent in writing of the Attorney General of Canada. 1953-54, c. 51, s. 229.

Assaults

Assault

244. A person commits an assault when

(a) without the consent of another person or with consent, where it is obtained by fraud, he applies force intentionally to the person of the other, directly or indirectly;

(b) he attempts or threatens, by an act or gesture, to apply force to the person of the other, if he has or causes the other to believe upon reasonable 24
grounds that he has present ability to effect his purpose; or

(c) while openly wearing or carrying a weapon or an imitation thereof, he accosts or impedes another person and begs. 1974-75-76, c. 93, s. 21. 2

2. In this Act

"offensive weapon" or "weapon" means

(a) anything that is designed to be used as a weapon, or

(b) anything that a person uses or intends to use as a weapon, whether or not it is designed to be used as a weapon,

and, without restricting the generality of the foregoing, includes any firearm as defined in section 82;

82. (1) For the purposes of this Part,

"firearm" means any barrelled weapon from which any shot, bullet or other missile can be discharged and that is capable of causing serious bodily injury or death to a person, and includes any frame or receiver of such a barrelled weapon and anything that can be adapted for use as a firearm;

Common assaults

Type 'A' Offence

245. (1) Every one who commits a common assault is guilty of an offence punishable on summary conviction. 722(1)

727. Where a defendant is charged with common assault and, before the defendant enters upon his defence, the summary conviction court is, from the evidence, of the opinion

(a) that the assault complained of was accompanied by an attempt to commit an indictable offence other than common assault or was committed in the course of the commission of an indictable offence other than common assault, or

(b) that the defendant should, for any reason, be prosecuted by indictment,

the summary conviction court shall not adjudicate thereon, but the proceedings shall be continued as for an indictable offence and the defendant shall be informed accordingly.

Causing bodily harm

Type 'B'(D) Offence

IPA offence 178.1

(2) Every one who unlawfully causes bodily harm to any person or commits an assault that causes bodily harm to any person

(a) is guilty of an indictable offence and is liable to imprisonment for five years; or

(b) is guilty of an offence punishable on summary conviction. 1974-75-76, c. 93, s. 22. 722(1)

228. Every one who, with intent

(a) to wound, maim or disfigure any person,

(b) to endanger the life of any person, or

(c) to prevent the arrest or detention of any person,

discharges a firearm, air gun or air pistol at or causes bodily harm in any way to any person, whether or not that person is the one mentioned in paragraph *(a)*, *(b)* or *(c)*, is guilty of an indictable offence and is liable to imprisonment for fourteen years.

32. (1) Every peace officer is justified in using or in ordering the use of as much force as he believes, in good faith and on reasonable and probable grounds,

(a) is necessary to suppress a riot, and

(b) is not excessive, having regard to the danger to be apprehended from the continuance of the riot.

(2) Every one who is bound by military law to obey the command of his superior officer is justified in obeying any command given by his superior officer for the suppression of a riot unless the order is manifestly unlawful.

(3) Every one is justified in obeying an order of a peace officer to use force to suppress a riot if

(a) he acts in good faith, and

(b) the order is not manifestly unlawful.

(4) Every one who, in good faith and on reasonable and probable grounds, believes that serious mischief will result from a riot before it is possible to secure the attendance of a peace officer is justified in using as much force as he believes in good faith and on reasonable grounds,

(a) is necessary to suppress the riot, and

(b) is not excessive, having regard to the danger to be apprehended from the continuance of the riot.

(5) For the purposes of this section the question whether an order is manifestly unlawful or not is a question of law.

33. (1) Where the proclamation referred to in section 68 has been made or an offence against paragraph 69*(a)* or *(b)* has been committed, it is the duty of a peace officer and of a person who is lawfully required by him to assist, to disperse or to arrest persons who do not comply with the proclamation.

(2) No civil or criminal proceedings lie against a peace officer or a person who is lawfully required by a peace officer to assist him in respect of any death or injury that by reason of resistance is caused as a result of the performance by the peace officer or that person of a duty that is imposed by subsection (1).

(3) Nothing in this section limits or affects any powers, duties or functions that are conferred or imposed by this Act with respect to the suppression of riots.

34. (1) Every one who is unlawfully assaulted without having provoked the assault is justified in repelling force by force if the force he uses is not intended to cause death or grievous bodily harm and is no more than is necessary to enable him to defend himself.

(2) Every one who is unlawfully assaulted and who causes death or grievous bodily harm in repelling the assault is justified if

(a) he causes it under reasonable apprehension of death or grievous bodily harm from the violence with which the assault was originally made or with which the assailant pursues his purposes, and

(b) he believes, on reasonable and probable grounds, that he cannot otherwise preserve himself from death or grievous bodily harm.

35. Every one who has without justification assaulted another but did not commence the assault with intent to cause death or grievous bodily harm, or has without justification provoked an assault upon himself by another, may justify the use of force subsequent to the assault if

(a) he uses the force

(i) under reasonable apprehension of death or grievous bodily harm from the violence of the person whom he has assaulted or provoked, and

(ii) in the belief, on reasonable and probable grounds, that it is necessary in order to preserve himself from death or grievous bodily harm;

(b) he did not, at any time before the necessity of preserving himself from death or grievous bodily harm arose, endeavour to cause death or grievous bodily harm; and

(c) he declined further conflict and quitted or retreated from it as far as it was feasible to do so before the necessity of preserving himself from death or grievous bodily harm arose.

36. Provocation includes, for the purposes of sections 34 and 35, provocation by blows, words or gestures.

37. (1) Every one is justified in using force to defend himself or any one under his protection from assault, if he uses no more force than is necessary to prevent the assault or the repetition of it.

(2) Nothing in this section shall be deemed to justify the wilful infliction of any hurt or mischief that is excessive, having regard to the nature of the assault that the force used was intended to prevent.

38. (1) Every one who is in peaceable possession of movable property, and every one lawfully assisting him, is justified

(a) in preventing a trespasser from taking it, or

(b) in taking it from a trespasser who has taken it,

if he does not strike or cause bodily harm to the trespasser.

(2) Where a person who is in peaceable possession of movable property lays hands upon it, a trespasser who persists in attempting to keep it or take it from him or from any one lawfully assisting him shall be deemed to commit an assault without justification or provocation.

39. (1) Every one who is in peaceable possession of movable property under a claim of right, and every one acting under his authority is protected from criminal responsibility for defending that possession, even against a person entitled by law to possession of it, if he uses no more force than is necessary.

(2) Every one who is in peaceable possession of movable property, but does not claim it as of right or does not act under the authority of a person who claims it as of right, is not justified or protected from criminal responsibility for defending his possession against a person who is entitled by law to possession of it.

40. Every one who is in peaceable possession of a dwelling-house, and every one lawfully assisting him or acting under his authority, is justified in using as much force as is necessary to prevent any person from forcibly breaking into or forcibly entering the dwelling-house without lawful authority.

41. (1) Every one who is in peaceable possession of a dwelling-house or real property and every one lawfully assisting him or acting under his authority is justified in using force to prevent any person from trespassing on the dwelling-house or real property, or to remove a trespasser therefrom, if he uses no more force than is necessary.

(2) A trespasser who resists an attempt by a person who is in peaceable possession of a dwelling-house or real property or a person lawfully assisting him or acting under his authority to prevent his entry or to remove him, shall be deemed to commit an assault without justification or provocation.

42. (1) Every one is justified in peaceably entering a dwelling-house or real property by day to take possession of it if he, or some person under whose authority he acts, is lawfully entitled to possession of it.

(2) Where a person

(a) not having peaceable possession of a dwelling-house or real property under a claim of right, or

(b) not acting under the authority of a person who has peaceable possession of a dwelling-house or real property under claim of right,

assaults a person who is lawfully entitled to possession of it and who is entering it peaceably by day to take possession of it, for the purpose of preventing him from entering, the assault shall be deemed to be without justification or provocation.

(3) Where a person

(a) having peaceable possession of a dwelling-house or real property under a claim of right, or

(b) acting under the authority of a person who has peaceable possession of a dwelling-house or real property under a claim of right,

assaults any person who is lawfully entitled to possession of it and who is entering it peaceably by day to take possession of it, for the purpose of preventing him from entering, the assault shall be deemed to be provoked by the person who is entering.

Assault with intent
Type 'D' Offence

246. (1) Every one who assaults a person with intent to commit an indictable offence is guilty of an indictable offence and is liable to imprisonment for five years.

230. Every one who, with intent to enable or assist himself or another person to commit an indictable offence,

(a) attempts, by any means, to choke, suffocate or strangle another person, or by any means calculated to choke, suffocate or strangle, attempts to render another person insensible, unconscious or incapable of resistance, or

(b) administers, or causes to be administered to any person, or attempts to administer to any person, or causes or attempts to cause any person to take a stupefying or overpowering drug, matter or thing,

is guilty of an indictable offence and is liable to imprisonment for life.

Other assaults
Type 'B' (D) Offence

(2) Every one who

(a) assaults a public officer or peace officer engaged in the execution of his duty, or a person acting in aid of such an officer; 2

(b) assaults a person with intent to resist or prevent the lawful arrest or detention of himself or another person; or

(c) assaults a person

(i) who is engaged in the lawful execution of a process against lands or goods or in making a lawful distress or seizure, or

(ii) with intent to rescue anything taken under a lawful process, distress or seizure,

is guilty of

(d) an indictable offence and is liable to imprisonment for five years, or

(e) an offence punishable on summary conviction. R.S., c. C-34, s. 246; 722(1)
1972, c. 13, s. 22.

118. Every one who

(a) resists or wilfully obstructs a public officer or peace officer in the execution of his duty or any person lawfully acting in aid of such an officer,

(b) omits, without reasonable excuse, to assist a public officer or peace officer in the execution of his duty in arresting a person or in preserving the peace, after having reasonable notice that he is required to do so, or

(c) resists or wilfully obstructs any person in the lawful execution of a process against lands or goods or in making a lawful distress or seizure,

is guilty of

(d) an indictable offence and is liable to imprisonment for two years, or

(e) an offence punishable on summary conviction.

228. Every one who, with intent

(a) to wound, maim or disfigure any person,

(b) to endanger the life of any person, or

(c) to prevent the arrest or detention of any person,

discharges a firearm, air gun or air pistol at or causes bodily harm in any way to any person, whether or not that person is the one mentioned in paragraph *(a)*, *(b)* or *(c)*, is guilty of an indictable offence and is liable to imprisonment for fourteen years.

2. In this Act

"peace officer" includes

(a) a mayor, warden, reeve, sheriff, deputy sheriff, sheriff's officer and justice of the peace,

(b) a warden, deputy warden, instructor, keeper, gaoler, guard and any other officer or permanent employee of a prison,

(c) a police officer, police constable, bailiff, constable, or other person employed for the preservation and maintenance of the public peace or for the service or execution of civil process,

(d) an officer or person having the powers of a customs or excise officer when performing any duty in the administration of the *Customs Act* or the *Excise Act*,

(d.1) a person appointed or designated as a fishery officer under the *Fisheries Act* when performing any of his duties or functions pursuant to that Act,

(e) the pilot in command of an aircraft

(i) registered in Canada under regulations made under the *Aeronautics Act*, or

(ii) leased without crew and operated by a person who is qualified under regulations made under the *Aeronautics Act* to be registered as owner of an aircraft registered in Canada under those regulations,

while the aircraft is in flight, and

(f) officers and men of the Canadian Forces who are

(i) appointed for the purposes of section 134 of the *National Defence Act*, or

(ii) employed on duties that the Governor in Council, in regulations made under the *National Defence Act* for the purposes of this paragraph, has prescribed to be of such a kind as to necessitate that the officers and men performing them have the powers of peace officers;

"public officer" includes

(a) an officer of customs or excise,

(b) an officer of the Canadian Forces,

(c) an officer of the Royal Canadian Mounted Police, and

(d) any officer while he is engaged in enforcing the laws of Canada relating to revenue, customs, excise, trade or navigation;

Kidnapping and Abduction

Kidnapping — *Type 'E' Offence* — *IPA offence 178.1*

247. (1) Every one who kidnaps a person with intent

(*a*) to cause him to be confined or imprisoned against his will,

(*b*) to cause him to be unlawfully sent or transported out of Canada against his will, or

(*c*) to hold him for ransom or to service against his will,

is guilty of an indictable offence and is liable to imprisonment for life.

Forcible confinement — *Type 'D' Offence*

(2) Every one who, without lawful authority, confines, imprisons or forcibly seizes another person is guilty of an indictable offence and is liable to imprisonment for five years.

Non-resistance

(3) In proceedings under this section the fact that the person in relation to whom the offence is alleged to have been committed did not resist is not a defence unless the accused proves that the failure to resist was not caused by threats, duress, force or exhibition of force. 1953-54, c. 51, s. 233.

Abduction of female — *Type 'E' Offence*

248. Every one who takes away or detains a female person, against her will, with intent

(*a*) to marry her or to have illicit sexual intercourse with her, or

(*b*) to cause her to marry or to have illicit sexual intercourse with a male person,

is guilty of an indictable offence and is liable to imprisonment for ten years. 1953-54, c. 51, s. 234.

Abduction of female under sixteen — *Type 'D' Offence*

249. (1) Every one who, without lawful authority, takes or causes to be
taken an unmarried female person under the age of sixteen years out of the 3(1)
possession of and against the will of her parent or guardian or of any other 196
person who has lawful care or charge of her is guilty of an indictable offence and
is liable to imprisonment for five years.

Matters not material

(2) For the purpose of proceedings under this section it is not material whether

(*a*) the female person is taken with her own consent or at her own suggestion, or

(*b*) the accused believes that the female person is sixteen years of age or more. 1953-54, c. 51, s. 235.

Abduction of child under fourteen — *Type 'E' Offence*

250. (1) Every one who, with intent to deprive a parent or guardian or any
other person who has lawful care or charge of a child under the age of fourteen 196
years of the possession of that child, or with intent to steal anything on or about
the person of such a child, unlawfully

(*a*) takes or entices away or detains the child, or

(*b*) receives or harbours the child,

is guilty of an indictable offence and is liable to imprisonment for ten years.

Claim of right in good faith

(2) This section does not apply to a person who, claiming in good faith a right to possession of a child, obtains possession of the child. 1953-54, c. 51, s. 236.

3. (1) For the purposes of this Act a person shall be deemed to have been of a given age when the anniversary of his birthday, the number of which corresponds to that age, is fully completed, and until then to have been under that age.

585. (1) In any proceedings to which this Act applies an entry or record of an incorporated society or its officers who have had the control or care of a child or young person at or about the time the child or young person was brought to Canada is evidence of the age of the child or young person if the entry or record was made before the time when the offence is alleged to have been committed.

(2) In the absence of other evidence, or by way of corroboration of other evidence, a jury, judge, justice or magistrate, as the case may be, may infer the age of a child or young person from his appearance.

196. In this Part

"child" includes an adopted child and an illegitimate child;

"guardian" includes a person who has in law or in fact the custody or control of a child.

Canada Evidence Act

4. (2) The wife or husband of a person charged with an offence against section 33 or 34 of the *Juvenile Delinquents Act* or with an offence against any of sections 143 to 146, 148, 150 to 155, 157, 166 to 169, 175, 195, 197, 200, 248 to 250, 255 to 258, 289, paragraph 423(1)(*c*) or an attempt to commit an offence under section 146 or 155 of the *Criminal Code,* is a competent and compellable witness for the prosecution without the consent of the person charged.

Abortion

Procuring miscarriage
Type 'E' Offence

251. (1) Every one who, with intent to procure the miscarriage of a female person, whether or not she is pregnant, uses any means for the purpose of carrying out his intention is guilty of an indictable offence and is liable to imprisonment for life. ss. (3) 26(6) Interp

Woman procuring her own miscarriage
Type 'D' Offence

(2) Every female person who, being pregnant, with intent to procure her own miscarriage, uses any means or permits any means to be used for the purpose of carrying out her intention is guilty of an indictable offence and is liable to imprisonment for two years. ss. (3)

"Means"

(3) In this section, "means" includes

(a) the administration of a drug or other noxious thing,

(b) the use of an instrument, and

(c) manipulation of any kind.

Exceptions

(4) Subsections (1) and (2) do not apply to

(a) a qualified medical practitioner, other than a member of a therapeutic abortion committee for any hospital, who in good faith uses in an accredited or approved hospital any means for the purpose of carrying out his intention to procure the miscarriage of a female person, or ss. (6) ss. (6) ss. (6)

(b) a female person who, being pregnant, permits a qualified medical practitioner to use in an accredited or approved hospital any means described in paragraph *(a)* for the purpose of carrying out her intention to procure her own miscarriage,

if, before the use of those means, the therapeutic abortion committee for that accredited or approved hospital, by a majority of the members of the committee and at a meeting of the committee at which the case of such female person has been reviewed,

(c) has by certificate in writing stated that in its opinion the continuation of the pregnancy of such female person would or would be likely to endanger her life or health, and

(d) has caused a copy of such certificate to be given to the qualified medical practitioner.

Information requirement

(5) The Minister of Health of a province may by order ss. (6)

(a) require a therapeutic abortion committee for any hospital in that province, or any member thereof, to furnish to him a copy of any certificate described in paragraph (4)*(c)* issued by that committee, together with such other information relating to the circumstances surrounding the issue of that certificate as he may require, or

(b) require a medical practitioner who, in that province, has procured the miscarriage of any female person named in a certificate described in paragraph (4)*(c)*, to furnish to him a copy of that certificate, together with such other information relating to the procuring of the miscarriage as he may require.

Interpretation Act

26. (6) Words importing male persons include female persons and corporations.

Definitions

(6) For the purposes of subsections (4) and (5) and this subsection

"accredited hospital"

"accredited hospital" means a hospital accredited by the Canadian Council on Hospital Accreditation in which diagnostic services and medical, surgical and obstetrical treatment are provided;

"approved hospital"

"approved hospital" means a hospital in a province approved for the purposes of this section by the Minister of Health of that province;

"board"

"board" means the board of governors, management or directors, or the trustees, commission or other person or group of persons having the control and management of an accredited or approved hospital;

"Minister of Health"

"Minister of Health" means

(a) in the Provinces of Ontario, Quebec, New Brunswick, Manitoba, Newfoundland and Prince Edward Island, the Minister of Health,

(a.1) in the Province of Alberta, the Minister of Hospitals and Medical Care, 1974-75-76, c. 93, s. 22.1.

(b) in the Province of British Columbia, the Minister of Health Services and Hospital Insurance,

(c) in the Provinces of Nova Scotia and Saskatchewan, the Minister of Public Health, and

(d) in the Yukon Territory and the Northwest Territories, the Minister of National Health and Welfare;

"qualified medical practitioner"

"qualified medical practitioner" means a person entitled to engage in the practice of medicine under the laws of the province in which the hospital referred to in subsection (4) is situated;

"therapeutic abortion committee"

"therapeutic abortion committee" for any hospital means a committee, comprised of not less than three members each of whom is a qualified medical practitioner, appointed by the board of that hospital for the purpose of considering and determining questions relating to terminations of pregnancy within that hospital.

Requirement of consent not affected

(7) Nothing in subsection (4) shall be construed as making unnecessary the obtaining of any authorization or consent that is or may be required, otherwise than under this Act, before any means are used for the purpose of carrying out an intention to procure the miscarriage of a female person. 1953-54, c. 51, s. 237; 1968-69, c. 38, s. 18.

Supplying noxious things

252. Every one who unlawfully supplies or procures a drug or other noxious thing or an instrument or thing, knowing that it is intended to be used or employed to procure the miscarriage of a female person, whether or not she is pregnant, is guilty of an indictable offence and is liable to imprisonment for two years. 1953-54, c. 51, s. 238.

159. (2) Every one commits an offence who knowingly, without lawful justification or excuse,

(c) offers to sell, advertises, publishes an advertisement of, or has for sale or disposal any means, instructions, medicine, drug or article intended or represented as a method of causing abortion or miscarriage, or

165. Every one who commits an offence under section 159, 161, 162, 163 or 164 is guilty of

(a) an indictable offence and is liable to imprisonment for two years, or

(b) an offence punishable on summary conviction.

Venereal Diseases

Venereal disease *Type 'A' Offence*

253. (1) Every one who, having venereal disease in a communicable form, communicates it to another person is guilty of an offence punishable on summary conviction. ss. (4) 722(1)

Defence

(2) No person shall be convicted of an offence under this section where he proves that he had reasonable grounds to believe and did believe that he did not have venereal disease in a communicable form at the time the offence is alleged to have been committed.

Corroboration

(3) No person shall be convicted of an offence under this section upon the evidence of only one witness, unless the evidence of that witness is corroborated in a material particular by evidence that implicates the accused.

"Venereal disease"

(4) For the purposes of this section, "venereal disease" means syphilis, gonorrhea or soft chancre. 1953-54, c. 51, s. 239.

159. (2) Every one commits an offence who knowingly, without lawful justification or excuse,

(d) advertises or publishes an advertisement of any means, instructions, medicine, drug or article intended or represented as a method for restoring sexual virility or curing venereal diseases or diseases of the generative organs.

Offences Against Conjugal Rights

Bigamy

254. (1) Every one commits bigamy who

(a) in Canada,

(i) being married, goes through a form of marriage with another person, 196

(ii) knowing that another person is married, goes through a form of marriage with that person, or

(iii) on the same day or simultaneously, goes through a form of marriage with more than one person; or

(b) being a Canadian citizen resident in Canada leaves Canada with intent to do anything mentioned in subparagraphs *(a)*(i) to (iii) and, pursuant thereto, does outside Canada anything mentioned in those subparagraphs in circumstances mentioned therein.

Matters of defence

(2) No person commits bigamy by going through a form of marriage if

(a) that person in good faith and on reasonable grounds believes that his spouse is dead, 26(6) Interp

(b) the spouse of that person has been continuously absent from him for seven years immediately preceding the time when he goes through the form of marriage, unless he knew that his spouse was alive at any time during those seven years,

(c) that person has been divorced from the bond of the first marriage, or

(d) the former marriage has been declared void by a court of competent jurisdiction.

Incompetency no defence

(3) Where a person is alleged to have committed bigamy, it is not a defence that the parties would, if unmarried, have been incompetent to contract marriage under the law of the place where the offence is alleged to have been committed.

Validity presumed

(4) Every marriage or form of marriage shall, for the purpose of this section, be deemed to be valid unless the accused establishes that it was invalid.

Act or omission by accused

(5) No act or omission on the part of an accused who is charged with bigamy invalidates a marriage or form of marriage that is otherwise valid. 1953-54, c. 51, s. 240.

196. In this Part

"form of marriage" includes a ceremony of marriage that is recognized as valid

(a) by the law of the place where it was celebrated, or

(b) by the law of the place where an accused is tried, notwithstanding that it is not recognized as valid by the law of the place where it was celebrated;

Interpretation Act

26. (6) Words importing male persons include female persons and corporations.

Type 'D' Offence

255. (1) Every one who commits bigamy is guilty of an indictable offence and is liable to imprisonment for five years.

Certificate of marriage

(2) For the purposes of this section a certificate of marriage issued under the authority of law is evidence of the marriage or form of marriage to which it relates without proof of the signature or official character of the person by whom it purports to be signed. 1953-54, c. 51, s. 241; 1968-69, c. 38, s. 92.

Procuring feigned marriage

Type 'D' Offence

256. (1) Every male person who

(a) procures, or

(b) knowingly aids in procuring,

a feigned marriage betweeen himself and a female person is guilty of an indictable offence and is liable to imprisonment for five years.

Corroboration

(2) No person shall be convicted of an offence under this section upon the evidence of only one witness unless the evidence of that witness is corroborated in a material particular by evidence that implicates the accused. 1953-54, c.51, s. 242.

Canada Evidence Act

4. (2) The wife or husband of a person charged with an offence against section 33 or 34 of the *Juvenile Delinquents Act* or with an offence against any of sections 143 to 146, 148, 150 to 155, 157, 166 to 169, 175, 195, 197, 200, 248 to 250, 255 to 258, 289, paragraph 423(1)*(c)* or an attempt to commit an offence under section 146 or 155 of the *Criminal Code,* is a competent and compellable witness for the prosecution without the consent of the person charged.

Polygamy

Type 'D' Offence

257. (1) Every one who

(a) practises or enters into or in any manner agrees or consents to practise or enter into

(i) any form of polygamy, or

(ii) any kind of conjugal union with more than one person at the same time,

whether or not it is by law recognized as a binding form of marriage; or

(b) celebrates, assists or is a party to a rite, ceremony, contract or consent that purports to sanction a relationship mentioned in subparagraph *(a)*(i) or (ii),

is guilty of an indictable offence and is liable to imprisonment for five years.

Evidence in case of polygamy

(2) Where an accused is charged with an offence under this section, no averment or proof of the method by which the alleged relationship was entered into, agreed to or consented to is necessary in the indictment or upon the trial of the accused, nor is it necessary upon the trial to prove that the persons who are alleged to have entered into the relationship had or intended to have sexual intercourse. 1953-54, c. 51, s. 243.

Canada Evidence Act

4. (2) The wife or husband of a person charged with an offence against section 33 or 34 of the *Juvenile Delinquents Act* or with an offence against any of sections 143 to 146, 148, 150 to 155, 157, 166 to 169, 175, 195, 197, 200, 248 to 250, 255 to 258, 289, paragraph 423(1)*(c)* or an attempt to commit an offence under section 146 or 155 of the *Criminal Code*, is a competent and compellable witness for the prosecution without the consent of the person charged.

Unlawful Solemnization of Marriage

Pretending to solemnize marriage

Type 'D' Offence

258. Every one who

(a) solemnizes or pretends to solemnize a marriage without lawful authority, the proof of which lies upon him, or

(b) procures a person to solemnize a marriage knowing that he is not lawfully authorized to solemnize the marriage,

is guilty of an indictable offence and is liable to imprisonment for two years. 1953-54, c. 51, s. 244.

Marriage contrary to law

Type 'D' Offence

259. Every one who, being lawfully authorized to solemnize marriage, knowingly and wilfully solemnizes a marriage in violation of the laws of the province in which the marriage is solemnized is guilty of an indictable offence and is liable to imprisonment for two years. 1953-54, c. 51, s. 245. 28 Interp

Interpretation Act

28. In every enactment

"province" means a province of Canada, and includes the Yukon Territory and the Northwest Territories;

Blasphemous Libel

Type 'D' Offence

260. (1) Every one who publishes a blasphemous libel is guilty of an indictable offence and is liable to imprisonment for two years.

Question of fact

(2) It is a question of fact whether or not any matter that is published is a blasphemous libel.

Saving

(3) No person shall be convicted of an offence under this section for expressing in good faith and in decent language, or attempting to establish by argument used in good faith and conveyed in decent language, an opinion upon a religious subject. 1953-54, c. 51, s. 246.

513. (1) No count for publishing a blasphemous, seditious or defamatory libel, or for selling or exhibiting an obscene book, pamphlet, newspaper or other written matter, is insufficient by reason only that it does not set out the words that are alleged to be libellous or the writing that is alleged to be obscene.

(2) A count for publishing a libel may charge that the published matter was written in a sense that by innuendo made the publication thereof criminal, and may specify that sense without any introductory assertion to show how the matter was written in that sense.

(3) It is sufficient, on the trial of a count for publishing a libel, to prove that the matter published was libellous, with or without innuendo.

Defamatory Libel

"Newspaper"

261. In sections 262 to 281, "newspaper" means any paper, magazine or periodical containing public news, intelligence or reports of events, or any remarks or observations thereon, printed for sale and published periodically or in parts or numbers, at intervals not exceeding thirty-one days between the publication of any two such papers, parts or numbers, and any paper, magazine or periodical printed in order to be dispersed and made public, weekly or more often, or at intervals not exceeding thirty-one days, that contains advertisements, exclusively or principally. 1953-54, c. 51, s. 247.

Definition

262. (1) A defamatory libel is matter published, without lawful justification or excuse, that is likely to injure the reputation of any person by exposing him to hatred, contempt or ridicule, or that is designed to insult the person of or concerning whom it is published.

Mode of expression

(2) A defamatory libel may be expressed directly or by insinuation or irony

(a) in words legibly marked upon any substance, or

(b) by any object signifying a defamatory libel otherwise than by words. 1953-54, c. 51, s. 248.

Publishing

263. A person publishes a libel when he

(a) exhibits it in public,

(b) causes it to be read or seen, or

(c) shows or delivers it, or causes it to be shown or delivered, with intent that it should be read or seen by the person whom it defames or by any other person. 1953-54, c. 51, s. 249.

Punishment of libel known to be false

Type 'D' Offence

264. Every one who publishes a defamatory libel that he knows is false is guilty of an indictable offence and is liable to imprisonment for five years. 1953-54, c. 51, s. 250.

Punishment for defamatory libel
Type 'D' Offence

265. Every one who publishes a defamatory libel is guilty of an indictable offence and is liable to imprisonment for two years. 1953-54, c. 51, c. 251.

Extortion by libel

266. (1) Every one commits an offence who, with intent

(a) to extort money from any person, or

(b) to induce a person to confer upon or procure for another person an appointment or office of profit or trust,

publishes or threatens to publish or offers to abstain from publishing or to prevent the publication of a defamatory libel.

Idem

(2) Every one commits an offence who, as the result of the refusal of any person to permit money to be extorted or to confer or procure an appointment or office of profit or trust, publishes or threatens to publish a defamatory libel.

Type 'D' Offence

(3) Every one who commits an offence under this section is guilty of an indictable offence and is liable to imprisonment for five years. 1953-54, c. 51, s. 252.

51. Intimidating Parliament or legislature
114. Influencing or negotiating appointments or dealing in offices
305. Extortion
381. Intimidation

Proprietor of newspaper presumed responsible

267. (1) The proprietor of a newspaper shall be deemed to publish defamatory matter that is inserted and published therein, unless he proves that the defamatory matter was inserted in the newspaper without his knowledge and without negligence on his part.

General authority to manager when negligence

(2) Where the proprietor of a newspaper gives to a person general authority to manage or conduct the newspaper as editor or otherwise, the insertion by that person of defamatory matter in the newspaper shall, for the purposes of subsection (1), be deemed not to be negligence on the part of the proprietor unless it is proved that

(a) he intended the general authority to include authority to insert defamatory matter in the newspaper, or

(b) he continued to confer general authority after he knew that it had been exercised by the insertion of defamatory matter in the newspaper.

Selling newspapers

(3) No person shall be deemed to publish a defamatory libel by reason only that he sells a number or part of a newspaper that contains a defamatory libel, unless he knows that the number or part contains defamatory matter or that defamatory matter is habitually contained in the newspaper. 1953-54,c.51,s.253.

Selling book containing defamatory libel

268. (1) No person shall be deemed to publish a defamatory libel by reason only that he sells a book, magazine, pamphlet or other thing, other than a newspaper that contains defamatory matter if, at the time of the sale, he does not know that it contains the defamatory matter.

Sale by servant

(2) Where a servant, in the course of his employment, sells a book, magazine, pamphlet or other thing, other than a newspaper, the employer shall be deemed not to publish any defamatory matter contained therein unless it is proved that the employer authorized the sale knowing that

(a) defamatory matter was contained therein, or

(b) defamatory matter was habitually contained therein, in the case of a periodical. 1953-54, c. 51, s. 254.

Publishing proceedings of courts of justice

269. No person shall be deemed to publish a defamatory libel by reason only that he publishes defamatory matter

(a) in a proceeding held before or under the authority of a court exercising judicial authority, or

(b) in an inquiry made under the authority of an Act or by order of Her Majesty, or under the authority of a public department or a department of the government of a province. 1953-54, c. 51, s. 255.

Parliamentary papers

270. No person shall be deemed to publish a defamatory libel by reason only that he

(a) publishes to the Senate or House of Commons or to a legislature, defamatory matter contained in a petition to the Senate or House of Commons or to the legislature, as the case may be,

(b) publishes by order or under the authority of the Senate or House of Commons or of a legislature, a paper containing defamatory matter, or

(c) publishes, in good faith and without ill-will to the person defamed, an extract from or abstract of a petition or paper mentioned in paragraph *(a)* or *(b)*. 1953-54, c. 51, s. 256.

Fair reports of parliamentary or judicial proceedings

271. (1) No person shall be deemed to publish a defamatory libel by reason only that he publishes in good faith, for the information of the public, a fair report of the proceedings of the Senate or House of Commons or a legislature, 28 Interp
or a committee thereof, or of the public proceedings before a court exercising judicial authority, or publishes, in good faith, any fair comment upon any such proceedings.

Divorce proceedings an exception

(2) This section does not apply to a person who publishes a report of evidence taken or offered in any proceeding before the Senate or House of Commons or any committee thereof, upon a petition or bill relating to any matter of marriage or divorce, if the report is published without authority from or leave of the House in which the proceeding is held or is contrary to any rule, order or practice of that House. 1953-54, c. 51, s. 257.

Fair report of public meeting

272. No person shall be deemed to publish a defamatory libel by reason only that he publishes in good faith, in a newspaper, a fair report of the proceedings of any public meeting if

(a) the meeting is lawfully convened for a lawful purpose and is open to the public,

(b) the report is fair and accurate,

(c) the publication of the matter complained of is for the public benefit, and

(d) he does not refuse to publish in a conspicuous place in the newspaper a reasonable explanation or contradiction by the person defamed in respect of the defamatory matter. 1953-54, c. 51, s. 258.

Public benefit

273. No person shall be deemed to publish a defamatory libel by reason only that he publishes defamatory matter that, on reasonable grounds, he believes is true, and that is relevant to any subject of public interest, the public discussion of which is for the public benefit. 1953-54, c. 51, s. 259.

Fair comment on public person or work of art

274. No person shall be deemed to publish a defamatory libel by reason only that he publishes fair comments

(a) upon the public conduct of a person who takes part in public affairs, or

(b) upon a published book or other literary production, or on any composition or work of art or performance publicly exhibited, or on any other communication made to the public on any subject, if the comments are confined to criticism thereof. 1953-54, c. 51, s. 260.

When truth a defence

275. No person shall be deemed to publish a defamatory libel where he proves that the publication of the defamatory matter in the manner in which it was published was for the public benefit at the time when it was published and that the matter itself was true. 1953-54, c. 51, s. 261.

434. (2) Every proprietor, publisher, editor or other person charged with the publication of a defamatory libel in a newspaper or with conspiracy to publish a defamatory libel in a newspaper shall be dealt with, indicted, tried and punished in the province where he resides or in which the newspaper is printed.

535. (2) An accused who is charged with defamatory libel may plead in accordance with sections 539 and 540.

539. (1) An accused who is charged with publishing a defamatory libel may plead that the defamatory matter published by him was true, and that it was for the public benefit that the matter should have been published in the manner in which and at the time when it was published.

(2) A plea that is made under subsection (1) may justify the defamatory matter in any sense in which it is specified in the count, or in the sense that the defamatory matter bears without being specified, or separate pleas justifying the defamatory matter in each sense may be pleaded separately to each count as if two libels had been charged in separate counts.

(3) A plea that is made under subsection (1) shall be in writing, and shall set out the particular facts by reason of which it is alleged to have been for the public good that the matter should have been published.

(4) The prosecutor may in his reply deny generally the truth of a plea that is made under this section.

540. (1) The truth of the matters charged in an alleged libel shall not be inquired into in the absence of a plea of justification under section 539 unless the accused is charged with publishing the libel knowing it to be false, in which case evidence of the truth may be given to negative the allegation that the accused knew that the libel was false.

(2) The accused may, in addition to a plea that is made under section 539, plead not guilty and the pleas shall be inquired into together.

(3) Where a plea of justification is pleaded and the accused is convicted, the court may, in pronouncing sentence, consider whether the guilt of the accused is aggravated or mitigated by the plea.

566. A prosecutor other than the Attorney General or counsel acting on his behalf is not entitled, on the trial of an indictment for the publication of a defamatory libel, to direct a juror to stand by.

Publication invited or necessary

276. No person shall be deemed to publish a defamatory libel by reason only that he publishes defamatory matter

(a) on the invitation or challenge of the person in respect of whom it is published, or

(b) that it is necessary to publish in order to refute defamatory matter published in respect of him by another person,

if he believes that the defamatory matter is true and it is relevant to the invitation, challenge or necessary refutation, as the case may be, and does not in any respect exceed what is reasonably sufficient in the circumstances. 1953-54, c. 51, s. 262.

Answer to inquiries

277. No person shall be deemed to publish a defamatory libel by reason only that he publishes, in answer to inquiries made to him, defamatory matter relating to a subject-matter in respect of which the person by whom or on whose behalf the inquiries are made has an interest in knowing the truth or who, on reasonable grounds, the person who publishes the defamatory matter believes has such an interest, if

(a) the matter is published, in good faith, for the purpose of giving information in answer to the inquiries,

(b) the person who publishes the defamatory matter believes that it is true,

(c) the defamatory matter is relevant to the inquires, and

(d) the defamatory matter does not in any respect exceed what is reasonably sufficient in the circumstances. 1953-54, c. 51, s. 263.

Giving information to person interested

278. No person shall be deemed to publish a defamatory libel by reason only that he publishes to another person defamatory matter for the purpose of giving information to that person with respect to a subject-matter in which the person to whom the information is given has, or is believed on reasonable grounds by the person who gives it to have, an interest in knowing the truth with respect to that subject-matter if

(a) the conduct of the person who gives the information is reasonable in the circumstances,

(b) the defamatory matter is relevant to the subject-matter, and

(c) the defamatory matter is true, or if it is not true, is made without ill-will toward the person who is defamed and is made in the belief, on reasonable grounds, that it is true. 1953-54, c. 51, s. 264.

Publication in good faith for redress of wrong

279. No person shall be deemed to publish a defamatory libel by reason only that he publishes defamatory matter in good faith for the purpose of seeking remedy or redress for a private or public wrong or grievance from a person who has, or who on reasonable grounds he believes has the right or is under an obligation to remedy or redress the wrong or grievance, if

(a) he believes that the defamatory matter is true,

(b) the defamatory matter is relevant to the remedy or redress that is sought, and

(c) the defamatory matter does not in any respect exceed what is reasonably sufficient in the circumstances. 1953-54, c. 51, s. 265.

Proving publication by order of legislature

280. (1) An accused who is alleged to have published a defamatory libel may, at any stage of the proceedings, adduce evidence to prove that the matter that is alleged to be defamatory was contained in a paper published by order or under the authority of the Senate or House of Commons or a legislature.

Directing verdict

(2) Where at any stage in proceedings referred to in subsection (1) the court, judge, justice or magistrate is satisfied that matter alleged to be defamatory was contained in a paper published by order or under the authority of the Senate or House of Commons or a legislature, he shall direct a verdict of not guilty to be entered and shall discharge the accused.

Certificate of order

(3) For the purposes of this section a certificate under the hand of the Speaker or clerk of the Senate or House of Commons or a legislature to the effect that the matter that is alleged to be defamatory was contained in a paper published by order or under the authority of the Senate, House of Commons or legislature, as the case may be, is conclusive evidence thereof. 1953-54,c.51,s.266.

Verdicts

Verdicts in cases of defamatory libel

281. Where, on the trial of an indictment for publishing a defamatory libel, a plea of not guilty is pleaded, the jury that is sworn to try the issue may give a general verdict of guilty or not guilty upon the whole matter put in issue upon the indictment, and shall not be required or directed by the judge to find the defendant guilty merely on proof of publication by the defendant of the alleged defamatory libel, and of the sense ascribed thereto in the indictment, but the judge may, in his discretion, give a direction or opinion to the jury on the matter in issue as in other criminal proceedings, and the jury may, on the issue, find a special verdict. 1953-54, c. 51, s. 267.

656. The person in whose favour judgment is given in proceedings by indictment for defamatory libel is entitled to recover from the opposite party costs in a reasonable amount to be fixed by order of the court.

657. Where costs that are fixed under section 656 are not paid forthwith the party in whose favour judgment is given may enter judgment for the amount of the costs by filing the order in the superior court of the province in which the trial was held, and that judgment is enforceable against the opposite party in the same manner as if it were a judgment rendered against him in that court in civil proceedings.

Hate Propaganda

Advocating genocide

Type 'D' Offence with consent ss. (3)

IPA offence 178.1

281.1 (1) Every one who advocates or promotes genocide is guilty of an indictable offence and is liable to imprisonment for five years.

"Genocide"

(2) In this section "genocide" means any of the following acts committed with intent to destroy in whole or in part any identifiable group, namely: ss. (4)

(a) killing members of the group, or

(b) deliberately inflicting on the group conditions of life calculated to bring about its physical destruction.

Consent

(3) No proceedings for an offence under this section shall be instituted without the consent of the Attorney General. 2

2. In this Act

"Attorney General" means the Attorney General or Solicitor General of a province in which proceedings to which this Act applies are taken and, with respect to

(a) the Northwest Territories and the Yukon Territory, and

(b) proceedings instituted at the instance of the Government of Canada and conducted by or on behalf of that Government in respect of a violation of or conspiracy to violate any Act of the Parliament of Canada or a regulation made thereunder other than this Act,

means the Attorney General of Canada, and except for the purposes of subsections 505(4) and 507(3), includes the lawful deputy of the said Attorney General, Solicitor General and Attorney General of Canada;

"Identifiable group"

(4) In this section "identifiable group" means any section of the public distinguished by colour, race, religion or ethnic origin. R.S., c. 11(1st Supp.),s.1.

Public incitement of hatred

Type 'B' (D) Offence

281.2 (1) Every one who, by communicating statements in any public place, incites hatred against any identifiable group where such incitement is likely to lead to a breach of the peace, is guilty of ss. (7) 281.1(4)

(a) an indictable offence and is liable to imprisonment for two years; or

(b) an offence punishable on summary conviction. 722(1)

Wilful promotion of hatred

Type 'B' (D) Offence with consent ss. (6)

(2) Every one who, by communicating statements, other than in private conversation, wilfully promotes hatred against any identifiable group is guilty of

(a) an indictable offence and is liable to imprisonment for two years; or

(b) an offence punishable on summary conviction. 722(1)

Defences

(3) No person shall be convicted of an offence under subsection (2)

(a) if he establishes that the statements communicated were true;

(b) if, in good faith, he expressed or attempted to establish by argument an opinion upon a religious subject;

(c) if the statements were relevant to any subject of public interest, the discussion of which was for the public benefit, and if on reasonable grounds he believed them to be true; or

(d) if, in good faith, he intended to point out, for the purpose of removal, matters producing or tending to produce feelings of hatred towards an identifiable group in Canada.

Forfeiture

(4) Where a person is convicted of an offence under section 281.1 or subsection (1) or (2) of this section, anything by means of or in relation to which the offence was committed, upon such conviction, may, in addition to any other punishment imposed, be ordered by the presiding magistrate or judge to be forfeited to Her Majesty in right of the province in which that person is convicted, for disposal as the Attorney General may direct. 2

Exemption from seizure of communication facilities

(5) Subsections 181(6) and (7) apply *mutatis mutandis* to section 281.1 or subsection (1) or (2) of this section.

181. (6) Nothing in this section or in section 445 authorizes the seizure, forfeiture or destruction of telephone, telegraph or other communication facilities or equipment that may be evidence of or that may have been used in the commission of an offence under section 185, 186, 187, 189, 190 or 193 and that is owned by a person engaged in providing telephone, telegraph or other communication service to the public or forming part of the telephone, telegraph or other communication service or system of such a person.

(7) Subsection (6) does not apply to prohibit the seizure, for use as evidence, of any facility or equipment described in that subsection that is designed or adapted to record a communication.

Consent

(6) No proceeding for an offence under subsection (2) shall be instituted without the consent of the Attorney General.

Definitions

(7) In this section

"communicating"

"communicating" includes communicating by telephone, broadcasting or other audible or visible means; 28 Interp

"identifiable group"

"identifiable group" has the same meaning as it has in section 281.1;

"public place"

"public place" includes any place to which the public have access as of right or by invitation, express or implied;

"statements"

"statements" includes words spoken or written or recorded electronically or electromagnetically or otherwise, and gestures, signs or other visible representations. R.S., c. 11(1st Supp.), s. 1.

Warrant of seizure

281.3 (1) A judge who is satisfied by information upon oath that there are reasonable grounds for believing that any publication, copies of which are kept for sale or distribution in premises within the jurisdiction of the court, is hate propaganda, shall issue a warrant under his hand authorizing seizure of the copies. ss. (8) ss. (8) ss. (8)

with consent ss. (7)

Summons to occupier

(2) Within seven days of the issue of the warrant, the judge shall issue a summons to the occupier of the premises requiring him to appear before the court and show cause why the matter seized should not be forfeited to Her Majesty. 28 Interp

Owner and author may appear

(3) The owner and the author of the matter seized and alleged to be hate propaganda may appear and be represented in the proceedings in order to oppose the making of an order for the forfeiture of the said matter.

Order of forfeiture

(4) If the court is satisfied that the publication is hate propaganda, it shall make an order declaring the matter forfeited to Her Majesty in right of the province in which the proceedings take place, for disposal as the Attorney General may direct.

Disposal of matter

(5) If the court is not satisfied that the publication is hate propaganda, it shall order that the matter be restored to the person from whom it was seized forthwith after the time for final appeal has expired.

Appeal

(6) An appeal lies from an order made under subsection (4) or (5) by any person who appeared in the proceedings

(a) on any ground of appeal that involves a question of law alone,

(b) on any ground of appeal that involves a question of fact alone, or

(c) on any ground of appeal that involves a question of mixed law and fact,

as if it were an appeal against conviction or against a judgment or verdict of acquittal, as the case may be, on a question of law alone under Part XVIII, and sections 601 to 624 apply *mutatis mutandis.*

mutatis mutandis — after the necessary changes in detail so that the text applies

Consent

(7) No proceeding under this section shall be instituted without the consent of the Attorney General.

Definitions

(8) In this section

"court"

"court" means

(a) in the Province of Quebec,

(i) the court of the sessions of the peace, or

(ii) where an application has been made to a judge of the provincial court for a warrant under subsection (1), that judge;

(a.1) in the Provinces of New Brunswick, Alberta and Saskatchewan, the Court of Queen's Bench;

(b) in the Province of Prince Edward Island, the Supreme Court; or

(c) in any other province, a county or district court;

"genocide"

"genocide" has the same meaning as it has in section 281.1;

"hate propaganda"

"hate propaganda" means any writing, sign or visible representation that advocates or promotes genocide or the communication of which by any person would constitute an offence under section 281.2; 2

"judge"

"judge" means a judge of a court or, in the Province of Quebec, a judge of the provincial court. R.S., C. 11(1st Supp.), s. 1; 1974-75-76, c. 48, s. 25(1); 1978-79, c. 11, s. 10, I. 6(9).

2. In this Act

"writing" includes a document of any kind and any mode in which, and any material on which, words or figures, whether at length or abridged, are written, printed or otherwise expressed, or a map or plan is inscribed.

PART VII

OFFENCES AGAINST RIGHTS OF PROPERTY

Interpretation

Definitions

282. In this Part

"break"

"break" means

(a) to break any part, internal or external, or

(b) to open any thing that is used or intended to be used to close or to cover an internal or external opening;

"document"

"document" means any paper, parchment or other material used for writing or printing, marked with matter capable of being read, but does not include trade marks on articles of commerce or inscriptions on stone or metal or other like material;

"exchequer bill"

"exchequer bill" means a bank note, bond, note, debenture or security that is issued or guaranteed by Her Majesty under the authority of the Parliament of Canada or the legislature of a province; 2

28 Interp

"exchequer bill paper"

"exchequer bill paper" means paper that is used to manufacture exchequer bills;

"false document"

"false document" means a document

(a) the whole or some material part of which purports to be made by or on behalf of a person

(i) who did not make it or authorize it to be made, or

(ii) who did not in fact exist;

(b) that is made by or on behalf of the person who purports to make it but is false in some material particular;

(c) that is made in the name of an existing person, by him or under his authority, with a fraudulent intention that it should pass as being made by some person, real or fictitious, other than the person who makes it or under whose authority it is made;

"revenue paper"

"revenue paper" means paper that is used to make stamps, licences or permits or for any purpose connected with the public revenue. 1953-54, c. 51, s. 268.

2. In this Act

"bank-note" includes any negotiable instrument

(a) issued by or on behalf of a person carrying on the business of banking in or out of Canada,

(b) issued under the authority of the Parliament of Canada or under lawful authority of the government of a state other than Canada,

intended to be used as money or as the equivalent of money, immediately upon issue or at some time subsequent thereto, and includes bank bills and bank post bills;

Interpretation Act

28. In every enactment

"legislature", "legislative council" or "legislative assembly" includes the Lieutenant Governor in Council and the Legislative Assembly of the Northwest Territories, as constituted before the 1st day of September 1905, the Commissioner in Council of the Yukon Territory, and the Commissioner in Council of the Northwest Territories;

"province" means a province of Canada, and includes the Yukon Territory and the Northwest Territories;

Theft

Theft

283. (1) Every one commits theft who fraudulently and without colour of right takes, or fraudulently and without colour of right converts to his use or to the use of another person, anything whether animate or inanimate, with intent,

(*a*) to deprive, temporarily or absolutely, the owner of it or a person who has a special property or interest in it, of the thing or of his property or interest in it,

(*b*) to pledge it or deposit it as security,

(*c*) to part with it under a condition with respect to its return that the person who parts with it may be unable to perform, or

(*d*) to deal with it in such a manner that it cannot be restored in the condition in which it was at the time it was taken or converted.

517. The real and personal property of which a person has, by law, the management, control or custody shall, for the purposes of an indictment or proceeding against any other person for an offence committed on or in respect of the property, be deemed to be the property of the person who has the management, control or custody of it.

Time when theft completed

(2) A person commits theft when, with intent to steal anything, he moves it or causes it to move or to be moved, or begins to cause it to become movable. 2

2. In this Act

"steal" means to commit theft;

Secrecy

(3) A taking or conversion of anything may be fraudulent notwithstanding that it is effected without secrecy or attempt at concealment.

Purpose of taking

(4) For the purposes of this Act the question whether anything that is converted is taken for the purpose of conversion, or whether it is, at the time it is converted, in the lawful possession of the person who converts it is not material.

Wild living creature

(5) For the purposes of this section a person who has a wild living creature in captivity shall be deemed to have a special property or interest in it while it is in captivity and after it has escaped from captivity. 1953-54, c. 51, s. 269.

Oysters

284. (1) Where oysters and oyster brood are in oyster beds, layings or fisheries that are the property of any person and are sufficiently marked out or known as the property of that person, he shall be deemed to have a special property or interest in them.

Oyster bed

(2) An indictment is sufficient if it describes an oyster bed, laying or fishery by name or in some other way, without stating that it is situated in a particular territorial division. 1953-54, c. 51, s. 270.

Theft by bailee of things under seizure

285. Every one who is a bailee of anything that is under lawful seizure by a peace officer or public officer in the execution of the duties of his office, and who is obliged by law or agreement to produce and deliver it to that officer or to another person entitled thereto at a certain time and place, or upon demand, steals it if he does not produce and deliver it in accordance with his obligation, but he does not steal it if his failure to produce and deliver it is not the result of a wilful act or omission by him. 1953-54, c. 51, s. 271. 2

2. In this Act

"public officer" includes

(a) an officer of customs or excise,

(b) an officer of the Canadian Forces,

(c) an officer of the Royal Canadian Mounted Police, and

(d) any officer while he is engaged in enforcing the laws of Canada relating to revenue, customs, excise, trade or navigation;

Agent pledging goods, when not theft

286. A factor or agent does not commit theft by pledging or giving a lien on goods or documents of title to goods that are entrusted to him for the purpose of sale or for any other purpose, if the pledge or lien is for an amount that does not exceed the sum of 2

(a) the amount due to him from his principal at the time the goods or documents are pledged or the lien is given, and

(b) the amount of any bill of exchange that he has accepted for or on account of his principal. 1953-54, c. 51, s. 272.

2. In this Act

"document of title to goods" includes a bought and sold note, bill of lading, warrant, certificate or order for the delivery or transfer of goods or any other valuable thing, and any other document used in the ordinary course of business as evidence of the possession or control of goods, authorizing or purporting to authorize, by endorsement or by delivery, the person in possession of the document to transfer or receive any goods thereby represented or therein mentioned or referred to;

Theft of telecommunication service

287. (1) Every one commits theft who fraudulently, maliciously, or without colour of right,

(a) abstracts, consumes or uses electricity or gas or causes it to be wasted or diverted, or

(b) uses any telecommunication facility or obtains any telecommunication service. ss. (2)

"Telecommunication" defined

(2) In this section and in section 287.1, "telecommunication" means any transmission, emission or reception of signs, signals, writing, images, sounds or intelligence of any nature by radio, visual, electronic or other electromagnetic system. 1974-75-76, c. 93, s. 23(1) and (2). 2

2. In this Act

"writing" includes a document of any kind and any mode in which, and any material on which, words or figures, whether at length or abridged, are written, printed or otherwise expressed, or a map or plan is inscribed.

Possession of device to obtain telecommunication facility or service

Type 'D' Offence

287.1 (1) Every one who, without lawful excuse, the proof of which lies upon him, manufactures, possesses, sells or offers for sale or distributes any instrument or device or any component thereof, the design of which renders it primarily useful for obtaining the use of any telecommunication facility or service, under circumstances that give rise to a reasonable inference that the device has been used or is or was intended to be used to obtain the use of any telecommunication facility or service without payment of a lawful charge therefor, is guilty of an indictable offence and liable to imprisonment for two years. 287(2)

Forfeiture

(2) Where a person is convicted of an offence under subsection (1) or paragraph 287(1)*(b)*, any instrument or device in relation to which the offence was committed or the possession of which constituted the offence, upon such conviction, in addition to any punishment that is imposed, may be ordered forfeited to Her Majesty whereupon it may be disposed of as the Attorney General directs.

Limitation

(3) No order for forfeiture shall be made under subsection (2) in respect of telephone, telegraph or other communication facilities or equipment owned by a person engaged in providing telephone, telegraph or other communication service to the public or forming part of the telephone, telegraph or other communication service or system of such a person by means of which an offence under subsection (1) has been committed if such person was not a party to the offence. 1974-75-76, c. 93, s. 24.

Theft by or from person having special property or interest

288. A person may be convicted of theft notwithstanding that anything that is alleged to have been stolen was stolen

(a) by the owner of it from a person who has a special property or interest in it;

(b) by a person who has a special property or interest in it from the owner of it;

(c) by a lessee of it from his reversioner;

(d) by one of several joint owners, tenants in common or partners of or in it from the other persons who have an interest in it; or

(e) by the directors, officers or members of a company, body corporate, unincorporated body or of a society associated together for a lawful purpose from the company, body corporate, unincorporated body or society, as the case may be. 1953-54, c. 51, s. 274.

Husband or wife

289. (1) Subject to subsection (2), no husband or wife, during cohabitation, commits theft of anything that is by law the property of the other.

Theft by spouse while living apart

(2) A husband or wife commits theft who, intending to desert or on deserting the other or while living apart from the other, fraudulently takes or converts anything that is by law the property of the other in a manner that, if it were done by another person, would be theft.

Assisting or receiving

(3) Every one commits theft who, during cohabitation of a husband and wife, knowingly,

(a) assists either of them in dealing with anything that is by law the property of the other in a manner that would be theft if they were not married, or

(b) receives from either of them anything that is by law the property of the other and has been obtained from the other by dealing with it in a manner that would be theft if they were not married. 1953-54, c. 51, s. 275.

Canada Evidence Act

4. (2) The wife or husband of a person charged with an offence against section 33 or 34 of the *Juvenile Delinquents Act* or with an offence against any of sections 143 to 146, 148, 150 to 155, 157, 166 to 169, 175, 195, 197, 200, 248 to 250, 255 to 258, 289, paragraph 423(1)(*c*) or an attempt to commit an offence under section 146 or 155 of the *Criminal Code,* is a competent and compellable witness for the prosecution without the consent of the person charged.

Theft by person required to account

290. (1) Every one commits theft who, having received anything from any person on terms that require him to account for or pay it or the proceeds of it or a part of the proceeds to that person or another person, fraudulently fails to account for or pay it or the proceeds of it or the part of the proceeds of it accordingly.

Effect of entry in account

(2) Where subsection (1) otherwise applies, but one of the terms is that the thing received or the proceeds or part of the proceeds of it shall be an item in a debtor and creditor account between the person who receives the thing and the person to whom he is to account for or to pay it, and that the latter shall rely only on the liability of the other as his debtor in respect thereof, a proper entry in that account of the thing received or the proceeds or part of the proceeds of it, as the case may be, is a sufficient accounting therefor, and no fraudulent conversion of the thing or the proceeds or part of the proceeds of it thereby accounted for shall be deemed to have taken place. 1953-54, c. 51, s. 276.

Theft by person holding power of attorney

291. Every one commits theft who, being entrusted, whether solely or jointly with another person, with a power of attorney for the sale, mortgage, pledge or other disposition of real or personal property, fraudulently sells, mortgages, pledges or otherwise disposes of the property or any part of it, or fraudulently converts the proceeds of a sale, mortgage, pledge or other disposition of the property, or any part of the proceeds, to some purpose other than that for which he was entrusted by the power of attorney. 1953-54, c. 51, s. 277.

Misappropriation of money held under direction

292. (1) Every one commits theft who, having received, either solely or jointly with another person, money or valuable security or a power of attorney 2
for the sale of real or personal property, with a direction that the money or 2
a part of it, or the proceeds or a part of the proceeds of the security or the property shall be applied to a purpose or paid to a person specified in the direction, fraudulently and contrary to the direction applies to any other purpose or pays to any other person the money or proceeds or any part of it.

Effect of entry in account

(2) This section does not apply where a person who receives anything mentioned in subsection (1) and the person from whom he receives it deal with each other on such terms that all money paid to the former would, in the absence of any such direction, be properly treated as an item in a debtor and creditor account between them, unless the direction is in writing. 1953-54, c. 51, s. 278.

2. In this Act

"property" includes

(a) real and personal property of every description and deeds and instruments relating to or evidencing the title or right to property, or giving a right to recover or receive money or goods,

(b) property originally in the possession or under the control of any person, and any property into or for which it has been converted or exchanged and anything acquired at any time by such conversion or exchange, and

(c) any postal card, postage stamp or other stamp issued or prepared for issue under the authority of the Parliament of Canada or of the legislature of a province for the payment to the Crown or a corporate body of any fee, rate or duty, whether or not it is in the possession of the Crown or of any person;

3. (2) For the purposes of this Act a postal card or stamp referred to in paragraph *(c)* of the definition "property" in section 2 shall be deemed to be a chattel, and to be equal in value to the amount of the postage, rate or duty expressed on its face.

2. In this Act

"valuable security" includes

(a) an order, exchequer acquittance or other security that entitles or evidences the title of any person

(i) to a share or interest in a public stock or fund or in any fund of a body corporate, company or society, or

(ii) to a deposit in a savings bank or other bank,

(b) a debenture, deed, bond, bill, note, warrant, order or other security for money or for payment of money,

(c) a document of title to lands or goods wherever situated,

(d) a stamp or writing that secures or evidences title to or an interest in a chattel personal, or that evidences delivery of a chattel personal, and

(e) a release, receipt, discharge or other instrument evidencing payment of money;

3. (3) For the purposes of this Act, the following rules apply for the purpose of determining the value of a valuable security where value is material, namely,

(a) where the valuable security is one mentioned in paragraph *(a)* or *(b)* of the definition "valuable security" in section 2, the value is the value of the share, interest, deposit or unpaid money, as the case may be, that is secured by the valuable security;

(b) where the valuable security is one mentioned in paragraph *(c)* or *(d)* of the definition "valuable security" in section 2, the value is the value of the lands, goods, chattel personal or interest in the chattel personal, as the case may be; and

(c) where the valuable security is one mentioned in paragraph *(e)* of the definition "valuable security" in section 2, the value is the amount of money that has been paid.

Taking ore for scientific purposes

293. No person commits theft by reason only that he takes, for the purpose of exploration or scientific investigation, a specimen of ore or mineral from land that is not enclosed and is not occupied or worked as a mine, quarry or digging. 1953-54, c. 51, s. 279.

583. In any proceeding in respect of theft of ores or minerals, the possession, contrary to any law in that behalf, of smelted gold or silver, gold-bearing quartz, or unsmelted or unmanufactured gold or silver, by an operator, workman or labourer actively engaged in or on a mine, is, in the absence of any evidence to the contrary, proof that the gold, silver or quartz was stolen by him.

Punishment for theft

294. Except where otherwise provided by law, every one who commits theft

Type 'E' Offence

IPA offence 178.1

(a) is guilty of an indictable offence and is liable to imprisonment for ten years, where the property stolen is a testamentary instrument or where the value of what is stolen exceeds two hundred dollars; or 2

Type 'B' (C) Offence

(b) is guilty

(i) of an indictable offence and is liable to imprisonment for two years, or

All Attempted Theft is a Type 'C' Offence 483(b)

(ii) of an offence punishable on summary conviction,

where the value of what is stolen does not exceed two hundred dollars. 1974-75-76, c. 93, s. 25.

2. In this Act

"testamentary instrument" includes any will, codicil or other testamentary writing or appointment, as well during the life of the testator whose testamentary disposition it purports to be as after his death, whether it relates to real or personal property, or to both;

300. Every one who, for a fraudulent purpose, destroys, cancels, conceals or obliterates

(a) a document of title to goods or lands,

(b) a valuable security or testamentary instrument, or

(c) a judicial or official document,

is guilty of an indictable offence and is liable to imprisonment for ten years.

485. (1) Where in any proceedings under this Part an accused is before a magistrate and it appears to the magistrate that for any reason the charge should be prosecuted by indictment, he may, at any time before the accused has entered upon his defence, decide not to adjudicate and shall thereupon inform the accused of his decision and continue the proceedings as a preliminary inquiry.

(2) Where an accused is before a magistrate charged with an offence mentioned in paragraph 483*(a)*, and, at any time before the magistrate makes an adjudication, the evidence establishes that the value of what was stolen, obtained, had in possession or attempted to be obtained, as the case may be, exceeds two hundred dollars, the magistrate shall put the accused to his election in accordance with subsection 484(2).

(3) Where an accused is put to his election pursuant to subsection (2), the following provisions apply, namely,

(a) if the accused does not elect to be tried by a magistrate, the magistrate shall continue the proceedings as a preliminary inquiry under Part XV, and, if he commits the accused for trial, he shall comply with paragraphs 484(3)*(a)* and *(b)*; and

(b) if the accused elects to be tried by a magistrate, the magistrate shall endorse on the information a record of the election and continue with the trial.

517. The real and personal property of which a person has, by law, the management, control or custody shall, for the purposes of an indictment or proceeding against any other person for an offence committed on or in respect of the property, be deemed to be the property of the person who has the management, control or custody of it.

Offences Resembling Theft

Taking motor vehicle or vessel without consent
Type 'A' Offence

295. Every one who, without the consent of the owner, takes a motor vehicle or vessel with intent to drive, use, navigate or operate it or cause it to be driven, used, navigated or operated is guilty of an offence punishable on summary conviction. R.S., c. C-34, s. 295; 1972, c. 13, s. 23. 2 239(10)

2. In this Act

"motor vehicle" means a vehicle that is drawn, propelled or driven by any means other than by muscular power, but does not include a vehicle of a railway that operates on rails;

240. (10) For the purposes of this section and sections 240.1, 240.2 and 295, "vessel" includes a machine designed to derive support in the atmosphere primarily from reactions against the earth's surface of air expelled from the machine.

Criminal breach of trust
Type 'E' Offence

296. Every one who, being a trustee of anything for the use or benefit, whether in whole or in part, of another person, or for a public or charitable purpose, converts, with intent to defraud and in violation of his trust, that thing or any part of it to a use that is not authorized by the trust is guilty of an indictable offence and is liable to imprisonment for fourteen years. 1953-54, c. 51, s. 282. 2

2. In this Act

"trustee" means a person who is declared by any Act to be a trustee or is, by the law of the province, a trustee, and without restricting the generality of the foregoing, includes a trustee on an express trust created by deed, will or instrument in writing, or by parol;

Public servant refusing to deliver property
Type 'E' Offence

297. Every one who, being or having been employed in the service of Her Majesty in right of Canada or in right of a province, or in the service of a municipality, and entrusted by virtue of that employment with the receipt, custody, management or control of anything, refuses or fails to deliver it to a person who is authorized to demand it and does demand it, is guilty of an indictable offence and is liable to imprisonment for fourteen years. 1953-54, c. 51, s. 283. 28 Interp 2

2. In this Act

"municipality" includes the corporation of a city, town, village, county, township, parish or other territorial or local division of a province, the inhabitants of which are incorporated or are entitled to hold property collectively for a public purpose;

Fraudulently taking cattle or defacing brand

Type 'D' Offence

298. (1) Every one who, without the consent of the owner,

(a) fraudulently takes, holds, keeps in his possession, conceals, receives, appropriates, purchases or sells, cattle that are found astray, or 3(4) 2

(b) fraudulently, in whole or in part,

(i) obliterates, alters or defaces, a brand or mark on cattle, or

(ii) makes a false or counterfeit brand or mark on cattle,

is guilty of an indictable offence and is liable to imprisonment for five years.

Punishment for theft of cattle

Type 'E' Offence

(1.1) Every one who commits theft of cattle is guilty of an indictable offence and is liable to imprisonment for ten years. 1974-75-76, c. 93, s. 26(1).

Evidence of property in cattle

(2) In any proceedings under this Act, evidence that cattle are marked with a brand or mark that is recorded or registered in accordance with any Act is, in the absence of any evidence to the contrary, proof that the cattle are owned by the registered owner of that brand or mark. 2

Presumption from possession

(3) Where an accused is charged with an offence under subsection (1) or (1.1), the burden of proving that the cattle came lawfully into the possession of the accused or his employee or into the possession of another person on behalf of the accused is on the accused, if the accused is not the registered owner of the brand or mark with which the cattle are marked, unless it appears that possession of the cattle by an employee of the accused or by another person on behalf of the accused was without the knowledge and authority, sanction or approval of the accused. 1953-54, c. 51, s. 284; 1968-69, c. 38, s. 92; 1974-75-76, c. 93, s. 26(2)

2. In this Act

"Act" includes

(a) an Act of the Parliament of Canada,

(b) an Act of the legislature of the former Province of Canada,

(c) an Act of the legislature of a province, and

(d) an Act or ordinance of the legislature of a province, territory or place in force at the time that province, territory or place became a province of Canada;

"cattle" means neat cattle or an animal of the bovine species by whatever technical or familiar name it is known, and includes a horse, mule, ass, pig, sheep or goat;

3. (4) For the purposes of this Act,

(a) a person has anything in possession when he has it in his personal possession or knowingly

(i) has it in the actual possession or custody of another person, or

(ii) has it in any place, whether or not that place belongs to or is occupied by him, for the use or benefit of himself or of another person; and

(b) where one of two or more persons, with the knowledge and consent of the rest, has anything in his custody or possession, it shall be deemed to be in the custody and possession of each and all of them.

Taking possession etc., of drift timber

Type 'D' Offence

299. (1) Every one is guilty of an indictable offence and is liable to imprisonment for five years who, without the consent of the owner,

(*a*) fraudulently takes, holds, keeps in his possession, conceals, receives, appropriates, purchases or sells, 3(4)

(*b*) removes, alters, obliterates or defaces a mark or number on, or

(*c*) refuses to deliver up to the owner or to the person in charge thereof on behalf of the owner or to a person authorized by the owner to receive it,

any lumber or lumbering equipment that is found adrift, cast ashore or lying upon or embedded in the bed or bottom, or on the bank or beach of a river, stream or lake in Canada, or in the harbours or any of the coastal waters of Canada. ss. (6)

Dealer in second-hand goods

Type 'A' Offence

(2) Every one who, being a dealer in second-hand goods of any kind, trades or traffics in or has in his possession for sale or traffic any lumbering equipment that is marked with the mark, brand, registered timber mark, name or initials of a person, without the written consent of that person, is guilty of an offence punishable on summary conviction.

Search for timber unlawfully detained

(3) A peace officer who suspects, on reasonable grounds, that any lumber owned by any person and bearing the registered timber mark of that person is kept or detained in or on any place without the knowledge or consent of that person, may enter into or upon that place to ascertain whether or not it is detained there without the knowledge or consent of that person. 2

Evidence of property in timber

(4) Where any lumber or lumbering equipment is marked with a timber mark or a boom chain brand registered under any Act, the mark or brand is, in proceedings under subsection (1), and, in the absence of any evidence to the contrary, proof that it is the property of the registered owner of the mark or brand.

Presumption from possession

(5) Where an accused or his servants or agents are in possession of lumber or lumbering equipment marked with the mark, brand, registered timber mark, name or initials of another person, the burden of proving that it came lawfully into his possession or into possession of his servants or agents is, in proceedings under subsection (1), on the accused.

Definitions

(6) In this section

"coastal waters of Canada"

"coastal waters of Canada" includes all of Queen Charlotte Sound, all the Strait of Georgia and the Canadian waters of the Strait of Juan de Fuca;

"lumber"

"lumber" means timber, mast, spar, shingle bolt, sawlog or lumber of any description;

"lumbering equipment"

"lumbering equipment" includes a boom chain, chain, line and shackle. 1953-54, c. 51, s. 285; 1968-69, c. 38, s. 92.

Destroying documents of title

Type 'E' Offence

300. Every one who, for a fraudulent purpose, destroys, cancels, conceals or obliterates

(a) a document of title to goods or lands, 2

(b) a valuable security or testamentary instrument, or 2

(c) a judicial or official document,

is guilty of an indictable offence and is liable to imprisonment for ten years. 1953-54, c. 51, s. 286.

2. In this Act

"document of title to goods" includes a bought and sold note, bill of lading, warrant, certificate or order for the delivery or transfer of goods or any other valuable thing, and any other document used in the ordinary course of business as evidence of the possession or control of goods, authorizing or purporting to authorize, by endorsement or by delivery, the person in possession of the document to transfer or receive any goods thereby represented or therein mentioned or referred to;

"document of title to lands" includes any writing that is or contains evidence of the title, or any part of the title to real property, or to any interest in real property, and any notarial or registrar's copy thereof, and any duplicate instrument, memorial, certificate or document authorized or required by any law in force in any part of Canada with respect to registration of titles, that relates to title to real property or to an interest in real property;

"testamentary instrument" includes any will, codicil or other testamentary writing or appointment, as well during the life of the testator whose testamentary disposition it purports to be as after his death, whether it relates to real or personal property, or to both;

"valuable security" includes

(a) an order, exchequer acquittance or other security that entitles or evidences the title of any person

(i) to a share or interest in a public stock or fund or in any fund of a body corporate, company or society, or

(ii) to a deposit in a savings bank or other bank,

(b) a debenture, deed, bond, bill, note, warrant, order or other security for money or for payment of money,

(c) a document of title to lands or goods wherever situated,

(d) a stamp or writing that secures or evidences title to or an interest in a chattel personal, or that evidences delivery of a chattel personal, and

(e) a release, receipt, discharge or other instrument evidencing payment of money;

3. (3) For the purposes of this Act, the following rules apply for the purpose of determining the value of a valuable security where value is material, namely,

(a) where the valuable security is one mentioned in paragraph *(a)* or *(b)* of the definition "valuable security" in section 2, the value is the value of the share, interest, deposit or unpaid money, as the case may be, that is secured by the valuable security;

(b) where the valuable security is one mentioned in paragraph *(c)* or *(d)* of the definition "valuable security" in section 2, the value is the value of the lands, goods, chattel personal or interest in the chattel personal, as the case may be; and

(c) where the valuable security is one mentioned in paragraph *(e)* of the definition "valuable security" in section 2, the value is the amount of money that has been paid.

Fraudulent concealment

Type 'D' Offence

301. Every one who, for a fraudulent purpose, takes, obtains, removes or conceals anything is guilty of an indictable offence and is liable to imprisonment for two years. 1953-54, c. 51, s. 287.

Theft, forgery, etc., of credit card

301.1 (1) Every one who

(a) steals a credit card, ss. (3)

(b) forges or falsifies a credit card, 324

(c) has in his possession, uses or deals in any other way with a credit card that he knows was obtained 3(4)

(i) by the commission in Canada of an offence, or

(ii) by an act or omission anywhere that, if it had occurred in Canada, would have constituted an offence, or

(d) uses a credit card that he knows has been revoked or cancelled

is guilty of

Type 'B' (E) Offence

(e) an indictable offence and is liable to imprisonment for ten years, or

(f) an offence punishable on summary conviction. 722(1)

Jurisdiction

(2) Where a person is alleged to have committed an offence under subsection (1), the offence is within the competence of and may be tried and punished by the court having jurisdiction in respect of similar offences in the territorial division where he is found in the same manner as if the offence had been committed in that territorial division or where he is alleged to have committed the offence.

"Credit card" defined

(3) For the purposes of this section, "credit card" means any card, plate, coupon book or other device issued or otherwise distributed for the purpose of being used upon presentation to obtain on credit money, goods, services or any other thing of value. 1974-75-76, c. 93, s. 27.

324. (1) Every one commits forgery who makes a false document, knowing it to be false, with intent

(a) that it should in any way be used or acted upon as genuine, to the prejudice of any one whether within Canada or not, or

(b) that some person should be induced, by the belief that it is genuine, to do or to refrain from doing anything, whether within Canada or not.

(2) Making a false document includes

(a) altering a genuine document in any material part,

(b) making a material addition to a genuine document or adding to it a false date, attestation, seal or other thing that is material, or

(c) making a material alteration in a genuine document by erasure, obliteration, removal or in any other way.

(3) Forgery is complete as soon as a document is made with the knowledge and intent referred to in subsection (1), notwithstanding that the person who makes it does not intend that any particular person should use or act upon it as genuine or be induced, by the belief that it is genuine, to do or refrain from doing anything.

(4) Forgery is complete notwithstanding that the false document is incomplete or does not purport to be a document that is binding in law, if it is such as to indicate that it was intended to be acted upon as genuine.

Robbery and Extortion

Robbery

302. Every one commits robbery who

(a) steals, and for the purpose of extorting whatever is stolen or to prevent or overcome resistence to the stealing, uses violence or threats of violence to a person or property; 2

(b) steals from any person and, at the time he steals or immediately before or immediately thereafter, wounds, beats, strikes or uses any personal violence to that person;

(c) assaults any person with intent to steal from him; or 244

(d) steals from any person while armed with an offensive weapon or imitation thereof. 1953-54, c. 51, s. 288. 2

Type 'E' Offence

IPA offence 178.1

303. Every one who commits robbery is guilty of an indictable offence and is liable to imprisonment for life. R.S., c. C-34, s. 303; 1972, c. 13, s. 70. 669

2. In this Act

"steal" means to commit theft;

"offensive weapon" or "weapon" means

(a) anything that is designed to be used as a weapon, or

(b) anything that a person uses or intends to use as a weapon, whether or not it is designed to be used as a weapon,

and, without restricting the generality of the foregoing, includes any firearm as defined in section 82;

82. (1) For the purposes of this Part,

"firearm" means any barrelled weapon from which any shot, bullet or other missile can be discharged and that is capable of causing serious bodily injury or death to a person, and includes any frame or receiver of such a barrelled weapon and anything that can be adapted for use as a firearm;

244. A person commits an assault when

(a) without the consent of another person or with consent, where it is obtained by fraud, he applies force intentionally to the person of the other, directly or indirectly;

(b) he attempts or threatens, by an act or gesture, to apply force to the person of the other, if he has or causes the other to believe upon reasonable grounds that he has present ability to effect his purpose; or

(c) while openly wearing or carrying a weapon or an imitation thereof, he accosts or impedes another and begs.

83. (1) Every one who uses a firearm

(a) while committing or attempting to commit an indictable offence, or

(b) during his flight after committing or attempting to commit an indictable offence,

whether or not he causes or means to cause bodily harm to any person as a result thereof, is guilty of an indictable offence and is liable to imprisonment

(c) in the case of a first offence under this subsection, except as provided in paragraph *(d)*, for not more than fourteen years and not less than one year; and

(d) in the case of a second or subsequent offence under this subsection, or in the case of a first such offence committed by a person who, prior to the coming into force of this subsection, was convicted of an indictable offence or an attempt to commit an indictable offence, in the course of which or during his flight after the commission or attempted commission of which he used a firearm, for not more than fourteen years and not less than three years.

(2) A sentence imposed on a person for an offence under subsection (1) shall be served consecutively to any other punishment imposed on him for an offence arising out of the same event or series of events and to any other sentence to which he is subject at the time the sentence is imposed on him for an offence under subsection (1).

Stopping mail with intent

Type 'E' Offence

304. Every one who stops a mail conveyance with intent to rob or search it is guilty of an indictable offence and is liable to imprisonment for life. 1953-54, c. 51, s. 290. 699

Section 314 — Theft from mail

Extortion

Type 'E' Offence

IPA offence 178.1

305. (1) Every one who, without reasonable justification or excuse and with intent to extort or gain anything, by threats, accusations, menaces or violence induces or attempts to induce any person, whether or not he is the person threatened, accused or menaced or to whom violence is shown, to do anything or cause anything to be done, is guilty of an indictable offence and is liable to imprisonment for fourteen years. 24

(2) A threat to institute civil proceedings is not a threat for the purposes of this section. 1953-54, c. 51, s. 291.

24. (1) Every one who, having an intent to commit an offence, does or omits to do anything for the purpose of carrying out his intention is guilty of an attempt to commit the offence whether or not it was possible under the circumstances to commit the offence.

(2) The question whether an act or omission by a person who has an intent to commit an offence is or is not mere preparation to commit the offence, and too remote to constitute an attempt to commit the offence, is a question of law.

266. (1) Every one commits an offence who, with intent

(a) to extort money from any person, or

(b) to induce a person to confer upon or procure for another person an appointment or office of profit or trust,

publishes or threatens to publish or offers to abstain from publishing or to prevent the publication of a defamatory libel.

(2) Every one commits an offence who, as the result of the refusal of any person to permit money to be extorted or to confer or procure an appointment or office of profit or trust, publishes or threatens to publish a defamatory libel.

(3) Every one who commits an offence under this section is guilty of an indictable offence and is liable to imprisonment for five years.

381. (1) Every one who, wrongfully and without lawful authority, for the purpose of compelling another person to abstain from doing anything that he has a lawful right to do, or to do anything that he has a lawful right to abstain from doing,

(a) uses violence or threats of violence to that person or to his wife or children, or injures his property,

(b) intimidates or attempts to intimidate that person or a relative of that person by threats that, in Canada or elsewhere, violence or other injury will be done to or punishment inflicted upon him or a relative of his, or that the property of any of them will be damaged,

(c) persistently follows that person about from place to place,

(d) hides any tools, clothes or other property owned or used by that person, or deprives him of them or hinders him in the use of them,

(e) with one or more other persons follows that person, in a disorderly manner, on a highway,

(f) besets or watches the dwelling-house or place where that person resides, works, carries on business or happens to be, or

(g) blocks or obstructs a highway,

is guilty of an offence punishable on summary conviction.

(2) A person who attends at or near or approaches a dwelling-house or place, for the purpose only of obtaining or communicating information, does not watch or beset within the meaning of this section.

Breaking and Entering

Breaking and entering with intent, committing offence or breaking out

Type 'E' Offence

IPA offence 178.1

306. (1) Every one who

(a) breaks and enters a place with intent to commit an indictable offence therein, 282 308 ss. (4)

(b) breaks and enters a place and commits an indictable offence therein, or

(c) breaks out of a place after

(i) committing an indictable offence therein, or

(ii) entering the place with intent to commit an indictable offence therein,

is guilty of an indictable offence and is liable

(d) to imprisonment for life, if the offence is committed in relation to a dwelling-house, or 669 2

(e) to imprisonment for fourteen years, if the offence is committed in relation to a place other than a dwelling-house.

(2) For the purposes of proceedings under this section, evidence that an accused

(a) broke and entered a place is, in the absence of any evidence to the contrary, proof that he broke and entered with intent to commit an indictable offence therein; or

(b) broke out of a place is, in the absence of any evidence to the contrary, proof that he broke out after

(i) committing an indictable offence therein, or

(ii) entering with intent to commit an indictable offence therein.

(3) Repealed. 1972, c. 13, s. 24.

(4) For the purposes of this section,

"place" means

(a) a dwelling-house;

(b) a building or structure or any part thereof, other than a dwelling-house;

(c) a railway vehicle, vessel, aircraft or trailer; or

(d) a pen or enclosure in which fur-bearing animals are kept in captivity for breeding or commercial purposes. R.S., c. C-34, s. 306; 1972, c. 13, s. 24.

2. In this Act

"dwelling-house" means the whole or any part of a building or structure that is kept or occupied as a permanent or temporary residence and includes

(a) a building within the curtilage of a dwelling-house that is connected to it by a doorway or by a covered and enclosed passageway, and

(b) a unit that is designed to be mobile and to be used as a permanent or temporary residence and that is being used as such a residence;

282. In this Part

"break" means

(a) to break any part, internal or external, or

(b) to open any thing that is used or intended to be used to close or to cover an internal or external opening;

Being unlawfully in dwelling-house
Type 'E' Offence

307. (1) Every one who without lawful excuse, the proof of which lies upon him, enters or is in a dwelling-house with intent to commit an indictable offence therein is guilty of an indictable offence and is liable to imprisonment for ten years. 308 2

Presumption

(2) For the purposes of proceedings under this section, evidence that an accused, without lawful excuse, entered or was in a dwelling-house is, in the absence of any evidence to the contrary, proof that he entered or was in the dwelling-house with intent to commit an indictable offence therein. 1953-54, c. 51, s. 293; 1968-69, c. 38, s. 92.

Entrance

308. For the purposes of sections 306 and 307,

(a) a person enters as soon as any part of his body or any part of an instrument that he uses is within any thing that is being entered; and

(b) a person shall be deemed to have broken and entered if

(i) he obtained entrance by a threat or artifice or by collusion with a person within, or

(ii) he entered without lawful justification or excuse, the proof of which lies upon him, by a permanent or temporary opening. 1953-54, c. 51, s. 294.

Possession of house-breaking instruments under suspicious circumstances
Type 'E' Offence

309. (1) Every one who, without lawful excuse, the proof of which lies upon him, has in his possession any instrument suitable for house-breaking, vault-breaking or safe-breaking, under circumstances that give rise to a reasonable inference that the instrument has been used or is or was intended to be used for house-breaking, vault-breaking or safe-breaking, is guilty of an indictable offence and is liable to imprisonment for fourteen years. 3(4)

3. (4) For the purposes of this Act,

(a) a person has anything in possession when he has it in his personal possession or knowingly

(i) has it in the actual possession or custody of another person, or

(ii) has it in any place, whether or not that place belongs to or is occupied by him, for the use or benefit of himself or of another person; and

(b) where one of two or more persons, with the knowledge and consent of the rest, has anything in his custody or possession, it shall be deemed to be in the custody and possession of each and all of them.

Disguise with intent
Type 'E' Offence

(2) Every one who, with intent to commit an indictable offence, has his face masked or coloured or is otherwise disguised is guilty of an indictable offence and is liable to imprisonment for ten years. R.S., c. C-34, s. 309; 1972, c. 13, s. 25.

Possession of instruments for breaking into coin-operated or currency exchange devices

Type 'D' Offence

310. Every one who, without lawful excuse, the proof of which lies upon him, has in his possession any instrument suitable for breaking into a coin-operated device or a currency exchange device, under circumstances that give rise to a reasonable inference that the instrument has been used or is or was intended to be used for breaking into a coin-operated device or a currency exchange device, is guilty of an indictable offence and is liable to imprisonment for two years. 1974-75-76, c. 93, s. 28. 3(4)

Selling, etc., automobile master key

Type 'D' Offence

311. (1) Every one who

(a) sells, offers for sale or advertises in a province an automobile master key otherwise than under the authority of a licence issued by the Attorney General of that province, or ss. (5)

(b) purchases or has in his possession in a province an automobile master key otherwise than under the authority of a licence issued by the Attorney General of that province,

is guilty of an indictable offence and is liable to imprisonment for two years.

Terms and conditions of licence

(2) A licence issued by the Attorney General of a province as described in paragraph (1)*(a)* or *(b)* may contain such terms and conditions relating to the sale, offering for sale, advertising, purchasing or having in possession of an automobile master key as the Attorney General of that province may prescribe.

Record to be kept

(3) Every one who sells an automobile master key

(a) shall keep a record of the transaction showing the name and address of the purchaser and particulars of the licence issued to the purchaser as described in paragraph (1)*(b)*, and

(b) shall produce such record for inspection at the request of a peace officer. 2

Failure to comply with ss. (3)

Type 'A' Offence

(4) Every one who fails to comply with subsection (3) is guilty of an offence punishable on summary conviction.

"Automobile master key"

(5) For the purposes of this section, "automobile master key" includes a key, pick, rocker key or other instrument designed or adapted to operate the ignition or other switches or locks of a series of motor vehicles. 1968-69, c. 38, s. 19. 2

2. In this Act

"motor vehicle" means a vehicle that is drawn, propelled or driven by any means other than by muscular power, but does not include a vehicle of a railway that operates on rails;

Having in Possession

3. (4) For the purposes of this Act,

(a) a person has anything in possession when he has it in his personal possession or knowingly

(i) has it in the actual possession or custody of another person, or

(ii) has it in any place, whether or not that place belongs to or is occupied by him, for the use or benefit of himself or of another person; and

(b) where one of two or more persons, with the knowledge and consent of the rest, has anything in his custody or possession, it shall be deemed to be in the custody and possession of each and all of them.

Possession of property obtained by crime

312. (1) Every one commits an offence who has in his possession any property or thing or any proceeds of any property or thing knowing that all or part of the property or thing or of the proceeds was obtained by or derived directly or indirectly from 316 3(4) 2

***(a)* the commission in Canada of an offence punishable by indictment; or**

***(b)* an act or omission anywhere that, if it had occurred in Canada, would have constituted an offence punishable by indictment.**

2. In this Act

"property" includes

(a) real and personal property of every description and deeds and instruments relating to or evidencing the title or right to property, or giving a right to recover or receive money or goods,

(b) property originally in the possession or under the control of any person, and any property into or for which it has been converted or exchanged and anything acquired at any time by such conversion or exchange, and

(c) any postal card, postage stamp or other stamp issued or prepared for issue under the authority of the Parliament of Canada or of the legislature of a province for the payment to the Crown or a corporate body of any fee, rate or duty, whether or not it is in the possession of the Crown or of any person;

3. (2) For the purposes of this Act a postal card or stamp referred to in paragraph *(c)* of the definition "property" in section 2 shall be deemed to be a chattel, and to be equal in value to the amount of the postage, rate or duty expressed on its face.

Obliterated vehicle identification number

(2) In proceedings in respect of an offence under subsection (1), evidence that a person has in his possession a motor vehicle the vehicle identification number of which has been wholly or partially removed or obliterated or a part of a motor vehicle being a part bearing a vehicle identification number that has been wholly or partially removed or obliterated is, in the absence of any evidence to the contrary, proof that the motor vehicle or part, as the case may be, was obtained, and that such person had the motor vehicle or part, as the case may be, in his possession knowing that it was obtained, ss. (3)

***(a)* by the commission in Canada of an offence punishable by indictment; or**

***(b)* by an act or omission anywhere that, if it had occurred in Canada, would have constituted an offence punishable by indictment.**

"Vehicle identification number" defined

(3) For the purposes of subsection (2), "vehicle identification number" means any number or other mark placed upon a motor vehicle for the purpose of distinguishing the motor vehicle from other similar motor vehicles. R.S., c. C-34, s. 312; 1972, c. 13, s. 27; 1974-75-76, c. 93, s. 29.

Punishment

Type 'E' Offence

IPA offence 178.1

313. Every one who commits an offence under section 312

(a) is guilty of an indictable offence and is liable to imprisonment for ten years, where the subject-matter of the offence is a testamentary instrument 2
or the value exceeds two hundred dollars; or

Type 'B' (C) Offence

(b) is guilty

(i) of an indictable offence and is liable to imprisonment for two years, or

(ii) of an offence punishable on summary conviction, 722(1)

where the value of what is in his possession does not exceed two hundred dollars. R.S., c. C-34, s. 313; 1972, c. 13, s. 28; 1974-75-76, c. 93, s. 30.

2. In this Act

"testamentary instrument" includes any will, codicil or other testamentary writing or appointment, as well during the life of the testator whose testamentary disposition it purports to be as after his death, whether it relates to real or personal property, or to both;

485. (1) Where in any proceedings under this Part an accused is before a magistrate and it appears to the magistrate that for any reason the charge should be prosecuted by indictment, he may, at any time before the accused has entered upon his defence, decide not to adjudicate and shall thereupon inform the accused of his decision and continue the proceedings as a preliminary inquiry.

(2) Where an accused is before a magistrate charged with an offence mentioned in paragraph 483*(a)*, and, at any time before the magistrate makes an adjudication, the evidence establishes that the value of what was stolen, obtained, had in possession or attempted to be obtained, as the case may be, exceeds two hundred dollars, the magistrate shall put the accused to his election in accordance with subsection 484(2).

(3) Where an accused is put to his election pursuant to subsection (2), the following provisions apply, namely,

(a) if the accused does not elect to be tried by a magistrate, the magistrate shall continue the proceedings as a preliminary inquiry under Part XV, and, if he commits the accused for trial, he shall comply with paragraphs 484(3)*(a)* and *(b)*; and

(b) if the accused elects to be tried by a magistrate, the magistrate shall endorse on the information a record of the election and continue with the trial.

517. The real and personal property of which a person has, by law, the management, control or custody shall, for the purposes of an indictment or proceeding against any other person for an offence committed on or in respect of the property, be deemed to be the property of the person who has the management, control or custody of it.

522. (1) Any number of persons may be charged in the same indictment with an offence under section 312 or paragraph 314(1)*(b)*, notwithstanding that

(a) the property was had in possession at different times; or

(b) the person by whom the property was obtained

(i) is not indicted with them, or

(ii) is not in custody or is not amenable to justice.

(2) Where, pursuant to subsection (1), two or more persons are charged in the same indictment with an offence referred to in that subsection, any one or more of those persons who separately committed the offence in respect of the property or any part of it may be convicted.

Theft from mail
Type 'E' Offence
IPA offence 178.1

314. (1) Every one who

(a) steals 2

(i) any thing sent by post, after it is deposited at a post office and before it is delivered,

(ii) a bag, sack or other container or covering in which mail is conveyed, whether it does or does not contain mail, or

(iii) a key suited to a lock adopted for use by the Canada Post Office, or

(b) has in his possession anything in respect of which he knows that an offence has been committed under paragraph *(a)*, 3(4)

is guilty of an indictable offence and is liable to imprisonment for ten years.

(2) In proceedings for an offence under this section it is not necessary to allege in the indictment or to prove on the trial that anything in respect of which the offence was committed had any value.

304. Every one who stops a mail conveyance with intent to rob or search it is guilty of an indictable offence and is liable to imprisonment for life.

3. (4) For the purposes of this Act,

(a) a person has anything in possession when he has it in his personal possession or knowingly

(i) has it in the actual possession or custody of another person, or

(ii) has it in any place, whether or not that place belongs to or is occupied by him, for the use or benefit of himself or of another person; and

(b) where one of two or more persons, with the knowledge and consent of the rest, has anything in his custody or possession, it shall be deemed to be in the custody and possession of each and all of them.

Interpretation Act

28. In every enactment

"bank" or "chartered bank" means a bank to which the *Bank Act* applies;

432. For the purposes of this Act,

(e) where an offence is committed in respect of a mail in the course of the door-to-door delivery of the mail, the offence shall be deemed to have been committed in any territorial division through which the mail was carried on that delivery

Interpretation Act

28. In every enactment

"bank" or "chartered bank" means a bank to which the *Bank Act* applies;

Bringing into Canada property obtained by crime

Type 'E' Offence

315. Every one who brings into or has in Canada anything that he has obtained outside of Canada by an act that, if it had been committed in Canada, would have been the offence of theft or an offence under section 312, is guilty of an indictable offence and is liable to imprisonment for ten years.1953-54,c.51,s.299.

Having in possession when complete

316. For the purposes of section 312 and paragraph 314(1)*(b)*, the offence of having in possession is complete when a person has, alone or jointly with another person, possession of or control over anything mentioned in those sections or when he aids in concealing or disposing of it, as the case may be. 1953-54, c. 51, s. 300.

Evidence

317. (1) Where an accused is charged with an offence under section 312 or paragraph 314(1)*(b)*, evidence is admissible at any stage of the proceedings to show that property other than the property that is the subject-matter of the 2
proceedings

(a) was found in the possession of the accused, and 316 3(4)

(b) was stolen within twelve months before the proceedings were commenced,

and that evidence may be considered for the purpose of proving that the accused knew that the property forming the subject-matter of the proceedings was stolen property.

Notice to accused

(2) Subsection (1) does not apply unless

(a) at least three days notice in writing is given to the accused that in the proceedings it is intended to prove that property other than the property that is the subject-matter of the proceedings was found in his possession, and

(b) the notice sets out the nature or description of the property and describes the person from whom it is alleged to have been stolen. 1953-54, c. 51, s. 301.

Evidence of previous conviction

318. (1) Where an accused is charged with an offence under section 312 or paragraph 314(1)*(b)* and evidence is adduced that the subject-matter of the proceedings was found in his possession, evidence that the accused was, within five years before the proceedings were commenced, convicted of an offence involving theft or an offence under section 312 is admissible at any stage of the proceedings and may be taken into consideration for the purpose of proving that the accused knew that the property that forms the subject-matter of the proceedings was unlawfully obtained.

Notice to accused

(2) Subsection (1) does not apply unless at least three days notice in writing is given to the accused that in the proceedings it is intended to prove the previous conviction. 1953-54, c. 51, s. 302.

False Pretences

False pretence

319. (1) A false pretence is a representation of a matter of fact either present or past, made by words or otherwise, that is known by the person who makes it to be false and that is made with a fraudulent intent to induce the person to whom it is made to act upon it.

Exaggeration

(2) Exaggerated commendation or depreciation of the quality of anything is not a false pretence unless it is carried to such an extent that it amounts to a fraudulent misrepresentation of fact.

Question of fact

(3) For the purposes of subsection (2) it is a question of fact whether commendation or depreciation amounts to a fraudulent misrepresentation of fact. 1953-54, c. 51, s. 303.

Fraud

338. (1) Every one who, by deceit, falsehood or other fraudulent means, whether or not it is a false pretence within the meaning of this Act, defrauds the public or any person, whether ascertained or not, of any property, money or valuable security, ...

(2) Every one who, by deceit, falsehood or other fraudulent means, whether or not it is a false pretence within the meaning of this Act, with intent to defraud, affects the public market price of stocks, shares, merchandise or anything that is offered for sale to the public, is guilty of an indictable offence and is liable to imprisonment for ten years.

False pretence or false statement

320. (1) Every one commits an offence who

(a) by a false pretence, whether directly or through the medium of a contract obtained by a false pretence, obtains anything in respect of which the offence of theft may be committed or causes it to be delivered to another person;

(b) obtains credit by a false pretence or by fraud; 338

(c) knowingly makes or causes to be made, directly or indirectly, a false statement in writing with intent that it should be relied upon, with respect to the financial condition or means or ability to pay of himself or any person, firm or corporation that he is interested in or that he acts for, for the purpose of procuring, in any form whatever, whether for his benefit or the benefit of that person, firm or corporation,

(i) the delivery of personal property,

(ii) the payment of money,

(iii) the making of a loan,

(iv) the extension of credit,

(v) the discount of an account receivable, or

(vi) the making, accepting, discounting or endorsing of a bill of exchange, cheque, draft, or promissory note; or ss. (5)

(d) knowing that a false statement in writing has been made with respect to the financial condition or means or ability to pay of himself or another person, firm or corporation that he is interested in or that he acts for, procures upon the faith of that statement, whether for his benefit or for the benefit of that person, firm or corporation, anything mentioned in subparagraphs *(c)*(i) to (vi).

Canada Evidence Act

29. (3) Where a cheque has been drawn on any financial institution or branch thereof by any person, an affidavit of the manager or accountant of the financial institution or branch, sworn before any commissioner or other person authorized to take affidavits, setting out that he is the manager or accountant, that he has made a careful examination and search of the books and records for the purpose of ascertaining whether or not such person has an account with the financial institution or branch, and that he has been unable to find such an account, shall be received in evidence as *prima facie* proof that such person has no account in the financial institution or branch.

Punishment

(2) Every one who commits an offence under paragraph (1)*(a)*

Type 'E' Offence

(a) is guilty of an indictable offence and is liable to imprisonment for ten years, where the property obtained is a testamentary instrument or where the value of what is obtained exceeds two hundred dollars; or 2

Type 'B' (C) Offence

(b) is guilty

(i) of an indictable offence and is liable to imprisonment for two years, or

(ii) of an offence punishable on summary conviction, 722(1)

where the value of what is obtained does not exceed two hundred dollars. 1974-75-76, c. 93, s. 31.

Type 'E' Offence

(3) Every one who commits an offence under paragraph (1)*(b)*, *(c)* or *(d)* is guilty of an indictable offence and is liable to imprisonment for ten years.

Presumption from cheque issued without funds

(4) Where, in proceedings under paragraph (1)*(a)*, it is shown that anything was obtained by the accused by means of a cheque that, when presented for payment within a reasonable time, was dishonoured on the ground that no funds or insufficient funds were on deposit to the credit of the accused in the bank or other institution on which the cheque was drawn, it shall be presumed to have been obtained by a false pretence, unless the court is satisfied by evidence that when the accused issued the cheque he had reasonable grounds to believe that it would be honoured if presented for payment within a reasonable time after it was issued. ss. (5) 28 Interp

"Cheque"

(5) In this section, "cheque" includes, in addition to its ordinary meaning, a bill of exchange drawn upon any institution that makes it a business practice to honour bills of exchange or any particular kind thereof drawn upon it by depositors. R.S., c. C-34, s. 320; 1972, c. 13, s. 29.

485. (1) Where in any proceedings under this Part an accused is before a magistrate and it appears to the magistrate that for any reason the charge should be prosecuted by indictment, he may, at any time before the accused has entered upon his defence, decide not to adjudicate and shall thereupon inform the accused of his decision and continue the proceedings as a preliminary inquiry.

(2) Where an accused is before a magistrate charged with an offence mentioned in paragraph 483*(a)*, and, at any time before the magistrate makes an adjudication, the evidence establishes that the value of what was stolen, obtained, had in possession or attempted to be obtained, as the case may be, exceeds two hundred dollars, the magistrate shall put the accused to his election in accordance with subsection 484(2).

(3) Where an accused is put to his election pursuant to subsection (2), the following provisions apply, namely,

(a) if the accused does not elect to be tried by a magistrate, the magistrate shall continue the proceedings as a preliminary inquiry under Part XV, and, if he commits the accused for trial, he shall comply with paragraphs 484(3)*(a)* and *(b)*; and

(b) if the accused elects to be tried by a magistrate, the magistrate shall endorse on the information a record of the election and continue with the trial.

515. No count that alleges false pretences, fraud or an attempt or conspiracy by fraudulent means, is insufficient by reason only that it does not set out in detail the nature of the false pretence, fraud or fraudulent means.

517. The real and personal property of which a person has, by law, the management, control or custody shall, for the purposes of an indictment or proceeding against any other person for an offence committed on or in respect of the property, be deemed to be the property of the person who has the management, control or custody of it.

2. In this Act

"testamentary instrument" includes any will, codicil or other testamentary writing or appointment, as well during the life of the testator whose testamentary disposition it purports to be as after his death, whether it relates to real or personal property, or to both;

Obtaining execution of valuable security by fraud

Type 'D' Offence

321. Every one who, with intent to defraud or injure another person, by a false pretence causes or induces any person

(*a*) to execute, make, accept, endorse or destroy the whole or any part of a valuable security, or 2

(*b*) to write, impress or affix a name or seal on any paper or parchment in order that it may afterwards be made or converted into or used or dealt with as a valuable security,

is guilty of an indictable offence and is liable to imprisonment for five years. 1953-54, c. 51, s. 305.

2. In this Act

"valuable security" includes

(*a*) an order, exchequer acquittance or other security that entitles or evidences the title of any person

(i) to a share or interest in a public stock or fund or in any fund of a body corporate, company or society, or

(ii) to a deposit in a savings bank or other bank, 28 Interp

(*b*) a debenture, deed, bond, bill, note, warrant, order or other security for money or for payment of money,

(*c*) a document of title to lands or goods wherever situated, 2

(*d*) a stamp or writing that secures or evidences title to or an interest in a chattel personal, or that evidences delivery of a chattel personal, and 2

(*e*) a release, receipt, discharge or other instrument evidencing payment of money;

3. (3) For the purposes of this Act, the following rules apply for the purpose of determining the value of a valuable security where value is material, namely,

(*a*) where the valuable security is one mentioned in paragraph (*a*) or (*b*) of the definition "valuable security" in section 2, the value is the value of the share, interest, deposit or unpaid money, as the case may be, that is secured by the valuable security;

(*b*) where the valuable security is one mentioned in paragraph (*c*) or (*d*) of the definition "valuable security" in section 2, the value is the value of the lands, goods, chattel personal or interest in the chattel personal, as the case may be; and

(*c*) where the valuable security is one mentioned in paragraph (*e*) of the definition "valuable security" in section 2, the value is the amount of money that has been paid.

3. (4) For the purposes of this Act,

(*a*) a person has anything in possession when he has it in his personal possession or knowingly

(i) has it in the actual possession or custody of another person, or

(ii) has it in any place, whether or not that place belongs to or is occupied by him, for the use or benefit of himself or of another person; and

(*b*) where one of two or more persons, with the knowledge and consent of the rest, has anything in his custody or possession, it shall be deemed to be in the custody and possession of each and all of them.

Fraudulently obtaining food and lodging

Type 'A' Offence

322. (1) Every one who fraudulently obtains food, lodging or other accomodation at an hotel or inn or at a lodging, boarding or eating house is guilty of an offence punishable on summary conviction.

Presumption

(2) In proceedings under this section, evidence that an accused obtained food, lodging or other accommodation at an hotel or inn or at a lodging, boarding or eating house, and did not pay for it and

(a) made a false or fictitious show or pretence of having baggage,

(b) had any false or pretended baggage,

(c) surreptitiously removed or attempted to remove his baggage or any material part of it,

(d) absconded or surreptitiously left the premises,

(e) knowingly made a false statement to obtain credit or time for payment, or

(f) offered a worthless cheque, draft or security in payment for his food, lodging or other accommodation, ss. (3)

is, in the absence of any evidence to the contrary, proof of fraud.

"Cheque"

(3) In this section "cheque" includes, in addition to its ordinary meaning, a bill of exchange drawn upon any institution that makes it a business practice to honour bills of exchange or any particular kind thereof drawn upon it by depositors. 1953-54, c. 51, s. 307; 1960-61, c. 43, s. 8; 1968-69, c. 38, s. 92.

Pretending to practise witchcraft, etc.

Type 'A' Offence

323. Every one who fraudulently

(a) pretends to exercise or to use any kind of witchcraft, sorcery, enchantment or conjuration,

(b) undertakes, for a consideration, to tell fortunes, or

(c) pretends from his skill in or knowledge of an occult or crafty science to discover where or in what manner anything that is supposed to have been stolen or lost may be found,

is guilty of an offence punishable on summary conviction. 1953-54, c. 51, s. 308.

Forgery and Offences Resembling Forgery

Forgery

324. (1) Every one commits forgery who makes a false document, knowing it to be false, with intent 282

(a) that it should in any way be used or acted upon as genuine, to the prejudice of any one whether within Canada or not, or

(b) that some person should be induced, by the belief that it is genuine, to do or to refrain from doing anything, whether within Canada or not.

Making a false document

(2) Making a false document includes 282

(a) altering a genuine document in any material part,

(b) making a material addition to a genuine document or adding to it a false date, attestation, seal or other thing that is material, or

(c) making a material alteration in a genuine document by erasure, obliteration, removal or in any other way.

When forgery complete

(3) Forgery is complete as soon as a document is made with the knowledge and intent referred to in subsection (1), notwithstanding that the person who makes it does not intend that any particular person should use or act upon it as genuine or be induced, by the belief that it is genuine, to do or refrain from doing anything.

Forgery complete though document incomplete

(4) Forgery is complete notwithstanding that the false document is incomplete or does not purport to be a document that is binding in law, if it is such as to indicate that it was intended to be acted upon as genuine. 1953-54, c. 51, s. 309.

282. In this Part

"document" means any paper, parchment or other material used for writing or printing, marked with matter capable of being read, but does not include trade marks on articles of commerce or inscriptions on stone or metal or other like material;

"false document" means a document

(a) the whole or some material part of which purports to be made by or on behalf of a person

(i) who did not make it or authorize it to be made, or

(ii) who did not in fact exist;

(b) that is made by or on behalf of the person who purports to make it but is false in some material particular;

(c) that is made in the name of an existing person, by him or under his authority, with a fraudulent intention that it should pass as being made by some person, real or fictitious, other than the person who makes it or under whose authority it is made;

Canada Evidence Act

35. Where any instrument that has been forged or fraudulently altered is admitted in evidence, the court or the judge or person who admits the instrument may, at the request of any person against whom it is admitted in evidence, direct that the instrument shall be impounded and be kept in the custody of some officer of the court or other proper person for such period and subject to such conditions, as to the court, judge or person admitting the instrument seem meet.

Type 'E' Offence

IPA offence 178.1

325. (1) Every one who commits forgery is guilty of an indictable offence and is liable to imprisonment for fourteen years.

Corroboration

(2) No person shall be convicted of an offence under this section upon the evidence of only one witness unless the evidence of that witness is corroborated in a material particular by evidence that implicates the accused. 1953-54, c. 51, s. 310.

Uttering forged document

Type 'E' Offence

IPA offence 178.1

326. (1) Every one who, knowing that a document is forged, 282

(a) uses, deals with, or acts upon it, or

(b) causes or attempts to cause any person to use, deal with, or act upon it, 24

as if the document were genuine, is guilty of an indictable offence and is liable to imprisonment for fourteen years.

Wherever forged

(2) For the purposes of proceedings under this section, the place where a document was forged is not material. 1953-54, c. 51, s. 311.

24. (1) Every one who, having an intent to commit an offence, does or omits to do anything for the purpose of carrying out his intention is guilty of an attempt to commit the offence whether or not it was possible under the circumstances to commit the offence.

(2) The question whether an act or omission by a person who has an intent to commit an offence is or is not mere preparation to commit the offence, and too remote to constitute an attempt to commit the offence, is a question of law.

Exchequer bill paper, public seals, etc.

327. Every one who, without lawful authority or excuse, the proof of which lies upon him,

(a) makes, uses or knowingly has in his possession 3(4)

(i) any exchequer bill paper, revenue paper, or paper that is used to make 282
bank notes, or 2

(ii) any paper that is intended to resemble paper mentioned in subparagraph (i),

(b) makes, offers or disposes of or knowingly has in his possession any plate, die, machinery, instrument or other writing or material that is adapted and 2
intended to be used to commit forgery, or

Type 'E' Offence

(c) makes, reproduces or uses a public seal of Canada or of a province, or the seal of a public body or authority in Canada, or of a court of law,

is guilty of an indictable offence and is liable to imprisonment for fourteen years. 1953-54, c. 51, s. 312.

2. In this Act

"bank-note" includes any negotiable instrument

(a) issued by or on behalf of a person carrying on the business of banking in or out of Canada,

(b) issued under the authority of the Parliament of Canada or under lawful authority of the government of a state other than Canada,

intended to be used as money or as the equivalent of money, immediately upon issue or at some time subsequent thereto, and includes bank bills and bank post bills;

"writing" includes a document of any kind and any mode in which, and any material on which, words or figures, whether at length or abridged, are written, printed or otherwise expressed, or a map or plan is inscribed.

282. In this Part

"exchequer bill" means a bank note, bond, note, debenture or security that is issued or guaranteed by Her Majesty under the authority of the Parliament of Canada or the legislature of a province;

"exchequer bill paper" means paper that is used to manufacture exchequer bills;

"revenue paper" means paper that is used to make stamps, licences or permits or for any purpose connected with the public revenue.

Counterfeit proclamation, etc.
Type 'D' Offence

328. Every one who knowingly

(a) prints a proclamation, order, regulation or appointment, or notice thereof, and causes it falsely to purport to have been printed by the Queen's Printer for Canada, or the Queen's Printer for a province, or

(b) tenders in evidence a copy of a proclamation, order, regulation or appointment that falsely purports to have been printed by the Queen's Printer for Canada or the Queen's Printer for a province,

is guilty of an indictable offence and is liable to imprisonment for five years. 1953-54, c. 51, s. 313.

Telegram, etc., in false name
Type 'D' Offence

329. Every one who, with intent to defraud, causes or procures a telegram, cablegram or radio message to be sent or delivered as being sent by the authority of another person, knowing that it is not sent by his authority and with intent that the message should be acted on as being sent by his authority, is guilty of an indictable offence and is liable to imprisonment for five years. 1953-54, c. 51, s. 314. 28 Interp

128. Every one who, with intent to mislead, causes a peace officer to enter upon an investigation by

(a) making a false statement that accuses some other person of having committed an offence,

(b) doing anything that is intended to cause some other person to be suspected of having committed an offence that he has not committed, or to divert suspicion from himself,

(c) reporting that an offence has been committed when it has not been committed, or

(d) reporting or in any other way making it known or causing it to be made known that he or some other person has died when he or that other person has not died,

is guilty of

(e) an indictable offence and is liable to imprisonment for five years, or

(f) an offence punishable on summary conviction.

False messages
Type 'D' Offence

330. (1) Every one who, with intent to injure or alarm any person, conveys or causes or procures to be conveyed by letter, telegram, telephone, cable, radio, or otherwise, information that he knows is false is guilty of an indictable offence and is liable to imprisonment for two years.

Interpretation Act

28. In every enactment

"radio" or "radiocommunication" means any transmission, emission or reception of signs, signals, writing, images, sounds or intelligence of any nature by means of electromagnetic waves of frequencies lower than three thousand Gigacycles per second propagated in space without artificial guide;

Indecent telephone calls
Type 'A' Offence

(2) Every one who, with intent to alarm or annoy any person, makes any indecent telephone call to such person is guilty of an offence punishable on summary conviction. 722(1)

Harassing telephone calls
Type 'A' Offence

(3) Every one who, without lawful excuse and with intent to harass any person, makes or causes to be made repeated telephone calls to such person is guilty of an offence punishable on summary conviction. 1960-61, c. 43, s. 9; 1968-69, c. 38, s. 22. 722(1)

722. (1) Except where otherwise expressly provided by law, every one who is convicted of an offence punishable on summary conviction is liable to a fine of not more than five hundred dollars or to imprisonment for six months or to both.

Threatening letters and telephone calls

IPA offence 178.1

331. (1) Every one commits an offence who by letter, telegram, telephone, cable, radio, or otherwise, knowingly utters, conveys or causes any person to receive a threat

(a) to cause death or injury to any person, or

(b) to burn, destroy or damage real or personal property, or

(c) to kill, maim, wound, poison or injure an animal or bird that is the property of any person.

Type 'F' Offence

(2) Every one who commits an offence under paragraph (1)*(a)* is guilty of an indictable offence and is liable to imprisonment for ten years.

Type 'B' (D) Offence

(3) Every one who commits an offence under paragraph (1)*(b)* or *(c)* is guilty of

(a) an indictable offence and is liable to imprisonment for two years, or

(b) an offence punishable on summary conviction. 1953-54, c. 51, s. 316; 1960-61, c. 43, s. 10.

Drawing document without authority, etc.

Type 'E' Offence

332. Every one who

(a) with intent to defraud and without lawful authority makes, executes, draws, signs, accepts or endorses a document in the name or on the account of another person by procuration or otherwise, or 282

(b) makes use of or utters a document knowing that it has been made, executed, signed, accepted or endorsed with intent to defraud and without lawful authority, in the name or on the account of another person, by procuration or otherwise,

is guilty of an indictable offence and is liable to imprisonment for fourteen years. 1953-54, c. 51, s. 317.

Obtaining, etc., by instrument based on forged document

Type 'E' Offence

333. Every one who demands, receives, or obtains anything, or causes or procures anything to be delivered or paid to any person under, upon, or by virtue of any instrument issued under the authority of law, knowing that it is based on a forged document, is guilty of an indictable offence and is liable to imprisonment for fourteen years. 1953-54, c. 51, s. 318.

282. In this Part

"document" means any paper, parchment or other material used for writing or printing, marked with matter capable of being read, but does not include trade marks on articles of commerce or inscriptions on stone or metal or other like material;

Counterfeiting stamp, etc.

Type 'E' Offence

334. (1) Every one who

(a) fraudulently uses, mutilates, affixes, removes or counterfeits a stamp or part thereof, ss. (3)

(b) knowingly and without lawful excuse, the proof of which lies upon him, has in his possession 3(4)

(i) a counterfeit stamp or a stamp that has been fraudulently mutilated, or

(ii) anything bearing a stamp of which a part has been fraudulently erased, removed or concealed, or

(c) without lawful excuse, the proof of which lies upon him, makes or knowingly has in his possession a die or instrument that is capable of making the impression of a stamp or part thereof,

is guilty of an indictable offence and is liable to imprisonment for fourteen years.

Counterfeiting mark

Type 'E' Offence

(2) Every one who, without lawful authority,

(a) makes a mark, ss. (3)

(b) sells, or exposes for sale, or has in his possession a counterfeit mark,

(c) affixes a mark to anything that is required by law to be marked, branded, sealed or wrapped other than the thing to which the mark was originally affixed or was intended to be affixed, or

(d) affixes a counterfeit mark to anything that is required by law to be marked, branded, sealed or wrapped,

is guilty of an indictable offence and is liable to imprisonment for fourteen years.

Definitions

(3) In this section

"mark"

"mark" means a mark, brand, seal, wrapper or design used by or on behalf of

(a) the Government of Canada or of a province,

(b) the government of a state other than Canada, or

(c) a department, board, commission or agent established by a government mentioned in paragraph *(a)* or *(b)* in connection with the service or business of that government;

"stamp"

"stamp" means an impressed or adhesive stamp used for the purpose of revenue by the Government of Canada or of a province or by the government of a state other than Canada. 1953-54, c. 51, s. 319.

3. (4) For the purposes of this Act,

(a) a person has anything in possession when he has it in his personal possession or knowingly

(i) has it in the actual possession or custody of another person, or

(ii) has it in any place, whether or not that place belongs to or is occupied by him, for the use or benefit of himself or of another person; and

(b) where one of two or more persons, with the knowledge and consent of the rest, has anything in his custody or possession, it shall be deemed to be in the custody and possession of each and all of them.

Damaging documents

Type 'E' Offence

335. (1) Every one who unlawfully

(a) destroys, defaces or injures a register, or any part of a register of births, baptisms, marriages, deaths or burials that is required or authorized by law to be kept in Canada, or a copy or any part of a copy of such a register that is required by law to be transmitted to a registrar or other officer,

(b) inserts or causes to be inserted in a register or copy referred to in paragraph *(a)* an entry, that he knows is false, of any matter relating to a birth, baptism, marriage, death or burial, or erases any material part from such register or copy,

(c) destroys, damages or obliterates an election document or causes an election document to be destroyed, damaged or obliterated, or ss. (2)

(d) makes or causes to be made an erasure, alteration or interlineation in or upon an election document,

is guilty of an indictable offence and is liable to imprisonment for five years.

"Election document"

(2) In this section, "election document" means any document or writing issued under the authority of an Act of the Parliament of Canada or of a legislature with respect to an election held pursuant to the authority of any such Act. 1953-54, c. 51, s. 320. 2

2. In this Act

"writing" includes a document of any kind and any mode in which, and any material on which, words or figures, whether at length or abridged, are written, printed or otherwise expressed, or a map or plan is inscribed.

Offences in relation to registers

Type 'D' Offence

336. Every one who

(a) being authorized or required by law to make or issue a certified copy of, extract from or certificate in respect of a register, record or document, knowingly makes or issues a false certified copy, extract or certificate, 282

(b) not being authorized or required by law to make or issue a certified copy of, extract from or certificate in respect of a register, record or document, fraudulently makes or issues a copy, extract or certificate that purports to be certified as authorized or required by law, or

(c) being authorized or required by law to make a certificate or declaration concerning any particular required for the purpose of making entries in a register, record or document, knowingly and falsely makes the certificate or declaration,

is guilty of an indictable offence and is liable to imprisonment for five years. 1953-54, c. 51, s. 321.

282. In this Part

"document" means any paper, parchment or other material used for writing or printing, marked with matter capable of being read, but does not include trade marks on articles of commerce or inscriptions on stone or metal or other like material;

—NOTES—

PART VIII

FRAUDULENT TRANSACTIONS RELATING TO CONTRACTS AND TRADE

Interpretation

Definitions

337. In this Part

"goods"

"goods" means anything that is the subject of trade or commerce;

"trading stamps"

"trading stamps" includes any form of cash receipt, receipt, coupon, premium ticket or other device, designed or intended to be given to the purchaser of goods by the vendor thereof or on his behalf, and to represent a discount on the price of the goods or a premium to the purchaser thereof

(a) that may be redeemed

(i) by any person other than the vendor, the person from whom the vendor purchased the goods, or the manufacturer of the goods,

(ii) by the vendor, the person from whom the vendor purchased the goods, or the manufacturer of the goods in cash or in goods that are not his property in whole or in part, or

(iii) by the vendor elsewhere than in the premises where the goods are purchased; or

(b) that does not show upon its face the place where it is delivered and the merchantable value thereof; or

(c) that may not be redeemed upon demand at any time;

but an offer, endorsed by the manufacturer upon a wrapper or container in which goods are sold, of a premium or reward for the return of that wrapper or container to the manufacturer is not a trading stamp. 1953-54, c. 51, s. 322.

Fraud

Fraud

338. (1) Every one who, by deceit, falsehood or other fraudulent means, whether or not it is a false pretence within the meaning of this Act, defrauds the public or any person, whether ascertained or not, of any property, money or valuable security, 2 2

Type 'E' Offence

IPA offence 178.1

(*a*) is guilty of an indictable offence and is liable to imprisonment for ten years, where the subject-matter of the fraud is a testamentary instrument or where the value thereof exceeds two hundred dollars; or 2

Type 'B' (C) Offence

(*b*) is guilty

(i) of an indictable offence and is liable to imprisonment for two years, or

(ii) of an offence punishable on summary conviction,

where the value of the property of which the public or any person is defrauded does not exceed two hundred dollars. 1974-75-76, c. 93, s. 32.

Affecting public market

Type 'E' Offence

(2) Every one who, by deceit, falsehood or other fraudulent means, whether or not it is a false pretence within the meaning of this Act, with intent to defraud, affects the public market price of stocks, shares, merchandise or anything that is offered for sale to the public, is guilty of an indictable offence and is liable to imprisonment for ten years. 1953-54, c. 51, s. 323. 319

319. (1) A false pretence is a representation of a matter of fact either present or past, made by words or otherwise, that is known by the person who makes it to be false and that is made with a fraudulent intent to induce the person to whom it is made to act upon it.

(2) Exaggerated commendation or depreciation of the quality of anything is not a false pretence unless it is carried to such an extent that it amounts to a fraudulent misrepresentation of fact.

(3) For the purposes of subsection (2) it is a question of fact whether commendation or depreciation amounts to a fraudulent misrepresentation of fact.

2. In this Act

"property" includes

(*a*) real and personal property of every description and deeds and instruments relating to or evidencing the title or right to property, or giving a right to recover or receive money or goods,

(*b*) property originally in the possession or under the control of any person, and any property into or for which it has been converted or exchanged and anything acquired at any time by such conversion or exchange, and

(*c*) any postal card, postage stamp or other stamp issued or prepared for issue under the authority of the Parliament of Canada or of the legislature of a province for the payment to the Crown or a corporate body of any fee, rate or duty, whether or not it is in the possession of the Crown or of any person;

3. (2) For the purposes of this Act a postal card or stamp referred to in paragraph (*c*) of the definition "property" in section 2 shall be deemed to be a chattel, and to be equal in value to the amount of the postage, rate or duty expressed on its face.

2. In this Act

"testamentary instrument" includes any will, codicil or other testamentary writing or appointment, as well during the life of the testator whose testamentary disposition it purports to be as after his death, whether it relates to real or personal property, or to both;

2. In this Act

"valuable security" includes

(a) an order, exchequer acquittance or other security that entitles or evidences the title of any person

(i) to a share or interest in a public stock or fund or in any fund of a body corporate, company or society, or

(ii) to a deposit in a savings bank or other bank,

(b) a debenture, deed, bond, bill, note, warrant, order or other security for money or for payment of money,

(c) a document of title to lands or goods wherever situated,

(d) a stamp or writing that secures or evidences title to or an interest in a chattel personal, or that evidences delivery of a chattel personal, and

(e) a release, receipt, discharge or other instrument evidencing payment of money;

3. (3) For the purposes of this Act, the following rules apply for the purpose of determining the value of a valuable security where value is material, namely,

(a) where the valuable security is one mentioned in paragraph *(a)* or *(b)* of the definition "valuable security" in section 2, the value is the value of the share, interest, deposit or unpaid money, as the case may be, that is secured by the valuable security;

(b) where the valuable security is one mentioned in paragraph *(c)* or *(d)* of the definition "valuable security" in section 2, the value is the value of the lands, goods, chattel personal or interest in the chattel personal, as the case may be; and

(c) where the valuable security is one mentioned in paragraph *(e)* of the definition "valuable security" in section 2, the value is the amount of money that has been paid.

485. (1) Where in any proceedings under this Part an accused is before a magistrate and it appears to the magistrate that for any reason the charge should be prosecuted by indictment, he may, at any time before the accused has entered upon his defence, decide not to adjudicate and shall thereupon inform the accused of his decision and continue the proceedings as a preliminary inquiry.

(2) Where an accused is before a magistrate charged with an offence mentioned in paragraph 483*(a)*, and, at any time before the magistrate makes an adjudication, the evidence establishes that the value of what was stolen, obtained, had in possession or attempted to be obtained, as the case may be, exceeds two hundred dollars, the magistrate shall put the accused to his election in accordance with subsection 484(2).

(3) Where an accused is put to his election pursuant to subsection (2), the following provisions apply, namely,

(a) if the accused does not elect to be tried by a magistrate, the magistrate shall continue the proceedings as a preliminary inquiry under Part XV, and, if he commits the accused for trial, he shall comply with paragraphs 484(3)*(a)* and *(b)*; and

(b) if the accused elects to be tried by a magistrate, the magistrate shall endorse on the information a record of the election and continue with the trial.

515. No count that alleges false pretences, fraud or an attempt or conspiracy by fraudulent means, is insufficient by reason only that it does not set out in detail the nature of the false pretence, fraud or fraudulent means.

517. The real and personal property of which a person has, by law, the management, control or custody shall, for the purposes of an indictment or proceeding against any other person for an offence committed on or in respect of the property, be deemed to be the property of the person who has the management, control or custody of it.

Using mails to defraud

Type 'D' Offence

IPA offence 178.1

339. Every one who makes use of the mails for the purpose of transmitting or delivering letters or circulars concerning schemes devised or intended to deceive or defraud the public, or for the purpose of obtaining money under false pretences, is guilty of an indictable offence and is liable to imprisonment for two years. 1953-54, c. 51, s. 324.

Fraudulent manipulation of stock exchange transactions

Type 'D' Offence

IPA offence 178.1

340. Every one who, through the facility of a stock exchange, curb market or other market, with intent to create a false or misleading appearance of active public trading in a security or with intent to create a false or misleading appearance with respect to the market price of a security,

(a) effects a transaction in the security that involves no change in the beneficial ownership thereof,

(b) enters an order for the purchase of the security, knowing that an order of substantially the same size at substantially the same time and at substantially the same price for the sale of the security has been or will be entered by or for the same or different persons, or

(c) enters an order for the sale of the security, knowing that an order of substantially the same size at substantially the same time and at substantially the same price for the purchase of the security has been or will be entered by or for the same or different persons,

is guilty of an indictable offence and is liable to imprisonment for five years. 1953-54, c. 51, s. 325.

Gaming in stocks or merchandise

Type 'D' Offence

341. (1) Every one is guilty of an indictable offence and is liable to imprisonment for five years who, with intent to make gain or profit by the rise or fall in price of the stock of an incorporated or unincorporated company or undertaking, whether in or out of Canada, or of any goods, wares or merchandise,

(a) makes or signs, or authorizes to be made or signed, any contract or agreement, oral or written, purporting to be for the purchase or sale of shares of stock or goods, wares or merchandise, without the *bona fide* intention of acquiring the shares, goods, wares or merchandise or of selling them, as the case may be; or

(b) makes or signs, or authorizes to be made or signed, any contract or agreement, oral or written, purporting to be for the sale or purchase of shares of stock or goods, wares or merchandise in respect of which no delivery of the thing sold or purchased is made or received, and without the *bona fide* intention of making or receiving delivery thereof, as the case may be;

but this section does not apply where a broker, on behalf of a purchaser, receives delivery, notwithstanding that the broker retains or pledges what is delivered as security for the advance of the purchase money or any part thereof.

Onus

(2) Where, in proceedings under this section, it is established that the accused made or signed a contract or agreement for the sale or purchase of shares of stock or goods, wares or merchandise, or acted, aided or abetted in the making or signing thereof, the burden of proof of a *bona fide* intention to acquire or to sell the shares, goods, wares or merchandise or to deliver or to receive delivery thereof, as the case may be, lies upon the accused. 1953-54, c. 51, s. 326.

Bona fide — In or with good faith, there is no pretence, it is actually so.

Broker reducing stock by selling for his own account

342. Every one is guilty of an indictable offence and is liable to imprisonment for five years who, being an individual, or a member or employee of a partnership, or a director, officer or employee of a corporation, where he or the partnership, or corporation is employed as a broker by any customer to buy and carry upon margin any shares of an incorporated or unincorporated company or undertaking, whether in or out of Canada, thereafter sells or causes to be sold shares of the company or undertaking for any account in which

(a) he or his firm or a partner thereof, or

(b) the corporation or a director thereof,

has a direct or indirect interest, if the effect of the sale is, otherwise than unintentionally, to reduce the amount of such shares in the hands of the broker or under his control in the ordinary course of business below the amount of such shares that the broker should be carrying for all customers. 1953-54, c. 51, s. 327.

Fraudulent concealment of title documents

Type 'D' Offence with consent ss. (2)

343. (1) Every one who, being a vendor or mortgagor of property or of a chose in action or being a solicitor for or agent of a vendor or mortgagor of property or a chose in action, is served with a written demand for an abstract of title by or on behalf of the purchaser or mortgagee before the completion of the purchase or mortgage, and who 2

(a) with intent to defraud and for the purpose of inducing the purchaser or mortgagee to accept the title offered or produced to him, conceals from him any settlement, deed, will or other instrument material to the title, or any encumbrance on the title, or

(b) falsifies any pedigree upon which the title depends,

is guilty of an indictable offence and is liable to imprisonment for two years.

(2) No proceedings shall be instituted under this section without the consent of the Attorney General. 1953-54, c. 51, s. 328.

Fraudulent registration of title

Type 'D' Offence

344. Every one who, as principal or agent, in a proceeding to register title to real property, or in a transaction relating to real property that is or is proposed to be registered, knowingly and with intent to deceive,

(a) makes a material false statement or representation,

(b) suppresses or conceals from a judge or registrar or any person employed by or assisting the registrar, any material document, fact, matter or information, or

(c) is privy to anything mentioned in paragraph *(a)* or *(b)*,

is guilty of an indictable offence and is liable to imprisonment for five years. 1953-54, c. 51, s. 329.

Fraudulent sale of real property

Type 'D' Offence

345. Every one who, knowing of an unregistered prior sale or of an existing unregistered grant, mortgage, hypothec, privilege or encumbrance of or upon real property, fraudulently sells the property or any part thereof is guilty of an indictable offence and is liable to imprisonment for two years. 1953-54, c. 51, s. 330.

Misleading receipt

Type 'D' Offence

346. Every one who wilfully

(a) with intent to mislead, injure or defraud any person, whether or not that person is known to him, gives to a person anything in writing that purports to be a receipt for or an acknowledgment of property that has been delivered to or received by him, before the property referred to in the purported receipt or acknowledgment has been delivered to or received by him, or

(b) accepts, transmits or uses a purported receipt or acknowledgment to which paragraph *(a)* applies,

is guilty of an indictable offence and is liable to imprisonment for two years. 1953-54, c. 51, s. 331.

Fraudulent disposal of goods on which money advanced

Type 'D' Offence

347. (1) Every one who

(a) having shipped or delivered to the keeper of a warehouse or to a factor, agent or carrier, anything upon which the consignee thereof has advanced money or has given valuable security, thereafter, with intent to deceive, 2
defraud or injure the consignee, disposes of it in a manner that is different from and inconsistent with any agreement that has been made in that behalf between him and the consignee, or

(b) knowingly and wilfully aids or assists any person to make a disposition of anything to which paragraph *(a)* applies for the purpose of deceiving, defrauding or injuring the consignee,

is guilty of an indictable offence and is liable to imprisonment for two years.

Saving

(2) No person is guilty of an offence under this section where, before disposing of anything in a manner that is different from and inconsistent with any agreement that has been made in that behalf between him and the consignee, he pays or tenders to the consignee the full amount of money or valuable security that the consignee has advanced. 1953-54, c. 51, s. 332.

Fraudulent receipts under *Bank Act*

Type 'D' Offence

348. Every one is guilty of an indictable offence and is liable to imprisonment for two years who

(a) wilfully makes a false statement in a receipt, certificate or acknowledgment for anything that may be used for a purpose mentioned in the *Bank Act*; or

(b) wilfully,

(i) after giving to another person,

(ii) after a person employed by him has, to his knowledge, given to another person, or

(iii) after obtaining and endorsing or assigning to another person,

a receipt, certificate or acknowledgment for anything that may be used for a purpose mentioned in the *Bank Act*, without the consent in writing of the holder or endorsee or the production and delivery of the receipt, certificate or acknowledgment, alienates or parts with, or does not deliver to the holder or owner the property mentioned in the receipt, certificate or acknowledgment. 1953-54, c. 51, s. 333.

Saving

349. Where an offence is committed under section 346, 347 or 348 by a person who acts in the name of a corporation, firm or partnership, no person other than the person who does the act by means of which the offence is committed or who is secretly privy to the doing of that act is guilty of the offence. 1953-54, c. 51, s. 334.

Disposal of property to defraud creditors

Type 'D' Offence

350. Every one who,

(a) with intent to defraud his creditors,

(i) makes or causes to be made a gift, conveyance, assignment, sale, transfer or delivery of his property, or 2

(ii) removes, conceals or disposes of any of his property, or

(b) with intent that any one should defraud his creditors, receives any property by means of or in relation to which an offence has been committed under paragraph *(a)*,

is guilty of an indictable offence and is liable to imprisonment for two years. 1953-54, c. 51, s. 335.

2. In this Act

"property" includes

(a) real and personal property of every description and deeds and instruments relating to or evidencing the title or right to property, or giving a right to recover or receive money or goods,

(b) property originally in the possession or under the control of any person, and any property into or for which it has been converted or exchanged and anything acquired at any time by such conversion or exchange, and

(c) any postal card, postage stamp or other stamp issued or prepared for issue under the authority of the Parliament of Canada or of the legislature of a province for the payment to the Crown or a corporate body of any fee, rate or duty, whether or not it is in the possession of the Crown or of any person;

3. (2) For the purposes of this Act a postal card or stamp referred to in paragraph *(c)* of the definition "property" in section 2 shall be deemed to be a chattel, and to be equal in value to the amount of the postage, rate or duty expressed on its face.

2. In this Act

"valuable security" includes

(a) an order, exchequer acquittance or other security that entitles or evidences the title of any person

(i) to a share or interest in a public stock or fund or in any fund of a body corporate, company or society, or

(ii) to a deposit in a savings bank or other bank,

(b) a debenture, deed, bond, bill, note, warrant, order or other security for money or for payment of money,

(c) a document of title to lands or goods wherever situated,

(d) a stamp or writing that secures or evidences title to or an interest in a chattel personal, or that evidences delivery of a chattel personal, and

(e) a release, receipt, discharge or other instrument evidencing payment of money;

3. (3) For the purposes of this Act, the following rules apply for the purpose of determining the value of a valuable security where value is material, namely,

(a) where the valuable security is one mentioned in paragraph *(a)* or *(b)* of the definition "valuable security" in section 2, the value is the value of the share, interest, deposit or unpaid money, as the case may be, that is secured by the valuable security;

(b) where the valuable security is one mentioned in paragraph *(c)* or *(d)* of the definition "valuable security" in section 2, the value is the value of the lands, goods, chattel personal or interest in the chattel personal, as the case may be; and

(c) where the valuable security is one mentioned in paragraph *(e)* of the definition "valuable security" in section 2, the value is the amount of money that has been paid.

Fraud in relation to fares, etc.

Type 'C' Offence

351. (1) Every one whose duty it is to collect a fare, toll, ticket or admission who wilfully

(*a*) fails to collect it,

(*b*) collects less than the proper amount payable in respect thereof, or

(*c*) accepts any valuable consideration for failing to collect it or for collecting less than the proper amount payable in respect thereof,

is guilty of an indictable offence and is liable to imprisonment for two years.

Idem

Type 'C' Offence

(2) Every one who gives or offers to a person whose duty it is to collect a fare, toll, ticket or admission fee, any valuable consideration

(*a*) for failing to collect it, or

(*b*) for collecting an amount less than the amount payable in respect thereof,

is guilty of an indictable offence and is liable to imprisonment for two years.

Fraudulently obtaining transportation

Type 'A' Offence

(3) Every one who, by any false pretence or fraud, unlawfully obtains transportation by land, water or air is guilty of an offence punishable on summary conviction. 1953-54, c. 51, s. 336. 319 338 722(1)

Fraud in relation to minerals

Type 'D' Offence

352. (1) Every one is guilty of an indictable offence and is liable to imprisonment for five years who

(*a*) being the holder of a lease or licence issued

(i) under an Act relating to the mining of precious metals, or

(ii) by the owner of land that is supposed to contain precious metals,

by a fraudulent device or contrivance defrauds or attempts to defraud any person of any precious metals or money payable or reserved by the lease or licence, or fraudulently conceals or makes a false statement with respect to the amount of precious metals procured by him; 24

(*b*) sells or purchases any rock, mineral, or other substance that contains precious metals or unsmelted, untreated, unmanufactured, or partly smelted, partly treated or partly manufactured precious metals, unless he establishes that he is the owner or agent of the owner or is acting under lawful authority; or

(*c*) has in his possession or knowingly has upon his premises 3(4)

(i) any rock or mineral of a value of twenty-five cents per pound or more,

(ii) any mica of a value of seven cents per pound or more, or

(iii) any precious metals,

that there is reasonable ground to believe have been stolen or have been dealt with contrary to this section, unless he establishes that he is lawfully in possession thereof.

583. In any proceeding in respect of theft of ores or minerals, the possession, contrary to any law in that behalf, of smelted gold or silver, gold-bearing quartz, or unsmelted or unmanufactured gold or silver, by an operator, workman or labourer actively engaged in or on a mine, is, in the absence of any evidence to the contrary, proof that the gold, silver or quartz was stolen by him.

24. (1) Every one who, having an intent to commit an offence, does or omits to do anything for the purpose of carrying out his intention is guilty of an attempt to commit the offence whether or not it was possible under the circumstances to commit the offence.

(2) The question whether an act or omission by a person who has an intent to commit an offence is or is not mere preparation to commit the offence, and too remote to constitute an attempt to commit the offence, is a question of law.

3. (4) For the purposes of this Act,

(a) a person has anything in possession when he has it in his personal possession or knowingly

(i) has it in the actual possession or custody of another person, or

(ii) has it in any place, whether or not that place belongs to or is occupied by him, for the use or benefit of himself or of another person; and

(b) where one of two or more persons, with the knowledge and consent of the rest, has anything in his custody or possession, it shall be deemed to be in the custody and possession of each and all of them.

Seizure and forfeiture

(2) Where a person is convicted of an offence under this section, the court may order anything by means of or in relation to which the offence was committed, upon such conviction, to be forfeited to Her Majesty in right of the province in which the proceedings take place. 1953-54, c. 51, s. 337.

Search for precious metals

353. (1) Where an information in writing is laid under oath before a justice by any person having an interest in a mining claim, that any precious metals or rock, mineral or other substance containing precious metals is unlawfully deposited in any place or held by any person contrary to law, the justice may issue a warrant to search any of the places or persons mentioned in the information. 28 Interp

Power to seize

(2) Where, upon search, anything mentioned in subsection (1) is found, it shall be seized and carried before the justice who shall order

(a) that it be detained for the purposes of an inquiry or trial, or

(b) if it is not detained for the purposes of an inquiry or trial,

(i) that it be restored to the owner, or

(ii) that it be forfeited to Her Majesty in right of the province in which the proceedings take place if the owner cannot be ascertained.

Appeal

(3) An appeal lies from an order made under paragraph (2)*(b)* in the manner in which an appeal lies in summary conviction proceedings under Part XXIV and the provisions of that Part relating to appeals apply to appeals under this subsection. 1953-54, c. 51, s. 338.

Offences in relation to mines

Type 'E' Offence

354. (1) Every one who

(a) adds anything to or removes anything from an existing or prospective mine, mining claim or oil well with a fraudulent intent to affect the result of an assay, test or valuation that has been made or is to be made with respect to the mine, mining claim or oil well, or

(b) adds anything to, removes anything from or tampers with a sample or material that has been taken or is being or is about to be taken from an existing or prospective mine, mining claim or oil well for the purpose of being assayed, tested or otherwise valued, with a fraudulent intent to affect the result of the assay, test or valuation,

is guilty of an indictable offence and is liable to imprisonment for ten years.

Presumption

(2) For the purposes of proceedings under subsection (1), evidence that

(a) something has been added to or removed from anything to which subsection (1) applies, or

(b) anything to which subsection (1) applies has been tampered with,

is, in the absence of any evidence to the contrary, proof of a fraudulent intent to affect the result of an assay, test or valuation. 1953-54, c. 51, s. 339; 1968-69, c. 38, s. 92.

Falsification of Books and Documents

Books and documents
Type 'D' Offence

355. (1) Every one who, with intent to defraud,

(a) destroys, mutilates, alters, falsifies, or makes a false entry in, or

(b) omits a material particular from, or alters a material particular in,

a book, paper, writing, valuable security or document is guilty of an indictable offence and is liable to imprisonment for five years. 2/2 [350]

Privy
Type 'D' Offence

(2) Every one who, with intent to defraud his creditors, is privy to the commission of an offence under subsection (1) is guilty of an indictable offence and is liable to imprisonment for five years. 1953-54, c. 51, s. 340.

2. In this Act

"writing" includes a document of any kind and any mode in which, and any material on which, words or figures, whether at length or abridged, are written, printed or otherwise expressed, or a map or plan is inscribed.

Falsifying employment record
Type 'A' Offence

356. Every one who, with intent to deceive, falsifies an employment record by any means, including the punching of a time clock, is guilty of an offence punishable on summary conviction. 1953-54, c. 51, s. 341. 722(1)

False return by public officer
Type 'D' Offence

357. Every one who, being entrusted with the receipt, custody or management of any part of the public revenues, knowingly furnishes a false statement or return of

(a) any sum of money collected by him or entrusted to his care, or

(b) any balance of money in his hands or under his control,

is guilty of an indictable offence and is liable to imprisonment for five years. 1953-54, c. 51, s. 342.

False prospectus etc.
Type 'E' Offence

358. (1) Every one who makes, circulates or publishes a prospectus, statement or account, whether written or oral, that he knows is false in a material particular, with intent

(a) to induce persons, whether ascertained or not, to become shareholders or partners in a company, ss. (2)

(b) to deceive or defraud the members, shareholders or creditors, whether ascertained or not, of a company,

(c) to induce any person to entrust or advance anything to a company, or

(d) to enter into any security for the benefit of a company,

is guilty of an indictable offence and is liable to imprisonment for ten years.

"Company"

(2) In this section, "company" means a syndicate, body corporate or company, whether existing or proposed to be created. 1953-54, c. 51, s. 343.

Obtaining carriage by false billing
Type 'A' Offence

359. (1) Every one who, by means of a false or misleading representation, knowingly obtains or attempts to obtain the carriage of anything by any person into a country, province, district or other place, whether or not within Canada, where the importation or transportation of it is, in the circumstances of the case, unlawful is guilty of an offence punishable on summary conviction. 722(1)

Forfeiture

(2) Where a person is convicted of an offence under subsection (1), anything by means of or in relation to which the offence was committed, upon such conviction, in addition to any punishment that is imposed, is forfeited to Her Majesty and shall be disposed of as the court may direct. 1953-54, c. 51, s. 344.

Trader failing to keep accounts

Type 'D' Offence

360. (1) Every one who, being a trader or in business,

(a) is indebted in an amount exceeding one thousand dollars,

(b) is unable to pay his creditors in full, and

(c) has not kept books of account that, in the ordinary course of the trade or business in which he is engaged, are necessary to exhibit or explain his transactions,

is guilty of an indictable offence and is liable to imprisonment for two years.

Saving

(2) No person shall be convicted of an offence under this section

(a) where, to the satisfaction of the court or judge, he

(i) accounts for his losses, and

(ii) shows that his failure to keep books was not intended to defraud his creditors; or

(b) where his failure to keep books occurred at a time more than five years prior to the day on which he was unable to pay his creditors in full. 1953-54, c. 51, s. 345.

Personation

Personation with intent

Type 'E' Offence

361. Every one who fraudulently personates any person, living or dead,

(a) with intent to gain advantage for himself or another person,

(b) with intent to obtain any property or an interest in any property, or 2 [350]

(c) with intent to cause disadvantage to the person whom he personates or another person,

is guilty of an indictable offence and is liable to imprisonment for fourteen years. 1953-54, c. 51, s. 346.

119. Every one who

(a) falsely represents himself to be a peace officer or a public officer, or

(b) not being a peace officer or public officer uses a badge or article of uniform or equipment in a manner that is likely to cause persons to believe that he is a peace officer or a public officer, as the case may be,

is guilty of an offence punishable on summary conviction.

Personation at examination

Type 'A' Offence

362. Every one who falsely, with intent to gain advantage for himself or some other person, personates a candidate at a competitive or qualifying examination held under the authority of law or in connection with a university, college or school or who knowingly avails himself of the results of such personation is guilty of an offence punishable on summary conviction. 1953-54, c. 51, s. 347. 722(1)

Acknowledging instrument in false name

Type 'D' Offence

363. Every one who, without lawful authority or excuse, the proof of which lies upon him, acknowledges in the name of another person before a court or a judge or other person authorized to receive the acknowledgment, a recognizance of bail, a confession of judgment, a consent to judgment or a judgment, deed or other instrument, is guilty of an indictable offence and is liable to imprisonment for five years. 1953-54, c. 51, s. 348.

Forgery of Trade Marks and Trade Descriptions

Forging trade mark

364. For the purposes of this Part, every one forges a trade mark who Trade Marks Act

(a) without the consent of the proprietor of the trade mark, makes or reproduces in any manner that trade mark or a mark so nearly resembling it as to be calculated to deceive, or

(b) falsifies, in any manner, a genuine trade mark. 1953-54, c. 51, s. 349.

Type 'B' (D) Offence 370

365. Every one commits an offence who, with intent to deceive or defraud the public or any person, whether ascertained or not, forges a trade mark. 1953-54, c. 51, s. 350.

Passing off

Type 'B' (D) Offence 370

366. Every one commits an offence who, with intent to deceive or defraud the public or any person, whether ascertain or not,

(a) passes off other wares or services as and for those ordered or required, or

(b) makes use, in association with wares or services, of any description that is false in a material respect as to

(i) the kind, quality, quantity or composition,

(ii) the geographical origin, or

(iii) the mode of the manufacture, production or performance

of such wares or services. 1953-54, c. 51, s. 351.

Instruments for forging trade mark

Type 'B' (D) Offence 370

367. (1) Every one commits an offence who makes, has in his possession or disposes of a die, block, machine or other instrument, designed or intended to be used in forging a trade mark.

Saving

(2) No person shall be convicted of an offence under this section where he proves that he acted in good faith in the ordinary course of his business or employment. 1953-54, c. 51, s. 352.

Other offences in relation to trade marks

Type 'B' (D) Offence 370

368. Every one commits an offence who, with intent to deceive or defraud,

(a) defaces, conceals or removes a trade mark or the name of another person from anything without the consent of that other person, or

(b) being a manufacturer, dealer, trader or bottler fills any bottle or siphon that bears the trade mark or name of another person, without the consent of that other person, with a beverage, milk, by-product of milk or other liquid commodity for the purpose of sale or traffic. 1953-54, c. 51, s. 353.

Used goods sold without disclosure

Type 'B' (D) Offence 370

369. Every one commits an offence who sells, exposes or has in his possession for sale, or advertises for sale, goods that have been used, reconditioned or remade and that bear the trade mark or the trade name of another person, without making full disclosure that the goods have been reconditioned, rebuilt or remade for sale and that they are not then in the condition in which they were originally made or produced. 1953-54, c. 51, s. 354. 3(4) [352]

Punishment
Type 'B' (D) Offence

370. (1) Every one who commits an offence under section 365, 366, 367, 368 or 369 is guilty of

(*a*) an indictable offence and is liable to imprisonment for two years, or

(*b*) an offence punishable on summary conviction. 722(1)

Forfeiture

(2) Anything by means of or in relation to which a person commits an offence under section 365, 366, 367, 368 or 369 is, unless the court otherwise orders, forfeited upon the conviction of that person for that offence. 1953-54, c. 51, s. 355.

Falsely claiming royal warrant
Type 'A' Offence

371. Every one who falsely represents that goods are made by a person holding a royal warrant, or for the service of Her Majesty, a member of the Royal Family or a public department is guilty of an offence punishable on summary conviction. 1953-54, c. 51, s. 356. 337 722(1)

337. In this Part

"goods" means anything that is the subject of trade or commerce;

Presumption from port of shipment

372. Where, in proceedings under this Part, the alleged offence relates to imported goods, evidence that the goods were shipped to Canada from a place outside Canada is, in the absence of any evidence to the contrary, proof that the goods were made or produced in the country from which they were shipped. 1953-54, c. 51, s. 357; 1968-69, c. 38, s. 92. 337

Wreck

Offences in relation to wreck
Type 'B' (D) Offence

373. Every one who

(*a*) secretes wreck, or defaces or obliterates the marks on wreck, or uses any means to disguise or conceal the fact that anything is wreck, or in any manner conceals the character of wreck, from a person who is entitled to inquire into the wreck, 2

(*b*) receives wreck, knowing that it is wreck, from a person other than the owner thereof or a receiver of wreck, and does not within forty-eight hours thereafter inform the receiver of wreck thereof,

(*c*) offers wreck for sale or otherwise deals with it, knowing that it is wreck, and not having a lawful authority to sell or deal with it,

(*d*) keeps wreck in his possession knowing that it is wreck, without lawful authority to keep it, for any time longer than the time reasonably necessary to deliver it to the receiver of wreck, or

(*e*) boards, against the will of the master, a vessel that is wrecked, stranded or in distress unless he is a receiver of wreck or a person acting under orders of a receiver of wreck,

is guilty of

(*f*) an indictable offence and is liable to imprisonment for two years, or

(*g*) an offence punishable on summary conviction. 1953-54, c. 51, s. 358. 722(1)

2. In this Act

"wreck" includes the cargo, stores and tackle of a vessel and all parts of a vessel separated from the vessel, and the property of persons who belong to, are on board or have quitted a vessel that is wrecked, stranded or in distress at any place in Canada;

Section 394 Interfering with saving of wrecked vessel

Public Stores

Distinguishing mark on public stores

374. The Governor in Council may, by notice to be published in the *Canada Gazette*, prescribe distinguishing marks that are appropriated for use on public stores to denote the property of Her Majesty therein, whether the stores belong to Her Majesty in right of Canada or to Her Majesty in any other right. 1953-54, c. 51, s. 359. 28 Interp 2

Applying or removing marks without authority

Type 'D' Offence

375. (1) Every one who,

(a) without lawful authority, the proof of which lies upon him, applies a distinguishing mark to anything, or ss. (3)

(b) with intent to conceal the property of Her Majesty in public stores, removes, destroys or obliterates, in whole or in part, a distinguishing mark,

is guilty of an indictable offence and is liable to imprisonment for two years.

Unlawful transactions in public stores

Type 'B' (D) Offence

(2) Every one who, without lawful authority, the proof of which lies upon him, receives, possesses, keeps, sells or delivers public stores that he knows bear 3(4)
a distinguishing mark is guilty of

(a) an indictable offence and is liable to imprisonment for two years, or

(b) an offence punishable of summary conviction. 722(1)

"Distinguishing mark"

(3) For the purposes of this section, "distinguishing mark" means a distinguishing mark that is appropriated for use on public stores pursuant to section 374. 1953-54, c. 51, s. 360.

Selling defective stores to Her Majesty

Type 'E' Offence

376. (1) Every one who knowingly sells or delivers defective stores to Her Majesty or commits fraud in connection with the sale, lease or delivery of stores 338
to Her Majesty or the manufacture of stores for Her Majesty is guilty of an 319
indictable offence and is liable to imprisonment for fourteen years.

Offences by officers and employees of corporations

Type 'E' Offence

(2) Every one who, being a director, officer, agent or employee of a corporation that commits, by fraud, an offence under subsection (1),

(a) knowingly takes part in the fraud, or

(b) knows or has reason to suspect that the fraud is being committed or has been or is about to be committed and does not inform the responsible government, or a department thereof, of Her Majesty,

is guilty of an indictable offence and is liable to imprisonment for fourteen years.

2. In this Act

"public stores" includes any movable property that is under the care, supervision, administration or control of a public department or of any person in the service of a public department;

3. (4) For the purposes of this Act,

(a) a person has anything in possession when he has it in his personal possession or knowingly

(i) has it in the actual possession or custody of another person, or

(ii) has it in any place, whether or not that place belongs to or is occupied by him, for the use or benefit of himself or of another person; and

(b) where one of two or more persons, with the knowledge and consent of the rest, has anything in his custody or possession, it shall be deemed to be in the custody and possession of each and all of them.

319. (1) A false pretence is a representation of a matter of fact either present or past, made by words or otherwise, that is known by the person who makes it to be false and that is made with a fraudulent intent to induce the person to whom it is made to act upon it.

(2) Exaggerated commendation or depreciation of the quality of anything is not a false pretence unless it is carried to such an extent that it amounts to a fraudulent misrepresentation of fact.

(3) For the purposes of subsection (2) it is a question of fact whether commendation or depreciation amounts to a fraudulent misrepresentation of fact.

338. (1) Every one who, by deceit, falsehood or other fraudulent means, whether or not it is a false pretence within the meaning of this Act, defrauds the public or any person, whether ascertained or not, of any property, money or valuable security, ...

682. (3) No person who is convicted of an offence under section 110, 113 or 376 has, after that conviction, capacity to contract with Her Majesty or to receive any benefit under a contract between Her Majesty and any other person or to hold office under Her Majesty.

722. (1) Except where otherwise expressly provided by law, every one who is convicted of an offence punishable on summary conviction is liable to a fine of not more than five hundred dollars or to imprisonment for six months or to both.

Unlawful use of military uniforms or certificates

Type 'A' Offence

377. Every one who without lawful authority, the proof of which lies upon him,

(a) wears a uniform of the Canadian Forces or any other naval, army or air force or a uniform that is so similar to the uniform of any of those forces that it is likely to be mistaken therefor, 2

(b) wears a distinctive mark relating to wounds received or service performed in war, or a military medal, ribbon, badge, chevron or any decoration or order that is awarded for war services, or any imitation thereof, or any mark or device or thing that is likely to be mistaken for any such mark, medal, ribbon, badge, chevron, decoration or order,

(c) has in his possession a certificate of discharge, certificate of release, statement of service or identity card from the Canadian Forces or any other naval, army or air force that has not been issued to and does not belong to him, or

(d) has in his possession a commission or warrant or a certificate of discharge, certificate of release, statement of service or identity card issued to an officer or person in or who has been in the Canadian Forces or any other naval, army or air force, that contains any alteration that is not verified by the initials of the officer who issued it, or by the initials of some officer thereto lawfully authorized, 3(4)

is guilty of an offence punishable on summary conviction. 1953-54, c. 51, s. 362. 722(1)

2. In this Act

"Canadian Forces" means the armed forces of Her Majesty raised by Canada;

3. (4) For the purposes of this Act,

(a) a person has anything in possession when he has it in his personal possession or knowingly

(i) has it in the actual possession or custody of another person, or

(ii) has it in any place, whether or not that place belongs to or is occupied by him, for the use or benefit of himself or of another person; and

(b) where one of two or more persons, with the knowledge and consent of the rest, has anything in his custody or possession, it shall be deemed to be in the custody and possession of each and all of them.

Military stores
Type 'B' (D) Offence

378. (1) Every one who buys, receives or detains from a member of the Canadian Forces or a deserter or absentee without leave therefrom any military stores that are owned by Her Majesty or for which the member, deserter or absentee without leave is accountable to Her Majesty is guilty of

(a) an indictable offence and is liable to imprisonment for five years, or

(b) an offence punishable on summary conviction. 722(1)

Exception

(2) No person shall be convicted of an offence under this section where he establishes that he did not know and had no reason to suspect that the military stores in respect of which the offence was committed were owned by Her Majesty or were military stores for which the member, deserter or absentee without leave was accountable to Her Majesty. 1953-54, c. 51, s. 363.

Evidence of enlistment

379. (1) In proceedings under sections 375 to 378, evidence that a person was at any time performing duties in the Canadian Forces is, in the absence of any evidence to the contrary, proof that his enrolment in the Canadian Forces prior to that time was regular.

Presumption when accused a dealer in stores

(2) An accused who is charged with an offence under subsection 375(2) shall be presumed to have known that the stores in respect of which the offence is alleged to have been committed bore a distinguishing mark within the meaning of that subsection at the time the offence is alleged to have been committed if he was, at that time, in the service or employment of Her Majesty or was a dealer in marine stores or in old metals. 1953-54, c. 51, s. 364; 1968-69, c. 38, s. 92.

722. (1) Except where otherwise expressly provided by law, every one who is convicted of an offence punishable on summary conviction is liable to a fine of not more than five hundred dollars or to imprisonment for six months or to both.

Breach of Contract, Intimidation and Discrimination Against Trade Unionists

Criminal breach of contract

Type 'B' (D) Offence with consent ss. (3)

380. (1) Every one who wilfully breaks a contract, knowing or having reasonable cause to believe that the probable consequences of doing so, whether alone or in combination with others, will be

(a) to endanger human life,

(b) to cause serious bodily injury,

(c) to expose valuable property, real or personal, to destruction or serious injury,

(d) to deprive the inhabitants of a city or place, or part thereof, wholly or to a great extent, of their supply of light, power, gas or water, or

(e) to delay or prevent the running of a locomotive engine, tender, freight or passenger train or car, on a railway that is a common carrier,

is guilty of

(f) an indictable offence and is liable to imprisonment for five years, or

(g) an offence punishable on summary conviction.

(2) No person wilfully breaks a contract within the meaning of subsection (1) by reason only that

(a) being the employee of an employer, he stops work as a result of the failure of his employer and himself to agree upon any matter relating to his employment, or,

(b) being a member of an organization of employees formed for the purpose of regulating relations between employers and employees, he stops work as a result of the failure of the employer and a bargaining agent acting on behalf of the organization to agree upon any matter relating to the employment of members of the organization,

if, before the stoppage of work occurs, all steps provided by law with respect to the settlement of industrial disputes are taken and any provision for the final settlement of differences, without stoppage of work, contained in or by law deemed to be contained in a collective agreement is complied with and effect given thereto.

(3) No proceedings shall be instituted under this section without the consent of the Attorney General. 1953-54, c. 51, s. 365.

199. Every one who undertakes to do an act is under a legal duty to do it if an omission to do the act is or may be dangerous to life.

202. (1) Every one is criminally negligent who

(a) in doing anything, or

(b) in omitting to do anything that it is his duty to do,

shows wanton or reckless disregard for the lives or safety of other persons.

(2) For the purposes of this section, "duty" means a duty imposed by law.

203. Every one who by criminal negligence causes death to another person is guilty of an indictable offence and is liable to imprisonment for life.

204. Every one who by criminal negligence causes bodily harm to another person is guilty of an indictable offence and is liable to imprisonment for ten years.

Intimidation

Type 'A' Offence

381. (1) Every one who, wrongfully and without lawful authority, for the purpose of compelling another person to abstain from doing anything that he has a lawful right to do, or to do anything that he has a lawful right to abstain from doing,

(a) uses violence or threats of violence to that person or to his wife or children, or injures his property,

(b) intimidates or attempts to intimidate that person or a relative of that person by threats that, in Canada or elsewhere, violence or other injury will be done to or punishment inflicted upon him or a relative of his, or that the property of any of them will be damaged, 24

(c) persistently follows that person about from place to place,

(d) hides any tools, clothes or other property owned or used by that person, or deprives him of them or hinders him in the use of them,

(e) with one or more other persons follows that person, in a disorderly manner, on a highway, 2

(f) besets or watches the dwelling-house or place where that person resides, works, carries on business or happens to be, or 2

(g) blocks or obstructs a highway,

is guilty of an offence punishable on summary conviction.

Exception

(2) A person who attends at or near or approaches a dwelling-house or place, for the purpose only of obtaining or communicating information, does not watch or beset within the meaning of this section. 1953-54, c. 51, s. 366.

305. (1) Every one who, without reasonable justification or excuse and with intent to extort or gain anything, by threats, accusations, menaces or violence induces or attempts to induce any person, whether or not he is the person threatened, accused or menaced or to whom violence is shown, to do anything or cause anything to be done, is guilty of an indictable offence and is liable to imprisonment for fourteen years.

(2) A threat to institute civil proceedings is not a threat for the purposes of this section.

2. In this Act

"dwelling-house" means the whole or any part of a building or structure that is kept or occupied as a permanent or temporary residence and includes

(a) a building within the curtilage of a dwelling-house that is connected to it by a doorway or by a covered and enclosed passageway, and

(b) a unit that is designed to be mobile and to be used as a permanent or temporary residence and that is being used as such a residence;

"highway" means a road to which the public has the right of access, and includes bridges over which or tunnels through which a road passes;

24. (1) Every one who, having an intent to commit an offence, does or omits to do anything for the purpose of carrying out his intention is guilty of an attempt to commit the offence whether or not it was possible under the circumstances to commit the offence.

(2) The question whether an act or omission by a person who has an intent to commit an offence is or is not mere preparation to commit the offence, and too remote to constitute an attempt to commit the offence, is a question of law.

51. Every one who does an act of violence in order to intimidate the Parliament of Canada or the legislature of a province is guilty of an indictable offence and is liable to imprisonment for fourteen years.

Threat to commit offences against internationally protected person

Type 'D' Offence

381.1 Every one who threatens to commit an offence against section 218, 244, 245, 246, 247 or 387.1 involving an internationally protected person is guilty of an indictable offence. 1974-75-76, c. 93, s. 33. 2 658

218 (Murder), 244 (Assault), 245 (Assault causing bodily harm), 246 (Assault with intent), 247 (Kidnapping), 387.1 (Attack on premises, residence or transport of internationally protected person)

2. In this Act

"internationally protected person" means

(a) a head of state, including any member of a collegial body performing the functions of a head of state under the constitution of the state concerned, a head of a government or a minister of foreign affairs, whenever such person is in a state other than the state in which he holds such position or office,

(b) a member of the family of a person described in paragraph *(a)* who accompanies that person in a state other than the state in which that person holds such position or office,

(c) a representative or official of a state or an official or agent of an international organization of an intergovernmental character who, at the time when and at the place where an offence referred to in subsection 6(1.2) is committed against his person or any property referred to in section 387.1 that is used by him, is entitled, pursuant to international law, to special protection from any attack on his person, freedom or dignity, or

(d) a member of the family of a representative, official or agent described in paragraph *(c)* who forms part of his household, if such representative, official or agent, at the time when and at the place where any offence referred to in subsection 6(1.2) is committed against the member of his family or any property referred to in section 387.1 that is used by that member, is entitled, pursuant to international law, to special protection from any attack on his person, freedom or dignity;

6. (8) If in any proceedings under this Act a question arises as to whether any person is a person who is entitled, pursuant to international law, to special protection from any attack on his person, freedom or dignity, a certificate purporting to have been issued by or under the authority of the Secretary of State for External Affairs containing any statement of fact relevant to that question is admissible in evidence in such proceedings and in the absence of evidence to the contrary is proof of the statements contained in the certificate.

6. (1.2) Notwithstanding anything in this Act or any other Act, every one who, outside Canada, commits an act or omission against the person of an internationally protected person or against any property referred to in section 387.1 used by him that if committed in Canada would be an offence against section 218, 219, 245, 246, 247, 381.1 or 387.1 shall be deemed to commit that act or omission in Canada if

(a) the act or omission is committed on a ship registered pursuant to any Act of Parliament;

(b) the act or omission is committed on an aircraft

(i) registered in Canada under regulations made under the *Aeronautics Act*, or

(ii) leased without crew and operated by a person who is qualified under regulations made under the *Aeronautics Act* to be registered as owner of an aircraft in Canada under such regulations;

(c) the person who commits the act or omission is a Canadian citizen or is present in Canada; or

(d) the Act or omission is against

(i) a person who enjoys his status as an internationally protected person by virtue of the functions he exercises on behalf of Canada, or

(ii) a member of the family of a person described in subparagraph (i) who qualifies under paragraph *(b)* or *(d)* of the definition "internationally protected person" in section 2.

658. Every one who is convicted of an indictable offence for which no punishment is specially provided is liable to imprisonment for five years.

Offences by employers

Type 'A' Offence

382. Every one who, being an employer or the agent of an employer, wrongfully and without lawful authority

(a) refuses to employ or dismisses from his employment any person for the reason only that the person is a member of a lawful trade union or of a lawful association or combination of workmen or employees formed for the purpose of advancing, in a lawful manner, their interests and organized for their protection in the regulation of wages and conditions of work,

(b) seeks by intimidation, threat of loss of position or employment, or by causing actual loss of position or employment, or by threatening or imposing any pecuniary penalty, to compel workmen or employees to abstain from belonging to a trade union, association or combination to which they have a lawful right to belong, or

(c) conspires, combines, agrees or arranges with any other employer or his agent to do anything mentioned in paragraph *(a)* or *(b)*,

is guilty of an offence punishable on summary conviction. 1953-54, c. 51, s. 367. 722(1)

Secret Commissions

Secret commissions

Type 'D' Offence

IPA offence 178.1

383. (1) Every one commits an offence who

(a) corruptly

(i) gives, offers or agrees to give or offer to an agent, or ss. (4)

(ii) being an agent, demands, accepts or offers or agrees to accept from any person,

a reward, advantage or benefit of any kind as consideration for doing or forbearing to do, or for having done or forborne to do, any act relating to the affairs or business of his principal or for showing or forbearing to show favour or disfavour to any person with relation to the affairs or business of his principal; or ss. (4)

(b) with intent to deceive a principal gives to an agent of that principal, or, being an agent, uses with intent to deceive his principal, a receipt, account, or other writing 2

(i) in which the principal has an interest,

(ii) that contains any statement that is false or erroneous or defective in any material particular, and

(iii) that is intended to mislead the principal.

Privy to offence

(2) Every one commits an offence who is knowingly privy to the commission of an offence under subsection (1).

Type 'D' Offence

IPA offence 178.1

(3) A person who commits an offence under this section is guilty of an indictable offence and is liable to imprisonment for two years.

Definitions

(4) In this section "agent" includes an employee, and "principal" includes an employer. 1953-54, c. 51, s. 368.

Trading Stamps

Issuing trading stamps

Type 'A' Offence

384. (1) Every one who, by himself or his employee or agent, directly or indirectly issues, gives, sells or otherwise disposes of, or offers to issue, give, sell or otherwise dispose of trading stamps to a merchant or dealer in goods for use 337
in his business is guilty of an offence punishable on summary conviction. 722(1)

Giving to purchaser of goods

(2) Every one who, being a merchant or dealer in goods, by himself or his employee or agent, directly or indirectly gives or in any way disposes of, or offers to give or in any way dispose of, trading stamps to a person who purchases goods from him is guilty of an offence punishable on summary conviction. 722(1)
1953-54, c. 51, s. 369.

337. In this Part

"goods" means anything that is the subject of trade or commerce;

"trading stamps" includes any form of cash receipt, receipt, coupon, premium ticket or other device, designed or intended to be given to the purchaser of goods by the vendor thereof or on his behalf, and to represent a discount on the price of the goods or a premium to the purchaser thereof

(a) that may be redeemed

(i) by any person other than the vendor, the person from whom the vendor purchased the goods, or the manufacturer of the goods,

(ii) by the vendor, the person from whom the vendor purchased the goods, or the manufacturer of the goods in cash or in goods that are not his property in whole or in part, or

(iii) by the vendor elsewhere than in the premises where the goods are purchased; or

(b) that does not show upon its face the place where it is delivered and the merchantable value thereof; or

(c) that may not be redeemed upon demand at any time;

but an offer, endorsed by the manufacturer upon a wrapper or container in which goods are sold, of a premium or reward for the return of that wrapper or container to the manufacturer is not a trading stamp.

PART IX

WILFUL AND FORBIDDEN ACTS IN RESPECT OF CERTAIN PROPERTY

Interpretation

"Property"

385. In this Part, "property" means real or personal corporeal property.

2. In this Act

"property" includes

(a) real and personal property of every description and deeds and instruments relating to or evidencing the title or right to property, or giving a right to recover or receive money or goods,

(b) property originally in the possession or under the control of any person, and any property into or for which it has been converted or exchanged and anything acquired at any time by such conversion or exchange, and

(c) any postal card, postage stamp or other stamp issued or prepared for issue under the authority of the Parliament of Canada or of the legislature of a province for the payment to the Crown or a corporate body of any fee, rate or duty, whether or not it is in the possession of the Crown or of any person;

Wilfully causing event to occur

386. (1) Every one who causes the occurrence of an event by doing an act or by omitting to do an act that it is his duty to do, knowing that the act or omission will probably cause the occurrence of the event and being reckless whether the event occurs or not, shall be deemed, for the purposes of this Part, wilfully to have caused the occurrence of the event.

Colour of right

(2) No person shall be convicted of an offence under sections 387 to 402 where he proves that he acted with legal justification or excuse and with colour of right.

Interest

(3) Where it is an offence to destroy or to damage anything,

(a) the fact that a person has a partial interest in what is destroyed or damaged does not prevent him from being guilty of the offence if he caused the destruction or damage, and

(b) the fact that a person has a total interest in what is destroyed or damaged does not prevent him from being guilty of the offence if he caused the destruction or damage with intent to defraud. 1953-54, c. 51, s. 371.

Mischief

Mischief

387. (1) Every one commits mischief who wilfully 386

(a) destroys or damages property, 385

(b) renders property dangerous, useless, inoperative or ineffective,

(c) obstructs, interrupts or interferes with the lawful use, enjoyment or operation of property, or

(d) obstructs, interrupts or interferes with any person in the lawful use, enjoyment or operation of property.

Type 'E' Offence

(2) Every one who commits mischief that causes actual danger to life is guilty of an indictable offence and is liable to imprisonment for life.

Type 'B' (E) Offence

(3) Every one who commits mischief in relation to public property is guilty of

(a) an indictable offence and is liable to imprisonment for fourteen years, or

(b) an offence punishable on summary conviction. 722(1)

Type 'B' (D) Offence

(4) Every one who commits mischief in relation to private property is guilty of

(a) an indictable offence and is liable to imprisonment for five years, or

(b) an offence punishable on summary conviction. 722(1)

Type 'B' (D) Offence

(5) Every one who wilfully does an act or wilfully omits to do an act that it is his duty to do is, if that act or omission is likely to constitute mischief causing actual danger to life, or to constitute mischief in relation to public property or private property, guilty of

(a) an indictable offence and is liable to imprisonment for five years, or

(b) an offence punishable on summary conviction. 722(1)

Saving

(6) No person commits mischief within the meaning of this section by reason only that

(a) he stops work as a result of the failure of his employer and himself to agree upon any matter relating to his employment,

(b) he stops work as a result of the failure of his employer and a bargaining agent acting on his behalf to agree upon any matter relating to his employment, or

(c) he stops work as a result of his taking part in a combination of workmen or employees for their own reasonable protection as workmen or employees.

Idem

(7) No person commits mischief within the meaning of this section by reason only that he attends at or near or approaches a dwelling-house or place for the purpose only of obtaining or communicating information. R.S., c. C-34, s. 387; 1972, c. 13, s. 30.

722. (1) Except where otherwise expressly provided by law, every one who is convicted of an offence punishable on summary conviction is liable to a fine of not more than five hundred dollars or to imprisonment for six months or to both.

Attack on premises, residence or transport of internationally protected person

Type 'D' Offence

387.1 Every one who commits an attack upon the official premises, private accommodation or means of transport of an internationally protected person that is likely to endanger the life or liberty of such person is guilty of an indictable offence. 1974-75-76, c. 93, s. 34. 2 [381.1] 658

6. (1.2) Notwithstanding anything in this Act or any other Act, every one who, outside Canada, commits an act or omission against the person of an internationally protected person or against any property referred to in section 387.1 used by him that if committed in Canada would be an offence against section 218, 219, 245, 246, 247, 381.1 or 387.1 shall be deemed to commit that act or omission in Canada if

(a) the act or omission is committed on a ship registered pursuant to any Act of Parliament;

(b) the act or omission is committed on an aircraft

(i) registered in Canada under regulations made under the *Aeronautics Act*, or

(ii) leased without crew and operated by a person who is qualified under regulations made under the *Aeronautics Act* to be registered as owner of an aircraft in Canada under such regulations;

(c) the person who commits the act or omission is a Canadian citizen or is present in Canada; or

(d) the Act or omission is against

(i) a person who enjoys his status as an internationally protected person by virtue of the functions he exercises on behalf of Canada, or

(ii) a member of the family of a person described in subparagraph (i) who qualifies under paragraph *(b)* or *(d)* of the definition "internationally protected person" in section 2.

658. Every one who is convicted of an indictable offence for which no punishment is specially provided is liable to imprisonment for five years.

Damage not more than fifty dollars

Type 'A' Offence

388. (1) Every one who wilfully destroys or damages property is, where actual danger to life is not involved, guilty of an offence punishable on summary conviction if the alleged amount of destruction or damage does not exceed fifty dollars. 386 385 722(1)

Compensation

(2) Where an accused is convicted of an offence under subsection (1) the summary conviction court may, in addition to any punishment that is imposed, order the accused to pay to a person aggrieved an amount not exceeding fifty dollars that appears to the summary conviction court to be reasonable compensation for the destruction or damage.

Imprisonment in default

(3) The summary conviction court may order that where an amount that is adjudged to be paid as compensation under subsection (2) is not paid forthwith or within the period that the summary conviction court appoints at the time of the conviction, the accused shall be imprisoned for a term not exceeding two months.

Idem

(4) The summary conviction court may order that terms of imprisonment that are imposed under this section shall take effect one after the other. 1953-54, c. 51, s. 373.

742. Where several persons join in committing the same offence and upon conviction each is adjudged to pay an amount to a person aggrieved, no more shall be paid to that person than an amount equal to the value of the property destroyed or injured or the amount of the injury done, together with costs, if any, and the residue of the amount adjudged to be paid shall be applied in the manner in which other penalties imposed by law are directed to be applied.

Arson and Other Fires

Arson
Type 'E' Offence
IPA offence 178.1

389. (1) Every one who wilfully sets fire to

(a) a building or structure, whether completed or not,

(b) a stack of vegetable produce or of mineral or vegetable fuel,

(c) a mine,

(d) a well of combustible substance,

(e) a vessel or aircraft, whether completed or not,

(f) timber or materials placed in a shipyard for building, repairing or fitting out a ship,

(g) military or public stores or munitions of war,

(h) a crop, whether standing or cut down, or

(i) any wood, forest, or natural growth, or any lumber, timber, log, float, boom, dam or slide,

is guilty of an indictable offence and is liable to imprisonment for fourteen years.

2. In this Act

"public stores" includes any movable property that is under the care, supervision, administration or control of a public department or of any person in the service of a public department;

Fraudulently burning personal property
Type 'D' Offence

(2) Every one who wilfully and for a fraudulent purpose sets fire to personal property not mentioned in subsection (1) is guilty of an indictable offence and is liable to imprisonment for five years. 1953-54, c. 51, s. 374.

Setting fire to other substance
Type 'D' Offence

390. Every one who

(a) wilfully sets fire to anything that is likely to cause anything mentioned in subsection 389(1) to catch fire; or

(b) wilfully and for a fraudulent purpose sets fire to anything that is likely to cause personal property not mentioned in subsection 389(1) to catch fire,

is guilty of an indictable offence and is liable to imprisonment for five years.

Presumption against holder of insurance

391. Where a person is charged with an offence under section 389 or 390, evidence that he is the holder of or is named as the beneficiary under a policy of fire insurance relating to the property in respect of which the offence is alleged to have been committed is, in the absence of any evidence to the contrary and where intent to defraud is material, proof of intent to defraud. 1953-54, c. 51, s. 376; 1968-69, c. 38, s. 92.

Setting a fire by negligence
Type 'D' Offence

392. (1) Every one who causes a fire

(a) wilfully, or

(b) by violating a law in force in the place where the fire occurs,

is, if the fire results in loss of life or destruction of or damage to property, guilty of an indictable offence and is liable to imprisonment for five years.

Presumption against person in control of premises

(2) For the purposes of this section, the person who owns, occupies or controls property in which a fire that results in loss of life or destruction of or damage to property originates or occurs shall be deemed wilfully to have caused the fire if he has failed to comply with any law that is intended to prevent fires or that requires the property to be equipped with apparatus for the purpose of extinguishing fires or for the purpose of enabling persons to escape in the event of fire, and if it is established that the fire, or the loss of life, or the whole or any substantial portion of the destruction of or damage to the property would not have occurred if he had complied with the law. 1953-54, c. 51, s. 377.

Other Interference with Property

False alarm of fire

Type 'B' (D) Offence

393. Every one who wilfully, without reasonable cause, by outcry, ringing bells, using a fire alarm, telephone or telegraph, or in any other manner, makes or circulates or causes to be made or circulated an alarm of fire is guilty of

(a) an indictable offence and is liable to imprisonment for two years, or

(b) an offence punishable on summary conviction. R.S., c. C-34, s. 393; 1972; 722(1)
c. 13, s. 31.

Interfering with saving of wrecked vessel

Type 'D' Offence

394. (1) Every one who wilfully prevents or impedes, or who wilfully endeavours to prevent or impede,

(a) the saving of a vessel that is wrecked, stranded, abandoned or in distress, or

(b) a person who attempts to save a vessel that is wrecked, stranded, abandoned or in distress,

is guilty of an indictable offence and is liable to imprisonment for five years.

Interfering with saving of wreck

Type 'A' Offence

(2) Every one who wilfully prevents or impedes or wilfully endeavours to prevent or impede the saving of wreck is guilty of an offence punishable on summary conviction. 1953-54, c. 51, s. 379. 722(1)

2. In this Act

"wreck" includes the cargo, stores and tackle of a vessel and all parts of a vessel separated from the vessel, and the property of persons who belong to, are on board or have quitted a vessel that is wrecked, stranded or in distress at any place in Canada;

Interfering with marine signal

Type 'A' Offence

395. (1) Every one who makes fast a vessel or boat to a signal, buoy or other sea mark that is used for purposes of navigation is guilty of an offence punishable on summary conviction. 722(1)

Idem

Type 'E' Offence

(2) Every one who wilfully alters, removes or conceals a signal, buoy or other sea mark that is used for purposes of navigation is guilty of an indictable offence and is liable to imprisonment for ten years. 1953-54, c. 51, s. 380.

Removing natural bar without permission

Type 'D' Offence

396. Every one who wilfully and without the written permission of the Minister of Transport, the burden of proof of which lies on the accused, removes any stone, wood, earth or other material that forms a natural bar necessary to the existence of a public harbour, or that forms a natural protection to such a bar, is guilty of an indictable offence and is liable to imprisonment for two years. 1953-54, c. 51, s. 381.

Occupant injuring building
Type 'D' Offence

397. Every one who, wilfully and to the prejudice of a mortgagee or owner, pulls down, demolishes or removes, all or any part of a dwelling-house or other building of which he is in possession or occupation, or severs from the freehold any fixture fixed therein or thereto is guilty of an indictable offence and is liable to imprisonment for five years. 1953-54, c. 51, s. 382. 386 2

Interfering with boundary lines
Type 'A' Offence

398. Every one who wilfully pulls down, defaces, alters or removes anything planted or set up as the boundary line or part of the boundary line of land is guilty of an offence punishable on summary conviction. 1953-54, c. 51, s. 383. 722(1)

Interfering with international boundary marks, etc.
Type 'D' Offence

399. (1) Every one who wilfully pulls down, defaces, alters or removes

(a) a boundary mark lawfully placed to mark an international, provincial, county or municipal boundary, or

(b) a boundary mark lawfully placed by a land surveyor to mark a limit, boundary or angle of a concession, range, lot or parcel of land,

is guilty of an indictable offence and is liable to imprisonment for five years.

Saving provision

(2) A land surveyor does not commit an offence under subsection (1) where, in his operations as a land surveyor,

(a) he takes up, when necessary, a boundary mark mentioned in paragraph (1)*(b)* and carefully replaces it as it was before he took it up, or

(b) he takes up a boundary mark mentioned in paragraph (1)*(b)* in the course of surveying for a highway or other work that, when completed, will make it impossible or impracticable for such boundary mark to occupy its original position, and he establishes a permanent record of the original position sufficient to permit such position to be ascertained. 1953-54, c. 51, s. 384; 1960-61, c. 43, s. 11.

Cattle and Other Animals

Injuring or endangering cattle
Type 'D' Offence

400. Every one who wilfully

(a) kills, maims, wounds, poisons or injures cattle, or 2

(b) places poison in such a position that it may easily be consumed by cattle,

is guilty of an indictable offence and is liable to imprisonment for five years. 1953-54, c. 51, s. 385.

2. In this Act

"cattle" means neat cattle or an animal of the bovine species by whatever technical or familiar name it is known, and includes a horse, mule, ass, pig, sheep or goat;

Injuring or endangering other animals
Type 'A' Offence

401. Every one who wilfully and without lawful excuse

(a) kills, maims, wounds, poisons or injures dogs, birds or animals that are not cattle and are kept for a lawful purpose, or

(b) places poison in such a position that it may easily be consumed by dogs, birds or animals that are not cattle and are kept for a lawful purpose,

is guilty of an offence punishable on summary conviction. 1953-54, c. 51, s. 386. 722(1)

Cruelty to Animals

Causing unnecessary suffering

402. (1) Every one commits an offence who

(a) wilfully causes or, being the owner, wilfully permits to be caused unnecessary pain, suffering or injury to an animal or bird, 386

(b) by wilful neglect causes damage or injury to animals or birds while they are being driven or conveyed,

(c) being the owner or the person having the custody or control of a domestic animal or bird or an animal or bird wild by nature that is in captivity, abandons it in distress or wilfully neglects or fails to provide suitable and adequate food, water, shelter and care for it,

(d) in any manner encourages, aids or assists at the fighting or baiting of animals or birds,

(e) wilfully, without reasonable excuse, administers a poisonous or injurious drug or substance to a domestic animal or bird or an animal or bird wild by nature that is kept in captivity or being the owner of such an animal or bird, wilfully permits a poisonous or injurious drug or substance to be administered to it,

(f) promotes, arranges, conducts, assists in, receives money for, or takes part in a meeting, competition, exhibition, pastime, practice, display, or event at or in the course of which captive birds are liberated by hand, trap, contrivance or any other means for the purpose of being shot when they are liberated, or

(g) being the owner, occupier, or person in charge of any premises, permits the premises or any part thereof to be used for a purpose mentioned in paragraph *(f)*.

Type 'A' Offence

(2) Every one who commits an offence under subsection (1) is guilty of an offence punishable on summary conviction. 722(1)

Failure to exercise reasonable care as evidence

(3) For the purposes of proceedings under paragraph (1)*(a)* or *(b)*, evidence that a person failed to exercise reasonable care or supervision of an animal or bird thereby causing it pain, suffering, damage or injury is, in the absence of any evidence to the contrary, proof that such pain, suffering, damage or injury was caused or was permitted to be caused wilfully or was caused by wilful neglect, as the case may be.

Presence at baiting as evidence

(4) For the purpose of proceedings under paragraph (1)*(d)*, evidence that an accused was present at the fighting or baiting of animals or birds is, in the absence of any evidence to the contrary, proof that he encouraged, aided or assisted at such fighting or baiting.

Order of prohibition

(5) Where an accused is convicted of an offence under subsection (1), the court may, in addition to any other sentence that may be imposed for the offence, make an order prohibiting the accused from owning or having the custody or control of an animal or bird during any period not exceeding two years. 1974-75-76, c. 93, s. 35.

Breach of order

Type 'A' Offence

(6) Every one who owns or has the custody or control of an animal or bird while he is prohibited from doing so by reason of an order made under subsection (5) is guilty of an offence punishable on summary conviction. 1953-54, c. 51, s. 387; 1968-69, c. 38, s. 23. 722(1)

Keeping cock-pit

403. (1) Every one who builds, makes, maintains or keeps a cock-pit on premises that he owns or occupies, or allows a cock-pit to be built, made, maintained or kept on such premises is guilty of an offence punishable on summary conviction.

Confiscation

(2) A peace officer who finds cocks in a cock-pit or on premises where a cock-pit is located shall seize them and take them before a justice who shall order them to be destroyed. 1953-54, c. 51, s. 388. 2 28 Interp

Interpretation Act

28. In every enactment

"shall" is to be construed as imperative;

404. Repealed. 1974-75-76, c. 86, s. 22.

405. Repealed. 1974-75-76, c. 86, s. 22.

PART X

OFFENCES RELATING TO CURRENCY

Interpretation

Definitions

406. In this Part

"counterfeit money"

"counterfeit money" includes

(a) a false coin or false paper money that resembles or is apparently intended to resemble or pass for a current coin or current paper money,

(b) a forged bank note or forged blank bank note, whether complete or incomplete, 2

(c) a genuine coin or genuine paper money that is prepared or altered to resemble or pass for a current coin or current paper money of a higher denomination,

(d) a current coin from which the milling is removed by filing or cutting the edges and on which new milling is made to restore its appearance,

(e) a coin cased with gold, silver or nickel, as the case may be, that is intended to resemble or pass for a current gold, silver or nickel coin, and

(f) a coin or a piece of metal or mixed metals washed or coloured by any means with a wash or material capable of producing the appearance of gold, silver or nickel and that is intended to resemble or pass for a current gold, silver or nickel coin;

"counterfeit token of value"

"counterfeit token of value" means a counterfeit excise stamp, postage stamp or other evidence of value, by whatever technical, trivial or deceptive designation it may be described, and includes genuine coin or paper money that has no value as money;

"current"

"current" means lawfully current in Canada or elsewhere by virtue of a law, proclamation or regulation in force in Canada or elsewhere as the case may be;

"utter"

"utter" includes sell, pay, tender and put off. 1953-54, c. 51, s. 391; 1967-68, c. 26, s. 8.

2. In this Act

"bank-note" includes any negotiable instrument

(a) issued by or on behalf of a person carrying on the business of banking in or out of Canada,

(b) issued under the authority of the Parliament of Canada or under lawful authority of the government of a state other than Canada,

intended to be used as money or as the equivalent of money, immediately upon issue or at some time subsequent thereto, and includes bank bills and bank post bills;

3. (4) For the purposes of this Act,

(a) a person has anything in possession when he has it in his personal possession or knowingly

(i) has it in the actual possession or custody of another person, or

(ii) has it in any place, whether or not that place belongs to or is occupied by him, for the use or benefit of himself or of another person; and

(b) where one of two or more persons, with the knowledge and consent of the rest, has anything in his custody or possession, it shall be deemed to be in the custody and possession of each and all of them.

Making

Making
Type 'E' Offence
IPA offence 178.1

407. Every one who makes or begins to make counterfeit money is guilty of an indictable offence and is liable to imprisonment for fourteen years. 1953-54, c. 51, s. 392. 406

Possession

Possession, etc., of counterfeit money
Type 'E' Offence
IPA offence 178.1

408. Every one who, without lawful justification or excuse, the proof of which lies upon him,

(a) buys, receives or offers to buy or receive,

(b) has in his custody or possession, or 3(4)

(c) introduces into Canada,

counterfeit money is guilty of an indictable offence and is liable to imprisonment for fourteen years. 1953-54, cl 51, s. 393.

Having clippings, etc.
Type 'E' Offence

409. Every one who, without lawful justification or excuse, the proof of which lies upon him, has in his custody or possession

(a) gold or silver filings or clippings,

(b) gold or silver bullion, or

(c) gold or silver in dust, solution or otherwise,

produced or obtained by impairing, diminishing or lightening a current gold or silver coin, knowing that it has been so produced or obtained, is guilty of an indictable offence and is liable to imprisonment for five years. 1953-54, c. 51, s. 394. 406

Uttering

Uttering, etc., counterfeit money
Type 'E' Offence
IPA offence 178.1

410. Every one who, without lawful justification or excuse, the proof of which lies upon him,

(a) utters or offers to utter counterfeit money or uses counterfeit money as if it were genuine, or 406

(b) exports, sends or takes counterfeit money out of Canada,

is guilty of an indictable offence and is liable to imprisonment for fourteen years. 1953-54, c. 51, s. 395.

Uttering coin
Type 'D' Offence

411. Every one who, with intent to defraud, knowingly utters

(a) a coin that is not current, or

(b) a piece of metal or mixed metals that resembles in size, figure or colour a current coin for which it is uttered,

is guilty of an indictable offence and is liable to imprisonment for two years. 1967-68, c. 26, s. 9.

Slugs and tokens
Type 'A' Offence

412. Every one who without lawful excuse, the proof of which lies upon him,

(a) manufactures, produces or sells, or

(b) has in his possession 3(4)

anything that is intended to be fraudulently used in substitution for a coin or token of value that any coin or token-operated device is designed to receive is guilty of an offence punishable on summary conviction. R.S., c. C-34, s. 412; 1972, c. 13, s. 32. 722(1)

Defacing and Impairing

Clipping and uttering clipped coin
Type 'E' Offence

413. Every one who

(a) impairs, diminishes or lightens a current gold or silver coin with intent that it should pass for a current gold or silver coin, or

(b) utters a coin, knowing that it has been impaired, diminished or lightened contrary to paragraph *(a)*,

is guilty of an indictable offence and is liable to imprisonment for fourteen years.

Defacing current coins
Type 'A' Offence

414. Every one who

(a) defaces a current coin, or

(b) utters a current coin that has been defaced,

is guilty of an offence punishable on summary conviction. 1967-68, c. 26, s. 10. 722(1)

Printing circulars, etc., in likeness of notes
Type 'A' Offence

415. (1) Every one who designs, engraves, prints or in any manner makes, executes, issues, distributes, circulates or uses a business or professional card, notice, placard, circular, handbill or advertisement in the likeness or appearance of

(a) a current bank note or current paper money, or 406 2

(b) any obligation or security of a government or a bank, 28 Interp

is guilty of an offence punishable on summary conviction. 722(1)

Printing anything in likeness of bank notes, etc.
Type 'A' Offence

(2) Every one who publishes or prints anything in the likeness or appearance of

(a) all or part of a current bank note or current paper money, or

(b) all or part of any obligation or security of a government or a bank,

is guilty of an offence punishable on summary conviction. 722(1)

When no conviction under subsection (2)

(3) No person shall be convicted of an offence under subsection (2) where it is established that, in publishing or printing anything to which that subsection applies,

(a) no photography was used at any stage for the purpose of publishing or printing it, except in connection with processes necessarily involved in transferring a finished drawing or sketch to a printed surface;

(b) except for the word "Canada", nothing having the appearance of a word, letter or numeral was a complete word, letter or numeral;

(c) no representation of a human face or figure was more than a general indication of features, without detail;

(d) no more than one colour was used; and

(e) nothing in the likeness or appearance of the back of a current bank note or current paper money was published or printed in any form. 1953-54, c. 51, s. 400.

Interpretation Act

28 In every enactment

"bank" or "chartered bank" means a bank to which the *Bank Act* applies;

Instruments or Materials

Making, having or dealing in instruments for counterfeiting
Type 'E' Offence

416. Every one who, without lawful justification or excuse, the proof of which lies upon him,

(*a*) makes or repairs,

(*b*) begins or proceeds to make or repair,

(*c*) buys or sells, or

(*d*) has in his custody or possession, 3(4)

a machine, engine, tool, instrument, material or thing that he knows has been used or that he knows is adapted and intended for use in making counterfeit money or counterfeit tokens of value is guilty of an indictable offence and is 406
liable to imprisonment for fourteen years. 1953-54, c. 51, s. 401.

327. Every one who, without lawful authority or excuse, the proof of which lies upon him,

(*a*) makes, uses or knowingly has in his possession

(i) any exchequer bill paper, revenue paper, or paper that is used to make bank notes, or

(ii) any paper that is intended to resemble paper mentioned in subparagraph (i),

is guilty of an indictable offence and is liable to imprisonment for fourteen years.

Conveying instruments for coining out of mint
Type 'E' Offence

417. Every one who, without lawful justification or excuse, the proof of which lies upon him, knowingly conveys out of any of Her Majesty's mints in Canada,

(*a*) a machine, engine, tool, instrument, material or thing used or employed in connection with the manufacture of coins,

(*b*) a useful part of anything mentioned in paragraph (*a*), or

(*c*) coin, bullion, metal or a mixture of metals,

is guilty of an indictable offence and is liable to imprisonment for fourteen years. 1953-54, c. 51, s. 402.

Advertising and Trafficking in Counterfeit Money or Counterfeit Tokens of Value

Advertising and dealing in counterfeit money, etc.
Type 'D' Offence

418. (1) Every one who

(*a*) by an advertisement or any other writing offers to sell, procure or dispose of counterfeit money or counterfeit tokens of value or to give information with respect to the manner in which or the means by which counterfeit money or counterfeit tokens of value may be sold, procured or disposed of, or 2

(*b*) purchases, obtains, negotiates or otherwise deals with counterfeit tokens of value, or offers to negotiate with a view to purchasing or obtaining them,

is guilty of an indictable offence and is liable to imprisonment for five years.

Fraudulent use of money genuine but valueless

(2) No person shall be convicted of an offence under subsection (1) in respect of genuine coin or genuine paper money that has no value as money unless, at the time when the offence is alleged to have been committed, he knew that the coin or paper money had no value as money and he had a fraudulent intent in his dealings with or with respect to the coin or paper money. 1953-54, c. 51, s. 403.

2. In this Act

"writing" includes a document of any kind and any mode in which, and any material on which, words or figures, whether at length or abridged, are written, printed or otherwise expressed, or a map or plan is inscribed.

Special Provisions as to Proof

When counterfeit complete

419. (1) Every offence relating to counterfeit money or counterfeit tokens of value shall be deemed to be complete notwithstanding that the money or tokens of value in respect of which the proceedings are taken are not finished or perfected or do not copy exactly the money or tokens of value that they are apparently intended to resemble or for which they are apparently intended to pass.

Certificate of examiner of counterfeit

(2) In any proceedings under this Part, a certificate signed by a person designated as an examiner of counterfeit by the Solicitor General of Canada, stating that any coin, paper money or bank note described therein is counterfeit money or that any coin, paper money or bank note described therein is genuine and is or is not, as the case may be, current in Canada or elsewhere, is evidence of the statements contained in the certificate without proof of the signature or the official character of the person appearing to have signed the certificate.

Cross-examination and notice

(3) Subsections 237(4) and (5) apply *mutatis mutandis* in respect of a certificate described in subsection (2). 1953-54, c. 51, s. 404; 1968-69, c. 38, s. 24.

mutatis mutandis — after the necessary changes in detail so that the text applies

237. (4) An accused against whom a certificate described in paragraph (1)*(d)*, *(e)* or *(f)* is produced may, with leave of the court, require the attendance of the analyst or of the qualified technician, as the case may be, for the purposes of cross-examination.

(5) No certificate shall be received in evidence pursuant to paragraph (1)*(d)*, *(e)* or *(f)* unless the party intending to produce it has, before the trial, given to the accused reasonable notice of his intention together with a copy of the certificate.

Forfeiture

Ownership

420. (1) Counterfeit money, counterfeit tokens of value and anything that is used or is intended to be used to make counterfeit money or counterfeit tokens of value belong to Her Majesty.

Seizure

(2) A peace officer may seize and detain 2

(a) counterfeit money,

(b) counterfeit tokens of value, and

(c) machines, engines, tools, instruments, materials or things that have been used or that have been adapted and are intended for use in making counterfeit money or counterfeit tokens of value;

and anything seized shall be sent to the Minister of Finance to be disposed of or dealt with as he may direct, but anything that is required as evidence in any proceedings shall not be sent to the Minister until it is no longer required in those proceedings. 1953-54, c. 51, s. 405.

3. (4) For the purposes of this Act,

(a) a person has anything in possession when he has it in his personal possession or knowingly

(i) has it in the actual possession or custody of another person, or

(ii) has it in any place, whether or not that place belongs to or is occupied by him, for the use or benefit of himself or of another person; and

(b) where one of two or more persons, with the knowledge and consent of the rest, has anything in his custody or possession, it shall be deemed to be in the custody and possession of each and all of them.

—NOTES—

PART XI

ATTEMPTS—CONSPIRACIES—ACCESSORIES

Attempts, accessories

421. Except where otherwise expressly provided by law, the following provisions apply in respect of persons who attempt to commit or are accessories after the fact to the commission of offences, namely, 24 23

Type 'E' 'F' or 'G' Offence 429.1 & 427

(a) every one who attempts to commit or is an accessory after the fact to the commission of an indictable offence for which, upon conviction, an accused is liable to be sentenced to death or to imprisonment for life, is guilty of an indictable offence and is liable to imprisonment for fourteen years;

Type 'B' 'C' 'D' or 'E' Offence 483

(b) every one who attempts to commit or is an accessory after the fact to the commission of an indictable offence for which, upon conviction, an accused is liable to imprisonment for fourteen years or less, is guilty of an indictable offence and is liable to imprisonment for a term that is one-half of the longest term to which a person who is guilty of that offence is liable; and

Type 'A' Offence

(c) every one who attempts to commit or is an accessory after the fact to the commission of an offence punishable on summary conviction is guilty of an offence punishable on summary conviction. 1953-54,c.51,s.406.

24. (1) Every one who, having an intent to commit an offence, does or omits to do anything for the purpose of carrying out his intention is guilty of an attempt to commit the offence whether or not it was possible under the circumstances to commit the offence.

(2) The question whether an act or omission by a person who has an intent to commit an offence is or is not mere preparation to commit the offence, and too remote to constitute an attempt to commit the offence, is a question of law.

23. (1) An accessory after the fact to an offence is one who, knowing that a person has been a party to the offence, receives, comforts or assists him for the purpose of enabling him to escape.

(2) No married person whose spouse has been a party to an offence is an accessory after the fact to that offence by receiving, comforting or assisting the spouse for the purpose of enabling the spouse to escape.

521. Any one who is charged with being an accessory after the fact to any offence may be indicted, whether or not the principal or any other party to the offence has been indicted or convicted or is or is not amenable to justice.

587. Where the complete commission of an offence charged is not proved but the evidence establishes an attempt to commit the offence, the accused may be convicted of the attempt.

588. (1) Where an attempt to commit an offence is charged but the evidence establishes the commission of the complete offence, the accused is not entitled to be acquitted, but the jury may convict him of the attempt unless the judge presiding at the trial, in his discretion, discharges the jury from giving a verdict and directs that the accused be indicted for the complete offence.

(2) An accused who is convicted under this section is not liable to be tried again for the offence that he was charged with attempting to commit.

589. (1) A count in an indictment is divisible and where the commission of the offence charged, as described in the enactment creating it or as charged in the count, includes the commission of another offence, whether punishable by indictment or on summary conviction, the accused may be convicted

(a) of an offence so included that is proved, notwithstanding that the whole offence that is charged is not proved, or

(b) of an attempt to commit an offence so included.

Counselling, etc., offence which is not committed

422. Except where otherwise expressly provided by law, the following provisions apply in respect of persons who counsel, procure or incite other persons to commit offences, namely,

(*a*) every one who counsels, procures or incites another person to commit an indictable offence is, if the offence is not committed, guilty of an indictable offence and is liable to the same punishment to which a person who attempts to commit that offence is liable; and 421

Type 'A' Offence

(*b*) every one who counsels, procures or incites another person to commit an offence punishable on summary conviction is, if the offence is not committed, guilty of an offence punishable on summary conviction. 1953-54,c.51,s.407.

22. (1) Where a person counsels or procures another person to be a party to an offence and that other person is afterwards a party to that offence, the person who counselled or procured is a party to that offence, notwithstanding that the offence was committed in a way different from that which was counselled or procured.

(2) Every one who counsels or procures another person to be a party to an offence is a party to every offence that the other commits in consequence of the counselling or procuring that the person who counselled or procured knew or ought to have known was likely to be committed in consequence of the counselling or procuring.

Conspiracy

423. (1) Except where otherwise expressly provided by law, the following provisions apply in respect of conspiracy, namely,

Type 'G' Offence 427(d)

(*a*) every one who conspires with any one to commit murder or to cause another person to be murdered, whether in Canada or not, is guilty of an indictable offence and is liable to imprisonment for fourteen years;

(*b*) every one who conspires with any one to prosecute a person for an alleged offence, knowing that he did not commit that offence, is guilty of an indictable offence and is liable

Type 'E' Offence

(i) to imprisonment for ten years, if the alleged offence is one for which, upon conviction, that person would be liable to be sentenced to death or to imprisonment for life or for fourteen years, or

Type 'D' Offence

(ii) to imprisonment for five years, if the alleged offence is one for which, upon conviction, that person would be liable to imprisonment for less than fourteen years;

Type 'D' Offence

(*c*) every one who conspires with any one to induce, by false pretences, false representations or other fraudulent means, a woman to commit adultery or fornication, is guilty of an indictable offence and is liable to imprisonment for two years; and

(*d*) every one who conspires with any one to commit an indictable offence not provided for in paragraph (*a*), (*b*) or (*c*) is guilty of an indictable offence and is liable to the same punishment as that to which an accused who is guilty of that offence would, upon conviction, be liable.

Canada Evidence Act

4. (2) The wife or husband of a person charged with an offence against section 33 or 34 of the *Juvenile Delinquents Act* or with an offence against any of sections 143 to 146, 148, 150 to 155, 157, 166 to 169, 175, 195, 197, 200, 248 to 250, 255 to 258, 289, paragraph 423(1)(*c*) or an attempt to commit an offence under section 146 or 155 of the *Criminal Code*, is a competent and compellable witness for the prosecution without the consent of the person charged.

Common law conspiracy

(2) Every one who conspires with any one

(a) to effect an unlawful purpose, or

(b) to effect a lawful purpose by unlawful means,

is guilty of an indictable offence and is liable to imprisonment for two years.

Conspiracy to commit offences

(3) Every one who, while in Canada, conspires with any one to do anything referred to in subsection (1) or (2) in a place outside Canada that is an offence under the laws of that place shall be deemed to have conspired to do in Canada that thing.

Idem

(4) Every one who, while in a place outside Canada, conspires with any one to do anything referred to in subsection (1) or (2) in Canada shall be deemed to have conspired in Canada to do that thing.

Jurisdiction

(5) Where a person has conspired to do anything that is an offence by virtue of subsection (3) or (4), the offence is within the competence of and may be tried and punished by the court having similar jurisdiction in respect of similar offences in the territorial division where he is found in the same manner as if the offence had been committed in that territorial division.

Where previously tried outside Canada

(6) Where, as a result of a conspiracy that is an offence by virtue of subsection (3) or (4), a person has been tried and convicted or acquitted outside Canada, he shall be deemed to have been tried and convicted or acquitted, as the case may be, in Canada. 1953-54,c.51,s.408; 1974-75-76,c.93,s.36.

Conspiracy in restraint of trade

424. (1) A conspiracy in restraint of trade is an agreement between two or more persons to do or to procure to be done any unlawful act in restraint of trade.

Trade union exception

(2) The purposes of a trade union are not, by reason only that they are in restraint of trade, unlawful within the meaning of subsection (1). 1953-54, c. 51, s. 409.

Saving

425. (1) No person shall be convicted of the offence of conspiracy by reason only that he

(a) refuses to work with a workman or for an employer, or

(b) does any act or causes any act to be done for the purpose of a trade combination, unless such act is an offence expressly punishable by law. ss (2)

"Trade combination"

(2) In this section, "trade combination" means any combination between masters or workmen or other persons for the purpose of regulating or altering the relations between masters or workmen, or the conduct of a master or workman in or in respect of his business, employment or contract of employment or service. 1953-54,c.51,s.410.

—NOTES—

PART XII

JURISDICTION

General

Superior court of criminal jurisdiction

426. Every superior court of criminal jurisdiction has jurisdiction to try any indictable offence. 1953-54, c. 51, s. 413(1). 2

2. In this Act

"court of criminal jurisdiction" means

(a) a court of general or quarter sessions of the peace, when presided over by a superior court judge or a county or district court judge, or in the cities of Montreal and Quebec, by a municipal judge of the city, as the case may be, or a judge of the sessions of the peace, and

(b) a magistrate or judge acting under Part XVI;

"superior court of criminal jurisdiction" means

(a) in the Province of Ontario, the Supreme Court,

(b) in the Province of Quebec, the Superior Court,

(c) in the Provinces of Nova Scotia, Prince Edward Island and Newfoundland respectively, the Supreme Court,

(d) in the Province of British Columbia, the Supreme Court or the Court of Appeal,

(e) in the Provinces of Manitoba, Saskatchewan, Alberta and New Brunswick, respectively, the Court of Appeal or the Court of Queen's Bench,

(f) in the Yukon Territory, the Supreme Court, and

(g) in the Northwest Territories, the Supreme Court;

Court of criminal jurisdiction

427. Every court of criminal jurisdiction has jurisdiction to try an indictable offence other than 2

(a) an offence under any of the following sections, namely,

Treason — (i) section 47,

Alarming Her Majesty — (ii) section 49,

Intimidating Parliament — (iii) section 51,

Inciting to mutiny — (iv) section 53,

Sedition — (v) section 62,

Piracy — (vi) section 75,

Piratical acts — (vii) section 76,

Murder — (viii) section 218, or

(ix) Repealed, 1974-75-76, c. 93, s. 37(1).

(x) to (xv) Repealed, 1972, c. 13, s. 33.

Accessories — *(b)* the offence of being an accessory after the fact to high treason or treason or murder,

Corrupting justice — *(c)* an offence under section 108 by the holder of a judicial office,

Attempts — *(d)* the offence of attempting to commit any offence mentioned in subparagraphs *(a)*(i) to (vii), or

Conspiracy — *(e)* the offence of conspiring to commit any offence mentioned in paragraph *(a)*. R.S., c. C-34, s. 427; 1972, c. 13, s. 33; 1974-75-76, c. 93, s. 37(2); 1974-75-76, c. 105, s. 29.

Jurisdiction over person

428. Subject to this Act, every superior court of criminal jurisdiction and every court of criminal jurisdiction that has power to try an indictable offence is competent to try an accused for that offence 2 / 2 [426]

(a) if the accused is found, is arrested or is in custody within the territorial jurisdiction of the court; or

(b) if the accused has been committed for trial to, or has been ordered to be tried by

(i) that court, or

(ii) any other court, the jurisdiction of which has by lawful authority been transferred to that court. 1953-54, c. 51, s. 414.

Trial by jury compulsory

429. Except where otherwise expressly provided by law, every accused who is charged with an indictable offence shall be tried by a court composed of a judge and jury. 1953-54, c. 51, s. 415.

Trial in superior court of criminal jurisdiction

429.1 Where an accused who is charged with

(a) an indictable offence under any of the following provisions, namely,

Bribery (i) section 109,

Rape (ii) section 144,

Attempted rape (iii) section 145,

Death by criminal negligence (iv) section 203,

Manslaughter (v) section 219,

Attempted murder (vi) section 222, or

Threat to murder (vii) paragraph 331(1)*(a)*,

Attempt *(b)* the offence of attempting to commit any offence referred to in paragraph *(a)*, other than an offence under section 145 or 222, or

Conspiring *(c)* the offence of conspiring to commit any offence referred to in paragraph *(a)*

elects under section 464 or 484 to be tried by a court composed of a judge and jury, then unless the accused

(d) at the time he so elects, under section 464 or 484, agrees to be tried by a court composed of a judge, who is not a judge of a superior court of criminal jurisdiction, and a jury, or

(e) subsequently re-elects under section 492,

the trial shall, subject to any requirement by the Attorney General under section 498, be conducted by a court composed of a judge of a superior court of criminal jurisdiction and a jury. 1974-75-76, c. 93, s. 38.

Trial without jury in Alberta

430. Notwithstanding anything in this Act, an accused who is charged with an indictable offence in the Province of Alberta may, with his consent, be tried by a judge of the superior court of criminal jurisdiction of Alberta without a jury. 1953-54, c. 51, s. 417.

Adjournment when no jury summoned

431. Where the competent authority has determined that a panel of jurors is not to be summoned for a term or sittings of the court for the trial of criminal cases in any territorial division, the clerk of the court may, on the day of the opening of the term or sittings, if a judge is not present to preside over the court, adjourn the court and the business of the court to a subsequent day. 1953-54, c. 51, s. 418.

2. In this Act

"clerk of the court" includes a person, by whatever name or title he may be designated, who from time to time performs the duties of a clerk of the court;

"territorial division" includes any province, county, union of counties, township, city, town, parish or other judicial division or place to which the context applies;

Accused absconding during trial

431.1 (1) Notwithstanding any other provision of this Act, where an accused, whether or not he is charged jointly with another, absconds during the course of his trial,

(a) he shall be deemed to have waived his right to be present at his trial, and

(b) the court may

(i) continue the trial and proceed to a judgment or verdict and, if it finds the accused guilty, impose a sentence on him in his absence, or

(ii) if a warrant in Form 7 is issued for the arrest of the accused, adjourn the trial to await his appearance,

but where the trial is adjourned pursuant to subparagraph *(b)*(ii), the court may, at any time, continue the trial if it is satisfied that it is no longer in the interests of justice to await the appearance of the accused.

Adverse inference

(2) Where a court continues a trial pursuant to subsection (1), it may draw an inference adverse to the accused from the fact that he has absconded.

Accused not entitled to re-opening

(3) Where an accused reappears at his trial that is continuing pursuant to subsection (1), he is not entitled to have any part of the proceedings that was conducted in his absence re-opened unless the court is satisfied that because of exceptional circumstances it is in the interests of justice to re-open the proceedings.

Counsel for accused may continue to act

(4) Where an accused has absconded during the course of his trial and the court continues the trial, counsel for the accused is not thereby deprived of any authority he may have to continue to act for the accused in the proceedings. 1974-75-76, c. 93, s. 39.

471.1 Accused absconding during inquiry

526.1 Election deemed to have been waived

Special Jurisdiction

Special jurisdictions

432. For the purposes of this Act,

(a) where an offence is committed in or upon any water or upon a bridge, between two or more territorial divisions, the offence shall be deemed to have been committed in any of the territorial divisions; 2

(b) where an offence is committed on the boundary of two or more territorial divisions or within five hundred yards of any such boundary, or the offence was commenced within one territorial division and completed within another, the offence shall be deemed to have been committed in any of the territorial divisions;

(c) where an offence is committed in or upon a vehicle employed in a journey, or on board a vessel employed on a navigable river, canal or inland water, the offence shall be deemed to have been committed in any territorial division through which the vehicle or vessel passed in the course of the journey or voyage on which the offence was committed, and where the center or other part of the road, or navigable river, canal or inland water on which the vehicle or vessel passed in the course of the journey or voyage is the boundary of two or more territorial divisions, the offence shall be deemed to have been committed in any of the territorial divisions;

(d) where an offence is committed in an aircraft in the course of a flight of that aircraft, it shall be deemed to have been committed

(i) in the territorial division in which the flight commenced,

(ii) in any territorial division over which the aircraft passed in the course of the flight, or

(iii) in the territorial division in which the flight ended; and

(e) where an offence is committed in respect of a mail in the course of the door-to-door delivery of the mail, the offence shall be deemed to have been committed in any territorial division through which the mail was carried on that delivery. 1953-54, c. 51, s. 419.

2. In this Act

"territorial division" includes any province, county, union of counties, township, city, town, parish or other judicial division or place to which the context applies;

Offences on territorial sea and waters off the coast

433. (1) Where an offence is committed by a person, whether or not he is a Canadian citizen, on the territorial sea of Canada or on internal waters between the territorial sea and the coast of Canada, whether or not it was committed on board or by means of a Canadian ship, the offence is within the competence of and shall be tried by the court having jurisdiction in respect of similar offences in the territorial division nearest to the place where the offence was committed, and shall be tried in the same manner as if the offence had been committed within that territorial division.

Consent

(2) No proceedings for an offence to which subsection (1) applies other than an offence for which the accused is punishable on summary conviction shall, where the accused is not a Canadian citizen, be instituted without the consent of the Attorney General of Canada. 1964-65, c. 22, s. 10; 1968-69, c. 38, s. 26.

Offence committed entirely in one province

434. (1) Subject to section 6, subsections (2) and (3) of this section and sections 665 and 666, nothing in this Act authorizes a court in a province to try an offence committed entirely in another province. 28 Interp

Exception

(2) Every proprietor, publisher, editor or other person charged with the publication of a defamatory libel in a newspaper or with conspiracy to publish 262 261 a defamatory libel in a newspaper shall be dealt with, indicted, tried and punished in the province where he resides or in which the newspaper is printed.

Exception

(3) Where an accused is charged with an offence that is alleged to have been committed in Canada outside the province in which he is, he may, if the offence 28 Interp is not an offence mentioned in section 427 and 427

(*a*) in the case of proceedings instituted at the instance of the Government of Canada and conducted by or on behalf of that Government, the Attorney General of Canada consents, or

(*b*) in any other case, the Attorney General of the province where the offence is alleged to have been committed consents,

appear before a court or person that would have had jurisdiction to try that offence if it had been committed in the province where the accused is, and where he signifies his consent to plead guilty and pleads guilty to that offence the court or person shall convict the accused and impose the punishment 28 Interp warranted by law, but where he does not signify his consent to plead guilty and plead guilty, he shall, if he was in custody prior to his appearance, be returned to custody and shall be dealt with according to law. 1974-75-76, c. 93, s. 40.

Where accused committed to stand trial

(4) Notwithstanding that an accused described in subsection (3) has been committed to stand trial or that an indictment has been preferred against him in respect of the offence to which he desires to plead guilty, he shall be deemed simply to stand charged of that offence without a preliminary inquiry having been conducted or an indictment having been preferred with respect thereto.

"Newspaper"

(5) In this section "newspaper" has the same meaning that it has in section 261. 1953-54, c. 51, s. 421(2),(5); 1960-61, c. 43, s. 12; 1968-69, c. 38, s. 27.

Offence outstanding in same province

435. Where an accused is charged with an offence that is alleged to have been committed in the province in which he is, he may, if the offence is not an offence mentioned in section 427, and

(*a*) in the case of proceedings instituted at the instance of the Government of Canada and conducted by or on behalf of that Government, the Attorney General of Canada consents, or

(*b*) in any other case, the Attorney General of the province where the offence is alleged to have been committed consents,

appear before a court or person that would not otherwise have jurisdiction to try that offence, but that would have had jurisdiction to try it if it had been committed in the place where he is, and where he signifies his consent to plead guilty and pleads guilty to that offence, the court or person shall convict the accused and impose the punishment warranted by law, but where he does not signify his consent to plead guilty and plead guilty, he shall, if he was in custody prior to his appearance, be returned to custody and shall be dealt with according to law. 1974-75-76, c. 93, s. 41.

Offence in unorganized territory

436. (1) Where an offence is committed in an unorganized tract of country in any province or on a lake, river or other water therein, not included in a territorial division or in a provisional judicial district, proceedings in respect thereof may be commenced and an accused may be charged, tried and punished in respect thereof within any territorial division or provisional judicial district of the province in the same manner as if the offence had been committed within that territorial division or provisional judicial district.

New territorial division

(2) Where a provisional judicial district or a new territorial division is constituted in an unorganized tract referred to in subsection (1), the jurisdiction conferred by that subsection continues until appropriate provision is made by law for the administration of criminal justice within the provisional judicial district or new territorial division. 1953-54, c. 51, s. 422.

Offence not in a province

437. Where an offence is committed in a part of Canada not in a province, proceedings in respect thereof may be commenced and the accused may be charged, tried and punished within any territorial division in any province in the same manner as if that offence has been committed in that territorial division. 1953-54, c. 51, s. 423.

Section 6 (Offences committed on aircraft — Offence against internationally protected person — Offences by Public Services employees — Jurisdiction), 665 (Transfer of probation order), 666 (Failure to comply with probation order)

427. Every court of criminal jurisdiction has jurisdiction to try an indictable offence other than

(a) an offence under any of the following sections, namely,
  (i) section 47,
  (ii) section 49,
  (iii) section 51,
  (iv) section 53,
  (v) section 62,
  (vi) section 75,
  (vii) section 76,
  (viii) section 218, or
  (ix) Repealed

(b) the offence of being an accessory after the fact to high treason or treason or murder,

(c) an offence under section 108 by the holder of a judicial office,

(d) the offence of attempting to commit any offence mentioned in subparagraphs *(a)*(i) to (vii), or

(e) the offence of conspiring to commit any offence mentioned in paragraph *(a)*.

Interpretation Act

28. In every enactment

"may" is to be construed as permissive;

"shall" is to be construed as imperative;

"province" means a province of Canada, and includes the Yukon Territory and the Northwest Territories;

Rules of Court

Power to make rules

438. (1) Every superior court of criminal jurisdiction and every court of appeal, respectively, may, at any time with the concurrence of a majority of the judges thereof present at a meeting held for the purpose, make rules of court not inconsistent with this Act or any other Act of the Parliament of Canada, and any rules so made apply to any prosecution, proceeding, action or appeal, as the case may be, within the jurisdiction of that court, instituted in relation to any matter of a criminal nature or arising from or incidental to any such prosecution, proceeding, action or appeal.

Idem

(1.1) Every court of criminal jurisdiction for a province that is not a court referred to in subsection (1) may, subject to the approval of the Lieutenant Governor in Council, make rules of court not inconsistent with this Act or any other Act of Parliament, and any rules so made apply to any prosecution, proceeding, action or appeal, as the case may be, within the jurisdiction of the court for which they are made, instituted in relation to any matter of a criminal nature or arising from or incidental to any such prosecution, proceeding, action or appeal. 1974-75-76, c. 93, s. 42.

Purpose of rules

(2) Rules under subsection (1) may be made

(a) generally to regulate the duties of the officers of the court and any other matter considered expedient to attain the ends of justice and carry into effect the provisions of the law;

(b) to regulate the sittings of the court or any division thereof, or of any judge of the court sitting in chambers, except in so far as they are regulated by law;

(c) to regulate in criminal matters the pleading, practice and procedure in the court including proceedings with respect to *mandamus, certiorari, habeas corpus*, prohibition, bail and costs, and the proceedings on an application to a summary conviction court to state a case for the opinion of the court with respect to a conviction, order, determination or other proceeding; and

(d) to carry out the provisions of this Act relating to appeals from conviction, acquittal or sentence on indictment and, without restricting the generality of this paragraph,

(i) for furnishing necessary forms and instructions in relation to notices of appeal or applications for leave to appeal to officials or other persons requiring or demanding them,

(ii) for ensuring the accuracy of notes taken at a trial and the verification of any copy or transcript,

(iii) for keeping writings, exhibits or other things connected with the proceedings on the trial,

(iv) for securing the safe custody of property during the period in which the operation of an order with respect to that property is suspended under subsection 616(1), and

(v) for providing that the Attorney General and counsel who acted for the Attorney General at the trial be supplied with certified copies of writings, exhibits and things connected with the proceedings that are required for the purposes of their duties.

Rules to continue

(3) Where in any province rules of court relating to criminal matters are in force on the 1st day of April 1955, they continue in force except in so far as they may be amended or repealed from time to time by the court authorized by this section to make rules.

Publication

(4) Rules of court that are made under the authority of this section shall be published in the *Canada Gazette*.

Regulations to secure uniformity

(5) Notwithstanding anything in this section, the Governor in Council may make such provision as he considers proper to secure uniformity in the rules of court in criminal matters, and all uniform rules made under the authority of this subsection prevail and have effect as if enacted by this Act. 1953-54, c. 51, s. 424.

PART XIII

SPECIAL PROCEDURE AND POWERS

General Powers of Certain Officials

Officials with powers of two justices

439. Every judge or magistrate authorized by the law of the province in which he is appointed to do anything that is required to be done by two or more justices may do alone anything that this Act or any other Act of the Parliament of Canada authorizes two or more justices to do. 1953-54, c. 51, s. 425. 2

2. In this Act

"justice" means a justice of the peace or a magistrate, and includes two or more justices where two or more justices are, by law, required to act or, by law, act or have jurisdiction;

"magistrate" means a magistrate, a police magistrate, a stipendiary magistrate, a district magistrate, a provincial magistrate, a judge of the sessions of the peace, a recorder, or any person having the power and authority of two or more justices of the peace, and includes

(a) with respect to the Provinces of Ontario, Quebec, New Brunswick and British Columbia, a judge of the provincial court,

(a.1) with respect to the Provinces of Alberta, Manitoba and Prince Edward Island, a provincial judge,

(a.2) with respect to the Province of Nova Scotia, a judge of the Provincial Magistrate's Court,

(b) with respect to the Province of Saskatchewan, a judge of the Magistrates' Courts, and;

(c) with respect to the Yukon Territory and the Northwest Territories, a judge of the Supreme Court,

and the lawful deputy of each of them;

Preserving order in court

440. Every judge or magistrate has the same power and authority to preserve order in a court over which he presides as may be exercised by the superior court of criminal jurisdiction of the province during the sittings thereof. 1953-54, c. 51, s. 426.

No loss of jurisdiction

440.1 (1) The validity of any proceedings before a court, judge, magistrate or justice is not affected by any failure to comply with the provisions of this Act relating to adjournments or remands, and where such failure has occurred and an accused or a defendant does not appear at any such proceeding or upon any adjournment thereof, the court, judge, magistrate or justice may issue a summons or, if it or he considers it necessary in the public interest, a warrant for the arrest of the accused or defendant.

Adjournment and order

(2) Where, in the opinion of the court, judge, magistrate or justice, an accused or a defendant who appears at a proceeding has been misled or prejudiced by reason of any matter referred to in subsection (1), the court, judge, magistrate or justice may adjourn the proceeding and may make such order as it or he considers proper.

Part XIV to apply

(3) The provisions of Part XIV apply *mutatis mutandis* where a summons or warrant is issued under subsection (1). 1974-75-76, c. 93, s. 43.

mutatis mutandis — after the necessary changes in detail so that the text applies

Part XIV — Compelling Appearance of Accused Before a Justice

Trial of juveniles to be without publicity

441. Where an accused is or appears to be under the age of sixteen years, his trial shall take place without publicity, whether he is charged alone or jointly with another person. 1953-54, c. 51, s. 427. 585(2)

585. (1) In the absence of other evidence, or by way of corroboration of other evidence, a jury, judge, justice or magistrate, as the case may be, may infer the age of a child or young person from his appearance.

Exclusion of public in certain cases

442. (1) Any proceedings against an accused that is a corporation or who is or appears to be sixteen years of age or more shall be held in open court, but where the presiding judge, magistrate or justice, as the case may be, is of the opinion that it is in the interest of public morals, the maintenance of order or the proper administration of justice to exclude all or any members of the public from the court room for all or part of the proceedings, he may so order.

Reasons to be stated

(2) Where an accused is charged with an offence mentioned in subsection 142(1) and the prosecutor or the accused makes an application for an order 2
under subsection (1) of this section, the presiding judge, magistrate or justice, as the case may be, shall, if no such order is made, state, by reference to the circumstances of the case, the reason for not making an order.

Order restricting publication of identity

(3) Where an accused is charged with an offence mentioned in subsection 142(1), the presiding judge, magistrate or justice shall, if application therefor is made by the prosecutor, make an order directing that the identity of the complainant and her evidence taken in the proceedings shall not be published 142(5)
in any newspaper or broadcast. ss. (5)
28
Interp [4

Type 'A' Offence

(4) Every one who fails to comply with an order made pursuant to subsection (3) is guilty of an offence punishable on summary conviction.

"Newspaper" defined

(5) In this section, "newspaper" has the same meaning as it has in section 261. 261
1974-75-76, c. 93, s. 44.

142. (1) Where an accused is charged with an offence under section 144 or 145 or subsection 146(1) or 149(1), no question shall be asked by or on behalf of the accused as to the sexual conduct of the complainant with a person other than the accused unless

(a) reasonable notice in writing has been given to the prosecutor by or on behalf of the accused of his intention to ask such question together with particulars of the evidence sought to be adduced by such question and a copy of such notice has been filed with the clerk of the court; and

(b) the judge, magistrate or justice, after holding a hearing *in camera* in the absence of the jury, if any, is satisfied that the weight of the evidence is such that to exclude it would prevent the making of a just determination of an issue of fact in the proceedings, including the credibility of the complainant.

(2) The notice given under paragraph (1)*(a)* and the evidence taken, the information given or the representations made at a hearing referred to in paragraph (1)*(b)* shall not be published in any newspaper or broadcast.

(3) Every one who, without lawful excuse the proof of which lies upon him, contravenes subsection (2) is guilty of an offence punishable on summary conviction.

(4) In this section, "newspaper" has the same meaning as it has in section 261.

(5) In this section and in section 442, "complainant" means the person against whom it is alleged that the offence was committed.

261. In sections 262 to 281, "newspaper" means any paper, magazine or periodical containing public news, intelligence or reports of events, or any remarks or observations thereon, printed for sale and published periodically or in parts or numbers, at intervals not exceeding thirty-one days between the publication of any two such papers, parts or numbers, and any paper, magazine or periodical printed in order to be dispersed and made public, weekly or more often, or at intervals not exceeding thirty-one days, that contains advertisements, exclusively or principally.

Information for search warrant

443. (1) A justice who is satisfied by information upon oath in Form 1, 2
that there is reasonable ground to believe that there is in a building, receptacle or place

(a) anything upon or in respect of which any offence against this Act has been or is suspected to have been committed,

(b) anything that there is reasonable ground to believe will afford evidence with respect to the commission of an offence against this Act, or

(c) anything that there is reasonable ground to believe is intended to be used for the purpose of committing any offence against the person for which a person may be arrested without warrant,

may at any time issue a warrant under his hand authorizing a person named
therein or a peace officer to search the building, receptacle or place for any such 2
thing, and to seize and carry it before the justice who issued the warrant or some
other justice for the same territorial division to be dealt with by him according 2
to law.

Endorsement of search warrant

(2) Where the building, receptable, or place in which anything mentioned in subsection (1) is believed to be is in some other territorial division, the justice may issue his warrant in like form modified according to the circumstances, and the warrant may be executed in the other territorial division after it has been endorsed, in Form 25, by a justice having jurisdiction in that territorial division.

Form

(3) A search warrant issued under this section may be in Form 5.

Effect of endorsement

(4) An endorsement that is made upon a warrant pursuant to subsection (2) is sufficient authority to the peace officers to whom it was originally directed and to all peace officers within the jurisdiction of the justice by whom it is endorsed to execute the warrant and to take the things to which it relates before the justice who issued the warrant or some other justice for the same territorial division. 1953-54, c. 51, s. 429.

Execution of search warrant

444. A warrant issued under section 443 shall be executed by day, unless the 2
justice, by the warrant, authorizes execution of it by night. 1953-54, c. 51, s. 430. 2

2. In this Act
"day" means the period between six o'clock in the forenoon and nine o'clock in the afternoon of the same day;

Seizure of things not specified

445. Every person who executes a warrant issued under section 443 may seize, in addition to the things mentioned in the warrant, anything that on reasonable grounds he believes has been obtained by or has been used in the commission of an offence, and carry it before the justice who issued the warrant or some other justice for the same territorial division, to be dealt with in accordance with section 446. 1953-54, c. 51, s. 431.

Canada Evidence Act

29. (7) Nothing in this section shall be construed as prohibiting any search of the premises of a financial institution under the authority of a warrant to search issued under any other Act of the Parliament of Canada, but unless the warrant is expressly endorsed by the person under whose hand it is issued as not being limited by this section, the authority conferred by any such warrant to search the premises of a financial institution and to seize and take away anything therein shall, as regards the books or records of such institution, be construed as limited to the searching of such premises for the purpose of inspecting and taking copies of entries in such books or records.

Detention of things seized

446. (1) Where anything that has been seized under section 445 or under a warrant issued pursuant to section 443 is brought before a justice, he shall, 2 [439]
unless the prosecutor otherwise agrees, detain it or order that it be detained, 2
taking reasonable care to ensure that it is preserved until the conclusion of any investigation or until it is required to be produced for the purposes of a preliminary inquiry or trial, but nothing shall be detained under the authority of this section for a period of more than three months after the time of the seizure unless, before the expiration of that period,

(a) a justice is satisfied on application that, having regard to the nature of the investigation, its further detention for a specified period is warranted and he so orders; or

(b) proceedings are instituted in which the thing detained may be required.

When accused committed for trial

(2) When an accused has been committed for trial the justice shall forward anything to which subsection (1) applies to the clerk of the court to which the 2
accused has been committed for trial to be detained by him and disposed of as the court directs.

Disposal of things seized in other cases

(3) Where a justice is satisfied that anything that has been seized under section 445 or under a warrant issued pursuant to section 443 will not be required for any purpose mentioned in subsection (1) or (2), he may,

(a) if possession of it by the person from whom it was seized is lawful, order it to be returned to that person, or

(b) if possession of it by the person from whom it was seized is unlawful,

(i) order it to be returned to the lawful owner or to the person who is entitled to possession of it, or

(ii) order it to be forfeited or otherwise dealt with in accordance with law, where the lawful owner or the person who is entitled to possession of it is not known.

Detention pending appeal, etc.

(4) Nothing shall be disposed of under subsection (3) pending any proceeding in which the right of seizure is questioned, or within thirty days after an order is made under that subsection.

Access to anything seized

(5) Where anything is detained under subsection (1), a judge of a superior court of criminal jurisdiction or of a court of criminal jurisdiction may, on 2 [426]
summary application on behalf of a person who has an interest in what is detained, after three clear days notice to the Attorney General, order that the 25(2) Interp
person by or on whose behalf the application is made be permitted to examine anything so detained.

Conditions

(6) An order that is made under subsection (5) shall be made on such terms as appear to the judge to be necessary or desirable to ensure that anything in respect of which the order is made is safeguarded and preserved for any purpose for which it may subsequently be required.

Appeal

(7) A person who considers himself aggrieved by an order made under subsection (3) may appeal from the order to the appeal court, as defined in section 747, and for the purposes of the appeal the provisions of sections 749 to 760 apply, *mutatis mutandis.* 1953-54, c. 51, s. 432; 1968-69, c. 38, s. 29.

mutatis mutandis — after the necessary changes in detail so that the text applies

Forfeiture of weapons

446.1 (1) Where it is determined by a court that a weapon was used in the commission of an offence and that weapon has been seized and detained, the weapon is, subject to subsection (2), forfeited and may be dealt with as the court that makes the determination directs. 2

Return of weapons to lawful owners

(2) If the court by which a determination referred to in subsection (1) is made is satisfied that the lawful owner of a weapon that, but for this subsection, would be forfeited by virtue of the determination, was not a party to the offence and had no reason to believe that the weapon would or might be used in the commission of an offence, the court shall order the weapon returned to the lawful owner thereof or the proceeds of any sale thereof to be paid to him.

Application of proceeds

(3) Where any weapon to which this section applies is sold, the proceeds of the sale shall be paid to the Attorney General or, where an order is made under subsection (2), to the person who was, immediately prior to the sale, the lawful owner of the weapon. 1972, c. 13, s. 37.

Seizure of explosives

447. (1) Every person who executes a warrant issued under section 443 may seize any explosive substance that he suspects is intended to be used for an unlawful purpose, and shall, as soon as possible, remove to a place of safety anything that he seizes by virtue of this section and detain it until he is ordered by a judge of a superior court to deliver it to some other person or an order is made pursuant to subsection (2). 2 28 Interp

Forfeiture

(2) Where an accused is convicted of an offence in respect of anything seized by virtue of subsection (1), it is forfeited and shall be dealt with as the court that makes the conviction may direct.

Application of proceeds

(3) Where anything to which this section applies is sold, the proceeds of the sale shall be paid to the Attorney General. 1953-54, c. 51, s. 433.

2. In this Act

"Attorney General" means the Attorney General or Solicitor General of a province in which proceedings to which this Act applies are taken and, with respect to

(a) the Northwest Territories and the Yukon Territory, and

(b) proceedings instituted at the instance of the Government of Canada and conducted by or on behalf of that Government in respect of a violation of or conspiracy to violate any Act of the Parliament of Canada or a regulation made thereunder other than this Act,

means the Attorney General of Canada, and except for the purposes of subsections 505(4) and 507(3), includes the lawful deputy of the said Attorney General, Solicitor General and Attorney General of Canada;

"clerk of the court" includes a person, by whatever name or title he may be designated, who from time to time performs the duties of a clerk of the court;

"explosive substance" includes

(a) anything intended to be used to make an explosive substance, and

(b) anything, or any part thereof, used or intended to be used, or adapted to cause, or to aid in causing an explosion in or with an explosive substance;

"territorial division" includes any province, county, union of counties, township, city, town, parish or other judicial division or place to which the context applies;

Interpretation Act

25. (2) Where there is a reference to a number of clear days or "at least" a number of days between two events, in calculating the number of days there shall be excluded the days on which the events happen.

2. In this Act

"offensive weapon" or "weapon" means

(a) anything that is designed to be used as a weapon, or

(b) anything that a person uses or intends to use as a weapon, whether or not it is designed to be used as a weapon,

and, without restricting the generality of the foregoing, includes any firearm as defined in section 82;

82. (1) For the purposes of this Part,

"firearm" means any barrelled weapon from which any shot, bullet or other missile can be discharged and that is capable of causing serious bodily injury or death to a person, and includes any frame or receiver of such a barrelled weapon and anything that can be adapted for use as a firearm;

Interpretation Act

28. In every enactment

"superior court" means

(a) in the Province of Ontario, Nova Scotia, Prince Edward Island or Newfoundland, the Supreme Court of the Province,

(b) in the Province of Quebec, the Court of Appeal and the Superior Court in and for the Province,

(c) in the Province of British Columbia, the Court of Appeal and the Supreme Court of the Province,

(d) in the Province of Manitoba, Saskatchewan, Alberta or New Brunswick, the Court of Appeal for the Province and the Court of Queen's Bench for the Province,

(e) in the Yukon Territory or the Northwest Territories, the Supreme Court thereof,

and includes the Supreme Court of Canada and the Federal Court of Canada;

"broadcasting" means any radiocommunication in which the transmissions are intended for direct reception by the general public;

"oath" includes a solemn affirmation or declaration, whenever the context applies to any person by whom and case in which a solemn affirmation or declaration may be made instead of an oath; and in like cases the expression "sworn" includes the expression "affirmed" or "declared";

PART XIV

COMPELLING APPEARANCE OF ACCUSED BEFORE A JUSTICE AND INTERIM RELEASE

Interpretation

Definitions

448. In this Part

"accused"

"accused" includes

(a) a person to whom a peace officer has issued an appearance notice under section 451, and 2

(b) a person arrested for a criminal offence;

"appearance notice"

"appearance notice" means a notice in Form 8.1 issued by a peace officer;

"judge"

"judge" means

(a) in the Province of Ontario, a judge of the superior court of criminal jurisdiction of the province or a judge or junior judge of a county or district court, 2

(b) in the Province of Quebec, a judge of the superior court of criminal jurisdiction of the province or three judges of the sessions of the peace or of the provincial court,

(c) in the Provinces of Nova Scotia, Manitoba and British Columbia, a judge of the superior court of criminal jurisdiction of the province or a judge of a county court,

(d) in the Province of Newfoundland, a judge of the superior court of criminal jurisdiction of the province or a judge of a district court,

(d.1) in the Provinces of New Brunswick, Alberta and Saskatchewan, a judge of the superior court of criminal jurisdiction of the province, 1978-79, c. 11, s. 10, Item 6(10).

(e) in the Province of Prince Edward Island, the Yukon Territory and the Northwest Territories, a judge of the Supreme Court;

"officer in charge"

"officer in charge" means the officer for the time being in command of the police force responsible for the lock-up or other place to which an accused is taken after arrest or a peace officer designated by him for the purposes of this Part who is in charge of such place at the time an accused is taken to that place to be detained in custody;

"promise to appear"

"promise to appear" means a promise in Form 8.2 given to an officer in charge;

"recognizance"

"recognizance", when used in relation to a recognizance entered into before an officer in charge, means a recognizance in Form 8.3, and when used in relation to a recognizance entered into before a justice or a judge, means a recognizance in Form 28;

"summons"

"summons" means a summons in Form 6 issued by a justice or a judge;

"undertaking"

"undertaking" means an undertaking in Form 9 given to a justice or a judge;

"warrant"

"warrant", when used in relation to a warrant for the arrest of a person, means a warrant in Form 7 and, when used in relation to a warrant for the committal of a person, means a warrant in Form 8.

R.S., c. C-34, s. 448; R.S., c. 2(2nd Supp.), s. 5; 1972, c. 17, s. 3; 1974-75-76, c. 48, s. 25(1).

2. In this Act

"justice" means a justice of the peace or a magistrate, and includes two or more justices where two or more justices are, by law, required to act or, by law, act or have jurisdiction;

"peace officer" includes

(a) a mayor, warden, reeve, sheriff, deputy sheriff, sheriff's officer and justice of the peace,

(b) a warden, deputy warden, instructor, keeper, gaoler, guard and any other officer or permanent employee of a prison,

(c) a police officer, police constable, bailiff, constable, or other person employed for the preservation and maintenance of the public peace or for the service or execution of civil process,

(d) an officer or person having the powers of a customs or excise officer when performing any duty in the administration of the *Customs Act* or the *Excise Act*,

(d.1) a person appointed or designated as a fishery officer under the *Fisheries Act* when performing any of his duties or functions pursuant to that Act,

(e) the pilot in command of an aircraft

(i) registered in Canada under regulations made under the *Aeronautics Act*, or

(ii) leased without crew and operated by a person who is qualified under regulations made under the *Aeronautics Act* to be registered as owner of an aircraft registered in Canada under those regulations,

while the aircraft is in flight, and

(f) officers and men of the Canadian Forces who are

(i) appointed for the purposes of section 134 of the *National Defence Act*, or

(ii) employed on duties that the Governor in Council, in regulations made under the *National Defence Act* for the purposes of this paragraph, has prescribed to be of such a kind as to necessitate that the officers and men performing them have the powers of peace officers;

"court of criminal jurisdiction" means

(a) a court of general or quarter sessions of the peace, when presided over by a superior court judge or a county or district court judge, or in the cities of Montreal and Quebec, by a municipal judge of the city, as the case may be, or a judge of the sessions of the peace, and

(b) a magistrate or judge acting under Part XVI;

"superior court of criminal jurisdiction" means

(a) in the Province of Ontario, the Supreme Court,

(b) in the Province of Quebec, the Superior Court,

(c) in the Provinces of Nova Scotia, Prince Edward Island and Newfoundland respectively, the Supreme Court,

(d) in the Province of British Columbia, the Supreme Court or the Court of Appeal,

(e) in the Provinces of Manitoba, Saskatchewan, Alberta and New Brunswick, respectively, the Court of Appeal or the Court of Queen's Bench,

(f) in the Yukon Territory, the Supreme Court, and

(g) in the Northwest Territories, the Supreme Court;

29. (1) It is the duty of every one who executes a process or warrant to have it with him, where it is feasible to do so, and to produce it when requested to do so.

(2) It is the duty of everyone who arrests a person, whether with or without warrant, to give notice to that person, where it is feasible to do so, of

(a) the process or warrant under which he makes the arrest, or

(b) the reason for the arrest.

(3) Failure to comply with subsection (1) or (2) does not of itself deprive a person who executes a process or warrant, or a person who makes an arrest, or those who assist them, of protection from criminal responsibility.

Arrest without Warrant and Release from Custody

Arrest without warrant by any person

449. (1) Any one may arrest without warrant

(a) a person whom he finds committing an indictable offence, or

(b) a person who, on reasonable and probable grounds, he believes

(i) has committed a criminal offence, and

(ii) is escaping from and freshly pursued by persons who have lawful authority to arrest that person.

Arrest by owner, etc. of property

(2) Any one who is

(a) the owner or a person in lawful possession of property, or

(b) a person authorized by the owner or by a person in lawful possession of property,

may arrest without warrant a person whom he finds committing a criminal offence on or in relation to that property.

Delivery to peace officer

(3) Any one other than a peace officer who arrests a person without warrant shall forthwith deliver the person to a peace officer. R.S., c. C-34, s. 449; R.S., c. 2(2nd Supp.), s. 5.

30. Every one who witnesses a breach of the peace is justified in interfering to prevent the continuance or renewal thereof and may detain any person who commits or is about to join in or to renew the breach of the peace, for the purpose of giving him into the custody of a peace officer, if he uses no more force than is reasonably necessary to prevent the continuance or renewal of the breach of the peace or than is reasonably proportioned to the danger to be apprehended from the continuance or renewal of the breach of the peace.

191. (1) Every one who obtains or attempts to obtain anything from any person by playing a game in a vehicle, aircraft or vessel used as a public conveyance for passengers is guilty of an indictable offence and is liable to imprisonment for two years.

(2) Every person in charge of a vehicle, aircraft or vessel and any person authorized by him may arrest, without warrant, a person who he has good reason to believe has committed or attempted to commit or is committing or attempting to commit an offence under this section.

29. (1) It is the duty of every one who executes a process or warrant to have it with him, where it is feasible to do so, and to produce it when requested to do so.

(2) It is the duty of everyone who arrests a person, whether with or without warrant, to give notice to that person, where it is feasible to do so, of

(a) the process or warrant under which he makes the arrest, or

(b) the reason for the arrest.

(3) Failure to comply with subsection (1) or (2) does not of itself deprive a person who executes a process or warrant, or a person who makes an arrest, or those who assist him, of protection from criminal responsibility.

Arrest without warrant by peace officer

450. (1) A peace officer may arrest without warrant

(a) a person who has committed an indictable offence or who, on reasonable and probable grounds, he believes has committed or is about to commit an indictable offence,

(b) a person whom he finds committing a criminal offence, or

(c) a person for whose arrest he has reasonable and probable grounds to believe that a warrant is in force within the territorial jurisdiction in which the person is found.

Limitation

(2) A peace officer shall not arrest a person without warrant for

(a) an indictable offence mentioned in section 483,

(b) an offence for which the person may be prosecuted by indictment or for which he is punishable on summary conviction, or

(c) an offence punishable on summary conviction,

in any case where

(d) he has reasonable and probable grounds to believe that the public interest, having regard to all the circumstances including the need to

(i) establish the identity of the person,

(ii) secure or preserve evidence of or relating to the offence, or

(iii) prevent the continuation or repetition of the offence or the commission of another offence,

may be satisfied without so arresting the person, and

(e) he has no reasonable grounds to believe that, if he does not so arrest the person, the person will fail to attend in court in order to be dealt with according to law.

Consequences of arrest without warrant

(3) Notwithstanding subsection (2), a peace officer acting under subsection (1) is deemed to be acting lawfully and in the execution of his duty for the purposes of

(a) any proceedings under this or any other Act of Parliament, and

(b) any other proceedings, unless in any such proceedings it is alleged and established by the person making the allegation that the peace officer did not comply with the requirements of subsection (2). R.S., c. C-34, s. 450; R.S., c. 2(2nd Supp.), s. 5.

31. (1) Every peace officer who witnesses a breach of the peace and every one who lawfully assists him is justified in arresting any person whom he finds committing the breach of the peace or who, on reasonable and probable grounds, he believes is about to join in or renew the breach of the peace.

(2) Every peace officer is justified in receiving into custody any person who is given into his charge as having been a party to a breach of the peace by one who has, or who on reasonable and probable grounds he believes has, witnessed the breach of the peace.

181. (2) A peace officer may, whether or not he is acting under a warrant issued pursuant to this section, take into custody any person whom he finds keeping a common gaming house and any person whom he finds therein, and may seize anything that may be evidence that such an offence is being committed and shall bring those persons and things before a justice having jurisdiction, to be dealt with according to law.

458. (2) Notwithstanding anything in this Act, a peace officer who has reasonable and probable grounds to believe that an accused

(a) has violated or is about to violate any summons, appearance notice, promise to appear, undertaking or recognizance that was issued or given to him or entered into by him, or

(b) has committed an indictable offence after any summons, appearance notice, promise to appear, undertaking or recognizance was issued or given to him or entered into by him,

may arrest the accused without warrant.

459. (4) If, following the hearing described in subsection (1), the judge is not satisfied that the continued detention of the accused in custody is justified within the meaning of subsection 457(7), he shall order that the accused be released from custody pending the trial of the charge,

(a) upon his giving an undertaking with such conditions as the judge directs, or

(b) upon his entering into a recognizance before the judge with or without sureties in such amount and with such conditions, if any, as the judge directs, but without deposit of money or other valuable security.

(6) Notwithstanding anything in this Act, a peace officer who has reasonable and probable grounds to believe that an accused who has been released from custody under subsection (4)

(a) has violated or is about to violate the undertaking or recognizance upon which he has been released, or

(b) has, after his release from custody upon his undertaking or recognizance, committed an indictable offence,

may arrest the accused without warrant and take him or cause him to be taken before a judge having jurisdiction in the province where the order for his release was made.

545. (1) Where an accused is, pursuant to this Part, found to be insane, the lieutenant governor of the province in which he is detained may make an order

(a) for the safe custody of the accused in a place and manner directed by him, or

(b) if in his opinion it would be in the best interest of the accused and not contrary to the interest of the public, for the discharge of the accused either absolutely or subject to such conditions as he prescribes.

(4) A peace officer who has reasonable and probable grounds to believe that an accused to whom paragraph (1)*(b)* applies has violated any condition prescribed in the order for his discharge may arrest the accused without warrant.

752. (2) The provisions of subsections 459(5), (6) and (7) apply *mutatis mutandis* in respect of a person who has been released from custody under subsection (1).

454. (3) A peace officer or officer in charge having the custody of a person who has been arrested without warrant as a person about to commit an indictable offence shall release that person unconditionally as soon as practicable after he is satisfied that the continued detention of that person in custody is no longer necessary in order to prevent the commission by him of an indictable offence.

Issue of appearance notice by peace officer

451. Where, by virtue of subsection 450(2), a peace officer does not arrest a person, he may issue an appearance notice to the person if the offence is

(a) an indictable offence mentioned in section 483,

(b) an offence for which the person may be prosecuted by indictment or for which he is punishable on summary conviction, or

(c) an offence punishable on summary conviction. R.S., c. 2(2nd Supp.), s. 5.

Release from custody by peace officer

452. (1) Where a peace officer arrests a person without warrant for

(a) an indictable offence mentioned in section 483,

(b) an offence for which the person may be prosecuted by indictment or for which he is punishable on summary conviction, or

(c) an offence punishable on summary conviction,

he shall, as soon as practicable,

(d) release the person from custody with the intention of compelling his appearance by way of summons, or

(e) issue an appearance notice to the person and thereupon release him,

unless

(f) he has reasonable and probable grounds to believe that it is necessary in the public interest, having regard to all the circumstances including the need to

(i) establish the identity of the person,

(ii) secure or preserve evidence of or relating to the offence, or

(iii) prevent the continuation or repetition of the offence or the commission of another offence,

that the person be detained in custody or that the matter of his release from custody be dealt with under another provision of this Part, or

(g) he has reasonable and probable grounds to believe that, if the person is released by him from custody, the person will fail to attend in court in order to be dealt with according to law.

Where subsection (1) does not apply

(2) Subsection (1) does not apply in respect of a person who has been arrested without warrant by a peace officer for an offence described in subsection 454(2).

Consequences of non-release

(3) A peace officer who has arrested a person without warrant for an offence described in subsection (1) and who does not release the person from custody as soon as practicable in the manner described in paragraph *(d)* or *(e)* of that subsection shall be deemed to be acting lawfully and in the execution of his duty for the purposes of

(a) any proceedings under this or any other Act of Parliament, and

(b) any other proceedings, unless in any such proceedings it is alleged and established by the person making the allegation that the peace officer did not comply with the requirements of subsection (1). R.S., c. 2(2nd Supp.), s. 5.

Release from custody by officer in charge

453. (1) Where a person who has been arrested without warrant by a peace officer is taken into custody, or where a person who has been arrested without warrant and delivered to a peace officer under subsection 449(3) is detained in custody under subsection 454(1) for

(a) an indictable offence mentioned in section 483,

(b) an offence for which the person may be prosecuted by indictment or for which he is punishable on summary conviction,

(c) an offence punishable on summary conviction, or

(d) any other offence that is punishable by imprisonment for five years or less,

and has not been taken before a justice or released from custody under any other provision of this Part, the officer in charge shall, as soon as practicable,

(e) release the person with the intention of compelling his appearance by way of summons,

(f) release the person upon his giving his promise to appear,

(g) release the person upon his entering into a recognizance before the officer in charge without sureties in such amount not exceeding five hundred dollars as the officer in charge directs, but without deposit of money or other valuable security, or

(h) if the person is not ordinarily resident in the province in which he is in custody or does not ordinarily reside within one hundred miles of the place in which he is in custody, release the person upon his entering into a recognizance before the officer in charge without sureties in such amount not exceeding five hundred dollars as the officer in charge directs and, if the officer in charge so directs, upon his depositing with the officer in charge such sum of money or other valuable security not exceeding in amount or value five hundred dollars, as the officer in charge directs,

unless

(i) he has reasonable and probable grounds to believe that it is necessary in the public interest, having regard to all the circumstances including the need to

(i) establish the identity of the person,

(ii) secure or preserve evidence of or relating to the offence, or

(iii) prevent the continuation or repetition of the offence or the commission of another offence,

that the person be detained in custody or that the matter of his release from custody be dealt with under another provision of this Part, or

(j) he has reasonable and probable grounds to believe that, if the person is released by him from custody, the person will fail to attend in court in order to be dealt with according to law.

Where subsection (1) does not apply

(2) Subsection (1) does not apply in respect of a person who has been arrested without warrant by a peace officer for an offence described in subsection 454(2).

Consequences of non-release

(3) An officer in charge who has the custody of a person taken into or detained in custody for an offence described in subsection (1) and who does not release the person from custody as soon as practicable in the manner described in paragraph *(e)*, *(f)*, *(g)* or *(h)* of that subsection shall be deemed to be acting lawfully and in the execution of his duty for the purposes of

(a) any proceedings under this or any other Act of Parliament, or

(b) any other proceedings, unless in any such proceedings it is alleged and established by the person making the allegation that the officer in charge did not comply with the requirements of subsection (1). R.S., c. 2(2nd Supp.), s. 5.

Release from custody by officer in charge where arrest made with warrant

453.1 Where a person who has been arrested with a warrant by a peace officer is taken into custody for

(a) an indictable offence mentioned in section 483,

(b) an offence for which the person may be prosecuted by indictment or for which he is punishable on summary conviction,

(c) an offence punishable on summary conviction, or

(d) any other offence that is punishable by imprisonment for five years or less,

the officer in charge may, if the warrant has been endorsed by a justice under subsection 455.3(6),

(e) release the person upon his giving his promise to appear,

(f) release the person upon his entering into a recognizance before the officer in charge without sureties in such amount not exceeding five hundred dollars as the officer in charge directs, but without deposit of money or other valuable security, or

(g) if the person is not ordinarily resident in the province in which he is in custody or does not ordinarily reside within one hundred miles of the place in which he is in custody, release the person upon his entering into a recognizance before the officer in charge without sureties in such amount not exceeding five hundred dollars as the officer in charge directs and, if the officer in charge so directs, upon his depositing with the officer in charge such sum of money or other valuable security not exceeding in amount or value five hundred dollars, as the officer in charge directs. R.S., c. 2(2nd Supp.), s. 5.

Money or other valuable security to be deposited with justice

453.2 Where a person has, pursuant to paragraph 453(1)*(h)* or paragraph 453.1*(g)*, deposited any sum of money or other valuable security with the officer in charge, the officer in charge shall, forthwith after the deposit thereof, cause the money or valuable security to be delivered to a justice for deposit with the justice. R.S., c. 2(2nd Supp.), s. 5.

Contents of appearance notice, promise to appear and recognizance

453.3 (1) An appearance notice or promise to appear or a recognizance entered into before an officer in charge shall

(a) set out the name of the accused,

(b) set out the substance of the offence that the accused is alleged to have committed, and

(c) state the time and place at which the accused is to attend court in order to be dealt with according to law.

Idem

(2) An appearance notice or promise to appear or a recognizance entered into before an officer in charge shall set out therein the text of subsections 133(5) and (6) and section 453.4.

Attendance for purposes of *Identification of Criminals Act*

(3) An appearance notice or promise to appear or a recognizance entered into before an officer in charge may, where the accused is alleged to have committed an indictable offence, require the accused to appear at a time and place stated therein for the purposes of the *Identification of Criminals Act*, and a person so appearing is deemed, for the purposes only of that Act, to be in lawful custody charged with an indictable offence.

Execution of appearance notice, promise to appear or recognizance

(4) An appearance notice or promise to appear or a recognizance entered into before an officer in charge shall be signed in duplicate by the accused, and one of the duplicates shall thereupon be given to him. 1974-75-76, c. 93, s. 45.

Proof of issue of appearance notice

(5) The issue of an appearance notice by any peace officer or officer in charge may be proved by the oral evidence, given under oath, of the officer who issued it or by his affidavit made before a justice or other person authorized to administer oaths or to take affidavits. R.S., c. 2(2nd Supp.), s. 5.

Interpretation Act

18. (2) Where power is conferred upon a justice of the peace to administer an oath or affirmation, or to take an affidavit or declaration, the power may be exercised by a notary public or a commissioner for taking oaths.

Failure to appear

453.4 Where an accused who is required by an appearance notice or promise to appear or by a recognizance entered into before an officer in charge to appear at a time and place stated therein for the purposes of the *Identification of Criminals Act* does not appear at that time and place, a justice may, where the appearance notice, promise to appear or recognizance has been confirmed by a justice under section 455.4, issue a warrant for the arrest of the accused for the offence with which he is charged. R.S., c. 2(2nd Supp.), s. 5.

133. (5) Every one who is named in an appearance notice or promise to appear, or in a recognizance entered into before an officer in charge, that has been confirmed by a justice under section 455.4 and who fails, without lawful excuse, the proof of which lies upon him, to appear at a time and place stated therein, if any, for the purposes of the *Identification of Criminals Act*, or to attend court in accordance therewith, is guilty of

(a) an indictable offence and is liable to imprisonment for two years, or

(b) an offence punishable on summary conviction.

Appearance of Accused before Justice

Taking before justice

454. (1) A peace officer who arrests a person with or without warrant or to whom a person is delivered under subsection 449(3) shall cause the person to be detained in custody and, in accordance with the following provisions, to be taken before a justice to be dealt with according to law, namely:

(a) where a justice is available within a period of twenty-four hours after the person has been arrested by or delivered to the peace officer, the person shall be taken before a justice without unreasonable delay and in any event within that period, and

(b) where a justice is not available within a period of twenty-four hours after the person has been arrested by or delivered to the peace officer, the person shall be taken before a justice as soon as possible,

unless, at any time before the expiration of the time prescribed in paragraph *(a)* or *(b)* for taking the person before a justice,

(c) the peace officer or officer in charge releases the person under any other provision of this Part, or

(d) the peace officer or officer in charge is satisfied that the person should be released from custody, whether unconditionally under subsection (3) or otherwise conditionally or unconditionally, and so releases him. 1974-75-76, c. 93, s. 46(1).

Conditional release

(1.1) Where a peace officer or an officer in charge is satisfied that a person described in subsection (1) should be released from custody conditionally, he may, unless the person is detained in custody for an offence mentioned in section 457.7, release that person in accordance with paragraphs 453(1)*(f)* to *(h)*. 1974-75-76, c. 93, s. 46(2).

Remand in custody for return to province where offence alleged to have been committed

(2) Where a person has been arrested without warrant for an indictable offence alleged to have been committed in Canada outside the province in which he was arrested, he shall, within the time prescribed in paragraphs (1)*(a)* and *(b)*, be taken before a justice within whose jurisdiction he was arrested and the justice,

(a) if he is not satisfied that there are reasonable and probable grounds to believe that the person arrested is the person alleged to have committed the offence, shall release him; or

(b) if he is satisfied that there are reasonable and probable grounds to believe that the person arrested is the person alleged to have committed the offence, may remand him to the custody of a peace officer to await execution of a warrant for his arrest in accordance with section 461, but if no warrant for his arrest is so executed within a period of six days after the time he is remanded to such custody, the person in whose custody he then is shall release him.

Release of person about to commit indictable offence

(3) A peace officer or officer in charge having the custody of a person who has been arrested without warrant as a person about to commit an indictable offence shall release that person unconditionally as soon as practicable after he is satisfied that the continued detention of that person in custody is no longer necessary in order to prevent the commission by him of an indictable offence.

Consequences of non-release

(4) Notwithstanding subsection (3), a peace officer or officer in charge having the custody of a person referred to in that subsection who does not release the person before the expiration of the time prescribed in paragraph (1)*(a)* or *(b)* for taking the person before the justice, shall be deemed to be acting lawfully and in the execution of his duty for the purposes of

(a) any proceedings under this or any other Act of Parliament, or

(b) any other proceedings, unless in such proceedings it is alleged and established by the person making the allegation that the peace officer or officer in charge did not comply with the requirements of subsection (3). R.S., c. 2(2nd Supp.), s. 5.

Information, Summons and Warrant

In what cases justice may receive information

455. Any one who, on reasonable and probable grounds, believes that a person has committed an indictable offence may lay an information in writing and under oath before a justice, and the justice shall receive the information, where it is alleged 27 Interp 28 Interp

(a) that the person has committed, anywhere, an indictable offence that may be tried in the province in which the justice resides, and that the person 2 [448]

(i) is or is believed to be, or

(ii) resides or is believed to reside,

within the territorial jurisdiction of the justice;

(b) that the person, wherever he may be, has committed an indictable offence within the territorial jurisdiction of the justice;

(c) that the person has, anywhere, unlawfully received property that was unlawfully obtained within the territorial jurisdiction of the justice; or 2

(d) that the person has in his possession stolen property within the territorial jurisdiction of the justice. R.S., c. 2(2nd Supp.), s. 5. 3(4)

2. In this Act

"property" includes

(a) real and personal property of every description and deeds and instruments relating to or evidencing the title or right to property, or giving a right to recover or receive money or goods,

(b) property originally in the possession or under the control of any person, and any property into or for which it has been converted or exchanged and anything acquired at any time by such conversion or exchange, and

(c) any postal card, postage stamp or other stamp issued or prepared for issue under the authority of the Parliament of Canada or of the legislature of a province for the payment to the Crown or a corporate body of any fee, rate or duty, whether or not it is in the possession of the Crown or of any person;

3. (2) For the purposes of this Act a postal card or stamp referred to in paragraph (c) of the definition "property" in section 2 shall be deemed to be a chattel, and to be equal in value to the amount of the postage, rate or duty expressed on its face.

Interpretation Act

27. (1) Where an enactment creates an offence,

(a) the offence shall be deemed to be an indictable offence if the enactment provides that the offender may be prosecuted for the offence by indictment;

28. In every enactment

"oath" includes a solemn affirmation or declaration, whenever the context applies to any person by whom and case in which a solemn affirmation or declaration may be made instead of an oath; and in like cases the expression "sworn" includes the expression "affirmed" or "declared";

"shall" is to be construed as imperative;

Time within which information to be laid in certain cases

455.1 Where

(a) an appearance notice has been issued to an accused under section 451, or

(b) an accused has been released from custody under section 452 or 453,

an information relating to the offence alleged to have been committed by the accused or relating to an included or other offence alleged to have been committed by him shall be laid before a justice as soon as practicable thereafter and in any event before the time stated in the appearance notice, promise to appear or recognizance issued to or given or entered into by the accused for his attendance in court. R.S., c. 2(2nd Supp.), s. 5.

Form

455.2 An information laid under section 455 or 455.1 may be in Form 2. R.S., c. 2(2nd Supp.), s. 5.

Justice to hear informant and witnesses

455.3 (1) A justice who receives an information, other than an information laid before him under section 455.1, shall

(a) hear and consider, *ex parte*,

(i) the allegations of the informant, and

(ii) the evidence of witnesses, where he considers it desirable or necessary to do so; and

(b) where he considers that a case for so doing is made out, issue, in accordance with this section, either a summons or a warrant for the arrest of the accused to compel the accused to attend before him to answer to a charge of an offence.

ex parte — in the absence of one side or party

Process compulsory

(2) No justice shall refuse to issue a summons or warrant by reason only that the alleged offence is one for which a person may be arrested without warrant.

Procedure when witnesses attend

(3) A justice who hears the evidence of a witness pursuant to subsection (1) shall

(a) take the evidence upon oath; and

(b) cause the evidence to be taken in accordance with section 468 in so far as that section is capable of being applied.

Summons to be issued except in certain cases

(4) Where the justice considers that a case is made out for compelling the accused to attend before him to answer to a charge of an offence, he shall issue a summons to the accused unless the allegations of the informant or the evidence of any witness or witnesses taken in accordance with subsection (3) disclose reasonable and probable grounds to believe that it is necessary in the public interest to issue a warrant for the arrest of the accused.

No process in blank

(5) A justice shall not sign a summons or warrant in blank.

Endorsement of warrant by justice

(6) Where a justice issues a warrant under this section, he may, where the offence is

(a) an indictable offence mentioned is section 483,

(b) an offence for which the person may be prosecuted by indictment or for which he is punishable on summary conviction,

(c) an offence punishable on summary conviction, or

(d) any other offence that is punishable by imprisonment for five years or less,

authorize the release of the accused pursuant to section 453.1 by making an endorsement on the warrant in Form 25.1.

Promise to appear or recognizance deemed to have been confirmed

(7) Where, pursuant to subsection (6), a justice authorizes the release of an accused pursuant to section 453.1, a promise to appear given by the accused or a recognizance entered into by the accused pursuant to that section shall be deemed, for the purposes of subsection 133(5), to have been confirmed by a justice under section 455.4. R.S., c. 2(2nd Supp.), s. 5.

Justice to hear informant and witnesses

455.4 (1) A justice who receives an information laid before him under section 455.1 shall

(a) hear and consider, *ex parte*,

(i) the allegations of the informant, and

(ii) the evidence of witnesses, where he considers it desirable or necessary to do so;

(b) where he considers that a case for so doing is made out, confirm the appearance notice, promise to appear or recognizance, as the case may be, whether the information relates to the offence alleged in the appearance notice, promise to appear or recognizance or to an included or other offence, and endorse the information accordingly; and

(c) where he considers that a case is not made out for the purposes of paragraph *(b)*, cancel the appearance notice, promise to appear or recognizance, as the case may be, and cause the accused to be notified forthwith of such cancellation.

ex parte — in the absence of one side or party

Procedure when witnesses attend

(2) A justice who hears the evidence of a witness pursuant to subsection (1) shall

(a) take the evidence upon oath; and 28 Interp

(b) cause the evidence to be taken in accordance with section 468 in so far as that section is capable of being applied. R.S., c. 2(2nd Supp.), s. 5.

Interpretation Act

28. In every enactment

"oath" includes a solemn affirmation or declaration, whenever the context applies to any person by whom and case in which a solemn affirmation or declaration may be made instead of an oath; and in like cases the expression "sworn" includes the expression "affirmed" or "declared";

Summons

455.5 (1) A summons issued under section 455.3 shall

(a) be directed to the accused;

(b) set out briefly the offence in respect of which the accused is charged; and

(c) require the accused to attend court at a time and place to be stated therein and to attend thereafter as required by the court in order to be dealt with according to law.

591. No indictment in respect of an offence for which, by reason of previous convictions, a greater punishment may be imposed shall contain any reference to previous convictions.

Service on individual

(2) A summons shall be served by a peace officer who shall deliver it personally to the person to whom it is directed or, if that person cannot conveniently be found, shall leave it for him at his last or usual place of abode with some inmate thereof who appears to be at least sixteen years of age. 2 [448]

629. (1) Subject to subsection (2), a subpoena shall be served in accordance with subsection 455.5(2).

3. (7) Where, pursuant to this Act, any summons, notice or other process is required to be or may be served upon a corporation, and no other method of service is provided, such service may be effected by delivering the process

(a) in the case of a municipal corporation, to the mayor, warden, reeve, or other chief officer of the corporation, or to the secretary, treasurer or clerk of the corporation, and

(b) in the case of any other corporation, to the manager, secretary or other executive officer of the corporation or of a branch thereof.

Proof of service

(3) Service of a summons may be proved by the oral evidence, given under oath, of the peace officer who served it or by his affidavit made before a justice or other person authorized to administer oaths or to take affidavits. 28 Interp / 18 Interp

Interpretation Act

18. (2) Where power is conferred upon a justice of the peace to administer an oath or affirmation, or to take an affidavit or declaration, the power may be exercised by a notary public or a commissioner for taking oaths.

28. In every enactment

"oath" includes a solemn affirmation or declaration, whenever the context applies to any person by whom and case in which a solemn affirmation or declaration may be made instead of an oath; and in like cases the expression "sworn" includes the expression "affirmed" or "declared";

Content of summons

(4) A summons shall set out therein the text of subsection 133(4) and section 455.6.

Attendance for purposes of *Identification of Criminals Act*

(5) A summons may, where the accused is alleged to have committed an indictable offence, require the accused to appear at a time and place stated therein for the purposes of the *Identification of Criminals Act*, and a person so appearing is deemed, for the purposes only of that Act, to be in lawful custody charged with an indictable offence. R.S., c. 2(2nd Supp.), s. 5.

Failure to appear

455.6 Where an accused who is required by a summons to appear at a time and place stated therein for the purposes of the *Identification of Criminals Act*, does not appear at that time and place, a justice may issue a warrant for the arrest of the accused for the offence with which he is charged. R.S., c. 2(2nd Supp.), s. 5.

133. (4) Every one who is served with a summons and who fails, without lawful excuse, the proof of which lies upon him, to appear at a time and place stated therein, if any, for the purposes of the *Identification of Criminals Act* or to attend court in accordance therewith, is guilty of

(a) an indictable offence and is liable to imprisonment for two years, or

(b) an offence punishable on summary conviction.

Contents of warrant to arrest

456. (1) A warrant issued under section 455.3 shall

(a) name or describe the accused,

(b) set out briefly the offence in respect of which the accused is charged, and

(c) order that the accused be forthwith arrested and brought before the justice who issued the warrant or before some other justice having jurisdiction in the same territorial division, to be dealt with according to law. 2

No return day

(2) A warrant issued under section 455.3 remains in force until it is executed, and need not be made returnable at any particular time. R.S., c. 2(2nd Supp.), s. 5.

Certain actions not to preclude issue of warrant

456.1 (1) A justice may, where he has reasonable and probable grounds to believe that it is necessary in the public interest to issue a warrant for the arrest of an accused, issue a warrant under section 455.3 for the arrest of the accused notwithstanding that

(a) an appearance notice or promise to appear or a recognizance entered into before an officer in charge has been confirmed or cancelled under subsection 455.4(1);

(b) a summons has previously been issued under subsection 455.3(4); or

(c) the accused has been released unconditionally or with the intention of compelling his appearance by way of summons.

Warrant in default of appearance

(2) Where

(a) service of a summons is proved and the accused fails to attend court in accordance with the summons,

(b) an appearance notice or promise to appear or a recognizance entered into before an officer in charge has been confirmed under subsection 455.4(1) and the accused fails to attend court in accordance therewith in order to be dealt with according to law, or

(c) it appears that a summons cannot be served because the accused is evading service,

a justice may issue a warrant for the arrest of the accused. R.S., c. 2(2nd Supp.), s. 5.

133. (4) Every one who is served with a summons and who fails, without lawful excuse, the proof of which lies upon him, to appear at a time and place stated therein, if any, for the purposes of the *Identification of Criminals Act* or to attend court in accordance therewith, is guilty of

(a) an indictable offence and is liable to imprisonment for two years, or

(b) an offence punishable on summary conviction.

Formalities of warrant

456.2 A warrant in accordance with this Part shall be directed to the peace officers within the territorial jurisdiction of the justice, judge or court by whom or by which it is issued. R. S., c. 2(2nd Supp.), s. 5.

Execution of warrant

456.3 (1) A warrant in accordance with this Part may be executed by arresting the accused

(a) wherever he is found within the territorial jurisdiction of the justice, judge or court by whom or by which the warrant was issued; or

(b) wherever he is found in Canada, in the case of fresh pursuit.

By whom warrant may be executed

(2) A warrant in accordance with this Part may be executed by a person who is one of the peace officers to whom it is directed, whether or not the place in which the warrant is to be executed is within the territory for which the person is a peace officer. R.S., c. 2(2nd Supp.), s. 5.

461. (1) Where a warrant for the arrest of an accused cannot be executed in accordance with section 456.3, a justice within whose jurisdiction the accused is or is believed to be shall, upon application, and upon proof on oath or by affidavit of the signature of the justice who issued the warrant, authorize the execution of the warrant within his jurisdiction by making an endorsement, which may be in Form 25, upon the warrant.

(2) An endorsement that is made upon a warrant pursuant to subsection (1) is sufficient authority to the peace officers to whom it was originally directed, and to all peace officers within the territorial jurisdiction of the justice by whom it is endorsed, to execute the warrant and to take the accused before the justice who issued the warrant or before some other justice for the same territorial division.

Judicial Interim Release

Order of release

457. (1) Subject to this section, where an accused who is charged with an offence other than an offence mentioned in section 457.7 and who is not required to be detained in custody in respect of any other matter is taken before a justice, the justice shall, unless a plea of guilty by the accused is accepted, order that the accused be released upon his giving an undertaking without conditions, unless the prosecutor, having been given a reasonable opportunity to do so, shows cause why the detention of the accused in custody is justified or why an order under any other provision of this section should be made. 1974-75-76, c. 93, s. 47(1).

Release on undertaking with conditions, etc.

(2) Where the justice does not make an order under subsection (1), he shall, unless the prosecutor shows cause why the detention of the accused is justified, order that the accused be released

(a) upon his giving an undertaking with such conditions as the justice directs,

(b) upon his entering into a recognizance before the justice, without sureties, in such amount and with such conditions, if any, as the justice directs but without deposit of money or other valuable security,

(c) upon his entering into a recognizance before the justice with sureties in such amount and with such conditions, if any, as the justice directs but without deposit of money or other valuable security,

(c.1) with the consent of the prosecutor, upon his entering into a recognizance before the justice, without sureties, in such amount and with such conditions, if any, as the justice directs and upon his depositing with the justice such sum of money or other valuable security as the justice directs, or
1974-75-76, c. 93, s. 47(2).

(d) if the accused is not ordinarily resident in the province in which he is in custody or does not ordinarily reside within one hundred miles of the place in which he is in custody, upon his entering into a recognizance before the justice with or without sureties in such amount and with such conditions, if any, as the justice directs, and upon his depositing with the justice such sum of money or other valuable security as the justice directs. 2

Idem

(3) The justice shall not make an order under any of paragraphs (2)*(b)* to *(d)* unless the prosecution shows cause why an order under the immediately preceding paragraph should not be made.

Conditions authorized

(4) The justice may direct as conditions under subsection (2) that the accused shall do any one or more of the following things as specified in the order, namely:

(a) report at times to be stated in the order to a peace officer or other person designated in the order;

(b) remain within a territorial jurisdiction specified in the order;

(c) notify the peace officer or other person designated under paragraph *(a)* of any change in his address or his employment or occupation;

(d) abstain from communicating with any witness or other person expressly named in the order except in accordance with such conditions specified in the order as the justice deems necessary;

(e) where the accused is the holder of a passport, deposit his passport as specified in the order; and

(f) comply with such other reasonable conditions specified in the order as the justice considers desirable.

Detention in custody

(5) Where the prosecutor shows cause why the detention of the accused in custody is justified, the justice shall order that the accused be detained in custody until he is dealt with according to law and shall include in the record a statement of his reasons for making the order.

Order of detention

(5.1) Notwithstanding any provision of this section, where an accused is charged

(a) with an indictable offence, other than an offence mentioned in section 457.7, that is alleged to have been committed while he was at large awaiting trial for another indictable offence,

(b) with an indictable offence, other than an offence mentioned in section 457.7 and is not ordinarily resident in Canada,

(c) with an offence under any of subsections 133(2) to (5) that is alleged to have been committed while he was at large awaiting trial for an offence, other than an offence mentioned in section 457.7, or

(d) with having committed an offence under section 4 or 5 of the *Narcotic Control Act* or the offence of conspiring to commit an offence under section 4 or 5 of the *Narcotic Control Act*,

the justice shall order that the accused be detained in custody until he is dealt with according to law, unless the accused, having been given a reasonable opportunity to do so, shows cause why his detention in custody is not justified, but where the justice orders that the accused be released, he shall include in the record a statement of his reasons for making the order.

Order of release

(5.2) Where an accused to whom paragraph (5.1)*(a)*, *(c)* or *(d)* applies shows cause why his detention in custody is not justified, the justice shall order that he be released upon his giving an undertaking or entering into a recognizance described in any of paragraphs (2)*(a)* to *(d)* with such conditions described in subsection (4) or, where the accused was at large upon an undertaking or recognizance with conditions, such additional conditions described in subsection (4), as the justice considers desirable, unless the accused, having been given a reasonable opportunity to do so, shows cause why such conditions or additional conditions should not be imposed.

Idem

(5.3) Where an accused to whom paragraph (5.1)*(b)* applies shows cause why his detention in custody is not justified, the justice shall order that he be released upon his giving an undertaking or entering into a recognizance described in any of paragraphs (2)*(a)* to *(d)* with such conditions, described in subsection (4), as the justice considers desirable. 1974-75-76, c. 93, s. 47(3).

Sufficiency of record

(6) For the purposes of subsections (5) and (5.1), it is sufficient if a record is made of the reasons in accordance with the provisions of Part XV relating to the taking of evidence at preliminary inquiries. 1974-75-76, c. 93, s. 47(4).

Justification for detention in custody

(7) For the purposes of this section, the detention of an accused in custody is justified only on either of the following grounds, namely:

(a) on the primary ground that his detention is necessary to ensure his attendance in court in order to be dealt with according to law; and

(b) on the secondary ground (the applicability of which shall be determined only in the event that and after it is determined that his detention is not justified on the primary ground referred to in paragraph *(a)*) that his detention is necessary in the public interest or for the protection or safety of the public, having regard to all the circumstances including any substantial likelihood that the accused will, if he is released from custody, commit a criminal offence or an interference with the administration of justice. 1974-75-76, c. 93, s. 47(5).

Detention in custody for offence mentioned in section 457.7

(8) Where an accused who is charged with an offence mentioned in section 457.7 is taken before a justice, the justice shall order that the accused be detained in custody until he is dealt with according to law and shall issue a warrant in Form 8 for the committal of the accused. 1974-75-76, c. 93, s. 47(6).

Remand in custody

457.1 A justice may, before or at any time during the course of any proceedings under section 457, upon application by the prosecutor or the accused, adjourn the proceedings and remand the accused to custody in prison by warrant in Form 14, but no such adjournment shall be for more than three clear days except with the consent of the accused. R.S., c. 2(2nd Supp.), s. 5.

Interpretation Act

25. (2) Where there is a reference to a number of clear days or "at least" a number of days between two events, in calculating the number of days there shall be excluded the days on which the events happen.

Order directing matters not to be published for specified period

457.2 (1) Where the prosecutor or the accused intends to show cause under section 457, he shall so state to the justice and the justice may, and shall upon application by the accused, before or at any time during the course of the proceedings under that section, make an order directing that the evidence taken, the information given or the representations made and the reasons, if any, given or to be given by the justice shall not be published in any newspaper or broadcast before such time as ss. (4)

28 Interp

(a) if a preliminary inquiry is held, the accused in respect of whom the proceedings are held is discharged, or

(b) if the accused in respect of whom the proceedings are held is tried or committed for trial, the trial is ended. 1974-75-76, c. 93, s. 48.

Failure to comply

Type 'A' Offence

(2) Every one who fails without lawful excuse, the proof of which lies upon him, to comply with an order made under subsection (1) is guilty of an offence punishable on summary conviction.

"Newspaper"

(3) In this section, "newspaper" has the same meaning as it has in sections 262 to 281 by virtue of section 261. R.S., c. 2(2nd Supp.), s. 5.

261. In sections 262 to 281, "newspaper" means any paper, magazine or periodical containing public news, intelligence or reports of events, or any remarks or observations thereon, printed for sale and published periodically or in parts or numbers, at intervals not exceeding thirty-one days between the publication of any two such papers, parts or numbers, and any paper, magazine or periodical printed in order to be dispersed and made public, weekly or more often, or at intervals not exceeding thirty-one days, that contains advertisements, exclusively or principally.

Interpretation Act

28. In every enactment

"broadcasting" means any radiocommunication in which the transmissions are intended for direct reception by the general public;

Inquiries to be made by justice and evidence

457.3 (1) In any proceedings under section 457,

(a) the justice may, subject to paragraph *(b)*, make such inquiries, on oath or otherwise, of and concerning the accused as he considers desirable;

(b) the accused shall not be examined or cross-examined by the justice or any other person as to the offence with which he is charged, and no inquiry shall be made of him as to that offence;

(c) the prosecutor may, in addition to any other relevant evidence, lead evidence

(i) to prove that the accused has previously been convicted of a criminal offence,

(ii) to prove that the accused has been charged with and is awaiting trial for another criminal offence,

(iii) to prove that the accused has previously committed an offence under section 133, or

(iv) to show the circumstances of the alleged offence, particularly as they relate to the probability of conviction of the accused; 1974-75-76,c.93,s.49.

(d) the justice may take into consideration any relevant matters agreed upon by the prosecutor and the accused or his counsel; and

(e) the justice may receive and base his decision upon evidence considered credible or trustworthy by him in the circumstances of each case.

Release pending sentence

(2) Where, before or at any time during the course of any proceedings under section 457, the accused pleads guilty and his plea is accepted, the justice may make any order provided for in this Part for the release of the accused until he is sentenced or a disposition in respect of him is made under paragraph 663(1)*(a)*. R.S., c. 2(2nd Supp.), s. 5.

Release of accused

457.4 (1) Where a justice makes an order under subsection 457(1), (2), (5.2) 2
or (5.3)

(*a*) if the accused thereupon complies with the order, the justice shall direct that he be released forthwith, and

(*b*) if the accused does not thereupon comply with the order, the justice who made the order or another justice having jurisdiction shall issue a warrant for the committal of the accused and may endorse thereon an authorization to the person having the custody of the accused to release the accused upon his complying with the order and, if the justice so endorses the warrant, he shall attach to it a copy of the order.

Discharge from custody

(2) Where the accused complies with an order referred to in paragraph (1)(*b*), the justice who made the order or another justice having jurisdiction shall, unless the accused has been released pursuant to an authorization referred to in that paragraph, issue an order for discharge in Form 35.

Warrant for committal

(3) Where the justice makes an order under subsection 457(5) or (5.1) for the detention of the accused, he shall issue a warrant for the committal of the accused. 1974-75-76, c. 93, s. 50(1) & (2).

Review of order of justice

457.5 (1) Where a justice makes an order under subsection 457(2), (5), (5.1), (5.2) or (5.3) the accused may, at any time before the trial of the charge, apply to a judge for a review of the order made by the justice. 1974-75-76, c.93, s.51(1).

Notice to prosecutor

(2) An application under this section shall not, unless the prosecutor otherwise consents, be heard by a judge unless the accused has given to the prosecutor at least two clear days notice in writing of the application. 25 Interp

Accused to be present

(3) If the judge so orders or the prosecutor or the accused or his counsel so requests, the accused shall be present at the hearing of an application under this section and, where the accused is in custody, the judge may order, in writing, the person having the custody of the accused to bring him before the court.

Adjournment of proceedings

(4) A judge may, before or at any time during the hearing of an application under this section, upon application by the prosecutor or the accused or his counsel, adjourn the proceedings, but if the accused is in custody no such adjournment shall be for more than three clear days except with the consent of the accused.

Failure of accused to attend

(5) Where an accused, other than an accused who is in custody, has been ordered by a judge to be present at the hearing of an application under this section and does not attend the hearing, the judge may issue a warrant for the arrest of the accused.

Execution

(6) A warrant issued under subsection (5) may be executed anywhere in Canada.

Evidence and powers of judge on review

(7) Upon the hearing of an application under this section, the judge may consider

(a) the transcript, if any, of the evidence of any witnesses heard by the justice,

(b) the exhibits, if any, filed in the proceedings before the justice, and

(c) such additional evidence or exhibits as may be tendered by the accused or the prosecutor,

and shall either

(d) dismiss the application, or

(e) if the accused shows cause, allow the application, vacate the order previously made by the justice and make any other order provided for in section 457, other than an order provided for in subsection (5) or (5.1) of that section, that he considers warranted. 1974-75-76, c. 93, s. 51(2).

Limitation of further applications

(8) Where an application under this section or section 457.6 has been heard, a further or other application under this section or section 457.6 shall not be made with respect to that same accused, except with leave of a judge, prior to the expiration of thirty days from the date of the decision of the judge who heard the previous application.

Application of ss. 457.2, 457.3 and 457.4

(9) The provisions of sections 457.2, 457.3 and 457.4 apply *mutatis mutandis* in respect of an application under this section. R.S., c. 2(2nd Supp.), s. 5.

mutatis mutandis — after the necessary changes in detail so that the text applies

Interpretation Act

25. (2) Where there is a reference to a number of clear days or "at least" a number of days between two events, in calculating the number of days there shall be excluded the days on which the events happen.

(3) Where there is a reference to a number of days, not expressed to be clear days, between two events, in calculating the number of days there shall be excluded the day on which the first event happens and there shall be included the day on which the second event happens.

Review of order by judge

457.6 (1) Where a justice makes an order under subsection 457(1), (2), (5.2) or (5.3), the prosecutor may, at any time before the trial of the charge, apply to a judge for a review of the order made by the justice. 1974-75-76, c. 93, s. 52.

Notice to accused

(2) An application under this section shall not be heard by a judge unless the prosecutor has given to the accused at least two clear days notice in writing of the application. 25 Interp

Accused to be present

(3) If the judge so orders or the prosecutor or the accused or his counsel so requests, the accused shall be present at the hearing of an application under this section and, where the accused is in custody, the judge may order, in writing, the person having the custody of the accused to bring him before the court.

Adjournment of proceedings

(4) A judge may, before or at any time during the hearing of an application under this section, upon application of the prosecutor or the accused or his counsel, adjourn the proceedings, but if the accused is in custody no such adjournment shall be for more than three clear days except with the consent of the accused.

Failure of accused to attend

(5) Where an accused, other than an accused who is in custody, has been ordered by a judge to be present at the hearing of an application under this section and does not attend the hearing, the judge may issue a warrant for the arrest of the accused.

Warrant for detention

(6) Where, pursuant to paragraph (8)*(e)*, the judge makes an order that the accused be detained in custody until he is dealt with according to law, he shall, if the accused is not in custody, issue a warrant for the committal of the accused.

Execution

(7) A warrant issued under subsection (5) or (6) may be executed anywhere in Canada.

Evidence and powers of judge on review

(8) Upon the hearing of an application under this section the judge may consider

(a) the transcript, if any, of the evidence of any witnesses heard by the justice,

(b) the exhibits, if any, filed in the proceedings before the justice, and

(c) such additional evidence or exhibits as may be tendered by the prosecutor or the accused,

and shall either

(d) dismiss the application, or

(e) if the prosecutor shows cause, allow the application, vacate the order previously made by the justice and make any other order provided for in section 457 that he considers to be warranted.

Limitation of further applications

(9) Where an application under this section or section 457.5 has been heard, a further or other application under this section or section 457.5 shall not be made with respect to the same accused, except with leave of a judge, prior to the expiration of thirty days from the date of the decision of the judge who heard the previous application.

Application of ss. 457.2, 457.3 and 457.4

(10) The provisions of sections 457.2, 457.3 and 457.4 apply *mutatis mutandis* in respect of an application under this section. R.S., c. 2(2nd Supp.), s. 5.

mutatis mutandis — after the necessary changes in detail so that the text applies

Interpretation Act

25. (2) Where there is a reference to a number of clear days or "at least" a number of days between two events, in calculating the number of days there shall be excluded the days on which the events happen.

Interim release by judge only

457.7 (1) Notwithstanding anything in this Act, where an accused is charged with an offence punishable by death, an offence under sections 50 to 53 or sections 76.1 to 76.3 or non-capital murder, no court, judge or justice, other than a judge of or a judge presiding in a superior court of criminal jurisdiction 2 [448] for the province in which the accused is so charged, may release the accused before or after committal for trial.

Interim release by judge only

(2) Where an accused is charged

(a) with an offence mentioned in subsection (1), other than the offence of having committed a murder,

(b) with an offence mentioned in subsection (1), other than the offence of having committed a murder, and the offence is alleged to have been committed while he was at large awaiting trial for another indictable offence,

(c) with an indictable offence mentioned in subsection (1), other than the offence of having committed murder, and is not ordinarily resident in Canada,

(d) with an offence under any of subsections 133(2) to (5) that is alleged to have been committed while he was at large awaiting trial for an offence mentioned in subsection (1), or

(d.1) with the offence of murder or the offence of conspiring to commit murder,

and he is not required to be detained in custody in respect of any other matter, a judge of or a judge presiding in a superior court of criminal jurisdiction for the province in which the accused is charged shall order that the accused be detained in custody unless

(e) in the case of an accused to whom paragraph *(a)* applies, the prosecutor having been given a reasonable opportunity to do so, fails to show cause why the detention of the accused in custody is justified within the meaning of subsection 457(7), or

(f) in the case of an accused to whom any of paragraphs *(b)*, *(c)*, *(d)* or *(d.1)* applies, the accused, having been given a reasonable opportunity to do so, shows cause why his detention in custody is not justified within the meaning of subsection 457(7).

Release of accused

(2.1) Where the judge does not order that the accused be detained in custody pursuant to subsection (2), he may order that the accused be released upon his giving an undertaking or entering into a recognizance described in any of paragraphs 457(2)*(a)* to *(d)* with such conditions described in subsection 457(4) or, where the accused was at large upon an undertaking or recognizance with conditions, such additional conditions described in subsection 457(4) as the judge considers desirable.

Order not reviewable except under s. 608.1

(2.2) An order made under this section is not subject to review, except as provided in section 608.1. 1974-75-76, c. 93, s. 53.

Application of sections 457.2, 457.3 and 457.4

(3) The provisions of sections 457.2, 457.3 except subsection (2) thereof, and 457.4 apply *mutatis mutandis* in respect of an application for an order under subsection (2). R.S., c. 2(2nd Supp.), s. 5; 1972, c. 13, s. 36(2).

mutatis mutandis — after the necessary changes in detail so that the text applies

Period for which appearance notice, etc., continues in force

457.8 (1) Where an accused has not been taken into custody or has been released from custody under or by virtue of any provision of this Part, the appearance notice, promise to appear, summons, undertaking or recognizance issued to or given or entered into by him continues in force, subject to its terms,

(a) where the accused was released from custody pursuant to an order of a judge made under subsection 457.7(2), until his trial is completed, or

(b) in any other case,

(i) until his trial is completed, and

(ii) where the accused is convicted at his trial, until he is sentenced or a disposition in respect of him is made under paragraph 663(1)*(a)* unless, at the time he is convicted, the court, judge or justice orders that the accused be taken into custody pending such sentence or disposition.

Order vacating previous order for release or detention

(2) Notwithstanding subsection (1),

(a) the court, judge or justice before whom an accused is being or is to be tried,

(b) the justice presiding at the preliminary inquiry in relation to an offence with which an accused is charged, other than an offence mentioned in section 457.7, or

(c) with the consent of the prosecutor and the accused,

(i) the justice by whom an order was made under this Part or any other justice, or

(ii) where the accused is charged with an offence mentioned in section 457.7, a judge presiding in a superior court of criminal jurisdiction for the province,

may, upon cause being shown, at any time vacate any order previously made under this Part for the interim release or detention of the accused and make any other order provided for in this Part for the detention or release of the accused until his trial is completed that the court, judge or justice considers to be warranted. 1974-75-76, c. 93, s. 54.

Arrest of Accused on Interim Release

Issue of warrant for arrest of accused

458. (1) Where a justice is satisfied that there are reasonable and probable grounds to believe that an accused

(a) has violated or is about to violate any summons, appearance notice, promise to appear, undertaking or recognizance that was issued or given to him or entered into by him, or

(b) has committed an indictable offence after any summons, appearance notice, promise to appear, undertaking or recognizance was issued or given to him or entered into by him, 27 Interp

he may issue a warrant for the arrest of the accused. 1974-75-76, c. 93, s. 55(1).

Interpretation Act

27. (1) Where an enactment creates an offence,

(a) the offence shall be deemed to be an indictable offence if the enactment provides that the offender may be prosecuted for the offence by indictment;

(b) the offence shall be deemed to be one for which the offender is punishable on summary conviction if there is nothing in the context to indicate that the offence is an indictable offence; and

(c) if the offence is one for which the offender may be prosecuted by indictment or for which he is punishable on summary conviction, no person shall be considered to have been convicted of an indictable offence by reason only of having been convicted of the offence on summary conviction.

Arrest of accused without warrant

(2) Notwithstanding anything in this Act, a peace officer who has reasonable and probable grounds to believe that an accused

(a) has violated or is about to violate any summons, appearance notice, promise to appear, undertaking or recognizance that was issued or given to him or entered into by him, or

(b) has committed an indictable offence after any summons, appearance notice, promise to appear, undertaking or recognizance was issued or given to him or entered into by him,

may arrest the accused without warrant. 1974-75-76, c. 93, s. 55(2).

Hearing

(3) Where an accused who has been arrested with a warrant issued under subsection (1), or who has been arrested under subsection (2), is taken before a justice, the justice shall

(a) where the accused was released from custody pursuant to an order made under subsection 457.7(2) by a judge of the superior court of criminal jurisdiction of any province, order that the accused be taken before a judge of that court, or

(b) in any other case, hear the prosecutor and his witnesses, if any, and the accused and his witnesses, if any.

Retention of accused

(4) Where an accused described in paragraph (3)*(a)* is taken before a judge and the judge finds

(a) that the accused has violated or had been about to violate his summons, appearance notice, promise to appear, undertaking or recognizance, or

(b) that there are reasonable and probable grounds to believe that the accused has committed an indictable offence after any summons, appearance notice, promise to appear, undertaking or recognizance was issued or given to him or entered into by him,

he shall cancel the summons, appearance notice, promise to appear, undertaking or recognizance and order that the accused be detained in custody unless the accused, having been given a reasonable opportunity to do so, shows cause why his detention in custody is not justified within the meaning of subsection 457(7).

Release of accused

(4.1) Where the judge does not order that the accused be detained in custody pursuant to subsection (4), he may order that the accused be released upon his giving an undertaking or entering into a recognizance described in any of paragraphs 457(2)*(a)* to *(d)* with such conditions described in subsection 457(4) or, where the accused was at large upon an undertaking or a recognizance with conditions, such additional conditions, described in subsection 457(4), as the judge considers desirable.

Order not reviewable

(4.2) Any order made under subsection (4) or (4.1) is not subject to review, except as provided in section 608.1.

Release of accused

(4.3) Where the judge does not make a finding under paragraph (4)*(a)* or *(b)*, he shall order that the accused be released from custody.

Powers of justice after hearing

(5) Where an accused described in subsection (3), other than an accused to whom paragraph *(a)* of that subsection applies, is taken before the justice and the justice finds

(a) that the accused has violated or had been about to violate his summons, appearance notice, promise to appear, undertaking or recognizance, or

(b) that there are reasonable and probable grounds to believe that the accused has committed an indictable offence after any summons, appearance notice, promise to appear, undertaking or recognizance was issued or given to him or entered into by him,

he shall cancel the summons, appearance notice, promise to appear, undertaking or recognizance and order that the accused be detained in custody unless the accused, having been given a reasonable opportunity to do so, shows cause why his detention in custody is not justified within the meaning of subsection 457(7).

Release of accused

(5.1) Where the accused shows cause why his detention in custody is not justified within the meaning of subsection 457(7), the justice shall order that the accused be released upon his giving an undertaking or entering into a recognizance described in any of paragraphs 457(2)*(a)* to *(d)* with such conditions, described in subsection 457(4), as the justice considers desirable.

Reasons

(6) Where the justice makes an order under subsection (5.1), he shall include in the record a statement of his reasons for making the order, and subsection 457(6) is applicable *mutatis mutandis* in respect thereof.

mutatis mutandis — after the necessary changes in detail so that the text applies

Where justice to order that accused be released

(7) Where the justice does not make a finding under paragraph (5)*(a)* or *(b)*, he shall order that the accused be released from custody.

Provisions applicable to proceedings under this section

(8) The provisions of sections 457.2, 457.3 and 457.4 apply *mutatis mutandis* in respect of any proceedings under this section, except that subsection 457.3(2) does not apply in respect of an accused who is charged with an offence mentioned in section 457.7.

Certain provisions applicable to order under this section

(9) Section 457.5 applies in respect of any order made under subsection (5) or (5.1) as though the order were an order made by a justice under subsection 457(2) or (5), and section 457.6 applies in respect of any order made under subsection (5.1) as though the order were an order made by a justice under subsection 457(2). 1974-75-76, c. 93, s. 55(1) to (6).

Review of Detention where Trial Delayed

Time for application to judge

459. (1) Where an accused who has been charged with an offence other than an offence mentioned in section 457.7 and who is not required to be detained in custody in respect of any other matter is being detained in custody pending his trial for that offence and the trial has not commenced

(a) in the case of an indictable offence, within ninety days from

(i) the day on which the accused was taken before a justice under section 454, or

(ii) where an order that the accused be detained in custody has been made under section 457.6 or 458, the day on which he was taken into custody under that order, or

(b) in the case of an offence for which the accused is being prosecuted in proceedings by way of summary conviction, within thirty days from

(i) the day on which the accused was taken before a justice under subsection 454(1), or

(ii) where an order that the accused be detained in custody has been made under section 457.6 or 458, the day on which he was taken into custody under that order,

the person having the custody of the accused shall, forthwith upon the expiration of those ninety or thirty days, as the case may be, apply to a judge having jurisdiction in the place in which the accused is in custody to fix a date for a hearing to determine whether or not the accused should be released from custody.

Notice of hearing

(2) Upon receiving an application under subsection (1), the judge shall fix a date for the hearing described therein of the question and direct that notice of the hearing be given to such persons, including the prosecutor and the accused, and in such manner as the judge may specify.

Matters to be considered on hearing

(3) Upon the hearing described in subsection (1), the judge may, in deciding whether or not the accused should be released from custody, take into consideration whether the prosecutor or the accused has been responsible for any unreasonable delay in the trial of the charge.

Order

(4) If, following the hearing described in subsection (1), the judge is not satisfied that the continued detention of the accused in custody is justified within the meaning of subsection 457(7), he shall order that the accused be released from custody pending the trial of the charge,

(a) upon his giving an undertaking with such conditions as the judge directs, or

(b) upon his entering into a recognizance before the judge with or without sureties in such amount and with such conditions, if any, as the judge directs, but without deposit of money or other valuable security.

Warrant of judge for arrest

(5) Where a judge having jurisdiction in the province where an order under subsection (4) for the release of an accused has been made is satisfied that there are reasonable and probable grounds to believe that the accused

(a) has violated or is about to violate the undertaking or recognizance upon which he has been released, or

(b) has, after his release from custody upon his undertaking or recognizance, committed an indictable offence,

he may issue a warrant for the arrest of the accused.

Arrest without warrant by peace officer

(6) Notwithstanding anything in this Act, a peace officer who has reasonable and probable grounds to believe that an accused who has been released from custody under subsection (4)

(a) has violated or is about to violate the undertaking or recognizance upon which he has been released, or

(b) has, after his release from custody upon his undertaking or recognizance, committed an indictable offence, 27 Interp

may arrest the accused without warrant and take him or cause him to be taken before a judge having jurisdiction in the province where the order for his release was made.

Hearing and order

(7) A judge before whom an accused is taken pursuant to a warrant issued under subsection (5) or pursuant to subsection (6) may, where the accused shows cause why his detention in custody is not justified within the meaning of subsection 457(7), order that the accused be released upon his giving an undertaking or entering into a recognizance described in any of paragraphs 457(2)*(a)* to *(d)* with such conditions, described in subsection 457(4), as the judge considers desirable. 1974-75-76, c. 93, s. 56.

Provisions applicable to proceedings

(8) The provisions of section 457.2, 457.3 and 457.4 apply *mutatis mutandis* in respect of any proceedings under this section.

mutatis mutandis — after the necessary changes in detail so that the text applies

Directions for expediting trial

(9) Where an accused is before a judge under this section, whether by virtue of an application under subsection (1) or otherwise, the judge may give such directions as he thinks necessary for expediting the trial of the accused. R.S., c. 2(2nd Supp.), s. 5.

Interpretation Act

27. (1) Where an enactment creates an offence,

(a) the offence shall be deemed to be an indictable offence if the enactment provides that the offender may be prosecuted for the offence by indictment;

(b) the offence shall be deemed to be one for which the offender is punishable on summary conviction if there is nothing in the context to indicate that the offence is an indictable offence; and

(c) if the offence is one for which the offender may be prosecuted by indictment or for which he is punishable on summary conviction, no person shall be considered to have been convicted of an indictable offence by reason only of having been convicted of the offence on summary conviction.

No application by way of *habeas corpus*

459.1 No application may be made by way of *habeas corpus* for the purpose of obtaining the making of any order under this Part, Part XVIII or Part XXIV relating to interim release or for the purpose of reviewing or varying any decision made thereunder relating to interim release or detention. R.S.,c.2(2nd Supp.),s.5.

habeas corpus — a writ directed to a person holding another in custody ordering him to bring the prisoner before the court for a particular purpose, usually to determine the legality of the detention or imprisonment.

Procedure to Procure Attendance of a Prisoner

Procuring attendance

460. (1) Where a person who is confined in a prison is required

(a) to attend at a preliminary inquiry into a charge against him,

(b) to stand his trial upon a charge that may be tried by indictment or on summary conviction, or

(c) to attend to give evidence in a proceeding to which this Act applies,

a judge of a superior court of criminal jurisdiction or of a county or district court may order in writing that the prisoner be brought before the court, judge, justice, or magistrate before whom his attendance is required, from day to day as 2
may be necessary, if

(d) the applicant for the order sets out the facts of the case in an affidavit and produces the warrant, if any, and

(e) the judge is satisfied that the ends of justice require that an order be made.

Magistrate's order

(2) A magistrate has the same powers for the purposes of subsection (1) as a judge has under that subsection where the person whose attendance is required is confined in a prison within the province in which the magistrate has jurisdiction.

Conveyance of prisoner

(3) An order that is made under subsection (1) or (2) shall be addressed to the person who has custody of the prisoner, and on receipt thereof that person shall

(a) deliver the prisoner to any person who is named in the order to receive him, or

(b) bring the prisoner before the court, judge, justice or magistrate, as the case may be, upon payment of his reasonable charges in respect thereof.

Detention of prisoner required as witness

(4) Where the prisoner is required as a witness, the judge or magistrate shall direct, in the order, the manner in which the prisoner shall be kept in custody and returned to the prison from which he is brought.

Detention in other cases

(5) Where the appearance of the prisoner is required for the purposes of paragraph (1)*(a)* or *(b)*, the judge or magistrate shall give appropriate directions in the order with respect to the manner in which the prisoner is

(a) to be kept in custody, if he is committed for trial; or

(b) to be returned, if he is discharged upon a preliminary inquiry or if he is acquitted of the charge against him.

Application of sections respecting sentence

(6) Sections 645 and 659 apply where a prisoner to whom this section applies is convicted and sentenced to imprisonment by the court, judge, justice or magistrate. 1953-54, c. 51, s. 446.

Endorsement of Warrant

Endorsing warrant

461. (1) Where a warrant for the arrest of an accused cannot be executed in accordance with section 456.3, a justice within whose jurisdiction the accused is or is believed to be shall, upon application, and upon proof on oath or by affidavit of the signature of the justice who issued the warrant, authorize the execution of the warrant within his jurisdiction by making an endorsement, which may be in Form 25, upon the warrant. 1974-75-76, c. 93, s. 57. 2 28 Interp

Effect of endorsement

(2) An endorsement that is made upon a warrant pursuant to subsection (1) is sufficient authority to the peace officers to whom it was originally directed, and to all peace officers within the territorial jurisdiction of the justice by whom it is endorsed, to execute the warrant and to take the accused before the justice who issued the warrant or before some other justice for the same territorial division. 1953-54, c. 51, s. 447.

2. In this Act

"justice" means a justice of the peace or a magistrate, and includes two or more justices where two or more justices are, by law, required to act or, by law, act or have jurisdiction;

"magistrate" means a magistrate, a police magistrate, a stipendiary magistrate, a district magistrate, a provincial magistrate, a judge of the sessions of the peace, a recorder, or any person having the power and authority of two or more justices of the peace, and includes

(a) with respect to the Provinces of Ontario, Quebec, New Brunswick and British Columbia, a judge of the provincial court,

(a.1) with respect to the Provinces of Alberta, Manitoba and Prince Edward Island, a provincial judge,

(a.2) with respect to the Province of Nova Scotia, a judge of the Provincial Magistrate's Court,

(b) with respect to the Province of Saskatchewan, a judge of the Magistrates' Courts, and;

(c) with respect to the Yukon Territory and the Northwest Territories, a judge of the Supreme Court,

and the lawful deputy of each of them;

Interpretation Act

28. In every enactment

"oath" includes a solemn affirmation or declaration, whenever the context applies to any person by whom and case in which a solemn affirmation or declaration may be made instead of an oath; and in like cases the expression "sworn" includes the expression "affirmed" or "declared";

Coroner's Warrant

Coroner's warrant and recognizance

462. (1) Where a person is alleged, by a verdict upon a coroner's inquisition, to have committed murder or manslaughter but he has not been charged with the offence, the coroner shall

(a) direct, by warrant under his hand, that the person be taken into custody and be conveyed, as soon as possible, before a justice, or

(b) direct the person to enter into a recognizance before him with or without sureties, to appear before a justice.

Transmitting depositions

(2) Where a coroner makes a direction under subsection (1) he shall transmit to the justice the evidence taken before him in the matter. 1953-54, c. 51, s. 448.

--NOTES--

PART XIV.1

LANGUAGE OF ACCUSED

Language of accused

462.1 (1) On application by an accused whose language is one of the official languages of Canada, made not later than

(a) the time of the appearance of the accused at which his trial date is set, if he is accused of an offence

(i) mentioned in section 483, or

(ii) punishable on summary conviction,

(b) the time of his election if he elects under subsection 464(3) or 484(1) to
be tried by a magistrate, or 2

(c) the time when he is committed to stand trial if he is charged with an offence mentioned in section 427 or if he has elected to be tried by a judge or a judge and jury,

a justice of the peace or magistrate shall grant an order directing that the accused
be tried before a justice of the peace, magistrate, judge or judge and jury, as the 2
case may be, who speak the official language of Canada that is the language of the accused or, if the circumstances warrant, who speak both official languages of Canada.

Idem

(2) On application by an accused whose language is not one of the official languages of Canada, made not later than whichever of the times referred to in paragraphs (1)*(a)* to *(c)* is applicable, a justice of the peace or magistrate may grant an order directing that the accused be tried before a justice of the peace, magistrate, judge or judge and jury, as the case may be, who speak the official language of Canada in which the accused, in the opinion of the justice or magistrate, can best give testimony or, if the circumstances warrant, who speak both official languages.

Accused to be advised of right

(3) The justice of the peace or magistrate before whom an accused first appears shall, if the accused is not represented by counsel, advise the accused of his right to apply for an order under subsection (1) or (2) and of the time before which such an application must be made.

Remand

(4) Where an accused fails to apply for an order under subsection (1) or (2) and the justice of the peace, magistrate or judge before whom the accused is to be tried (in this Part referred to as "the court") is satisfied that it is in the best interests of justice that the accused be tried before a justice of the peace, magistrate, judge or judge and jury who speak the official language of Canada that is the language of the accused or, if the language of the accused is not one of the official languages of Canada, the official language of Canada in which the accused, in the opinion of the court, can best give testimony, the court may, if it does not speak that language, by order remand the accused to be tried by a justice of the peace, magistrate, judge or judge and jury, as the case may be, who speak that language or, if the circumstances warrant, who speak both official languages.

Variation of order

(5) An order under this section that an accused be tried before a justice of the peace, magistrate, judge or judge and jury who speak the official language of Canada that is the language of the accused or the official language of Canada in which the accused can best give testimoney may, if the circumstances warrant, be varied by the court to require that the accused be tried before a justice of the peace, magistrate, judge or judge and jury who speak both official languages.

Part XIV.1 in force in the Province of New Brusnwick and the Yukon and Northwest Territories only.

Change of venue

462.2 Notwithstanding any other provision of this Act but subject to any regulations made pursuant to section 462.4, the court shall order that the trial of an accused be held in a territorial division in the same province other than that in which the offence would otherwise be tried if an order has been made that the accused be tried before a justice of the peace, magistrate, judge or judge and jury who speak the official language of Canada that is the language of the accused or the official language of Canada in which the accused can best give testimony or both official languages and such order cannot be conveniently complied with in the territorial division in which the offence would otherwise be 2
tried.

Saving

462.3 Nothing in this Part or the *Official Languages Act* derogates from or otherwise adversely affects any right afforded by a law of a province in force on the coming into force of this Part in that province or thereafter coming into force relating to the language of proceedings or testimony in criminal matters that is not inconsistent with this Part or that Act.

Regulations

462.4 The Lieutenant Governor in Council of a province may make 28 Interp
regulations generally for carrying into effect the purposes and provisions of this Part in the province and the Commissioner of the Yukon Territory and the Commissioner of the Northwest Territories may make regulations generally for carrying into effect the purposes and provisions of this Part in the Yukon Territory and the Northwest Territories, respectively.

2. In this Act

"magistrate" means a magistrate, a police magistrate, a stipendiary magistrate, a district magistrate, a provincial magistrate, a judge of the sessions of the peace, a recorder, or any person having the power and authority of two or more justices of the peace, and includes

(a) with respect to the Provinces of Ontario, Quebec, New Brunswick and British Columbia, a judge of the provincial court,

(a.1) with respect to the Provinces of Alberta, Manitoba and Prince Edward Island, a provincial judge,

(a.2) with respect to the Province of Nova Scotia, a judge of the Provincial Magistrate's Court,

(b) with respect to the Province of Saskatchewan, a judge of the Magistrates' Courts, and

(c) with respect to the Yukon Territory and the Northwest Territories, a judge of the Supreme Court,

and the lawful deputy of each of them;

"territorial division" includes any province, county, union of counties, township, city, town, parish or other judicial division or place to which the context applies;

Interpretation Act

28. In every enactment

"lieutenant governor in council" means the lieutenant governor, or person administering the government of the province indicated by the enactment, for the time being, acting by and with the advice of, or by and with the advice and consent of, or in conjuction with the executive council of such province and, in relation to the Yukon Territory or the Northwest Territories, means the Commissioner thereof;

PART XV

PROCEDURE ON PRELIMINARY INQUIRY

Jurisdiction

Inquiry by justice

463. Where an accused who is charged with an indictable offence is before a justice, the justice shall, in accordance with this Part, inquire into that charge and any other charge against that person. 1953-54, c. 51, s. 449.

2. In this Act

"justice" means a justice of the peace or a magistrate, and includes two or more justices where two or more justices are, by law, required to act or, by law, act or have jurisdiction;

"magistrate" means a magistrate, a police magistrate, a stipendiary magistrate, a district magistrate, a provincial magistrate, a judge of the sessions of the peace, a recorder, or any person having the power and authority of two or more justices of the peace, and includes

(a) with respect to the Provinces of Ontario, Quebec, New Brunswick and British Columbia, a judge of the provincial court,

(a.1) with respect to the Provinces of Alberta, Manitoba and Prince Edward Island, a provincial judge,

(a.2) with respect to the Province of Nova Scotia, a judge of the Provincial Magistrate's Court,

(b) with respect to the Province of Saskatchewan, a judge of the Magistrates' Courts, and;

(c) with respect to the Yukon Territory and the Northwest Territories, a judge of the Supreme Court,

and the lawful deputy of each of them;

"prosecutor" means the Attorney General or, where the Attorney General does not intervene, means the person who institutes proceedings to which this Act applies, and includes counsel acting on behalf of either of them;

"territorial division" includes any province, county, union of counties, township, city, town, parish or other judicial division or place to which the context applies;

482. In this Part

"magistrate" means

(a) a person appointed under the law of a province, by whatever title he may be designated, who is specially authorized by the terms of his appointment to exercise the jurisdiction conferred upon a magistrate by this Part, but does not include two or more justices of the peace sitting together,

(b) with respect to the Yukon Territory, a judge of the Supreme Court or a magistrate or deputy magistrate appointed under an Ordinance of the Territory, and

(c) with respect to the Northwest Territories, a judge of the Supreme Court or a magistrate or deputy magistrate appointed under an Ordinance of the Territories.

Interpretation Act

27. (1) Where an enactment creates an offence,

(a) the offence shall be deemed to be an indictable offence if the enactment provides that the offender may be prosecuted for the offence by indictment;

(b) the offence shall be deemed to be one for which the offender is punishable on summary conviction if there is nothing in the context to indicate that the offence is an indictable offence; and

(c) if the offence is one for which the offender may be prosecuted by indictment or for which he is punishable on summary conviction, no person shall be considered to have been convicted of an indictable offence by reason only of having been convicted of the offence on summary conviction.

Remand by justice to magistrate in certain cases

464. (1) Where an accused is before a justice other than a magistrate as defined in Part XVI charged with an offence over which a magistrate, under 2 & 48
that Part, has absolute jurisdiction, the justice shall remand the accused to 483
appear before a magistrate having absolute jurisdiction over that offence in the territorial division in which the offence is alleged to have been committed. 2

Election before justice in certain cases

(2) Where an accused is before a justice other than a magistrate as defined in Part XVI charged with an offence other than an offence that is mentioned in section 427, and the offence is not one over which a magistrate has absolute jurisdiction under section 483, the justice shall, after the information has been read to the accused, put him to his election in the following words:

> You have the option to elect to be tried by a magistrate without a jury; or you may elect to be tried by a judge without a jury; or you may elect to be tried by a court composed of a judge and jury. How do you elect to be tried?

Procedure where accused elects trial by magistrate

(3) Where an accused elects to be tried by a magistrate, the justice shall endorse on the information a statement that the accused has so elected and shall remand the accused to appear and plead to the charge before a magistrate having jurisdiction over that offence in the territorial division in which the offence is alleged to have been committed.

Procedure when accused does not elect trial by magistrate

(4) Where an accused does not elect to be tried by a magistrate, the justice shall hold a preliminary inquiry into the charge and if the accused is committed for trial or, where the accused is a corporation, is ordered to stand trial, the justice shall

(a) endorse on the information a statement showing the nature of the election or that the accused did not elect, and

(b) state in the warrant of committal, if any, that the accused

(i) elected to be tried by a judge without a jury,

(ii) elected to be tried by a court composed of a judge and jury, or

(iii) did not elect. 1953-54, c. 51, s. 450; 1968-69, c. 38, s. 32.

Powers of Justice

Powers of justice

465. (1) A justice acting under this Part may

(a) Repealed. R.S., c. 2(2nd Supp.), s. 6.

(b) adjourn the inquiry from time to time and change the place of hearing, where it appears to be desirable to do so by reason of the absence of a witness, the inability of a witness who is ill to attend at the place where the justice usually sits, or for any other sufficient reason, but no such adjournment shall be for more than eight clear days unless 25(2) Interp

(i) the accused, whether or not he is in custody, and the prosecutor consent to the proposed adjournment, or 2

(ii) the accused is remanded for observation under subparagraph *(c)*(i);

(c) by order in writing,

(i) direct an accused to attend, at a place or before a person specified in the order and within a time specified therein, for observation, or

(ii) remand an accused to such custody as the justice directs for observation for a period not exceeding thirty days, where, in his opinion, supported by the evidence, or where the prosecutor and the accused consent, by the report in writing, of at least one duly qualified medical practitioner, there is reason to believe that

(iii) the accused may be mentally ill, or

(iv) the balance of the mind of the accused may be disturbed, where the accused is a female person charged with an offence arising out of the death
of her newly-born child. 1974-75-76, c. 93, s. 58(1). 2

(d) except where the accused is authorized pursuant to Part XIV to be at large, remand the accused to custody in a prison by warrant in Form 14;

(e) resume an inquiry before the expiration of a period for which it has been
adjourned with the consent of the prosecutor and the accused or his counsel; 2

(f) order in writing, in Form 26, that the accused be brought before him, or
any other justice for the same territorial division, at any time before the 2
expiration of the time for which the accused has been remanded;

(g) Repealed. R.S., c. 2(2nd Supp.), s. 6.

(h) grant or refuse permission to the prosecutor or his counsel to address him in support of the charge, by way of opening or summing up or by way of reply upon any evidence that is given on behalf of the accused;

(i) receive evidence on the part of the prosecutor or the accused, as the case may be, after hearing any evidence that has been given on behalf of either of them;

(j) order that no person other than the prosecutor, the accused and their counsel shall have access to or remain in the room in which the inquiry is held, where it appears to him that the ends of justice will be best served by so doing; and

(k) regulate the course of the inquiry in any way that appears to him to be desirable and that is not inconsistent with this Act.

Remand for observation

(2) Notwithstanding paragraph (1)(c), a justice acting under this Part may remand an accused in accordance with that paragraph

(a) for a period not exceeding thirty days without having heard the evidence or considered the report of a duly qualified medical practitioner where compelling circumstances exist for so doing and where a medical practitioner is not readily available to examine the accused and give evidence or submit a report; and

(b) for a period of more than thirty days but not exceeding sixty days where he is satisfied that observation for such a period is required in all the circumstances of the case and his opinion is supported by the evidence or, where the prosecutor and the accused consent, by the report in writing, of at least one duly qualified medical practitioner.

Direct issue to be tried

(3) Where, as a result of observations made pursuant to an order issued under
paragraph (1)*(c)*, it appears to a justice that there is sufficient reason to doubt 2
that the accused is, on account of insanity, capable of conducting his defence, 16
the justice shall direct that an issue be tried whether the accused is then, on account of insanity, unfit to conduct his defence at the preliminary inquiry.

Section 543 applicable

(4) Where the justice directs the trial of an issue under subsection (3), he shall 2
proceed in accordance with section 543 in so far as that section may be applied. 1974-75-76,c.93,s.58(2).

Corporation

466. Where an accused is a corporation, subsections 486(1) and (2) apply, *mutatis mutandis.* 1953-54, c. 51, s. 452. 20 Interp

486. (1) An accused that is a corporation shall appear by its counsel or agent.

(2) Where an accused corporation does not appear pursuant to a summons and service of the summons upon the corporation is proved, the magistrate 3(7) & 455.5(3)

(a) may, if the charge is one over which he has absolute jurisdiction, proceed with the trial of the charge in the absence of the accused corporation, and

(b) shall, if the charge is not one over which he has absolute jurisdiction, hold a preliminary inquiry in accordance with Part XV.

(3) Where an accused corporation appears but does not make any election under subsection 484(2), the magistrate shall hold a preliminary inquiry in accordance with Part XV.

Taking Evidence of Witnesses

Order restricting publication of evidence taken at preliminary inquiry

467. (1) Prior to the commencement of the taking of evidence at a preliminary inquiry, the justice holding the inquiry shall, if application therefor is made by the accused or, where there is more than one accused, by any one of them, make an order directing that the evidence taken at the inquiry shall not be published in any newspaper or broadcast before such time as 2 ss. (4) 28 Interp

(a) the accused who made the application is discharged, or

(b) if the accused who made the application is committed for trial or ordered to stand trial, the trial is ended.

Accused to be informed of right to apply for order

(2) Where an accused is not represented by counsel at a preliminary inquiry, the justice holding the inquiry shall, prior to the commencement of the taking of evidence at the inquiry, inform the accused of his right to make application under subsection (1). 2 2

Type 'A' Offence

(3) Every one who fails to comply with an order made pursuant to subsection (1) is guilty of an offence punishable on summary conviction.

"Newspaper"

(4) In this section, "newspaper" has the same meaning as it has in sections 262 to 281 by virtue of section 261. 1968-69,c.38,s.33.

261. In sections 262 to 281, "newspaper" means any paper, magazine or periodical containing public news, intelligence or reports of events, or any remarks or observations thereon, printed for sale and published periodically or in parts or numbers, at intervals not exceeding thirty-one days between the publication of any two such papers, parts or numbers, and any paper, magazine or periodical printed in order to be dispersed and made public, weekly or more often, or at intervals not exceeding thirty-one days, that contains advertisements, exclusively or principally.

Taking evidence

468. (1) Where the accused is before a justice holding a preliminary inquiry, the justice shall 2

(a) take the evidence under oath, in the presence of the accused, of the witnesses called on the part of the prosecution and allow the accused or his counsel to cross-examine them; and 28 Interp 2

(b) cause a record of the evidence of each witness to be taken

(i) by a stenographer appointed by him, or in legible writing, in the form of a deposition, in Form 27, or

(ii) in a province where a sound recording apparatus is authorized by or under provincial legislation for use in civil cases, by the type of apparatus so authorized and in accordance with the requirements of the provincial legislation.

Reading and signing depositions

(2) Where a deposition is taken down in writing, the justice shall, in the presence of the accused, before asking the accused if he wishes to call witnesses, 2

(a) cause the deposition to be read to the witness,

(b) cause the deposition to be signed by the witness, and

(c) sign the deposition himself.

Authentication by justice

(3) Where depositions are taken down in writing the justice may sign 2

(a) at the end of each deposition, or

(b) at the end of several or of all the depositions in a manner that will indicate that his signature is intended to authenticate each deposition.

Stenographer to be sworn

(4) Where the stenographer appointed to take down the evidence is not a duly sworn court stenographer he shall make oath that he will truly and faithfully report the evidence. 28 Interp

Authentication of transcript

(5) Where the evidence is taken down by a stenographer appointed by the justice, it need not be read to or signed by the witnesses, but the evidence shall be transcribed by the stenographer and the transcript shall be signed by the justice and shall be accompanied by 2

(a) an affidavit of the stenographer that it is a true report of the evidence, or

(b) a certificate that it is a true report of the evidence if the stenographer is a duly sworn court stenographer.

Transcription of record taken by sound recording apparatus

(6) Where, in accordance with this Act, a record is taken in any proceedings under this Act by a sound recording apparatus, the record so taken shall be dealt with and transcribed and the transcription certified and used in accordance with the provincial legislation *mutatis mutandis* mentioned in subsection (1). 1953-54,c.51,s.453;1960,c.37,s.2.

Accused to be addressed

469. (1) When the evidence of the witnesses called on the part of the prosecution has been taken down and, where required by this Part, has been read, the justice shall address the accused as follows or to the like effect:

Having heard the evidence, do you wish to say anything in answer to the charge? You are not bound to say anything, but whatever you do say will be taken down in writing and may be given in evidence against you at your trial. You must clearly understand that you have nothing to hope from any promise of favour and nothing to fear from any threat that may have been held out to you to induce you to make any admission or confession of guilt, but whatever you now say may be given in evidence against you at your trial notwithstanding the promise or threat.

Statement of accused

(2) Where the accused says anything in answer to the address made by the justice pursuant to subsection (1), his answer shall be taken down in writing and shall be signed by the justice and kept with the evidence of the witnesses and dealt with in accordance with this Part.

Witnesses for accused

(3) When subsections (1) and (2) have been complied with the justice shall ask the accused if he wishes to call any witnesses.

Depositions of such witnesses

(4) The justice shall hear each witness called by the accused who testifies to any matter relevant to the inquiry, and for the purposes of this subsection, section 468 applies, *mutatis mutandis.* 1953-54,c.51,s.454.

584. A statement made by an accused under subsection 469(2) and purporting to be signed by the justice before whom it was made may be given in evidence against the accused at his trial without proof of the signature of the justice, unless it is proved that the justice by whom the statement purports to be signed did not sign it.

Confession or admission of accused

470. (1) Nothing in this Act prevents a prosecutor giving in evidence at a preliminary inquiry any admission, confession or statement made at any time by the accused that by law is admissible against him.

Restriction of publication of reports of preliminary inquiry

Type 'A' Offence

(2) Every one who publishes in any newspaper, or broadcasts, a report that any admission or confession was tendered in evidence at a preliminary inquiry or a report of the nature of such admission or confession so tendered in evidence unless

(a) the accused has been discharged, or

(b) if the accused has been committed for trial, the trial has ended,

is guilty of an offence punishable on summary conviction.

(3) In this section "newspaper" has the same meaning that it has in sections 262 to 281 by virtue of section 261. 1953-54,c.51,s.455; 1959,c.41,s.18.

261. In sections 262 to 281, "newspaper" means any paper, magazine or periodical containing public news, intelligence or reports of events, or any remarks or observations thereon, printed for sale and published periodically or in parts or numbers, at intervals not exceeding thirty-one days between the publication of any two such papers, parts or numbers, and any paper, magazine or periodical printed in order to be dispersed and made public, weekly or more often, or at intervals not exceeding thirty-one days, that contains advertisements, exclusively or principally.

mutatis mutandis — after the necessary changes in detail so that the text applies

Remand Where Offence Committed in Another Jurisdiction

Order that accused appear or be taken before justice where offence committed

471. (1) Where an accused is charged with an offence alleged to have been committed out of the limits of the jurisdiction in which he has been charged, the justice before whom he appears or is brought may, at any stage of the inquiry after hearing both parties,

(a) order the accused to appear, or

(b) if the accused is in custody, issue a warrant in Form 10 to convey the accused

before a justice having jurisdiction in the place where the offence is alleged to have been committed, who shall continue and complete the inquiry.

Transmission of transcript and documents and effect of order or warrant

(2) Where a justice makes an order or issues a warrant pursuant to subsection (1), he shall cause the transcript of any evidence given before him in the inquiry and all documents that were then before him and that are relevant to the inquiry to be transmitted to a justice having jurisdiction in the place where the offence is alleged to have been committed and

(a) any evidence the transcript of which is so transmitted shall be deemed to have been taken by the justice to whom it is transmitted; and

(b) Any appearance notice, promise to appear, undertaking or recognizance issued to or given or entered into by the accused under Part XIV shall be deemed to have been issued, given or entered into in the jurisdiction where the offence is alleged to have been committed and to require the accused to appear before the justice to whom the transcript and documents are transmitted at the time provided in the order made in respect of the accused under paragraph (1)*(a)*. R.S., c. C-34, s. 471; R.S., c. 2(2nd Supp.), s. 7.

Absconding Accused

Accused absconding during inquiry

471.1 (1) Notwithstanding any other provision of this Act, where an accused, whether or not he is charged jointly with another, absconds during the course of a preliminary inquiry into an offence with which he is charged,

(*a*) he shall be deemed to have waived his right to be present at the inquiry; and

(*b*) the justice 2

(i) may continue the inquiry and, when all the evidence has been taken, shall dispose of the inquiry in accordance with section 475, or

(ii) if a warrant is issued for the arrest of the accused, may adjourn the inquiry to await his appearance,

but where the inquiry is adjourned pursuant to subparagraph (*b*)(ii), the justice may continue it at any time pursuant to subparagraph (*b*)(i) if he is satisfied that it would no longer be in the interests of justice to await the appearance of the accused.

Adverse inference

(2) Where the justice continues a preliminary inquiry pursuant to subsection (1), he may draw an inference adverse to the accused from the fact that he has absconded.

Accused not entitled to re-opening

(3) Where an accused reappears at a preliminary inquiry that is continuing pursuant to subsection (1), he is not entitled to have any part of the proceedings that was conducted in his absence re-opened unless the justice is satisfied that because of exceptional circumstances it is in the interests of justice to re-open the inquiry.

Counsel for accused may continue to act

(4) Where the accused has absconded during the course of a preliminary inquiry and the justice continues the inquiry, counsel for the accused is not 2
thereby deprived of any authority he may have to continue to act for the accused in the proceedings.

Provisions of subsections 469(1) and (2) not applicable

(5) Where, at the conclusion of the evidence on the part of the prosecution at a preliminary inquiry that has been continued pursuant to subsection (1), the accused is absent, the provisions of subsections 469(1) and (2) do not apply but, if counsel for the accused is present, he shall be given an opportunity to call witnesses on behalf of the accused and the provisions of subsection 469(4) apply *mutatis mutandis*. 1974-75-76,c.93,s.59.

Section 431.1 Accused absconding during trial
Section 526.1 Election deemed to have been waived

2. In this Act

"counsel" means a barrister or solicitor, in respect of the matters or things that barristers and solicitors, respectively, are authorized by the law of the province to do or perform in relation to legal proceedings;

"justice" means a justice of the peace or a magistrate, and includes two or more justices where two or more justices are, by law, required to act or, by law, act or have jurisdiction;

mutatis mutandis — after the necessary changes in detail so that the text applies

Interpretation Act

25. (2) Where there is a reference to a number of clear days or "at least" a number of days between two events, in calculating the number of days there shall be excluded the days on which the events happen.

Procedure Where Witness Refuses to Testify

Witness refusing to be examined

472. (1) Where a person, being present at a preliminary inquiry and being required by the justice to give evidence, 2

(a) refuses to be sworn,

(b) having been sworn, refuses to answer the questions that are put to him,

(c) fails to produce any writings that he is required to produce, or

(d) refuses to sign his deposition,

without offering a reasonable excuse for his failure or refusal, the justice may adjourn the inquiry and may, by warrant in Form 16, commit the person to prison for a period not exceeding eight clear days or for the period during which the inquiry is adjourned, whichever is the lesser period. 25(2) Interp

Further commitment

(2) Where a person to whom subsection (1) applies is brought before the justice upon the resumption of the adjourned inquiry and again refuses to do what is required of him, the justice may again adjourn the inquiry for a period not exceeding eight clear days and commit him to prison for the period of adjournment or any part thereof, and may adjourn the inquiry and commit the person to prison from time to time until the person consents to do what is required of him. 2 25(2) Interp

Saving

(3) Nothing is this section shall be deemed to prevent the justice from sending the case for trial upon any other sufficient evidence taken by him. 1953-54,c.51,s.457. 2

Remedial Provisions

Irregularity or variance not to affect validity

473. The validity of any proceeding at or subsequent to a preliminary inquiry is not affected by

(a) any irregularity or defect in the substance or form of the summons or warrant,

(b) any variance between the charge set out in the summons or warrant and the charge set out in the information, or

(c) any variance between the charge set out in the summons, warrant or information and the evidence adduced by the prosecution at the inquiry. 1953-54,c.51,s.458.

Adjournment if accused misled

474. Where it appears to the justice that the accused has been deceived or misled by any irregularity, defect or variance mentioned in section 473, he may adjourn the inquiry and may remand the accused or grant him interim release in accordance with Part XIV. 1974-75-76,c.93,s.59.1. 2

Adjudication and Recognizances

Committal, dismissal, etc.

475. (1) When all the evidence has been taken by the justice he shall, 2

(a) if in his opinion the evidence is sufficient to put the accused on trial,

(i) commit the accused for trial, or

(ii) order the accused, where it is a corporation, to stand trial in the court having criminal jurisdiction; or

(b) discharge the accused, if in his opinion upon the whole of the evidence no sufficient case is made out to put the accused on trial. R.S.,c.C-34,s.475; R.S.,c.2(2nd Supp.),s.8.

(2) Repealed,R.S.,c.2(2nd Supp.),s.8.

Committal for trial at any stage of inquiry with consent

476. (1) Notwithstanding any other provision of this Act, the justice may, 2
at any stage of a preliminary inquiry, with the consent of the accused and the
prosecutor, commit the accused for trial or order the accused, where it is a 2
corporation, to stand trial in the court having criminal jurisdiction, without
taking or recording any evidence or further evidence.

Proceedings where accused committed under ss(1)

(2) Where an accused is committed for trial or ordered to stand trial under
subsection (1), the justice shall endorse on the information a statement of the 2
consent of the accused and the prosecutor, and the accused shall thereafter be 2
dealt with in all respects as if committed for trial or ordered to stand trial
under section 475. 1968-69,c.38,s.35.

Recognizance of witness

477. (1) Where an accused is committed for trial or is ordered to stand trial,
the justice who held the preliminary inquiry may require any witness whose 2
evidence is, in his opinion, material to enter into a recognizance to give evidence at the trial of the accused and to comply with such reasonable conditions prescribed in the recognizance as the justice considers desirable for securing the attendance of the witness to give evidence at the trial of the accused. 1974-75-76,c.93,s.60.

Form

(2) The recognizance may be in Form 28, and may be set out at the end of a deposition or be separate therefrom.

Sureties or deposit for appearance of witness

(3) A justice may, for any reason satisfactory to him, require any witness entering into a recognizance pursuant to this section

(a) to produce one or more sureties in such amount as he may direct, or 28 Interp

(b) to deposit with him a sum of money sufficient in his opinion to ensure that the witness will appear and give evidence.

Witness refusing to be bound

(4) Where a witness does not comply with subsection (1) or (3) when
required to do so by a justice, he may be committed by the justice, by warrant
in Form 21, to a prison in the territorial division where the trial is to be held, 2
there to be kept until he does what is required of him or until the trial is
concluded.

Discharge

(5) Where a witness has been committed to prison pursuant to subsection (4), the court before which the witness appears or a justice having jurisdiction in the territorial division where the prison is situated may, by order in Form 35, discharge the witness from custody when the trial is concluded. 1953-54, c. 51, s. 461.

Transmission of Record

Material to be transmitted to clerk of court

478. Where a justice commits an accused for trial or orders an accused to stand trial, he shall forthwith send to the clerk or other proper officer of the court by which the accused is to be tried, the information, the evidence, the exhibits, the statement if any of the accused, any promise to appear, undertaking or recognizance given or entered into in accordance with Part XIV, and any evidence taken before a coroner, that are in the possession of the justice. R.S., c. C-34, s. 478; R.S., c. 2(2nd Supp.), s. 9.

479. to 481. Repealed. R.S., c. 2(2nd Supp.), s. 9.

PART XVI

Indictable Offences—Trial without Jury

Interpretation

Definitions

482. In this Part

"judge"

"judge" means,

(a) in the Province of Ontario, a judge of the superior court of criminal jurisdiction of the Province or a judge or junior judge of a county or district court, 2

(b) in the Province of Quebec, a judge of the sessions of the peace or a judge of the provincial court,

(c) in the Province of Nova Scotia, a judge of a county court,

(c.1) in the Province of New Brunswick, a judge of the Court of Queen's Bench, 1978-79, c. 11, s. 10, I. 6(11).

(d) in the Province of Manitoba, the Chief Justice, or a puisne judge of the Court of Queen's Bench, or a judge of a county court,

(e) in the Province of British Columbia, the Chief Justice or a puisne judge of the Supreme Court, or a judge of a county court,

(f) in the Provinces of Saskatchewan and Alberta, a judge of the superior court of criminal jurisdiction of the province, 1978-79, c. 11, s. 10, I. 6(12). 2

(g) in the Province of Newfoundland, a judge of the Supreme Court or of a district court,

(h) in the Province of Prince Edward Island, the Yukon Territory and the Northwest Territories, a judge of the Supreme Court;

"magistrate"

"magistrate" means

(a) a person appointed under the law of a province, by whatever title he may be designated, who is specially authorized by the terms of his appointment to exercise the jurisdiction conferred upon a magistrate by this Part, but does not include two or more justices of the peace sitting together,

(b) with respect to the Yukon Territory, a judge of the Supreme Court or a magistrate or deputy magistrate appointed under an Ordinance of the Territory, and

(c) with respect to the Northwest Territories, a judge of the Supreme Court or a magistrate or deputy magistrate appointed under an Ordinance of the Territories. R.S., c. C-34, s. 482; 1972, c. 13, s. 39; 1972, c. 17, s. 2; 1974-75-76, c. 48, s. 25(1); 1974-75-76, c. 93, s. 61; 1978-79, c. 11, s. 10.

2. In this Act

"superior court of criminal jurisdiction" means

(a) in the Province of Ontario, the Supreme Court,

(b) in the Province of Quebec, the Superior Court,

(c) in the Provinces of Nova Scotia, Prince Edward Island and Newfoundland respectively, the Supreme Court,

(d) in the Province of British Columbia, the Supreme Court or the Court of Appeal,

(e) in the Provinces of Manitoba, Saskatchewan, Alberta and New Brunswick, respectively, the Court of Appeal or the Court of Queen's Bench,

(f) in the Yukon Territory, the Supreme Court, and

(g) in the Northwest Territories, the Supreme Court;

Jurisdiction of Magistrates

Absolute Jurisdiction

Absolute jurisdiction

483. The jurisdiction of a magistrate to try an accused is absolute and does not depend upon the consent of the accused where the accused is charged in an information 482

(*a*) with

(i) theft, other than theft of cattle, 294(b)

(ii) obtaining money or property by false pretences, 320(2)(

(iii) unlawfully having in his possession any property or thing or any proceeds of any property or thing knowing that all or a part of the property or thing or of the proceeds was obtained by or derived directly or indirectly from the commission in Canada of an offence punishable by indictment, or

(iv) having, by deceit, falsehood or other fraudulent means, defrauded the public or any person, whether ascertained or not, of any property, money or valuable security, 338(1)(

where the subject-matter of the offence is not a testamentary instrument and where the alleged value thereof does not exceed two hundred dollars;

(*b*) with an attempt to commit any offence referred in paragraph (*a*); or

(*c*) with an offence under

Gaming house — (i) section 185,

Bookmaking etc. — (ii) section 186,

Betting — (iii) section 187,

Lotteries — (iv) section 189,

Cheating at play — (v) section 192,

Bawdy-house — (vi) section 193,

Driving while disqualified — (vii) subsection 238(3), or

(viii) and (ix) Repealed, 1972,c.13,s.40,

Fraud in relation to fares, etc. — (x) section 351. R.S.,c. C-34,s.483; 1972,c.13,s.40; 1974-75-76,c.93,s.62.

Magistrate's Jurisdiction with Consent

Trial by magistrate with consent

484. (1) Where an accused is charged in an information with an indictable offence other than an offence that is mentioned in section 427, and the offence "G" is not one over which a magistrate has absolute jurisdiction under section 483, a "C" magistrate may try the accused if the accused elects to be tried by a magistrate.

Election

(2) An accused to whom this section applies shall, after the information has been read to him, be put to his election in the following words:

You have the option to elect to be tried by a magistrate without a jury; or you may elect to be tried by a judge without a jury; or you may elect to be tried by a court composed of a judge and jury. How do you elect to be tried?

Procedure where accused does not consent

(3) Where an accused does not elect to be tried by a magistrate, the magistrate shall hold a preliminary inquiry in accordance with Part XV, and if the accused is committed for trial or, in the case of a corporation is ordered to stand trial, the magistrate shall 482

(*a*) endorse on the information a statement showing the nature of the election or that the accused did not elect, and

(*b*) state in the warrant of committal, if any, that the accused

(i) elected to be tried by a judge without a jury, 482

(ii) elected to be tried by a court composed of a judge and jury, or

(iii) did not elect.

Procedure where accused consents

(4) Where an accused elects to be tried by a magistrate, the magistrate shall

(a) endorse on the information a record of the election, and

(b) call upon the accused to plead to the charge, and if the accused does not plead guilty the magistrate shall proceed with the trial or fix a time for the trial. 1953-54, c.51, s.468.

Magistrate may decide to hold preliminary inquiry

485. (1) Where in any proceedings under this Part an accused is before a magistrate and it appears to the magistrate that for any reason the charge should be prosecuted by indictment, he may, at any time before the accused has entered upon his defence, decide not to adjudicate and shall thereupon inform the accused of his decision and continue the proceedings as a preliminary inquiry. 482

Where value more than two hundred dollars

(2) Where an accused is before a magistrate charged with an offence mentioned in paragraph 483*(a)*, and, at any time before the magistrate makes an adjudication, the evidence establishes that the value of what was stolen, obtained, had in possession or attempted to be obtained, as the case may be, exceeds two hundred dollars, the magistrate shall put the accused to his election in accordance with subsection 484(2).

Continuing proceedings

(3) Where an accused is put to his election pursuant to subsection (2), the following provisions apply, namely,

(a) if the accused does not elect to be tried by a magistrate, the magistrate shall continue the proceedings as a preliminary inquiry under Part XV, and, if he commits the accused for trial, he shall comply with paragraphs 484(3)*(a)* and *(b)*; and

(b) if the accused elects to be tried by a magistrate, the magistrate shall endorse on the information a record of the election and continue with the trial. R.S.,c.C-34,s.485;

Corporation

486. (1) An accused that is a corporation shall appear by its counsel or agent. 28 Interp

Non-appearance

(2) Where an accused corporation does not appear pursuant to a summons and service of the summons upon the corporation is proved, the magistrate 3(7) & 455.5(3)

(a) may, if the charge is one over which he has absolute jurisdiction, proceed with the trial of the charge in the absence of the accused corporation, and

(b) shall, if the charge is not one over which he has absolute jurisdiction, hold a preliminary inquiry in accordance with Part XV.

Corporation not electing

(3) Where an accused corporation appears but does not make any election under subsection 484(2), the magistrate shall hold a preliminary inquiry in accordance with Part XV. 1953-54,c.51,s.470.

3. (7) Where, pursuant to this Act, any summons, notice or other process is required to be or may be served upon a corporation, and no other method of service is provided, such service may be effected by delivering the process

(a) in the case of a municipal corporation, to the mayor, warden, reeve, or other chief officer of the corporation, or to the secretary, treasurer or clerk of the corporation, and

(b) in the case of any other corporation, to the manager, secretary or other executive officer of the corporation or of a branch thereof.

455.5 (3) Service of a summons may be proved by the oral evidence, given under oath, of the peace officer who served it or by his affidavit made before a justice or other person authorized to administer oaths or to take affidavits.

Taking evidence

487. Where an accused is tried by a magistrate in accordance with this Part, the evidence of witnesses for the prosecutor and the accused shall be taken in accordance with the provisions of Part XV relating to preliminary inquiries. 1953-54,c.51,s.471.

Jurisdiction of Judges

Trial by judge with consent

488. An accused who is charged with an indictable offence other than an offence that is mentioned in section 427 shall, where he elects under section 464, 484 or 492 to be tried by a judge without a jury, be tried, subject to this
Part, by a judge without a jury. 1953-54,c.51,s.472. 482

Court of record

489. (1) A judge who holds a trial under this Part shall, for all purposes thereof and proceedings connected therewith or relating thereto, be a court of record.

(2) The record of a trial that a judge holds under this Part shall be kept in the court over which the judge presides. 1953-54,c.51,s.473.

Election

Duty of judge

490. (1) Where an accused elects, under section 464 or 484, to be tried by a
judge without a jury, a judge having jurisdiction shall, 482

(*a*) upon receiving a written notice from the sheriff or other person having custody of the accused stating that the accused is in custody and setting out the nature of the charge against him, or

(*b*) upon being notified by the clerk of the court that the accused is not in 2
custody and of the nature of the charge against him,

fix a time and place for the trial of the accused.

Notice by sheriff, when given

(2) The sheriff or other person having custody of the accused shall give the notice mentioned in paragraph (1)(*a*) within twenty-four hours after the accused is committed for trial, if he is in custody pursuant to that committal or if, at the time of committal, he is in custody for any other reason.

Duty of sheriff when date set for trial

(3) Where, pursuant to subsection (1), a time and place is fixed for the trial of an accused who is in custody, the accused

(*a*) shall be notified forthwith by the sheriff or other person having custody of the accused of the time and place so fixed, and

(*b*) shall be produced at the time and place so fixed.

Duty of accused when not in custody

(4) Where an accused is not in custody the duty of ascertaining from the clerk of the court the time and place fixed for the trial, pursuant to subsection (1), is on the accused, and he shall attend for his trial at the time and place so fixed.

Further election

(5) Where an accused has elected under section 464 or 484 to be tried by a
judge without a jury he may, at any time before a time has been fixed for his 482
trial or thereafter with the consent in writing of the Attorney General or counsel 2
acting on his behalf, re-elect to be tried by a judge and jury by filing with the
clerk of the court an election in writing and the consent, if consent is required, 2
and where an election is filed in accordance with this subsection the accused shall be tried before a court of competent jurisdiction with a jury and not otherwise. 1953-54,c.51,s.474; 1968-69,c.38,s.37.

Re-election where previous election to be tried by judge without jury

491. (1) Where an accused has elected under section 464 or 484 to be tried by a judge without a jury he may, at any time before his trial, with the consent in writing of the Attorney General or counsel acting on his behalf, notify a magistrate having jurisdiction that he wishes to re-elect under this section.

Time and place for re-election

(2) A magistrate who receives a notice and consent pursuant to subsection (1) 482
shall forthwith fix a time and place for the accused to re-elect and shall cause notice thereof to be given to the accused.

Form of election

(3) The accused shall attend or, if he is in custody, shall be produced at the time and place fixed under subsection (2) and shall, after the charge upon which he has been committed for trial or ordered to stand trial has been read to him, be put to his election in the following words:

You have elected to be tried by a judge without a jury. Do you now elect to be tried by a magistrate without a jury?

Proceedings on election

(4) Where an accused elects under this section to be tried by a magistrate 482
without a jury, the magistrate shall proceed with the trial or fix a time and place for the trial. 1968-69,c.38,s.38.

Re-election where previous election to be tried by judge and jury

492. (1) Where an accused has elected or is deemed to have elected to be
tried by a court composed of a judge and jury, the accused may notify the 482
sheriff in the territorial division in which he is to be tried that he desires to 2
re-elect under this section,

(a) to be tried by a judge without a jury; or

(b) if he has the consent in writing of the Attorney General or counsel acting 2
on his behalf, to be tried by a magistrate without a jury. 482

Time and place for re-election

(2) A sheriff who receives a notice and a consent, if required, pursuant to subsection (1) shall forthwith inform a judge or magistrate having jurisdiction and the judge or magistrate, as the case may be, shall fix a time and place for the accused to re-elect and shall cause notice thereof to be given to the accused.

Form of election

(3) The accused shall attend or, if he is in custody, shall be produced at the time and place fixed under subsection (2) and shall, after the charge upon which he has been committed for trial or ordered to stand trial has been read to him,

(a) if the notice states that the accused desires to re-elect to be tried by a judge without a jury, be put to his election in the following words:

You have elected or are deemed to have elected to be tried by a court composed of a judge and jury. Do you now elect to be tried by a judge without a jury?;

or

(b) if the notice states that the accused desires to re-elect to be tried by a magistrate without a jury, be put to his election in the following words:

You have elected or are deemed to have elected to be tried by a court composed of a judge and jury. Do you now elect to be tried by a magistrate without a jury?

Proceedings on election

(4) Where an accused elects under this section to be tried by a judge without a jury or a magistrate without a jury, the judge or magistrate, as the case may be, shall proceed with the trial or fix a time and place for the trial.

Limit of time for re-election

(5) Where an accused who desires to re-elect to be tried by a judge without a jury does not notify the sheriff in accordance with subsection (1) more than fourteen days before the day fixed for the opening of the sittings or session of the court sitting with a jury by which he is to be tried, no election may be made under this section unless the Attorney General or counsel acting on his behalf consents in writing. 1960-61,c.43,s.19; 1968-69,c.38,s.39.

Proceedings on re-election to be tried by magistrate without jury

493. Where an accused elects under section 491 or 492 to be tried by a magistrate without a jury, 482

(a) the accused shall be tried upon the information that was before the justice 2
at the preliminary inquiry, subject to any amendments thereto that may be allowed by the magistrate by whom the accused is tried; and

(b) the magistrate before whom the election is made shall endorse on the information a record of the election. 1968-69,c.38,s.40.

Consent by Crown to re-election in certain cases

494. Where an accused, being charged with an offence that, under this Part, may be tried by a judge without a jury, is committed for trial or, in the case of a corporation, is ordered to stand trial, within fourteen days of the opening of the sittings or session of the court composed of a judge and jury by which the accused is to be tried, the accused is not entitled to elect, under section 492, to be tried under this Part by a judge without a jury unless the Attorney General or 2
counsel acting on his behalf consents in writing. 1953-54,c.51,s.476.

Election deemed to have been made in certain cases

495. Where an accused is committed for trial or ordered to stand trial for an offence that, under this Part, may be tried by a judge without a jury, he shall, for the purposes of the provisions of this Part relating to election and re-election, be deemed to have elected to be tried by a court composed of a judge and jury if

(a) he did not elect when he was put to his election under section 464 or 484, or

(b) he was committed for trial or ordered to stand trial by a magistrate who, pursuant to section 485, continued the proceedings before him as a preliminary inquiry. 1953-54,c.51,s.477; 1960,c.43,s.20.

Trial

Preferring charge

496. (1) Where an accused elects under section 464, 484 or 492 to be tried by a judge without a jury, an indictment in Form 4 shall be preferred by the 482
Attorney General or his agent, or by any person who has the written consent of the Attorney General, and in the Province of British Columbia may be preferred by the clerk of the peace.

What offences may be included

(2) An indictment that is preferred under subsection (1) may contain any number of counts, and there may be joined in the same indictment 2

(a) counts relating to offences in respect of which the accused elected to be tried by a judge without a jury and for which the accused was committed for trial, whether or not the offences were included in one information, and

(b) counts relating to offences disclosed by the evidence taken on the preliminary inquiry, in addition to or in substitution for any offence for which the accused was committed for trial.

Consent of Attorney General or accused in certain cases

(3) An indictment that is preferred under subsection (1) may include an offence that is not referred to in paragraph (2)*(a)* or *(b)* if the accused consents, and that offence may be dealt with, tried and determined and punished in all respects as if the offence were one in respect of which the accused had been committed for trial, but if that offence was committed wholly in a province other than that in which the accused is before the court, subsection 434(3) applies. 1953-54,c.51,s.478; 1968-69,c.38,s.41.

434. (3) Where an accused is charged with an offence that is alleged to have been committed in Canada outside the province in which he is, he may, if the offence is not an offence mentioned in section 427 and

(a) in the case of proceedings instituted at the instance of the Government of Canada and conducted by or on behalf of that Government, the Attorney General of Canada consents, or

(b) in any other case, the Attorney General of the province where the offence is alleged to have been committed consents,

appear before a court or person that would have had jurisdiction to try that offence if it had been committed in the province where the accused is, and where he signifies his consent to plead guilty and pleads guilty to that offence the court or person shall convict the accused and impose the punishment warranted by law, but where he does not signify his consent to plead guilty and plead guilty, he shall, if he was in custody prior to his appearance, be returned to custody and shall be dealt with according to law.

General

Discretion of judge or magistrate where more than one accused

497. Where two or more persons are charged with the same offence the following provisions apply, namely,

(*a*) if one or more of them, but not all, elect under section 464 to be tried by a judge without a jury, a judge may, in his discretion, decline to fix a time for 482
the trial pursuant to section 490 and may require all the persons to be tried by a court composed of a judge and jury;

(*b*) if one or more of them, but not all, elect under section 484 to be tried by a magistrate or by a judge without a jury, as the case may be, the magistrate 482
may, in his discretion, decline to record the election and if he does so, shall hold a preliminary inquiry;

(*c*) if one or more of them, but not all, elect under section 491 to be tried by a magistrate without a jury the magistrate may, in his discretion, decline to fix a time for the trial pursuant to section 491 and may require all of the persons to be tried by a judge without a jury, subject to the right of any of them to re-elect under subsection 490(5); and

(*d*) if one or more of them, but not all, elect under section 492 to be tried by a judge without a jury or by a magistrate without a jury the judge or magistrate, as the case may be, may in his discretion require all the persons to be tried by a court composed of a judge and jury. 1953-54,c.51,s.479; 1968-69,c.38,s.42.

Attorney General may require trial by jury

498. The Attorney General may, notwithstanding that an accused elects 2
under section 464, 484, 491 or 492 to be tried by a judge or magistrate, as the case may be, require the accused to be tried by a court composed of a judge and jury, unless the alleged offence is one that is punishable with imprisonment for
five years or less, and where the Attorney General so requires, a judge or "D"
magistrate has no jurisdiction to try the accused under this Part and a magistrate shall hold a preliminary inquiry unless a preliminary inquiry has been held prior to the requirement by the Attorney General that the accused be tried by a court composed of a judge and jury. 1968-69,c.38,s.43.

Continuance of proceedings where judge or magistrate unable to act

499. (1) Where an accused is being tried under this Part by a judge or magistrate, as the case may be, and the judge or magistrate before whom the accused is being tried dies or is for any reason unable to continue, the proceedings may, subject to this section, be continued before another judge or magistrate, as the case may be, who has jurisdiction to try the accused under this Part.

Where adjudication made

(2) Where an adjudication was made by a judge or magistrate before whom the trial was commenced, the judge or magistrate, as the case may be, before whom the proceedings are continued shall, without further election by the accused, impose the punishment or make the order that, in the circumstances, is authorized by law.

Where no adjudication by judge

(3) Where the trial was commenced before a judge but he did not make an adjudication, the judge before whom the proceedings are continued shall, without further election by the accused, commence the trial again as a trial *de novo*.

Where no adjudication by magistrate

(4) Where the trial was commenced before a magistrate but he did not make an adjudication, the magistrate before whom the proceedings are continued shall put the accused to his election in accordance with section 484, and the proceedings shall, in all respects, be continued in accordance with this Part as if the accused were appearing before a magistrate for the first time upon the charge laid against him. 1953-54, c. 51, s. 481; 1959, c. 41, s. 21.

Record of conviction or order

500. (1) Where an accused who is tried under this Part is convicted or an order is made in relation to him, the judge or magistrate, as the case may be, shall endorse the information accordingly and shall sentence the accused or otherwise deal with him in the manner authorized by law, and upon request by the accused, the prosecutor or a peace officer, shall cause a conviction in Form 31 and a certified copy thereof, or an order and a certified copy thereof, to be drawn up and shall deliver the certified copy to the person making the request.

Discharge and record of acquittal

(2) Where an accused who is tried under this Part is found not guilty of an offence with which he is charged, the judge or magistrate, as the case may be, shall immediately discharge him in respect of that offence and shall cause an order in Form 33 to be drawn up, and upon request shall make out and deliver to the accused a certified copy of the order.

Transmission of record by magistrate

(3) Where an accused elects to be tried by a magistrate under this Part, the magistrate shall transmit the written charge, the memorandum of adjudication and the conviction, if any, into such custody as the Attorney General may direct.

Proof of conviction or dismissal

(4) A copy of a conviction or of an order, certified by the judge or by the proper officer of the court, or by the magistrate, as the case may be, or proved to be a true copy, is, upon proof of the identity of the person, sufficient evidence in any legal proceedings to prove the conviction of that person or the dismissal of a charge against him, as the case may be, for the offence mentioned therein.

Warrant of committal

(5) Where an accused other than a corporation is convicted, the judge or magistrate, as the case may be, shall issue or cause to be issued a warrant of committal in Form 18, and section 461 applies in respect of a warrant of committal issued under this subsection. R.S., c. C-34, s. 500; 1972, c. 13, s. 42.

461. (1) Where a warrant for the arrest of an accused cannot be executed in accordance with section 456.3, a justice within whose jurisdiction the accused is or is believed to be shall, upon application, and upon proof on oath or by affidavit of the signature of the justice who issued the warrant, authorize the execution of the warrant within his jurisdiction by making an endorsement, which may be in Form 25, upon the warrant.

(2) An endorsement that is made upon a warrant pursuant to subsection (1) is sufficient authority to the peace officers to whom it was originally directed, and to all peace officers within the territorial jurisdiction of the justice by whom it is endorsed, to execute the warrant and to take the accused before the justice who issued the warrant or before some other justice for the same territorial division.

456.3 (1) A warrant in accordance with this Part may be executed by arresting the accused *(Part XIV*

(a) wherever he is found within the territorial jurisdiction of the justice, judge or court by whom or by which the warrant was issued; or

(b) wherever he is found in Canada, in the case of fresh pursuit.

(2) A warrant in accordance with this Part may be executed by a person who is one of the peace officers to whom it is directed, whether or not the place in which the warrant is to be executed is within the territory for which the person is a peace officer.

Adjournment

501. A judge or magistrate acting under this Part may from time to time adjourn a trial until it is finally terminated. 1953-54, c. 51, s. 483.

Application of Parts XIV, XV, XVII and XX

502. The provisions of Part XIV, the provisions of Part XV relating to transmission of the record by a magistrate where he holds a preliminary inquiry, and the provisions of Parts XVII and XX, in so far as they are not inconsistent with this Part, apply, *mutatis mutandis*, to proceedings under this Part. R.S., c. C-34, s. 502; R.S., c. 2(2nd Supp.), s. 10.

PART XVII

PROCEDURE BY INDICTMENT

Preferring Indictment

Finding indictment

503. For the purposes of this Part, finding an indictment includes

(a) preferring an indictment, and

(b) presentment of an indictment by a grand jury. 1953-54, c. 51, s. 485.

Prosecutor may prefer indictment

504. The prosecutor may prefer, before a court constituted with a grand jury, 2
a bill of indictment against any person who has been committed for trial at that court in respect of

(a) the charge on which that person was committed for trial, or

(b) any charge founded on the facts disclosed by the evidence taken on the preliminary inquiry. 1953-54, c. 51, s. 486.

Others who may prefer indictment

505. (1) A bill of indictment may be preferred

(a) by the Attorney General or anyone by his direction, before the grand 2
jury of any court constituted with a grand jury,

(b) by anyone who has the written consent of the Attorney General, or the written consent of a judge of a court constituted with a grand jury, before the grand jury of the court specified in the consent, or

(c) by order of a court constituted with a grand jury, before the grand jury of that court.

Consent need not be averred

(2) No reference is necessary in an indictment to a consent that is given or an order that is made under this section.

Savings

(3) No objection shall be taken to an indictment for want of a consent or order required by this section unless it is taken by motion to quash the indictment before the accused is given in charge to the jury.

Indictment not to be preferred except with consent of judge or by Attorney General

(4) Notwithstanding anything in this section, where

(a) a preliminary inquiry has not been held, or

(b) a preliminary inquiry has been held and the accused has been discharged, a bill of indictment shall not be preferred except with the written consent of a judge of a court constituted with a grand jury, before the grand jury of the court specified in the consent, or by the Attorney General before the grand jury of any court constituted with a grand jury. 1953-54, c. 51, s. 487; 1968-69, c. 38, s. 44.

2. In this Act

"Attorney General" means the Attorney General or Solicitor General of a province in which proceedings to which this Act applies are taken and, with respect to

(a) the Northwest Territories and the Yukon Territory, and

(b) proceedings instituted at the instance of the Government of Canada and conducted by or on behalf of that Government in respect of a violation of or conspiracy to violate any Act of the Parliament of Canada or a regulation made thereunder other than this Act,

means the Attorney General of Canada, and except for the purposes of subsections 505(4) and 507(3), includes the lawful deputy of the said Attorney General, Solicitor General and Attorney General of Canada;

No indictment except as provided

506. (1) Except as provided in this Part no bill of indictment shall be preferred.

Criminal information

(2) No criminal information shall be laid or granted.

Coroner's inquisition

(3) No person shall be tried upon a coroner's inquisition. 1953-54, c. 51, s. 488.

Preferring indictment in certain provinces

507. (1) In the Provinces of Newfoundland, Prince Edward Island, New Brunswick, Quebec, Ontario, Manitoba, Saskatchewan, Alberta and British Columbia and in the Yukon Territory and Northwest Territories it is not necessary to prefer a bill of indictment before a grand jury, but it is sufficient if the trial of an accused is commenced by an indictment in writing setting forth the offence with which he is charged. 1974-75-76, c. 93, s. 63.

Indictment not to be preferred except with consent of judge or by Attorney General

(2) An indictment under subsection (1) may be preferred by the Attorney General or his agent, or by any person with the written consent of a judge of the court or of the Attorney General or, in any province to which this section applies, by order of the court. 2

Idem

(3) Notwithstanding anything in this section, where

(a) a preliminary inquiry has not been held, or

(b) a preliminary inquiry has been held and the accused has been discharged,

an indictment under subsection (1) shall not be preferred except with the written consent of a judge of the court, or by the Attorney General. see 505(4)
1959, c. 41, s. 22; 1968-69, c. 38, s. 45.

Summons or warrant

507.1 (1) Where an indictment has been presented to a court, a judge of the court, if he considers it necessary, may issue 2

(a) a summons addressed to the accused, or

(b) a warrant for the arrest of the accused to compel the accused to attend before him to answer the charge described in the indictment.

Part XIV to apply

(2) The provisions of Part XIV apply *mutatis mutandis* where a summons or warrant is issued under subsection (1). 1974-75-76, c. 93, s. 64.

mutatis mutandis — after the necessary changes in detail so that the text applies

Attorney General may direct stay

508. (1) The Attorney General or counsel instructed by him for the purpose may, at any time after an indictment has been found and before judgment, direct the clerk of the court to make an entry on the record that the proceedings are stayed by his direction, and when the entry is made all proceedings on the indictment shall be stayed accordingly and any recognizance relating to the proceedings is vacated.

Recommencement of proceedings

(2) Proceedings stayed in accordance with subsection (1) may be recommenced, without laying a new charge or preferring a new indictment, as the case may be, by the Attorney General or counsel instructed by him for the purpose giving notice of the recommencement to the clerk of the court in which the stay of proceedings was entered, but where no such notice is given within one year after the entry of the stay of proceedings, the proceedings shall be deemed never to have been commenced. R.S., c. C-34, s. 508; 1972, c. 13, s. 43.

Form of indictment

509. An indictment is sufficient if it is on paper and is in Form 3 or 4, as the case may be. 1953-54, c. 51, s. 491.

General Provisions as to Counts

Substance of offence

510. (1) Each count in an indictment shall in general apply to a single transaction and shall contain and is sufficient if it contains in substance a statement that the accused committed an indictable offence therein specified. 2

Form of statement

(2) The statement referred to in subsection (1) may be

(a) in popular language without technical averments or allegations of matters that are not essential to be proved,

(b) in the words of the enactment that describes the offence or declares the matters charged to be an indictable offence, or

(c) in words that are sufficient to give to the accused notice of the offence with which he is charged.

Details of circumstances

(3) A count shall contain sufficient detail of the circumstances of the alleged offence to give to the accused reasonable information with respect to the act or omission to be proved against him and to identify the transaction referred to, but otherwise the absence or insufficiency of details does not vitiate the count.

Indictment for treason

(4) Where an accused is charged with an offence under section 47 or sections 49 to 53, every overt act that is to be relied upon shall be stated in the indictment.

Reference to section

(5) A count may refer to any section, subsection, paragraph or subparagraph of the enactment that creates the offence charged, and for the purpose of determining whether a count is sufficient, consideration shall be given to any such reference.

General provisions not restricted

(6) Nothing in this Part relating to matters that do not render a count insufficient shall be deemed to restrict or limit the application of this section. 1953-54, c. 51, s. 492.

High treason and first degree murder

511. No person shall be convicted for the offence of high treason or first degree murder unless in the indictment charging the offence he is specifically charged with that offence. 1974-75-76, c. 105, s. 6.

Certain omissions not grounds for objection

512. No count in an indictment is insufficient by reason of the absence of details where, in the opinion of the court, the count otherwise fulfils the requirements of section 510 and, without restricting the generality of the foregoing, no count in an indictment is insufficient by reason only that

(a) it does not name the person injured or intended or attempted to be injured,

(b) it does not name the person who owns or has a special property or interest in property mentioned in the count,

(c) it charges an intent to defraud without naming or describing the person whom it was intended to defraud,

(d) it does not set out any writing that is the subject of the charge,

(e) it does not set out the words used where words that are alleged to have been used are the subject of the charge,

(f) it does not specify the means by which the alleged offence was committed,

(g) it does not name or describe with precision any person, place or thing, or

(h) it does not, where the consent of a person, official or authority is required before proceedings may be instituted for an offence, state that the consent has been obtained. 1953-54, c. 51, s. 493.

Special Provisions as to Counts

Sufficiency of count charging libel

513. (1) No count for publishing a blasphemous, seditious or defamatory libel, or for selling or exhibiting an obscene book, pamphlet, newspaper or other written matter, is insufficient by reason only that it does not set out the words that are alleged to be libellous or the writing that is alleged to be obscene. 260-262

Specifying sense

(2) A count for publishing a libel may charge that the published matter was written in a sense that by innuendo made the publication thereof criminal, and may specify that sense without any introductory assertion to show how the matter was written in that sense.

Proof

(3) It is sufficient, on the trial of a count for publishing a libel, to prove that the matter published was libellous, with or without innuendo. 1953-54, c. 51, s. 494.

Sufficiency of count charging perjury, etc.

514. No count that charges

(*a*) perjury, 121

(*b*) the making of a false oath or a false statement, 124 122.1

(*c*) fabricating evidence, or 125

(*d*) procuring the commission of an offence mentioned in paragraph (*a*), (*b*) or (*c*),

is insufficient by reason only that it does not state the nature of the authority of the tribunal before which the oath or statement was taken or made, or the subject of the inquiry, or the words used or the evidence fabricated, or that it does not expressly negative the truth of the words used. 1953-54, c. 51, s. 495.

Sufficiency of count relating to fraud

515. No count that alleges false pretences, fraud or an attempt or conspiracy by fraudulent means, is insufficient by reason only that it does not set out in detail the nature of the false pretence, fraud or fraudulent means. 1953-54, c. 51, s. 496. 319 338

Particulars

What may be ordered

516. (1) The court may, where it is satisfied that it is necessary for a fair trial, order the prosecutor to furnish particulars and, without restricting the generality of the foregoing, may order the prosecutor to furnish particulars

(*a*) of what is relied upon in support of a charge of perjury, the making of a false oath or of a false statement, fabricating evidence or counselling or procuring the commission of any of those offences;

(*b*) of any false pretence or fraud that is alleged;

(*c*) of any alleged attempt or conspiracy by fraudulent means;

(*d*) setting out the passages in a book, pamphlet, newspaper or other printing or writing that are relied upon in support of a charge of selling or exhibiting an obscene book, pamphlet, newspaper, printing or writing;

(*e*) further describing any writing or words that are the subject of a charge;

(*f*) further describing the means by which an offence is alleged to have been committed; or

(*g*) further describing a person, place or thing referred to in an indictment.

Regard to evidence

(2) For the purpose of determining whether or not a particular is required, the court may give consideration to any evidence that has been taken.

Particular

(3) Where a particular is delivered pursuant to this section,

(a) a copy shall be given without charge to the accused or his counsel,

(b) the particular shall be entered in the record, and

(c) the trial shall proceed in all respects as if the indictment had been amended to conform with the particular. 1953-54, c. 51, s. 497.

Ownership of Property

Ownership

517. The real and personal property of which a person has, by law, the management, control or custody shall, for the purposes of an indictment or proceeding against any other person for an offence committed on or in respect of the property, be deemed to be the property of the person who has the management, control or custody of it. 1953-54, c. 51, s. 498.

Joinder or Severance of Counts

Count for murder

518. No count that charges an offence other than murder shall be joined in an indictment to a count that charges murder. 1953-54, c. 51, s. 499.

Offences may be charged in the alternative

519. (1) A count is not objectionable by reason only that

(a) it charges in the alternative several different matters, acts or omissions that are stated in the alternative in an enactment that describes as an indictable offence the matters, acts or omissions charged in the count, or

(b) it is double or multifarious.

Application to amend or divide counts

(2) An accused may at any stage of his trial apply to the court to amend or to divide a count that

(a) charges in the alternative different matters, acts or omissions that are stated in the alternative in the enactment that describes the offence or declares that the matters, acts or omissions charged are an indictable offence, or

(b) is double or multifarious,

on the ground that, as framed, it embarrasses him in his defence.

Order

(3) The court may, where it is satisfied that the ends of justice require it, order that a count be amended or divided into two or more counts, and thereupon a formal commencement may be inserted before each of the counts into which it is divided. 1953-54, c. 51, s. 500.

Joinder of counts

520. (1) Subject to section 518, any number of counts for any number of indictable offences may be joined in the same indictment, but the counts shall be distinguished in the manner shown in Forms 3 and 4.

Each count separate

(2) Where there is more than one count in an indictment, each count may be treated as a separate indictment.

Separate trial

(3) The court may, where it is satisfied that the ends of justice require it, direct that the accused be tried separately upon one or more of the counts.

Order for severance

(4) An order for the separate trial of one or more counts in an indictment may be made before or during the trial, but if the order is made during the trial the jury shall be discharged from giving a verdict on the counts on which the trial does not proceed.

Subsequent procedure

(5) The counts in respect of which a jury is discharged pursuant to subsection (4) may subsequently be proceeded upon in all respects as if they were contained in a separate indictment. 1953-54, c. 51, s. 501.

Joinder of Accused in Certain Cases

Accessories after the fact

521. Any one who is charged with being an accessory after the fact to any 23
offence may be indicted, whether or not the principal or any other party to the offence has been indicted or convicted or is or is not amenable to justice. 1953-54, c. 51, s. 502.

Trial of persons jointly for having in possession

522. (1) Any number of persons may be charged in the same indictment with an offence under section 312 or paragraph 314(1)*(b)*, notwithstanding that

(a) the property was had in possession at different times; or

(b) the person by whom the property was obtained

(i) is not indicted with them, or

(ii) is not in custody or is not amenable to justice.

Conviction of one or more

(2) Where, pursuant to subsection (1), two or more persons are charged in the same indictment with an offence referred to in that subsection, any one or more of those persons who separately committed the offence in respect of the property or any part of it may be convicted. 1953-54, c. 51, s. 503.

Proceedings before Grand Jury

Evidence under oath

523. Every person who appears before a grand jury to give evidence in support of a bill of indictment shall be examined on the matters in question
upon oath to be administered by the foreman of the grand jury or by any 28 Interp
member who acts on his behalf. 1953-54, c. 51, s. 504.

Endorsing bill of indictment

524. The name of every witness who is examined or whom it is intended to examine shall be endorsed on the bill of indictment and submitted to the grand jury by the prosecutor, and no other witnesses shall be examined by or before the grand jury unless the presiding judge otherwise orders in writing. 1953-54, c. 51, s. 505.

Foreman to initial names

525. The foreman of the grand jury or any member of the grand jury who acts on his behalf shall write his initials against the name of each witness who is sworn and examined with respect to the bill of indictment. 1953-54, c. 51, s. 506.

23. (1) An accessory after the fact to an offence is one who, knowing that a person has been a party to the offence, receives, comforts or assists him for the purpose of enabling him to escape.

(2) No married person whose spouse has been a party to an offence is an accessory after the fact to that offence by receiving, comforting or assisting the spouse for the purpose of enabling the spouse to escape.

Interpretation Act

28. In every enactment

"oath" includes a solemn affirmation or declaration, whenever the context applies to any person by whom and case in which a solemn affirmation or declaration may be made instead of an oath; and in like cases the expression "sworn" includes the expression "affirmed" or "declared";

Proceedings when Person Indicted is at Large

Bench Warrant

526. (1) Where an indictment has been found against a person who is at large, and that person does not appear or remain in attendance for his trial, the court before which the accused should have appeared or remained in attendance may issue a warrant in Form 7 for his arrest. 503

503. For the purposes of this Part, finding an indictment includes
(*a*) preferring an indictment, and
(*b*) presentment of an indictment by a grand jury.

Execution

(2) A warrant issued under subsection (1) may be executed anywhere in Canada. R.S., c. C-34, s. 526; R.S., c. 2(2nd Supp.), s. 11.

Interim release

(3) Where an accused is arrested under a warrant issued under subsection (1), a judge of the court that issued the warrant may order that the accused be released upon his giving an undertaking that he will do any one or more of the following things as specified in the order, namely,

(*a*) report at times to be stated in the order to a peace officer or other person designated in the order;

(*b*) remain within a territorial jurisdiction specified in the order; 2

(*c*) notify the peace officer or other person designated under paragraph (*a*) of any change in his address or his employment or occupation;

(*d*) abstain from communicating with any witness or other person expressly named in the order except in accordance with such conditions specified in the order as the judge deems necessary;

(*e*) where the accused is the holder of a passport, deposit his passport as specified in the order; and

(*f*) comply with such other reasonable conditions specified in the order as the judge considers desirable. 1974-75-76, c. 93, s. 64.1.

Election deemed to be waived

526.1 (1) Notwithstanding anything in this Act, where a person to whom subsection 526(1) applies has elected or is deemed to have elected to be tried by a court composed of a judge and jury and, at the time he failed to appear or to remain in attendance for his trial, he had not re-elected to be tried by a court composed of a judge without a jury or a magistrate without a jury, he shall not be tried by a court composed of a judge and jury unless

(*a*) he establishes to the satisfaction of a judge of the court in which he is indicted that there was a legitimate excuse for his failure to appear or remain in attendance for his trial; or

(*b*) the Attorney General requires pursuant to section 498 that the accused be tried by a court composed of a judge and jury.

Idem

(2) An accused who may not be tried by a court composed of a judge and jury, pursuant to subsection (1), is deemed to have elected under section 464 to be tried by a judge of the court in which he is indicted without a jury and subsection 490(5) does not apply. 1974-75-76, c. 93, s. 65.

Change of Venue

Reasons for change of venue

527. (1) A court before which an accused is or may be indicted, at any term or sittings thereof, or a judge who may hold or sit in that court, may at any time before or after an indictment is found, upon the application of the prosecutor or the accused, order the trial to be held in a territorial division in the same province other than that in which the offence would otherwise be tried if

(*a*) it appears expedient to the ends of justice, or

(*b*) a competent authority has directed that a jury is not to be summoned at the time appointed in a territorial division where the trial would otherwise by law be held.

Reasons to be stated

(1.1) Where an accused is charged with an offence mentioned in subsection 142(1) and no order is made pursuant to an application under subsection (1) of this section, the court or judge, as the case may be, shall state, by reference to the circumstances of the case, the reason for not making the order. **1974-75-76, c. 93, s. 66.**

142. (1) Where an accused is charged with an offence under section 144 or 145 or subsection 146(1) or 149(1), no question ....

Conditions as to expense

(2) The court or judge may, in an order made upon an application by the prosecutor under subsection (1), prescribe conditions that he thinks proper with respect to the payment of additional expenses caused to the accused as a result of the change of venue.

Transmission of record

(3) Where an order is made under subsection (1), the officer who has custody of the indictment, if any, and the writings and exhibits relating to the prosecution, shall transmit them forthwith to the clerk of the court before which the trial is ordered to be held, and all proceedings in the case shall be held or, if previously commenced, shall be continued in that court.

Idem

(4) Where the writings and exhibits referred to in subsection (3) have not been returned to the court in which the trial was to be held at the time an order is made to change the place of trial, the person who obtains the order shall serve a true copy thereof upon the person in whose custody they are and that person shall thereupon transmit them to the clerk of the court before which the trial is to be held. **1953-54, c. 51, s. 508.**

Order is authority to remove prisoner

528. An order that is made under section 527 is sufficient warrant, justification and authority to all sheriffs, keepers of prisons and peace officers for the removal, disposal and reception of an accused in accordance with the terms of the order, and the sheriff may appoint and authorize any peace officer to convey the accused to a prison in the territorial division in which the trial is ordered to be held. **1953-54, c. 51, s. 509.**

Amendment

Amending defective indictment or count

529. (1) An objection to an indictment or to a count in an indictment for a defect apparent on the face thereof shall be taken by motion to quash the indictment or count before the accused has pleaded, and thereafter only by leave of the court or judge before whom the trial takes place, and a court or judge before whom an objection is taken under this section may, if it is considered necessary, order the indictment or count to be amended to cure the defect.

Amendment where variance

(2) A court may, upon the trial of an indictment, amend the indictment or a count thereof or a particular that is furnished under section 516, to make the indictment, count or particular conform to the evidence, where there appears to be a variance between the evidence and

(*a*) the charge in a count in the indictment as found; or

(*b*) the charge in a count in the indictment

(i) as amended, or

(ii) as it would have been if it had been amended in conformity with any particular that has been furnished pursuant to section 516.

Amending indictment

(3) A court shall, upon the arraignment of an accused, or at any stage of the trial, amend the indictment or a count thereof as may be necessary where it appears

(*a*) that the indictment has been preferred

(i) under another Act of the Parliament of Canada instead of this Act, or

(ii) under this Act instead of another Act of the Parliament of Canada;

(*b*) that the indictment or a count thereof

(i) fails to state or states defectively anything that is requisite to constitute the offence,

(ii) does not negative an exception that should be negatived,

(iii) is in any way defective in substance,

and the matters to be alleged in the proposed amendment are disclosed by the evidence taken on the preliminary inquiry or on the trial; or

(*c*) that the indictment or a count thereof is in any way defective in form.

Matters to be considered by the court

(4) The court shall, in considering whether or not an amendment should be made, consider

(*a*) the matters disclosed by the evidence taken on the preliminary inquiry,

(*b*) the evidence taken on the trial, if any,

(*c*) the circumstances of the case,

(*d*) whether the accused has been misled or prejudiced in his defence by a variance, error or omission mentioned in subsection (2) or (3), and

(*e*) whether, having regard to the merits of the case, the proposed amendment can be made without injustice being done.

Adjournment if accused prejudiced

(5) Where, in the opinion of the court, the accused has been misled or prejudiced in his defence by a variance, error or omission in an indictment or a count thereof, the court may, if it is of opinion that the misleading or prejudice may be removed by an adjournment, adjourn the trial to a subsequent day in the same sittings or to the next sittings of the court and may make such an order with respect to the payment of costs resulting from the necessity for amendment as it considers desirable.

Question of law

(6) The question whether an order to amend an indictment or a count thereof should be granted or refused is a question of law.

Endorsing indictment

(7) An order to amend an indictment or a count thereof shall be endorsed on the indictment as part of the record and the trial shall proceed as if the indictment or count had been originally found as amended.

Mistakes not material

(8) A mistake in the heading of an indictment shall be corrected as soon as it is discovered but, whether corrected or not, is not material.

Limitation

(9) The authority of a court to amend indictments does not authorize the court to add to the overt acts stated in an indictment for high treason or treason or for an offence against any provision in sections 49, 50, 51 and 53. 1953-54, c. 51, s. 510; 1974-75, c. 105, s. 29.

Amended indictment need not be presented to grand jury

530. Where a grand jury returns a true bill in respect of an indictment and the indictment is subsequently amended in accordance with section 529, it is not necessary, unless the judge otherwise directs, to present the amended indictment to the grand jury, but the indictment, as amended, shall be deemed to be as valid in all respects for all purposes of the proceedings as if it had been returned by the grand jury in its amended form. 1953-54, c. 51, s. 511.

Inspection and Copies of Documents

Right of accused

531. An accused is entitled, after he has been committed for trial or at his trial,

(a) to inspect without charge the indictment, his own statement, the evidence and the exhibits, if any; and

(b) to receive, on payment of a reasonable fee determined in accordance with a tariff of fees fixed or approved by the Attorney General of the province, a copy

(i) of the evidence,

(ii) of his own statement, if any, and

(iii) of the indictment;

but the trial shall not be postponed to enable the accused to secure copies unless the court is satisfied that the failure of the accused to secure them before the trial is not attributable to lack of diligence on the part of the accused. 1953-54, c. 51, s. 512; 1974-75-76, c. 93, s. 67.

Delivery of documents in case of treason, etc.

532. (1) An accused who is indicted for high treason or treason or for being an accessory after the fact to high treason or treason is entitled to receive, after 23
the indictment has been found and at least ten days before his arraignment, 503 25(2) Interp

(a) a copy of the indictment,

(b) a list of the witnesses to be produced on the trial to prove the indictment, and

(c) a copy of the panel of jurors who are to try him, returned by the sheriff.

Details

(2) The list of the witnesses and the copy of the panel of the jurors referred to in subsection (1) shall mention the names, occupations and places of abode of the witnesses and jurors respectively.

Witness to delivery

(3) The writings referred to in subsection (1) shall be given to the accused at the same time and in the presence of at least two witnesses.

Exception

(4) This section does not apply to the offence of high treason by killing Her Majesty, or to the offence of high treason where the overt act alleged in an attempt to injure the person of Her Majesty in any manner or to the offence of being an accessory after the fact in such a case of high treason. 1953-54, c. 51, s. 513; 1974-75-76, c. 105, s. 29.

23. (1) An accessory after the fact to an offence is one who, knowing that a person has been a party to the offence, receives, comforts or assists him for the purpose of enabling him to escape.

(2) No married person whose spouse has been a party to an offence is an accessory after the fact to that offence by receiving, comforting or assisting the spouse for the purpose of enabling the spouse to escape.

Interpretation Act

25. (2) Where there is a reference to a number of clear days or "at least" a number of days between two events, in calculating the number of days there shall be excluded the days on which the events happen.

Release of exhibits for testing

533. (1) A judge of a superior court of criminal jurisdiction or a court of criminal jurisdiction may, on summary application on behalf of the accused or the prosecutor, after three days notice to the accused or prosecutor, as the case may be, order the release of any exhibit for the purpose of a scientific or other test or examination, subject to such terms as appear to be necessary or desirable to ensure the safeguarding of the exhibit and its preservation for use at the trial. 2 2 2

Disobeying orders

(2) Every one who fails to comply with the terms of an order that is made under subsection (1) is guilty of contempt of court and may be dealt with summarily by the judge or magistrate who made the order or before whom the trial of the accused takes place. 1953-54, c. 51, s. 514; 1960-61, c. 43, s. 21.

9. (1) Where a court, judge, justice or magistrate summarily convicts a person for a contempt of court committed in the face of the court and imposes punishment in respect thereof, that person may appeal

(a) from the conviction, or

(b) against the punishment imposed.

(3) An appeal under this section lies to the court of appeal of the province in which the proceedings take place, and, for the purposes of this section, the provisions of Part XVIII apply, *mutatis mutandis.*

2. In this Act

"court of criminal jurisdiction" means

(a) a court of general or quarter sessions of the peace, when presided over by a superior court judge or a county or district court judge, or in the cities of Montreal and Quebec, by a municipal judge of the city, as the case may be, or a judge of the sessions of the peace, and

(b) a magistrate or judge acting under Part XVI;

"superior court of criminal jurisdiction" means

(a) in the Province of Ontario, the Supreme Court,

(b) in the Province of Quebec, the Superior Court,

(c) in the Provinces of Nova Scotia, Prince Edward Island and Newfoundland respectively, the Supreme Court,

(d) in the Province of British Columbia, the Supreme Court or the Court of Appeal,

(e) in the Provinces of Manitoba, Saskatchewan, Alberta and New Brunswick, respectively, the Court of Appeal or the Court of Queen's Bench,

(f) in the Yukon Territory, the Supreme Court, and

(g) in the Northwest Territories, the Supreme Court;

"prosecutor" means the Attorney General or, where the Attorney General does not intervene, means the person who institutes proceedings to which this Act applies, and includes counsel acting on behalf of either of them;

503. For the purposes of this Part, finding an indictment includes

(a) preferring an indictment, and

(b) presentment of an indictment by a grand jury

Pleas

Pleas permitted

534. (1) An accused who is called upon to plead may plead guilty or not guilty, or the special pleas authorized by this Part and no others.

Refusal to plead

(2) Where an accused refuses to plead or does not answer directly, the court shall order the clerk of the court to enter a plea of not guilty.

Allowing time

(3) An accused is not entitled as of right to have his trial postponed but the court may, if it considers that the accused should be allowed further time to plead, move to quash, or prepare for his defence or for any other reason, adjourn the trial to a later time in the session or sittings of the court, or to the next of any subsequent session or sittings of the court, upon such terms as the court considers proper.

Included or other offence

(4) Notwithstanding any other provision of this Act, where an accused pleads not guilty of the offence charged but guilty of an included or other offence, the court may in its discretion with the consent of the prosecutor accept such plea of guilty and, if such plea is accepted, shall find the accused not guilty of the offence charged. 1974-75-76, c. 105, s. 7.

Special pleas

535. (1) An accused may plead the special pleas of

(a) *autrefois acquit*,

(b) *autrefois convict*, and

(c) pardon.

In case of libel

(2) An accused who is charged with defamatory libel may plead in accordance with sections 539 and 540.

Disposal

(3) The pleas of *autrefois acquit*, *autrefois convict* and pardon shall be disposed of by the judge without a jury before the accused is called upon to plead further.

Pleading over

(4) When the pleas referred to in subsection (3) are disposed of against the accused, he may plead guilty or not guilty. 1974-75-76, c. 105, s. 8.

Statement sufficient

(5) Where an accused pleads *autrefois acquit* or *autrefois convict* it is sufficient if he

(a) states that he has been lawfully acquitted or convicted, as the case may be, of the offence charged in the count to which the plea relates, and

(b) indicates the time and place of the acquittal or conviction. 1953-54, c. 51, s. 516; 1960-61, c. 44, s. 5.

Evidence of identity of charges

536. Where an issue on a plea of *autrefois acquit* or *autrefois convict* is tried, the evidence and adjudication and the notes of the judge and official stenographer on the former trial and the record transmitted to the court pursuant to section 478 on the charge that is pending before that court, are admissible in evidence to prove or to disprove the identity of the charges. 1953-54, c. 51, s. 517.

What determines identity

537. (1) Where an issue on a plea of *autrefois acquit* or *autrefois convict* to a count is tried and it appears

(a) that the matter on which the accused was given in charge on the former trial is the same in whole or in part as that on which it is proposed to give him in charge, and

(b) that on the former trial, if all proper amendments had been made that might then have been made, he might have been convicted of all the offences of which he may be convicted on the count to which the plea of *autrefois acquit* or *autrefois convict* is pleaded,

the judge shall give judgment discharging the accused in respect of that count.

Allowance of special plea in part

(2) The following provisions apply where an issue on a plea of *autrefois acquit* or *autrefois convict* is tried, namely,

(*a*) where it appears that the accused might on the former trial have been convicted of an offence of which he may be convicted on the count in issue, the judge shall direct that the accused shall not be found guilty of any offence of which he might have been convicted on the former trial, and

(*b*) where it appears that the accused may be convicted on the count in issue of an offence of which he could not have been convicted on the former trial, the accused shall plead guilty or not guilty with respect to that offence. 1953-54, c. 51, s. 518.

Circumstances of aggravation

538. (1) Where an indictment charges substantially the same offence as that charged in an indictment on which an accused was previously convicted or acquitted, but adds a statement of intention or circumstances of aggravation tending, if proved, to increase the punishment, the previous conviction or acquittal bars the subsequent indictment.

Effect of previous charge of murder or manslaughter

(2) A conviction or acquittal on an indictment for murder bars a subsequent indictment for the same homicide charging it as manslaughter or infanticide, and a conviction or acquittal on an indictment for manslaughter or infanticide bars a subsequent indictment for the same homicide charging it as murder.

Previous charges of first degree murder

(3) A conviction or acquittal on an indictment for first degree murder bars a subsequent indictment for the same homicide charging it as second degree murder, and a conviction or acquittal on an indictment for second degree murder bars a subsequent indictment for the same homicide charging it as first degree murder. 1974-75-76, c. 105, s. 9.

Effect of previous charge of infanticide or manslaughter

(4) A conviction or acquittal on an indictment for infanticide bars a subsequent indictment for the same homicide charging it as manslaughter, and a conviction or acquittal on an indictment for manslaughter bars a subsequent indictment for the same homicide charging it as infanticide. 1953-54, c. 51, s. 519; 1960-61, c. 44, s. 6.

Libel, plea of justification

539. (1) An accused who is charged with publishing a defamatory libel may plead that the defamatory matter published by him was true, and that it was for the public benefit that the matter should have been published in the manner in which and at the time when it was published.

Where more than one sense alleged

(2) A plea that is made under subsection (1) may justify the defamatory matter in any sense in which it is specified in the count, or in the sense that the defamatory matter bears without being specified, or separate pleas justifying the defamatory matter in each sense may be pleaded separately to each count as if two libels had been charged in separate counts.

Plea in writing

(3) A plea that is made under subsection (1) shall be in writing, and shall set out the particular facts by reason of which it is alleged to have been for the public good that the matter should have been published.

Reply

(4) The prosecutor may in his reply deny generally the truth of a plea that is made under this section. 1953-54, c. 51, s. 520.

Plea of justification necessary

540. (1) The truth of the matters charged in an alleged libel shall not be inquired into in the absence of a plea of justification under section 539 unless the accused is charged with publishing the libel knowing it to be false, in which case evidence of the truth may be given to negative the allegation that the accused knew that the libel was false.

Not guilty, in addition

(2) The accused may, in addition to a plea that is made under section 539, plead not guilty and the pleas shall be inquired into together.

Effect of plea on punishment

(3) Where a plea of justification is pleaded and the accused is convicted, the court may, in pronouncing sentence, consider whether the guilt of the accused is aggravated or mitigated by the plea. 1953-54, c. 51, s. 521.

Plea of not guilty

541. Any ground of defence for which a special plea is not provided by this Act may be relied upon under the plea of not guilty. 1953-54, c. 51, s. 522.

16. (1) No person shall be convicted of an offence in respect of an act or omission on his part while he was insane.

(2) For the purposes of this section a person is insane when he is in a state of natural imbecility or has disease of the mind to an extent that renders him incapable of appreciating the nature and quality of an act or omission or of knowing that an act or omission is wrong.

(3) A person who has specific delusions, but is in other respects sane, shall not be acquitted on the ground of insanity unless the delusions caused him to believe in the existence of a state of things that, if it existed, would have justified or excused his act or omission.

(4) Every one shall, until the contrary is proved, be presumed to be and to have been sane.

Defence of Insanity

Insanity of accused when offence committed

542. (1) Where, upon the trial of an accused who is charged with an indictable offence, evidence is given that the accused was insane at the time the offence was committed and the accused is acquitted, 16

(a) the jury, or

(b) the judge or magistrate, where there is no jury,

shall find whether the accused was insane at the time the offence was committed and shall declare whether he is acquitted on account of insanity.

Custody after finding

(2) Where the accused is found to have been insane at the time the offence was committed, the court, judge or magistrate before whom the trial is held shall order that he be kept in strict custody in the place and in the manner that the court, judge or magistrate directs, until the pleasure of the lieutenant governor of the province is known. 1953-54, c. 51, s. 523.

Insanity at time of trial

543. (1) A court, judge or magistrate may, at any time before verdict, where it appears that there is sufficient reason to doubt that the accused is, on account of insanity, capable of conducting his defence, direct that an issue be tried whether the accused is then, on account of insanity, unfit to stand his trial.

577. (2) The court may

(c) cause the accused to be removed and to be kept out of court during the trial of an issue as to whether the accused is, on account of insanity, unfit to stand his trial where it is satisfied that failure to do so might have an adverse effect on the mental health of the accused.

Direction or remand for observation

(2) A court, judge or magistrate may, at any time before verdict or sentence, when of the opinion, supported by the evidence or, where the prosecutor and the accused consent, by the report in writing, of at least one duly qualified medical practitioner, that there is reason to believe that

(a) an accused is mentally ill, or

(b) the balance of the mind of an accused is disturbed, where the accused is a female person charged with an offence arising out of the death of her 216
newly-born child, 2

by order in writing

(c) direct the accused to attend, at a place or before a person specified in the order and within a time specified therein, for observation, or

(d) remand the accused to such custody as the court, judge or magistrate directs for observation for a period not exceeding thirty days.

Direction or remand for observation

(2.1) Notwithstanding subsection (2), a court, judge or magistrate may remand an accused in accordance with that subsection

(a) for a period not exceeding thirty days without having heard the evidence or considered the report of a duly qualified medical practitioner where compelling circumstances exist for so doing and where a medical practitioner is not readily available to examine the accused and give evidence or submit a report; and

(b) for a period of more than thirty days but not exceeding sixty days where he is satisfied that observation for such a period is required in all the circumstances of the case and his opinion is supported by the evidence or, where the prosecutor and the accused consent, by the report in writing, of at least one duly qualified medical practitioner. 1974-75-76, c. 93, s. 68.

Court shall assign counsel

(3) Where it appears that there is sufficient reason to doubt that the accused is, on account of insanity, capable of conducting his defence, the court, judge or magistrate shall, if the accused is not represented by counsel, assign counsel to act on behalf of the accused.

Trial of issue

(4) For the purposes of subsection (1), the following provisions apply, namely,

(a) where the issue arises before the close of the case of the prosecution, the court, judge or magistrate may postpone directing the trial of the issue until any time up to the opening of the case for the defence;

(b) where the trial is held or is to be held before a court composed of a judge and jury,

(i) if the judge directs the issue to be tried before the accused is given in charge to a jury for trial on the indictment, it shall be tried by twelve jurors, or in the Yukon Territory and the Northwest Territories, by six jurors, and

(ii) if the judge directs the issue to be tried after the accused has been given in charge to a jury for trial on the indictment, the jury shall be sworn to try that issue in addition to the issue on which they are already sworn; and

(c) where the trial is held before a judge or magistrate, he shall try the issue and render a verdict.

If sane, trial proceeds

(5) Where the verdict is that the accused is not unfit on account of insanity to stand his trial, the arraignment or the trial shall proceed as if no such issue had been directed.

If insane, order for custody

(6) Where the verdict is that the accused is unfit on account of insanity to stand his trial, the court, judge or magistrate shall order that the accused be kept in custody until the pleasure of the lieutenant governor of the province is known, and any plea that has been pleaded shall be set aside and the jury shall be discharged.

Where accused acquitted

(7) Where the court, judge or magistrate has postponed directing the trial of the issue pursuant to paragraph (4)*(a)* and the accused is acquitted at the close of the case for the prosecution, the issue shall not be tried.

Subsequent trial

(8) No proceeding pursuant to this section shall prevent the accused from being tried subsequently on the indictment unless the trial of the issue was postponed pursuant to paragraph (4)*(a)* and the accused was acquitted at the close of the case for the prosecution. R.S., c. C-34, s. 543; 1972, c. 13, s. 44.

Insanity of accused to be discharged for want of prosecution

544. Where an accused who is charged with an indictable offence is brought before a court, judge or magistrate to be discharged for want of prosecution and the accused appears to be insane, the court, judge or magistrate shall proceed in accordance with section 543 in so far as that section may be applied. 1953-54, c. 51, s. 525.

Supervision of insane persons

545. (1) Where an accused is, pursuant to this Part, found to be insane, the lieutenant governor of the province in which he is detained may make an order

(a) for the safe custody of the accused in a place and manner directed by him, or

(b) if in his opinion it would be in the best interest of the accused and not contrary to the interest of the public, for the discharge of the accused either absolutely or subject to such conditions as he prescribes. R.S., c. C-34, s. 545; 1972, c. 13, s. 45.

Warrant for transfer

(2) An accused to whom paragraph (1)*(a)* applies may, by warrant signed by an officer authorized for that purpose by the lieutenant governor of the province in which he is detained, be transferred for the purposes of his rehabilitation to any other place in Canada specified in the warrant with the consent of the person in charge of such place.

Transfer of accused

(3) A warrant mentioned in subsection (2) is sufficient authority for any person who has custody of the accused to deliver the accused to the person in charge of the place specified in the warrant and for such last mentioned person to detain the accused in the manner specified in the order mentioned in subsection (1).

Arrest of accused

(4) A peace officer who has reasonable and probable grounds to believe that an accused to whom paragraph (1)*(b)* applies has violated any condition prescribed in the order for his discharge may arrest the accused without warrant.

Taking before a justice

(5) Where an accused has been arrested pursuant to subsection (4), he shall be dealt with in accordance with the following provisions:

(a) where a justice having jurisdiction in the territorial division in which the accused has been arrested is available within a period of twenty-four hours after the arrest of the accused by a peace officer, the accused shall be taken before a justice without unreasonable delay and in any event within that period; and

(b) where a justice having jurisdiction in the territorial division in which the accused has been arrested is not available within a period of twenty-four hours after the arrest of the accused by a peace officer, the accused shall be taken before a justice as soon as possible.

Order of justice

(6) A justice before whom an accused is taken pursuant to subsection (5) may make any order that to him seems desirable in the circumstances respecting the detention of the accused pending a decision of the lieutenant governor of the province referred to in subsection (1) and shall cause notice of such order to be given to that lieutenant governor. 1974-75-76, c. 93, s. 69.

Prisoner mentally ill

546. (1) The lieutenant governor of a province may, upon evidence satisfactory to him that a person who is insane, mentally ill, mentally deficient or feeble-minded is serving a sentence in a prison in that province, order that the person be removed to a place of safekeeping to be named in the order. 1974-75-76, c. 93, s. 70. ss. (5)

Custody in safe-keeping

(2) A person who is removed to a place of safe-keeping under an order made pursuant to subsection (1) shall, subject to subsections (3) and (4), be kept in that place or in any other place of safe-keeping in which, from time to time, he may be ordered by the lieutenant governor to be kept.

Order for imprisonment or discharge

(3) Where the lieutenant governor is satisfied that a person to whom subsection (2) applies has recovered, he may order that the person

(a) be returned to the prison from which he was removed pursuant to subsection (1), if he is liable to further custody in prison, or

(b) be discharged, if he is not liable to further custody in prison.

Order for transfer to custody of minister of health

(4) Where the lieutenant governor is satisfied that a person to whom subsection (2) applies has partially recovered, he may, where the person is not liable to further custody in prison, order that the person shall be subject to the direction of the minister of health for the province, or such other person as the lieutenant governor may designate, and the minister of health or other person designated may make any order or direction in respect of the custody and care of the person that he considers proper.

"prison"

(5) In this section "prison" means a prison other than a penitentiary, and includes a reformatory school or industrial school. 1953-54, c. 51, s. 527.

Appointment of board of review

547. (1) The lieutenant governor of a province may appoint a board to review the case of every person in custody in a place in that province by virtue of an order made pursuant to section 545 or subsection 546(1) or (2).

Constitution of board

(2) The board referred to in subsection (1) shall consist of not less than three and not more than five members of whom one member shall be designated chairman by the members of the board, if no chairman has been designated by the lieutenant governor.

Idem

(3) At least two members of the board shall be duly qualified psychiatrists entitled to engage in the practice of medicine under the laws of the province for which the board is appointed, and at least one member of the board shall be a member of the bar of the province.

Quorum

(4) Three members of the board of review, at least one of whom is a psychiatrist described in subsection (3) and one of whom is a member of the bar of the province, constitute a quorum of the board.

Periodic review and report to be made on case of each person in custody

(5) The board shall review the case of every person referred to in subsection (1)

(a) not later than six months after the making of the order referred to in that subsection relating to that person, and

(b) at least once in every twelve month period following the review required pursuant to paragraph *(a)* so long as the person remains in custody under the order,

and forthwith after each review the board shall report to the lieutenant governor setting out fully the results of such review and stating

(c) where the person in custody was found unfit on account of insanity to stand his trial, whether, in the opinion of the board, that person has recovered sufficiently to stand his trial,

(d) where the person in custody was found not guilty on account of insanity, whether, in the opinion of the board, that person has recovered and, if so, whether in its opinion it is in the interest of the public and of that person for the lieutenant governor to order that he be discharged absolutely or subject to such conditions as the lieutenant governor may prescribe,

(e) where the person in custody was removed from a prison pursuant to subsection 546(1), whether, in the opinion of the board, that person has recovered or partially recovered, or

(f) any recommendations that it considers desirable in the interests of recovery of the person to whom such review relates and that are not contrary to the public interest.

Review and report to be made when requested by lieutenant governor

(6) In addition to any review required to be made under subsection (5), the board shall review any case referred to in subsection (1) when requested to do so by the lieutenant governor and shall forthwith after such review report to the lieutenant governor in accordance with subsection (5). 1968-69, c. 38, s. 48.

Powers

(7) For the purposes of a review under this section, the chairman of a board has all the powers that are conferred by sections 4 and 5 of the *Inquiries Act* on commissioners appointed under Part I of that Act. 1974-75-76, c. 93, s. 71.

Corporations

Appearance by attorney

548. Every corporation against which an indictment is found shall appear and plead by counsel or agent. 1953-54, c. 51, s. 528. 20 Interp

Notice to corporation

549. (1) The clerk of the court shall, where an indictment is found against a corporation, cause a notice of the indictment to be served upon the corporation.

Contents of notice

(2) A notice of an indictment referred to in subsection (1) shall set out the nature and purport of the indictment and advise that, unless the corporation appears and pleads within seven days after service of the notice, a plea of not guilty will be entered for the accused by the court, and that the trial of the indictment will be proceeded with as though the corporation had appeared and pleaded. 1953-54, c. 51, s. 529; 1960-61, c. 43, s. 23.

Procedure on default of appearance

550. Where a corporation does not appear in the court in which an indictment is found and plead within the time specified in the notice referred to in section 549, the presiding judge may, on proof by affidavit of service of the notice, order the clerk of the court to enter a plea of not guilty on behalf of the corporation, and the plea has the same force and effect as if the corporation had appeared by its counsel or agent and pleaded that plea. 1953-54, c. 51, s. 530.

Trial of corporation

551. Where the corporation appears and pleads to the indictment or a plea of not guilty is entered by order of the court pursuant to section 550, the court shall proceed with the trial of the indictment and, where the corporation is convicted, section 647 applies. 1953-54, c. 51, s. 531.

647. Notwithstanding subsection 646(2), a corporation that is convicted of an offence is liable, in lieu of any imprisonment that is prescribed as punishment for that offence,

(a) to be fined in an amount that is in the discretion of the court, where the offence is an indictable offence, or

(b) to be fined in an amount not exceeding one thousand dollars, where the offence is a summary conviction offence.

Record of Proceedings

How recorded

552. (1) It is sufficient, in making up the record of a conviction or acquittal on an indictment, to copy the indictment and the plea that was pleaded, without a formal caption or heading.

Record of proceedings

(2) The court shall keep a record of every arraignment and of proceedings subsequent to arraignment. 1953-54, c. 51, s. 532.

Form of record in case of amendment

553. Where it is necessary to draw up a formal record in proceedings in which the indictment has been amended, the record shall be drawn up in the form in which the indictment remained after the amendment, without reference to the fact that the indictment was amended. 1953-54, c. 51, s. 533.

Juries

Qualification of juror

554. (1) A person who is qualified and summoned as a grand or petit juror according to the laws in force for the time being in a province is qualified to serve as a grand or petit juror, as the case may be, in criminal proceedings in that province.

Majority of panel may find bill

(2) Where a panel of grand jurors is not more than thirteen, a majority of the panel may find a true bill. 1953-54, c. 51, s. 534.

No person to be disqualified on grounds of sex

(3) Notwithstanding subsection (1), no person may be disqualified, exempted or excused from serving as a grand or petit juror in criminal proceedings on the ground of his or her sex. R.S., c. C-34, s. 554; 1972, c. 13, s. 46.

Mixed Juries

Mixed juries in Quebec

555. (1) In those districts in the Province of Quebec in which the sheriff is required by law to return a panel of petit jurors composed one-half of persons who speak the English language and one-half of persons who speak the French language, he shall in his return specify in separate lists those jurors whom he returns as speaking the English language and those whom he returns as speaking the French language, and the names of the jurors summoned shall be called alternately from those lists.

Motion by accused

(2) In any district referred to in subsection (1) the accused may, upon arraignment, move that he be tried by a jury composed entirely of jurors who speak the language of the accused if that language is English or French.

Order for panel

(3) Where a motion is made under subsection (2), the judge may order the sheriff to summon a sufficient panel of jurors who speak the language of the accused unless, in his discretion, it appears that the ends of justice are better served by empanelling a mixed jury. 1953-54,c.51,s.535.

Mixed juries in Manitoba

556. (1) Where an accused who is arraigned before the Court of Queen's Bench for Manitoba demands a jury composed at least half of persons who speak the language of the accused, if that language is either English or French, he shall be tried by a jury composed at least of one-half of the persons whose names stand first in succession upon the general panel and who, not being lawfully challenged, are found, in the judgment of the court, to speak the language of the accused.

When panel exhausted

(2) Where, as a result of challenges or any other cause there is, in proceedings to which this section applies, a deficiency of persons who speak the language of the accused, the court shall fix another time for the trial, and the sheriff shall remedy the deficiency by summoning, for the time so fixed, the additional number of jurors who speak the language of the accused that the court orders and whose names appear next in succession on the list of petit jurors. 1953-54, c. 51, s. 536.

Challenging the Array

Objection to constitution of grand jury

557. Where an objection is taken to the constitution of a grand jury it shall be taken by motion to the court, but an indictment shall be quashed pursuant thereto only if the judge is of opinion that

(a) the objection is well founded, and

(b) the accused has suffered or may suffer prejudice in the circumstances of which he complains. 1953-54,c.51,s.537.

Challenging the array

558. (1) The accused or the prosecutor may challenge the array of petit jurors only on the ground of partiality, fraud or wilful misconduct on the part of the sheriff or his deputies by whom the panel was returned.

In writing

(2) A challenge under subsection (1) shall be in writing and shall state that the person who returned the panel was partial or fraudulent or that he wilfully misconducted himself, as the case may be.

Form

(3) A challenge under this section may be in Form 36. 1953-54,c.51,s.538.

Trying ground of challenge

559. Where a challenge is made under section 558, the judge shall determine whether the alleged ground of challenge is true or not, and where he is satisfied that the alleged ground of challenge is true he shall direct a new panel to be returned. 1953-54,c.51,s.539.

Empanelling Jury

Names of jurors on cards

560. (1) The name of each juror on a panel of petit jurors that has been returned, his number on the panel and the place of his abode, shall be written on a separate card, and all the cards shall, as far as possible, be of equal size.

To be placed in box

(2) The sheriff or other officer who returns the panel shall deliver the cards referred to in subsection (1) to the clerk of the court who shall cause them to be placed together in a box to be provided for the purpose and to be thoroughly shaken together.

To be drawn by clerk of court

(3) Where

(a) the array is not challenged, or

(b) the array is challenged but the judge does not direct a new panel to be returned,

the clerk of the court shall, in open court, draw out the cards referred to in subsection (2) one after another, and shall call out the name and number upon each card as it is drawn, until the number of persons who have answered to their names is, in the opinion of the judge, sufficient to provide a full jury after allowing for challenges and directions to stand by.

Jurors to be sworn

(4) The clerk of the court shall swear each member of the jury in the order in which the names of the jurors were drawn.

Drawing additional names if necessary

(5) Where the number of persons who answer to their names is not sufficient to provide a full jury, the clerk of the court shall proceed in accordance with subsections (3) and (4) until twelve jurors are sworn. 1953-54, c. 51, s. 540.

Challenges by accused in Territories

561. Notwithstanding anything in this Act, six jurors shall be sworn in the Yukon Territory and the Northwest Territories, and in those Territories the accused is entitled to half the number of challenges provided for in section 562, and the prosecutor may not direct more than twenty-four jurors to stand by unless the presiding judge, for special cause to be shown, so orders. 1968-69, c. 38, s. 49.

Peremptory challenges by accused

562. (1) An accused who is charged with high treason or first degree murder is entitled to challenge twenty jurors peremptorily.

Idem

(2) An accused who is charged with an offence, not being high treason or first degree murder, for which he may be sentenced to imprisonment for more than five years is entitled to challenge twelve jurors peremptorily. 1974-75-76, c. 105, s. 10.

Idem

(3) An accused who is charged with an offence that is not referred to in subsection (1) or (2) is entitled to challenge four jurors peremptorily. 1953-54, c. 51, s. 542.

Challenge by prosecutor

563. (1) The prosecutor is entitled to challenge four jurors peremptorily, and may direct any number of jurors who are not challenged peremptorily by the accused to stand by until all the jurors have been called who are available for the purpose of trying the indictment.

Limitation

(2) Notwithstanding subsection (1), the prosecutor may not direct more than forty-eight jurors to stand by unless the presiding judge for special cause to be shown, so orders.

Accused to challenge first if required

(3) The accused may be called upon to declare whether he challenges a juror peremptorily or for cause before the prosecutor is called upon to declare whether he requires the juror to stand by, or challenges him peremptorily or for cause. 1953-54, c. 51, s. 543.

Peremptory challenges in case of mixed jury

564. Where an accused who is charged with an offence for which he is entitled to twenty or twelve peremptory challenges in accordance with this Part is to be tried pursuant to section 555 or 556 by a jury composed of one-half of persons who speak the language of the accused, he is entitled to exercise one-half of those challenges in respect of the jurors who speak English and one-half in respect of the jurors who speak French. 1953-54, c. 51, s. 544.

Challenges where tried jointly

565. Where two or more accused persons are jointly charged in an indictment and it is proposed to try them together, each may make his challenges in the same manner as if he were to be tried alone. 1953-54, c. 51, s. 545.

Standing by in libel cases

566. A prosecutor other than the Attorney General or counsel acting on his behalf is not entitled, on the trial of an indictment for the publication of a defamatory libel, to direct a juror to stand by. 1953-54, c. 51, s. 546.

Challenge for cause

567. (1) A prosecutor or an accused is entitled to any number of challenges on the ground that

(a) the name of a juror does not appear on the panel, but no misnomer or misdescription is a ground of challenge where it appears to the court that the description given on the panel sufficiently designates the person referred to,

(b) a juror is not indifferent between the Queen and the accused,

(c) a juror has been convicted of an offence for which he was sentenced to death or to a term of imprisonment exceeding twelve months,

(d) a juror is an alien,

(e) a juror is physically unable to perform properly the duties of a juror, or

(f) a juror does not speak the official language of Canada that is the language of the accused or the official language of Canada in which the accused can best give testimony or both official languages of Canada, where the accused is required by reason of an order under section 462.1 to be tried before a judge and jury who speak the official language of Canada that is the language of the accused or the official language of Canada in which the accused can best give testimony or who speak both official languages of Canada, as the case may be. 1977-78, c. 36, s. 5.

No other ground

(2) No challenge for cause shall be allowed on a ground not mentioned in subsection (1). 1953-54, c. 51, s. 547.

Challenge in writing

568. (1) Where a challenge is made on a ground mentioned in section 567, the court may, in its discretion, require the party that challenges to put the challenge in writing.

Form

(2) A challenge may be in Form 37.

Denial

(3) A challenge may be denied by the other party to the proceedings on the ground that it is not true. 1953-54, c. 51, s. 548.

Objection that name not on panel

569. (1) Where the ground of a challenge is that the name of a juror does not appear on the panel, the issue shall be tried by the judge on the *voir dire* by the inspection of the panel, and such other evidence that the judge thinks fit to receive.

Other grounds

(2) Where the ground of a challenge is one not mentioned in subsection (1), the two jurors who were last sworn, or if no jurors have then been sworn, two persons present whom the court may appoint for the purpose, shall be sworn to determine whether the ground of challenge is true.

If challenge not sustained, or if sustained

(3) Where the finding, pursuant to subsection (1) or (2) is that the ground of challenge is not true, the juror shall be sworn, but if the finding is that the ground of challenge is true, the juror shall not be sworn.

Disagreement of triers

(4) Where, after what the court considers to be a reasonable time, the two persons who are sworn to determine whether the ground of challenge is true are unable to agree, the court may discharge them from giving a verdict and may direct two other persons to be sworn to determine whether the ground of challenge is true. 1953-54, c. 51, s. 549.

Calling jurors who have stood by

570. (1) Where, as a result of challenges and directions to stand by, a full jury has not been sworn and no names remain to be called, the names of those who have been directed to stand by shall be called again in the order in which their names were drawn and they shall be sworn, unless challenged by the accused, or unless the prosecutor challenges them or shows cause why they should not be sworn.

Other jurors becoming available

(2) Where, before a juror is sworn pursuant to subsection (1), other jurors in the panel become available, the prosecutor may require the names of those jurors to be put into and drawn from the box in accordance with section 560, and those jurors shall be challenged, ordered to stand by or sworn, as the case may be, before the names of the jurors who were originally ordered to stand by are called again. 1953-54, c. 51, s. 550.

Summoning other jurors when panel exhausted

571. (1) Where a full jury cannot be provided notwithstanding that the relevant provisions of this Part have been complied with, the court may, at the request of the prosecutor, order the sheriff or other proper officer forthwith to summon as many persons, whether qualified jurors or not, as the court directs for the purpose of providing a full jury.

Orally

(2) Jurors may be summoned under subsection (1) by word of mouth, if necessary.

Adding names to panel

(3) The names of the persons who are summoned under this section shall be added to the general panel for the purposes of the trial, and the same proceedings shall be taken with respect to calling and challenging those persons and directing them to stand by as are provided in this Part with respect to the persons named in the original panel. 1953-54, c. 51, s. 551.

Who shall be jury

572. (1) The twelve jurors, or in the Yukon Territory and the Northwest Territories the six jurors, whose names are drawn and who are sworn in accordance with this Part, shall be the jury to try the issues of the indictment, and the names of the jurors so drawn and sworn shall be kept apart until the jury gives its verdict or until it is discharged, whereupon the names shall be returned to the box as often as occasion arises, as long as an issue remains to be tried before a jury.

Same jury may try another issue by consent

(2) The court may try an issue with the same jury in whole or in part that previously tried or was drawn to try another issue, without the jurors being sworn again, but if the prosecutor or the accused objects to any of the jurors or the court excuses any of the jurors, the court shall order those persons to withdraw and shall direct that the required number of names to make up a full jury be drawn and, subject to the provisions of this Part relating to challenges and directions to stand by, the persons whose names are drawn shall be sworn.

Sections directory

(3) No omission to follow the directions of this section or section 560 or 570 affects the validity of a proceeding. 1953-54,c.51,s.552; 1968-69,c.38.s50.

Discharge of juror

573. (1) Where in the course of a trial the judge is satisfied that a juror should not, because of illness or other reasonable cause, continue to act, the judge may discharge the juror.

Trial may continue

(2) Where in the course of a trial a member of the jury dies or is discharged pursuant to subsection (1), the jury shall, unless the judge otherwise directs and if the number of jurors is not reduced below ten, or in the Yukon Territory and the Northwest Territories below five, be deemed to remain properly constituted for all purposes of the trial and the trial shall proceed and a verdict may be given accordingly. R.C., c. C-34, s. 573; 1972, c. 13, s. 47.

Trial

Trial continuous

574. (1) The trial of an accused shall proceed continuously subject to adjournment by the court.

Adjournment

(2) The judge may adjourn the trial from time to time in the same sittings.

Formal adjournment unnecessary

(3) No formal adjournment of trial or entry thereof is required.

Questions reserved for decision

(4) The judge, in any case tried without a jury, may reserve his final decision on any question raised at the trial, and his decision, when given, shall be deemed to have been given at the trial. 1953-54,c.51,s.554.

Taking evidence

575. On the trial of an accused for an indictable offence the evidence of the witnesses for the prosecutor and the accused and the addresses of the prosecutor and the accused or counsel for the accused by way of summing up shall be taken in accordance with the provisions of Part XV relating to the taking of evidence at preliminary inquiries. 1959,c.41,s.24; 1960,c.37,s.3.

Separation of jurors

576. (1) The judge may, at any time before the jury retires to consider its verdict, permit the members of the jury to separate.

Keeping in charge

(2) Where permission to separate cannot be given or is not given the jury shall be kept under the charge of an officer of the court as the judge directs, and that officer shall prevent the jurors from communicating with anyone other than himself or another member of the jury without leave of the judge.

Non-compliance with subsection (2)

(3) Failure to comply with subsection (2) does not affect the validity of the proceedings.

Empanelling new jury in certain cases

(4) Where the fact that there has been a failure to comply with this section or section 576.1 is discovered before the verdict of the jury is returned the judge may, if he considers that the failure to comply might lead to a miscarriage of justice, discharge the jury and

(a) direct that the accused be tried with a new jury during the same session or sittings of the court, or

(b) postpone the trial on such terms as justice may require

(c) postpone the trial on such terms as justice may require.

Refreshment and accommodation

(5) The judge shall direct the sheriff to provide the jurors who are sworn with suitable and sufficient refreshment, food and lodging while they are together until they have given their verdict. R.S.,c. C-34,s.576; 1972,c.13,s.48.

Restriction on publication

576.1 (1) Where permission to separate is given to members of a jury under subsection 576(1), no information regarding any portion of the trial at which the jury is not present shall be published, after the permission is granted, in any newspaper or broadcast before the jury retires to consider its verdict. ss (3) 28 Interp

Type 'A' Offence

(2) Every one who fails to comply with subsection (1) is guilty of an offence punishable on summary conviction.

"Newspaper"

(3) In this section, "newspaper" has the same meaning as it has in sections 262 to 281 by virtue of section 261. 1972,c.13,s.49.

261. In sections 262 to 281, "newspaper" means any paper, magazine or periodical containing public news, intelligence or reports of events, or any remarks or observations thereon, printed for sale and published periodically or in parts or numbers, at intervals not exceeding thirty-one days between the publication of any two such papers, parts or numbers, and any paper, magazine or periodical printed in order to be dispersed and made public, weekly or more often, or at intervals not exceeding thirty-one days, that contains advertisements, exclusively or principally.

Interpretation Act

28. In every enactment

"broadcasting" means any radiocommunication in which the transmissions are intended for direct reception by the general public;

"radio" or "radiocommunication" means any transmission, emission or reception of signs, signals, writing, images, sounds or intelligence of any nature by means of electromagnetic waves of frequencies lower than three thousand Gigacycles per second propagated in space without artifical guide;

Disclosure of jury proceedings

576.2 Every member of a jury who, except for the purposes of

(a) an investigation of an alleged offence under subsection 127(2) in relation to a juror, or

(b) giving evidence in criminal proceedings in relation to such an offence,

Type 'A' Offence

discloses any information relating to the proceedings of the jury when it was absent from the courtroom that was not subsequently disclosed in open court is guilty of an offence punishable on summary conviction. 1972,c.13,s.49.

127. (2) Every one who wilfully attempts in any manner other than a manner described in subsection (1) to obstruct, pervert or defeat the course of justice is guilty of an indictable offence and is liable to imprisonment for ten years.

Accused to be present

577. (1) Subject to subsection (2), an accused other than a corporation shall be present in court during the whole of his trial. 28 Interp

Exceptions

(2) The court may

(a) cause the accused to be removed and to be kept out of court, where he misconducts himself by interrupting the proceedings so that to continue the proceedings in his presence would not be feasible,

(b) permit the accused to be out of court during the whole or any part of his trial on such conditions as the court considers proper, or

(c) cause the accused to be removed and to be kept out of court during the trial of an issue as to whether the accused is, on account of insanity, unfit to stand his trial where it is satisfied that failure to do so might have an adverse effect on the mental health of the accused.

To make defence

(3) An accused is entitled, after the close of the case for the prosecution, to make full answer and defence personally or by counsel. R.S.,c. C-34,s.577; 1972, c.13,s.50.

Summing up by prosecutor

578. (1) Where an accused, or any one of several accused being tried together, is defended by counsel, the counsel shall, at the end of the case for the prosecution, declare whether or not he intends to adduce evidence on behalf of the accused for whom he appears and if he does not announce his intention to adduce evidence, the prosecutor may address the jury by way of summing up.

Summing up by accused

(2) Counsel for the accused or the accused, where he is not defended by counsel, is entitled, if he thinks fit, to open the case for the defence, and after the conclusion of that opening to examine such witnesses as he thinks fit, and when all the evidence is concluded to sum up the evidence.

Accused's right of reply

(3) Where no witnesses are examined for an accused, he or his counsel is entitled to address the jury last, but otherwise counsel for the prosecution is entitled to address the jury last.

Prosecutor's right of reply where more than one accused

(4) Where two or more accused are tried jointly and witnesses are examined for any of them, all the accused or their respective counsel are required to address the jury before it is addressed by the prosecutor. 1953-54, c. 51, s. 558; 1968-69, c. 38, s. 52.

View

579. (1) The judge may, where it appears to be in the interests of justice, at any time after the jury has been sworn and before they give their verdict, direct the jury to have a view of any place, thing or person, and shall give directions as to the manner in which, and the persons by whom, the place, thing or person shall be shown to the jury, and may for that purpose adjourn the trial.

Directions to prevent communication

(2) Where a view is ordered under subsection (1), the judge shall give any directions that he considers necessary for the purpose of preventing undue communication by any person with members of the jury, but failure to comply with any directions given under this subsection does not affect the validity of the proceedings.

Who shall attend

(3) Where a view is ordered under subsection (1) the accused and the judge shall attend. 1953-54,c.51,s.559.

Disagreement of jury

580. (1) Where the judge is satisfied that the jury is unable to agree upon its verdict and that further detention of the jury would be useless, he may in his discretion discharge that jury and direct a new jury to be empanelled during the sittings of the court, or may adjourn the trial on such terms as justice may require.

Discretion not reviewable

(2) A discretion that is exercised under subsection (1) by a judge is not reviewable. 1953-54, c. 51, s. 560.

Proceeding on Sunday, etc., not invalid

581. The taking of the verdict of a jury and any proceeding incidental thereto is not invalid by reason only that it is done on Sunday or on a holiday. 28 Interp

Evidence on Trial

Admissions at trial

582. Where an accused is on trial for an indictable offence he or his counsel may admit any fact alleged against him for the purpose of dispensing with proof thereof. 1953-54,c.51,s.562.

Evidence of stealing ores or minerals

583. In any proceeding in respect of theft of ores or minerals, the possession, contrary to any law in that behalf, of smelted gold or silver, gold-bearing quartz, or unsmelted or unmanufactured gold or silver, by an operator, workman or labourer actively engaged in or on a mine, is, in the absence of any evidence to the contrary, proof that the gold, silver or quartz was stolen by him. 1953-54, c. 51, s. 563; 1968-69, c. 38, s. 92.

Use in evidence of statement by accused

584. A statement made by an accused under subsection 469(2) and purporting to be signed by the justice before whom it was made may be given in evidence against the accused at his trial without proof of the signature of the justice, unless it is proved that the justice by whom the statement purports to be signed did not sign it. 1953-54, c. 51, s. 564.

Children and Young Persons

Proof of age

585. (1) In any proceedings to which this Act applies an entry or record of an incorporated society or its officers who have had the control or care of a child or young person at or about the time the child or young person was brought to Canada is evidence of the age of the child or young person if the entry or record was made before the time when the offence is alleged to have been committed.

Inference from appearance

(2) In the absence of other evidence, or by way of corroboration of other evidence, a jury, judge, justice or magistrate, as the case may be, may infer the age of a child or young person from his appearance. 1953-54,c.51,s.565: 1968-69,c.38,s.92.

3. (1) For the purposes of this Act a person shall be deemed to have been of a given age when the anniversary of his birthday, the number of which corresponds to that age, is fully completed, and until then to have been under that age.

Corroboration

Unsworn evidence of child

586. No person shall be convicted of an offence upon the unsworn evidence of a child unless the evidence of the child is corroborated in a material particular by evidence that implicates the accused. 1953-54,c.51,s.566.

Canada Evidence Act

16. (1) In any legal proceeding where a child of tender years is offered as a witness, and such child does not, in the opinion of the judge, justice or other presiding officer, understand the nature of an oath, the evidence of such child may be received, though not given upon oath, if, in the opinion of the judge, justice or other presiding officer, as the case may be, the child is possessed of sufficient intelligence to justify the reception of the evidence, and understands the duty of speaking the truth.

(2) No case shall be decided upon such evidence alone, and it must be corroborated by some other material evidence.

Verdicts

Full offence charged, attempt proved

587. Where the complete commission of an offence charged is not proved but the evidence establishes an attempt to commit the offence, the accused may 24
be convicted of the attempt. 1953-54,c.51,s.567.

24. (1) Every one who, having an intent to commit an offence, does or omits to do anything for the purpose of carrying out his intention is guilty of an attempt to commit the offence whether or not it was possible under the circumstances to commit the offence.

(2) The question whether an act or omission by a person who has an intent to commit an offence is or is not mere preparation to commit the offence, and too remote to constitute an attempt to commit the offence, is a question of law.

Attempt charged, full offence proved

588. (1) Where an attempt to commit an offence is charged but the evidence establishes the commission of the complete offence, the accused is not entitled to be acquitted, but the jury may convict him of the attempt unless the judge presiding at the trial, in his discretion, discharges the jury from giving a verdict and directs that the accused be indicted for the complete offence.

Conviction at bar

(2) An accused who is convicted under this section is not liable to be tried again for the offence that he was charged with attempting to commit. 1953-54, c.51,s.568.

Offence charged, part only proved

589. (1) A count in an indictment is divisible and where the commission of the offence charged, as described in the enactment creating it or as charged in the count, includes the commission of another offence, whether punishable by indictment or on summary conviction, the accused may be convicted 2

(a) of an offence so included that is proved, notwithstanding that the whole offence that is charged is not proved, or

(b) of an attempt to commit an offence so included.

First degree murder charged

(2) For greater certainty and without limiting the generality of subsection (1), where a count charges first degree murder and the evidence does not prove first degree murder but proves second degree murder or an attempt to commit second degree murder, the jury may find the accused not guilty of first degree murder but guilty of second degree murder or an attempt to commit second degree murder, as the case may be. 1974-75-76,c.105,s.11.

Conviction for infanticide or manslaughter on charge of murder

(3) Subject to subsection (4), where a count charges murder and the evidence proves manslaughter or infanticide but does not prove murder, the jury may find the accused not guilty of murder but guilty of manslaughter or infanticide, but shall not on that count find the accused guilty of any other offence.

Conviction for concealing body of child where murder or infanticide charged

(4) Where a count charges the murder of a child or infanticide and the evidence proves the commission of an offence under section 227 but does not prove murder or infanticide, the jury may find the accused not guilty of murder or infanticide, as the case may be, but guilty of an offence under section 227.

Conviction for dangerous driving, etc., where criminal negligence or manslaughter charged

(5) Where a count charges an offence under section 203, 204 or 219 arising out of the operation of a motor vehicle or the navigation or operation of a vessel, or an offence under subsection 233(1), and the evidence does not prove such offence but does prove an offence under subsection 233(4) or 240(1), the accused may be convicted of an offence under subsection 233(4) or 240(1), as the case may be. 1953-54,c.51,s.569; 1960-61,c.43,s.24; 1960-61,c.44,s.7.

534. (4) Notwithstanding any other provision of this Act, where an accused pleads not guilty of the offence charged but guilty of an included or other offence, the court may in its discretion with the consent of the prosecutor accept such plea of guilty and, if such plea is accepted, shall find the accused not guilty of the offence charged.

No acquittal unless act or omission not wilful

590. Where a female person is charged with infanticide and the evidence establishes that she caused the death of her child but does not establish that, at the time of the act or omission by which she caused the death of the child,

(a) she was not fully recovered from the effects of giving birth to the child or from the effect of lactation consequent on the birth of the child, and

(b) the balance of her mind was, at that time, disturbed by reason of the effect of giving birth to the child or of the effect of lactation consequent on the birth of the child,

she may be convicted unless the evidence establishes that the act or omission was not wilful. 1953-54,c.51,s.570.

Previous Convictions

No reference to previous conviction

591. No indictment in respect of an offence for which, by reason of previous convictions, a greater punishment may be imposed shall contain any reference to previous convictions. 1953-54,c.51,s.571. 2

2. In this Act

"indictment" includes

(a) information, presentment and a count therein,

(b) a plea, replication or other pleading, and

(c) any record;

Previous conviction

592. (1) Where an accused is convicted of an offence for which a greater punishment may be imposed by reason of previous convictions, no greater punishment shall be imposed upon him by reason thereof unless the prosecutor 2
satisfies the court that the accused, before making his plea, was notified that a greater punishment would be sought by reason thereof.

Procedure where previous conviction alleged

(2) Where an accused is convicted of an offence for which a greater punishment may be imposed by reason of previous convictions, the court shall, upon application by the prosecutor and upon being satisfied that the accused was notified in accordance with subsection (1), ask the accused whether he was previously convicted and, if he does not admit that he was previously convicted, evidence of previous convictions may be adduced.

Corporations

(3) Where, pursuant to section 551, the court proceeds with the trial of an accused corporation that has not appeared and pleaded to an indictment, the court may, if the accused is convicted, make inquiries with respect to previous convictions whether or not the accused was notified that a greater punishment would be sought by reason thereof. 1953-54,c.51,s.572.

Evidence of character

593. Where, at a trial, the accused adduces evidence of his good character the prosecutor may, in answer thereto, before a verdict is returned, adduce evidence of the previous conviction of the accused for any offences, including any previous conviction by reason of which a greater punishment may be imposed. 1953-54, c. 51, s. 573.

Proof of previous conviction

594. (1) In any proceedings,

(a) a certificate setting out with reasonable particularity the conviction or the conviction and sentence in Canada of a person for an indictable offence, signed by

(i) the person who made the conviction,

(ii) the clerk of the court in which the conviction was made, or 2

(iii) a fingerprint examiner, ss (4)

is, upon proof that the accused is the person referred to in the certificate, evidence that the accused was so convicted or so convicted and sentenced without proof of the signature or the official character of the person appearing to have signed the certificate;

(b) evidence that the fingerprints of the accused are the same as the fingerprints of the person whose fingerprints are reproduced in a certificate issued under subparagraph *(a)*(iii) is, in the absence of any evidence to the contrary, proof that the accused is the person referred to in that certificate;

(c) a certificate of a fingerprint examiner stating that he has compared the fingerprints attached to that certificate with the fingerprints reproduced in a certificate issued under subparagraph *(a)*(iii) and that they are those of the same person is evidence of the statements contained in the certificate without proof of the signature or the official character of the person appearing to have signed the certificate; and

(d) a certificate under subparagraph *(a)*(iii) may be in Form 42, and a certificate under paragraph *(c)* may be in Form 43.

Idem

(2) In any proceedings, a copy of the summary conviction in Canada of an accused, signed by the person who made the conviction or by the clerk of the court in which the conviction was made, is, upon proof of the identity of the accused, evidence of the conviction of the accused without proof of the signature or the official character of the person appearing to have signed it.

Attendance and right to cross-examine

(3) An accused against whom a certificate issued under subparagraph (1)*(a)*(iii) or paragraph (1)*(c)* is produced may, with leave of the court, require the attendance of the person who signed the certificate for the purposes of cross-examination.

Notice of intention to produce certificate

(3.1) No certificate issued under subparagraph (1)(*a*)(iii) or paragraph (1)(*c*) shall be received in evidence unless the party intending to produce it has given to the accused reasonable notice of his intention together with a copy of the certificate.

"Fingerprint examiner"

(4) In this section "fingerprint examiner" means a person designated as such for the purposes of this section by the Solicitor General of Canada. R.S.,c C-34, s.594; 1972,c.13,s.51.

Sentence

Accused found guilty may speak to sentence

595. Where a jury finds an accused guilty, or where an accused pleads guilty, the judge who presides at the trial shall ask the accused whether he has anything to say before sentence is passed upon him, but an omission to comply with this section does not affect the validity of the proceedings. 1953-54,c.51,s.575.

Sentence justified by any count

596. Where one sentence is passed upon a verdict of guilty on two or more counts of an indictment, the sentence is good if any of the counts would have justified the sentence. 1953-54,c.51,s.576.

597. Repealed. 1974-75-76, c. 105, s. 12.

Formal Defects in Jury Process

Judgment not to be stayed on certain grounds

598. Judgment shall not be stayed or reversed after verdict upon an indictment

(*a*) by reason of any irregularity in the summoning or empanelling of the jury, or

(*b*) because a person who served upon the jury was not returned as a juror by a sheriff or other officer. 1953-54,c.51,s.578.

Directions as to jury or jurors directory

599. No omission to observe the directions contained in any Act with respect 2
to the qualification, selection, balloting or distribution of jurors, the preparation of the jurors' book, the selecting of jury lists, or the drafting of panels from the jury lists, is a ground for impeaching or quashing a verdict rendered in criminal proceedings. 1953-54,c.51,s.579.

2. In this Act

"Act" includes

(*a*) an Act of the Parliament of Canada,

(*b*) an Act of the legislature of the former Province of Canada,

(*c*) an Act of the legislature of a province, and

(*d*) an Act or ordinance of the legislature of a province, territory or place in force at the time that province, territory or place became a province of Canada;

Saving powers of court

600. Nothing in this Act alters, abridges or affects any power or authority that a court or judge had immediately before the 1st day of April 1955, or any practice or form that existed immediately before the 1st day of April 1955, with respect to trials by jury, jury process, juries or jurors, except where the power or authority, practice or form is expressly altered by or is inconsistent with this Act. 1953-54,c.51,s.580.

PART XVIII

APPEALS—INDICTABLE OFFENCES

Definitions

601. In this Part

"court of appeal"

"court of appeal" means the court of appeal, as defined by the definition "court of appeal" in section 2, for the province or territory in which the trial of a person by indictment is held;

2. In this Act

"court of appeal" means

- *(a)* in the Province of Ontario, the Court of Appeal,
- *(b)* in the Province of Quebec, the Court of Appeal,
- *(c)* in the Province of Nova Scotia, the Appeal Division of the Supreme Court,
- *(d)* in the Province of New Brunswick, the Court of Appeal,
- *(e)* in the Province of British Columbia, the Court of Appeal,
- *(f)* in the Province of Prince Edward Island, the Supreme Court,
- *(g)* in the Province of Manitoba, the Court of Appeal,
- *(h)* in the Province of Saskatchewan, the Court of Appeal,
- *(i)* in the Province of Alberta, the Court of Appeal,
- *(j)* in the Province of Newfoundland, the Court of Appeal,
- *(k)* in the Yukon Territory, the Court of Appeal, and
- *(l)* in the Northwest Territories, the Court of Appeal;

"indictment"

"indictment" includes an information or charge in respect of which a person has been tried for an indictable offence under Part XVI;

"registrar"

"registrar" means the registrar or clerk of the court of appeal;

"sentence"

"sentence" includes a declaration made under subsection 181(3), an order made under subsection 98(1) or (2), subsection 178.21(1) or 218(6), section 653, 654 or 655 and a disposition made under subsection 234(2), 236(2), 662.1(1), 663(1) or 664(3) or (4);

"trial court"

"trial court" means the court by which an accused was tried and includes a judge or a magistrate acting under Part XVI. R.S., c. C-34, s. 601; 1972, c. 13, s. 52; 1973, c. 38, s. 6.1; 1973-74, c. 50, s. 3; 1974-75-76, c. 93, s. 72; 1976-77, c. 53, s. 4(1).

Procedure abolished

602. No proceedings other than those authorized by this Part and Part XXIII shall be taken by way of appeal in proceedings in respect of indictable offences. 1953-54, c. 51, s. 582.

Right of appeal of person convicted

603. (1) A person who is convicted by a trial court in proceedings by indictment may appeal to the court of appeal

(a) against his conviction

(i) on any ground of appeal that involves a question of law alone,

(ii) on any ground of appeal that involves a question of fact or a question of mixed law and fact, with leave of the court of appeal or a judge thereof or upon the certificate of the trial judge that the case is a proper case for appeal, or

(iii) on any ground of appeal not mentioned in subparagraph (i) or (ii) that appears to the court of appeal to be a sufficient ground of appeal, with leave of the court of appeal; or

(b) against the sentence passed by the trial court, with leave of the court of 601
appeal or a judge thereof unless that sentence is one fixed by law.

Appeal against absolute term in excess of ten years

(1.1) A person who has been convicted of second degree murder and sentenced to imprisonment for life without eligibility for parole for a specified number of years in excess of ten may appeal to the court of appeal against the number of years in excess of ten of his imprisonment without eligibility for parole. 1974-75-76, c. 105, s. 13.

Appeal against verdict of unfit or special verdict of insanity

(2) A person who

(a) is found unfit, on account of insanity, to stand his trial may appeal to the court of appeal against that verdict, or

(b) is found not guilty on account of insanity may appeal to the court of appeal against that special verdict,

on any ground of appeal mentioned in subparagraph (1)*(a)*(i), (ii) or (iii) and subject to the conditions prescribed therein.

Where application for leave to appeal refused by judge

(3) Where a judge of the court of appeal refuses leave to appeal under this section otherwise than under paragraph (1)*(b)*, the appellant may, by filing
notice in writing with the court of appeal within seven days after such refusal, 25(1) Interp
have the application for leave to appeal determined by the court of appeal. 1968-69, c. 38. s. 55.

604. Repealed. 1974-75-76, c. 105, s. 14.

Interpretation Act

25. (1) Where the time limited for the doing of a thing expires or falls upon a holiday, the thing may be done on the day next following that is not a holiday.

(3) Where there is a reference to a number of days, not expressed to be clear days, between two events, in calculating the number of days there shall be excluded the day on which the first event happens and there shall be included the day on which the second event happens.

Right of Attorney General to appeal

605. (1) The Attorney General or counsel instructed by him for the purpose may appeal to the court of appeal

(a) against a judgment or verdict of acquittal of a trial court in proceedings by indictment on any ground of appeal that involves a question of law alone, or

(b) with leave of the court of appeal or a judge thereof, against the sentence passed by a trial court in proceedings by indictment, unless that sentence is one fixed by law.

Acquittal

(2) For the purposes of this section a judgment or verdict of acquittal includes an acquittal in respect of an offence specifically charged where the accused has on the trial thereof been convicted of an included or other offence.

Appeal against verdict of unfit

(3) The Attorney General or counsel instructed by him for the purpose may appeal to the court of appeal against a verdict that an accused is unfit, on account of insanity, to stand his trial, on any ground of appeal that involves a question of law alone. 1953-54, c. 51, s. 584; 1960-61, c. 43, s. 25; 1968-69, c. 38, s. 56.

Appeal against ineligible parole period

(4) The Attorney General or counsel instructed by him for the purpose may appeal to the court of appeal in respect of a conviction for second degree murder, against the number of years of imprisonment without eligibility for parole, being less than twenty-five, that has been imposed as a result of that conviction. 1974-75-76, c. 105, s. 15.

Specifying grounds of dissent

606. Where an appeal is dismissed by the court of appeal and a judge of that court expresses an opinion dissenting from the judgment of the court, the formal judgment of the court shall specify any grounds in law upon which the dissent, in whole or in part, is based. 1953-54, c. 51, s. 585.

Procedure on Appeals

Notice of appeal

607. (1) An appellant who proposes to appeal to the court of appeal or to obtain the leave of that court to appeal shall give notice of appeal or notice of his application for leave to appeal, in such manner and within such period as may be directed by rules of court.

Extension of time

(2) The court of appeal or a judge thereof may at any time extend the time within which notice of appeal or notice of an application for leave to appeal may be given. 1974-75-76, c. 105, s. 16.

Release pending determination of appeal

608. (1) A judge of the court of appeal may, in accordance with this section, release an appellant from custody pending the determination of his appeal if,

(a) in the case of an appeal to the court of appeal against conviction, the appellant has given notice of appeal or, where leave is required, notice of his application for leave to appeal pursuant to section 607, ss (3)

(b) in the case of an appeal to the court of appeal against sentence only, the appellant has been granted leave to appeal, or ss (4)

(c) in the case of an appeal or an application for leave to appeal to the Supreme Court of Canada, the appellant has filed and served his notice of appeal or, where leave is required, his application for leave to appeal. ss (3)

Notice of application for release

(2) Where an appellant applies to a judge of the court of appeal to be released pending the determination of his appeal, he shall give written notice of the application to the prosecutor or to such other person as a judge of the court of appeal directs.

Circumstances in which appellant may be released

(3) In the case of an appeal referred to in paragraph (1)(*a*) or (*c*), the judge of the court of appeal may order that the appellant be released pending the determination of his appeal if the appellant establishes that

(a) the appeal or application for leave to appeal is not frivolous,

(b) he will surrender himself into custody in accordance with the terms of the order, and

(c) his detention is not necessary in the public interest.

Idem

(4) In the case of an appeal referred to in paragraph (1)*(b)*, the judge of the court of appeal may order that the appellant be released pending the determination of his appeal or until otherwise ordered by a judge of the court of appeal if the appellant establishes that

(a) the appeal has sufficient merit that, in the circumstances, it would cause unnecessary hardship if he were detained in custody,

(b) he will surrender himself into custody in accordance with the terms of the order, and

(c) his detention is not necessary in the public interest.

Conditions of order

(5) Where the judge of the court of appeal does not refuse the application of the appellant, he shall order that the appellant be released

(a) upon his giving an undertaking to the judge, without conditions or with such conditions as the judge directs, to surrender himself into custody in accordance with the order,

(b) upon his entering into a recognizance without sureties in such amount, with such conditions, if any, and before such justice as the judge directs, but without deposit of money or other valuable security, or

(c) upon his entering into a recognizance with or without sureties in such amount, with such conditions, if any, and before such justice as the judge directs, and upon his depositing with that justice such sum of money or other valuable security, as the judge directs,

and the person having the custody of the appellant shall, where the appellant complies with the order, forthwith release the appellant.

Application of certain provisions of s. 459

(6) The provisions of subsections 459(5), (6) and (7) apply *mutatis mutandis* in respect of a person who has been released from custody under subsection (5) of this section.

459. (5) Where a judge having jurisdiction in the province where an order under subsection (4) for the release of an accused has been made is satisfied that there are reasonable and probable grounds to believe that the accused

(*a*) has violated or is about to violate the undertaking or recognizance upon which he has been released, or

(*b*) has, after his release from custody upon his undertaking or recognizance, committed an indictable offence,

he may issue a warrant for the arrest of the accused.

(6) Notwithstanding anything in this Act, a peace officer who has reasonable and probable grounds to believe that an accused who has been released from custody under subsection (4)

(*a*) has violated or is about to violate the undertaking or recognizance upon which he has been released, or

(*b*) has, after his release from custody upon his undertaking or recognizance, committed an indictable offence,

may arrest the accused without warrant and take him or cause him to be taken before a judge having jurisdiction in the province where the order for his release was made.

(7) A judge before whom an accused is taken pursuant to a warrant issued under subsection (5) or pursuant to subsection (6) may, where the accused shows cause why his detention in custody is not justified within the meaning of subsection 457(7), order that the accused be released upon his giving an undertaking or entering into a recognizance described in any of paragraphs 457(2)(*a*) to (*d*) with such conditions, described in subsection 457(4), as the judge considers desirable.

Release or detention pending new trial, new hearing or hearing of reference

(7) Where, with respect to any person, the court of appeal or the Supreme Court of Canada orders a new trial or new hearing or the Minister of Justice gives a direction or makes a reference under section 617, this section applies to the release or detention of that person pending the new trial or new hearing or the hearing and determination of the reference, as the case may be, as though that person were an appellant in an appeal described in paragraph (1)(*a*).

Application to appeals on summary conviction proceedings

(8) This section applies to applications for leave to appeal and appeals to the Supreme Court of Canada in summary conviction proceedings.

Form of undertaking or recognizance

(9) An undertaking under this section may be in Form 9 and a recognizance under this section may be in Form 28.

Directions for expediting appeal, new trial, etc.

(10) A judge of the court of appeal, where upon the application of an appellant he does not make an order under subsection (5) or where he cancels an order previously made under this section, or a judge of the Supreme Court of Canada upon application by an appellant in the case of an appeal to that Court, may give such directions as he thinks necessary for expediting the hearing of the appellant's appeal or for expediting the new trial or new hearing or the hearing of the reference, as the case may be. R.S., c. 2(2nd Supp.), s. 12.

Review by court of appeal

608.1 (1) A decision made by a judge under section 457.7 or subsection 458(4) or (4.1) or a decision made by a judge of the court of appeal under section 608 may, upon the direction of the chief justice or acting chief justice of the court of appeal, be reviewed by that court and that court may, if it does not confirm the decision,

(a) vary the decision; or

(b) substitute such other decision as, in its opinion, should have been made.

Enforcement of decision

(2) A decision as varied by the court of appeal under paragraph (1)*(a)* or a decision made by the court of appeal under paragraph (1)*(b)* shall have effect and may be enforced in all respects as though it were the decision made by the judge under section 457.7 or subsection 458(4) or (4.1) or by the judge of the court of appeal under section 608, as the case may be. 1974-75, c. 93, s. 73.

Direction or remand for observation

608.2 (1) A judge of the court of appeal may, by order in writing,

(a) direct an appellant to attend, at a place or before a person specified in the order and within a time specified therein, for observation, or

(b) remand an appellant to such custody as the judge directs for observation for a period not exceeding thirty days,

where, in his opinion, supported by the evidence or, where the appellant and the respondent consent, by the report in writing, of at least one duly qualified medical practitioner, there is reason to believe that

(c) the appellant may be mentally ill, or

(d) the balance of the mind of the appellant is disturbed, where the appellant
is a female person charged with an offence arising out of the death of her 220
newly-born child. 2

Idem

(2) Notwithstanding subsection (1), a judge of the court of appeal may remand an appellant in accordance therewith

(a) for a period not exceeding thirty days without having heard the evidence or considered the report of a duly qualified medical practitioner where compelling circumstances exist for so doing and where a medical practitioner is not readily available to examine the accused and give evidence or submit a report; and

(b) for a period of more than thirty days but not exceeding sixty days where he is satisfied that observation for such a period is required in all the circumstances of the case and his opinion is supported by the evidence or, where the appellant and the respondent consent, by the report in writing, of at least one duly qualified medical practitioner. 1972, c. 13, s. 54; 1974-75-76, c. 93, s. 74.

Report by judge

609. (1) Where, under this Part, an appeal is taken or an application for leave to appeal is made, the judge or magistrate who presided at the trial shall, at the request of the court of appeal or a judge thereof, in accordance with rules of court, furnish to it or him a report on the case or on any matter relating to the case that is specified in the request.

Transcript of evidence

(2) A copy or transcript of

(a) the evidence taken at the trial,

(b) the charge to the jury, if any,

(c) the reasons for judgment, if any, and

(d) the addresses of the prosecutor and the accused or counsel for the accused by way of summing up, if

(i) a ground for the appeal is based upon either of the addresses, or

(ii) the appeal is pursuant to section 604,

shall be furnished to the court of appeal, except in so far as it is dispensed with by order of a judge of that court.

Notes of proceedings

(3) A copy of the charge to the jury, if any, and any objections that were made to it shall, before the copy or transcript is transmitted to the court of appeal pursuant to subsection (2), be submitted to the judge who presided at the trial, and if the judge refuses to certify that the charge and objections are accurately set out, he shall immediately certify to the court of appeal

(a) the reasons for his refusal, and

(b) the charge that was given to the jury, if any, and any objections that were made to it.

Copies to interested parties

(4) A party to an appeal is entitled to receive, upon payment of any charges that are fixed by rules of court, a copy or transcript of any material that is prepared under subsections (1), (2) and (3). 1974-75-76, c. 105, s. 17.

(5) The Minister of Justice is entitled, upon request, to receive a copy or transcript of any material that is prepared under subsections (1), (2) and (3). R.S., c. C-34, s. 609; 1972, c. 13, s. 55.

Powers of court of appeal

610. (1) For the purposes of an appeal under this Part the court of appeal may, where it considers it in the interests of justice,

(a) order the production of any writing, exhibit, or other thing connected 2
with the proceedings;

(b) order any witness who would have been a compellable witness at the trial, whether or not he was called at the trial,

(i) to attend and be examined before the court of appeal, or

(ii) to be examined in the manner provided by rules of court before a judge of the court of appeal, or before any officer of the court of appeal or justice of the peace or other person appointed by the court of appeal for the purpose;

(c) admit, as evidence, an examination that is taken under subparagraph *(b)*(ii);

(d) receive the evidence, if tendered, of any witness, including the appellant, who is a competent but not compellable witness;

(e) order that any question arising on the appeal that

(i) involves prolonged examination of writings or accounts, or scientific or local investigation, and

(ii) cannot in the opinion of the court of appeal conveniently be inquired into before the court of appeal,

be referred for inquiry and report, in the manner provided by rules of court, to a special commissioner appointed by the court of appeal; and

(f) act upon the report of a commissioner who is appointed under paragraph *(e)* in so far as the court of appeal thinks fit to do so.

Parties entitled to adduce evidence and be heard

(2) In proceedings under this section the parties or their counsel are entitled to examine or cross-examine witnesses and, in an inquiry under paragraph (1)*(e)*, are entitled to be present during the inquiry and to adduce evidence and to be heard.

Other powers

(3) A court of appeal may exercise in relation to proceedings in the court any powers not mentioned in subsection (1) that may be exercised by the court on appeals in civil matters, and may issue any process that is necessary to enforce the orders or sentences of the court but no costs shall be allowed to the appellant or respondent on the hearing and determination of an appeal or on any proceedings preliminary or incidental thereto.

Execution of process

(4) Any process that is issued by the court of appeal under this section may be executed anywhere in Canda. 1953-54, c. 51, s. 589.

Legal assistance for appellant

611. A court of appeal or a judge of that court may, at any time, assign counsel to act on behalf of an accused who is a party to an appeal or to proceedings preliminary or incidental to an appeal where, in the opinion of the court or judge, it appears desirable in the interests of justice that the accused should have legal aid and where it appears that the accused has not sufficient means to obtain that aid. 1953-54, c. 51, s. 590.

Summary determination of frivolous appeals

612. Where it appears to the registrar that a notice of appeal, which purports 601
to be on a ground of appeal that involves a question of law alone, does not show a substantial ground of appeal, the registrar may refer the appeal to the court of appeal for summary determination, and, where an appeal is referred under this section, the court of appeal may, if it considers that the appeal is frivolous or vexatious and can be determined without being adjourned for a full hearing, dismiss the appeal summarily, without calling on any person to attend the hearing or to appear for the respondent on the hearing. 1968-69,c.38,s.59.

Powers of the Court of Appeal

Powers

613. (1) On the hearing of an appeal against a conviction or against a verdict that the appellant is unfit, on account of insanity, to stand his trial, or against a special verdict of not guilty on account of insanity, the court of appeal

(a) may allow the appeal where it is of the opinion that

(i) the verdict should be set aside on the ground that it is unreasonable or cannot be supported by the evidence,

(ii) the judgment of the trial court should be set aside on the ground of a 601
wrong decision on a question of law, or

(iii) on any ground there was a miscarriage of justice;

(b) may dismiss the appeal where

(i) the court is of the opinion that the appellant, although he was not
properly convicted on a count or part of the indictment, was properly 601
convicted on another count or part of the indictment,

(ii) the appeal is not decided in favour of the appellant on any ground mentioned in paragraph *(a)*, or

(iii) notwithstanding that the court is of the opinion that on any ground mentioned in subparagraph *(a)*(ii) the appeal might be decided in favour of the appellant, it is of the opinion that no substantial wrong or miscarriage of justice has occurred;

(c) may refuse to allow the appeal where it is of the opinion that the trial
court arrived at a wrong conclusion as to the effect of a special verdict, and
may order the conclusion to be recorded that appears to the court to be
required by the verdict, and may pass a sentence that is warranted in law in 601
substitution for the sentence passed by the trial court; 601

(d) may set aside a conviction and find the appellant not guilty on account of insanity and order the appellant to be kept in safe custody to await the pleasure of the lieutenant governor where it is of the opinion that, although the appellant committed the act or made the omission charged against him, he was insane at the time the act was committed or the omission was made, so that he was not criminally responsible for his conduct; or

(e) may set aside the conviction and find the appellant unfit, on account of insanity, to stand his trial and order the appellant to be kept in safe custody to await the pleasure of the lieutenant governor.

Order to be made

(2) Where a court of appeal allows an appeal under paragraph (1)*(a)*, it shall quash the conviction and

(a) direct a judgment or verdict of acquittal to be entered, or

(b) order a new trial.

Substituting verdict

(3) Where a court of appeal dismisses an appeal under subparagraph (1)(*b*)(i), it may substitute the verdict that in its opinion should have been found and affirm the sentence passed by the trial court or impose a sentence that is warranted in law.

Appeal from acquittal

(4) Where an appeal is from an acquittal the court of appeal may

(a) dismiss the appeal; or

(b) allow the appeal, set aside the verdict and

(i) order a new trial, or

(ii) except where the verdict is that of a court composed of a judge and jury, enter a verdict of guilty with respect to the offence of which, in its opinion, the accused should have been found guilty but for the error in law, and pass a sentence that is warranted in law. 1974-75-76,c.93,s.75.

New trial under Part XVI

(5) Where an appeal is taken in respect of proceedings under Part XVI and the court of appeal orders a new trial under this Part, the following provisions apply, namely,

(a) if the accused, in his notice of appeal or notice of application for leave to appeal, requested that the new trial, if ordered, should be held before a court composed of a judge and jury, the new trial shall be held accordingly;

(b) if the accused, in his notice of appeal or notice of application for leave to appeal, did not request that the new trial, if ordered, should be held before a court composed of a judge and jury, the new trial shall, without further election by the accused, be held before a judge or magistrate, as the case may be, acting under Part XVI, other than a judge or magistrate who tried the accused in the first instance, unless the court of appeal directs that the new trial be held before the judge or magistrate who tried the accused in the first instance;

(c) if the court of appeal orders that the new trial shall be held before a court composed of a judge and jury it is not necessary, in any province of Canada, to prefer a bill of indictment before a grand jury in respect of the charge upon which the new trial was ordered, but it is sufficient if the new trial is commenced by an indictment in writing setting forth the offence with which the accused is charged and in respect of which the new trial was ordered; and

(d) notwithstanding paragraph *(a)*, if the conviction against which the accused appealed was for an offence mentioned in section 483 and was made by a magistrate, the new trial shall be held before a magistrate acting under Part XVI, other than the magistrate who tried the accused in the first instance, unless the court of appeal directs that the new trial be held before the magistrate who tried the accused in the first instance.

Where appeal against verdict of insanity allowed

(6) Where a court of appeal allows an appeal against a verdict that the accused is unfit, on account of insanity, to stand his trial it shall, subject to subsection (7), order a new trial.

Appeal court may set aside verdict of insanity and direct acquittal

(7) Where the verdict that the accused is unfit, on account of insanity, to stand his trial was returned after the close of the case for the prosecution, the court of appeal may, notwithstanding that the verdict is proper, if it is of opinion that the accused should have been acquitted at the close of the case for the prosecution, allow the appeal, set aside the verdict and direct a judgment or verdict of acquittal to be entered.

Additional powers

(8) Where a court of appeal exercises any of the powers conferred by subsection (2), (4), (6) or (7), it may make any order, in addition, that justice requires. 1953-54,c.51,s.592; 1960-61,c.43,s.26; 1968-69,c.38,s.60.

Powers of court on appeal against sentence

614. (1) Where an appeal is taken against sentence the court of appeal shall, 601
unless the sentence is one fixed by law, consider the fitness of the sentence appealed against, and may upon such evidence, if any, as it thinks fit to require or to receive,

(a) vary the sentence with the limits prescribed by law for the offence of which the accused was convicted, or

(b) dismiss the appeal.

Effect of judgment

(2) A judgment of a court of appeal that varies the sentence of an accused who was convicted has the same force and effect as if it were a sentence passed by the trial court. 1953-54,c.51,s.593.

Right of appellant to attend

615. (1) Subject to subsection (2), an appellant who is in custody is entitled, if he desires, to be present at the hearing of the appeal.

Appellant represented by counsel

(2) An appellant who is in custody and who is represented by counsel is not entitled to be present

(a) at the hearing of the appeal, where the appeal is on a ground involving a question of law alone,

(b) on an application for leave to appeal, or

(c) on any proceedings that are preliminary or incidental to an appeal,

unless rules of court provide that he is entitled to be present or the court of appeal or a judge thereof gives him leave to be present.

Argument may be oral or in writing

(3) An appellant may present his case on appeal and his argument in writing instead of orally, and the court of appeal shall consider any case of argument so presented.

Sentence in absence of appellant

(4) The power of a court of appeal to impose sentence may be exercised notwithstanding that the appellant is not present. 1953-54,c.51,s.594; 1968-69, c.38,s.61.

Restitution of property

616. (1) Where an order for compensation or for the restitution of property is made by the trial court under section 653, 654 or 655, the operation of the order is suspended

(a) until the expiration of the period prescribed by rules of court for the giving of notice of appeal or of notice of application for leave to appeal, unless the accused waives an appeal, and

(b) until the appeal or application for leave to appeal has been determined, where an appeal is taken or application for leave to appeal is made.

Annulling or varying order

(2) The court of appeal may by order annul or vary an order made by the 601
trial court with respect to compensation or the restitution of property within 601
the limits prescribed by the provision under which the order was made by the trial court, whether or not the conviction is quashed. 1953-54,c.51,s.595.

Powers of Minister of Justice

Powers of Minister of Justice

617. The Minister of Justice may, upon an application for the mercy of the Crown by or on behalf of a person who has been convicted in proceedings by indictment or who has been sentenced to preventive detention under Part XXI,

(a) direct, by order in writing, a new trial or, in the case of a person under sentence of preventive detention, a new hearing, before any court that he thinks proper, if after inquiry he is satisfied that in the circumstances a new trial or hearing, as the case may be, should be directed;

(b) refer the matter at any time to the court of appeal for hearing and determination by that court as if it were an appeal by the convicted person or the person under sentence of preventive detention, as the case may be; or

(c) refer to the court of appeal at any time, for its opinion, any question upon which he desires the assistance of that court, and the court shall furnish its opinion accordingly. 1968-69,c.38,s.62.

608. (7) Where, with respect to any person, the court of appeal or the Supreme Court of Canada orders a new trial or new hearing or the Minister of Justice gives a direction or makes a reference under section 617, this section applies to the release or detention of that person pending the new trial or new hearing or the hearing and determination of the reference, as the case may be, as though that person were an appellant in an appeal described in paragraph (1)*(a)*.

Appeals to the Supreme Court of Canada

Appeal from conviction

618. (1) A person who is convicted of an indictable offence and whose conviction is affirmed by the court of appeal may appeal to the Supreme Court of Canada 601

(a) on any question of law on which a judge of the court of appeal dissents, or

(b) on any question of law, if leave to appeal is granted by the Supreme Court of Canada within twenty-one days after the judgment appealed from is pronounced or within such extended time as the Supreme Court of Canada or a judge thereof may, for special reasons, allow.

Appeal where acquittal set aside

(2) A person

(a) who is acquitted of an indictable offence other than by reason of the special verdict of not guilty on account of insanity and whose acquittal is set aside by the court of appeal, or

(b) who is tried jointly with a person referred to in paragraph *(a)* and is convicted and whose conviction is sustained by the court of appeal,

may appeal to the Supreme Court of Canada on a question of law. 1953-54, c.51,s.597; 1956,c.48,s.19; 1960-61,c.43,s.27; 1968-69,c.38,s.63; 1974-75-76, c.105,s.18.

619. Repealed. 1974-75-76, c.105, s.19.

Appeal against affirmation of special verdict of insanity

620. (1) A person who has been found not guilty on account of insanity and

(a) whose acquittal is affirmed on that ground by the court of appeal, or

(b) against whom a verdict of guilty is entered by the court of appeal under subparagraph 613(4)*(b)*(i),

may appeal to the Supreme Court of Canada.

Appeal against affirmation of verdict of unfit

(2) A person who is found unfit, on account of insanity, to stand his trial and against whom that verdict is affirmed by the court of appeal may appeal to the Supreme Court of Canada.

Grounds of appeal

(3) An appeal under subsection (1) or (2) may be

(a) on any question of law on which a judge of the court of appeal dissents, or

(b) on any question of law, if leave to appeal is granted by the Supreme Court of Canada within twenty-one days after the judgment appealed from is pronounced or within such extended time as the Supreme Court of Canada or a judge thereof may, for special reasons, allow. 1968-69,c. 38,s.64.

Appeal by Attorney General

621. (1) Where a judgment of a court of appeal sets aside a conviction pursuant to an appeal taken under section 603 or 604 or dismisses an appeal taken pursuant to paragraph 605(1)*(a)* or subsection 605(3), the Attorney General may appeal to the Supreme Court of Canada

(a) on any question of law on which a judge of the court of appeal dissents, or

(b) on any question of law, if leave to appeal is granted by the Supreme Court of Canada within twenty-one days after the judgment appealed from is pronounced or within such extended time as the Supreme Court of Canada or a judge thereof may, for special reasons, allow.

Terms

(2) Where leave to appeal is granted under paragraph (1)*(b)*, the Supreme Court of Canada may impose such terms as it sees fit. 1953-54,c.51,s.598; 1956, c.48,s.20; 1960-61,c.44,s.12; 1968-69,c.38,s.65.

Notice of appeal

622. No appeal lies to the Supreme Court of Canada unless notice of appeal in writing is served by the appellant upon the respondent within fifteen days 25(3) Interp

(a) after the judgment of the court of appeal is pronounced where the appeal may be taken without leave, or

(b) after leave to appeal is granted, where leave is required,

unless before or after the expiration of that period further time is allowed by the Supreme Court of Canada or a judge thereof. 1953-54,c.51,s.599.

Order of Supreme Court of Canada

623. (1) The Supreme Court of Canada may, on an appeal under this Part, make any order that the court of appeal might have made and may make any rule or order that is necessary to give effect to its judgment.

When appeal presumed abandoned

(2) An appeal to the Supreme Court of Canada that is not brought on for hearing by the appellant at the session of that court during which the judgment appealed from is pronounced by the court of appeal, or during the next session thereof, shall be deemed to be abandoned, unless otherwise ordered by the Supreme Court of Canada or a judge thereof. 1953-54,c.51,s.600.

Appeals by Attorney General of Canada

Right of Attorney General of Canada to appeal

624. The Attorney General of Canada has the same rights of appeal in proceedings instituted at the instance of the Government of Canada and conducted by or on behalf of that Government as the Attorney General of a province has under this Part. 1953-54,c.51,s.601.

608. (8) This section applies to applications for leave to appeal and appeals to the Supreme Court of Canada in summary conviction proceedings.

—NOTES—

PART XIX

PROCURING ATTENDANCE OF WITNESSES

Application

Application

625. Except where section 460 applies, this Part applies where a person is required to attend to give evidence in a proceeding to which this Act applies. 1953-54, c. 51, s. 602.

460. (1) Where a person who is confined in a prison is required

(a) to attend at a preliminary inquiry into a charge against him,

(b) to stand his trial upon a charge that may be tried by indictment or on summary conviction, or

(c) to attend to give evidence in a proceeding to which this Act applies,

a judge of a superior court of criminal jurisdiction or of a county or district court may order in writing that the prisoner be brought before the court, judge, justice, or magistrate before whom his attendance is required, from day to day as may be necessary, if

(d) the applicant for the order sets out the facts of the case in an affidavit and produces the warrant, if any, and

(e) the judge is satisfied that the ends of justice require that an order be made.

(2). A magistrate has the same powers for the purposes of subsection (1) as a judge has under that subsection where the person whose attendance is required is confined in a prison within the province in which the magistrate has jurisdiction.

(3) An order that is made under subsection (1) or (2) shall be addressed to the person who has custody of the prisoner, and on receipt thereof that person shall

(a) deliver the prisoner to any person who is named in the order to receive him, or

(b) bring the prisoner before the court, judge, justice or magistrate, as the case may be, upon payment of his reasonable charges in respect thereof.

(4) Where the prisoner is required as a witness, the judge or magistrate shall direct, in the order, the manner in which the prisoner shall be kept in custody and returned to the prison from which he is brought.

(5) Where the appearance of the prisoner is required for the purposes of paragraph (1)*(a)* or *(b)*, the judge or magistrate shall give appropriate directions in the order with respect to the manner in which the prisoner is

(a) to be kept in custody, if he is committed for trial; or

(b) to be returned, if he is discharged upon a preliminary inquiry or if he is acquitted of the charge against him.

(6) Sections 645 and 659 apply where a prisoner to whom this section applies is convicted and sentenced to imprisonment by the court, judge, justice or magistrate.

Process

Subpoena

626. (1) Where a person is likely to give material evidence in a proceeding to which this Act applies, a subpoena may be issued in accordance with this Part requiring that person to attend to give evidence.

Warrant in Form 12

(2) Where it is made to appear that a person who is likely to give material evidence

(*a*) will not attend in response to a subpoena if a subpoena is issued, or

(*b*) is evading service of a subpoena,

a court, justice or magistrate having power to issue a subpoena to require the attendance of that person to give evidence may issue a warrant in Form 12 to cause that person to be arrested and to be brought to give evidence.

Subpoena issued first

(3) Except where paragraph (2)(*a*) applies, a warrant in Form 12 shall not be issued unless a subpoena has been first been issued. 1953-54, c. 51, s. 603.

How subpoena issued

627. (1) Where a person is required to attend to give evidence before a
superior court of criminal jurisdiction, a court of appeal, an appeal court or a 2
court of criminal jurisdiction other than a magistrate acting under Part XVI, the 2
subpoena directed to that person shall be issued out of the court before which the attendance of that person is required.

Who may issue

(2) Where a person is required to attend to give evidence before a magistrate acting under Part XVI, or a summary conviction court under Part XXIV or in
proceedings over which a justice has jurisdiction, a subpoena directed to that 2
person shall be issued

(*a*) by a justice or magistrate, as the case may be, where the person whose
attendance is required is within the province in which the proceedings were 28 Interp
instituted, or

(*b*) out of a superior court of criminal jurisdiction or a county or district court of the province in which the proceedings were instituted, where the person whose attendance is required is not within the province.

Order of judge

(3) A subpoena shall not be issued pursuant to paragraph (2)(*b*), except pursuant to an order of a judge of the court made upon application by a party to the proceedings.

Seal

(4) A subpoena or warrant that is issued by a court under this Part shall be under the seal of the court and shall be signed by a judge of the court or by the
clerk of the court. 2

Signature

(5) A subpoena or warrant that is issued by a justice or magistrate under this Part shall be signed by the justice or magistrate.

Form

(6) A subpoena issued under this Part may be Form 11. 1953-54, c. 51, s. 604; 1960-61, c. 43, s. 28.

Contents of subpoena

628. (1) A subpoena shall require the person to whom it is directed to attend, at a time and place to be stated in the subpoena, to give evidence and, if required, to bring with him any writings that he has in his possession or under his control relating to the subject-matter of the proceedings.

Witness to appear and remain

(2) A person who is served with a subpoena issued under this Part shall attend and shall remain in attendance throughout the proceedings unless he is excused by the presiding judge, justice or magistrate. 1953-54, c. 51, s. 605.

636. (1) A person who, being required by law to attend or remain in attendance for the purpose of giving evidence fails, without lawful excuse, to attend or remain in attendance accordingly is guilty of contempt of court.

(2) A court, judge, justice or magistrate may deal summarily with a person who is guilty of contempt of court under this section and that person is liable to a fine of one hundred dollars or to imprisonment for ninety days or to both, and may be ordered to pay the costs that are incident to the service of any process under this Part and to his detention, if any.

(3) A conviction under this section may be in Form 34 and a warrant of committal in respect of a conviction under this section may be in Form 22.

Execution or Service of Process

Service

629. (1) Subject to subsection (2), a subpoena shall be served in accordance with subsection 455.5(2).

455.5. (2) A summons shall be served by a peace officer who shall deliver it personally to the person to whom it is directed or, if that person cannot conveniently be found, shall leave it for him at his last or usual place of abode with some inmate thereof who appears to be at least sixteen years of age.

Personal service

(2) A subpoena that is issued pursuant to paragraph 627(2)*(b)* shall be served personally upon the person to whom it is directed.

Proof of service

(3) Service of a subpoena may be proved by the affidavit of the person who effected service. R.S., c. C-34, s. 629; 1972, c. 13, s. 56(2).

Subpoena effective throughout Canada

630. (1) A subpoena that is issued out of a superior court of criminal jurisdiction, a court of appeal, an appeal court or a court of criminal jurisdiction other than a magistrate acting under Part XVI has effect anywhere in Canada according to its terms.

Subpoena effective throughout province

(2) A subpoena that is issued by a justice or magistrate has effect anywhere in the province in which it is issued. 1953-54, c. 51, s. 607; 1960-61, c. 43, s. 29.

Warrant effective throughout Canada

631. (1) A warrant that is issued out of a superior court of criminal jurisdiction, a court of appeal, an appeal court or a court of criminal jurisdiction other than a magistrate acting under Part XVI may be executed anywhere in Canada.

Warrant effective throughout province

(2) Subject to subsection 633(3), a warrant that is issued by a justice or magistrate may be executed anywhere in the province in which it is issued. 1953-54, c. 51, s. 608; 1960-61, c. 43, s. 30.

Defaulting or Absconding Witness

Warrant for absconding witness

632. (1) Where a person is bound by recognizance to give evidence in any proceedings, a justice who is satisfied upon information being made before him in writing and under oath that the person is about to abscond or has absconded, may issue his warrant in Form 13 directing a peace officer to arrest that person and to bring him before the court, judge, justice or magistrate before whom he is bound to appear. 28 Interp

Endorsement of warrant

(2) Section 461 applies, *mutatis mutandis*, to a warrant issued under this section.

mutatis mutandis — after the necessary changes in detail so that the text applies

461 (1) Where a warrant for the arrest of an accused cannot be executed in accordance with section 456.3, a justice within whose jurisdiction the accused is or is believed to be shall, upon application, and upon proof on oath or by affidavit of the signature of the justice who issued the warrant, authorize the execution of the warrant within his jurisdiction by making an endorsement, which may be in Form 25, upon the warrant.

(2) An endorsement that is made upon a warrant pursuant to subsection (1) is sufficient authority to the peace officers to whom it was originally directed, and to all peace officers within the territorial jurisdiction of the justice by whom it is endorsed, to execute the warrant and to take the accused before the justice who issued the warrant or before some other justice for the same territorial division.

Copy of information

(3) A person who is arrested under this section is entitled, upon request, to receive a copy of the information upon which the warrant for his arrest was issued. 1953-54, c. 51, s. 609.

Warrant when witness does not attend

633. (1) Where a person who has been served with a subpoena to give evidence in a proceeding does not attend or remain in attendance, the court, judge, justice or magistrate before whom that person was required to attend may, if it is established

(*a*) that the subpoena has been served in accordance with this Part, and

(*b*) that the person is likely to give material evidence,

issue or cause to be issued a warrant in Form 12 for the arrest of that person.

Warrant where witness bound by recognizance

(2) Where a person who has been bound by a recognizance to attend to give evidence in any proceeding does not attend or does not remain in attendance, the court, judge, justice or magistrate before whom that person was bound to attend may issue or cause to be issued a warrant in Form 12 for the arrest of that person.

Warrant effective throughout Canada

(3) A warrant that is issued by a justice or magistrate pursuant to subsection (1) or (2) may be executed anywhere in Canada. 1953-54, c. 51, s. 610.

Order where witness arrested under warrant

634. Where a person is brought before a court, judge, justice or magistrate under a warrant issued pursuant to subsection 626(2), or pursuant to section 632 or 633, the court, judge, justice or magistrate may order that the person 2

(*a*) be detained in custody, or

(*b*) be released on recognizance in Form 28, with or without sureties, 28 Interp

to appear and give evidence when required. 1953-54, c. 51, s. 611.

Maximum period for detention of witness

635. (1) No person shall be detained in custody under the authority of any provision of this Act, for the purpose only of appearing and giving evidence when required as a witness, for any period exceeding thirty days unless prior to the expiration of those thirty days he has been brought before a judge of a superior court of criminal jurisdiction in the province in which he is being detained.

Application by witness to judge

(2) Where at any time prior to the expiration of the thirty days referred to in subsection (1), a witness being detained in custody as described in that subsection applies to be brought before a judge of a court described therein, the judge before whom the application is brought shall fix a time prior to the expiration of those thirty days for the hearing of the application and shall cause notice of the time so fixed to be given to the witness, the person having custody of the witness and such other persons as the judge may specify, and at the time so fixed for the hearing of the application the person having custody of the witness shall cause the witness to be brought before a judge of the court for that purpose.

Review of detention

(3) If the judge before whom a witness is brought under this section is not satisfied that the continued detention of the witness is justified, he shall order him to be discharged, or to be released on recognizance in Form 28, with or without sureties, to appear and to give evidence when required, but if the judge is satisfied that the continued detention of the witness is justified, he may order his continued detention until the witness does what is required of him pursuant to section 477 or the trial is concluded, or until the witness appears and gives evidence when required, as the case may be, except that the total period of detention of the witness from the time he was first detained in custody shall not in any case exceed ninety days. 1968-69, c. 38, s. 66.

Contempt

636. (1) A person who, being required by law to attend or remain in attendance for the purpose of giving evidence fails, without lawful excuse, to attend or remain in attendance accordingly is guilty of contempt of court.

Punishment

(2) A court, judge, justice or magistrate may deal summarily with a person who is guilty of contempt of court under this section and that person is liable to a fine of one hundred dollars or to imprisonment for ninety days or to both, and may be ordered to pay the costs that are incident to the service of any process under this Part and to his detention, if any.

Form

(3) A conviction under this section may be in Form 34 and a warrant of committal in respect of a conviction under this section may be in Form 22. 1953-54, c. 51, s. 612.

Evidence on Commission

Order appointing commissioner

637. A party to a proceeding to which this Act applies may apply for an order appointing a commissioner to take the evidence of a witness who

(a) is, by reason of

(i) physical disability arising out of illness, or

(ii) some other good and sufficient cause,

not likely to be able to attend at the time the trial is held, or

(b) is out of Canada. 1953-54, c. 51, s. 613.

Application where witness is ill

638. (1) An application under paragraph 637*(a)* shall be made

(a) to a judge of a superior court of the province, or 28 Interp [6

(b) to a judge of a county or district court in the territorial division where the proceedings are taken.

Evidence of medical practitioner

(2) An application under subparagraph 637*(a)*(i) may be granted on the evidence of a registered medical practitioner. 1953-54, c. 51, s. 614.

Reading evidence of witness who is ill

639. Where the evidence of a witness mentioned in subparagraph 637*(a)*(i) is taken by a commissioner appointed under section 638, it may be read in evidence in the proceedings if

(a) it is proved by oral evidence or by affidavit that the witness is, by reason of death or physical disability arising out of illness, unable to attend,

(b) the transcript of the evidence is signed by the commissioner by or before whom it purports to have been taken, and

(c) it is proved to the satisfaction of the court that reasonable notice of the time for taking the evidence was given to the other party, and that the accused or his counsel, or the prosecutor or his counsel, as the case may be, had or might have had full opportunity to cross-examine the witness. 1953-54, c. 51, s. 615.

Application for order when witness out of Canada

640. (1) An application that is made under paragraph 637*(b)* shall be made

(a) to a judge of a superior court of criminal jurisdiction or of a court of criminal jurisdiction before which the accused is to be tried, or

(b) to a magistrate acting under Part XVI, where the accused is to be tried by a magistrate acting under that Part.

Reading evidence of witness out of Canada

(2) Where the evidence of a witness is taken by a commissioner appointed under this section, it may be read in evidence in the proceedings.

Reading evidence to grand jury

(3) Subject to section 642, evidence that is taken by a commissioner appointed under this section may, where the presiding judge directs, be read in evidence before a grand jury. 1953-54, c. 51, s. 616.

Providing for presence of accused counsel

641. (1) A judge or magistrate who appoints a commissioner may make provision in the order to enable an accused to be present or represented by counsel when the evidence is taken, but failure of the accused to be present or to be represented by counsel in accordance with the order does not prevent the reading of the evidence in the proceedings if the evidence has otherwise been taken in accordance with the order and with this Part.

Return of evidence

(2) An order for the taking of evidence by commission shall indicate the officer of the court to whom the evidence that is taken under the order shall be returned. 1953-54, c. 51, s. 617.

Rules and practice same as in civil cases

642. Except where otherwise provided by this Part or by rules of court, the practice and procedure in connection with the appointment of commissioners under this Part, the taking of evidence by commissioners, the certifying and return thereof, and the use of the evidence in the proceedings shall, as far as possible, be the same as those that govern like matters in civil proceedings in the superior court of the province in which the proceedings are taken. 1953-54, c. 51, s. 618.

Evidence Previously Taken

Evidence at preliminary inquiry may be read at trial in certain cases

643. (1) Where, at the trial of an accused, a person whose evidence was given at a previous trial upon the same charge, or whose evidence was taken in the investigation of the charge against the accused or upon the preliminary inquiry into the charge, refuses to be sworn or to give evidence, or if facts are proved upon oath from which it can be inferred reasonably that the person

(*a*) is dead,

(*b*) has since become and is insane,

(*c*) is so ill that he is unable to travel or testify, or

(*d*) is absent from Canada,

and where it is proved that his evidence was taken in the presence of the accused, it may be read as evidence in the proceedings without further proof, if the evidence purports to be signed by the judge or justice before whom it purports to have been taken, unless the accused proves that it was not in fact signed by that judge or justice or that he did not have full opportunity to cross-examine the witness.

Idem

(2) Evidence that has been taken on the preliminary inquiry or other investigation of a charge against an accused may be read as evidence in the prosecution of the accused for any other offence upon the same proof and in the same manner in all respects, as it might, according to law, be read in the prosecution of the offence with which the accused was charged when the evidence was taken. 1953-54, c. 51, s. 619; 1968-69, c. 38. s. 67.

Absconding accused deemed present

(3) For the purposes of this section, where evidence was taken at a previous trial of an accused in the absence of the accused, who was absent by reason of having absconded, he shall be deemed to have been present during the taking of the evidence and to have had full opportunity to cross-examine the witness. 1074-75-76, c. 93, s. 76.

PART XX

PUNISHMENTS, FINES, FORFEITURES, COSTS AND RESTITUTION OF PROPERTY

Punishment Generally

"Court" defined

644. In this Part, except as provided in section 667, "court" means a court, judge, justice or magistrate and includes a person who is authorized to exercise the powers of a court, judge, justice or magistrate to impose punishment. 1974-75-76, c. 93, s. 77.

Degrees of punishment

645. (1) Where an enactment prescribes different degrees or kinds of punishment in respect of an offence, the punishment to be imposed is, subject to the limitations prescribed in the enactment, in the discretion of the court that convicts a person who commits the offence.

Discretion as to punishment

(2) Where an enactment prescribes a punishment in respect of an offence, the punishment to be imposed is, subject to the limitations prescribed in the enactment, in the discretion of the court that convicts a person who commits the offence, but no punishment is a minimum punishment unless it is declared to be a minimum punishment.

Imprisonment in default where term not specified

(3) Where an accused is convicted of an offence punishable with both fine and imprisonment and a term of imprisonment in default of payment of the fine is not specified in the enactment that prescribed the punishment to be imposed, the imprisonment that may be imposed in default of payment shall not exceed the term of imprisonment that is prescribed in respect of the offence.

Cumulative punishments

(4) Where an accused

(a) is convicted while under sentence for an offence, and a term of imprisonment, whether in default of payment of a fine or otherwise, is imposed;

(b) is convicted of an offence punishable with both fine and imprisonment, and both are imposed with a direction that, in default of payment of the fine, the accused shall be imprisoned for a term certain; or

(c) is convicted of more offences than one before the same court at the same sittings, and

(i) more than one fine is imposed with a direction in respect of each of them that, in default of payment thereof, the accused shall be imprisoned for a term certain,

(ii) terms of imprisonment for the respective offences are imposed, or

(iii) a term of imprisonment is imposed in respect of one offence and a fine is imposed in respect of another offence with a direction that, in default of payment, the accused shall be imprisoned for a term certain,

the court that convicts the accused may direct that the terms of imprisonment shall be served one after the other. 1953-54, c. 51, s. 621.

Fine in lieu of other punishment

646. (1) An accused who is convicted of an indictable offence punishable with imprisonment for five years or less may be fined in addition to or in lieu of any other punishment that is authorized, but an accused shall not be fined in lieu of imprisonment where the offence of which he is convicted is punishable by a minimum term of imprisonment. 'C' & 'D' offences

Fine in addition to other punishment

(2) An accused who is convicted of an indictable offence punishable with imprisonment for more than five years may be fined in addition to, but not in lieu of, any other punishment that is authorized. 'E', 'F' & 'G' offences

Imprisonment in default of payment

(3) Where a fine is imposed under this section, a term of imprisonment may be imposed in default of payment of the fine, but no such term shall exceed ss. (12)

(a) two years, where the term of imprisonment that may be imposed for the offence is less than five years, or

(b) five years, where the term of imprisonment that may be imposed for the offence is five years or more.

Time for payment

(4) Subject to the provisions of this section, where an accused is convicted of an indictable offence and is fined, the court that convicts the accused may direct that the fine 644

(a) be paid forthwith, or

(b) be paid at such time and on such terms as the court may fix.

What to be considered

(5) Where a court imposes a fine, the court shall not, at the time the sentence is imposed, direct that the fine be paid forthwith unless

(a) the court is satisfied that the convicted person is possessed of sufficient means to enable him to pay the fine forthwith,

(b) upon being asked by the court whether he desires time for payment, the convicted person does not request such time, or

(c) for any other special reason, the court deems it expedient that no time should be allowed.

Idem

(6) The court, in considering whether time should be allowed for payment and, if so, for what period, shall consider any representation made by the accused but any time allowed shall be not less than fourteen clear days from the date sentence is imposed. 25(2) Interp

Interpretation Act

25. (2) Where there is a reference to a number of clear days or "at least" a number of days between two events, in calculating the number of days there shall be excluded the days on which the events happen.

Warrant of committal

(7) Where time has been allowed for payment the court shall not issue a warrant of committal in default of payment of the fine until the expiration of the time allowed for payment.

Reasons for committal

(8) Where no time has been allowed for payment and a warrant of committal in default of payment of a fine of the accused is issued the court shall state in the warrant the reason for immediate committal.

Surrender by accused

(9) Notwithstanding subsection (7), where, before the expiration of the time allowed for payment, the accused appears before a court as defined in section 644, and signifies in writing that he prefers to be committed immediately rather than to await the expiration of the time allowed, the court may forthwith issue a warrant committing the accused to prison.

Young offenders

(10) Where a person who has been allowed time for payment appears to the court to be not less than sixteen nor more than twenty-one years of age, the court shall, before issuing a warrant committing the person to prison for default of payment of the fine, obtain and consider a report concerning the conduct and means to pay of the accused.

Extension of time

(11) Where time has been allowed for payment under subsection (4) the court that imposed the sentence may, upon an application by or on behalf of the accused, allow further time for payment, subject to any rules made by the court under section 438.

"Fine"

(12) In this section "fine" includes a pecuniary penalty or other sum of money. 1953-54, c. 51, s. 622; 1959, c. 41, s. 27.

Fines on corporations

647. Notwithstanding subsection 646(2), a corporation that is convicted of an offence is liable, in lieu of any imprisonment that is prescribed as punishment for that offence,

(a) to be fined in an amount that is in the discretion of the court, where the offence is an indictable offence, or

(b) to be fined in an amount not exceeding one thousand dollars, where the offence is a summary conviction offence. 1953-54, c. 51, s. 623; 1968-69, c. 38, s. 68; 1974-75-76, c. 93, s. 78.

Enforcement of fines on corporations

648. Where a fine that is imposed on a corporation is not paid forthwith the prosecutor may, by filing the conviction, enter as a judgment the amount of the fine and costs, if any, in the superior court of the province in which the trial was held, and that judgment is enforceable against the corporation in the same manner as if it were a judgment rendered against the corporation in that court in civil proceedings. 1968-69, c. 38, s. 69. 28 Interp

Interpretation Act

28. In every enactment

"superior court" means

(a) in the Province of Ontario, Nova Scotia, Prince Edward Island or Newfoundland, the Supreme Court of the Province,

(b) in the Province of Quebec, the Court of Appeal and the Superior Court in and for the Province,

(c) in the Province of British Columbia, the Court of Appeal and the Supreme Court of the Province,

(d) in the Province of Manitoba, Saskatchewan, Alberta or New Brunswick, the Court of Appeal for the Province and the Court of Queen's Bench for the Province,

(e) in the Yukon Territory or the Northwest Territories, the Supreme Court thereof,

and includes the Supreme Court of Canada and the Federal Court of Canada;

Commencement of sentence

649. (1) A sentence commences when it is imposed, except where a relevant enactment otherwise provides.

Convicted person lawfully at large

(2) Any time during which a convicted person is lawfully at large on interim release granted pursuant to any provision of this Act does not count as part of any term of imprisonment imposed pursuant to his conviction.

Determination of sentence

(2.1) In determining the sentence to be imposed on a person convicted of an offence, a justice, magistrate or judge may take into account any time spent in custody by the person as a result of the offence.

When time begins to run

(3) Notwithstanding subsection (1), a term of imprisonment, whether imposed by a trial court or the court appealed to, commences or shall be deemed to be resumed, as the case requires, on the day on which the convicted person is arrested and taken into custody under the sentence.

Where fine imposed

(4) Notwithstanding subsection (1), where the sentence that is imposed is a fine with a term of imprisonment in default of payment, no time prior to the day of execution of the warrant of committal counts as part of the term of imprisonment.

Application for leave to appeal

(5) An application for leave to appeal is an appeal for the purposes of this section. R.S., c. C-34, s. 649; R.S., c. 2(2nd Supp.), s. 13.

Reduction of imprisonment on part payment

650. (1) Where a term of imprisonment is imposed in default of payment of a penalty, the term shall, upon payment of a part of the penalty, whether the payment was made before or after the issue of a warrant of committal, be reduced by the number of days that bears the same proportion to the number of days in the term as the part paid bears to the total penalty.

Minimum which can be accepted

(2) No amount offered in part payment of a penalty shall be accepted unless it is sufficient to secure reduction of sentence of one day, or some multiple thereof, and where a warrant of committal has been issued, no part payment shall be accepted until any fee that is payable in respect of the warrant or its execution has been paid.

To whom payment made

(3) Payment may be made under this section to the person who has lawful custody of the prisoner or to such other person as the Attorney General directs.

Application of money paid

(4) A payment under this section shall, unless the order imposing the penalty otherwise provides, be applied to the payment in full of costs and charges, and thereafter to payment in full of compensation or damages that are included in the penalty, and finally to payment in full of any part of the penalty that remains unpaid. ss. (5)

"Penalty"

(5) In this section, "penalty" means all the sums of money, including fines, in default of payment of which a term of imprisonment is imposed and includes the costs and charges of committing the defaulter and of conveying him to prison. 1953-54, c. 51, 625; 1959, c. 41, s. 29.

Fines and penalties go to provincial treasurer

651. (1) Where a fine, penalty or forfeiture is imposed or a recognizance is forfeited and no provision, other than this section, is made by law for the application of the proceeds thereof, the proceeds belong to Her Majesty in right of the province in which the fine, penalty or forfeiture was imposed or the recognizance was forfeited, and shall be paid by the person who receives them to the treasurer of that province.

Exception

(2) Where

(a) a fine, penalty or forfeiture is imposed

(i) in respect of a violation of a revenue law of Canada,

(ii) in respect of a breach of duty or malfeasance in office by an officer or employee of the Government of Canada, or

(iii) in respect of any proceedings instituted at the instance of the Government of Canada in which that government bears the costs of prosecution; or

(b) a recognizance in connection with proceedings mentioned in paragraph *(a)* is forfeited,

the proceeds of the fine, penalty, forfeiture or recognizance belong to Her Majesty in right of Canada and shall be paid by the person who receives them to the Receiver General.

Direction for payment to municipality

(3) Where a provincial, municipal or local authority bears, in whole or in part, the expense of administering the law under which a fine, penalty or forfeiture is imposed or under which proceedings are taken in which a recognizance is forfeited,

(a) the lieutenant governor in council may, from time to time, direct that the proceeds of a fine, penalty, forfeiture or recognizance that belongs to Her Majesty in right of the province shall be paid to that authority, and 28 Interp

(b) the Governor in Council may, from time to time, direct that the proceeds of a fine, penalty, forfeiture or recognizance that belongs to Her Majesty in right of Canada shall be paid to that authority. 1953-54, c. 51, s. 626; 1968-69, c. 38, s. 71. 28 Interp

Recovery of penalties

652. (1) Where a fine, pecuniary penalty or forfeiture is imposed by law and no other mode is prescribed for the recovery thereof, the fine, pecuniary penalty or forfeiture is recoverable or enforceable in civil proceedings by Her Majesty, but by no other person.

Limitation

(2) No proceedings under subsection (1) shall be instituted more than two years after the time when the cause of action arose or the offence was committed in respect of which the fine, pecuniary penalty or forfeiture was imposed. 1953-54, c. 51, s. 627.

Interpretation Act

28. In every enactment

"Governor in Council", or "Governor General in Council" means the Governor General of Canada, or person administering the Government of Canada for the time being, acting by and with the advice of, or by and with the advice and consent of, or in conjunction with the Queen's Privy Council for Canada;

"lieutenant governor in council" means the lieutenant governor, or person administering the government of the province indicated by the enactment, for the time being, acting by and with the advice of, or by and with the advice and consent of, or in conjuction with the executive council of such province and, in relation to the Yukon Territory or the Northwest Territories, means the Commissioner thereof;

Compensation for loss of property

653. (1) A court that convicts an accused of an indictable offence may, upon 616(1)
the application of a person aggrieved, at the time sentence is imposed, order the accused to pay to that person an amount by way of satisfaction or compensation for loss of or damage to property suffered by the applicant as a result of the 2
commission of the offence of which the accused is convicted.

Enforement

(2) Where an amount that is ordered to be paid under subsection (1) is not paid forthwith the applicant may, by filing the order, enter as a judgment, in the superior court of the province in which the trial was held, the amount ordered to be paid, and that judgment is enforceable against the accused in the same manner as if it were a judgment rendered against the accused in that court in civil proceedings.

Moneys found on accused

(3) All or any part of an amount that is ordered to be paid under subsection (1) may, if the court making the order is satisfied that ownership of or right to possession of those moneys is not disputed by claimants other than the accused and the court so directs, be taken out of moneys found in the possession of the accused at the time of his arrest. 1953-54, c. 51, s. 628; 1968-69, c. 38, s. 72.

616. (1) Where an order for compensation or for the restitution of property is made by the trial court under section 653, 654 or 655, the operation of the order is suspended

(a) until the expiration of the period prescribed by rules of court for the giving of notice of appeal or of notice of application for leave to appeal, unless the accused waives an appeal, and

(b) until the appeal or application for leave to appeal has been determined, where an appeal is taken or application for leave to appeal is made.

Compensation to *bona fide* purchasers

654. (1) Where an accused is convicted of an indictable offence and any 616(1)
property obtained as a result of the commission of the offence has been sold to an innocent purchaser, the court may, upon the application of the purchaser after restitution of the property to its owner, order the accused to pay to the purchaser an amount not exceeding the amount paid by the purchaser for the property.

Enforcement

(2) Where an amount that is ordered to be paid under subsection (1) is not paid forthwith the applicant may, by filing the order, enter as a judgment, in the superior court of the province in which the trial was held, the amount ordered to be paid, and that judgment is enforceable against the accused in the same manner is if it were a judgment rendered against the accused in that court in civil proceedings.

Moneys found on accused

(3) All or any part of an amount that is ordered to be paid under subsection (1) may, if the court making the order is satisfied that ownership of or right to possession of those moneys is not disputed by claimants other than the accused and the court so directs, be taken out of moneys found in the possession of the accused at the time of his arrest.

742. Where several persons join in committing the same offence and upon conviction each is adjudged to pay an amount to a person aggrieved, no more shall be paid to that person than an amount equal to the value of the property destroyed or injured or the amount of the injury done, together with costs, if any, and the residue of the amount adjudged to be paid shall be applied in the manner in which other penalties imposed by law are directed to be applied.

Order for restitution of property

655. (1) Where an accused is convicted of an indictable offence the court shall order that any property obtained by the commission of the offence shall be restored to the person entitled to it, if at the time of the trial the property is before the court or has been detained so that it can be immediately restored to that person under the order. 616(1)

Where no conviction

(2) Where an accused is tried for an indictable offence but is not convicted, and the court finds that an indictable offence has been committed, the court may order that any property obtained by the commission of the offence shall be restored to the person entitled to it, if at the time of the trial the property is before the court or has been detained, so that it can be immediately restored to that person under the order.

When order not to be made

(3) An order shall not be made under this section in respect of

(a) property to which an innocent purchaser for value has acquired lawful title,

(b) a valuable security that has been paid or discharged in good faith by a person who was liable to pay or discharge it, 2

(c) a negotiable instrument that has, in good faith, been taken or received by transfer or delivery for valuable consideration by a person who had no notice and no reasonable cause to suspect that an indictable offence had been committed, or

(d) property in respect of which there is a dispute as to ownership or right of possession by claimants other than the accused.

By whom order executed

(4) An order made under this section shall be executed by the peace officers by whom the process of the court is ordinarily executed.

Saving

(5) This section does not apply to proceedings against a trustee, banker, merchant, attorney, factor, broker or other agent entrusted with the possession of goods or documents of title to goods, for an offence under section 290, 291, 292 or 296. 1953-54, c. 51, s. 630. 2

Costs to successful party in case of libel

656. The person in whose favour judgment is given in proceedings by indictment for defamatory libel is entitled to recover from the opposite party costs in a reasonable amount to be fixed by order of the court. 1953-54, c. 51, s. 631.

How recovered

657. Where costs that are fixed under section 656 are not paid forthwith the party in whose favour judgment is given may enter judgment for the amount of the costs by filing the order in the superior court of the province in which the trial was held, and that judgment is enforceable against the opposite party in the same manner as if it were a judgment rendered against him in that court in civil proceedings. 1953-54, c. 51, s. 632. 28 Interp [648]

Imprisonment

Imprisonment when no other provision

658. Every one who is convicted of an indictable offence for which no punishment is specially provided is liable to imprisonment for five years. 1953-54, c. 51, s. 633.

115. Every one who, without lawful excuse, contravenes an Act of the Parliament of Canada by wilfully doing anything that it forbids or by wilfully omitting to do anything that it requires to be done is, unless some penalty or punishment is expressly provided by law, guilty of an indictable offence and is liable to imprisonment for two years.

722. (1) Except where otherwise expressly provided by law, every one who is convicted of an offence punishable on summary conviction is liable to a fine of not more than five hundred dollars or to imprisonment for six months or to both.

Imprisonment for life or more than two years

659. (1) Except where otherwise provided, a person who is sentenced to imprisonment for

(a) life,

(b) a term of two years or more, or

(c) two or more terms of less than two years each that are to be served one after the other and that, in the aggregate, amount to two years or more,

shall be sentenced to imprisonment in a penitentiary.

Subsequent term less than two years

(2) Where a person who is sentenced to imprisonment in a penitentiary is, before the expiration of that sentence, sentenced to imprisonment for a term of less than two years, he shall be sentenced to and shall serve that term in a penitentiary, but if the previous sentence of imprisonment in a penitentiary is set aside, he shall serve that term in accordance with subsection (3). 1974-75-76, c. 93, s. 79.

Imprisonment for term less than two years

(3) A person who is sentenced to imprisonment and who is not required to be sentenced as provided in subsection (1) or (2) shall, unless a special prison is prescribed by law, be sentenced to imprisonment in a prison or other place of confinement within the province in which he is convicted, other than a penitentiary, in which the sentence of imprisonment may be lawfully executed. ss. (7)

Sentence to penitentiary of person serving sentence elsewhere

(4) Where a person is sentenced to imprisonment in a penitentiary while he is lawfully imprisoned in a place other than a penitentiary he shall, except where otherwise provided, be sent immediately to the penitentiary and shall serve in the penitentiary the unexpired portion of the term of imprisonment that he was serving when he was sentenced to the penitentiary as well as the term of imprisonment for which he was sentenced to the penitentiary.

Transfer to penitentiary

(5) Where, at any time, a person who is imprisoned in a prison or place of confinement other than a penitentiary is subject to two or more terms of imprisonment, each of which is for less than two years, that are to be served one after the other, and the aggregate of the unexpired portions of those terms at that time amounts to two years or more, he shall be transferred to a penitentiary to serve those terms; but if any one or more of such terms is set aside and the unexpired portions of the remaining term or terms on the day on which he was transferred under this section amounted to less than two years, he shall serve that term or terms in accordance with subsection (3).

Only definite portion of certain sentences to be counted

(6) For the purposes of this section, where a person is sentenced to imprisonment for a definite term and an indeterminate period thereafter, such sentence shall be deemed to be for a term of less than two years and only the definite term thereof shall be taken into account in determining whether he is required to be sentenced to imprisonment in a penitentiary or to be committed or transferred to a penitentiary under subsection (5).

Idem

(6.1) Where, either before or after the coming into force of this subsection, a person has been sentenced, committed or transferred to a penitentiary, otherwise than pursuant to an agreement made under subsection 15(1) of the *Penitentiary Act*, any indeterminate portion of his sentence shall, for all purposes, be deemed not to have been imposed. 1976-77, c. 53, s. 13.

Exceptions

(7) For the purposes of subsection (3) "penitentiary" does not, until a day to be fixed by proclamation of the Governor in Council, include the penitentiary mentioned in section 82 of the *Penitentiary Act*, chapter 206 of the Revised Statutes of Canada, 1952. 1953-54, c. 51, s. 634; 1968-69, c. 38, s. 74.

Sentence served according to regulations

660. (1) A sentence of imprisonment shall be served in accordance with the enactments and rules that govern the institution to which the prisoner is sentenced, and a reference to hard labour in a conviction or sentence shall be deemed to be a reference to the employment of prisoners that is provided for in the enactments or rules.

Hard labour improperly ordered

(2) A conviction or sentence that imposes hard labour shall not be quashed or set aside on the ground only that the enactment that creates the offence does not authorize the imposition of hard labour, but shall be amended accordingly. 1953-54, c. 51, s. 635.

Delivery of Accused to Keeper of Prison

Execution of warrant of committal

661. A peace officer or other person to whom a warrant of committal authorized by this Act or any other Act of the Parliament of Canada is directed shall convey the person named or described therein to the prison mentioned in the warrant and deliver him, together with the warrant, to the keeper of the prison who shall thereupon give to the peace officer or other person who delivers the prisoner a receipt in Form 39 setting out the state and condition of the prisoner when delivered into his custody. 1953-54, c. 51, s. 636.

Absolute and Conditional Discharges, Suspended Sentences Intermittent Sentences and Probation

Report by probation officer

662. (1) Where an accused, other than a corporation, pleads guilty to or is found guilty of an offence, a probation officer shall, if required to do so by a court, prepare and file with the court a report in writing relating to the accused for the purpose of assisting the court in imposing sentence or in determining whether the accused should be discharged pursuant to section 662.1.

Copies to be provided

(2) Where a report is filed with the court under subsection (1), the clerk of the court shall forthwith cause a copy of the report to be provided to the accused or his counsel and to the prosecutor. R.S., c. C-34, s. 662; 1972,c. 13, s. 57.

Conditional and absolute discharge

662.1 (1) Where an accused, other than a corporation, pleads guilty to or is found guilty of an offence, other than an offence for which a minimum punishment is prescribed by law or an offence punishable, in the proceedings commenced against him, by imprisonment for fourteen years or for life, the court before which he appears may, if it considers it to be in the best interests of the accused and not contrary to the public interest, instead of convicting the accused, by order direct that the accused be discharged absolutely or upon the conditions prescribed in a probation order. 1974-75-76, c. 105, s. 20.

Period for which appearance notice, etc. continues in force

(2) Subject to the provisions of Part XIV, where an accused who has not been taken into custody or who has been released from custody under or by virtue of any provision of Part XIV pleads guilty to or is found guilty of an offence but is not convicted, the appearance notice, promise to appear, summons, undertaking or recognizance issued to or given or entered into by him continues in force, subject to its terms, until a disposition in respect of him is made under subsection (1) unless, at the time he pleads guilty or is found guilty, the court, judge or justice orders that he be taken into custody pending such a disposition.

Effect of discharge

(3) Where a court directs under subsection (1) that an accused be discharged, the accused shall be deemed not to have been convicted of the offence to which he pleaded guilty or of which he was found guilty and to which the discharge relates except that

(a) the accused may appeal from the direction that the accused be discharged as if that direction were a conviction in respect of the offence to which the discharge relates;

(a.1) the Attorney General may appeal from the direction that the accused be discharged, as if that direction were a judgment or verdict of acquittal referred to in paragraph 605(1)*(a)*; and

(b) the accused may plead *autrefois convict* in respect of any subsequent charge relating to the offence to which the discharge relates.

Where person bound by probation order convicted of offence

(4) Where an accused who is bound by the conditions of a probation order made at a time when he was directed to be discharged under this section is convicted of an offence, including an offence under section 666, the court that made the probation order may, in addition to or in lieu of exercising its authority under subsection 664(4), at any time when it may take action under that subsection, revoke the discharge, convict the accused of the offence to which the discharge relates and impose any sentence that could have been imposed if the accused had been convicted at the time he was discharged, and no appeal lies from a conviction under this subsection where an appeal was taken from the order directing that the accused be discharged. 1972, c. 13, s. 57; 1974-75-76, c. 93, s. 80.

Making of probation order

663. (1) Where an accused is convicted of an offence the court may, having regard to the age and character of the accused, the nature of the offence and the circumstances surrounding its commission,

(a) in the case of an offence other than one for which a minimum punishment is prescribed by law, suspend the passing of sentence and direct that the accused be released upon the conditions prescribed in a probation order;

(b) in addition to fining the accused or sentencing him to imprisonment, whether in default of payment of a fine or otherwise, for a term not exceeding two years, direct that the accused comply with the conditions prescribed in a probation order; or

(c) where it imposes a sentence of imprisonment on the accused, whether in default of payment of a fine or otherwise, that does not exceed ninety days, order that the sentence be served intermittently at such times as are specified in the order and direct that the accused, at all times when he is not in confinement pursuant to such order, comply with the conditions prescribed in a probation order. 1974-75-76,c.93,s.81.

Conditions in probation order

(2) The following conditions shall be deemed to be prescribed in a probation order, namely, that the accused shall keep the peace and be of good behaviour and shall appear before the court when required to do so by the court, and, in 667
addition, the court may prescribe as conditions in a probation order that the accused shall do any one or more of the following things as specified in the order, namely,

(a) report to and be under the supervision of a probation officer or other person designated by the court;

(b) provide for the support of his spouse or any other dependants whom he is liable to support; 26(6) Interp

(c) abstain from the consumption of alcohol either absolutely or on such terms as the court may specify;

(d) abstain from owning, possessing or carrying a weapon; 2

(e) make restitution or reparation to any person aggrieved or injured by the commission of the offence for the actual loss or damage sustained by that person as a result thereof;

(f) remain within the jurisdiction of the court and notify the court or the probation officer or other person designated under paragraph *(a)* of any change in his address or his employment or occupation;

(g) make reasonable efforts to find and maintain suitable employment; and

(h) comply with such other reasonable conditions as the court considers desirable for securing the good conduct of the accused and for preventing a repetition by him of the same offence or the commission of other offences.

Form and period of order

(3) A probation order may be in Form 44, and the court that makes the probation order shall specify therein the period for which it is to remain in force.

Proceedings on making of order

(4) Where the court makes a probation order, it shall 667

(a) cause the order to be read by or to the accused;

(b) cause a copy of the order to be given to the accused; and

(c) inform the accused of the provisions of subsection 664(4) and the provisions of section 666. R.S.,c.C-34,s.663; 1972,c.13,s.58.

Coming into force of order

664. (1) A probation order comes into force

(*a*) on the date on which the order is made, or

(*b*) where the accused is sentenced to imprisonment under paragraph 663(1)(*b*) otherwise than in default of payment of a fine, upon the expiration of that sentence.

Duration of order and limit on term of order

(2) Subject to subsection (4),

(*a*) where an accused who is bound by a probation order is convicted of an offence, including an offence under section 666, or is imprisoned under paragraph 663(1)(*b*) in default of payment of a fine, the order continues in force except in so far as the sentence renders it impossible for the accused for the time being to comply with the order; and

(*b*) no probation order shall continue in force for more than three years from the date on which the order came into force.

Modification of order

(3) Where a court has made a probation order, the court may at any time, 667
upon application by the accused or the prosecutor, require the accused to 2
appear before it and, after hearing the accused and the prosecutor,

(*a*) make any changes in or additions to the conditions prescribed in the order that in the opinion of the court are rendered desirable by a change in the circumstances since the conditions were prescribed,

(*b*) relieve the accused, either absolutely or upon such terms or for such period as the court deems desirable, of compliance with any condition described in any of paragraphs 663(2)(*a*) to (*h*) that is prescribed in the order, or

(*c*) decrease the period for which the probation order is to remain in force,

and the court shall thereupon endorse the probation order accordingly and, if it changes or adds to the conditions prescribed in the order, inform the accused of its action and give him a copy of the order so endorsed.

Modification of order where person bound convicted of offence

(4) Where an accused who is bound by a probation order is convicted of an offence, including an offence under section 666, and

(*a*) the time within which an appeal may be taken against that conviction has expired and he has not taken an appeal,

(*b*) he has taken an appeal against that conviction and the appeal has been dismissed, or

(*c*) he has given written notice to the court that convicted him that he elects not to appeal his conviction or has abandoned his appeal, as the case may be,

in addition to any punishment that may be imposed for that offence the court that made the probation order may, upon application by the prosecutor, require the accused to appear before it and, after hearing the prosecutor and the accused,

(*d*) where the probation order was made under paragraph 663(1)(*a*), revoke the order and impose any sentence that could have been imposed if the passing of sentence had not been suspended, or

(*e*) make such changes in or additions to the conditions prescribed in the order as the court deems desirable or extend the period for which the order is to remain in force for such period, not exceeding one year, as the court deems desirable,

and the court shall thereupon endorse the probation order accordingly and, if it changes or adds to the conditions prescribed in the order or extends the period for which the order is to remain in force, inform the accused of its action and give him a copy of the order so endorsed.

Compelling appearance of person bound

(5) The provisions of Parts XIV and XV with respect to compelling the appearance of an accused before a justice apply *mutatis mutandis* to proceedings under subsections (3) and (4). 1968-69, c. 38, s. 75.

Transfer of order

665. (1) Where an accused who is bound by a probation order becomes a resident of, or is convicted of an offence including an offence under section 666 in a territorial division, other than the territorial division where the order was made, the court that made the order may, upon the application of the 667
prosecutor, and, if both such territorial divisions are not in the same province, with the consent of

(*a*) the Attorney General of Canada, in the case of proceedings in relation to an offence that were instituted at the instance of the Government of Canada and conducted by or on behalf of that Government, or

(*b*) in any other case, the Attorney General of the province in which the order was made,

transfer the order to a court in that other territorial division that would, having regard to the mode of trial of the accused, have had jurisdiction to make the order in that other territorial division if the accused had been tried and convicted there of the offence in respect of which the order was made, and the order may thereafter be dealt with and enforced by the court to which it is so transferred in all respects as if that court had made the order. 1974-75-76, c. 93, s. 82.

Where court unable to act

(2) Where a court that has made a probation order or to which a probation order has been transferred pursuant to subsection (1) is for any reason unable to act, the powers of that court in relation to the probation order may be exercised by any other court that has equivalent jurisdiction in the same province. 1968-69, c. 38, s. 75.

Type 'A' Offence

666. (1) An accused who is bound by a probation order and who wilfully fails or refuses to comply with that order is guilty of an offence punishable on summary conviction.

Where accused may be tried and punished

(2) An accused who is charged with an offence under subsection (1) may be tried and punished by any court having jurisdiction to try that offence in the place where the offence is alleged to have been committed or in the place where the accused is found, is arrested or is in custody, but where the place where the accused is found, is arrested or is in custody is outside the province in which the offence is alleged to have been committed, no proceedings in respect of that offence shall be instituted in that place without the consent of Attorney General of such province. 1968-69, c. 38, s. 75.

"Court"

667. For the purposes of sections 662 to 666, "court" means

(*a*) a superior court of criminal jurisdiction,

(*b*) a court of criminal jurisdiction,

(*c*) a justice or magistrate acting as a summary conviction court under Part XXIV, or

(*d*) a court that hears an appeal. 1968-69, c. 38, s. 75.

688. Repealed. 1972, c. 13, s. 59.

Sentence of life imprisonment

669. The sentence to be pronounced against a person who is to be sentenced to imprisonment for life shall be,

(a) in respect of a person who has been convicted of high treason or first degree murder, that he be sentenced to imprisonment for life without eligibility for parole until he has served twenty-five years of his sentence;

(b) in respect of a person who has been convicted of second degree murder, that he be sentenced to imprisonment for life without eligibility for parole until he has served at least ten years of his sentence or such greater number of years, not being more than twenty-five years, as has been substituted therefor pursuant to section 671; and

(c) in respect of a person who has been convicted of any other offence, that he be sentenced to imprisonment for life with normal eligibility for parole. 1974-75-76, c. 105, s. 21.

Recommendation by jury

670. Where a jury finds an accused guilty of second degree murder, the judge who presides at the trial shall, before discharging the jury, put to them the following question:

"You have found the accused guilty of second degree murder and the law requires that I now pronounce a sentence of imprisonment for life against him. Do you wish to make any recommendation with respect to the number of years that he must serve before he is eligible for release on parole? You are not required to make any recommendation but if you do, your recommendation will be considered by me when I am determining whether I should substitute for the ten year period, which the law would otherwise require the accused to serve before he is eligible to be considered for release on parole, a number of years that is more than ten but not more than twenty-five."

Ineligibility for parole

671. At the time of the sentencing of an accused under section 669 who is convicted of second degree murder, the judge presiding at the trial of the accused or, if that judge is unable to do so, any judge of the same court may, having regard to the character of the accused, the nature of the offence and the circumstances surrounding its commission, and to any recommendation made pursuant to section 670, by order, substitute for ten years a number of years of imprisonment, (being more than ten but not more than twenty-five) without eligibility for parole, as he deems fit in the circumstances.

Application for judicial review

672. (1) Where a person has served at least fifteen years of his sentence

(a) in the case of a person who has been convicted of high treason or first degree murder, or

(b) in the case of a person convicted of second degree murder who has been sentenced to imprisonment for life without eligibility for parole until he has served more than fifteen years of his sentence,

he may apply to the appropriate Chief Justice in the province or territory in which the conviction took place for a reduction in his number of years of imprisonment without eligibility for parole.

Judicial hearing

(2) Upon receipt of an application under subsection (1), the appropriate Chief Justice shall designate a judge of the superior court of criminal jurisdiction to empanel a jury to hear the application and determine whether the applicant's number of years of imprisonment without eligibility for parole ought to be reduced having regard to the character of the applicant, his conduct while serving his sentence, the nature of the offence for which he was convicted and such other matters as the judge deems relevant in the circumstances and such determination shall be made by no less than two-thirds of such jury.

Renewal of application

(3) Where the jury hearing an application under subsection (1) determine that the applicant's number of years of imprisonment without eligibility for parole ought not to be reduced, the jury shall set another time at or after which an application may again be made by the applicant to the appropriate Chief Justice for a reduction in his number of years of imprisonment without eligibility for parole.

Reduction

(4) Where the jury hearing an application under subsection (1) determine that the applicant's number of years of imprisonment without eligibility for parole ought to be reduced, the jury may, by order,

(a) substitute a lesser number of years of imprisonment without eligibility for parole than that then applicable; or

(b) terminate the ineligibility for parole.

Rules

(5) The appropriate Chief Justice in each province or territory may make such rules in respect of applications and hearings under this section as are required for the purposes of this section.

Appropriate Chief Justice

(6) For the purposes of this section, the "appropriate Chief Justice" is

(a) in relation to

(i) the Provinces of British Columbia and Prince Edward Island, respectively, the Chief Justice of the Supreme Court,

(ii) the Provinces of Nova Scotia and Newfoundland, respectively, the Chief Justice of the Supreme Court, Trial Division,

(iii) the Provinces of Saskatchewan, Manitoba, Alberta and New Brunswick, respectively, the Chief Justice of the Court of Queen's Bench,

(iv) Repealed. 1978-79, c. 11, s. 10, I. 6(13).

(v) in the Province of Ontario, the Chief Justice of the High Court of Justice, and

(vi) the Province of Quebec, the Chief Justice of the Superior Court;

(b) in relation to the Yukon Territory, the Chief Justice of the Court of Appeal thereof, and

(c) in relation to the Northwest Territories, the Chief Justice of the Court of Appeal thereof.

Territories

(7) For the purposes of this section, when the appropriate Chief Justice is designating a judge of the superior court of criminal jurisdiction to empanel a jury to hear an application in respect of a conviction that took place in the Yukon Territory or the Northwest Territories, the appropriate Chief Justice may designate the judge from the Court of Appeal or the Supreme Court of the Yukon Territory or Northwest Territories, as the case may be.

Time spent in custody

673. In calculating the period of imprisonment served for the purposes of section 669, 671 or 672, there shall be included any time spent in custody between,

(a) in the case of a sentence of imprisonment for life imposed after the commencement of the *Criminal Law Amendment Act (No. 2), 1976*, the day on which that person was arrested and taken into custody in respect of the offence for which he was sentenced to imprisonment for life and the day the sentence was imposed; or

(b) in the case of a sentence of death that has been or is deemed to have been commuted to a sentence of imprisonment for life, the day on which that person was arrested and taken into custody in respect of the offence for which he was sentenced to death and the day the sentence was commuted or deemed to have been commuted to a sentence of imprisonment for life.

Parole prohibited

674. (1) Unless the Parliament of Canada otherwise provides by an enactment making express reference to this section, no person who has been sentenced to imprisonment for life without eligibility for parole for a specified number of years pursuant to this Act shall be considered for parole or released pursuant to the terms of a grant of parole under the *Parole Act* or any other Act of the Parliament of Canada until the expiration or termination of his specified number of years of imprisonment without eligibility for parole.

Temporary absence or day parole

(2) Notwithstanding the *Penitentiary Act* and the *Parole Act*, in the case of any person sentenced to imprisonment for life without eligibility for parole for a specified number of years pursuant to this Act, until the expiration of all but three years of his number of years of imprisonment without eligibility for parole, no absence without escort may be authorized under the *Penitentiary Act*, no absence with escort for humanitarian and rehabilitative reasons may be authorized under the *Penitentiary Act* without the approval of the National Parole Board and no day parole may be granted under the *Parole Act*.

675—681. Repealed. 1974-75-76, c. 105, s. 21.

Disabilities

Public office vacated on conviction

682. (1) Where a person is convicted of an indictable offence for which he is sentenced to imprisonment for a term exceeding five years and holds, at the time he is convicted, an office under the Crown or other public employment, the office or employment forthwith becomes vacant. 1974-75-76, c. 105, s. 22.

When disability ceases

(2) A person to whom subsection (1) applies is, until he undergoes the punishment imposed upon him or the punishment substituted therefor by competent authority or receives a free pardon from Her Majesty, incapable of holding any office under the Crown or other public employment, or of being elected or sitting or voting as a member of the Parliament of Canada or of a legislature or of exercising any right of suffrage.

Disability to contract

(3) No person who is convicted of an offence under section 110, 113 or 376 has, after that conviction, capacity to contract with Her Majesty or to receive any benefit under a contract between Her Majesty and any other person or to hold office under Her Majesty.

Application for restoration of privileges

(3.1) A person to whom subsection (3) applies may, at any time before a pardon is granted to him under section 4 of the *Criminal Records Act*, apply to the Governor in Council for the restoration of one or more of the capacities lost by him by virtue of that subsection. 28 Interp

Order of restoration

(3.2) Where an application is made under subsection (3.1), the Governor in Council may order that the capacities lost by the applicant by virtue of subsection (3) be restored to him in whole or in part and subject to such conditions as he considers desirable in the public interest. 1974-75-76, c. 93, s. 83.

Removal of disability

(4) Where a conviction is set aside by competent authority any disability imposed by this section is removed. 1953-54, c. 51, s. 654.

Interpretation Act

28. In every enactment

"Governor in Council", or "Governor General in Council" means the Governor General of Canada, or person administering the Government of Canada for the time being, acting by and with the advice of, or by and with the advice and consent of, or in conjunction with the Queen's Privy Council for Canada;

Pardon

To whom pardon may be granted

683. (1) Her Majesty may extend the royal mercy to a person who is sentenced to imprisonment under the authority of an Act of the Parliament of Canada, even if the person is imprisoned for failure to pay money to another person.

Free or conditional pardon

(2) The Governor in Council may grant a free pardon or a conditional pardon to any person who has been convicted of an offence. 28 Interp

Effect of free pardon

(3) Where the Governor in Council grants a free pardon to a person, that person shall be deemed thereafter never to have committed the offence in respect of which the pardon is granted.

Punishment for subsequent offence not affected

(4) No free pardon or conditional pardon prevents or mitigates the punishment to which the person might otherwise be lawfully sentenced on a subsequent conviction for an offence other than that for which the pardon was granted. 1953-54, c. 51, s. 655.

684. Repealed. 1974-75-76, c. 105, s. 23.

Remission by Governor in Council

685. (1) The Governor in Council may order the remission, in whole or in part, of a pecuniary penalty, fine or forfeiture imposed under an Act of the Parliament of Canada, whoever the person may be to whom it is payable or however it may be recoverable.

Terms of remission

(2) An order for remission under subsection (1) may include the remission of costs incurred in the proceedings, but no costs to which a private prosecutor is entitled shall be remitted. 1953-54, c. 51, s. 657.

Royal prerogative

686. Nothing in this Act in any manner limits or affects Her Majesty's royal prerogative of mercy. 1953-54, c. 51, s. 658.

Interpretation Act

28. In every enactment

"Governor in Council", or "Governor General in Council" means the Governor General of Canada, or person administering the Government of Canada for the time being, acting by and with the advice of, or by and with the advice and consent of, or in conjunction with the Queen's Privy Council for Canada;

PART XXI

DANGEROUS OFFENDERS

Interpretation

Definitions

687. In this Part,

"court"

"court" means the court by which an offender in relation to whom an application under this Part is made was convicted, or a superior court of criminal jurisdiction; 2

"serious personal injury offence"

"serious personal injury offence" means

(a) an indictable offence (other than high treason, treason, first degree murder or second degree murder) involving

(i) the use or attempted use of violence against another person, or

(ii) conduct endangering or likely to endanger the life or safety of another person or inflicting or likely to inflict severe psychological damage upon another person,

and for which the offender may be sentenced to imprisonment for ten years or more, or

(b) an offence mentioned in section 144 (rape) or 145 (attempted rape) or an offence or attempt to commit an offence mentioned in section 146 (sexual intercourse with a female under fourteen or between fourteen and sixteen), 149 (indecent assault on a female), 156 (indecent assault on a male) or 157 (gross indecency). 1976-77, c. 53, s. 14.

Dangerous Offenders

Application for finding

688. Where, upon an application made under this Part following the conviction of a person for an offence but before the offender is sentenced therefor, it is established to the satisfaction of the court 687

(a) that the offence for which the offender has been convicted is a serious personal injury offence described in paragraph *(a)* of the definition of that expression in section 687 and the offender constitutes a threat to the life, safety or physical or mental well-being of other persons on the basis of evidence establishing

(i) a pattern of repetitive behaviour by the offender, of which the offence for which he has been convicted forms a part, showing a failure to restrain his behaviour and a likelihood of his causing death or injury to other persons, or inflicting severe psychological damage upon other persons, through failure in the future to restrain his behaviour,

(ii) a pattern of persistent aggressive behaviour by the offender, of which the offence for which he has been convicted forms a part, showing a substantial degree of indifference on the part of the offender as to the reasonably foreseeable consequences to other persons of his behaviour, or

(iii) any behaviour by the offender, associated with the offence for which he has been convicted, that is of such a brutal nature as to compel the conclusion that his behaviour in the future is unlikely to be inhibited by normal standards of behavioural restraint, or

(b) that the offence for which the offender has been convicted is a serious personal injury offence described in paragraph *(b)* of the definition of that expression in section 687 and the offender, by his conduct in any sexual matter including that involved in the commission of the offence for which he has been convicted, has shown a failure to control his sexual impulses and a likelihood of his causing injury, pain or other evil to other persons through failure in the future to control his sexual impulses,

the court may find the offender to be a dangerous offender and may thereupon impose a sentence of detention in a penitentiary for an indeterminate period, in lieu of any other sentence that might be imposed for the offence for which the offender has been convicted.

Hearing of application

689. (1) Where an application under this Part has been made, the Court shall hear and determine the application except that no such application shall be heard unless 687

(a) the Attorney General of the province in which the offender was tried has, either before or after the making of the application, consented to the application; 2

(b) at least seven days notice has been given to the offender by the prosecutor, following the making of the application, outlining the basis on which it is intended to found the application; and

(c) a copy of the notice has been filed with the clerk of the court or the 2
magistrate, as the case may be. 2

By court alone

(2) An application under this Part shall be heard and determined by the court without a jury.

When proof unnecessary

(3) For the purposes of an application under this Part, where an offender admits any allegations contained in the notice referred to in paragraph (1)*(b)*, no proof of those allegations is required.

Proof of consent

(4) The production of a document purporting to contain any nomination or consent that may be made or given by the Attorney General under this Part and purporting to be signed by the Attorney General is, in the absence of any evidence to the contrary, proof of that nomination or consent without proof of the signature or the official character of the person appearing to have signed the document.

Evidence of dangerous offender status

690. (1) On the hearing of an application under this Part, the court shall hear the evidence of at least two psychiatrists and all other evidence that, in its opinion, is relevant, including the evidence of any psychologist or criminologist called as a witness by the prosecution or the offender.

Nomination of psychiatrists

(2) One of the psychiatrists referred to in subsection (1) shall be nominated by the prosecution and one shall be nominated by the offender.

Nomination by court

(3) If the offender fails or refuses to nominate a psychiatrist pursuant to this section, the court shall nominate a psychiatrist on behalf of the offender.

Saving

(4) Nothing in this section shall be construed to enlarge the number of expert witnesses that may be called without the leave of the court or judge under section 7 of the *Canada Evidence Act.*

Direction or remand for observation

691. (1) A court to which an application is made under this Part may, by order in writing, 687

(a) direct the offender in relation to whom the application is made to attend, at a place or before a person specified in the order and within a time specified therein, for observation, or

(b) remand the offender in such custody as the court directs, for a period not exceeding thirty days, for observation,

where in its opinion, supported by the evidence of, or where the prosecutor and the offender consent, supported by the report in writing of, at least one duly qualified medical practitioner, there is reason to believe that evidence might be obtained as a result of such observation that would be relevant to the application.

Idem

(2) Notwithstanding subsection (1), a court to which an application is made under this Part may remand the offender to which that application relates in accordance with that subsection

(a) for a period not exceeding thirty days without having heard the evidence or considered the report of a duly qualified medical practitioner where compelling circumstances exist for so doing and where a medical practitioner is not readily available to examine the offender and give evidence or submit a report; and

(*b*) for a period of more than thirty but not more than sixty days where it is satisfied that observation for such a period is required in all the circumstances of the case and its opinion is supported by the evidence of, or where the prosecutor and the offender consent, by the report in writing of, at least one duly qualified medical practitioner.

Evidence of character

692. Without prejudice to the right of the offender to tender evidence as to his character and repute, evidence of character and repute may, if the court thinks fit, be admitted on the question whether the offender is or is not a dangerous offender.

Presence of accused at hearing of application

693. (1) The offender shall be present at the hearing of the application under this Part and if at the time the application is to be heard

(*a*) he is confined in a prison, the court may order, in writing, the person having the custody of the accused to bring him before the court; or

(*b*) he is not confined in a prison, the court shall issue a summons or a warrant to compel the accused to attend before the court and the provisions of Part XIV relating to summons and warrant are applicable *mutatis mutandis.*

Exception

(2) Notwithstanding subsection (1), the court may 687

(*a*) cause the offender to be removed and to be kept out of court, where he misconducts himself by interrupting the proceedings so that to continue the proceedings in his presence would not be feasible; or

(*b*) permit the offender to be out of court during the whole or any part of the hearing on such conditions as the court considers proper.

Appeal

694. (1) A person who is sentenced to detention in a penitentiary for an indeterminate period under this part may appeal to the court of appeal against that sentence on any ground of law or fact or mixed law and fact.

Appeal by Attorney General

(2) The Attorney General may appeal to the court of appeal against the dismissal of an application for an order under this Part on any ground of law.

Disposition of appeal

(3) On an appeal against a sentence of detention in a penitentiary for an indeterminate period the court of appeal may 2

(*a*) quash such sentence and impose any sentence that might have been imposed in respect of the offence for which the appellant was convicted, or order a new hearing; or

(*b*) dismiss the appeal.

Idem

(4) On an appeal against the dismissal of an application for an order under this Part the court of appeal may

(*a*) allow the appeal, set aside any sentence imposed in respect of the offence for which the respondent was convicted and impose a sentence of detention in a penitentiary for an indeterminate period, or order a new hearing; or

(*b*) dismiss the appeal.

Effect of judgment

(5) A judgment of the court of appeal imposing a sentence pursuant to this section has the same force and effect as if it were a sentence passed by the trial court.

Commencement of sentence

(6) Notwithstanding subsection 649(1), a sentence imposed on an offender by the court of appeal pursuant to this section shall be deemed to have commenced when the offender was sentenced by the court by which he was convicted.

Part XVIII applies re appeals

(7) The provisions of Part XVIII with respect to procedure on appeals apply, *mutatis mutandis*, to appeals under this section.

Disclosure to Solicitor General

695. Where a court, pursuant to section 688, finds an offender to be a dangerous offender and imposes a sentence of detention in a penitentiary for an indeterminate period, the court shall order that a copy of all reports or testimony given by psychiatrists, psychologists or criminologists and any observations of the court with respect to the reasons for the sentence, together with a transcript of the trial of the dangerous offender be forwarded to the Solicitor General of Canada for his information. 687

Review for parole

695.1 (1) Subject to subsection (2), where a person is in custody under a sentence of detention in a penitentiary for an indeterminate period, the National Parole Board shall, forthwith after the expiration of three years from the day on which that person was taken into custody and not later than every two years thereafter, review the condition, history and circumstances of that person for the purpose of determining whether he should be granted parole under the *Parole Act* and, if so, on what conditions.

Idem

(2) Where a person is in custody under a sentence of detention in a penitentiary for an indeterminate period that was imposed before the *Criminal Law Amendment Act, 1977* came into force, the National Parole Board shall, at least once in every year, review the condition, history and circumstances of that person for the purpose of determining whether he should be granted parole under the *Parole Act* and, if so, on what conditions. 1976-77,c.35,s.14.

Criminal Law Amendment Act, 1977

15. (1) Where, on the day that section 14 comes into force, an application is pending before a court under Part XXI of the *Criminal Code* for the preventive detention of a dangerous sexual offender or an habitual criminal within the meaning of that Part as it read immediately before that day, all proceedings thereon shall be continued and disposed of in all respects as if section 14 had not been enacted.

(2) Sections 693 to 695 of the *Criminal Code,* as enacted by section 14 apply to a person who, before the coming into force of that section, was sentenced to preventive detention under Part XXI of the *Criminal Code* as if the references in those sections to "a sentence of detention in a penitentiary for an indeterminate period" were references to "a sentence of preventive detention". 1976,c.35,s.15.

2.1 Where, in any provision of this Act, a reference to another provision of this Act or a provision of any other Act is followed by words in parenthesis that are or purport to be descriptive of the subject-matter of the provision referred to, the words in parenthesis form no part of the provision in which they occur but shall be deemed to have been inserted for convenience of reference only.

PART XXII

EFFECT AND ENFORCEMENT OF RECOGNIZANCES

Applications for forfeiture of recognizances

696. (1) Applications for the forfeiture of recognizances shall be made to the courts, designated in column II of the schedule, of the respective provinces ss (2)
designated in column I of the schedule.

Definitions

(2) In this Part

"clerk of the court"

"clerk of the court" means the officer designated in column III of the schedule in respect of the court designated in column II of the schedule;

"schedule"

"schedule" means the schedule to this Part. 1953-54,c.51,s.668.

Recognizance binding

697. Where a person is bound by recognizance to appear before a court, justice or magistrate for any purpose and the session or sittings of that court or 2
the proceedings are adjourned or an order is made changing the place of trial, that person and his sureties continue to be bound by the recognizance in like 28 Interp
manner as if it had been entered into with relation to the resumed proceedings or the trial at the time and place at which the proceedings are ordered to be resumed or the trial is ordered to be held. 1953-54,c.51,s.669.

Responsibility of sureties

698. (1) Where an accused is bound by recognizance to appear for trial, his arraignment or conviction does not discharge the recognizance, but it continues to bind him and his sureties, if any, for his appearance until he is discharged or sentenced, as the case may be.

Committal or new sureties

(2) Notwithstanding subsection (1), the court, justice or magistrate may commit an accused to prison or may require him to furnish new or additional sureties for his appearance until he is discharged or sentenced, as the case may be.

Effect of committal

(3) The sureties of an accused who is bound by recognizance to appear for trial are discharged if he is committed to prison pursuant to subsection (2).

Endorsement on recognizance

(4) The provisions of section 697 and subsections (1), (2) and (3) of this section shall be endorsed on any recognizance entered into pursuant to this Act. 1953-54,c.51,s.670.

Effect of subsequent arrest

699. Where an accused is bound by recognizance to appear for trial, his arrest upon another charge does not vacate the recognizance, but it continues to bind him and his sureties, if any, for his appearance until he is discharged or sentenced, as the case may be, in respect of the offence to which the recognizance relates. 1953-54,c.51,s.671.

Render of accused by sureties

700. (1) A surety for a person who is bound by recognizance to appear may, by an application in writing to a court, justice or magistrate apply to be relieved of his obligation under the recognizance, and the court, justice or magistrate shall thereupon issue an order in writing for committal of that person to the prison nearest to the place where he was, under the recognizance, bound to appear.

Arrest

(2) An order under subsection (1) shall be given to the surety and upon receipt thereof he or any peace officer may arrest the person named in the order and deliver him with the order to the keeper of the prison named therein, and the keeper shall receive and imprison him until he is discharged according to law.

Certificate and entry of render

(3) Where a judge, justice or magistrate who issues an order under subsection (1) receives from the sheriff a certificate that the person named in the order has been committed to prison pursuant to subsection (2), he shall order an entry of the committal to be endorsed on the recognizance.

Discharge of sureties

(4) An endorsement under subsection (3) vacates the recognizance and discharges the sureties. 1953-54,c.51,s.672.

Render of accused in court by sureties

701. A surety for a person who is bound by recognizance to appear may bring that person into the court at which he is required to appear at any time during the sittings thereof and before his trial and the surety may discharge his obligation under the recognizance by giving that person into the custody of the court, and the court shall thereupon commit that person to prison until he is discharged according to law. 1953-54,c.51,s.673.

Rights of surety preserved

702. Nothing is this Part limits or restricts any right that a surety has of taking and giving into custody any person for whom, under a recognizance, he is a surety. 1953-54,c.51,s.674.

Application of judicial interim release provisions

703. Where a surety for a person has rendered him into custody and that person has been committed to prison, the provisions of Parts XIV, XVIII and XXIV relating to judicial interim release apply, *mutatis mutandis*, in respect of him and he shall forthwith be taken before a justice or judge as an accused charged with an offence or as an appellant, as the case may be, for the purposes of those provisions. R.S.,c. C-34,s.703; R.S.,c.2(2nd Supp.),s.14.

Default to be endorsed

704. (1) Where, in proceedings to which this Act applies, a person who is bound by recognizance does not comply with a condition of the recognizance, a court, justice or magistrate having knowledge of the facts shall endorse or cause to be endorsed on the back of the recognizance a certificate in Form 29 setting out

(a) the nature of the default,

(b) the reason for the default, if it is known,

(c) whether the ends of justice have been defeated or delayed by reason of the default, and

(d) the names and addresses of the principal and sureties.

Transmission to clerk of court

(2) A recognizance that has been endorsed pursuant to subsection (1) shall be sent to the clerk of the court and shall be kept by him with the records of the court. 696

Certificate is evidence

(3) A certificate that has been endorsed on a recognizance pursuant to subsection (1) is evidence of the default to which it relates.

Transmission of deposit

(4) Where, in proceedings to which this section applies, the principal or surety has deposited money as security for the performance of a condition of a recognizance, that money shall be sent to the clerk of the court with the defaulted recognizance, to be dealt with in accordance with this Part. 1953-54, c.51,s.676; 1968-69,c.38,s.92.

Proceedings in case of default

705. (1) Where a recognizance has been endorsed with a certificate pursuant to section 704 and has been received by the clerk of the court pursuant to that section,

(a) a judge of the court shall, upon the request of the clerk of the court or the Attorney General or counsel acting on his behalf, fix a time and place for the hearing of an application for the forfeiture of the recognizance, and 707(5)

(b) the clerk of the court shall, not less than ten days before the time fixed under paragraph *(a)* for the hearing, send by registered mail to each principal and surety named in the recognizance, directed to him at the address set out in the certificate, a notice requiring him to appear at the time and place fixed by the judge to show cause why the recognizance should not be forfeited.

Order of judge

(2) Where subsection (1) has been complied with, the judge may, after giving the parties an opportunity to be heard, in his discretion grant or refuse the application and make any order with respect to the forfeiture of the recognizance that he considers proper.

Fieri facias to issue

(3) Where, pursuant to subsection (2), the judge orders forfeiture of a recognizance, the principal and his sureties become judgment debtors of the Crown, each in the amount that he has pledged himself to pay, and the clerk of the court or, in the Province of Quebec, the prothonotary, shall issue a writ of *fieri facias* in Form 30 and deliver it to the sheriff of each of the territorial divisions in which any of the principal and his sureties resides, carries on business or has property.

Transfer of deposit

(4) Where a deposit has been made by a person against whom an order for forfeiture of a recognizance has been made, no writ of *fieri facias* shall issue, but the amount of the deposit shall be transferred by the person who has custody of it to the person who is entitled by law to receive it. R.S.,c. C-34,s.705; 1972, c.13,s.60.

Levy under writ

706. (1) Where a writ of *fieri facias* is issued pursuant to section 705, the sheriff to whom it is delivered shall execute the writ and deal with the proceeds thereof in the same manner in which he is authorized to execute and deal with the proceeds of writs of *fieri facias* issued out of superior courts in the province in civil proceedings.

Costs

(2) Where this section applies the Crown is entitled to the costs of execution and of proceedings incidental thereto that are fixed, in the Province of Quebec, by any tariff applicable in the Superior Court in civil proceedings, and in any other province, by any tariff applicable in the superior court of the province in civil proceedings, as the judge may direct. 1953-54,c.51,s.678.

Committal when writ not satisfied

707. (1) Where a writ of *fieri facias* has been issued under this Part and it appears from a certificate in a return made by the sheriff that sufficient goods and chattels, lands and tenements cannot be found to satisfy the writ, or that the proceeds of the execution of the writ are not sufficient to satisfy it, a judge of the court may, upon the application of the Attorney General or counsel acting on his behalf, fix a time and place for the sureties to show cause why a warrant of committal should not be issued in respect of them.

Notice

(2) Seven clear days notice of the time and place fixed for the hearing pursuant to subsection (1) shall be given to the sureties. 25(2) Interp

Hearing

(3) The judge shall, at the hearing referred to in subsection (1), inquire into the circumstances of the case and may in his discretion

(a) order the discharge of the amount for which the surety is liable, or

(b) make any order with respect to the surety and to his imprisonment that he considers proper in the circumstances and issue a warrant of committal in Form 24.

Warrant of committal

(4) A warrant of committal issued pursuant to this section authorizes the sheriff to take into custody the person in respect of whom the warrant was issued and to confine him in a prison in the territorial division in which the writ was issued or in the prison nearest to the court, until satisfaction is made or until the period of imprisonment fixed by the judge has expired.

"Attorney General"

(5) In this section and in section 705, "Attorney General" means, where subsection 651(2) applies, the Attorney General of Canada. 1953-54,c.51,s.679.

651. (2) Where

(a) a fine, penalty or forfeiture is imposed

(i) in respect of a violation of a revenue law of Canada,

(ii) in respect of a breach of duty or malfeasance in office by an officer or employee of the Government of Canada, or

(iii) in respect of any proceedings instituted at the instance of the Government of Canada in which that government bears the costs of prosecution; or

(b) a recognizance in connection with proceedings mentioned in paragraph *(a)* is forfeited,

the proceeds of the fine, penalty, forfeiture or recognizance belong to Her Majesty in right of Canda and shall be paid by the person who receives them to the Receiver General.

SCHEDULE

Column I	Column II	Column III
Ontario	The Supreme Court, in respect of a recognizance for the appearance of a person before that court.	The Registrar or Local Registra of the Supreme Court
	A judge of the Court of Appeal in respect of a recognizance for the appearance of a person before that court.	The Registrar of the Suprem Court
	A court of the General Sessions of the Peace in respect of a recognizance for the appearance of a person before that court, a judge acting under Part XVI, a justice or a magistrate.	Clerk of the Peace
Quebec	The Superior Court, exercising civil jurisdiction.	The Clerk of the Peace
Nova Scotia	A judge of the Supreme Court in respect of a recognizance for the appearance of a person before the Appeal Division.	The Prothonotary at Halifax
	A judge of the County Court in respect of a recognizance for the appearance of a person before a judge of the Supreme Court, a judge of the County Court, a judge acting under Part XVI, a justice or a magistrate.	The Clerk of the County Cour
New Brunswick	The Court of Queen's Bench	The Registrar of the Court o Queen's Bench
Manitoba	The Court of Queen's Bench	The Clerk or Deputy Clerk o the Crown and Pleas
British Columbia	The Supreme Court in respect of a recognizance for the appearance of a person before that court or the Court of Appeal.	The District Registrar of th Supreme Court
	A County Court in respect of a recognizance for the appearance of a person before that court or a judge acting under Part XVI.	The Clerk of the County Cour
	A Provincial Court in respect of a recognizance for the appearance of a person before a judge of that court or a justice.	The Clerk of the Provinci Court
Prince Edward Island	The Supreme Court	The Prothonotary
Saskatchewan	The Court of Queen's Bench	The Local Registrar of the Cour of Queen's Bench
Alberta	The Court of Queen's Bench	The Clerk of the Court of Queen' Bench
Newfoundland	The Supreme Court	The Registrar of the Suprem Court
Yukon Territory	The Supreme Court	The Clerk of the Court
Northwest Territories	The Supreme Court	The Clerk of the Court

R.S., c. C-34, Schedule to Part XXII; 1972, c. 17, s. 3; 1974-75-76, c. 93, s. 84; 1978-79, c. 11, s. 10.

PART XXIII

EXTRAORDINARY REMEDIES

Application of Part

708. This Part applies to proceedings in criminal matters by way of *certiorari*, *habeas corpus*, *mandamus* and prohibition. 1953-54,c.51,s.680.

Detention on inquiry to determine legality of imprisonment

709. Where proceedings to which this Part applies have been instituted before a judge or court having jurisdiction, by or in respect of a person who is in custody by reason that he is charged with or has been convicted of an offence, to have the legality of his imprisonment determined, the judge or court may, without determining the question, make an order for the further detention of that person and direct the judge, justice or magistrate under whose warrant he is in custody, or any other judge, justice or magistrate to take any proceedings, hear such evidence or do any other thing that, in the opinion of the judge or court, will best further the ends of justice. 1968-69,c.38,s.81.

Where conviction or order not reviewable

710. No conviction or order shall be removed by *certiorari*

(a) where an appeal was taken, whether or not the appeal has been carried to a conclusion, or

(b) where the defendant appeared and pleaded and the merits were tried, and an appeal might have been taken, but the defendant did not appeal. 1953-54, c.51,s.682.

Conviction or order remediable, when

711. (1) No conviction, order or warrant for enforcing a conviction or order shall, on being removed by *certiorari*, be held to be invalid by reason of any irregularity, informality or insufficiency therein, where the court before which or the judge before whom the question is raised, upon perusal of the evidence, is satisfied

(a) that an offence of the nature described in the conviction, order or warrant, as the case may be, was committed,

(b) that there was jurisdiction to make the conviction or order or issue the the warrant, as the case may be, and

(c) that the punishment imposed, if any, was not in excess of the punishment that might lawfully have been imposed,

but the court or judge has the same powers to deal with the proceedings in the manner that he considers proper that are conferred upon a court to which an appeal might have been taken.

Correcting punishment

(2) Where, in proceedings to which subsection (1) applies, the court or judge is satisfied that a person was properly convicted of an offence but the punishment that was imposed is greater than the punishment that might lawfully have been imposed, the court or judge

(a) shall correct the sentence,

(i) where the punishment is a fine, by imposing a fine that does not exceed the maximum fine that might lawfully have been imposed,

(ii) where the punishment is imprisonment, and the person has not served a term of imprisonment under the sentence that is equal to or greater than the term of imprisonment that might lawfully have been imposed, by imposing a term of imprisonment that does not exceed the maximum term of imprisonment that might lawfully have been imposed, or

(iii) where the punishment is a fine and imprisonment, by imposing a punishment in accordance with subparagraph (i) or (ii), as the case requires, or

(b) shall remit the matter to the judge, justice or magistrate and direct him to impose a punishment that is not greater than the punishment that may be lawfully imposed.

Amendment

(3) Where an adjudication is varied pursuant to subsection (1) or (2), the conviction and warrant of committal, if any, shall be amended to conform with the adjudication as varied.

Sufficiency of statement

(4) Any statement that appears in a conviction and is sufficient for the purpose of the conviction is sufficient for the purposes of an information, summons, order or warrant in which it appears in the proceedings. 1953-54, c.51,s.683.

Irregularities within section 711

712. Without restricting the generality of section 711, that section shall be deemed to apply where

(a) the statement of the adjudication or of any other matter or thing is in the past tense instead of in the present tense,

(b) the punishment imposed is less than the punishment that might by law have been imposed for the offence that appears by the evidence to have been committed, or

(c) there has been an omission to negative circumstances, the existence of which would make the act complained of lawful, whether those circumstances are stated by way of exception or otherwise in the provision under which the offence is charged, or are stated in another provision. 1953-54,c.51,s.684.

General order for security by recognizance

713. (1) A court that has authority to quash a conviction, order or other proceeding on *certiorari* may prescribe by general order that no motion to quash any such conviction, order or other proceeding removed to the court by *certiorari,* shall be heard unless the defendant has entered into a recognizance with one or more sufficient sureties, before one or more justices of the territorial division in which the conviction or order was made, or before a judge or other officer, or has made a deposit to be prescribed with a condition that the defendant will prosecute the writ of *certiorari* at his own expense, without wilful delay, and, if ordered, will pay to the person in whose favour the conviction, order or other proceeding is affirmed, his full costs and charges to be taxed according to the practice of the court where the conviction, order or proceeding is affirmed.

Provisions of Part XXII

(2) The provisions of Part XXII relating to forfeiture of recognizances apply to a recognizance entered into under this section. 1953-54,c.51,s.685.

Effect of order dismissing application to quash

714. Where a motion to quash a conviction, order or other proceeding is refused, the order of the court refusing the application is sufficient authority for the clerk of the court forthwith to return the conviction, order or proceeding 2
to the court from which or the person from whom it was removed, and for proceedings to be taken with respect thereto for the enforcement thereof. 1953-54,c.51,s.686.

Want of proof of order in council

715. (1) No order, conviction or other proceeding shall be quashed or set aside, and no defendant shall be discharged, by reason only that evidence has not been given

(a) of a proclamation or order of the Governor in Council or the lieutenant governor in council; 28 Interp

(b) of rules, regulations or by-laws, made by the Governor in Council under an Act of the Parliament of Canada or by the lieutenant governor in council under an Act of the legislatue of the province; or

(c) of the publication of a proclamation, order, rule, regulation or by-law in the *Canada Gazette* or in the official gazette for the province.

Judicial notice

(2) Proclamations, orders, rules, regulations and by-laws mentioned in subsection (1) and the publication thereof shall be judicially noticed. 1953-54, c.51,s.687. 17 CEA

Defect in form

716. No warrant of committal shall, on *certiorari* or *habeas corpus*, be held to be void by reason only of any defect therein, where

(a) it is alleged in the warrant that the defendant was convicted, and

(b) there is a valid conviction to sustain the warrant. 1953-54,c.51,s.688.

No action against official when conviction, etc., quashed

717. Where an application is made to quash a conviction, order or other proceeding made or held by a magistrate acting under Part XVI or a justice on the ground that he exceeded his jurisdiction, the court to which or the judge to whom the application is made may in quashing the conviction, order or other proceeding, order that no civil proceedings shall be taken against the justice or magistrate or against any officer who acted under the conviction, order or other proceeding or under any warrant issued to enforce it. 1953-54,c.51,s.689.

718. Repealed. R.S., c.44(1st Supp.), s.10.

Appeal in *mandamus*, etc.

719. (1) An appeal lies to the court of appeal from a decision granting 2
or refusing the relief sought in proceedings by way of *mandamus*, *certiorari* or prohibition.

Application of Part XVIII

(2) Except as hereinafter in this section provided, the provisions of Part XVIII apply, *mutatis mutandis*, to appeals under this section.

Refusal of application, and appeal

(3) Where an application for a writ of *habeas corpus ad subjiciendum* is refused by a judge of a court having jurisdiction therein, no application may again be made on the same grounds whether to the same or to another court or judge, unless fresh evidence is adduced, but an appeal from such refusal shall lie to the court of appeal, and where on such appeal the application is refused a further appeal shall lie to the Supreme Court of Canada.

Where writ granted

(4) Where a writ of *habeas corpus ad subjiciendum* is granted by any judge no appeal therefrom shall lie at the instance of any party including the Attorney General of the province concerned or the Attorney General of Canada.

Appeal from judgment on return of writ

(5) Where a judgment is issued on the return of a writ of *habeas corpus ad subjiciendum*, an appeal therefrom lies to the court of appeal, and from a judgment of the court of appeal to the Supreme Court of Canada, with the leave of that court, at the instance of the applicant or the Attorney General of the province concerned or the Attorney General of Canada, but not at the instance of any other party.

Hearing of appeal

(6) An appeal in *habeas corpus* matters shall be heard by the court to which the appeal is directed at an early date, whether in or out of the prescribed sessions of the court. 1953-54,c.51,s.691; 1964-65,c.53,s.1.

--NOTES—

PART XXIV

SUMMARY CONVICTIONS

Interpretation

Definitions **720.** (1) In this Part

"informant" "informant" means a person who lays an information;

"information" "information" includes

(*a*) a count in an information, and 2

(*b*) a complaint in respect of which a justice is authorized by an Act of the 2
Parliament of Canada or an enactment made thereunder to make an order;

"order" "order" means any order, including an order for the payment of money;

"proceedings" "proceedings" means

(*a*) proceedings in respect of offences that are declared by an Act of the Parliament of Canada or an enactment made thereunder to be punishable on summary conviction, and

(*b*) proceedings where a justice is authorized by an Act of the Parliament of Canada or an enactment made thereunder to make an order;

"prosecutor" "prosecutor" means an informant or the Attorney General or their respective counsel or agents;

"sentence" "sentence" includes an order made under subsection 98(1) or (2) or a disposition made under subsection 234(2), 236(2), 662.1(1), 663(1) or 664(3) or (4);

"summary conviction court" "summary conviction court" means a person who has jurisdiction in the
territorial division where the subject-matter of the proceedings is alleged to 2
have arisen and who

(*a*) is given jurisdiction over the proceedings by the enactment under which the proceedings are taken,

(*b*) is a justice or magistrate, where the enactment under which the 2
proceedings are taken does not expressly give jurisdiction to any person or class of persons, or

(*c*) is a magistrate, where the enactment under which the proceedings are taken gives jurisdiction in respect thereof to two or more justices;

"trial" "trial" includes the hearing of a complaint.

"Clerk of the appeal court" (2) For the purposes of this Part, the expression "clerk of the appeal court" includes a local clerk of the appeal court. R.S., c. C-34, s. 720; 1972, c. 13, s. 61; 1974-75-76, c. 93, s. 85; 1976-77, c. 53, s. 4(1).

2. In this Act

"Attorney General" means the Attorney General or Solicitor General of a province in which proceedings to which this Act applies are taken and, with respect to

(*a*) the Northwest Territories and the Yukon Territory, and

(*b*) proceedings instituted at the instance of the Government of Canada and conducted by or on behalf of that Government in respect of a violation of or conspiracy to violate any Act of the Parliament of Canada or a regulation made thereunder other than this Act,

means the Attorney General of Canada and, except for the purposes of subsections 505(4) and 507(3), includes the lawful deputy of the said Attorney General, Solicitor General and Attorney General of Canada;

"counsel" means a barrister or solicitor, in respect of the matters or things that barristers and solicitors, respectively, are authorized by the law of the province to do or perform in relation to legal proceedings;

"count" means a charge in an information or indictment;

"justice" means a justice of the peace or a magistrate, and includes two or more justices where two or more justices are, by law, required to act or, by law, act or have jurisdiction;

"magistrate" means a magistrate, a police magistrate, a stipendiary magistrate, a district magistrate, a provincial magistrate, a judge of the sessions of the peace, a recorder, or any person having the power and authority of two or more justices of the peace, and includes

(a) with respect to the Provinces of Ontario, Quebec, New Brunswick and British Columbia, a judge of the provincial court,

(a.1) with respect to the Provinces of Alberta, Manitoba and Prince Edward Island, a provincial judge,

(a.2) with respect to the Province of Nova Scotia, a judge of the Provincial Magistrate's Court,

(b) with respect to the Province of Saskatchewan, a judge of the Magistrates' Courts, and;

(c) with respect to the Yukon Territory and the Northwest Territories, a judge of the Supreme Court,

and the lawful deputy of each of them;

Application of part

721. (1) Except where otherwise provided by law, this Part applies to proceedings as defined in this Part. 720

Limitation

(2) No proceedings shall be instituted more than six months after the time when the subject-matter of the proceedings arose. 1953-54, c. 51, s. 693.

Interpretation Act

25. (1) Where the time limited for the doing of a thing expires or falls upon a holiday, the thing may be done on the day next following that is not a holiday.

(7) Where there is a reference to a period of time consisting of a number of months after or before a specified day, the number of months shall be counted from, but not so as to include, the month in which the specified day falls, and the period shall be reckoned as being limited by and including

(a) the day immediately after or before the specified day, according as the period follows or precedes the specified day; and

(b) the day in the last month so counted having the same calendar number as the specified day, but if such last month has no day with the same calendar number, then the last day of that month.

Punishment

General penalty

722. (1) Except where otherwise expressly provided by law, every one who is convicted of an offence punishable on summary conviction is liable to a fine of not more than five hundred dollars or to imprisonment for six months or to both. ss. 11

647. Notwithstanding subsection 646(2), a corporation that is convicted of an offence is liable, in lieu of any imprisonment that is prescribed as punishment for that offence,

(a) to be fined in an amount that is in the discretion of the court, where the offence is an indictable offence, or

(b) to be fined in an amount not exceeding one thousand dollars, where the offence is a summary conviction offence.

Imprisonment in default where not otherwise specified

(2) Where the imposition of a fine or the making of an order for the payment of money is authorized by law, but the law does not provide that imprisonment may be imposed in default of payment of the fine or compliance with the order, the court may order that in default of payment of the fine or compliance with the order, as the case may be, the defendant shall be imprisoned for a period of not more than six months.

Time for payment

(3) A summary conviction court may direct, subject to the provisions of this section, that any fine adjudged to be paid shall

(a) be paid forthwith, or

(b) be paid at such time and on such terms as the summary conviction court may fix.

What to be considered

(4) Where a summary conviction court directs that an accused pay a fine, the court shall not, at the time the sentence is imposed, direct that the fine be paid forthwith unless

(a) the court is satisfied that the convicted person is possessed of sufficient means to enable him to pay the fine forthwith,

(b) upon being asked by the court whether he desires time for payment, the convicted person does not request such time, or

(c) for any other special reason, the court deems it expedient that no time should be allowed.

Idem

(5) The court in considering whether time should be allowed for payment and, if so, for what period, shall consider any representation made by the accused but any time allowed shall be not less than fourteen clear days from the date sentence is imposed. 25(2) Interp

Interpretation Act

25. (2) Where there is a reference to a number of clear days or "at least" a number of days between two events, in calculating the number of days there shall be excluded the days on which the events happen.

Warrant of committal

(6) Where time has been allowed for payment the court shall not issue a warrant of committal in default of payment of the fine until the expiration of the time allowed for payment.

Reasons for committal

(7) Where no time has been allowed for payment and a warrant of committal in default of payment of a fine of the accused is issued the court shall state in the warrant the reason for immediate committal.

Surrender by accused

(8) Notwithstanding subsection (6), where, before the expiration of the time allowed for payment, the accused appears before a summary conviction court and signifies in writing that he prefers to be committed immediately rather than to await the expiration of the time allowed, the court may forthwith issue a warrant committing the accused to prison.

Young offenders

(9) Where a person who has been allowed time for payment appears to the court to be not less than sixteen nor more than twenty-one years of age, the court shall, before issuing a warrant committing the person to prison for default of payment of the fine, obtain and consider a report concerning the conduct and means to pay of the accused.

Extension of time

(10) Where time has been allowed for payment under subsection (3) the court that imposed the sentence may, upon application by or on behalf of the accused, allow further time for payment.

"Fine"

(11) In this section "fine" includes a pecuniary penalty or other sum of money. 1953-54, c. 51, s. 694; 1959, c. 41, s. 31.

Information

Commencement of proceedings

723. (1) Proceedings under this Part shall be commenced by laying an information in Form 2.

One justice may act before the trial

(2) Notwithstanding any other law that requires an information to be laid before or to be tried by two or more justices, one justice may

(a) receive the information,

(b) issue a summons or warrant with respect to the information, and

(c) do all other things preliminary to the trial. 1953-54, c. 51, s. 695.

Formalities of information

724. (1) In proceedings to which this Part applies, the information

(a) shall be in writing and under oath, and 28 Interp

(b) may charge more than one offence or relate to more than one matter of complaint, but where more than one offence is charged or the information relates to more than one matter of complaint, each offence or matter of complaint, as the case may be, shall be set out in a separate count.

No reference to previous convictions

(2) No information in respect of an offence for which, by reason of previous convictions, a greater punishment may be imposed shall contain any reference to previous convictions. 1953-54, c. 51, s. 696.

Any justice may act before and after trial

725. (1) Nothing in this Act or any other law shall be deemed to require a justice before whom proceedings are commenced or who issues process before or after the trial, to be the justice or one of the justices before whom the trial is held.

Two or more justices

(2) Where two or more justices have jurisdiction with respect to proceedings they shall be present and act together at the trial, but one justice may thereafter do anything that is required or is authorized to be done in connection with the proceedings.

Adjournment

(3) Subject to section 726, in proceedings under this Part no summary conviction court other than the summary conviction court by which the plea of an accused is taken has jurisdiction for the purposes of the hearing and adjudication, but any justice may

(a) adjourn the proceedings at any time before the plea of the accused is taken, or

(b) adjourn the proceedings at any time after the plea of the accused is taken for the purpose of enabling the proceedings to be continued before the summary conviction court by which the plea was taken.

Jurisdiction

(4) Where the summary conviction court by which the plea of the accused was taken has not commenced to hear evidence, any summary conviction court having jurisdiction to the try the accused has jurisdiction for the purposes of the hearing and adjudication. 1953-54, c. 51, s. 697; 1959, c. 41, s. 32; 1960-61, c. 43, s. 41; 1974-75-76, c. 93, s. 86(1).

(5) Repealed. 1974-75-76, c. 93, s. 86(2).

Inability of justice to continue

726. (1) Where a trial under this Part is commenced before a summary conviction court and a justice who is, or is a member of, that summary conviction court dies or is, for any reason, unable to continue the trial, another justice who is authorized to be, or to be a member of, a summary conviction court for the same territorial division may act in the place of the justice before whom the trial 2
was commenced.

Continuing trial

(2) A justice who, pursuant to subsection (1), acts in the place of a justice before whom a trial was commenced

(*a*) shall, if an adjudication has been made by the summary conviction court, impose the punishment or make the order that, in the circumstances, is authorized by law, or

(*b*) shall, if an adjudication has not been made by the summary conviction court, commence the trial again as a trial *de novo*. 1953-54, c. 51, s. 698.

Duty of court where common assault is charged

727. Where a defendant is charged with common assault and, before the defendant enters upon his defence, the summary conviction court is, from the evidence, of the opinion

(*a*) that the assault complained of was accompanied by an attempt to commit an indictable offence other than common assault or was committed in the course of the commission of an indictable offence other than common assault, or

(*b*) that the defendant should, for any reason, be prosecuted by indictment,

the summary conviction court shall not adjudicate thereon, but the proceedings shall be continued as for an indictable offence and the defendant shall be informed accordingly. 1953-54, c. 51, s. 699.

Summons and Warrant

Compelling appearance

728. (1) The provisions of Parts XIV and XV with respect to compelling the appearance of an accused before a justice apply, *mutatis mutandis*, to proceedings under this Part.

mutatis mutandis — after the necessary changes in detail so that the text applies

Copy of warrant to be served

(2) Where a warrant is issued in the first instance for the arrest of a defendant, a copy thereof shall be served on the person who is arrested thereunder. 1953-54, c. 51, s. 700.

29. (1) It is the duty of every one who executes a process or warrant to have it with him, where it is feasible to do so, and to produce it when requested to do so.

(2) It is the duty of every one who arrests a person, whether with or without warrant, to give notice to that person, where it is feasible to do so, of

(*a*) the process or warrant under which he makes the arrest, or

(*b*) the reason for the arrest.

(3) Failure to comply with subsection (1) or (2) does not of itself deprive a person who executes a process or warrant, or a person who makes an arrest, or those who assist them, of protection from criminal responsibility.

Interpretation Act

28. In every enactment

"oath" includes a solemn affirmation or declaration, whenever the context applies to any person by whom and case in which a solemn affirmation or declaration may be made instead of an oath; and in like cases the expression "sworn" includes the expression "affirmed" or "declared";

Defects and Objections

General provisions as to counts

729. (1) Sections 510 and 512 apply, *mutatis mutandis*, to informations in respect of proceedings as defined in this Part.

mutatis mutandis — after the necessary changes in detail so that the text applies

510. (1) Each count in an indictment shall in general apply to a single transaction and shall contain and is sufficient if it contains in substance a statement that the accused committed an indictable offence therein specified.

(2) The statement referred to in subsection (1) may be

(a) in popular language without technical averments or allegations of matters that are not essential to be proved,

(b) in the words of the enactment that describes the offence or declares the matters charged to be an indictable offence, or

(c) in words that are sufficient to give to the accused notice of the offence with which he is charged.

(3) A count shall contain sufficient detail of the circumstances of the alleged offence to give to the accused reasonable information with respect to the act or omission to be proved against him and to identify the transaction referred to, but otherwise the absence or insufficiency of details does not vitiate the count.

(5) A count may refer to any section, subsection, paragraph or subparagraph of the enactment that creates the offence charged, and for the purpose of determining whether a count is sufficient, consideration shall be given to any such reference.

(6) Nothing in this Part relating to matters that do not render a count insufficient shall be deemed to restrict or limit the application of this section.

512. No count in an indictment is insufficient by reason of the absence of details where, in the opinion of the court, the count otherwise fulfils the requirements of section 510 and, without restricting the generality of the foregoing, no count in an indictment is insufficient by reason only that

(a) it does not name the person injured or intended or attempted to be injured,

(b) it does not name the person who owns or has a special property or interest in property mentioned in the count,

(c) it charges an intent to defraud without naming or describing the person whom it was intended to defraud,

(d) it does not set out any writing that is the subject of the charge,

(e) it does not set out the words used where words that are alleged to have been used are the subject of the charge,

(f) it does not specify the means by which the alleged offence was committed,

(g) it does not name or describe with precision any person, place or thing, or

(h) it does not, where the consent of a person, official or authority is required before proceedings may be instituted for an offence, state that the consent has been obtained.

Particulars

(2) The summary conviction court may, if it is satisfied that it is necessary for a fair trial, order that a particular, further describing any matter relevant to the proceedings, be furnished to the defendant. 1953-54, c. 51, s. 701.

No need to negative exception, etc.

730. (1) No exception, exemption, proviso, excuse or qualification prescribed by law is required to be set out or negatived, as the case may be, in an information.

Burden of proving exception, etc.

(2) The burden of proving that an exception, exemption, proviso, excuse or qualification prescribed by law operates in favour of the defendant is on the defendant, and the prosecutor is not required, except by way of rebuttal, to prove that the exception, exemption, proviso, excuse or qualification does not operate in favour of the defendant, whether or not it is set out in the information. 1953-54, c. 51, s. 702.

Process not objectionable on certain other grounds

731. No information, summons, conviction, order or process shall be deemed to charge two offences or to be uncertain by reason only that it states that the alleged offence was committed

***(a)* in different modes, or**

(b) in respect of one or other of several articles, either conjunctively or disjunctively. 1953-54, c. 51, s. 703.

Amending defective information

732. (1) An objection to an information for a defect apparent on its face shall be taken by motion to quash the information before the defendant has pleaded, and thereafter only by leave of the summary conviction court before which the trial takes place.

Amendment where variance

(2) A summary conviction court may, upon the trial of an information, amend the information or a particular that is furnished under section 729, to make the information or particular conform to the evidence if there appears to be a variance between the evidence and

(a) the charge in the information, or

(b) the charge in the information

(i) as amended, or

(ii) as it would have been if amended in conformity with any particular that has been furnished pursuant to section 729.

Amending information

(3) A summary conviction court may, at any stage of the trial, amend the information as may be necessary if it appears

(a) that the information has been laid

(i) under another Act of the Parliament of Canada instead of this Act, or

(ii) under this Act instead of another Act of the Parliament of Canada; or

(b) that the information

(i) fails to state or states defectively anything that is requisite to constitute the offence,

(ii) does not negative an exception that should be negatived, or

(iii) is in any way defective in substance,

and the matters to be alleged in the proposed amendment are disclosed by the evidence taken on the trial; or

(c) that the information is in any way defective in form.

Variance not material

(4) A variance between the information and the evidence taken on the trial is not material with respect to

(a) the time when the offence is alleged to have been committed, if it is proved that the information was laid within the prescribed period of limitation, or

(b) the place where the subject-matter of the proceedings is alleged to have arisen, if it is proved that it arose within the territorial jurisdiction of the summary conviction court that holds the trial.

What to be considered

(5) The summary conviction court shall, in considering whether or not an amendment should be made, consider

(a) the evidence taken on the trial, if any,

(b) the circumstances of the case,

(c) whether the defendant has been misled or prejudiced in his defence by a variance, error or omission mentioned in subsection (2) or (3), and

(d) whether, having regard to the merits of the case, the proposed amendment can be made without injustice being done.

Adjournment if defendant prejudiced

(6) Where in the opinion of the summary conviction court the defendant has been misled or prejudiced in his defence by an error or omission in the information, the summary conviction court may adjourn the trial and may make such an order with respect to the payment of costs resulting from the necessity of amendment as it considers desirable. 1953-54, c. 51, s. 704.

Stay of Proceedings

Attorney General may direct stay

732.1 (1) The Attorney General or counsel instructed by him for the purpose may, at any time after proceedings are commenced and before judgment, direct the clerk of the court to make an entry on the record that the proceedings are stayed by his direction and when the entry is made the proceedings shall be stayed accordingly and any recognizance relating to the proceedings is vacated. 2

Recommencement of proceedings

(2) Proceedings stayed in accordance with subsection (1) may be recommenced, without laying a new information, by the Attorney General or counsel instructed by him for the purpose giving notice of the recommencement to the clerk of the court in which the stay of proceedings was entered, but where no such notice is given within one year after the entry of the stay of proceedings or before the expiration of the time within which the proceedings could have been instituted, whichever is the earlier, the proceedings shall be deemed never to have been commenced. 1972, c. 13, s. 62. Interp

Interpretation Act

25. (1) Where the time limited for the doing of a thing expires or falls upon a holiday, the thing may be done on the day next following that is not a holiday.

28. In every enactment

"year" means any period of twelve consecutive months, except that a reference to a "calendar year" means a period of twelve consecutive months commencing on the first day of January and a reference by number to a Dominical year means the period of twelve consecutive months commencing on the first day of January of that year.

Trial

Jurisdiction

733. Every summary conviction court has jurisdiction to try, determine and adjudge proceedings to which this Part applies in the territorial division over which the person who constitutes that court has jurisdiction. 1953-54, c. 51, s. 705. 2

Non-appearance of prosecutor

734. Where, in proceedings to which this Part applies, the defendant appears for the trial and the prosecutor, having had due notice, does not appear, the summary conviction court may dismiss the information or may adjourn the trial to some other time upon such terms as it considers proper. 1953-54, c. 51, s. 706. 2

When both parties appear

735. (1) Where the prosecutor and defendant appear, the summary conviction court shall proceed to hold the trial.

Counsel or agent

(2) A defendant may appear personally or by counsel or agent, but the summary conviction court may require the defendant to appear personally and may, if it thinks fit, issue a warrant in Form 7 for the arrest of the defendant, and adjourn the trial to await his appearance pursuant thereto. 2

Appearance by corporation

(3) Where the defendant is a corporation it shall appear by counsel or agent, and if it does not appear, the summary conviction court may, upon proof of service of the summons, proceed *ex parte* to hold the trial. 1953-54, c. 51, s. 707.

ex parte — in the absence of one side or party

Arraignment

736. (1) Where the defendant appears, the substance of the information shall be stated to him, and he shall be asked,

(*a*) whether he pleads guilty or not guilty to the information, where the proceedings are in respect of an offence that is punishable on summary conviction, or

(*b*) whether he has cause to show why an order should not be made against him, in proceedings where a justice is authorized by law to make an order.

Conviction or order if charge admitted

(2) Where the defendant pleads guilty or does not show sufficient cause why an order should not be made against him, as the case may be, the summary conviction court shall convict him or make an order against him accordingly.

Procedure if charge not admitted

(3) Where the defendant pleads not guilty or states that he has cause to show why an order should not be made against him, as the case may be, the summary conviction court shall proceed with the trial, and shall take the evidence of witnesses for the prosecutor and the defendant in accordance with the provisions of Part XV relating to preliminary inquiries.

Separating trial of counts

(4) The summary conviction court may, before or during the trial, where it is satisfied that the ends of justice require it, direct that the defendant be tried separately upon one or more of the counts in the information. 2

Admission by defendant

(5) A defendant may admit any fact alleged against him for the purpose of dispensing with proof thereof. 1953-54, c. 51, s. 708.

Right to make full answer and defence

737. (1) The prosecutor is entitled personally to conduct his case, and the defendant is entitled to make his full answer and defence.

Examination of witnesses

(2) The prosecutor or defendant, as the case may be, may examine and cross-examine witnesses personally or by counsel or agent.

On oath

(3) Every witness at a trial in proceedings to which this Part applies shall be examined under oath. 1953-54, c. 51, s. 709. 28 Interp

2. In this Act

"clerk of the court" includes a person, by whatever name or title he may be designated, who from time to time performs the duties of a clerk of the court;

"counsel" means a barrister or solicitor, in respect of the matters or things that barristers and solicitors, respectively, are authorized by the law of the province to do or perform in relation to legal proceedings;

"count" means a charge in an information or indictment;

"justice" means a justice of the peace or a magistrate, and includes two or more justices where two or more justices are, by law, required to act or, by law, act or have jurisdiction;

"prosecutor" means the Attorney General or, where the Attorney General does not intervene, means the person who institutes proceedings to which this Act applies, and includes counsel acting on behalf of either of them;

"territorial division" includes any province, county, union of counties, township, city, town, parish or other judicial division or place to which the context applies;

Interpretation Act

28. In every enactment

"oath" includes a solemn affirmation or declaration, whenever the context applies to any person by whom and case in which a solemn affirmation or declaration may be made instead of an oath; and in like cases the expression "sworn" includes the expression "affirmed" or "declared";

Adjournment

738. (1) The summary conviction court may, in its discretion, before or during the trial, adjourn the trial to a time and place to be appointed and stated in the presence of the parties or their counsels or agents, but no such adjournment shall be for more than eight clear days unless both parties or their counsel or agents consent to the proposed adjournment whether or not the defendant is in custody. 1974-75-76, c. 93, s. 87(1). 25(2) Interp

Interpretation Act

25. (2) Where there is a reference to a number of clear days or "at least" a number of days between two events, in calculating the number of days there shall be excluded the days on which the events happen.

(2) Repealed. R.S., c. 2(2nd Supp.), s. 15.

Non-appearance of defendant

(3) Where a defendant to whom an appearance notice that has been confirmed by a justice under section 455.4 has been issued or who has been served with a summons does not appear at the time and place appointed for the trial and the issue of the appearance notice or service of the summons within a reasonable time before the appearance was required is proved, or where a defendant does not appear for the resumption of a trial that has been adjourned in accordance with subsection (1), the summary conviction court

(a) may proceed *ex parte* to hear and determine the proceedings in the absence of the defendant as fully and effectually as if the defendant had appeared, or

(b) may, if it thinks fit, issue a warrant in Form 7 for the arrest of the defendant, and adjourn the trial to await his appearance pursuant thereto.

455.5 (3) Service of a summons may be proved by the oral evidence, given under oath, of the peace officer who served it or by his affidavit made before a justice or other person authorized to administer oaths or to take affidavits.

740. (3) A summary conviction court that holds a trial pursuant to subsection 738(3) may, if it convicts the defendant, make inquiries with respect to previous convictions, whether or not the defendant was notified that a greater punishment would be sought by reason thereof.

Consent of Attorney General required

(3.1) Where, at the trial of a defendant, the summary conviction court proceeds in the manner described in paragraph (3)*(a)*, no proceedings under section 133 arising out of the failure of the defendant to appear at the time and place appointed for the trial or for the resumption of the trial shall be instituted or if instituted shall be proceeded with, except with the consent of the Attorney General.

133. (4) Every one who is served with a summons and who fails, without lawful excuse, the proof of which lies upon him, to appear at a time and place stated therein, if any, for the purposes of the *Identification of Criminals Act* or to attend court in accordance therewith, is guilty of

(a) an indictable offence and is liable to imprisonment for two years, or

(b) an offence punishable on summary conviction.

Non-appearance of prosecutor

(4) Where the prosecutor does not appear at the time and place appointed for the resumption of an adjourned trial, the summary conviction court may dismiss the information with or without costs.

Direction or remand for observation

(5) Notwithstanding subsection (1), the summary conviction court may, at any time before convicting a defendant or making an order against him or dismissing the information, as the case may be, when of the opinion, supported by the evidence, or, where the prosecutor and defendant consent, by the report in writing, of at least one duly qualified medical practioner, that there is reason to believe that the defendant is mentally ill, by order in writing,

(a) direct the defendant to attend, at a place or before a person specified in the order and within a time specified therein, for observation; or

(b) remand the defendant to such custody as the court directs for observation for a period not exceeding thirty days.

Idem

(6) Notwithstanding subsection (5), a summary conviction court may remand the defendant in accordance therewith

(a) for a period not exceeding thirty days without having heard the evidence or considered the report of a duly qualified medical practitioner where compelling circumstances exist for so doing and where a medical practitioner is not readily available to examine the accused and give evidence or submit a report; and

(b) for a period of more than thirty days but not exceeding sixty days where it is satisfied that observation for such a period is required in all the circumstances of the case and that opinion is supported by the evidence or, where the prosecutor and the accused consent, by the report in writing, of at least one duly qualified medical practitioner.

Court may order trial of issue

(7) Where, as a result of observations made pursuant to an order issued under subsection (5), it appears to a summary conviction court that there is sufficient reason to doubt that a defendant is, on account of insanity, capable of conducting his defence, the summary conviction court shall direct that an issue be tried as to whether the defendant is then, on account of insanity, unfit to stand his trial.

Section 543 applicable

(8) Where a summary conviction court directs the trial of an issue under subsection (7), it shall proceed in accordance with section 543 in so far as that section may be applied. R.S., c. C-34, s. 738; R.S., c. 2(2nd Supp.), s. 15; 1972, c. 13, s. 63; 1974-75-76, c. 93, s. 87(1) to (4).

Adjudication

Conviction, order or dismissal

739. When the summary conviction court has heard the prosecutor, defendant and witnesses it shall, after considering the matter, convict the defendant or make an order against him or dismiss the information, as the case may be. 1953-54, c. 51, s. 711.

Previous conviction

740. (1) Where a defendant is convicted of an offence for which a greater punishment may be imposed by reason of previous convictions, no greater punishment shall be imposed upon him by reason thereof unless the prosecutor satisfies the summary conviction court that the defendant, before making his plea, was notified that a greater punishment would be sought by reason thereof.

Procedure where previous conviction charged

(2) Where a defendant is convicted of an offence for which a greater punishment may be imposed by reason of previous convictions, the summary conviction court shall, upon application by the prosecutor, and upon being satisfied that the defendant was notified in accordance with subsection (1), ask the defendant whether he was previously convicted, and if he does not admit that he was previously convicted, evidence of previous convictions may be adduced.

Where hearing *ex parte*

(3) A summary conviction court that holds a trial pursuant to subsection 738(3) may, if it convicts the defendant, make inquiries with respect to previous convictions, whether or not the defendant was notified that a greater punishment would be sought by reason thereof.

Proof of previous conviction

(4) For the purposes of this section, a previous conviction may be proved in the manner prescribed by section 594. 1953-54, c. 51, s. 712.

594. (1) In any proceedings,

(a) a certificate setting out with reasonable particularity the conviction or the conviction and sentence in Canada of a person for an indictable offence, signed by

(i) the person who made the conviction,

(ii) the clerk of the court in which the conviction was made, or

(iii) a fingerprint examiner,

is, upon proof that the accused is the person referred to in the certificate, evidence that the accused was so convicted or so convicted and sentenced without proof of the signature or the official character of the person appearing to have signed the certificate;

(b) evidence that the fingerprints of the accused are the same as the fingerprints of the person whose fingerprints are reproduced in a certificate issued under subparagraph *(a)*(iii) is, in the absence of any evidence to the contrary, proof that the accused is the person referred to in that certificate;

(c) a certificate of a fingerprint examiner stating that he has compared the fingerprints attached to that certificate with the fingerprints reproduced in a certificate issued under subparagraph *(a)*(iii) and that they are those of the same person is evidence of the statements contained in the certificate without proof of the signature or the official character of the person appearing to have signed the certificate; and

(d) a certificate under subparagraph *(a)*(iii) may be in Form 42, and a certificate under paragraph *(c)* may be in Form 43.

(2) In any proceedings, a copy of the summary conviction in Canada of an accused, signed by the person who made the conviction or by the clerk of the court in which the conviction was made, is, upon proof of the identity of the accused, evidence of the conviction of the accused without proof of the signature or the official character of the person appearing to have signed it.

(3) An accused against whom a certificate issued under subparagraph (1)*(a)*(iii) or paragraph (1)*(c)* is produced may, with leave of the court, require the attendance of the person who signed the certificate for the purposes of cross-examination.

(3.1) No certificate issued under subparagraph (1)*(a)*(iii) or paragraph (1)*(c)* shall be received in evidence unless the party intending to produce it has given to the accused reasonable notice of his intention together with a copy of the certificate.

(4) In this section "fingerprint examiner" means a person designated as such for the purposes of this section by the Solicitor General of Canada.

Memo of conviction or order

741. (1) Where a defendant is convicted or where an order is made in relation to him, a minute or memorandum of the conviction or order shall be made by the summary conviction court, without fee, indicating that the matter was dealt with under this Part and, upon request by the accused or the prosecutor, the court shall cause a conviction or order in Form 31 or 32, as the case may be, and a certified copy thereof to be drawn up and shall deliver the certified copy to the person making the request.

Warrant of committal

(2) Where a defendant is convicted or an order is made against him, the summary conviction court shall issue a warrant of committal in Form 18 or 19, and section 461 applies in respect of a warrant of committal issued under this subsection. R.S., c. C-34, s. 741; 1972, c. 13, s. 64.

461. (1) Where a warrant for the arrest of an accused cannot be executed in accordance with section 456.3, a justice within whose jurisdiction the accused is or is believed to be shall, upon application, and upon proof on oath or by affidavit of the signature of the justice who issued the warrant, authorize the execution of the warrant within his jurisdiction by making an endorsement, which may be in Form 25, upon the warrant.

(2) An endorsement that is made upon a warrant pursuant to subsection (1) is sufficient authority to the peace officers to whom it was originally directed, and to all peace officers within the territorial jurisdiction of the justice by whom it is endorsed, to execute the warrant and to take the accused before the justice who issued the warrant or before some other justice for the same territorial division.

Disposal of penalties when joint offenders

742. Where several persons join in committing the same offence and upon conviction each is adjudged to pay an amount to a person aggrieved, no more shall be paid to that person than an amount equal to the value of the property destroyed or injured or the amount of the injury done, together with costs, if any, and the residue of the amount adjudged to be paid shall be applied in the manner in which other penalties imposed by law are directed to be applied. 1953-54, c. 51, s. 714.

Order of dismissal

743. (1) Where the summary conviction court dismisses an information it may, if requested by the defendant, draw up an order of dismissal, and shall give to the defendant a certified copy of the order of dismissal.

Effect of certificate

(2) A copy of an order of dismissal, certified in accordance with subsection (1) is, without further proof, a bar to any subsequent proceedings against the defendant in respect of the same cause. 1953-54, c. 51, s. 715.

Costs

744. (1) The summary conviction court may in its discretion award and order such costs as it considers reasonable and not inconsistent with such of the fees established by section 772 as may be taken or allowed in proceedings before that summary conviction court, to be paid

(a) to the informant by the defendant, where the summary conviction court convicts or makes an order against the defendant, or

(b) to the defendant by the informant, where the summary conviction court dismisses an information.

Order set out

(2) An order under subsection (1) shall be set out in the conviction, order or order of dismissal, as the case may be.

Costs are part of fine

(3) Where a fine or sum of money or both are adjudged to be paid by a defendant, and a term of imprisonment in default of payment is imposed, the defendant is, in default of payment, liable to serve the term of imprisonment imposed, and for the purposes of this subsection, any costs that are awarded against the defendant shall be deemed to be part of the fine or sum of money adjudged to be paid.

Where no fine imposed

(4) Where no fine or sum of money is adjudged to be paid by a defendant, but costs are awarded against the defendant or informant, the person who is liable to pay them is, in default of payment, liable to imprisonment for one month.

"Costs"

(5) In this section, "costs" includes the costs and charges, after they have been ascertained, of committing and conveying to prison the person against whom costs have been awarded. 1953-54, c. 51, s. 716; 1968-69, c. 38, s. 83.

Sureties to Keep the Peace

Where injury or damage feared

745. (1) Any person who fears that another person will cause personal injury to him or his wife or child or will damage his property may lay an information before a justice.

Interpretation Act

26. (6) Words importing male persons include female persons and corporations.

Duty of justice

(2) A justice who receives an information under subsection (1) shall cause the parties to appear before him or before a summary conviction court having jurisdiction in the same territorial division.

Adjudication

(3) The justice or the summary conviction court before which the parties appear may, if satisfied by the evidence adduced that the informant has reasonable grounds for his fears,

(a) order that the defendant enter into a recognizance, with or without sureties, to keep the peace and be of good behaviour for any period that does not exceed twelve months, and comply with such other reasonable conditions prescribed in the recognizance as the court considers desirable for securing the good conduct of the defendant, or

(b) commit the defendant to prison for a term not exceeding twelve months if he fails or refuses to enter into the recognizance.

Forms

(4) A recognizance and committal to prison in default of recognizance under subsection (3) may be in Forms 28 and 20, respectively.

Procedure

(5) The provisions of this Part apply, *mutatis mutandis*, to proceedings under this section. 1953-54, c. 51, s. 717; 1974-75-76, c. 93, s. 88.

mutatis mutandis — after the necessary changes in detail so that the text applies

Breach of recognizance

Type 'A' Offence

746. A person bound by recognizance under section 745 who commits a breach of the recognizance is guilty of an offence punishable on summary conviction. 1953-54, c. 51, s. 718.

Appeals

"Appeal court"

747. For the purposes of sections 748 to 760 "appeal court" means

(a) in the Province of Prince Edward Island, the Supreme Court,

(b) in the Province of Newfoundland, the district court of the judicial district where the cause of the proceedings arose,

(c) in the Provinces of Nova Scotia and Manitoba, the county court of the district or county where the cause of the proceedings arose,
1978-79, c. 11, s. 10, I. 6(17).

(d) in the Province of Quebec, the Superior Court,

(e) in the Province of Ontario, the county court of the district or county or group of counties where the adjudication was made,

(f) in the Provinces of Alberta, New Brunswick and Saskatchewan, the Court of Queen's Bench, 1978-79, c. 11, s. 10, I. 6(18).

(g) Repealed. 1978-79, c. 11, s. 10, I. 6(18).

(h) in the Province of British Columbia, the county court of the county where the adjudication was made, and

(i) in the Yukon Territory and Northwest Territories, a judge of the Supreme Court thereof. R.S., c. C-34, s. 747; 1972, c. 13, s. 65; 1972, c. 17, s. 2; 1974-75, c. 19, s. 1; 1978-79, c. 11, s. 10, I. 6.

Appeal by defendant, informant or Attorney General

748. Except where otherwise provided by law,

(a) the defendant in proceedings under this Part may appeal to the appeal court

(i) from a conviction or order made against him, or

(ii) against a sentence passed upon him; and

(b) the informant, the Attorney General or his agent in proceedings under this Part may appeal to the appeal court

(i) from an order dismissing an information, or

(ii) against a sentence passed upon a defendant,

and the Attorney General of Canada or his agent has the same rights of appeal in proceedings instituted at the instance of the Government of Canada and conducted by or on behalf of that government as the Attorney General of a province or his agent has under this paragraph. 1959, c. 41, s. 34.

753. (1) A person does not waive his right of appeal under section 748 by reason only that he pays the fine imposed upon conviction, without in any way indicating an intention to appeal or reserving the right to appeal.

(2) A conviction, order or sentence shall be deemed not to have been appealed against until the contrary is shown.

770. (1) Every person for whom a case is stated in respect of an adjudication of a summary conviction court from which he is entitled to an appeal under section 748 shall be taken to have abandoned all his rights of appeal under that section.

Alberta

749. (1) In the Province of Alberta an appeal under section 748 shall be heard at the sittings of the appeal court that is held nearest to the place where the cause of the proceedings arose, but the judge of the appeal court may, on the application of one of the parties, appoint another place for the hearing of the appeal.

Saskatchewan

(2) In the Province of Saskatchewan an appeal under section 748 shall be heard at the sittings of the appeal court at the judicial centre nearest to the place where the adjudication was made, but the judge of the appeal court may, on the application of one of the parties, appoint another place for the hearing of the appeal.

British Columbia

(3) In the Province of British Columbia an appeal under section 748 shall be heard at the sittings of the appeal court that is held nearest to the place where the adjudication was made, but the judge of the appeal court may, on the application of one of the parties, appoint another place for the hearing of the appeal.

Yukon, Northwest Territories

(4) In the Yukon Territory and the Northwest Territories, an appeal under section 748 shall be heard at the place where the cause of the proceedings arose or at the place nearest thereto where a court is appointed to be held. 1960-61, c. 43, s. 43; 1968-69, c. 38, s. 85.

Notice of appeal

750. (1) An appellant who proposes to appeal to the appeal court shall give notice of appeal in such manner and within such period as may be directed by rules of court.

Extension of time

(2) The appeal court or a judge thereof may at any time extend the time within which notice of appeal may be given. R.S., c. C-34, s. 750; 1972, c. 18, s. 66; 1974-75-76, c. 93, s. 89.

751. Repealed. 1974-75-76, c. 93, s. 90.

Interim Release of Appellant

Undertaking or recognizance of appellant

752. (1) A person who was the defendant in proceedings before a summary conviction court and by whom an appeal is taken under section 748 shall, if he 720
is in custody, remain in custody unless the appeal court at which the appeal is 747
to be heard orders that the accused be released

(a) upon his giving an undertaking to the appeal court, without conditions or with such conditions as the appeal court directs, to surrender himself into custody in accordance with the order,

(b) upon his entering into a recognizance without sureties in such amount, with such conditions, if any, as the appeal court directs, but without deposit of money or other valuable security, or 2

(c) upon his entering into a recognizance with or without sureties in such amount, with such conditions, if any, as the appeal court directs, and upon his depositing with that appeal court such sum of money or other valuable security as the appeal court directs,

and the person having the custody of the appellant shall, where the appellant complies with the order, forthwith release the appellant.

Application of certain provisions of section 459

(2) The provisions of subsections 459(5), (6) and (7) apply *mutatis mutandis* in respect of a person who has been released from custody under subsection (1). 1974-75-76, c. 93, s. 91.

mutatis mutandis — after the necessary changes in detail so that the text applies

459. (5) Where a judge having jurisdiction in the province where an order under subsection (4) for the release of an accused has been made is satisfied that there are reasonable and probable grounds to believe that the accused

(a) has violated or is about to violate the undertaking or recognizance upon which he has been released, or

(b) has, after his release from custody upon his undertaking or recognizance, committed an indictable offence,

he may issue a warrant for the arrest of the accused.

(6) Notwithstanding anything in this Act, a peace officer who has reasonable and probable grounds to believe that an accused who has been released from custody under subsection (4)

(a) has violated or is about to violate the undertaking or recognizance upon which he has been released, or

(b) has, after his release from custody upon his undertaking or recognizance, committed an indictable offence,

may arrest the accused without warrant and take him or cause him to be taken before a judge having jurisdiction in the province where the order for his release was made.

(7) A judge before whom an accused is taken pursuant to a warrant issued under subsection (5) or pursuant to subsection (6) may, where the accused shows cause why his detention in custody is not justified within the meaning of subsection 457(7), order that the accused be released upon his giving an undertaking or entering into a recognizance described in any of paragraphs 457(2)*(a)* to *(d)* with such conditions, described in subsection 457(4), as the judge considers desirable.

Undertaking or recognizance of prosecutor

752.1 (1) The prosecutor in proceedings before a summary conviction court by whom an appeal is taken under section 748 shall, forthwith after filing the notice of appeal and proof of service thereof in accordance with section 750, appear before a justice, and the justice shall, after giving the prosecutor and the respondent a reasonable opportunity to be heard, order that the prosecutor

(*a*) give an undertaking as prescribed in this section, or

(*b*) enter into a recognizance in such amount with or without sureties and with or without deposit of money or other valuable security as the justice directs.

Condition

(2) The condition of an undertaking or recognizance given or entered into under this section is that the prosecutor will appear personally or by counsel at the sittings of the appeal court at which the appeal is to be heard.

Appeals by Attorney General

(3) This section does not apply in respect of an appeal taken by the Attorney General or by counsel acting on behalf of the Attorney General.

Form of undertaking or recognizance

(4) An undertaking under this section may be in Form 9.2 and a recognizance under this section may be in Form 28. R.S., c. 2(2nd Supp.), s. 16.

Application to appeal court for review

752.2 (1) Where a justice makes an order under section 752.1, either the appellant or the respondent may, before or at any time during the hearing of the appeal, apply to the appeal court for a review of the order made by the justice. 1974-75-76, c. 93, s. 91.1.

Disposition of application by appeal court

(2) Upon the hearing of an application under this section, the appeal court, after giving the appellant and the respondent a reasonable opportunity to be heard, shall

(*a*) dismiss the application, or

(*b*) if the person applying for the review shows cause, allow the application, vacate the order made by the justice and make the order that in the opinion of the appeal court should have been made.

Effect of order

(3) An order made under this section shall have the same force and effect as if it had been made by the justice. R.S., c. 2(2nd Supp.), s. 16.

Application to fix date for hearing of appeal

752.3 (1) Where, in the case of an appellant who has been convicted by a summary conviction court and who is in custody pending the hearing of his appeal, the hearing of his appeal has not commenced within thirty days from the day on which notice of his appeal was given in accordance with the rules referred to in section 750, the person having the custody of the appellant shall, forthwith upon the expiration of those thirty days, apply to the appeal court to fix a date for the hearing of the appeal.

Order fixing date

(2) Upon receiving an application under subsection (1), the appeal court shall, after giving the prosecutor a reasonable opportunity to be heard, fix a date for the hearing of the appeal and give such directions as it thinks necessary for expediting the hearing of the appeal. 1974-75-76, c. 93, s. 92.

Payment of fine not a waiver of appeal

753. (1) A person does not waive his right of appeal under section 748 by reason only that he pays the fine imposed upon conviction, without in any way indicating an intention to appeal or reserving the right to appeal.

Presumption

(2) A conviction, order or sentence shall be deemed not to have been appealed against until the contrary is shown. 1953-54, c. 51, s. 725.

Procedure on Appeal

Notification and transmission of conviction, etc.

754. (1) Where a notice of appeal has been given in accordance with the rules referred to in section 750, the clerk of the appeal court shall notify the summary conviction court that made the conviction or order appealed from or imposed the sentence appealed against of the appeal and upon receipt of such notification that summary conviction court shall transmit the conviction, order or order of dismissal and all other material in its possession in connection with the proceedings to the appeal court before the time when the appeal is to be heard, or within such further time as the appeal court may direct, and the material shall be kept by the clerk of the appeal court with the records of the appeal court. 1974-75-76, c. 93, s. 93(1).

Saving

(2) An appeal shall not be dismissed by the appeal court by reason only that some person other than the appellant failed to comply with the provisions of this Part relating to appeals.

Appellant to furnish transcript of evidence

(3) Where the evidence upon a trial before a summary conviction court has been taken by a stenographer duly sworn or by a sound recording apparatus, the appellant shall, unless the appeal court otherwise orders or the rules referred to in section 750 otherwise provide, cause a transcript thereof, certified by the stenographer or in accordance with subsection 468(6), as the case may be, to be furnished to the appeal court and the respondent for use upon the appeal. R.S., c. C-34, s. 754; 1972, c. 13, s. 67; 1974-75-76, c. 93, s. 93(2).

468. (1) Where the accused is before a justice holding a preliminary inquiry, the justice shall

(a) take the evidence under oath, in the presence of the accused, of the witnesses called on the part of the prosecution and allow the accused or his counsel to cross-examine them; and

(b) cause a record of the evidence of each witness to be taken

(i) by a stenographer appointed by him or in legible writing, in the form of a deposition, in Form 27, or

(ii) in a province where a sound recording apparatus is authorized by or under provincial legislation for use in civil cases, by the type of apparatus so authorized and in accordance with the requirements of the provincial legislation.

(6) Where, in accordance with this Act, a record is taken in any proceedings under this Act by a sound recording apparatus, the record so taken shall be dealt with and transcribed and the transcription certified and used in accordance with the provincial legislation *mutatis mutandis* mentioned in subsection (1).

mutatis mutandis — after the necessary changes in detail so that the text applies

Certain sections applicable to appeals

755. (1) Where an appeal is taken under section 748 in respect of any conviction, acquittal, sentence or order, the provisions of section 610 to 616, 720
with the exception of subsections 610(3) and 613(5), apply *mutatis mutandis*.

New trial

(2) Where an appeal court orders a new trial, it shall be held before a summary 747
conviction court other than the court that tried the defendant in the first instance, unless the appeal court directs that the new trial be held before the summary conviction court that tried the accused in the first instance.

Order of detention or release

(3) Where an appeal court orders a new trial, it may make such order for the release or detention of the appellant pending such trial as may be made by a justice pursuant to section 457 and the order may be enforced in the same manner as if it had been made by a justice under that section and the provisions of Part XIV apply *mutatis mutandis* to the order.

Trial *de novo*

(4) Notwithstanding subsections (1) to (3), where an appeal is taken under section 748 and where, because of the condition of the record of the trial in the summary conviction court or for any other reason, the appeal court, upon application of the defendant, the informant, the Attorney General or his agent, is of the opinion that the interests of justice would be better served by hearing and determining the appeal by holding a trial *de novo*, the appeal court may order that the appeal shall be heard by way of trial *de novo* in accordance with such rules as may be made under subsection 438(1.1) and for this purpose the provisions of sections 729 to 744 apply *mutatis mutandis.*

Former evidence

(5) The appeal court may, for the purpose of hearing and determining an appeal under subsection (4), permit the evidence of any witness taken before the summary conviction court to be read if that evidence has been authenticated in accordance with section 468 and if

(a) the appellant and respondent consent,

(b) the appeal court is satisfied that the attendance of the witness cannot reasonably be obtained, or

(c) by reason of the formal nature of the evidence or otherwise the court is satisfied that the opposite party will not be prejudiced,

and any evidence that is read under the authority of this subsection has the same force and effect as if the witness had given the evidence before the appeal court.

Appeal against sentence

(6) Where an appeal is taken under subsection (4) against sentence, the appeal court shall, unless the sentence is one fixed by law, consider the fitness of the sentence appealed against and may, upon such evidence, if any, as it thinks fit to require or receive, by order,

(a) dismiss the appeal, or

(b) vary the sentence within the limits prescribed by law for the offence of which the defendant was convicted;

and in making any order under paragraph *(b)* the appeal court may take into account any time spent in custody by the defendant as a result of the offence.

General provisions re appeals

(7) The following provisions apply in respect of appeals under subsection (4), namely,

(a) where an appeal is based on an objection to an information or any process, judgment shall not be given in favour of the appellant

(i) for any alleged defect therein in substance or in form, or

(ii) for any variance between the information or process and the evidence adduced at the trial,

unless it is shown

(iii) that the objection was taken at the trial, and

(iv) that an adjournment of the trial was refused notwithstanding that the variance referred to in subparagraph (ii) had deceived or misled the appellant; and

(b) where an appeal is based on a defect in a conviction or an order, judgment shall not be given in favour of the appellant, but the court shall make an order curing the defect. 1953-54, c. 51, s. 727; 1974-75-76, c. 93, s. 94.

Provisions of s. 608.2 applicable

755.1 The provisions of section 608.2, with the exception of paragraph (1)*(b)* thereof, apply *mutatis mutandis* in respect of an appellant who was a defendant and who has taken an appeal under section 748. 1974-75-76, c. 93, s. 95.

mutatis mutandis — after the necessary changes in detail so that the text applies

608.2 (1) A judge of the court of appeal may, by order in writing,

(a) direct an appellant to attend, at a place or before a person specified in the order and within a time specified therein, for observation, or

(b) remand an appellant to such custody as the judge directs for observation for a period not exceeding thirty days,

where, in his opinion, supported by the evidence or, where the appellant and the respondent consent, by the report in writing, of at least one duly qualified medical practitioner, there is reason to believe that

(c) the appellant may be mentally ill, or

(d) the balance of the mind of the appellant is disturbed, where the appellant is a female person charged with an offence arising out of the death of her newly-born child.

(2) Notwithstanding subsection (1), a judge of the court of appeal may remand an appellant in accordance therewith

(a) for a period not exceeding thirty days without having heard the evidence or considered the report of a duly qualified medical practitioner where compelling circumstances exist for so doing and where a medical practitioner is not readily available to examine the accused and give evidence or submit a report; and

(b) for a period of more than thirty days but not exceeding sixty days where he is satisfied that observation for such a period is required in all the circumstances of the case and his opinion is supported by the evidence or, where the appellant and the respondent consent, by the report in writing, of at least one duly qualified medical practitioner. 1972, c. 13, s. 54; 1974-75-76, c. 93, s. 74.

NOTE: Subsection 608.2(1) as enacted by 1972, c. 13, s. 54, repealed and amended by 1974-75-76, c. 93, s. 74, read as follows;

608.2 (1) A judge of the court of appeal may remand an appellant by order in writing, to such custody as he directs for observation for a period not exceeding thirty days where, in his opinion, supported by the evidence of at least one duly qualified medical practitioner, there is reason to believe that

(a) the appellant is mentally ill, or

(b) the balance of the mind of the appellant is disturbed, where the appellant is a female person charged with or convicted of an offence arising out of the death of her newly-born child.

Interpretation Act

36. Where an enactment (in this section called the "former enactment") is repealed and another enactment (in this section called the "new enactment") is substituted therefor,

(h) any reference in an unrepealed enactment to the former enactment shall, as regards a subsequent transaction, matter or thing, be read and construed as a reference to the provisions of the new enactment relating to the same subject-matter as the former enactment, but where there are no provisions in the new enactment relating to the same subject-matter, the former enactment shall be read as unrepealed in so far as is necessary to maintain or give effect to the unrepealed enactment.

Adjournment

756. The appeal court may adjourn the hearing of the appeal from time to time as may be necessary. 1953-54, c. 51, s. 728.

Dismissal for failure to appear or want of prosecution

757. The appeal court may, upon proof that notice of an appeal has been 747
given and that

(a) the appellant has failed to comply with any order made under section 752 or 752.1 or with the conditions of any undertaking or recognizance given or entered into as prescribed in either of those sections, or

(b) the appeal has not been proceeded with or has been abandoned,

order that the appeal be dismissed. R.S., c. C-34, s. 757; R.S., c. 2 (2nd Supp.), s. 18.

Costs

758. Where an appeal is heard and determined or is abandoned or is dismissed for want of prosecution, the appeal court may make any order with respect to costs that it considers just and reasonable. 1953-54, c. 51, s. 730.

To whom costs payable, and when

759. (1) Where the appeal court orders the appellant or respondent to pay
costs, the order shall direct that the costs be paid to the clerk of the court, 2
to be paid by him to the person entitled to them, and shall fix the period within which the costs shall be paid.

Certificate of non-payment of costs

(2) Where the costs are not paid in full within the period fixed for payment and the person who has been ordered to pay them has not been bound by a recognizance to pay them, the clerk of the court shall, upon application by the person entitled to the costs, or by any person on his behalf, and upon payment of any fee to which the clerk of the court is entitled, issue a certificate in Form 38 certifying that the costs or a part thereof, as the case may be, have not been paid.

Committal

(3) A justice having jurisdiction in the territorial division in which a certificate has been issued under subsection (2) may, upon production of the certificate, by warrant in Form 23, commit the defaulter to imprisonment for a term not exceeding one month, unless the amount of the costs and, where the justice thinks fit so to order, the costs of the committal and of conveying the defaulter to prison are sooner paid. 1953-54, c. 51, s. 731; 1968-69, c. 38, s. 89.

Enforcement of conviction or order by court of appeal

760. (1) A conviction or order made by the appeal court may be enforced

(a) in the same manner as if it had been made by the summary conviction 720
court, or

(b) by process of the appeal court.

Enforcement by justice

(2) Where an appeal taken against a conviction or order adjudging payment of a sum of money is dismissed, the summary conviction court that made the conviction or order or a justice for the same territorial division may issue a warrant of committal as if no appeal had been taken.

Duty of clerk of court

(3) Where a conviction or order that has been made by an appeal court is to be enforced by a justice, the clerk of the appeal court shall send to the justice the conviction or order and all writings relating thereto, except the notice of intention to appeal and any recognizance. 1953-54, c. 51, s. 732.

2. In this Act

"justice" means a justice of the peace or a magistrate, and includes two or more justices where two or more justices are, by law, required to act or, by law, act or have jurisdiction;

"territorial division" includes any province, county, union of counties, township, city, town, parish or other judicial division or place to which the context applies;

Stated Case

"Superior court"

761. For the purposes of sections 762 to 770, "superior court" means the superior court of criminal jurisdiction for the province in which the proceedings in respect of which a case is sought to be stated are carried on. 1953-54,c.51,s.733. 2

Application for stated case

762. (1) A party to proceedings to which this Part applies or the Attorney General may appeal against a conviction, order, determination or other proceeding of a summary conviction court on the ground that 720 720 720

(a) it is erroneous in point of law, or

(b) it is in excess of jurisdiction,

by applying to the summary conviction court to state a case setting forth the facts as found by that court and the grounds on which the proceedings are questioned.

Rules of court, if any, to apply

(2) An application to state a case shall be made and the case shall be stated within the period and in the manner directed by rules of court, if any, and where there are no rules of court otherwise providing, the following rules apply, namely,

(a) the application

(i) shall be in writing and be directed to the summary conviction court,

(ii) shall be served upon the summary conviction court by leaving with that court a copy thereof within thirty clear days after the time when the adjudication that is questioned was made; 25(1)(2) Interp

(b) the case shall be stated and signed by the summary conviction court within one month after the time when the application was made; and 25(7) Interp

(c) the appellant shall, within fifteen clear days after receiving the stated case,

(i) give to the respondent a notice in writing of the appeal with a copy of the stated case, and

(ii) transmit the stated case to the superior court.

Right of Attorney General of Canada to appeal

(3) The Attorney General of Canada has the same rights of appeal in proceedings instituted at the instance of the Government of Canada and conducted by or on behalf of that Government as the Attorney General of a province has under this section. R.S., c. C-34, s. 762; R.S., c. 2(2nd Supp.), s. 19.

Application of ss. 752, 752.1, 752.3 and 757

763. The provisions of sections 752, 752.1, 752.3 and 757 apply *mutatis mutandis* in respect of an appeal under section 762, except that

(a) in the application of section 752.3 in respect thereof, the period of thirty days therein referred to shall be read as one month from the time when the application to state a case was made to the summary conviction court; and

(b) upon receiving an application by the person having the custody of an appellant described in section 752.3 to fix a date for the hearing of the appeal, the superior court shall, after giving the prosecutor a reasonable opportunity to be heard, give such directions as it thinks necessary for expediting the hearing thereof. R.S., c. C-34, s. 763; R.S., c. 2(2nd Supp.), s. 20. 2

Procedure when justice dies or quits office

764. (1) Where, pending an application for a stated case, a justice who was, or was a member of, the summary conviction court dies, quits office or is unable to act, the appellant may, upon giving notice to the respondent, apply to the superior court to state a case, and if a case is thereupon stated it shall be dealt with as if it had been stated by the summary conviction court.

Undertaking, etc., to be given by appellant before case stated

(2) The superior court may, upon receiving an application under subsection (1) and before stating a case, order that the appellant appear before a justice and give an undertaking or enter into a recognizance as provided in

(a) section 752, where the defendant is the appellant, or

(b) section 752.1, in any other case.

Where appellant is Attorney General

(3) Subsection (2) does not apply where the appellant is the Attorney General
or counsel acting on behalf of the Attorney General. R.S., c. C-34, s. 764; R.S., 2
c. 2(2nd Supp.), s. 21.

Refusal to state a case

765. Where a summary conviction court, to which an application to state a case is made, considers that the application is frivolous, it may refuse to state a case and shall, at the request of the appellant, issue to him a certificate of the refusal, but the summary conviction court shall not refuse to state a case where the application is made by or at the direction of the Attorney General of Canada or the Attorney General of a province or counsel acting on behalf of either of them. 1953-54, c. 51, s. 737.

Compelling statement of case

766. (1) Where a summary conviction court refuses to state a case, the
appellant may apply to the superior court, upon an affidavit setting out the 761
facts, for an order directing the summary conviction court and the respondent to show cause why a case should not be stated.

Order

(2) Where an application is made under subsection (1), the superior court may make the order or dismiss the application, with or without payment of costs by the appellant or the summary conviction court, as it considers appropriate in the circumstances.

Case to be stated

(3) Where the superior court pursuant to an application made under subsection (1) determines that a case should be stated, it shall so order and the summary conviction court shall, upon being served with a copy of the order, state a case accordingly.

Undertaking, etc., to be given by appellant before cause ordered to be shown

(4) The superior court may, upon receiving an application under subsection (1) and before making any order described in that subsection, order that the appellant appear before a justice and give an undertaking or enter into a recognizance as provided in

(a) section 752, where the defendant is the appellant, or

(b) section 752.1, in any other case.

When appellant Attorney General

(5) Subsection (4) does not apply where the appellant is the Attorney General or counsel acting on behalf of the Attorney General. R.S., c. C-34, s. 766; R.S., c. 2(2nd Supp.), s. 22.

No *certiorari* required

767. No writ of *certiorari* or other writ is required to remove any conviction, order or other determination in relation to which a case is stated for the purpose 2
of obtaining the judgment, determination or opinion of the superior court. 761
1953-54, c. 51, s. 739.

Powers of court hearing appeal

768. (1) Where a case is stated under this Part, the superior court shall hear and determine the grounds of appeal and may

(*a*) affirm, reverse or modify the conviction, order or determination,

(*b*) cause the case to be sent back to the summary conviction court for 720
amendment and deliver judgment after it has been amended, or

(*c*) remit the matter to the summary conviction court with the opinion of the superior court,

and may make

(*d*) any other order in relation to the matter that it considers proper, and

(*e*) any order, with respect to costs, that it considers proper, but except as provided in subsection 766(2), no order for the payment of costs shall be made against a summary conviction court that states a case.

Authority of judge

(2) The authority and jurisdiction of the superior court to which a case is stated may, where that authority and jurisdiction may be exercised by a judge of that court, subject to any rules of court in relation thereto, be exercised by a judge of the court sitting in chambers as well in vacation as in term time. 1953-54, c. 51, s. 740.

Enforcement of adjudication

769. (1) Where the superior court has rendered its decision on a stated case, the summary conviction court in relation to whose adjudication the case has been stated or a justice exercising the same jurisdiction has the same authority to enforce a conviction, order or determination that has been affirmed, amended or made by the superior court as the summary conviction court would have had if a case had not been stated.

Idem

(2) An order of the superior court may be enforced by its own process. 1953-54, c. 51, s. 741.

Statement of case precludes appeal

770. (1) Every person for whom a case is stated in respect of an adjudication of a summary conviction court from which he is entitled to an appeal under section 748 shall be taken to have abandoned all his rights of appeal under that section.

No case to be stated when no appeal

(2) Where it is provided by law that no appeal lies from a conviction or order, no appeal by way of a stated case lies from such a conviction or order. 1953-54, c. 51, s. 742.

2. In this Act

"superior court of criminal jurisdiction" means

(*a*) in the Province of Ontario, the Supreme Court,

(*b*) in the Province of Quebec, the Superior Court,

(*c*) in the Provinces of Nova Scotia, Prince Edward Island and Newfoundland respectively, the Supreme Court,

(*d*) in the Province of British Columbia, the Supreme Court or the Court of Appeal,

(*e*) in the Provinces of Manitoba, Saskatchewan, Alberta and New Brunswick, respectively, the Court of Appeal or the Court of Queen's Bench,

(*f*) in the Yukon Territory, the Supreme Court, and

(*g*) in the Northwest Territories, the Supreme Court;

Appeals to Court of Appeal

On question of law

771. (1) An appeal to the court of appeal, as defined in section 601 may, with leave of that court, be taken on any ground that involves a question of law alone, against

(*a*) a decision of a court in respect of an appeal under section 755, or

(*b*) a decision of a superior court in respect of a stated case under section 768, except where the superior court to which the case was stated is the court of appeal.

601. In this Part

"court of appeal" means the court of appeal, as defined by the definition "court of appeal" in section 2, for the province or territory in which the trial of a person by indictment is held;

2. In this Act

"court of appeal" means

(*a*) in the Province of Ontario, the Court of Appeal,

(*b*) in the Province of Quebec, the Court of Appeal,

(*c*) in the Province of Nova Scotia, the Appeal Division of the Supreme Court,

(*d*) in the Province of New Brunswick, the Court of Appeal,

(*e*) in the Province of British Columbia, the Court of Appeal,

(*f*) in the Province of Prince Edward Island, the Supreme Court,

(*g*) in the Province of Manitoba, the Court of Appeal,

(*h*) in the Province of Saskatchewan, the Court of Appeal,

(*i*) in the Province of Alberta, the Court of Appeal,

(*j*) in the Province of Newfoundland, the Court of Appeal,

(*k*) in the Yukon Territory, the Court of Appeal, and

(*l*) in the Northwest Territories, the Court of Appeal;

Sections applicable

(2) Sections 601 to 616 apply *mutatis mutandis* to an appeal under this section.

mutatis mutandis — after the necessary changes in detail so that the text applies

Costs

(3) Notwithstanding subsection (2), the court of appeal may make any order with respect to costs that it considers proper in relation to an appeal under this section.

Enforcement of decision

(4) The decision of the court of appeal may be enforced in the same manner as if it had been made by the summary conviction court before which the proceedings were originally heard and determined.

Right of Attorney General of Canada to appeal

(5) The Attorney General of Canada has the same rights of appeal in proceedings instituted at the instance of the Government of Canada and conducted by or on behalf of that Government as the Attorney General of a province has under this Part. 1953-54, c. 61, s. 743; 1959, c. 41, s. 38; 1960-61, c. 43, s. 45.

Fees and Allowances

Fees and allowances

772. (1) Subject to subsection (2), the fees and allowances mentioned in the schedule to this Part and no others are the fees and allowances that may be taken or allowed in proceedings before summary conviction courts and justices under this Part. 720 2[720]

Order of lieutenant governor in council

(2) The lieutenant governor in council of a province may order that all or any of the fees and allowances mentioned in the schedule to this Part shall not be taken or allowed in proceedings before summary conviction courts and justices under this Part in that province. 1968-69, c. 38, s. 91. 28 Interp

Interpretation Act

28. In every enactment

"lieutenant governor in council" means the lieutenant governor, or person administering the government of the province indicated by the enactment, for the time being, acting by and with the advice of, or by and with the advice and consent of, or in conjuction with the executive council of such province and, in relation to the Yukon Territory or the Northwest Territories, means the Commissioner thereof;

"province" means a province of Canada, and includes the Yukon Territory and the Northwest Territories;

SCHEDULE

FEES AND ALLOWANCES THAT MAY BE CHARGED BY SUMMARY CONVICTION COURTS AND JUSTICES

1. Information $1.00
2. Summons or warrant 0.50
3. Warrant where summons issued in first instance. 0.30
4. Each necessary copy of summons or warrant 0.30
5. Each subpoena or warrant to or for witnesses 0.30
   (A subpoena may contain any number of names. Only one subpoena may be issued on behalf of a party in any proceeding, unless the summary conviction court or the justice considers it necessary or desirable that more than one subpoena be issued.)
6. Information for warrant for witness and warrant for witness 1.00
7. Each necessary copy of subpoena to or warrant for witness 0.20
8. Each recognizance 1.00
9. Hearing and determining proceeding 1.00
10. Where hearing lasts more than two hours 2.00
11. Where two or more justices hear and determine a proceeding, each is entitled to the fee authorized by item 9.
12. Each warrant of committal 0.50
13. Making up record of conviction or order upon request of a party to the proceedings. 1.00
14. Copy of a writing other than a conviction or order, upon request of a party to the proceeding; for each folio of one hundred words 0.10
15. Bill of costs, when made out in detail upon request of a party to the proceedings 0.20
    (Items 14 and 15 may be charged only where there has been an adjudication.)
16. Attending to remand prisoner 1.00
17. Attending to take recognizance of bail 1.00

FEES AND ALLOWANCES THAT MAY BE ALLOWED TO PEACE OFFICERS

18. Arresting a person upon a warrant or without a warrant 1.50
19. Serving summons or subpoena. 0.50
20. Mileage to serve summons or subpoena or to make an arrest, both ways, for each mile 0.10
    (Where a public conveyance is not used, reasonable costs of transportation may be allowed.)
21. Mileage where service cannot be effected, upon proof of a diligent attempt to effect service, each way, for each mile 0.10
22. Returning with prisoner after arrest to take him before a summary conviction court or justice at a place different from the place where the peace officer received the warrant to arrest, if the journey is of necessity over a route different from that taken by the peace officer to make the arrest, each way, for each mile. 0.10
23. Taking a prisoner to prison on remand or committal, each way, for each mile 0.10
    (Where a public conveyance is not used, reasonable costs of transportation may be allowed. No charge may be made under this item in respect of a service for which a charge is made under item 22.)
24. Attending summary conviction court or justice on summary conviction proceedings, for each day necessarily employed 2.00
    (No more than $2.00 may be charged under this item in respect of any day notwithstanding the number of proceedings that the peace officer attended on that day before that summary conviction court or justice.)

FEES AND ALLOWANCES THAT MAY BE ALLOWED TO WITNESSES

25. Each day attending trial 4.00
26. Mileage travelled to attend trial, each way, for each mile. 0.10

FEES AND ALLOWANCES THAT MAY BE ALLOWED TO INTERPRETERS

27. Each half day attending trial. 2.50
28. Actual living expenses when away from ordinary place of residence, not to exceed per day 10.00
29. Mileage travelled to attend trial, each way, for each mile. 0.10

Schedule to Part XXIV

—NOTES—

PART XXV

FORMS

Forms

773. (1) The forms set out in this Part varied to suit the case or forms to the like effect shall be deemed to be good, valid and sufficient in the circumstances for which, respectively, they are provided.

Seal not required

(2) No justice is required to attach or affix a seal to any writing or process that he is authorized to issue and in respect of which a form is provided by this Part. 1953-54, c. 51, s. 753.

Interpretation Act

26. (5) Where a form is prescribed, deviations therefrom, not affecting the substance or calculated to mislead, do not invalidate the form used.

FORM 1

INFORMATION TO OBTAIN A SEARCH WARRANT
(Section 443)

Canada,
Province of ,
(*territorial division*) .

This is the information of A.B., of in the said (*territorial division*), (*occupation*), hereinafter called the informant, taken before me.

The informant says that (*describe things to be searched for and offence in respect of which search is to be made*), and that he has reasonable grounds for believing that the said things, or some part of them are in the (*dwelling-house, etc.*), of C.D., of in the said (*territorial division*) (*here add the grounds of belief, whatever they may be*).

Wherefore the informant prays that a search warrant may be granted to search the said (*dwelling-house, etc.*), for the said things.

Sworn before me
this day of
A.D. ,
at .

....
Signature of Informant

....
A Justice of the Peace in and for

FORM 2

INFORMATION (Sections 455, 455.1 and 723)

Canada,
Province of ,
(*territorial division*) .

This is the information of C.D., of , (*occupation*), hereinafter called the informant.

The informant says that (*if the informant has not personal knowledge state that he has reasonable and probable grounds to believe and does believe and state the offence.*)

Sworn before me
this day of
A.D. ,
at .

....
Signature of Informant

....
A Justice of the Peace in and for

FORM 3

HEADING OF INDICTMENT (Sections 509 and 520)

Canada,
Province of ,
(*territorial division*) .

In the (*set out name of the court*)

Her Majesty the Queen
against
(*name of accused*)

1. The jurors for Her Majesty the Queen present that
2. The said jurors further present that

FORM 4

HEADING OF INDICTMENT (Sections 496, 509 and 520)

Canada,
Province of ,
(*territorial division*) .

In the (*set out name of the court*)

Her Majesty the Queen
against
(*name of accused*)

(*Name of accused*) stands charged

1. That he (*state offence*).
2. That he (*state offence*).

Dated this day of A.D.
at

....
(*Signature of signing officer, Agent of Attorney General, etc., as the case may be*)

FORM 5

WARRANT TO SEARCH (Section 443)

Canada,
Province of ,
(*territorial division*) .

To the peace officers in the said (*territorial division*):

Whereas it appears on the oath of A.B., of that there are reasonable grounds for believing that (*describe things to be searched for and offence in respect of which search is to be made*) are in at , hereinafter called the premises:

This is, therefore, to authorize and require you between the hours of (*as the justice may direct*) to enter into the said premises and to search for the said things and to bring them before me or some other justice.

Dated this day of A.D.
at

....
A Justice of the Peace in and for

FORM 6

SUMMONS TO A PERSON CHARGED WITH AN OFFENCE
(Sections 455.3, 455.5 and 728)

Canada,
'rovince of ,
territorial division) .

'o A.B., of (occupation):

Whereas you have this day been charged before me that (*set ut briefly the offence in respect of which the accused is charged*);

This is therefore to command you, in Her Majesty's name:

1. to attend court on , the day of A.D. , at o'clock in the noon, at or before any justice for the aid (*territorial division*) who is there, and to attend thereafter s required by the court, in order to be dealt with according to aw; and

2. to appear on , the day of .D. , at o'clock in the oon, at , for the purposes of the *Identification of 'riminals Act*. (*Ignore, if not filled in*).

You are warned that failure without lawful excuse to attend ourt in accordance with this summons is an offence under subection 133(4) of the *Criminal Code*.

Subsection 133(4) of the *Criminal Code* states as follows:

"(4) Every one who is served with a summons and who fails, without lawful excuse, the proof of which lies upon him, to attend court in accordance therewith, is guilty of

(*a*) an indictable offence and is liable to imprisonment for two years, or
(*b*) an offence punishable on summary conviction."

Section 455.6 of the *Criminal Code* states as follows:

"**455.6** Where an accused who is required by a summons to appear at a time and place stated therein for the purposes of the *Identification of Criminals Act*, does not appear at that time and place, a justice may issue a warrant for the arrest of the accused for the offence with which he is charged."

Dated this day of A.D. ,
t .

....
A Justice of the Peace in and for or Judge

FORM 7

WARRANT FOR ARREST

Canada,
Province of ,
(*territorial division*) .

To the peace officers in the said (*territorial division*):

This warrant is issued for the arrest of A.B., of , (*occupation*) , hereinafter called the accused.

Whereas the accused has been charged that (*set out briefly the offence in respect of which the accused is charged*);

And whereas:*

1. there are reasonable and probable grounds to believe that it is necessary in the public interest to issue this warrant for the arrest of the accused [455.3(4); 456.1(1)];

2. the accused failed to attend court in accordance with the summons served upon him [456.1(2)];

3. an (appearance notice *or* promise to appear *or* a recognizance entered into before an officer in charge) (*delete whichever are inapplicable*) was confirmed and the accused failed to attend court in accordance therewith [456.1(2)];

4. it appears that a summons cannot be served because the accused is evading service [456.1(2)];

5. the accused was ordered to be present at the hearing of an application for a review of an order made by a justice and did not attend the hearing [457.5(5); 457.6(5)];

6. there are reasonable and probable grounds to believe that the accused has violated or is about to violate the (promise to appear *or* undertaking *or* recognizance) (*delete whichever are inapplicable*) upon which he was released [458(1); 459(5); 608(6)];

7. there are reasonable and probable grounds to believe that the accused has since his release from custody on (a promise to appear *or* an undertaking *or* a recognizance) (*delete whichever are inapplicable*) committed an indictable offence [458(1); 459(5); 608(6)];

8. the accused was required by (an appearance notice *or* a promise to appear *or* a recognizance entered into before an officer in charge *or* a summons) (*delete whichever are inapplicable*) to attend at a time and place stated therein for the purposes of the *Identification of Criminals Act* and did not appear at that time and place [453.4; 455.6];

9. an indictment has been found against the accused and the accused has not appeared or remained in attendance before the court for his trial [526];

10.**

This is, therefore, to command you, in Her Majesty's name, forthwith to arrest the said accused and to bring him before (*state court, judge or justice*) , to be dealt with according to law.

Dated this day of A.D. ,
at .

....
Judge, Clerk of the Court, Magistrate or Justice

***For any case not covered by recitals 1 to 9, insert recital in the words of the statute authorizing the warrant.*

Form 8

WARRANT FOR COMMITTAL

Canada,
Province of
(*territorial division*)

To the peace officers in the said (*territorial division*) and to the keeper of the (*prison*) at :

This warrant is issued for the committal of A.B., of , (*occupation*), hereinafter called the accused.

Whereas the accused has been charged that (*set out briefly the offence in respect of which the accused is charged*);

And whereas:*

1. the prosecutor has shown cause why the detention of the accused in custody is justified [457(5)];

2. an order has been made that the accused be released upon (giving an undertaking *or* entering into a recognizance) (*delete whichever is inapplicable*) but the accused has not yet complied with the order [457.4(1); 457.5(9); 457.6(10); 458(8); 459(8)];**

3. the application by the prosecutor for a review of the order of a justice in respect of the interim release of the accused has been allowed and that order has been vacated, and the prosecutor has shown cause why the detention of the accused in custody is justified [457.6];

4. the accused has violated or was about to violate his (promise to appear *or* undertaking *or* recognizance) (*delete whichever are inapplicable*) and the same was cancelled, and the detention of the accused in custody is justified or seems proper in the circumstances [458(4); 458(5)];

5. there are reasonable and probable grounds to believe that the accused has after his release from custody on (a promise to appear *or* an undertaking *or* a recognizance) *delete whichever are inapplicable*) committed an indictable offence and the detention of the accused in custody is justified or seems proper in the circumstances [458(4); 458(5)];

6. the accused has violated or was about to violate the (undertaking *or* recognizance) (*delete whichever is inapplicable*) on which he was released and the detention of the accused in custody seems proper in the circumstances [459(7); 608(6)];

7. there are reasonable and probable grounds to believe that the accused has after his release from custody on (an undertaking *or* a recognizance) (*delete whichever is inapplicable*) committed an indictable offence and the detention of the accused in custody seems proper in the circumstances [459(7); 608(6)];

8.***

This is, therefore, to command you, in Her Majesty's name, to take the accused and convey him safely to the (*prison*) at , and there deliver him to the keeper thereof, with the following precept:

I do hereby command you the said keeper to receive the accused in your custody in the said prison and keep him safely there until he is delivered by due course of law.

Dated this day of A.D. , at .

....
Judge, Clerk of the Court,
Magistrate or Justice

Initial applicable recital.

***If the person having custody of the accused is authorized under paragraph 457.4(1) to release him upon his complying with an order, endorse the authorization on this warrant and attach a copy of the order.*

****For any case not covered by recitals 1 to 7, insert recital in the words of the statute authorizing the warrant.*

Form 8.1

APPEARANCE NOTICE ISSUED BY A PEACE OFFICER TO A PERSON NOT YET CHARGED WITH AN OFFENCE (Sections 451 and 452)

Canada,
Province of
(*territorial division*)

To A.B., of
(*occupation*):

You are alleged to have committed (*set out substance of offence*).

1. You are required to attend court on day the day of A.D. , at o'clock in the noon, in court room No. , at court, in the municipality of , and to attend thereafter as required by the court in order to be dealt with according to law.

2. You are also required to appear on day, the day of A.D. , at o'clock in the noon, at , (*police station*) (*address*) , for the purposes of the *Identification of Criminals Act*. (*Ignore, if not filled in*).

You are warned that failure to attend court in accordance with this appearance notice is an offence under subsection 133(5) of the *Criminal Code*.

Subsections 133(5) and (6) of the *Criminal Code* state as follows:

"(5) Every one who is named in an appearance notice or promise to appear, or in a recognizance entered into before an officer in charge, that has been confirmed by a justice under section 455.4 and who fails, without lawful excuse, the proof of which lies upon him to attend court in accordance therewith, is guilty of

(*a*) an indictable offence and is liable to imprisonment for two years, or

(*b*) an offence punishable on summary conviction.

(6) For the purposes of subsection (5), it is not a lawful excuse that an appearance notice, promise to appear or recognizance states defectively the substance of the alleged offence."

Section 453.4 of the *Criminal Code* states as follows:

"**453.4** Where an accused who is required by an appearance notice or promise to appear or by a recognizance entered into before an officer in charge to appear at a time and place stated therein for the purposes of the *Identification of Criminals Act* does not appear at that time and place, a justice may, where the appearance notice, promise to appear or recognizance has been confirmed by a justice under section 455.4, issue a warrant for the arrest of the accused for the offence with which he is charged."

Issued at a.m./p.m. this day of A.D. , at

....
Signature of peace officer

Form 8.2

PROMISE TO APPEAR (Sections 453 and 453.1)

Canada,
Province of ,
(*territorial division*) .

I, A.B., of , (*occupation*), understand that it is alleged that I have committed (*set out substance of offence*).

In order that I may be released from custody,

1. I promise to attend court on day, the day of A.D. , at o'clock in the noon, in courtroom No. , at court in the municipality of , and to attend thereafter as required by the court, in order to be dealt with according to law.

2. I also promise to appear on day, the day of A.D. , at o'clock in the noon, at , (*police station*) (*address*) for the purposes of the *Identification of Criminals Act* (*Ignore if not filled in*).

I understand that failure without lawful excuse to attend court in accordance with this promise to appear is an offence under subsection 133(5) of the *Criminal Code*.

Subsections 133(5) and (6) of the *Criminal Code* state as follows:

"(5) Every one who is named in an appearance notice or promise to appear, or in a recognizance entered into before an officer in charge, that has been confirmed by a justice under section 455.4 and who fails, without lawful excuse, the proof of which lies upon him, to attend court in accordance therewith, is guilty of

(*a*) an indictable offence and is liable to imprisonment for two years, or

(*b*) an offence punishable on summary conviction.

(6) For the purposes of subsection (5), it is not a lawful excuse that an appearance notice, promise to appear or recognizance states defectively the substance of the alleged offence."

Section 453.4 of the *Criminal Code* states as follows:

"453.4 Where an accused who is required by an appearance notice or promise to appear or by a recognizance, entered into before an officer in charge to appear at a time and place stated therein for the purposes of the *Identification of Criminals Act* does not appear at that time and place, a justice may, where the appearance notice, promise to appear or recognizance has been confirmed by a justice under section 455.4, issue a warrant for the arrest of the accused for the offence with which he is charged."

Dated this day of A.D. , at .

....
Signature of accused

Form 8.3

RECOGNIZANCE ENTERED INTO BEFORE AN OFFICER IN CHARGE
(Sections 453 and 453.1)

Canada,
Province of ,
(*territorial division*) .

I, A.B., of , (*occupation*), understand that it is alleged that I have committed (*set out substance of offence*).

In order that I may be released from custody, I hereby acknowledge that I owe $ (*not exceeding $500*) to Her Majesty the Queen to be levied on my real and personal property if I fail to attend court as hereinafter required.

(*or, for a person not ordinarily resident in the province in which he is in custody or within one hundred miles of the place in which he is in custody:*)

In order that I may be released from custody, I hereby acknowledge that I owe $ (*not exceeding $500*) to Her Majesty the Queen and deposit herewith (*money or other valuable security not exceeding in amount or value $500*) to be forfeited if I fail to attend court as hereinafter required.

1. I acknowledge that I am required to attend court on day, the day of A.D. , at o'clock in the noon, in courtroom No. , at court, in the municipality of , and to attend thereafter as required by the court, in order to be dealt with according to law.

2. I acknowledge that I am also required to appear on day, the day of A.D. , at o'clock in the noon, at (*police station*) (*address*) for the purposes of the *Identification of Criminals Act*. (*Ignore if not filled in*).

I understand that failure without lawful excuse to attend court in accordance with this recognizance is an offence under subsection 133(5) of the *Criminal Code*.

Subsections 133(5) and (6) of the *Criminal Code* state as follows:

"(5) Every one who is named in an appearance notice or promise to appear, or in a recognizance entered into before an officer in charge, that has been confirmed by a justice under section 455.4 and who fails, without lawful excuse, the proof of which lies upon him, to attend court in accordance therewith, is guilty of

(*a*) an indictable offence and is liable to imprisonment for two years, or

(*b*) an offence punishable on summary conviction.

(6) For the purposes of subsection (5), it is not a lawful excuse that an appearance notice, promise to appear or recognizance states defectively the substance of the alleged offence."

Section 453.4 of the *Criminal Code* states as follows:

"453.4 Where an accused who is required by an appearance notice or promise to appear or by a recognizance entered into before an officer in charge to appear at a time and place stated therein for the purposes of the *Identification of Criminals Act* does not appear at that time and place, a justice may, where the appearance notice, promise to appear or recognizance has been confirmed by a justice under section 455.4, issue a warrant for the arrest of the accused for the offence with which he is charged."

Dated this day of A.D. , at .

....
Signature of accused

FORM 9

UNDERTAKING GIVEN TO A JUSTICE OR A JUDGE
(Sections 457, 457.5, 457.6, 457.7, 458, 459, 608 and 608.1)

Canada,
Province of ,
(*territorial division*) .

I, A.B., of , (*occupation*), understand that I have been charged that (*set out briefly the offence in respect of which accused is charged*).

In order that I may be released from custody, I undertake to attend court on day, the day of A.D. , and to attend thereafter as required by the court in order to be dealt with according to law *or* (*where date and place of appearance before court are not known at the time undertaking is given*) to attend at the time and place fixed by the court and thereafter as required by the court in order to be dealt with according to law.

(*and where applicable*)

I also undertake to (*insert any conditions that are directed*)

(*a*) report at (*state times*) to (*name of peace officer or other person designated*),

(*b*) remain within (*designated territorial jurisdiction*),

(*c*) notify (*name of peace officer or other person designated*) of any change in my address, employment or occupation,

(*d*) abstain from communication with (*name of witness or other person*) except in accordance with the following conditions:

(*as the justice or judge specifies*),

(*e*) deposit my passport (*as the justice or judge directs*), and

(*f*) (*any other reasonable conditions*).

I understand that failure without lawful excuse to attend court in accordance with this undertaking is an offence under subsection 133(2) of the *Criminal Code*.

Subsections 133(2) and (3) of the *Criminal Code* state as follows:

"(2) Every one who, being at large on his undertaking or recognizance given to or entered into before a justice or a judge, fails, without lawful excuse, the proof of which lies upon him, to attend court in accordance therewith or to surrender himself in accordance with an order of the judge, as the case may be, is guilty of

(*a*) an indictable offence and is liable to imprisonment for two years, or

(*b*) an offence punishable on summary conviction.

(3) Every one who, being at large on his undertaking or recognizance given to or entered into before a justice or a judge and being bound to comply with a condition of that undertaking or recognizance directed by a justice or a judge, fails, without lawful excuse, the proof of which lies upon him, to comply with that condition, is guilty of

(*a*) an indictable offence and is liable to imprisonment for two years, or

(*b*) an offence punishable on summary conviction."

Dated this day of A.D. ,
at .

....
Signature of accused

FORM 9.1

UNDERTAKING BY APPELLANT (DEFENDANT)
(Sections 752, 763, 764 and 766)

Canada,
Province of ,
(*territorial division*) .

I, A.B., of , (*occupation*), being the appellant against conviction (*or* against sentence *or* against an order *or* by way of stated case) in respect of the following matter (*set out the offence, subject matter of order or question of law*)
undertake to appear personally at the sittings of the appeal court at which the appeal is to be heard.

(*and where applicable*)

I also undertake to (*insert any conditions that are directed*)

(*a*) report at (*state times*) to (*name of peace officer or other person designated*),

(*b*) remain within (*designated territorial jurisdiction*),

(*c*) notify (*name of peace officer or other person designated*) of any change in my address, employment or occupation,

(*d*) abstain from communicating with (*name of witness or other person*) except in accordance with the following conditions:

(*as the justice or judge specifies*),

(*e*) deposit my passport (*as the justice or judge directs*), and

(*f*) (*any other reasonable conditions*).

Dated this day of A.D. ,
at .

....
Signature of appellant

FORM 9.2

UNDERTAKING BY APPELLANT (PROSECUTOR)
(Sections 752.1, 763, 764 and 766)

Canada,
Province of ,
(*territorial division*) .

I, A.B., of , (*occupation*), being the appellant against an order of dismissal (*or* against sentence) in respect of the following charge (*set out the name of the defendant and the offence, subject matter of order or question of law*)
undertake to appear personally or by counsel at the sittings of the appeal court at which the appeal is to be heard.

Dated this day of A.D. ,
at .

....
Signature of appellant

Form 10

WARRANT TO CONVEY ACCUSED BEFORE JUSTICE OF ANOTHER TERRITORIAL DIVISION (Section 471)

Canada,
Province of ,
(*territorial division*) .

To the peace officers in the said (*territorial division*):

Whereas A.B., of hereinafter called the accused, has been charged that (*state place of offence and charge*);

And Whereas I have taken the deposition of X.Y. in respect of the said charge;

And Whereas the charge is for an offence committed in the (*territorial division*):

This is to command you, in Her Majesty's name, to convey the said A.B., before a justice of the (*last-mentioned territorial division*).

Dated this day of A.D. , at .

....
A Justice of the Peace in and for

Form 11

SUBPOENA TO A WITNESS (Section 627)

Canada,
Province of ,
(*territorial division*) .

To E.F., of , (*occupation*):

Whereas A.B. has been charged that (*state offence as in the information*), and it has been made to appear that you are likely to give material evidence for (the prosecution *or* the defence):

This is therefore to command you to attend before (*set out court or justice*), on the day of A.D. , at o'clock in the noon at to give evidence concerning the said charge.*

**Where a witness is required to produce documents add the following:*
and to bring with you any writings in your possession or under your control that relate to the said charge, and more particularly the following: (*specify any writings required*).

Dated this day of A.D. , at .

(*Seal if required*)

....
A Justice *or* clerk of the court

Form 12

WARRANT FOR WITNESS (Sections 626 and 633)

Canada,
Province of ,
(*territorial division*) .

To the peace officers in the (*territorial division*):

Whereas A.B. of , has been charged that (*state offence as in the information*);

And Whereas it has been made to appear that E.F. of , hereinafter called the witness, is likely to give material evidence for (the prosecution *or* the defence) and that*

**Insert whichever of the following is appropriate:*

(*a*) the said E.F. will not attend unless compelled to do so;

(*b*) the said E.F. is evading service of a subpoena;

(*c*) the said E.F. was duly served with a subpoena and has neglected (to attend at the time and place appointed therein *or* to remain in attendance);

(*d*) the said E.F. was bound by a recognizance to attend and give evidence and has neglected (to attend *or* to remain in attendance).

This is therefore to command you, in Her Majesty's name, to bring the witness forthwith before (*set out court or justice*) to be dealt with in accordance with section 634 of the *Criminal Code.*

Dated this day of A.D. , at .

Seal if required)

....
A Justice *or* Clerk of the Court

Form 13

WARRANT TO ARREST AN ABSCONDING WITNESS (Section 632)

Canada,
Province of ,
(*territorial division*) .

To the peace officers in the (*territorial division*):

Whereas A.B. of , has been charged that (*state offence as in the information*);

And Whereas I am satisfied by information in writing and under oath that C.D. of , hereinafter called the witness, is bound by recognizance to give evidence upon the trial of the accused upon the said charge, and that the witness (has absconded *or* is about to abscond):

This is therefore to command you, in Her Majesty's name, to arrest the witness and bring him forthwith before (*the court, judge, justice or magistrate before whom the witness is bound to appear*) to be dealt with in accordance with section 634 of the *Criminal Code.*

Dated this day of A.D. , at .

....
A Justice of the Peace in and for

Form 14

WARRANT REMANDING A PRISONER (Sections 457.1 and 465)

Canada,
Province of ,
(*territorial division*) .

To the peace officers in the (*territorial division*):

You are hereby commanded forthwith to convey to the (*prison*) at the persons named in the following schedule each of whom has been remanded to the time mentioned in the schedule:

Person charged	Offence	Remanded to

And I hereby command you, the keeper of the said prison, to receive each of the said persons into your custody in the prison and keep him safely until the day when his remand expires and then to have him before me or any other justice at at o'clock in the noon of the said day, there to answer to the charge and to be dealt with according to law, unless you are otherwise ordered before that time.

Dated this day of A.D. , at .

....
A Justice of the Peace in and for

Form 16

WARRANT OF COMMITTAL OF WITNESS FOR REFUSING TO BE SWORN OR TO GIVE EVIDENCE (Section 472)

Canada,
Province of ,
(*territorial division*) .

To the peace officers in the (*territorial division*):

Whereas A.B. of , hereinafter called the accused, has been charged that (*set out offence as in the information*);

And Whereas E.F. of , hereinafter called the witness, attending before me to give evidence for (the prosecution *or* the defence) concerning the charge against the accused (refused to be sworn *or* being duly sworn as a witness refused to answer certain questions concerning the charge that were put to him *or* refused or neglected to produce the following writings, namely *or* refused to sign his deposition) having been ordered to do so, without offering any just excuse for such refusal or neglect:

This is therefore to command you, in Her Majesty's name, to take the witness and convey him safely to the prison at , and there deliver him to the keeper thereof, together with the following precept:

I do hereby command you, the said keeper, to receive the said witness into your custody in the said prison and safely keep him there for the term of days, unless he sooner consents to do what was required of him, and for so doing this is a sufficient warrant.

Dated this day of A.D. , at .

....
A Justice of the Peace in and for

Form 18

WARRANT OF COMMITTAL UPON CONVICTION (Sections 500 and 741)

Canada,
Province of ,
(*territorial division*) .

To the peace officers in the (*territorial division*) and to the keeper of the (*prison*) at :

Whereas A.B., hereinafter called the accused, was this day convicted upon a charge that (*state offence as in the information*), and it was adjudged that the accused for his offence*

* *Use whichever of the following forms of sentence is applicable:*

(*a*) be imprisoned in the (*prison*) at for the term of ;

(*b*) forfeit and pay the sum of dollars to be applied according to law, and also pay to the sum of dollars in respect of costs and in default of payment of the said sums (forthwith *or within a time fixed, if any*) be imprisoned in the (*prison*) at for the term of unless the said sums and costs and charges of the committal and of conveying the accused to the said prison are sooner paid;

(*c*) be imprisoned in (*prison*) at for the term of , and in addition (*as in* (*b*) *above*).

You are hereby commanded, in Her Majesty's name, to take the accused and convey him safely to the (*prison*) at and deliver him to the keeper thereof, together with the following precept:

You, the said keeper, are hereby commanded to receive the accused into custody in the said prison and imprison him there**

** *Complete in accordance with the adjudication.*

and for so doing this is a sufficient warrant.

Dated this day of A.D. , at .

(*Seal, if required*)

....
Clerk of the Court, Justice *or* Magistrate

Form 19

WARRANT OF COMMITTAL UPON AN ORDER FOR THE PAYMENT OF MONEY (Section 741)

Canada,
Province of ,
(*territorial division*) .

To the peace officers in the (*territorial division*) and to the keeper of the (*prison*) at :

Whereas A.B., hereinafter called the defendant, was tried upon an information alleging that (*set out matter of complaint*), and it was ordered that (*set out the order made*), and in default that the defendant be imprisoned in the (*prison*) at for a term of :

I hereby command you, in Her Majesty's name, to take the defendant and convey him safely to the (*prison*) at , and deliver him to the keeper thereof together with the following precept:

I hereby command you, the keeper of the said prison, to receive the defendant into your custody in the said prison and imprison him there for the term of , unless the said amounts and the costs and charges of the committal and of conveying the defendant to the said prison are sooner paid, and for so doing this is a sufficient warrant.

Dated this day of A.D. , at

....
A Justice of the Peace in and for

Form 20

WARRANT OF COMMITTAL FOR FAILURE TO FURNISH RECOGNIZANCE TO KEEP THE PEACE (Section 745)

Canada,
Province of ,
(*territorial division*) .

To the peace officers in the (*territorial division*) and to the keeper of the (*prison*) at :

Whereas A.B., hereinafter called the accused, has been ordered to enter into a recognizance to keep the peace and be of good behaviour, and has (refused *or* failed) to enter into a recognizance accordingly:

You are hereby commanded, in Her Majesty's name, to take the accused and convey him safely to the (*prison*) at and deliver him to the keeper thereof together with the following precept:

You, the said keeper, are hereby commanded to receive the accused into your custody in the said prison and imprison him there until he enters into a recognizance as aforesaid or until he is discharged in due course of law.

Dated this day of A.D. , at

....
(*Seal, if required*) Clerk of the Court, Justice *or* Magistrate

Form 21

WARRANT OF COMMITTAL OF WITNESS FOR FAILURE TO ENTER INTO RECOGNIZANCE (Section 477)

Canada,
Province of ,
(*territorial division*) .

To the peace officers in the (*territorial division*) and to the keeper of the (*prison*) at :

Whereas A.B., hereinafter called the accused, was committed for trial on a charge that (*state offence as in the information*);

And Whereas E.F., hereinafter called the witness, having appeared as a witness on the preliminary inquiry into the said charge, and being required to enter into a recognizance to appear as a witness on the trial of the accused on the said charge, has (failed *or* refused) to do so:

This is therefore to command you, in Her Majesty's name, to take and safely convey the said witness to the (*prison*) at and there deliver him to the keeper thereof, together with the following precept:

I do hereby command you, the said keeper, to receive the witness into your custody in the said prison and keep him there safely until the trial of the accused upon the said charge, unless before that time the witness enters into the said recognizance.

Dated this day of A.D. , at

....
A Justice of the Peace in and for

Form 22

WARRANT OF COMMITTAL FOR CONTEMPT (Section 636)

Canada,
Province of ,
(*territorial division*) .

To the peace officers in the said (*territorial division*) and to the keeper of the (*prison*) at :

Whereas E.F. of , hereinafter called the defaulter, was on the day of A.D. , at , convicted before for contempt in that he did not attend before to give evidence on the trial of a charge that (*state offence as in the information*) against A.B. of , although (duly subpoenaed *or* bound by recognizance to appear and give evidence in that behalf, *as the case may be*) and did not show any sufficient excuse for his default;

And Whereas in and by the said conviction it was adjudged that the defaulter (*set out punishment adjudged*);

And Whereas the defaulter has not paid the amounts adjudged to be paid; (*delete if not applicable*)

This is therefore to command you, in Her Majesty's name, to take the defaulter and convey him safely to the prison at and there deliver him to the keeper thereof, together with the following precept:

I do hereby command you, the said keeper, to receive the defaulter into your custody in the said prison and imprison him there* and for so doing this is a sufficient warrant.

**Insert whichever of the following is applicable:*

(*a*) for the term of ,

(*b*) for the term of unless the said sums and the costs and charges of the committal and of conveying the defaulter to the said prison are sooner paid, *or*

(*c*) for the term of and for the term of (*if consecutive so state*) unless the said sums and costs and charges of the committal and of conveying the defaulter to the said prison are sooner paid.

Dated this day of A.D. , at

....

(*Seal, if required*). A Justice *or* Clerk of the Court

Form 23

WARRANT OF COMMITTAL IN DEFAULT OF PAYMENT OF COSTS OF AN APPEAL (Section 759)

Canada,
Province of ,
(*territorial division*) .

To the peace officers of (*territorial division*) and to the keeper of the (*prison*) at :

Whereas it appears that upon the hearing of an appeal before the (*set out court*), it was adjudged that A.B., of , hereinafter called the defaulter, should pay to the Clerk of the Court the sum of dollars in respect of costs;

And Whereas the Clerk of the Court has certified that the defaulter has not paid the sum within the time limited therefor:

I do hereby command you, the said peace officers, in Her Majesty's name, to take the defaulter and safely convey him to the (*prison*) at and deliver him to the keeper thereof, together with the following precept:

I do hereby command you, the said keeper, to receive the defaulter into your custody in the said prison and imprison him for the term of , unless the said sum and the costs of the committal and of conveying the defaulter to prison are sooner paid, and for so doing this is a sufficient warrant.

Dated this day of A.D. , at

....
A Justice of the Peace in and for

Form 24

WARRANT OF COMMITTAL ON FORFEITURE OF A RECOGNIZANCE (Section 707)

Canada,
Province of ,
(*territorial division*) .

To the sheriff of (*territorial division*) and to the keeper of the (*prison*) at :

You are hereby commanded to take (A.B. and C.D. *as the case may be*) hereinafter called the defaulters, and to convey them safely to the (*prison*) at and deliver them to the keeper thereof, together with the following precept:

You, the said keeper, are hereby commanded to receive the defaulters into your custody in the said prison and imprison them for a period of or until satisfaction is made of a judgment debt of dollars due to Her Majesty the Queen in respect of the forfeiture of a recognizance entered into by on the day of A.D.

Dated this day of A.D.

....

(*Seal*) Clerk of the

Form 25

ENDORSEMENT OF WARRANT
(Subsection 443(2) and sections 461 and 741)

Canada,
Province of ,
(*territorial division*) .

Pursuant to application this day made to me, I hereby authorize the execution of this warrant within the said (*territorial division*).

Dated this day of A.D. , at .

....
A Justice of the Peace in and for

Form 25.1

ENDORSEMENT OF WARRANT
(Section 453.1 and subsection 455.3(6))

Canada,
Province of ,
(*territorial division*) .

Whereas this warrant is issued in respect of an offence mentioned in subsection 453(1) of the *Criminal Code*, I hereby authorize the release of the accused pursuant to section 453.1 thereof.

Dated this day of A.D. , at .

....
A Justice of the Peace in and for

Form 26

ORDER FOR ACCUSED TO BE BROUGHT BEFORE JUSTICE PRIOR TO EXPIRATION OF PERIOD OF REMAND (Section 465)

Canada,
Province of ,
(*territorial division*) .

To the keeper of the (*prison*) at :

Whereas by warrant dated the day of A.D. , I committed A.B., hereinafter called the accused, to your custody and required you safely to keep until the day of A.D. , and then to have him before me or any other justice at at o'clock in the noon to answer to the charge against him and to be dealt with according to law unless you should be ordered otherwise before that time:

Now, therefore, I order and direct you to have the accused before at at o'clock in the noon to answer to the charge against him and to be dealt with according to law.

Dated this day of A.D. , at .

....
A Justice of the Peace in and for

Form 27

DEPOSITION OF A WITNESS (Section 468)

Canada,
Province of ,
(*territorial division*) .

These are the depositions of X.Y., of , and M.N., of , taken before me, this day of A.D., at , in the presence and hearing of A.B., hereinafter called the accused, who stands charged (*state offence as in the information*).

X.Y., having been duly sworn, deposes as follows: (*insert deposition as nearly as possible in words of witness*).

M.N., having been duly sworn, deposes as follows:

I certify that the depositions of X.Y., and M.N., written on the several sheets of paper hereto annexed to which my signature is affixed, were taken in the presence and hearing of the accused (and signed by them respectively, in his presence, *where they are required to be signed by witness*). In witness whereof I have hereto signed my name.

....
A Justice of the Peace in and for

FORM 28

RECOGNIZANCE

Canada,
Province of ,
(*territorial division*)

Be it remembered that on this day the persons named in the following schedule personally came before me and severally acknowledged themselves to owe to Her Majesty the Queen the several amounts set opposite their respective names, namely,

Name	Address	Occupation	Amount
A.B.			
C.D.			
E.F.			

to be made and levied of their several goods and chattels, lands and tenements, respectively, to the use of Her Majesty the Queen, if the said A.B. fails in any of the conditions hereunder written.

Taken and acknowledged before me on the day of A.D. , at .

....
Judge, Clerk of the Court, Magistrate or Justice

1. Whereas the said ,
hereinafter called the accused, has been charged that (*set out the offence in respect of which the accused has been charged*);

Now, therefore, the condition of this recognizance is that if the accused attends court on day, the day of A.D. , at o'clock in the noon and attends thereafter as required by the court in order to be dealt with according to law *or* (*where date and place of appearance before court are not known at the time recognizance is entered into*) if the accused attends at the time and place fixed by the court and attends thereafter as required by the court in order to be dealt with according to law [457; 457.5; 457.6; 457.7; 457.8; 458; 459; 608.1];

And further, if the appellant (*insert in Schedule of Conditions any additional conditions that are directed*),
the said recognizance is void, otherwise it stands in full force and effect.

2. Whereas the said ,
hereinafter called the appellant, is an appellant against his conviction (*or* against his sentence) in respect of the following charge (*set out the offence for which the appellant was convicted*) [608; 608.1]:

Now, therefore, the condition of this recognizance is that if the appellant attends as required by the court in order to be dealt with according to law;

And further, if the appellant (*insert in Schedule of Conditions any additional conditions that are directed*),
the said recognizance is void, otherwise it stands in full force and effect.

3. Whereas the said ,
hereinafter called the appellant, is an appellant against his conviction (*or* against his sentence *or* against an order *or* by way of stated case) in respect of the following matter (*set out offence, subject matter of order or question of law*) [752; 763; 764; 766]:

Now, therefore, the condition of this recognizance is that if the appellant appears personally at the sittings of the appeal court at which the appeal is to be heard;

And further, if the appellant (*insert in Schedule of Conditions any additional conditions that are directed*),
the said recognizance is void, otherwise it stands in full force and effect.

4. Whereas the said ,
hereinafter called the appellant, is an appellant against an order of dismissal (*or* against sentence) in respect of the following charge (*set out the name of the defendant and the offence, subject matter of order or question of law*) [752.1; 763; 764; 766]:

Now, therefore, the condition of this recognizance is that if the appellant appears personally or by counsel at the sittings of the appeal court at which the appeal is to be heard the said recognizance is void, otherwise it stands in full force and effect.

5. Whereas the said ,
hereinafter called the accused, was committed for trial on a charge that (*set out the offence in respect of which the accused has been charged*);

And whereas A.B. appeared as a witness on the preliminary inquiry into the said charge [477; 634; 635];

Now, therefore, the condition of this recognizance is that if the said A.B. appears at the time and place fixed for the trial of the accused to give evidence upon the indictment that is found against the accused, the said recognizance is void, otherwise it stands in full force and effect.

6. The condition of the above written recognizance is that if A.B. keeps the peace and is of good behaviour for the term of commencing on , the said recognizance is void, otherwise it stands in full force and effect [745].

Schedule of Conditions

(*a*) reports at (*state times*) to (*name of peace officer or other person designated*),

(*b*) remains within (*designated territorial jurisdiction*),

(*c*) notifies (*name of peace officer or other person designated*) of any change in his address, employment or occupation,

(*d*) abstains from communicating with (*name of witness or other person*) except in accordance with the following conditions: (*as the justice or judge specifies*),

(*e*) deposits his passport (*as the justice or judge directs*), and

(*f*) (*any other reasonable conditions*).

Note: The provisions of section 697 and subsections 698(1), (2) and (3) must be endorsed on a recognizance. See subsection 698(4).

Form 29

CERTIFICATE OF DEFAULT TO BE ENDORSED ON RECOGNIZANCE (Section 704)

I hereby certify that A.B. has not appeared as required by his recognizance and that by reason thereof the ends of justice have been (defeated *or* delayed, *as the case may be*).

The reason for the default is (*state reason if known*).

The names and addresses of the principal and sureties are as follows:

Dated this day of A.D. , at

(*Seal, if required*) .... Clerk of the Court, Judge, Justice *or* Magistrate

Form 30

WRIT OF FIERI FACIAS (Section 705)

Elizabeth II by the Grace of God, etc.

To the sheriff of (*territorial division*), GREETING.

You are hereby commanded to levy of the goods and chattels, lands and tenements of each of the following persons the amount set opposite the name of each:

Name	Address	Occupation	Amount

And you are further commanded to make a return of what you have done in execution of this writ.

Dated this day of A.D. , at .

(*Seal*) .... Clerk of the

Form 31

CONVICTION (Sections 500 and 741)

Canada,
Province of ,
(*territorial division*) .

Be it remembered that on the day of at , A.B., hereinafter called the accused, was tried under Part (XVI *or* XXIV) of the *Criminal Code* upon the charge that (*state fully the offence of which accused was convicted*), was convicted of the said offence and the following punishment was imposed upon him, namely,*

**Use whichever of the following forms of sentence is applicable:*

(*a*) That the said accused be imprisoned in the (*prison*) at for the term of .

(*b*) That the said accused forfeit and pay the sum of dollars to be applied according to law and also pay to the sum of dollars in respect of costs and in default of payment of the said sums (forthwith *or within a time fixed, if any*) to be imprisoned in the (*prison*) at for the term of unless the said sums and costs and charges of the committal and of conveying the accused to the said prison are sooner paid.

(*c*) That the said accused be imprisoned in the (*prison*) at for the term of and in addition forfeit and pay the sum of dollars to be applied according to law and also pay to the sum of dollars in respect of costs and in default of payment of the said sums (forthwith *or within a time fixed, if any*) to be imprisoned in the (*prison*) at for the term of (*if sentence to be consecutive, state accordingly*) unless the said sums and costs and charges of the committal and of conveying the accused to the said prison are sooner paid.

Dated this day of A.D. , at .

(*Seal, if required*) .... Clerk of the Court, Justice *or* Magistrate

Form 32

ORDER AGAINST A DEFENDANT (Section 741)

Canada,
Province of ,
(*territorial division*) .

Be it remembered that on the day of A.D. , at , A.B., of , was tried upon an information alleging that (*set out matter of complaint*), and it was ordered and adjudged that (*set out the order made*).

Dated this day of A.D. , at .

.... A Justice of the Peace in and for

Form 33

ORDER ACQUITTING ACCUSED (Section 500)

Canada,
Province of ,
(*territorial division*) .

Be it remembered that on the day of A.D. , at A.B., of (*occupation*), was tried upon the charge that (*state fully the offence of which accused was acquitted*) and was found not guilty of the said offence.

Dated this day of A.D. , at .

(*Seal, if required*) .... Magistrate *or* Clerk of the Court

Form 34

CONVICTION FOR CONTEMPT (Section 636)

Canada,
Province of ,
(*territorial division*) .

Be it remembered that on the day of A.D. , at in the (*territorial division*), E.F. of , hereinafter called the defaulter, is convicted by me for contempt in that he did not attend before (set out court *or* justice) to give evidence on the trial of a charge that (*state fully offence with which accused was charged*), although (duly subpoenaed *or* bound by recognizance to attend to give evidence, *as the case may be*) and has not shown before me any sufficient excuse for his default;

Wherefore I adjudge the defaulter for his said default, (*set out punishment as authorized and determined in accordance with section 636*).

Dated this day of A.D. , at .

(*Seal, if required*) .... A Justice *or* Clerk of the Court (*as the case may be*)

Form 35

ORDER FOR DISCHARGE OF A PERSON IN CUSTODY
(Sections 457.4, 752, 763, 764 and 766)

Canada,
Province of ,
(*territorial division*) .

To the keeper of the (*prison*) at :

I hereby direct you to release E.F., detained by you under a (warrant of committal *or* order) dated the day of A.D. , if the said E.F. is detained by you for no other cause.

(*Seal, if required*)

....
A Judge, Justice *or* Clerk of the Court

Form 36

CHALLENGE TO ARRAY (Section 558)

Canada,
Province of ,
(*territorial division*) .

The Queen
v.
C.D.

The (prosecutor *or* accused) challenges the array of the panel on the ground that X.Y., (sheriff *or* deputy sheriff), who returned the panel, was guilty of (partiality *or* fraud *or* wilful misconduct) on returning it.

Dated this day of A.D. , at .

....
Counsel for (prosecutor *or* accused)

Form 37

CHALLENGE FOR CAUSE (Section 568)

Canada,
Province of ,
(*territorial division*) .

The Queen
v.
C.D.

The (prosecutor *or* accused) challenges G.H. on the ground that (*set out ground of challenge in accordance with subsection 567(1)*).

....
Counsel for (prosecutor *or* accused)

Form 38

CERTIFICATE OF NON-PAYMENT OF COSTS OF APPEAL (Section 759)

In the Court of

(*Style of Cause*)

I hereby certify that A.B. (the appellant *or* respondent, *as the case may be*) in this appeal, having been ordered to pay costs in the sum of dollars, has failed to pay the said costs within the time limited for the payment thereof.

Dated this day of A.D. , at .

(*Seal*)

....
Clerk of the Court of

Form 39

GAOLER'S RECEIPT TO PEACE OFFICER FOR PRISONER (Section 661)

I hereby certify that I have received from X.Y., a peace officer for (*territorial division*) one A.B., together with a (warrant *or* order) issued by (*set out court or justice, as the case may be*).*

*(*Add a statement of the condition of the prisoner*)

Dated this day of A.D. , at .

....
Keeper of (*prison*)

Form 42
(Section 594)

I, (*name*) , a fingerprint examiner designated as such for the purposes of section 594 of the *Criminal Code* by the Solicitor General of Canada, do hereby certify that (*name*) also known as (*aliases if any*) , FPS Number , whose fingerprints are shown reproduced below (*reproduction of fingerprints*) has been convicted or has been convicted and sentenced in Canada as follows:

(*record*)

Dated this day of A.D. , at .

....
Fingerprint Examiner

Form 43
(Section 594)

I, (*name*) , a fingerprint examiner designated as such for the purposes of section 594 of the *Criminal Code* by the Solicitor General of Canada, do hereby certify that I have compared the fingerprints attached marked exhibit A with the fingerprints reproduced in the certificate in Form 42 attached marked exhibit B and that they are those of the same person.

Dated this day of A.D. , at .

....
Fingerprint Examiner

FORM 44

PROBATION ORDER (Sections 662.1 and 663)

Canada,
Province of ,
(*territorial division*).

Whereas on the day of at ,
A.B., hereinafter called the accused, (*pleaded guilty to or was tried under* (*here insert Part XVI, XVII or XXIV, as the case may be*) *of the Criminal Code and was* (*here insert convicted or found guilty, as the case may be*) *upon the charge that* (*here state the offence to which the accused pleaded guilty or for which the accused was found guilty or convicted, as the case may be*));

And whereas on the day of
the court adjudged*

*(*Use whichever of the following forms of disposition is applicable*):

(*a*) that the accused be discharged upon the conditions hereinafter prescribed:

(*b*) that the passing of sentence upon the accused be suspended and that the said accused be released upon the conditions hereinafter prescribed:

(*c*) that the accused forfeit and pay the sum of dollars to be applied according to law and in default of payment of the said sum (*forthwith or within a time fixed, if any*) be imprisoned in the (*prison*) at for the term of unless the said sum and charges of the committal and of conveying the said accused to the said prison are sooner paid, and in addition thereto, that the said accused comply with the conditions hereinafter prescribed:

(*d*) that the accused be imprisoned in the (*prison*) at for the term of and, in addition thereto, that the said accused comply with the conditions hereinafter prescribed:

Now therefore the said accused shall, for the period of from the date of this order or, where paragraph (*d*) is applicable, the date of expiration of his sentence of imprisonment, comply with the following conditions, namely, that the said accused shall keep the peace and be of good behaviour and appear before the court when required to do so by the court, and, in addition

(*a*) etc. (*here state any additional conditions prescribed pursuant to subsection 663(2)*).

Dated this day of A.D. ,
at

....
Clerk of the Court,
Justice *or* Magistrate

R.S., c. C-34, Part XXV; R.S., c. 2(2nd Supp.), s. 23; 1972, c. 13, s. 68.

—NOTES—

INDEX

Index

Index

Index

Index

Index

Index

—NOTES—

SELECTED FEDERAL STATUTES

Interpretation Act

Bill of Rights

Identification of Criminals Act

Canada Evidence Act

Juvenile Delinquents Act

Food and Drugs Act

Narcotic Control Act

War Measures Act

INTERPRETATION ACT

CHAPTER I-23

An Act respecting the interpretation of statutes

SHORT TITLE

Short title 1. This Act may be cited as the *Interpretation Act.* 1967-68, c. 7, s. 1.

INTERPRETATION

Definitions 2. (1) In this Act

"Act" "Act" means an Act of the Parliament of Canada;

"enact" "enact" includes to issue, make or establish;

"enactment" "enactment" means an Act or regulation or any portion of an Act or regulation;

"public officer" "public officer" includes any person in the public service of Canada

(*a*) who is authorized by or under an enactment to do or enforce the doing of an act or thing or to exercise a power, or

(*b*) upon whom a duty is imposed by or under an enactment;

"regulation" "regulation" includes an order, regulation, order in council, order prescribing regulations, rule, rule of court, form, tariff of costs or fees, letters patent, commission, warrant, proclamation, by-law, resolution or other instrument issued, made or established

(*a*) in the execution of a power conferred by or under the authority of an Act, or

(*b*) by or under the authority of the Governor in Council; 28

"repeal" "repeal" includes revoke or cancel.

Expired enactment (2) For the purposes of this Act, an enactment that has expired or lapsed or otherwise ceased to have effect shall be deemed to have been repealed. 1967-68, c. 7, s. 2. ss (1)

APPLICATION

Application 3. (1) Every provision of this Act extends and applies, unless a contrary intention appears, to every enactment, whether enacted before or after the commencement of this Act. 2

Application to this Act (2) The provisions of this Act apply to the interpretation of this Act.

Rules of construction not excluded (3) Nothing in this Act excludes the application to an enactment of a rule of construction applicable thereto and not inconsistent with this Act. 1967-68, c. 7, s. 3.

ENACTING CLAUSE OF ACTS

Enacting clause 4. (1) The enacting clause of an Act may be in the following form:

"Her Majesty, by and with the advice and consent of the Senate and House of Commons of Canada, enacts as follows:"

Order of clauses (2) The enacting clause of an Act shall follow the preamble, if any, and the various provisions within the purview or body of the Act shall follow in a concise and enunciative form. 1967-68, c. 7, s. 4.

OPERATION

Royal Assent

Royal assent and date of commencement

5. (1) The Clerk of the Parliaments shall endorse on every Act, immediately after the title thereof, the day, month and year when the Act was assented to in Her Majesty's name; such endorsement shall be taken to be a part of the Act, and the date of such assent shall be the date of the commencement of the Act, if no other date of commencement is therein provided. 28

Commencement provision

(2) Where an Act contains a provision that the Act or any portion thereof is to come into force on a day later than the date of assent to the Act, such provision shall be deemed to have come into force on the date of assent to the Act.

Commencement when no date fixed

(3) Where an Act provides that certain provisions thereof are to come or shall be deemed to have come into force on a day other than the date of assent to the Act, the remaining provisions of the Act shall be deemed to have come into force on the date of assent to the Act. 1967-68, c. 7, s. 5.

Day Fixed for Commencement or Repeal

Operation when date fixed for commencement or repeal

6. (1) Where an enactment is expressed to come into force on a particular day, 2
it shall be construed as coming into force upon the expiration of the previous day; and where an enactment is expressed to expire, lapse or otherwise cease to have effect on a particular day, it shall be construed as ceasing to have effect upon the commencement of the following day.

When no date fixed

(2) Every enactment that is not expressed to come into force on a particular day shall be construed as coming into force

(a) in the case of an Act, upon the expiration of the day immediately before 2
the day the Act was enacted;

(b) in the case of a regulation of a class that is not exempted from the application of subsection 5(1) of the *Statutory Instruments Act*, upon the expiration of the day immediately before the day the regulation was registered pursuant to section 6 of that Act; and

(c) in the case of a regulation of a class that is exempted from the application 2
of subsection 5(1) of the *Statutory Instruments Act*, upon the expiration of the day immediately before the day the regulation was made. R.S., c. I-23, s. 6; R.S., c.29(2nd Supp.), s. 1.

Regulation Prior to Commencement

Preliminary proceedings

7. Where an enactment is not in force and it contains provisions conferring 2
power to make regulations or do any other thing, that power may, for the
purpose of making the enactment effective upon its commencement, be 28
exercised at any time before its commencement, but a regulation so made or a thing so done has no effect until the commencement of the enactment except in so far as may be necessary to make the enactment effective upon its commencement. 1967-68, c. 7, s. 7.

Territorial Operation

Territorial operation

8. (1) Every enactment applies to the whole of Canada, unless it is otherwise 2
expressed therein.

Amending enactment

(2) Where an enactment that does not apply to the whole of Canada is amended, no provision in the amending enactment applies to any part of Canada to which the amended enactment does not apply, unless it is therein provided that the amending enactment applies to such part of Canada or to the whole of Canada.

Extra-territorial operation

(3) Every Act of the Parliament of Canada now in force enacted prior to the 11th day of December 1931 that in terms or by necessary or reasonable implication was intended, as to the whole or any part thereof, to have extra-territorial operation, shall be construed as if at the date of its enactment the Parliament of Canada then had full power to make laws having extra-territorial operation as provided by the *Statute of Westminster, 1931.* R.S., c. 107, s. 2; 1967-68, c. 7, s. 8.

RULES OF CONSTRUCTION

Private Acts

Provisions in private Acts

9. No provision in a private Act affects the rights of any person, except only as therein mentioned or referred to. 1967-68, c. 7, s. 9.

Law Always Speaking

Law always speaking

10. The law shall be considered as always speaking, and whenever a matter or thing is expressed in the present tense, it shall be applied to the circumstances
as they arise, so that effect may be given to the enactment and every part 2
thereof according to its true spirit, intent and meaning. 1967-68, c. 7, s.10.

Enactments Remedial

Enactments deemed remedial

11. Every enactment shall be deemed remedial, and shall be given such fair, large and liberal construction and interpretation as best ensures the attainment of its objects. 1967-68, c. 7, s. 11.

Preambles and Marginal Notes

Preamble

12. The preamble of an enactment shall be read as a part thereof intended to assist in explaining its purport and object. 196-68, c. 7, s. 12.

Marginal notes

13. Marginal notes and references to former enactments in an enactment after the end of a section or other division thereof form no part of the enactment, but shall be deemed to have been inserted for convenience of reference only. 1967-68, c. 7, s. 13.

Application of Definitions

Application of interpretation provisions

14. (1) Definitions or rules of interpretation contained in an enactment apply to the construction of the provisions of the enactment that contain those definitions or rules of interpretation, as well as to the other provisions of the enactment.

Interpretation sections subject to exceptions

(2) Where an enactment contains an interpretation section or provision, it shall be read and construed

(a) as being applicable only if the contrary intention does not appear, and

(b) as being applicable to all other enactments relating to the same subject-matter unless the contrary intention appears. 1967-68, c. 7, s. 14.

Words in regulations

15. Where an enactment confers power to make regulations, expressions used in the regulations have the same respective meanings as in the enactment conferring the power. 1967-68, c. 7, s. 15.

Her Majesty

Her Majesty not bound or affected unless stated

16. No enactment is binding on Her Majesty or affects Her Majesty or Her Majesty's rights or prerogatives in any manner, except only as therein mentioned or referred to. 1967-68, c. 7, s. 16.

Proclamations

Proclamation

17. (1) Where an enactment authorizes the issue of a proclamation, the 2
proclamation shall be understood to be a proclamation of the Governor in 28
Council.

Proclamation to be issued on advice

(2) Where the Governor General is authorized to issue a proclamation, the
proclamation shall be understood to be a proclamation issued under an order of 28
the Governor in Council, but it is not necessary to mention in the proclamation that it is issued under such order.

Date of proclamation

(3) Where the Governor in Council has authorized the issue of a proclamation, the proclamation may purport to have been issued on the day its issue was so authorized, and the day on which it so purports to have been issued shall be deemed to be the day on which the proclamation takes effect.

Judicial notice of proclamation

(4) Where an enactment is expressed to come into force on a day to be fixed by proclamation, judicial notice shall be taken of the issue of the proclamation and the day fixed thereby without being specially pleaded. 1967-68, c. 7, s.17.

Oaths

Administration of oaths

18. (1) Where by an enactment or by a rule of the Senate or House of
Commons, evidence under oath is authorized or required to be taken, or an oath 28
is authorized or directed to be made, taken or administered, the oath may be administered, and a certificate of its having been made, taken or administered may be given by any one authorized by the enactment or rule to take the evidence, or by a judge of any court, a notary public, a justice of the peace, or a commissioner for taking affidavits, having authority or jurisdiction within the place where the oath is administered.

Where justice of the peace empowered

(2) Where power is conferred upon a justice of the peace to administer an oath or affirmation, or to take an affidavit or declaration, the power may be exercised by a notary public or a commissioner for taking oaths. 1967-68, c. 7, s. 18.

Reports to Parliament

Reports to Parliament

19. Where an Act requires a report or other document to be laid before 2
Parliament and, in compliance with the Act, a particular report or document has been laid before Parliament at a session thereof, nothing in the Act shall be construed as requiring the same report or document to be laid before Parliament at any subsequent session thereof. 1967-68, c. 7, s. 19.

Corporations

Powers vested in corporations

20. (1) Words establishing a corporation shall be construed

(a) to vest in the corporation power to sue and be sued, to contract and be contracted with by its corporate name, to have a common seal and to alter or change it at pleasure, to have perpetual succession, to acquire and hold personal property or movables for the purposes for which the corporation is established and to alienate the same at pleasure;

(b) in the case of a corporation having a name consisting of an English and a French form or a combined English and French form, to vest in the corporation power to use either the English or the French form of its name or both forms and to show on its seal both the English and French forms of its name or to have two seals, one showing the English and the other showing the French form of its name;

(c) to vest in a majority of the members of the corporation the power to bind the others by their acts; and

(d) to exempt from personal liability for its debts, obligations or acts such individual members of the corporation as do not contravene the provisions of the enactment establishing the corporation.

Corporate name

(2) Where an enactment establishes a corporation and in each of the English 2
and French versions of the enactment the name of the corporation is in the form only of the language of that version, the name of the corporation shall consist of the form of its name in each of the versions of the enactment.

Banking business

(3) No corporation shall be deemed to be authorized to carry on the business of banking unless such power is expressly conferred upon it by the enactment establishing the corporation. 1967-68, c. 7, s. 20.

Majority and Quorum

Majorities

21. (1) Where an act or thing is required or authorized to be done by more than two persons, a majority of them may do it.

Quorum of board, court, commission, etc.

(2) Where an enactment establishes a board, court, commission or other body consisting of three or more members (in this section called an "association"),

(a) at a meeting of the association, a number of members of the association equal to

(i) at least one-half of the number of members provided for by the enactment, if that number is a fixed number, and

(ii) if the number of members provided for by the enactment is not a fixed number but is within a range having a maximum or minimum, at least one-half of the number of members in office if that number is within the range,

constitutes a quorum;

(b) an act or thing done by a majority of the members of the association present at a meeting, if the members present constitute a quorum, shall be deemed to have been done by the association; and

(c) a vacancy in the membership of the association does not invalidate the constitution of the association or impair the right of the members in office to act, if the number of members in office is not less than a quorum. 1967-68, c. 7, s. 21.

Appointment, Retirement and Powers of Officers

Public officers hold office during pleasure

22. (1) Every public officer appointed before, on or after the 1st day of 2
September 1967, by or under the authority of an enactment or otherwise, shall be deemed to have been appointed to hold office during pleasure only, unless it is otherwise expressed in the enactment or in his commission or appointment.

Effective day of appointments

(2) Where an appointment is made by instrument under the Great Seal, the 28
instrument may purport to have been issued on or after the day its issue was authorized, and the day on which it so purports to have been issued shall be deemed to be the day on which the appointment takes effect.

Appointment or engagement otherwise than under Great Seal

(3) Where in any enactment there is authority to appoint a person to a 2
position or to engage the services of a person, otherwise than by instrument under the Great Seal, the instrument of appointment or engagement may be expressed to be effective on or after the day on which such person commenced the performance of the duties of the position or commenced the performance of the services, and the day on which it is so expressed to be effective, unless that day is more than sixty days before the day on which the instrument is issued, shall be deemed to be the day on which the appointment or engagement takes effect.

Remuneration

(4) Where a person is appointed to an office, the appointing authority may fix, vary or terminate his remuneration.

Commencement of appointments or retirements

(5) Where a person is appointed to an office effective on a specified day, or where the appointment of a person is terminated effective on a specified day, the appointment or termination, as the case may be, shall be deemed to have been effected immediately upon the expiration of the previous day. 1967-68, c. 7, s. 22.

Implied powers respecting public officers

23. (1) Words authorizing the appointment of a public officer to hold office 2
during pleasure include the power of

(a) terminating his appointment or removing or suspending him,

(b) re-appointing or reinstating him, and

(c) appointing another in his stead or to act in his stead,

in the discretion of the authority in whom the power of appointment is vested.

Powers of acting Minister, successor or deputy

(2) Words directing or empowering a Minister of the Crown to do an act or thing, or otherwise applying to him by his name of office, include a Minister acting for him, or, if the office is vacant, a Minister designated to act in the office by or under the authority of an order in council, and also his successors in the office, and his or their deputy, but nothing in this subsection shall be construed to authorize a deputy to exercise any authority conferred upon a Minister to make a regulation as defined in the *Statutory Instruments Act.*

Successors to and deputy of public officer

(3) Words directing or empowering any other public officer to do any act or thing, or otherwise applying to him by his name of office, include his successors in the office and his or their deputy.

Powers of holder of public office

(4) Where a power is conferred or a duty imposed on the holder of an office as such, the power may be exercised and the duty shall be performed by the person for the time being charged with the execution of the powers and duties of the office. R.S., c. I-23, s.23; R.S., c. 29(2nd Supp.), s. 1.

Evidence

Documentary evidence

24. (1) Where an enactment provides that a document is evidence of a fact without anything in the context to indicate that the document is conclusive evidence, then, in any judicial proceedings, the document is admissible in evidence and the fact shall be deemed to be established in the absence of any evidence to the contrary.

Queen's Printer

(2) Every copy of an enactment having printed thereon what purports to be the name or title of the Queen's Printer and Controller of Stationery or the Queen's Printer shall be deemed to be a copy purporting to be printed by the Queen's Printer for Canada. 1967-68, c. 7, s. 24; 1968-69, c. 28, s. 105.

Computation of Time

Time limits and holidays

25. (1) Where the time limited for the doing of a thing expires or falls upon a holiday, the thing may be done on the day next following that is not a holiday. 28

Clear days

(2) Where there is a reference to a number of clear days or "at least" a number of days between two events, in calculating the number of days there shall be excluded the days on which the events happen.

Not clear days

(3) Where there is a reference to a number of days, not expressed to be clear days, between two events, in calculating the number of days there shall be excluded the day on which the first event happens and there shall be included the day on which the second event happens.

Beginning and ending of prescribed periods

(4) Where a time is expressed to begin or end at, on or with a specified day, or to continue to or until a specified day, the time includes that day.

After specified day

(5) Where a time is expressed to begin after or to be from a specified day, the time does not include that day.

Within a time

(6) Where anything is to be done within a time after, from, of or before a specified day, the time does not include that day.

Calculation of a period of months after or before a specified day

(7) Where there is a reference to a period of time consisting of a number of months after or before a specified day, the number of months shall be counted from, but not so as to include, the month in which the specified day falls, and the period shall be reckoned as being limited by and including

(*a*) the day immediately after or before the specified day, according as the period follows or precedes the specified day; and

(*b*) the day in the last month so counted having the same calendar number as the specified day, but if such last month has no day with the same calendar number, then the last day of that month.

Time of the day

(8) Where there is a reference to time expressed as a specified time of the day, the time shall be taken to mean standard time.

Time when specified age attained

(9) A person shall be deemed not to have attained a specified number of years of age until the commencement of the anniversary, of the same number, of the day of his birth. 1967-68, c. 7, s. 25.

Miscellaneous Rules

Reference to magistrate, etc.

26. (1) Where anything is required or authorized to be done by or before a judge, magistrate, justice of the peace, or any functionary or officer, it shall be done by or before one whose jurisdiction or powers extend to the place where such thing is to be done.

Ancillary powers

(2) Where power is given to a person, officer or functionary, to do or enforce the doing of any act or thing, all such powers shall be deemed to be also given as are necessary to enable the person, officer or functionary to do or enforce the doing of the act or thing.

Powers to be exercised as required

(3) Where a power is conferred or a duty imposed the power may be exercised and the duty shall be performed from time to time as occasion requires.

Power to appeal

(4) Where a power is conferred to make regulations, the power shall be 2
construed as including a power, exercisable in the like manner, and subject to
the like consent and conditions, if any, to repeal, amend or vary the regulations 2
and make others.

Forms

(5) Where a form is prescribed, deviations therefrom, not affecting the substance or calculated to mislead, do not invalidate the form used.

Gender

(6) Words importing male persons include female persons and corporations.

Number

(7) Words in the singular include the plural, and words in the plural include the singular.

Parts of speech and grammatical forms

(8) Where a word is defined, other parts of speech and grammatical forms of the same word have corresponding meanings. 1967-68, c. 7, s. 26.

Offences

Indictable and summary conviction offences

27. (1) Where an enactment creates an offence,

(a) the offence shall be deemed to be an indictable offence if the enactment 2
provides that the offender may be prosecuted for the offence by indictment;

(b) the offence shall be deemed to be one for which the offender is punishable on summary conviction if there is nothing in the context to indicate that the offence is an indictable offence; and

(c) if the offence is one for which the offender may be prosecuted by indictment or for which he is punishable on summary conviction, no person shall be considered to have been convicted of an indictable offence by reason only of having been convicted of the offence on summary conviction.

***Criminal Code* to apply**

(2) All the provisions of the *Criminal Code* relating to indictable offences apply to indictable offences created by an enactment, and all the provisions of the *Criminal Code* relating to summary conviction offences apply to all other offences created by an enactment, except to the extent that the enactment otherwise provides.

Documents similarly construed

(3) In a commission, proclamation, warrant or other document relating to criminal law or procedure in criminal matters

(a) a reference to an offence for which the offender may be prosecuted by indictment shall be construed as a reference to an indictable offence; and

(b) a reference to any other offence shall be construed as a reference to an offence for which the offender is punishable on summary conviction. 1967-68, c. 7, s. 27.

DEFINITIONS

28. In every enactment

"Act" "Act", as meaning an Act of a legislature, includes an ordinance of the Yukon Territory or of the Northwest Territories;

"bank" "bank" or "chartered bank" means a bank to which the *Bank Act* applies;

"broadcasting" "broadcasting" means any radiocommunication in which the transmissions are intended for direct reception by the general public;

"commencement" "commencement", when used with reference to an enactment, means the time at which the enactment comes into force;

"Commonwealth" "Commonwealth", "British Commonwealth", "Commonwealth of Nations" or "British Commonwealth of Nations" means the association of countries named in the schedule, which schedule may be amended from time to time by proclamation of the Governor in Council

(*a*) by adding thereto the name of any country recognized by such proclamation to be a member of the Commonwealth, or

(*b*) by deleting therefrom the name of any country recognized by such proclamation to be no longer a member of the Commonwealth;

and "Commonwealth country" means a country that is a member of the association of such countries;

"Commonwealth and Dependent Territories" "Commonwealth and Dependent Territories" means the several Commonwealth countries and their colonies, possessions, dependencies, protectorates, protected states, condominiums and trust territories;

"county" "county" includes two or more counties united for purposes to which the enactment relates;

"county court" "county court" in its application to the Province of Ontario includes, and in its application to the Province of Newfoundland means, "district court"; 1978-79, c. 11, s. 10, I. 15(1).

"diplomatic or consular officer" "diplomatic or consular officer" includes an ambassador, envoy, minister, charge d'affaires, counsellor, secretary, attache, consul-general, consul, vice-consul, pro-consul, consular agent, acting consul-general, acting consul, acting vice-consul, acting consular agent, high commissioner, permanent delegate, adviser, acting high commissioner, and acting permanent delegate;

"Federal Court" "Federal Court" means the Federal Court of Canada;

"Federal Court—Appeal Division" "Federal Court—Appeal Division" or "Federal Court of Appeal" means that division of the Federal Court of Canada called the Federal Court—Appeal Division or referred to as the Federal Court of Appeal by the *Federal Court Act*;

"Federal Court—Trial Division" "Federal Court—Trial Division" means that division of the Federal Court of Canada so named by the *Federal Court Act*;

"fiscal year" "fiscal year" or "financial year" means, in relation to money provided by Parliament, or the Consolidated Revenue Fund, or the accounts, taxes or finances of Canada, the period beginning on and including the 1st day of April in one year and ending on and including the 31st day of March in the next year;

"Governor" "Governor", "Governor of Canada", or "Governor General" means the Governor General for the time being of Canada, or other chief executive officer or administrator for the time being carrying on the Government of Canada on behalf and in the name of the Sovereign, by whatever title he is designated;

"Governor in Council" "Governor in Council", or "Governor General in Council" means the Governor General of Canada, or person administering the Government of Canada for the time being, acting by and with the advice of, or by and with the advice and consent of, or in conjunction with the Queen's Privy Council for Canada;

"Great Seal" "Great Seal" means the Great Seal of Canada;

"Her Majesty" "Her Majesty", "His Majesty", "the Queen", "the King" or "the Crown" means the Sovereign of the United Kingdom, Canada and Her other Realms and Territories, and Head of the Commonwealth;

"Her Majesty's Realms and Territories" "Her Majesty's Realms and Territories" means all realms and territories under the sovereignty of Her Majesty;

"herein" "herein" used in any section shall be understood to relate to the whole enactment, and not to that section only;

"holiday" "holiday" means any of the following days, namely, Sunday; New Year's Day; Good Friday; Easter Monday; Christmas Day; the birthday or the day fixed by proclamation for the celebration of the birthday of the reigning Sovereign; Victoria Day; Dominion Day; the first Monday in September, designated Labour Day; Remembrance Day; any day appointed by proclamation to be observed as a day of general prayer or mourning or day of public rejoicing or thanksgiving; and any of the following additional days, namely:

(a) in any province, any day appointed by proclamation of the lieutenant governor of the province to be observed as a public holiday or as a day of general prayer or mourning or day of public rejoicing or thanksgiving within the province, and any day that is a non-juridical day by virtue of an Act of the legislature of the province, and

(b) in any city, town, municipality or other organized district, any day appointed as a civic holiday by resolution of the council or other authority charged with the administration of the civic or municipal affairs of the city, town, municipality or district;

SOR/57-55

QUEEN'S BIRTHDAY

Proclaimed for Celebration

Whereas Our birthday falling on the twenty-first day of April it is thought fit to appoint the first Monday immediately preceding the twenty-fifth day of May as the day upon which Our birthday is to be officially celebrated in Canada in 1957 and each year thereafter.

Now Know Ye that we do hereby proclaim and declare by this Our Proclamation that the first Monday immediately preceding the twenty-fifth day of May is hereby fixed for the celebration in Canada of Our birthday in the year of Our Lord one thousand nine hundred and fifty-seven and each year thereafter.

SOR/57-56

THANKSGIVING DAY

Proclaimed for Observance

Whereas it hath pleased Almighty God in His great goodness to vouchsafe many blessings throughout the years to the people of Canada;

We Therefore considering that these blessings vouchsafed to the people of Canada do call for a solemn and public acknowledgment have thought fit, by and with the advice of Our Privy Council for Canada, to appoint the second Monday in October in each and every year as a day of general thanksgiving; and We do hereby appoint the second Monday in October, in the year of Our Lord one thousand nine hundred and fifty-seven and each year thereafter as a day of general thanksgiving to Almighty God for the blessings with which the people of Canada have been favoured; and We do hereby invite all Our people of Canada to observe the said day each year as a day of general thanksgiving.

NOTE: SOR/57-55 and SOR/57-56 were not consolidated and were not revoked by the 1978 Consolidation. Noted on page 190 of the 1978 Consolidation.

"legislature" "legislature", "legislative council" or "legislative assembly" includes the Lieutenant Governor in Council and the Legislative Assembly of the Northwest Territories, as constituted before the 1st day of September 1905, the Commissioner in Council of the Yukon Territory, and the Commissioner in Council of the Northwest Territories;

"lieutenant governor" "lieutenant governor" means the lieutenant governor for the time being, or other chief executive officer or administrator for the time being, carrying on the government of the province indicated by the enactment, by whatever title he is designated, and, in relation to the Yukon Territory or the Northwest Territories, means the Commissioner thereof;

"lieutenant governor in council" "lieutenant governor in council" means the lieutenant governor, or person administering the government of the province indicated by the enactment, for the time being, acting by and with the advice of, or by and with the advice and consent of, or in conjunction with the executive council of such province and, in relation to the Yukon Territory or the Northwest Territories, means the Commissioner thereof;

"local time" "local time", in relation to any place, means the time observed in that place for the regulation of business hours;

"may" "may" is to be construed as permissive;

"military" "military" shall be construed as relating to all or any part of the Canadian Forces;

"month" "month" means a calendar month;

"now" "now" or "next" shall be construed as having reference to the time when the enactment was enacted;

"oath" "oath" includes a solemn affirmation or declaration, whenever the context applies to any person by whom and case in which a solemn affirmation or declaration may be made instead of an oath; and in like cases the expression "sworn" includes the expression "affirmed" or "declared";

"person" "person" or any word or expression descriptive of a person, includes a corporation;

"proclamation" "proclamation" means a proclamation under the Great Seal;

"province" "province" means a province of Canada, and includes the Yukon Territory and the Northwest Territories;

"radio" or "radiocommunication" "radio" or "radiocommunication" means any transmission, emission or reception of signs, signals, writing, images, sounds or intelligence of any nature by means of electromagnetic waves of frequencies lower than three thousand Gigacycles per second propagated in space without artificial guide;

"regular force" "regular force" means the component of the Canadian Forces that is referred to in the *National Defence Act* as the regular force;

"reserve force" "reserve force" means the component of the Canadian Forces that is referred to in the *National Defence Act* as the reserve force;

"shall" "shall" is to be construed as imperative;

"standard time" "standard time", except as otherwise provided by any proclamation of the Governor in Council which may be issued for the purposes of this definition in relation to any province or territory or any part thereof, means

(a) in relation to the Province of Newfoundland, Newfoundland standard time, being three hours and thirty minutes behind Greenwich time,

(b) in relation to the Provinces of Nova Scotia, New Brunswick and Prince Edward Island, those parts of the Province of Quebec lying east of the sixty-third meridian of west longitude, and those parts of the Northwest Territories lying east of the sixty-eighth meridian of west longitude, Atlantic standard time, being four hours behind Greenwich time,

(c) in relation to those parts of the province of Quebec lying west of the sixty-third meridian of west longitude, and those parts of the Province of Ontario lying between the ninetieth and the sixty-eighth meridians of west longitude, Southampton Island and the islands adjacent to Southampton Island, and that part of the Northwest Territories lying between the sixty-eighth and the eighty-fifth meridians of west longitude, eastern standard time, being five hours behind Greenwich time,

(d) in relation to that part of the Province of Ontario lying west of the ninetieth meridian of west longitude, the Province of Manitoba, and that part of the Northwest Territories, except Southampton Island and the islands adjacent to Southampton Island, lying between the eighty-fifth and the one hundred and second meridians of west longitude, central standard time, being six hours behind Greenwich time,

(e) in relation to the Province of Saskatchewan, the Province of Alberta, and that part of the Northwest Territories lying west of the one hundred and second meridian of west longitude, mountain standard time, being seven hours behind Greenwich time,

(f) in relation to the Province of British Columbia, Pacific standard time, being eight hours behind Greenwich time, and

(g) in relation to the Yukon Territory, Yukon standard time, being nine hours behind Greenwich time;

"statutory declaration" "statutory declaration" means a solemn declaration made by virtue of the *Canada Evidence Act*;

"superior court" "superior court" means

(a) in the Province of Ontario, Nova Scotia, Prince Edward Island or Newfoundland, the Supreme Court of the Province,

(b) in the Province of Quebec, the Court of Appeal and the Superior Court in and for the Province,

(c) in the Province of British Columbia, the Court of Appeal and the Supreme Court of the Province,

(d) in the Province of Manitoba, Saskatchewan, Alberta or New Brunswick, the Court of Appeal for the Province and the Court of Queen's Bench for the Province,

(e) in the Yukon Territory or the Northwest Territories, the Supreme Court thereof,

and includes the Supreme Court of Canada and the Federal Court of Canada.

"sureties" "sureties" means sufficient sureties, and the expression "security" means sufficient security; and, whenever these words are used, one person is sufficient therefor, unless otherwise expressly required;

"telecommunication" "telecommunication" means any transmission, emission or reception of signs, signals, writing, images or sounds or intelligence of any nature by wire, radio, visual or other electromagnetic system;

"two justices" "two justices" means two or more justices of the peace, assembled or acting together;

"United Kingdom" "United Kingdom" means the United Kingdom of Great Britain and Northern Ireland;

"United States" "United States" means the United States of America;

"writing" "writing", or any term of like import, includes words printed, typewritten, painted, engraved, lithographed, photographed, or represented or reproduced by any mode of representing or reproducing words in visible form;

"year" "year" means any period of twelve consecutive months, except that a reference to a "calendar year" means a period of twelve consecutive months commencing on the first day of January and a reference by number to a Dominical year means the period of twelve consecutive months commencing on the first day of January of that year. R.S., c. I-23, s. 28; R.S., c. 10(2nd Supp.), s. 65; 1972, c. 17, s. 2; 1974-75, c. 19, s. 2; 1978-79, c. 11, s. 10.

Affirmative and negative resolutions

28.1 (1) In every Act

(a) the expression "subject to affirmative resolution of Parliament", when used in relation to any regulation, means that such regulation shall be laid 2
before Parliament within fifteen days after it is made or, if Parliament is not 25(3)
then sitting, on any of the first fifteen days next thereafter that Parliament is sitting and shall not come into force unless and until it is affirmed by a resolution of both Houses of Parliament introduced and passed in accordance with the rules of those Houses;

(b) the expression "subject to affirmative resolution of the House of Commons", when used in relation to any regulation, means that such regulation shall be laid before the House of Commons within fifteen days after it is made or, if the House is not then sitting, on any of the first fifteen days next thereafter that the House is sitting and shall not come into force unless and until it is affirmed by a resolution of the House of Commons introduced and passed in accordance with the rules of that House;

(c) the expression "subject to negative resolution of Parliament", when used in relation to any regulation, means that such regulation shall be laid before Parliament within fifteen days after it is made or, if Parliament is not then sitting, on any of the first fifteen days next thereafter that Parliament is sitting and may be annulled by a resolution of both Houses of Parliament introduced and passed in accordance with the rules of those Houses; and

(d) the expression "subject to negative resolution of the House of Commons", when used in relation to any regulation, means that such regulation shall be laid before the House of Commons within fifteen days after it is made or, if the House is not then sitting, on any of the first fifteen days next thereafter that Parliament is sitting and may be annulled by a resolution of the House of Commons introduced and passed in accordance with the rules of that House.

Effect of negative resolution

(2) Where a regulation is annulled by a resolution of Parliament or of the House of Commons, as the case may be, it shall be deemed to have been revoked on the day the resolution is passed and any law that was revoked or amended by the making of that regulation shall be deemed to be revived on the day the resolution is passed but the validity of any action taken or not taken in compliance with a regulation so deemed to have been revoked shall not be affected by the resolution. R.S., c. 29(2nd Supp.), s. 1.

"Telegraph"

29. The expression "telegraph" and its derivatives in an enactment or in an Act of the legislature of any province enacted before that province became part of Canada on any subject that is within the legislative powers of the Parliament of Canada, shall be deemed not to include the word "telephone" or its derivatives. 1967-68, c. 7, s. 30.

Common names

30. The name commonly applied to any country, place, body, corporation, society, officer, functionary, person, party or thing, means the country, place, body, corporation, society, officer, functionary, person, party or thing to which the name is commonly applied, although the name is not the formal or extended designation thereof. 1967-68, c. 7, s. 31.

Power to define year

31. Where in an enactment relating to the affairs of Parliament or the Government of Canada there is a reference to a period of a year without anything in the context to indicate beyond doubt whether a fiscal year, or any period of twelve consecutive months or a period of twelve consecutive months commencing on the first day of January is intended, the Governor in Council may prescribe which of such periods of twelve consecutive months shall constitute a year for the purposes of the enactment. 1967-68, c. 7, s. 32.

REFERENCES AND CITATIONS

Citation of enactment

32. (1) In an enactment or document

(a) an Act may be cited by reference to its chapter number in the Revised Statutes, by reference to its chapter number in the volume of Acts for the year or regnal year in which it was enacted, or by reference to its long title or short title, with or without reference to its chapter number; and

(b) a regulation may be cited by reference to its long title or short title, by reference to the Act under which it was made or by reference to the number or designation under which it was registered by the Clerk of the Privy Council.

Citation includes amendment

(2) A citation of or reference to an enactment shall be deemed to be a citation of or reference to the enactment as amended. 1967-68, c. 7, s. 33.

Reference to two or more parts, etc.

33. (1) A reference in an enactment by number or letter to two or more parts, divisions, sections, subsections, paragraphs, subparagraphs, clauses, subclauses, schedules, appendices or forms shall be read as including the number or letter first mentioned and the number or letter last mentioned.

Reference in enactments to parts, etc.

(2) A reference in an enactment to a part, division, section, schedule, appendix or form shall be read as a reference to a part, division, section, schedule, appendix or form of the enactment in which the reference occurs.

Reference in enactment to subsections, etc.

(3) A reference in an enactment to a subsection, paragraph, subparagraph, clause or subclause shall be read as a reference to a subsection, paragraph, subparagraph, clause or subclause of the section, subsection, paragraph, subparagraph or clause, as the case may be, in which the reference occurs.

Reference to regulations

(4) A reference in an enactment to regulations shall be read as a reference to regulations made under the enactment in which the reference occurs.

Reference to another enactment

(5) A reference in an enactment by number or letter to any section, subsection, paragraph, subparagraph, clause, subclause or other division or line of another enactment shall be read as a reference to the section, subsection, paragraph, subparagraph, clause, subclause or other division or line of such other enactment as printed by authority of law. 1967-68, c. 7, s. 34.

REPEAL AND AMENDMENT

Power of repeal or amendment reserved

34. (1) Every Act shall be so construed as to reserve to Parliament the power 2
of repealing or amending it, and of revoking, restricting or modifying any power, privilege or advantage thereby vested in or granted to any person.

Amendment or repeal at same session

(2) An Act may be amended or repealed by an Act passed in the same session of Parliament.

Amendment part of enactment

(3) An amending enactment, as far as consistent with the tenor thereof, shall 2
be construed as part of the enactment that it amends. 1967-68, c. 7, s. 35.

Effect of repeal

35. Where an enactment is repealed in whole or in part, the repeal does not 2

(a) revive any enactment or anything not in force or existing at the time when the repeal takes effect;

(b) affect the previous operation of the enactment so repealed or anything duly done or suffered thereunder;

(c) affect any right, privilege, obligation or liability acquired, accrued, accruing or incurred under the enactment so repealed;

(d) affect any offence committed against or a violation of the provisions of the enactment so repealed, or any penalty, forfeiture or punishment incurred under the enactment so repealed; or

(e) affect any investigation, legal proceeding or remedy in respect of any such right, privilege, obligation, liability, penalty, forfeiture or punishment;

and an investigation, legal proceeding or remedy as described in paragraph *(e)* may be instituted, continued or enforced, and the penalty, forfeiture or punishment may be imposed as if the enactment had not been so repealed. 1967-68, c.7,s.36.

Repeal and substitution

36. Where an enactment (in this section called the "former enactment") is 2
repealed and another enactment (in this section called the "new enactment") is substituted therefor,

(a) every person acting under the former enactment shall continue to act, as if appointed under the new enactment, until another is appointed in his stead;

(b) every bond and security given by a person appointed under the former enactment remains in force, and all books, papers, forms and things made or used under the former enactment shall continue to be used as before the repeal so far as they are consistent with the new enactment;

(c) every proceeding taken under the former enactment shall be taken up and continued under and in conformity with the new enactment so far as it may be done consistently with the new enactment;

(d) the procedure established by the new enactment shall be followed as far as it can be adapted thereto in the recovery or enforcement of penalties and forfeitures incurred, and in the enforcement of rights, existing or accruing under the former enactment or in a proceeding in relation to matters that have happened before the repeal;

(e) when any penalty, forfeiture or punishment is reduced or mitigated by the new enactment, the penalty, forfeiture or punishment if imposed or adjudged after the repeal shall be reduced or mitigated accordingly;

(f) except to the extent that the provisions of the new enactment are not in substance the same as those of the former enactment, the new enactment shall not be held to operate as new law, but shall be construed and have effect as a consolidation and as declaratory of the law as contained in the former enactment;

(g) all regulations made under the repealed enactment remain in force and 2
shall be deemed to have been made under the new enactment, in so far as they are not inconsistent with the new enactment, until they are repealed or others are made in their stead; and

(h) any reference in an unrepealed enactment to the former enactment shall, as regards a subsequent transaction, matter or thing, be read and construed as a reference to the provisions of the new enactment relating to the same subject-matter as the former enactment, but where there are no provisions in the new enactment relating to the same subject-matter, the former enactment shall be read as unrepealed in so far as is necessary to maintain or give effect to the unrepealed enactment. 1967-68, c. 7, s. 37.

Repeal does not imply enactment was in force

37. (1) The repeal of an enactment in whole or in part shall not be deemed to 2
be or to involve a declaration that such enactment was or was considered by Parliament or other body or person by whom the enactment was enacted to have been previously in force.

Amendment does not imply change in law

(2) The amendment of an enactment shall not be deemed to be or to involve a declaration that the law under such enactment was or was considered by Parliament or other body or person by whom the enactment was enacted to have been different from the law as it is under the enactment as amended.

Repeal does not declare previous law

(3) The repeal or amendment of an enactment in whole or in part shall not be 2
deemed to be or to involve any declaration as to the previous state of the law.

Judicial construction not adopted

(4) A re-enactment, revision, consolidation or amendment of an enactment shall not be deemed to be or to involve an adoption of the construction that has by judicial decision or otherwise been placed upon the language used in the enactment or upon similar language. 1967-68, c. 7, s. 38.

DEMISE OF CROWN

Effect of demise

38. (1) Where there is a demise of the Crown,

(a) the demise does not effect the holding of any office under the Crown in right of Canada; and

(b) it is not necessary by reason of such demise that the holder of any such office again be appointed thereto or that, having taken an oath of office or allegiance before such demise, he again take such oath.

Continuation of proceedings

(2) No writ, action or other process or proceeding, civil or criminal, in or issuing out of any court established by an Act of the Parliament of Canada is, by reason of a demise of the Crown, determined, abated, discontinued or affected, but every such writ, action, process or proceeding remains in full force and may be enforced, carried on or otherwise proceeded with or completed as though there had been no such demise. 1967-68, c. 7, s. 39.

SCHEDULE

Australia
The Bahamas
Bangladesh
Barbados
Botswana
Canada
Cyprus
Fiji
Gambia
Ghana
Grenada
Guyana
India
Jamaica
Kenya
Lesotho
Malawi
Malaysia
Malta
Mauritius
Nauru
New Zealand
Nigeria
Papua New Guinea
Seychelles
Sierra Leone
Singapore
Sri Lanka
Swaziland
Tanzania
Tonga
Trinidad and Tobago
Uganda
United Kingdom
Western Samoa
Zambia

R.S., c. I-23, Sch.; SI/72-93; SOR/74-287; SOR/77-394.

CANADIAN BILL OF RIGHTS

An Act for the Recognition and Protection of Human Rights and Fundamental Freedoms

Preamble

The Parliament of Canada, affirming that the Canadian Nation is founded upon principles that acknowledge the supremacy of God, the dignity and worth of the human person and the position of the family in a society of free men and free institutions;

Affirming also that men and institutions remain free only when freedom is founded upon respect for moral and spiritual values and the rule of law;

And being desirous of enshrining these principles and the human rights and fundamental freedoms derived from them, in a Bill of Rights which shall reflect the respect of Parliament for its constitutional authority and which shall ensure the protection of these rights and freedoms in Canada:

Therefore Her Majesty, by and with the advice and consent of the Senate and House of Commons of Canada, enacts as follows:

PART I

BILL OF RIGHTS

Recognition and declaration of rights and freedoms

1. It is hereby recognized and declared that in Canada there have existed and shall continue to exist without discrimination by reason of race, national origin, colour, religion or sex, the following human rights and fundamental freedoms, namely,

(a) the right of the individual to life, liberty, security of the person and enjoyment of property, and the right not to be deprived thereof except by due process of law;

(b) the right of the individual to equality before the law and the protection of the law;

(c) freedom of religion;

(d) freedom of speech;

(e) freedom of assembly and association; and

(f) freedom of the press.

Construction of law

2. Every law of Canada shall, unless it is expressly declared by an Act of the Parliament of Canada that it shall operate notwithstanding the *Canadian Bill of Rights*, be so construed and applied as not to abrogate, abridge or infringe or to authorize the abrogation, abridgment or infringement of any of the rights or freedoms herein recognized and declared, and in particular, no law of Canada shall be construed or applied so as to

(a) authorize or effect the arbitrary detention, imprisonment or exile of any person;

(b) impose or authorize the imposition of cruel and unusual treatment or punishment;

(c) deprive a person who has been arrested or detained

(i) of the right to be informed promptly of the reason for his arrest or detention,

(ii) of the right to retain and instruct counsel without delay, or

(iii) of the remedy by way of *habeas corpus* for the determination of the validity of his detention and for his release if the detention is not lawful;

(d) authorize a court, tribunal, commission, board or other authority to compel a person to give evidence if he is denied counsel, protection against self crimination or other constitutional safeguards;

(e) deprive a person of the right to a fair hearing in accordance with the principles of fundamental justice for the determination of his rights and obligations;

(f) deprive a person charged with a criminal offence of the right to be presumed innocent until proved guilty according to law in a fair and public hearing by an independent and impartial tribunal, or of the right to reasonable bail without just cause; or

(g) deprive a person of the right to the assistance of an interpreter in any proceedings in which he is involved or in which he is a party or a witness, before a court, commission, board or other tribunal, if he does not understand or speak the language in which such proceedings are conducted.

Duties of Minister of Justice

3. The Minister of Justice shall, in accordance with such regulations as may be prescribed by the Governor in Council, examine every regulation transmitted to the Clerk of the Privy Council for registration pursuant to the *Statutory Instruments Act* and every Bill introduced in or presented to the House of Commons, in order to ascertain whether any of the provisions thereof are inconsistent with the purposes and provisions of this Part and he shall report any such inconsistency to the House of Commons at the first convenient opportunity. 1970-71-72, c. 38, s. 29.

Short title

4. The provisions of this Part shall be known as the *Canadian Bill of Rights.*

PART II

Savings

5. (1) Nothing in Part I shall be construed to abrogate or abridge any human right or fundamental freedom not enumerated therein that may have existed in Canada at the commencement of this Act.

"Law of Canada" defined

(2) The expression "law of Canada" in Part I means an Act of the Parliament of Canada enacted before or after the coming into force of this Act, any order, rule or regulation thereunder, and any law in force in Canada or in any part of Canada at the commencement of this Act that is subject to be repealed, abolished or altered by the Parliament of Canada.

Jurisdiction of Parliament

(3) The provisions of Part I shall be construed as extending only to matters coming within the legislative authority of the Parliament of Canada.

REGULATIONS RESPECTING THE EXAMINATION OF BILLS AND REGULATIONS PURSUANT TO THE CANADIAN BILL OF RIGHTS

Short Title

1. These Regulations may be cited as the *Canadian Bill of Rights Examination Regulations.*

Interpretation

2. In these Regulations, "Minister" means the Minister of Justice.

Examination of Bills

3. In the case of every Bill introduced in or presented to the House of Commons the Minister shall, forthwith upon receipt of two copies of the Bill from the Clerk of the House of Commons,

(a) examine the Bill in order to determine whether any of the provisions thereof are inconsistent with the purposes and provisions of the *Canadian Bill of Rights;* and

(b) cause to be affixed to each of the copies thereof so received from the Clerk of the House of Commons a certificate, in a form approved by the Minister and signed by the Deputy Minister of Justice, stating that the Bill has been examined as required by the *Canadian Bill of Rights;*

and one each of the copies thereof so certified shall thereupon be transmitted to the Clerk of the House of Commons and the Clerk of the Privy Council.

Examination of Regulations

4. The Clerk of the Privy Council shall, upon receipt of a regulation transmitted to him for registration pursuant to the *Statutory Instruments Act*, forward a copy thereof to the Minister.

5. The Minister shall, forthwith upon receipt of a copy of a regulation forwarded to him by the Clerk of the Privy Council pursuant to section 4,

(a) examine the regulation in order to determine whether any of the provisions thereof are inconsistent with the purposes and provisions of the *Canadian Bill of Rights;* and

(b) cause to be affixed to the copy thereof so received from the Clerk of the Privy Council a certificate, in a form approved by the Minister and signed by the Deputy Minister of Justice, stating that the regulation has been examined as required by the *Canadian Bill of Rights;*

and the copy so certified shall thereupon be returned to the Clerk of the Privy Council.

Report to the Minister

6. Where any of the provisions of any Bill examined by the Minister pursuant to section 3 or any of the provisions of any regulation examined by him pursuant to section 5 are ascertained by the Minister to be inconsistent with the purposes and provisions of the *Canadian Bill of Rights*, the Minister shall make a report in writing of the inconsistency and shall cause such report to be deposited with the Clerk of the House of Commons in accordance with Standing Order 41 of the House of Commons at the earliest convenient opportunity.

7. A copy of every report made by the Minister pursuant to section 6 shall, where such report relates to a regulation, be transmitted to the Clerk of the Privy Council forthwith upon the making thereof.

—NOTES—

IDENTIFICATION OF CRIMINALS ACT

CHAPTER I-1

An Act respecting the identification of criminals

Short title

1. This Act may be cited as the *Identification of Criminals Act.*

Bertillon Signaletic System

2. (1) Any person in lawful custody, charged with, or under conviction of an indictable offence, or who has been apprehended under the *Extradition Act* or the *Fugitive Offenders Act*, may be subjected, by or under the direction of those in whose custody he is, to the measurements, processes and operations practised under the system for the identification of criminals commonly known as the Bertillon Signaletic System, or to any measurements, processes or operations sanctioned by the Governor in Council having the like object in view. 28 Interp

Use of force

(2) Such force may be used as is necessary to the effectual carrying out and application of such measurements, processes and operations.

Publication of cards

(3) The signaletic cards and other results thereof may be published for the purpose of affording information to officers and others engaged in the execution or administration of the law.

No liability for acting under Act

3. No one having the custody of any such person, and no one acting in his aid or under his direction, and no one concerned in such publication, incurs any liability, civil or criminal, for anything lawfully done under this Act.

Interpretation Act

28. In every enactment

"Governor in Council" or "Governor General in Council" means the Governor General of Canada, or person administering the Government of Canada for the time being, acting by and with the advice of, or by and with the advice and consent of, or in conjuction with the Queen's Privy Council for Canada;

P. C. 1954-1109

MEASUREMENTS PROCESSES OR OPERATIONS OF FINGERPRINTING AND PHOTOGRAPHY SANCTIONED

For the purposes of the *Identification of Criminals Act*, the measurements, processes or operations of fingerprinting and photography are hereby sanctioned.

NOTE: P. C. 1954-1109, noted on page 1855 of the 1955 Consolidation of the Revised Regulations of Canada was not consolidated and was not revoked by the 1978 Consolidated Regulations of Canada. It is noted on page 107 of the 1978 Consolidation.

—NOTES—

CANADA EVIDENCE ACT

CHAPTER E-10

An Act respecting witnesses and evidence

SHORT TITLE

Short title

1. This Act may be cited as the *Canada Evidence Act*.

PART I

Application

Application

2. This Part applies to all criminal proceedings, and to all civil proceedings and other matters whatever respecting which the Parliament of Canada has jurisdiction in this behalf.

Witnesses

Interest or crime

3. A person is not incompetent to give evidence by reason of interest or crime.

Accused and spouse

4. (1) Every person charged with an offence, and, except as otherwise provided in this section, the wife or husband, as the case may be, of the person so charged, is a competent witness for the defence, whether the person so charged is charged solely or jointly with any other person.

Idem

(2) The wife or husband of a person charged with an offence against section 33 or 34 of the *Juvenile Delinquents Act* or with an offence against any of sections 143 to 146, 148, 150 to 155, 157, 166 to 169, 175, 195, 197, 200, 248 to 250, 255 to 258, 289, paragraph 423(1)*(c)* or an attempt to commit an offence under section 146 or 155 of the *Criminal Code*, is a competent and compellable witness for the prosecution without the consent of the person charged.

Communications during marriage

(3) No husband is compellable to disclose any communication made to him by his wife during their marriage, and no wife is compellable to disclose any communication made to her by her husband during their marriage.

Saving

(4) Nothing in this section affects a case where the wife or husband of a person charged with an offence may at common law be called as a witness without the consent of that person.

Failure to testify

(5) The failure of the person charged, or of the wife or husband of such person, to testify, shall not be made the subject of comment by the judge, or by counsel for the prosecution. 1953-54, c. 51, s. 749.

143 (Rape); 144 (Punishment for rape); 145 (Attempt to commit rape); 146 (Sexual intercourse with female under fourteen and Sexual intercourse with female between fourteen and sixteen); 148 (Sexual intercourse with feeble-minded); 150 (Incest); 151 (Seduction of female between sixteen and eighteen); 152 (Seduction under promise of marriage); 153 (Sexual intercourse with step-daughter, etc., or female employee); 154 (Seduction of female passengers on vessels); 155 (Buggery or bestiality); 157 (Acts of gross indecency); 166 (Parent or guardian procuring defilement); 167 (Householder permitting defilement); 168 (Corrupting children); 169 (Indecent acts); 175 (Vagrancy); 195 (Procuring); 197 (Duty of persons to provide necessaries); 200 (Abandoning child); 248 (Abduction of female); 249 (Abduction of female under sixteen); 250 (Abduction of child under fourteen); 255 (Bigamy); 256 (Procuring feigned marriage); 257 (Polygamy); 258 (Pretending to solemnize marriage); 289 (Husband and wife - theft); 423(1)*(a)* (Conspiracy to commit murder);

Incriminating questions

5. (1) No witness shall be excused from answering any question upon the ground that the answer to such question may tend to criminate him, or may tend to establish his liability to a civil proceeding at the instance of the Crown or of any person.

Answer not receivable against witness

(2) Where with respect to any question a witness objects to answer upon the ground that his answer may tend to criminate him, or may tend to establish his liability to a civil proceeding at the instance of the Crown or of any person, and if but for this Act, or the Act of any provincial legislature, the witness would therefore have been excused from answering such question, then although the witness is by reason of this Act, or by reason of such provincial Act, compelled to answer, the answer so given shall not be used or receivable in evidence against him in any criminal trial, or other criminal proceeding against him thereafter taking place, other than a prosecution for perjury in the giving of such evidence.

Criminal Code

120. Every one commits perjury who, being a witness in a judicial proceeding, with intent to mislead gives false evidence, knowing that the evidence is false.

Evidence of mute

6. A witness who is unable to speak may give his evidence in any other manner in which he can make it intelligible.

Expert witnesses

7. Where, in any trial or other proceeding, criminal or civil, it is intended by the prosecution or the defence, or by any party, to examine as witnesses professional or other experts entitled according to the law or practice to give opinion evidence, not more than five of such witnesses may be called upon either side without the leave of the court or judge or person presiding. 1968-69, c.14, s.1.

Handwriting comparison

8. Comparison of a disputed writing with any writing proved to the satisfaction of the court to be genuine shall be permitted to be made by witnesses; and such writings, and the evidence of witnesses respecting such writings, may be submitted to the court and jury as proof of the genuineness or otherwise of the writing in dispute. 28 Interp

Interpretation Act

28. In every enactment

"writing", or any term of like import, includes words printed, typewritten, painted, engraved, lithographed, photographed, or represented or reproduced by any mode of representing or reproducing words in visible form;

Adverse witnesses

9. (1) A party producing a witness shall not be allowed to impeach his credit by general evidence of bad character, but if the witness, in the opinion of the court, proves adverse, such party may contradict him by other evidence, or, by leave of the court, may prove that the witness made at other times a statement inconsistent with his present testimony; but before such last mentioned proof can be given the circumstances of the supposed statement, sufficient to designate the particular occasion, shall be mentioned to the witness, and he shall be asked whether or not he did make such statement.

Previous statements in writing by witness not proved adverse

(2) Where the party producing a witness alleges that the witness made at other times a statement in writing, or reduced to writing, inconsistent with his present testimony, the court may, without proof that the witness is adverse, grant leave to that party to cross-examine the witness as to the statement and the court may consider such cross-examination in determining whether in the opinion of the court the witness is adverse. 1968-69, c. 14, s. 2.

Cross-examination as to previous statements in writing

10. (1) Upon any trial a witness may be cross-examined as to previous statements made by him in writing, or reduced to writing, relative to the subject-matter of the case, without such writing being shown to him; but, if it is intended to contradict the witness by the writing, his attention must, before such contradictory proof can be given, be called to those parts of the writing that are to be used for the purpose of so contradicting him; the judge, at any time during the trial, may require the production of the writing for his inspection, and thereupon make such use of it for the purposes of the trial as he thinks fit.

Deposition of witness in criminal investigation

(2) A deposition of the witness, purporting to have been taken before a justice on the investigation of a criminal charge and to be signed by the witness and the justice, returned to and produced from the custody of the proper officer, shall be presumed *prima facie* to have been signed by the witness.

prima facie — evidence which, if not rebutted, is sufficient to raise the probability of guilt

Cross-examination as to previous oral statements

11. Where a witness upon cross-examination as to a former statement made by him relative to the subject-matter of the case and inconsistent with his present testimony, does not distinctly admit that he did make such statement, proof may be given that he did in fact make it; but before such proof can be given the circumstances of the supposed statement, sufficient to designate the particular occasion, shall be mentioned to the witness, and he shall be asked whether or not he did make such statement.

Examination as to previous conviction

12. (1) A witness may be questioned as to whether he has been convicted of any offence, and upon being so questioned, if he either denies the fact or refuses to answer, the opposite party may prove such conviction.

How conviction proved

(2) The conviction may be proved by producing

(a) a certificate containing the substance and effect only, omitting the formal part, of the indictment and conviction, if it is for an indictable offence, or a copy of the summary conviction, if for an offence punishable upon summary conviction, purporting to be signed by the clerk of the court or other officer having the custody of the records of the court in which the conviction, if upon indictment, was had, or to which the conviction, if summary, was returned; and

(b) proof of identity.

Oaths and affirmations

Who may administer oaths

13. Every court and judge, and every person having, by law or consent of parties, authority to hear and receive evidence, has power to administer an oath to every witness who is legally called to give evidence before that court, judge or person. 18 & 28 Interp

Interpretation Act

18. (1) Where by an enactment or by a rule of the Senate or House of Commons, evidence under oath is authorized or required to be taken, or an oath is authorized or directed to be made, taken or administered, the oath may be administered, and a certificate of its having been made, taken or administered may be given by any one authorized by the enactment or rule to take the evidence, or by a judge of any court, a notary public, a justice of the peace, or a commissioner for taking affidavits, having authority or jurisdiction within the place where the oath is administered.

(2) Where power is conferred upon a justice of the peace to administer an oath or affirmation, or to take an affidavit or declaration, the power may be exercised by a notary public or a commissioner for taking oaths.

28. In every enactment

"oath" includes a solemn affirmation or declaration, whenever the context applies to any person by whom and case in which a solemn affirmation or declaration may be made instead of an oath; and in like cases the expression "sworn" includes the expression "affirmed" or "declared";

Affirmation by witness instead of oath

14. (1) Where a person called or desiring to give evidence objects, on grounds of conscientious scruples, to take an oath, or is objected to as incompetent to take an oath, such person may make the following affirmation:

I solemnly affirm that the evidence to be given by me shall be the truth, the whole truth, and nothing but the truth.

Effect

(2) Upon the person making such solemn affirmation, his evidence shall be taken and have the same effect as if taken under oath.

Affirmation by deponent

15. (1) Where a person required or desiring to make an affidavit or deposition in a proceeding or on an occasion whereon or concerning a matter respecting which an oath is required or is lawful, whether on the taking of office or otherwise, refuses or is unwilling to be sworn, on grounds of conscientious scruples, the court or judge, or other officer or person qualified to take affidavits or depositions, shall permit such person, instead of being sworn, to make his solemn affirmation in the words following, namely: "I, A.B., do solemnly affirm, etc."; and this solemn affirmation shall be of the same force and effect as if such person had taken an oath in the usual form.

Effect

(2) Any witness whose evidence is admitted or who makes an affirmation under this section or section 14 is liable to indictment and punishment for perjury in all respects as if he had been sworn.

Criminal Code

120. Every one commits perjury who, being a witness in a judicial proceeding, with intent to mislead gives false evidence, knowing that the evidence is false.

Evidence of child

16. (1) In any legal proceeding where a child of tender years is offered as a witness, and such child does not, in the opinion of the judge, justice or other presiding officer, understand the nature of an oath, the evidence of such child may be received, though not given upon oath, if, in the opinion of the judge, justice or other presiding officer, as the case may be, the child is possessed of sufficient intelligence to justify the reception of the evidence, and understands the duty of speaking the truth.

Must be corroborated

(2) No case shall be decided upon such evidence alone, and it must be corroborated by some other material evidence.

Criminal Code

586. No person shall be convicted of an offence upon the unsworn evidence of a child unless the evidence of the child is corroborated in a material particular by evidence that implicates the accused.

Judicial Notice

Imperial Acts, etc.

17. Judicial notice shall be taken of all Acts of the Imperial Parliament, of all ordinances made by the Governor in Council, or the lieutenant governor in council of any province or colony that, or some portion of which, now forms or hereafter may form part of Canada, and of all the Acts of the legislature of any such province or colony, whether enacted before or after the passing of the *British North America Act, 1867.* 28 Interp

Interpretation Act

28. In every enactment

"Governor in Council", or "Governor General in Council" means the Governor General of Canada, or person administering the Government of Canada for the time being, acting by and with the advice of, or by and with the advice and consent of, or in conjunction with the Queen's Privy Council for Canada;

"lieutenant governor in council" means the lieutenant governor, or person administering the government of the province indicated by the enactment, for the time being, acting by and with the advice of, or by and with the advice and consent of, or in conjuction with the executive council of such province and, in relation to the Yukon Territory or the Northwest Territories, means the Commissioner thereof;

"province" means a province of Canada, and includes the Yukon Territory and the Northwest Territories;

Acts of Canada

18. Judicial notice shall be taken of all Acts of the Parliament of Canada, public or private, without being specially pleaded. 1967-68, c. 7, s. 40.

Documentary Evidence

Copies by Queen's Printer

19. Every copy of any Act of the Parliament of Canada, public or private, printed by the Queen's Printer, is evidence of such Act and of its contents; and every copy purporting to be printed by the Queen's Printer shall be deemed to be so printed, unless the contrary is shown.

Imperial proclamations etc.

20. Imperial proclamations, orders in council, treaties, orders, warrants, licences, certificates, rules, regulations, or other Imperial official records, Acts or documents may be proved

(a) in the same manner as they may from time to time be provable in any court in England;

(b) by the production of a copy of the *Canada Gazette*, or a volume of the Acts of the Parliament of Canada purporting to contain a copy of the same or a notice thereof; or

(c) by the production of a copy thereof purporting to be printed by the Queen's Printer.

Proclamations, etc., of Governor General

21. Evidence of any proclamation, order, regulation or appointment, made or issued by the Governor General or by the Governor in Council, or by or under the authority of any minister or head of any department of the Government of Canada and evidence of a treaty to which Canada is a party, may be given in all or any of the modes following, that is to say: 28 Interp [17]

(a) by the production of a copy of the *Canada Gazette*, or a volume of the Acts of the Parliament of Canada purporting to contain a copy of such treaty, proclamation, order, regulation, or appointment or a notice thereof;

(b) by the production of a copy of such proclamation, order, regulation or appointment, purporting to be printed by the Queen's Printer;

(b.1) by the production of a copy of such treaty purporting to be printed by the Queen's Printer or by Information Canada; and 1976-77, c. 28, s. 14.

(c) by the production, in the case of any proclamation, order, regulation or appointment made or issued by the Governor General or by the Governor in Council, of a copy or extract purporting to be certified to be true by the clerk, or assistant or acting clerk of the Queen's Privy Council for Canada; and in the case of any order, regulation or appointment made or issued by or under the authority of any such minister or head of a department, by the production of a copy or extract purporting to be certified to be true by the minister, or by his deputy or acting deputy, or by the secretary or acting secretary of the department over which he presides.

Proclamations, etc., of lieutenant governor

22. (1) Evidence of any proclamation, order, regulation, or appointment made or issued by a lieutenant governor or lieutenant governor in council of any province, or by or under the authority of any member of the executive council, being the head of any department of the government of the province, may be given in all or any of the modes following, that is to say: 28 Interp [17]

(a) by the production of a copy of the official gazette for the province, purporting to contain a copy of such proclamation, order, regulation or appointment, or a notice thereof;

(b) by the production of a copy of such proclamation, order, regulation or appointment, purporting to be printed by the government or Queen's Printer for the province; and

(c) by the production of a copy or extract of such proclamation, order, regulation or appointment, purporting to be certified to be true by the clerk or assistant or acting clerk of the executive council, or by the head of any department of the government of a province, or by his deputy or acting deputy as the case may be.

In the case of the Territories

(2) *Prima facie* evidence of any proclamation, order, regulation or appointment made by the Lieutenant Governor or Lieutenant Governor in Council of the Northwest Territories, as constituted prior to the 1st day of September 1905, or of the Commissioner in Council of the Northwest Territories or of the Commissioner in Council of the Yukon Territory, may also be given by the production of a copy of the *Canada Gazette* purporting to contain a copy of such proclamation, order, regulation or appointment, or a notice thereof.

prima facie — assumed to be proved and true unless evidence is given to disprove it

Evidence of judicial proceedings, etc.

23. (1) Evidence of any proceeding or record whatever of, in, or before any court in Great Britain or the Supreme or Federal Courts of Canada, or any court in any province of Canada, or any court in any British colony or possession, or any court of record of the United States of America, or of any state of the United States of America, or of any other foreign country, or before any justice of the peace or coroner in any province of Canada, may be given in any action or proceeding by an exemplification or certified copy thereof, purporting to be under the seal of such court, or under the hand or seal of such justice or coroner, as the case may be, without any proof of the authenticity of such seal or of the signature of such justice or coroner, or other proof whatever.

Certificate where court has no seal

(2) Where any such court, justice or coroner has no seal, or so certifies, such evidence may be made by a copy purporting to be certified under the signature of a judge or presiding magistrate of such court or of such justice or coroner, without any proof of the authenticity of the signature, or other proof whatever.

Certified copies

24. In every case in which the original record could be received in evidence,

(a) a copy of any official or public document of Canada or of any province, purporting to be certified under the hand of the proper officer or person in whose custody such official or public document is placed, or

(b) a copy of a document, by-law, rule, regulation or proceeding, or a copy of any entry in any register or other book of any municipal or other corporation, created by charter or Act of Canada or of any province, purporting to be certified under the seal of the corporation, and the hand of the presiding officer, clerk or secretary thereof,

is receivable in evidence without proof of the seal of the corporation, or of the signature or of the official character of the person or persons appearing to have signed the same, and without further proof thereof.

Books and documents

25. Where a book or other document is of so public a nature as to be admissible in evidence on its mere production from the proper custody, and no other Act exists that renders its contents provable by means of a copy, a copy thereof or extract therefrom is admissible in evidence in any court of justice, or before a person having, by law or by consent of parties, authority to hear, receive and examine evidence, if it is proved that it is a copy or extract purporting to be certified to be true by the officer to whose custody the original has been entrusted.

Books kept in offices under Government of Canada

26. (1) A copy of any entry in any book kept in any office or department of the Government of Canada, or in any commission, board or other branch of the public service of Canada, shall be received as evidence of such entry, and of the matters, transactions and accounts therein recorded, if it is proved by the oath or affidavit of an officer of such department, commission, board or other branch of the public service, that the book was, at the time of the making of the entry, one of the ordinary books kept in such office, department, commission, board or other branch of the public service, that the entry was made in the usual and ordinary course of business of such office, department, commission, board or other branch of the public service, and that such copy is a true copy thereof. 28 Interp

Interpretation Act

28. In every enactment

"oath" includes a solemn affirmation or declaration, whenever the context applies to any person by whom and case in which a solemn affirmation or declaration may be made instead of an oath; and in like cases the expression "sworn" includes the expression "affirmed" or "declared";

Proof of non-issue of licence or document

(2) Where by any Act of Canada or regulation thereunder provision is made for the issue by a department, commission, board or other branch of the public service, of a licence requisite to the doing or having of any act or thing or for the issue of any other document, an affidavit of an officer of the department, commission, board or other branch of the public service, sworn before any commissioner or other person authorized to take affidavits, that he has charge of the appropriate records and that after careful examination and search of such records he has been unable to find in any given case that any such licence or other document has been issued, shall be received in evidence as *prima facie* proof that in such case no licence or other document has been issued.

prima facie — assumed to be proved and true unless evidence is given to disprove it

Proof of mailing departmental matter

(3) Where by any Act of Canada or regulation thereunder provision is made for sending by mail any request for information, notice or demand by a department or other branch of the public service, an affidavit of an officer of the department or other branch of the public service sworn before any commissioner or other person authorized to take affidavits setting out that he has charge of the appropriate records, that he has a knowledge of the facts in the particular case, that such a request, notice or demand was sent by registered letter on a named date to the person or firm to whom it was addressed (indicating such address) and that he identifies as exhibits attached to such affidavit the post office certificate of registration of such letter and a true copy of such request, notice or demand, shall, upon production and proof of the post office receipt for the delivery of such registered letter to the addressee, be received in evidence as *prima facie* proof of such sending and of such request, notice or demand.

Proof of official character

(4) Where proof is offered by affidavit pursuant to this section it is not necessary to prove the official character of the person making the affidavit if that information is set out in the body of the affidavit.

Notarial acts in Quebec

27. Any document purporting to be a copy of a notarial act or instrument made, filed or registered in the Province of Quebec, and to be certified by a notary or prothonotary to be a true copy of the original in his possession as such notary or prothonotary, shall be received in evidence in the place and stead of the original, and has the same force and effect as the original would have if produced and proved; but it may be proved in rebuttal that there is no such original, or that the copy is not a true copy of the original in some material particular, or that the original is not an instrument of such nature as may, by the law of the Province of Quebec, be taken before a notary or be filed, enrolled or registered by a notary in the said Province.

Notice of production of book or document

28. (1) No copy of any book or other document shall be received in evidence, under the authority of section 23, 24, 25, 26 or 27, upon any trial, unless the party intending to produce the same has before the trial given to the party against whom it is intended to be produced reasonable notice of such intention.

Not less than 7 days

(2) The reasonableness of the notice shall be determined by the court, judge or other person presiding, but the notice shall not in any case be less than seven days. 25(3) Interp

Interpretation Act

25. (3) Where there is a reference to a number of days, not expressed to be clear days, between two events, in calculating the number of days there shall be excluded the day on which the first event happens and there shall be included the day on which the second event happens.

Copies of entries

29. (1) Subject to this section, a copy of any entry in any book or record kept in any financial institution shall in all legal proceedings be received in evidence as *prima facie* proof of such entry and of the matters, transactions and accounts therein recorded. ss. (8)

Reception of evidence

(2) A copy of an entry in such book or record shall not be received in evidence under this section unless it is first proved that the book or record was, at the time of the making of the entry, one of the ordinary books or records of the financial institution, that the entry was made in the usual and ordinary course of business, that the book or record is in the custody or control of the financial institution and that such copy is a true copy thereof; and such proof may be given by the manager or accountant of the financial institution and may be given orally or by affidavit sworn before any commissioner or other person authorized to take affidavits.

Cheques, proof of "no account"

(3) Where a cheque has been drawn on any financial institution or branch thereof by any person, an affidavit of the manager or accountant of the financial institution or branch, sworn before any commissioner or other person authorized to take affidavits, setting out that he is the manager or accountant, that he has made a careful examination and search of the books and records for the purpose of ascertaining whether or not such person has an account with the financial institution or branch, and that he has been unable to find such an account, shall be received in evidence as *prima facie* proof that such person has no account in the financial institution or branch.

Proof of official character

(4) Where evidence is offered by affidavit pursuant to this section it is not necessary to prove the signature or official character of the person making the affidavit if the official character of that person is set out in the body of the affidavit.

Compulsion of production or appearance

(5) A financial institution or officer of a financial institution is not in any legal proceedings to which the financial institution is not a party compellable to produce any book or record, the contents of which can be proved under this section, or to appear as a witness to prove the matters, transactions and accounts therein recorded unless by order of the court made for special cause.

Order to inspect and copy

(6) On the application of any party to a legal proceeding the court may order that such party be at liberty to inspect and take copies of any entries in the books or records of a financial institution for the purposes of the legal proceeding; and the person whose account is to be inspected shall be notified of the application at least two clear days before the hearing thereof, and if it is shown to the satisfaction of the court that he cannot be notified personally, the notice may be given by addressing it to the financial institution. ss. (8) 25(2) Interp

Warrants to search

(7) Nothing in this section shall be construed as prohibiting any search of the premises of a financial institution under the authority of a warrant to search issued under any other Act of the Parliament of Canada, but unless the warrant is expressly endorsed by the person under whose hand it is issued as not being limited by this section, the authority conferred by any such warrant to search the premises of a financial institution and to seize and take away anything therein shall, as regards the books or records of such institution, be construed as limited to the searching of such premises for the purpose of inspecting and taking copies of entries in such books or records.

Definitions

(8) In this section

"court"

"court" means the court, judge, arbitrator or person before whom a legal proceeding is held or taken;

"financial institution"

"financial institution" means the Bank of Canada, the Federal Business Development Bank and any institution incorporated in Canada that accepts deposits of money from its members or the public, and includes a branch, agency or office of any such Bank or institution; 1974-75-76, c. 14, s. 57.

"legal proceeding"

"legal proceeding" means any civil or criminal proceeding or inquiry in which evidence is or may be given, and includes an arbitration.

Computation of time

(9) Holidays shall be excluded from the computation of time under this section. 1968-69, c. 14, s. 3.

prima facie — assumed to be proven and true unless evidence is given to disprove

Interpretation Act

25. (2) Where there is a reference to a number of clear days or "at least" a number of days between two events, in calculating the number of days there shall be excluded the days on which the events happen.

Business records to be received in evidence

30. (1) Where oral evidence in respect of a matter would be admissible in a legal proceeding, a record made in the usual and ordinary course of business that contains information in respect of that matter is admissible in evidence under this section in the legal proceeding upon production of the record. ss. (12)

Inference where information not in business record

(2) Where a record made in the usual and ordinary course of business does not contain information in respect of a matter the occurrence or existence of which might reasonably be expected to be recorded in that record, the court may upon production of the record admit the record for the purpose of establishing that fact and may draw the inference that such matter did not occur or exist.

Copy of records

(3) Where it is not possible or reasonably practicable to produce any record described in subsection (1) or (2), a copy of the record accompanied by an affidavit setting out the reasons why it is not possible or reasonably practicable to produce the record and an affidavit of the person who made the copy setting out the source from which the copy was made and attesting to its authenticity, each affidavit having been sworn before a commissioner or other person authorized to take affidavits, is admissible in evidence under this section in the same manner as if it were the original of such record. ss. (12)

Where record kept in form requiring explanation

(4) Where production of any record or of a copy of any record described in subsection (1) or (2) would not convey to the court the information contained in the record by reason of its having been kept in a form that requires explanation, a transcript of the explanation of the record or copy prepared by a person qualified to make the explanation, accompanied by an affidavit of that person setting forth his qualifications to make the explanation, attesting to the accuracy of the explanation and sworn before any commissioner or other person authorized to take affidavits, is admissible in evidence under this section in the same manner as if it were the original of such record. ss. (12)

Court may order other part of record to be produced

(5) Where part only of a record is produced under this section by any party, the court may examine any other part of the record and direct that, together with the part of the record previously so produced, the whole or any part of such other part thereof be produced by that party as the record produced by him.

Court may examine record and hear evidence

(6) For the purpose of determining whether any provision of this section applies, or for the purpose of determining the probative value, if any, to be given to information contained in any record received in evidence under this section, the court may, upon production of any record, examine the record, receive any evidence in respect thereof given orally or by affidavit including evidence as to the circumstances in which the information contained in the record was written, recorded, stored or reproduced, and draw any reasonable inference from the form or content of the record.

Notice of intention to produce record or affidavit

(7) Unless the court orders otherwise, no record or affidavit shall be received in evidence under this section unless the party producing the record or affidavit has, at least seven days before its production, given notice of his intention to produce it to each other party to the legal proceeding and has, within five days after receiving any notice in that behalf given by any such party, produced it for inspection by such party.

Not necessary to prove signature and official character

(8) Where evidence is offered by affidavit under this section it is not necessary to prove the signature or official character of the person making the affidavit if the official character of that person is set out in the body of the affidavit.

Examination on record with leave of court

(9) Subject to section 4, any person who has or may reasonably be expected to have knowledge of the making or contents of any record produced or received in evidence under this section may, with leave of the court, be examined or cross-examined thereon by any party to the legal proceeding.

Evidence inadmissible under section

(10) Nothing in this section renders admissible in evidence in any legal proceeding

(a) such part of any record as is proved to be

(i) a record made in the course of an investigation or inquiry,

(ii) a record made in the course of obtaining or giving legal advice or in contemplation of a legal proceeding,

(iii) a record in respect of the production of which any privilege exists and is claimed, or

(iv) a record of or alluding to a statement made by a person who is not, or if he were living and of sound mind would not be, competent and compellable to disclose in the legal proceeding a matter disclosed in the record;

(b) any record the production of which would be contrary to public policy; or

(c) any transcript or recording of evidence taken in the course of another legal proceeding.

Construction of section

(11) The provisions of this section shall be deemed to be in addition to and not in derogation of

(a) any other provision of this or any other Act of the Parliament of Canada respecting the admissibility in evidence of any record or the proof of any matter, or

(b) any existing rule of law under which any record is admissible in evidence or any matter may be proved.

Definitions

(12) In this section

"business"

"business" means any business, profession, trade, calling, manufacture or undertaking of any kind carried on in Canada or elsewhere whether for profit or otherwise, including any activity or operation carried on or performed in Canada or elsewhere by any government, by any department, branch, board, commission or agency of any government, by any court or other tribunal or by any other body or authority performing a function of government;

"copy" and "photographic film"

"copy", in relation to any record, includes a print, whether enlarged or not, from a photographic film of such record, and "photographic film" includes a photographic plate, microphotographic film or photostatic negative;

"court"

"court" means the court, judge, arbitrator or person before whom a legal proceeding is held or taken;

"legal proceeding"

"legal proceeding" means any civil or criminal proceeding or inquiry in which evidence is or may be given, and includes an arbitration;

"record"

"record" includes the whole or any part of any book, document, paper, card, tape or other thing on or in which information is written, recorded, stored or reproduced, and, except for the purposes of subsections (3) and (4), any copy or transcript received in evidence under this section pursuant to subsection (3) or (4). 1968-69, c. 14, s. 4.

Definitions

31. (1) In this section

"corporation"

"corporation" means the Bank of Canada, the Federal Business Development Bank and any bank to which the *Bank Act* applies, or to which the *Quebec Savings Banks Act* applies, and each of the following carrying on business in Canada, namely, every railway, express, telegraph and telephone company (except a street railway and tramway company), insurance company or society, trust company and loan company (except a company subject to Part II of the *Small Loans Act*); 1974-75-76, c. 14, s. 57.

"government"

"government" means the government of Canada or of any province of Canada and includes any department, commission, board or branch of any such government;

"photographic film"

"photographic film" includes any photographic plate, microphotographic film and photostatic negative.

When print admissible in evidence

(2) A print, whether enlarged or not, from any photographic film of,

(a) an entry in any book or record kept by any government or corporation and destroyed, lost, or delivered to a customer after such film was taken,

(b) any bill of exchange, promissory note, cheque, receipt, instrument or document held by any government or corporation and destroyed, lost, or delivered to a customer after such film was taken, or

(c) any record, document, plan, book or paper belonging to or deposited with any government or corporation,

is admissible in evidence in all cases in which and for all purposes for which the object photographed would have been received upon proof that

(d) while such book, record, bill of exchange, promissory note, cheque, receipt, instrument or document, plan, book or paper was in the custody or control of the government or corporation, the photographic film was taken thereof in order to keep a permanent record thereof, and

(e) the object photographed was subsequently destroyed by or in the presence of one or more of the employees of the government or corporation, or was lost or was delivered to a customer.

Evidence of compliance with conditions

(3) Evidence of compliance with the conditions prescribed by this section may be given by any one or more of the employees of the government or corporation, having knowledge of the taking of the photographic film, of such destruction, loss, or delivery to a customer, or of the making of the print, as the case may be, either orally or by affidavit sworn in any part of Canada before any notary public or commissioner for oaths.

Proof by notarial copy

(4) Unless the court otherwise orders, a notarial copy of an affidavit under subsection (3) is admissible in evidence in lieu of the original affidavit.

Order signed by Secretary of State

32. (1) An order in writing, signed by the Secretary of State of Canada, and purporting to be written by command of the Governor General, shall be received in evidence as the order of the Governor General.

Copies printed in *Canada Gazette*

(2) All copies of official and other notices, advertisements and documents printed in the *Canada Gazette* are admissible in evidence as *prima facie* proof of the originals, and of the contents thereof.

prima facie — assumed to be proved and true unless evidence is given to disprove

Proof of handwriting of person certifying

33. (1) No proof shall be required of the handwriting or official position of any person certifying, in pursuance of this Act, to the truth of any copy of or extract from any proclamation, order, regulation, appointment, book or other document.

Printed or written

(2) Any such copy or extract may be in print or in writing, or partly in print and partly in writing.

Attesting witness

34. (1) It is not necessary to prove by the attesting witness any instrument to the validity of which attestation is not requisite.

Instrument, how proved

(2) Such instrument may be proved by admission or otherwise as if there had been no attesting witness thereto.

Impounding of forged instrument

35. Where any instrument that has been forged or fraudulently altered is admitted in evidence, the court or the judge or person who admits the instrument may, at the request of any person against whom it is admitted in evidence, direct that the instrument shall be impounded and be kept in the custody of some officer of the court or other proper person for such period and subject to such conditions, as to the court, judge or person admitting the instrument seem meet.

Construction

36. This Part shall be deemed to be in addition to and not in derogation of any powers of proving documents given by any existing Act, or existing at law.

Provincial Laws of Evidence

How applicable

37. In all proceedings over which the Parliament of Canada has legislative authority, the laws of evidence in force in the province in which such proceedings are taken, including the laws of proof of service of any warrant, summons, subpoena or other document, subject to this and other Acts of the Parliament of Canada, apply to such proceedings.

Statutory Declarations

Solemn declaration

38. Any judge, notary public, justice of the peace, police or stipendiary magistrate, recorder, mayor or commissioner authorized to take affidavits to be used either in the provincial or federal courts, or any other functionary authorized by law to administer an oath in any matter, may receive the solemn declaration of any person voluntarily making the declaration before him, in the following form, in attestation of the execution of any writing, deed or instrument, or of the truth of any fact, or of any account rendered in writing:

I, A.B., solemnly declare that (*state the fact or facts declared to*), and I make this solemn declaration conscientiously believing it to be true, and knowing that it is of the same force and effect as if made under oath.

Declared before me...at ....this ....day of...................................19.....

Insurance Proofs

Affidavits, etc.

39. Any affidavit, affirmation or declaration required by any insurance company authorized by law to do business in Canada, in regard to any loss of, or injury to person, property or life insured or assured therein, may be taken before any commissioner or other person authorized to take affidavits or before any justice of the peace, or before any notary public for any province of Canada; and such officer is hereby required to take such affidavit, affirmation or declaration.

PART II

Application

Foreign courts

40. This Part applies to the taking of evidence relating to proceedings in courts out of Canada.

Interpretation

Definitions

41. In this Part

"cause" — "cause" includes a proceeding against a criminal;

"court" — "court" means the Supreme Court of Canada, and any superior court in any province of Canada; 28 Interp

"judge" — "judge" means any judge of the Supreme Court of Canada and any judge of any superior court in any province of Canada;

"oath" — "oath" includes affirmation in cases in which, by the law of Canada, or of the province, as the case may be, an affirmation is allowed instead of an oath.

Interpretation Act

28. In every enactment

"oath" includes a solemn affirmation or declaration, whenever the context applies to any person by whom and case in which a solemn affirmation or declaration may be made instead of an oath; and in like cases the expression "sworn" includes the expression "affirmed" or "declared";

"superior court" means

(a) in the Province of Ontario, Nova Scotia, Prince Edward Island or Newfoundland, the Supreme Court of the Province,

(b) in the Province of Quebec, the Court of Appeal and the Superior Court in and for the Province,

(c) in the Province of British Columbia, the Court of Appeal and the Supreme Court of the Province,

(d) in the Province of Manitoba, Saskatchewan, Alberta or New Brunswick, the Court of Appeal for the Province and the Court of Queen's Bench for the Province,

(e) in the Yukon Territory or the Northwest Territories, the Supreme Court thereof,

and includes the Supreme Court of Canada and the Federal Court of Canada;

Construction

42. This Part shall not be so construed as to interfere with the right of legislation of the legislature of any province requisite or desirable for the carrying out of the objects hereof.

Interpretation Act

28. In every enactment

"Commonwealth", "British Commonwealth", "Commonwealth of Nations" or "British Commonwealth of Nations" means the association of countries named in the schedule, which schedule may be amended from time to time by proclamation of the Governor in Council [51]

(a) by adding thereto the name of any country recognized by such proclamation to be a member of the Commonwealth, or

(b) by deleting therefrom the name of any country recognized by such proclamation to be no longer a member of the Commonwealth;

and "Commonwealth country" means a country that is a member of the association of such countries;

"writing", or any term of like import, includes words printed, typewritten, painted, engraved, lithographed, photographed, or represented or reproduced by any mode of representing or reproducing words in visible form;

Procedure

Order for examination of witness in Canada

43. Where, upon an application for that purpose, it is made to appear to any court or judge, that any court or tribunal of competent jurisdiction, in the Commonwealth and Dependent Territories, or in any foreign country, before which any civil, commercial or criminal matter is pending, is desirous of obtaining the testimony in relation to such matter, of a party or witness within the jurisdiction of such first mentioned court, or of the court to which such judge belongs, or of such judge, the court or judge may, in its or his discretion, order the examination upon oath upon interrogatories, or otherwise, before any person or persons named in the order, of such party or witness accordingly, and by the same or any subsequent order may command the attendance of such party or witness for the purpose of being examined, and for the production of any writings or other documents mentioned in the order, and of any other writings or documents relating to the matter in question that are in the possession or power of such party or witness.

41
28 Interp
28 Interp

Enforcement of the order

44. Upon the service upon the party or witness of an order referred to in section 43, and of an appointment of a time and place for the examination of such party or witness signed by the person named in the order for taking the examination, or, if more than one person is named, then by one of the persons named, and upon payment or tender of the like conduct money as is properly payable upon attendance at a trial, the order may be enforced in like manner as an order made by the court or judge in a cause pending in such court or before such judge. 41

Expenses and conduct money

45. Every person whose attendance is required in the manner aforesaid is entitled to the like conduct money and payment for expenses and loss of time as upon attendance at a trial.

Administering oath

46. Upon any examination of parties or witnesses, under the authority of any order made in pursuance of this Part, the oath shall be administered by the person authorized to take the examination, or, if more than one, then by one of such persons.

Right of refusal to answer or produce document

47. (1) Any person examined under any order made under this Part has the like right to refuse to answer questions tending to criminate himself, or other questions, as a party or witness, as the case may be, would have in any cause pending in the court by which, or by a judge whereof, the order is made.

Nature of right

(2) No person shall be compelled to produce, under any such order, any writing or other document that he could not be compelled to produce at a trial of such a cause.

Rules of court

48. (1) The court may frame rules and orders in relation to procedure, to the evidence to be produced in support of the application for an order for examination of parties and witnesses under this Part, and generally for carrying this Part into effect.

Letters rogatory

(2) In the absence of any order in relation to such evidence, letters rogatory from any court of justice in the Commonwealth and Dependent Territories, or from any foreign tribunal, in which such civil, commercial or criminal matter is pending, shall be deemed and taken to be sufficient evidence in support of such application.

PART III

THE TAKING OF AFFIDAVITS ABROAD

Application of Part III

49. This Part extends to the following classes of persons:

(a) officers of any of Her Majesty's diplomatic or consular services while exercising their functions in any foreign country, including ambassadors, envoys, ministers, charges d'affaires, counsellors, secretaries, attaches, consuls general, consuls, vice-consuls, pro-consuls, consular agents, acting consuls general, acting consuls, acting vice-consuls and acting consular agents;

(b) officers of the Canadian diplomatic, consular and representative services while exercising their functions in any foreign country or in any part of the Commonwealth and Dependent Territories other than Canada, including, in addition to the diplomatic and consular officers mentioned in paragraph *(a)*, high commissioners, permanent delegates, acting high commissioners, acting permanent delegates, counsellors and secretaries; and 28 Interp

(c) Canadian Government Trade Commissioners and Assistant Canadian Government Trade Commissioners while exercising their functions in any foreign country or in any part of the Commonwealth and Dependent Territories other than Canada.

Oaths taken abroad

50. Oaths, affidavits, affirmations or declarations administered, taken or received outside of Canada by any person mentioned in section 49, are as valid and effectual and are of the like force and effect to all intents and purposes as if they had been administered, taken or received in Canada by a person authorized to administer, take or receive oaths, affidavits, affirmations or declarations therein that are valid and effectual under this Act.

Documents to be admitted in evidence

51. Any document that purports to have affixed, impressed or subscribed thereon or thereto, the signature of any person authorized by this Part to administer, take or receive oaths, affidavits, affirmations or declarations, together with his seal or with the seal or stamp of his office, or the office to which he is attached, in testimony of any oath, affidavit, affirmation or declaration being administered, taken or received by him, shall be admitted in evidence, without proof of the seal or stamp or of his signature or of his official character.

INTERPRETATION ACT

SCHEDULE

Australia
The Bahamas
Bangladesh
Barbados
Botswana
Canada
Cyprus
Fiji
Gambia
Ghana
Grenada
Guyana
India
Jamaica
Kenya
Lesotho
Malawi
Malaysia
Malta
Mauritius
Nauru
New Zealand
Nigeria
Papua New Guinea
Seychelles
Sierra Leone
Singapore
Sri Lanka
Swaziland
Tanzania
Tonga
Trinidad and Tobago
Uganda
United Kingdom
Western Samoa
Zambia

JUVENILE DELINQUENTS ACT

CHAPTER J-3

An Act respecting juvenile delinquents

Short title

1. This Act may be cited as the *Juvenile Delinquents Act.*

Definitions

2. (1) In this Act

"child"

"child" means any boy or girl apparently or actually under the age of sixteen years, or such other age as may be directed in any province pursuant to subsection (2); 25(9) Interp

Interpretation Act

25. (9) A person shall be deemed not to have attained a specified number of years of age until the commencement of the anniversary, of the same number, of the day of his birth.

"court"

"court" or "juvenile court" means any court duly established under any provincial statute for the purpose of dealing with juvenile delinquents, or specially authorized by provincial statute, the Governor in Council, or the lieutenant governor in council, to deal with juvenile delinquents; 28 Interp

"court of appeal"

"court of appeal" has the same meaning as it has in the *Criminal Code;*

Criminal Code

2. In this Act

"court of appeal" means

(a) in the Province of Ontario, the Court of Appeal,
(b) in the Province of Quebec, the Court of Appeal,
(c) in the Province of Nova Scotia, the Appeal Division of the Supreme Court
(d) in the Province of New Brunswick, the Court of Appeal,
(e) in the Province of British Columbia, the Court of Appeal,
(f) in the Province of Prince Edward Island, the Supreme Court,
(g) in the Province of Manitoba, the Court of Appeal,
(h) in the Province of Saskatchewan, the Court of Appeal,
(i) in the Province of Alberta, the Court of Appeal,
(j) in the Province of Newfoundland, the Court of Appeal,
(k) in the Yukon Territory, the Court of Appeal, and
(l) in the Northwest Territories, the Court of Appeal;

"guardian"

"guardian" includes any person who has in law or in fact the custody or control of any child;

"industrial school"

"industrial school" means any industrial school or juvenile reformatory or other reformative institution or refuge for children duly approved by provincial statute or by the lieutenant governor in council in any province, and includes such an institution in a province other than that in which the committal is made, when such institution is otherwise available;

"judge"

"judge" means the judge of a juvenile court seized of the case, or the justice, specially authorized by federal or provincial authority to deal with juvenile delinquents, seized of the case;

"justice"

"justice" except in section 5 has the same meaning as it has in the *Criminal Code;*

Criminal Code

2. In this Act

"justice" means a justice of the peace or a magistrate, and includes two or more justices where two or more justices are, by law, required to act or, by law, act or have jurisdiction;

"juvenile delinquent"

"juvenile delinquent" means any child who violates any provision of the *Criminal Code* or of any federal or provincial statute, or of any by-law or ordinance of any municipality, or who is guilty of sexual immorality or any similar form of vice, or who is liable by reason of any other act to be committed to an industrial school or juvenile reformatory under any federal or provincial statute;

"magistrate"

"magistrate", except in subsections 13(1) and (4), and except in section 14, means two or more justices of the peace and also a police magistrate, a stipendiary magistrate and any other person having the power or authority of two or more justices of the peace;

"probation officer"

"probation officer" means any probation officer for juvenile delinquents duly appointed under any provincial statute or this Act;

"superintendent"

"superintendent" means a superintendent of neglected children, or of neglected and delinquent children, or a superintendent or director of child welfare, or a commissioner of the Bureau of Child Protection, or, in general, any officer, whatever is his designation, who is appointed by any provincial government to have the general charge or supervision of work in the province dealing with delinquent children, and also the lawful deputy of such officer;

"supreme court judge"

"supreme court judge" means

(a) in the Province of Ontario, a judge of the Supreme Court of Ontario;

(b) in the Province of Quebec, a judge of the Superior Court;

(c) in the Province of Nova Scotia, a judge of the Supreme Court of Nova Scotia;

(d) in the Province of New Brunswick, a judge of the Court of Queen's Bench of New Brunswick; 1978-79, c. 11, s. 10, I. 17(1).

(e) in the Province of British Columbia, a judge of the Supreme Court of British Columbia;

(f) in the Province of Prince Edward Island, a judge of the Supreme Court of Prince Edward Island;

(g) in the Province of Manitoba, a judge of the Court of Queen's Bench;

(h) in the Province of Saskatchewan, a judge of the Court of Queen's Bench;

(i) in the Province of Alberta, a judge of the Court of Queen's Bench of Alberta; 1978-79, c. 11, s. 10, I. 17(2).

(j) in the Province of Newfoundland, a judge of the Supreme Court of Newfoundland; and

(k) in the Yukon Territory, a judge of the Supreme Court of the Yukon Territory.

Alteration of definition "child"

(2) The Governor in Council may from time to time by proclamation

(a) direct that in any province the expression "child" in this Act means any boy or girl apparently or actually under the age of eighteen years, and any such proclamation may apply either to boys only or to girls only or to both boys and girls, and

(b) revoke any direction made with respect to any province by a proclamation under this section, and thereupon the expression "child" in this Act in that province means any boy or girl apparently or actually under the age of sixteen years. 1972, c. 17, s. 2.

Delinquency

3. (1) The commission by a child of any of the acts enumerated in the definition "juvenile delinquent" in subsection 2(1), constitutes an offence to be known as a delinquency, and shall be dealt with as hereinafter provided.

How child dealt with

(2) Where a child is adjudged to have committed a delinquency he shall be dealt with, not as an offender, but as one in a condition of delinquency and therefore requiring help and guidance and proper supervision.

Court's jurisdiction

4. Except as provided in section 9, the juvenile court has exclusive jurisdiction in cases of delinquency including cases where, after the committing of the delinquency, the child has passed the age limit mentioned in the definition "child" in subsection 2(1). 2

Summary trials

5. (1) Except as hereinafter provided, prosecutions and trials under this Act shall be summary and shall, *mutatis mutandis*, be governed by the provisions of the *Criminal Code* relating to summary convictions in so far as such provisions are applicable, whether or not the act constituting the offence charged would be in the case of an adult triable summarily, except that

(*a*) the provisions relating to appeals do not apply to any proceeding in a juvenile court, and

(*b*) the provisions prescribing a time limit for making a complaint or laying an information in respect of offences punishable on summary conviction where no time is specially limited for making any complaint or laying any information in the Act or law relating to the particular case, do not apply to any such proceeding other than a proceeding against an adult, except when an adult is dealt with under section 4 of this Act. 33(5)

Time for commencement

(2) The provisions of the *Criminal Code* prescribing a time limit for the commencement of prosecutions for offences against the *Criminal Code* apply, *mutatis mutandis*, to all proceedings in the juvenile court.

mutatis mutandis — after the necessary changes in detail so that the text applies

"Justice"

(3) Whenever in such provisions the expression "justice" occurs, it shall be taken in the application of such provisions to proceedings under this Act to mean "judge of the juvenile court, or justice specially authorized by federal or provincial authority to deal with juvenile delinquents".

Powers of judge

6. (1) Every judge of a juvenile court in the exercise of his jurisdiction as such has all the powers of a magistrate.

Idem

(2) In addition to those expressly mentioned in this Act, the juvenile court judge has all the powers and duties, with respect to juvenile offenders, vested in, or imposed on a judge, stipendiary magistrate, justice or justices, by or under the *Prisons and Reformatories Act*.

Discretion of court

(3) The discretion of the juvenile court judge as to the term for which a juvenile delinquent may be committed is not affected by this section.

Appointment of deputy judge

7. (1) The judge of a juvenile court may with the approval of the attorney general of the province in which such court is situated appoint a deputy judge, who has all the powers and authority of a judge of a juvenile court in case of the absence or illness or other disability of such judge.

Tenure of office

(2) A deputy judge so appointed holds office during pleasure and is removable at any time by the attorney general or by the judge, with the approval of the attorney general, without cause.

Resignation

(3) The resignation of a deputy judge may be accepted by either the judge by whom he was appointed, or the attorney general.

All cases to go to juvenile court

8. (1) When any child is arrested, with or without a warrant, such child shall, 2
instead of being taken before a justice, be taken before the juvenile court; and, if a child is taken before a justice, upon a summons or under a warrant or for any other reason, it is the duty of the justice to transfer the case to the juvenile court, and of the officer having the child in charge to take the child before that court, and in any such case the juvenile court shall hear and dispose of the case in the same manner as if the child had been brought before it upon information originally laid therein.

Exception

(2) Subsection (1) does not apply to any justice who is a judge of the juvenile court or who has power to act as such under any Act in force in the province.

Exceptional procedure when offence is indictable

9. (1) Where the act complained of is, under the provisions of the *Criminal Code* or otherwise, an indictable offence, and the accused child is apparently or 27(1)(a Interp
actually over the age of fourteen years, the court may, in its discretion, order the child to be proceeded against by indictment in the ordinary courts in accordance with the provisions of the *Criminal Code* in that behalf; but such course shall in no case be followed unless the court is of the opinion that the good of the child and the interest of the community demand it.

Order may be rescinded

(2) The court may, in its discretion, at any time before any proceeding has been initiated against the child in the ordinary criminal courts, rescind an order so made.

Notices to parents

10. (1) Due notice of the hearing of any charge of delinquency shall be served on the parent or parents or the guardian of the child, or if there is neither parent nor guardian, or if the residence of the parent or parents or guardian is unknown, then on some near relative, if any, living in the city, town or county, whose whereabouts is known, and any person so served has the right to be present at 22(4)
the hearing.

Service of notice

(2) The judge may give directions as to the persons to be served under this section, and such directions are conclusive as to the sufficiency of any notice given in accordance therewith.

Powers of clerk

11. (1) The clerk of every juvenile court has power *ex officio* to administer oaths and also, in the absence of the judge and deputy judge, to adjourn any hearing for a definite period not to exceed ten days.

ex officio — by virtue of the office; because one is elected, appointed or holds a particular office, they, by virtue of that office, also hold the other office or appointment

Duties of clerk

(2) It is the duty of the clerk of the juvenile court to notify the probation officer or the chief probation officer, in advance, when any child is to be brought before the court for trial.

Private trials

12. (1) The trials of children shall take place without publicity and separately and apart from the trials of other accused persons, and at suitable times to be designated and appointed for that purpose.

Place of trials

(2) Such trials may be held in the private office of the judge or in some other private room in the court house or municipal building, or in the detention home, or if no such room or place is available, then in the ordinary court room, but when held in the ordinary court room an interval of half an hour shall be allowed to elapse between the close of the trial or examination of any adult and the beginning of the trial of a child.

Names not to be published or identity of child indicated

(3) No report of a delinquency committed, or said to have been committed, by a child, or of the trial or other disposition of a charge against a child, or of a charge against an adult brought in the juvenile court under section 33 or under section 35, in which the name of the child or of the child's parent or guardian or of any school or institution that the child is alleged to have been attending or of which the child is alleged to have been an inmate is disclosed, or in which the identity of the child is otherwise indicated, shall without the special leave of the court, be published in any newspaper or other publication.

Application to newspapers

(4) Subsection (3) applies to all newspapers and other publications published anywhere in Canada, whether or not this Act is otherwise in force in the place of publication.

Detention home

13. (1) No child, pending a hearing under this Act, shall be held in confinement in any county or other gaol or other place in which adults are or may be imprisoned, but shall be detained at a detention home or shelter used exclusively for children or under other charge approved of by the judge or, in his absence, by the sheriff, or, in the absence of both the judge and the sheriff, by the mayor or other chief magistrate of the city, town, county or place.

Type 'A' Offence

(2) Any officer or person violating subsection (1) is liable on summary conviction before a juvenile court or a magistrate to a fine not exceeding one hundred dollars, or to imprisonment not exceeding thirty days, or to both.

Exception

(3) This section does not apply to a child as to whom an order has been made pursuant to section 9.

Idem

(4) This section does not apply to a child apparently over the age of fourteen years who, in the opinion of the judge, or, in his absence, of the sheriff, or, in the absence of both the judge and the sheriff, of the mayor or other chief magistrate of the city, town, county or place, cannot safely be confined in any place other than a gaol or lock-up.

2. In this Act

"magistrate", except in subsections 13(1) and (4), and except in section 14, means two or more justices of the peace and also a police magistrate, a stipendiary magistrate and any other person having the power or authority of two or more justices of the peace;

Where there is no detention home

14. (1) Where a warrant has issued for the arrest of a child, or where a child has been arrested without a warrant, in a county or district in which there is no detention home used exclusively for children, no incarceration of the child shall be made or had unless in the opinion of the judge of the court, or, in his absence, of the sheriff, or, in the absence of both the judge and the sheriff, of the mayor or other chief magistrate of the city, town, county or place, such course is necessary in order to insure the attendance of such child in court.

Promise to attend may be accepted

(2) In order to avoid, if possible, such incarceration, the verbal or written promise of the person served with notice of the proceedings as aforesaid, or of any other proper person, to be responsible for the presence of such child when required, may be accepted; and in case the child fails to appear, at such time or times as the court requires, the person or persons assuming responsibility as aforesaid, shall be deemed guilty of contempt of court, unless in the opinion of the court there is reasonable cause for such failure to appear.

Bail may be accepted

15. Pending the hearing of a charge of delinquency the court may accept bail for the appearance of the child charged at the trial as in the case of other accused persons.

Court may adjourn or postpone hearing

16. The court may postpone or adjourn the hearing of a charge of delinquency for such period or periods as the court may deem advisable, or may postpone or adjourn the hearing *sine die.*

sine die — without naming a day, an indefinite period

Proceedings may be informal

17. (1) Proceedings under this Act with respect to a child, including the trial and disposition of the case, may be as informal as the circumstances will permit, consistent with a due regard for a proper administration of justice.

Not affected by irregularities

(2) No adjudication or other action of a juvenile court with respect to a child shall be quashed or set aside because of any informality or irregularity where it appears that the disposition of the case was in the best interests of the child.

Service of process in another jurisdiction

(3) Except as provided in subsection (5), if a person, whether a child or an adult, against whom any warrant has issued out of a juvenile court cannot be found within the jurisdiction of the juvenile court out of which the warrant was so issued, but is or is suspected to be in any other part of Canada, any judge or deputy judge of a juvenile court within whose jurisdiction such person is or is suspected to be, or if there is no juvenile court having jurisdiction in such place, then any justice within whose jurisdiction such person is or is suspected to be, upon proof being made on oath or affirmation of the handwriting of the juvenile court judge or other officer who issued the warrant, shall make an endorsement on the warrant, signed with his name, authorizing the execution thereof within his jurisdiction.

Authority to arrest

(4) Such endorsement is sufficient authority to the person bringing such warrant, and to all other persons to whom the warrant was originally directed, and also to all probation officers, constables and other peace officers of the juvenile court or of the territorial division where the warrant has been so endorsed, to execute the warrant therein and to carry the person against whom the warrant issued when apprehended, before the juvenile court out of which the warrant issued.

Child outside of jurisdiction

(5) Where a child who has been before a juvenile court and is still under the surveillance of such court has been caused by the court to be placed in a foster home outside of the jurisdiction of such court or has been committed by the court to the care or custody of a probation officer or other suitable person or to an industrial school, outside of the jurisdiction of such court, the court may take any action with respect to such child that it could take were the child within the jurisdiction of such court, and for any such purpose any warrant or other process issued with respect to such child may be executed or served in any place in Canada outside of the jurisdiction of such court without the necessity of complying with subsection (3).

Seal not required

18. It is not necessary to its validity that any seal should be attached or affixed to any information, summons, warrant, conviction, order or other process or document filed, issued or entered in any proceeding had or taken under this Act.

Child's oath may be dispensed with

19. (1) When in a proceeding before a juvenile court a child of tender years who is called as a witness does not, in the opinion of the judge, understand the nature of an oath, the evidence of such child may be received, though not given under oath, if in the opinion of the judge the child is possessed of sufficient intelligence to justify the reception of the evidence and understands the duty of speaking the truth.

Corroborative evidence

(2) No person shall be convicted upon the evidence of a child of tender years not under oath unless such evidence is corroborated in some material respect.

Release on probation

20. (1) In the case of a child adjudged to be a juvenile delinquent the court may, in its discretion, take either one or more of the several courses of action hereinafter in this section set out, as it may in its judgment deem proper in the circumstances of the case:

(a) suspend final disposition;

(b) adjourn the hearing or disposition of the case from time to time for any definite or indefinite period;

(c) impose a fine not exceeding twenty-five dollars, which may be paid in periodical amounts or otherwise; 22(2)

(d) commit the child to the care or custody of a probation officer or of any other suitable person;

(e) allow the child to remain in its home, subject to the visitation of a probation officer, such child to report to the court or to the probation officer as often as may be required;

(f) cause the child to be placed in a suitable family home as a foster home, subject to the friendly supervision of a probation officer and the further order of the court;

(g) impose upon the delinquent such further or other conditions as may be deemed advisable;

(h) commit the child to the charge of any children's aid society, duly organized under an Act of the legislature of the province and approved by the lieutenant governor in council, or, in any municipality in which there is no children's aid society, to the charge of the superintendent, if there is one; or

(i) commit the child to an industrial school duly approved by the lieutenant governor in council.

Support of child

(2) In every such case it is within the power of the court to make an order upon the parent or parents of the child, or upon the municipality to which the child belongs, to contribute to the child's support such sum as the court may determine, and where such order is made upon the municipality, the municipality may from time to time recover from the parent or parents any sum or sums paid by it pursuant to such order.

Return of juvenile delinquent to court

(3) Where a child has been adjudged to be a juvenile delinquent and whether or not such child has been dealt with in any of the ways provided for in subsection (1), the court may at any time, before such juvenile delinquent has reached the age of twenty-one years and unless the court has otherwise ordered, cause by notice, summons, or warrant, the delinquent to be brought before the court, and the court may then take any action provided for in subsection (1), or may make an order with respect to such child under section 9, or may discharge the child on parole or release the child from detention, but in a province in which there is a superintendent, no child shall be released by the judge from an industrial school without a report from such superintendent recommending such release, and where an order is made by a court releasing a juvenile delinquent from an industrial school or transferring such delinquent from an industrial school to a foster home or from one foster home to another under this subsection, it is not necessary for such delinquent to be before the court at the time that such order is made.

Evidence on hearing

(4) When a child is returned to the court, as provided in subsection (3), the court may deal with the case on the report of the probation officer or other person in whose care such child has been placed, or of the secretary of a children's aid society, or of the superintendent, or of the superintendent of the industrial school to which the child has been committed, without the necessity of hearing any further or other evidence.

Child's own good

(5) The action taken shall, in every case, be that which the court is of opinion the child's own good and the best interests of the community require.

May be dealt with under provincial law

21. (1) Whenever an order has been made under section 20 committing a child to a children's aid society, or to a superintendent, or to an industrial school, if so ordered by the provincial secretary, the child may thereafter be dealt with under the laws of the province in the same manner in all respects as if an order had been lawfully made in respect of a proceeding instituted under authority of a statute of the province; and from and after the date of the issuing of such order except for new offences, the child shall not be further dealt with by the court under this Act.

Order in advance

(2) The order of the provincial secretary may be made in advance and to apply to all cases of commitment mentioned in this section.

Parent or guardian may be ordered to pay fine, damages or costs

22. (1) Where a child is adjudged to have been guilty of an offence and the court is of the opinion that the case would be best met by the imposition of a fine, damages or costs, whether with or without restitution or any other action, the court may, if satisfied that the parent or guardian has conduced to the commission of the offence by neglecting to exercise due care of the child or otherwise, order that the fine, damages or costs awarded be paid by the parent or guardian of the child, instead of by the child.

Limit of amount

(2) Where a fine is imposed and ordered to be paid by the parent or guardian, the limit of amount imposed by subsection 20(1) does not apply, but shall in no case exceed the amount fixed for a similar offence under the *Criminal Code.*

Recovery of amount

(3) Where, under the provisions of this section or of section 20, a sum of money is ordered to be paid, the court may adjudge, either by the order respecting the payment of such sum or by an order made subsequently, that the money shall be recoverable by distress and sale of the goods and chattels of the party and in default of such distress by imprisonment, and the amount is so recoverable or is recoverable in the same manner as a fine imposed under any provision of the *Criminal Code* is recoverable, or is recoverable as provided in any Act of the legislature of the province making provision for the recovery of fines.

Parent or guardian to be heard

(4) No order shall be made under this section without giving the parent or guardian an opportunity of being heard; but a parent or guardian who has been duly served with notice of the hearing pursuant to section 10 shall be deemed to have had such opportunity, notwithstanding the fact that he has failed to attend the hearing.

Appeal

(5) A parent or guardian has the same right of appeal from an order made under this section as if the order had been made on the conviction of the parent or guardian.

Additional action

(6) Any action taken under this section may be additional to any action taken under section 20.

Religion of child to be respected

23. (1) No Protestant child dealt with under this Act shall be committed to the care of any Roman Catholic children's aid society or be placed in any Roman Catholic family as his foster home; nor shall any Roman Catholic child dealt with under this Act be committed to the care of any Protestant children's aid society, or be placed in any Protestant family as his foster home; but this section does not apply to the placing of children in a temporary home or shelter for children, established under the authority of a statute of the province, or, in a municipality where there is but one children's aid society, to such children's aid society.

Order to enforce preceding provision

(2) If a Protestant child is committed to the care of a Roman Catholic children's aid society or placed in a Roman Catholic family as his foster home or if a Roman Catholic child is committed to the care of a Protestant children's aid society or placed in a Protestant family as his foster home, contrary to this section, the court shall, on the application of any person in that behalf, make an order providing for the proper commitment or placing of the child pursuant to subsection (1).

Children of religious faith other than Protestant or Roman Catholic

(3) No child of a religious faith other than the Protestant or Roman Catholic shall be committed to the care of either a Protestant or Roman Catholic children's aid society or be placed in any Protestant or Roman Catholic family as his foster home unless there is within the municipality no children's aid society or no suitable family of the same religious faith as that professed by the child or by his family, and, if there is no children's aid society or suitable family of such faith to which the care of such child can properly be given, the disposition of such child is in the discretion of the court.

Children not allowed to be in court

24. (1) No child, other than an infant in arms, shall be permitted to be present in court during the trial of any person charged with an offence or during any proceedings preliminary thereto, and if so present the child shall be ordered to be removed unless he is the person charged with the alleged offence, or unless the child's presence is required, as a witness or otherwise, for the purposes of justice.

Exception

(2) This section does not apply to messengers, clerks and other persons required to attend at any court for the purposes connected with their employment.

Children under twelve

25. It is not lawful to commit a juvenile delinquent apparently under the age of twelve years to any industrial school, unless and until an attempt has been made to reform such child in his own home or in a foster home or in the charge of a children's aid society, or of a superintendent, and unless the court finds that the best interests of the child and the welfare of the community require such commitment.

Children to be separated from adults

26. (1) No juvenile delinquent shall, under any circumstances, upon or after conviction, be sentenced to or incarcerated in any penitentiary, or county or other gaol, or police station, or any other place in which adults are or may be imprisoned.

Exception

(2) This section does not apply to a child who has been proceeded against under section 9.

Juvenile court committee

27. (1) There shall be in connection with the juvenile court a committee of citizens, serving without remuneration, to be known as the "juvenile court committee".

Juvenile court committee *ex officio*

(2) Where there is a children's aid society in a city or town in which this Act is in force, the committee of such society or a sub-committee thereof shall be the juvenile court committee; and where there is both a Protestant and a Roman Catholic children's aid society then the committee of the Protestant children's aid society or a sub-committee thereof shall be the juvenile court committee as regards Protestant children, and the committee of the Roman Catholic children's aid society or a sub-committee thereof shall be the juvenile court committee as regards Roman Catholic children.

Appointment by court

(3) Where there is no children's aid society in a city or town in which this Act is in force, the court may, and, upon a petition signed by fifty residents of the municipality in question, shall appoint three or more persons to be the juvenile court committee with respect to Protestant children, and three or more other persons to be the juvenile court committee with respect to Roman Catholic children; and the persons so appointed may in their discretion sit as one joint committee.

When child of religious faith other than Protestant or Roman Catholic

(4) In the case of a child of a religious faith other than Protestant or Roman Catholic, the court shall appoint three or more suitable persons to be the juvenile court committee as regards such child, such persons to be of the same religious faith as the child if there are such suitable persons resident within the municipality willing to act, and if in the opinion of the court they are desirable persons to be such committee.

Duties of committee

28. (1) It is the duty of the juvenile court committee to meet as often as may be necessary and consult with the probation officers with regard to juvenile delinquents, to offer, through the probation officers and otherwise, advice to the court as to the best mode of dealing with such delinquents, and, generally, to facilitate by every means in its power, the reformation of juvenile delinquents.

Representatives may be present

(2) Representatives of the juvenile court committee, who are members of that committee, may be present at any session of the juvenile court.

Certain cases reserved for judge

(3) No deputy judge shall hear and determine any case that a juvenile court committee desires should be reserved for hearing and determination by the judge of the juvenile court.

Court may appoint probation officer

29. Where no probation officer has been appointed under provincial authority and remuneration for a probation officer has been provided by municipal grant, public subscription or otherwise, the court shall, with the concurrence of the juvenile court committee, appoint one or more suitable persons as probation 27
officers.

Powers of a probation officer

30. Every probation officer duly appointed under this Act or of any provincial statute has in the discharge of his or her duties as such probation officer all the powers of a constable, and shall be protected from civil actions for anything done in *bona fide* exercise of the powers conferred by this Act.

bona fide — in or with good faith, there is no pretence, it is actually so

Duties of probation officer

31. It is the duty of a probation officer 2

(*a*) to make such investigation as may be required by the court;

(*b*) to be present in court in order to represent the interests of the child when the case is heard;

(*c*) to furnish to the court such information and assistance as may be required; and

(*d*) to take such charge of any child, before or after trial, as may be directed by the court.

Probation officers under control of judge

32. Every probation officer, however appointed, is under the control and subject to the directions of the judge of the court with which such probation 2
officer is connected, for all purposes of this Act.

Adults liable who contribute to delinquency

Type 'A' Offence ss. (5)

33. (1) Any person, whether the parent or guardian of the child or not, who, knowingly or wilfully,

(*a*) aids, causes, abets or connives at the commission by a child of a delinquency, or 3(1)

(*b*) does any act producing, promoting, or contributing to a child's being or becoming a juvenile delinquent or likely to make any child a juvenile 2
delinquent,

is liable on summary conviction before a juvenile court or a magistrate to a fine not exceeding five hundred dollars or to imprisonment for a period not exceeding two years, or to both.

Liability of parents and guardians

Type 'A' Offence ss. (5)

(2) Any person who, being the parent or guardian of the child and being able to do so, knowingly neglects to do that which would directly tend to prevent the child being or becoming a juvenile delinquent or to remove the conditions that render or are likely to render the child a juvenile delinquent is liable on summary conviction before a juvenile court or a magistrate to a fine not exceeding five hundred dollars or to imprisonment for a period not exceeding two years, or to both.

Adjournment

(3) The court or magistrate may postpone or adjourn the hearing of a charge under this section for such periods as the court may deem advisable or may postpone or adjourn the hearing *sine die* and may impose conditions upon any person found guilty under this section and suspend sentence subject to those conditions, and on proof at any time that those conditions have been violated may pass sentence on such person.

sine die — without naming a day, an indefinite period

No defence if child does not become delinquent

(4) It is not a valid defence to a prosecution under this section either that the child is of too tender years to understand or appreciate the nature or effect of the conduct of the accused, or that notwithstanding the conduct of the accused the child did not in fact become a juvenile delinquent.

Limitation

(5) Notwithstanding anything to the contrary in section 5 or in the provisions of the *Criminal Code* referred to in paragraph 5(1)*(b)*, any prosecution for an offence under this section may be commenced within one year from the time when the offence is alleged to have been committed.

Canada Evidence Act

4. (2) The wife or husband of a person charged with an offence against section 33 or 34 of the *Juvenile Delinquents Act* or with an offence against any of sections 143 to 146, 148, 150 to 155, 157, 166 to 169, 175, 195, 197, 200, 248 to 250, 255 to 258, 289, paragraph 423(1)(*c*) or an attempt to commit an offence under section 146 or 155 of the *Criminal Code*, is a competent and compellable witness for the prosecution without the consent of the person charged.

Penalty for inducing, etc., child to leave home, etc.

Type 'A' Offence

34. Any person who induces or attempts to induce any child to leave any 2
detention home, industrial school, foster home or any other institution or place 2
where such child has been placed under this Act or who removes or attempts to remove such child therefrom, without the authority of the court, or who, when a child has unlawfully left the custody of an institution or foster home knowingly harbours or conceals such child without notice of the child's whereabouts to the court or to the institution or to the local police authorities, is guilty of an offence and is liable upon summary conviction before a juvenile court or before a magistrate to a fine not exceeding one hundred dollars or to imprisonment for a period not exceeding one year, or to both.

No preliminary hearing

35. (1) Prosecutions against adults for offences against any provisions of the
Criminal Code in respect of a child may be brought in the juvenile court without 2
the necessity of a preliminary hearing before a justice, and may be summarily 2
disposed of where the offence is triable summarily, or otherwise dealt with as in the case of a preliminary hearing before a justice.

Application of *Criminal Code*

(2) All provisions of the *Criminal Code* not inconsistent with this Act that would apply to similar proceedings if brought before a justice apply to prosecutions brought before the juvenile court under this section.

Contempt of court

36. (1) Every juvenile court has such and like powers and authority to preserve order in court during the sittings thereof and by the like ways and means as now by law are or may be exercised and used in like cases and for the like purposes by any court in Canada and by the judges thereof, during the sittings thereof.

Enforcing of process

(2) Every judge of a juvenile court, whenever any resistance is offered to the execution of any summons, warrant of execution or other process issued by him, may enforce the due execution of the process by the means provided by the law for enforcing the execution of the process of other courts in like cases.

Appeals by special leave

37. (1) A supreme court judge may, in his discretion, on special grounds, grant 2
special leave to appeal from any decision of the juvenile court or a magistrate; in 2
any case where such leave is granted the procedure upon appeal shall be such as is provided in the case of a conviction on indictment, and the provisions of the *Criminal Code* relating to appeals from conviction on indictment *mutatis mutandis* apply to such appeal, save that the appeal shall be to a supreme court judge instead of to the court of appeal, with a further right of appeal to the
court of appeal by special leave of that court. 2

When leave to appeal may be granted

(2) No leave to appeal shall be granted under this section unless the judge or court granting such leave considers that in the particular circumstances of the case it is essential in the public interest or for the due administration of justice that such leave be granted.

Application for leave to appeal

(3) Application for leave to appeal under this section shall be made within 25(3) Interp
ten days of the making of the conviction or order complained of, or within such further time, not exceeding an additional twenty days, as a supreme court judge may see fit to fix, either before or after the expiration of the said ten days.

Interpretation Act

25. (3) Where there is a reference to a number of days, not expressed to be clear days, between two events, in calculating the number of days there shall be excluded the day on which the first event happens and there shall be included the day on which the second event happens.

Act to be liberally construed

38. This Act shall be liberally construed in order that its purpose may be carried out, namely, that the care and custody and discipline of a juvenile delinquent shall approximate as nearly as may be that which should be given by his parents, and that as far as practicable every juvenile delinquent shall be treated, not as criminal, but as a misdirected and misguided child, and one needing aid, encouragement, help and assistance.

Not to affect provincial statutes

39. Nothing in this Act shall be construed as having the effect of repealing or overriding any provision of any provincial statute intended for the protection or benefit of children; and when a juvenile delinquent, who has not been guilty of an act that is under the provisions of the *Criminal Code* an indictable offence, comes within the provisions of a provincial statute, he may be dealt with either under such statute or under this Act as may be deemed to be in the best interests of the child.

Repeal of former law

40. Whenever and so soon as this Act goes into force in any province, city, town, or other portion of a province, every provision of the *Criminal Code* or of any other Act of the Parliament of Canada inconsistent with the provisions of this Act, stands repealed as regards such province, city, town, or other portion of a province.

Sections in force in Canada

41. Subsections 12(4) and 17(3) and (5), and section 34 shall be in force in all parts of Canada, whether this Act is otherwise in force or not.

When Act shall be enforced

42. Subject to section 41, this Act may be put in force in any province, or in any portion of a province, by proclamation, after the passing of an Act by the legislature of any province providing for the establishment of juvenile courts, or designating any existing courts as juvenile courts, and of detention homes for children.

Any city or town may ask for this law

43. (1) Subject to section 41, this Act may be put in force in any city, town, or other portion of a province, by proclamation, notwithstanding that the provincial legislature has not passed an Act such as referred to in section 42, if the Governor in Council is satisfied that proper facilities for the due carrying out of the provisions of this Act have been provided in such city, town, or other portion of a province, by the municipal council thereof or otherwise.

Special appointment of judge

(2) The Governor in Council may designate a superior court or county court judge or a justice, having jurisdiction in the city, town, or other portion of a province, in which the Act is so put in force, to act as juvenile court judge for such city, town, or other portion of a province, and the judge or justice so designated or appointed has and shall exercise in such city, town, or other portion of a province, all the powers by this Act conferred on the juvenile court. 28 Interp

Enforcement of Act

44. This Act shall go into force only when and as proclamations declaring it in force in any province, city, town or other portion of the province are issued and published in the *Canada Gazette.*

Operation of Act

45. Notwithstanding section 44, this Act shall be in force in every part of Canada in which the *Juvenile Delinquents Act*, chapter 108 of the Revised Statutes of Canada, 1927, was in force on the 14th day of June 1929.

Interpretation Act

28. In every enactment

"Governor in Council", or "Governor General in Council" means the Governor General of Canada, or person administering the Government of Canada for the time being, acting by and with the advice of, or by and with the advice and consent of, or in conjunction with the Queen's Privy Council for Canada;

—NOTES—

FOOD AND DRUGS ACT

CHAPTER F-27

An Act respecting food, drugs, cosmetics and therapeutic devices

SHORT TITLE

Short title

1. This Act may be cited as the *Food and Drugs Act.*

INTERPRETATION

Definitions

2. In this Act

"advertisement"

"advertisement" includes any representation by any means whatever for the purpose of promoting directly or indirectly the sale or disposal of any food, drug, cosmetic or device;

"analyst"

"analyst" means any person designated as a Food and Drug Analyst under subsection 25(3);

"contraceptive device"

"contraceptive device" means

(a) any instrument, apparatus or contrivance, and

(b) any substance not being a drug,

that is manufactured, sold or represented for use in the prevention of conception;

"cosmetic"

"cosmetic" includes any substance or mixture of substances manufactured, sold or represented for use in cleansing, improving or altering the complexion, skin, hair or teeth, and includes deodorants and perfumes;

"Department"

"Department" means the Department of National Health and Welfare;

"device"

"device" means any article, instrument, apparatus or contrivance, including any component, part or accessory thereof, manufactured, sold or represented for use in

(a) the diagnosis, treatment, mitigation or prevention of a disease, disorder or abnormal physical state, or the symptoms thereof, in man or animal,

(b) restoring, correcting or modifying a body function or the body structure of man or animal,

(c) the diagnosis of pregnancy in humans or animals, or

(d) the care of humans or animals during pregnancy and at and after birth of the offspring, including care of the offspring,

and includes a contraceptive device but does not include a drug;

"drug"

"drug" includes any substance or mixture of substances manufactured, sold or represented for use in

(a) the diagnosis, treatment, mitigation or prevention of a disease, disorder, abnormal physical state, or the symptoms thereof, in man or animal,

(b) restoring, correcting or modifying organic functions in man or animal, or

(c) disinfection in premises in which food is manufactured, prepared or kept, or for the control of vermin in such premises;

"food"

"food" includes any article manufactured, sold or represented for use as food or drink for man, chewing gum, and any ingredient that may be mixed with food for any purpose whatever;

"inspector" "inspector" means any person designated as a Food and Drug Inspector under subsection 25(4);

"label" "label" includes any legend, word or mark attached to, included in, belonging to or accompanying any food, drug, cosmetic, device or package;

"Minister" "Minister" means the Minister of National Health and Welfare;

"package" "package" includes any thing in which any food, drug, cosmetic or device is wholly or partly contained, placed or packed;

"prescribed" "prescribed" means prescribed by the regulations;

"sell" "sell" includes sell, offer for sale, expose for sale, have in possession for sale, and distribute;

"unsanitary" conditions" "unsanitary conditions" means such conditions or circumstances as might contaminate a food, drug or cosmetic with dirt or filth or render the same injurious to health. 1968-69, c. 41, s. 1.

PART I

FOODS, DRUGS, COSMETICS AND DEVICES

General

Prohibited advertising

3. (1) No person shall advertise any food, drug, cosmetic or device to the 2
general public as a treatment, preventative or cure for any of the diseases, disorders or abnormal physical states mentioned in Schedule A.

Idem

(2) No person shall sell any food, drug, cosmetic or device 2

(*a*) that is represented by label, or

(*b*) that he advertises to the general public

as a treatment, preventative or cure for any of the diseases, disorders or abnormal physical states mentioned in Schedule A.

Advertising of contraceptive device prohibited

(3) Except as authorized by regulation, no person shall advertise to the
general public any contraceptive device or any drug manufactured, sold or 2
represented for use in the prevention of conception.

Food

Prohibited sales of food

4. No person shall sell an article of food that 2

(*a*) has in or upon it any poisonous or harmful substance;

(*b*) is unfit for human consumption;

(*c*) consists in whole or in part of any filthy, putrid, disgusting, rotten, decomposed or diseased animal or vegetable substance;

(*d*) is adulterated; or

(*e*) was manufactured, prepared, preserved, packaged or stored under unsanitary conditions.

Deception

5. (1) No person shall label, package, treat, process, sell or advertise any food in a manner that is false, misleading or deceptive or is likely to create an erroneous impression regarding its character, value, quantity, composition, merit or safety.

Idem

(2) An article of food that is not labelled or packaged as required by the regulations, or is labelled or packaged contrary to the regulations, shall be deemed to be labelled or packaged contrary to subsection (1).

Where standard prescribed

6. Where a standard has been prescribed for a food, no person shall label, package, sell or advertise any article in such a manner that it is likely to be mistaken for such food, unless the article complies with the prescribed standard.

Unsanitary conditions

7. No person shall manufacture, prepare, preserve, package or store for sale
any food under unsanitary conditions. 2

Drugs

Prohibited sales of drugs

8. No person shall sell any drug that 2

(*a*) was manufactured, prepared, preserved, packed or stored under unsanitary conditions; or

(*b*) is adulterated.

Deception

9. (1) No person shall label, package, treat, process, sell or advertise any drug 2
in a manner that is false, misleading or deceptive or is likely to create an erroneous impression regarding its character, value, quantity, composition, merit or safety.

Idem

(2) A drug that is not labelled or packaged as required by the regulations, or is labelled or packaged contrary to the regulations, shall be deemed to be labelled or packaged contrary to subsection (1).

Where standard prescribed

10. (1) Where a standard has been prescribed for a drug, no person shall label, package, sell or advertise any substance in such a manner that it is likely to be mistaken for such drug, unless the substance complies with the prescribed standard.

Trade standards

(2) Where a standard has not been prescribed for a drug, but a standard for the drug is contained in any publication mentioned in Schedule B, no person shall label, package, sell or advertise any substance in such a manner that it is likely to be mistaken for such drug, unless the substance complies with such standard.

Professed standards

(3) Where a standard for a drug has not been prescribed and no standard for the drug is contained in any publication mentioned in Schedule B, no person shall sell such drug, unless

(*a*) it is in accordance with the professed standard under which it is sold, and

(*b*) it does not resemble, in a manner likely to deceive, any drug for which a standard has been prescribed or is contained in any publication mentioned in Schedule B.

Unsanitary conditions

11. No person shall manufacture, prepare, preserve, package or store for sale any drug under unsanitary conditions.

Indicating safe conditions

12. No person shall sell any drug described in Schedule C or D unless the
Minister has, in prescribed form and manner, indicated that the premises in which 2
the drug was manufactured and the process and conditions of manufacture therein are suitable to ensure that the drug will not be unsafe for use.

Idem

13. No person shall sell any drug described in Schedule E unless the Minister has, in prescribed form and manner, indicated that the batch from which the drug was taken is not unsafe for use.

Samples

14. (1) No person shall distribute or cause to be distributed any drug as a sample.

Exception

(2) Subsection (1) does not apply to the distribution, under prescribed conditions, of samples of drugs to physicians, dentists, veterinary surgeons or pharmacists.

Sale prohibited

15. No person shall sell any drug described in Schedule F. 2

Cosmetics

Prohibited sales of cosmetics

16. No person shall sell any cosmetic that 2

(a) has in or upon it any substance that may cause injury to the health of the user when the cosmetic is used,

(i) according to the directions on the label or accompanying such cosmetic, or

(ii) for such purposes and by such methods of use as are customary or usual therefor;

(b) consists in whole or in part of any filthy or decomposed substance or of any foreign matter; or

(c) was manufactured, prepared, preserved, packed or stored under unsanitary conditions.

Where standard prescribed

17. Where a standard has been prescribed for a cosmetic, no person shall label, package, sell or advertise any article in such a manner that it is likely to be mistaken for such cosmetic, unless the article complies with the prescribed standard.

18. No person shall manufacture, prepare, preserve, package or store for sale any cosmetic under unsanitary conditions.

Devices

Prohibited sales of devices

19. No person shall sell any device that, when used according to directions or under such conditions as are customary or usual, may cause injury to the health of the purchaser or user thereof. 2

Deception

20. (1) No person shall label, package, treat, process, sell or advertise any device in a manner that is false, misleading or deceptive or is likely to create an erroneous impression regarding its design, construction, performance, intended use, quantity, character, value, composition, merit or safety. 1976-77, c. 28, s. 16.

Idem

(2) A device that is not labelled or packaged as required by the regulations, or is labelled or packaged contrary to the regulations, shall be deemed to be labelled or packaged contrary to subsection (1).

Where standard prescribed

21. Where a standard has been prescribed for a device, no person shall label, package, sell or advertise any article in such a manner that it is likely to be mistaken for such device, unless the article complies with the prescribed standard.

—NOTES—

PART II

ADMINISTRATION AND ENFORCEMENT

Powers of Inspectors

Powers of inspectors

22. (1) An inspector may at any reasonable time

(*a*) enter any place where on reasonable grounds he believes any article to which this Act or the regulations apply is manufactured, prepared, preserved, packaged or stored, examine any such article and take samples thereof, and examine anything that he reasonably believes is used or capable of being used for such manufacture, preparation, preservation, packaging or storing; ss. (2)

(*b*) open and examine any receptacle or package that on reasonable grounds he believes contains any article to which this Act or the regulations apply;

(*c*) examine any books, documents or other records found in any place mentioned in paragraph (*a*) that on reasonable grounds he believes contain any information relevant to the enforcement of this Act with respect to any article to which this Act or the regulations apply and make copies thereof or extracts therefrom; and

(*d*) seize and detain for such time as may be necessary any article by means of or in relation to which he reasonably believes any provision of this Act or the regulations has been violated.

Definition

(2) For the purposes of subsection (1), the expression "article to which this Act or the regulations apply" includes

(*a*) any food, drug, cosmetic or device,

(*b*) anything used for the manufacture, preparation, preservation, packaging or storing thereof, and

(*c*) any labelling or advertising material.

Certificate of appointment

(3) An inspector shall be furnished with a prescribed certificate of designation and on entering any place pursuant to subsection (1) shall if so required produce the certificate to the person in charge thereof.

Assistance to inspector

(4) The owner or person in charge of a place entered by an inspector pursuant to subsection (1) and every person found therein shall give the inspector all reasonable assistance in his power and furnish him with such information as he may reasonably require.

Obstructing inspector

(5) No person shall obstruct an inspector in the carrying out of his duties under this Act or the regulations.

False statements

(6) No person shall knowingly make any false or misleading statement either verbally or in writing to any inspector engaged in carrying out his duties under this Act or the regulations.

Interference

(7) No person shall remove, alter or interfere in any way with any article seized under this Act without the authority of an inspector.

Storing of seized articles

(8) Any article seized under this Act may at the option of an inspector be kept or stored in the building or place where it was seized or may at the direction of an inspector be removed to any other proper place.

Forfeiture

Release of seized articles

23. (1) An inspector shall release any article seized by him under this Act when he is satisfied that all the provisions of this Act and the regulations with respect thereto have been complied with.

Destruction with consent

(2) Where an inspector has seized an article under this Act and the owner thereof or the person in whose possession the article was at the time of seizure consents to the destruction thereof, the article is thereupon forfeited to Her Majesty and may be destroyed or otherwise disposed of as the Minister or the Minister of Consumer and Corporate Affairs may direct.

Forfeiture upon conviction

(3) Where a person has been convicted of a violation of this Act or the regulations, the court or judge may order that any article by means of or in relation to which the offence was committed or anything of a similar nature belonging to or in the possession of the accused or found with such article, be forfeited, and upon such order being made, such articles and things are forfeited to Her Majesty and may be disposed of as the Minister or the Minister of Consumer and Corporate Affairs may direct.

Order for forfeiture

(4) Without prejudice to the operation of subsection (3), a judge of a superior, county or district court of the province in which any article was seized under this Act may, on the application of an inspector and on such notice to such persons as the judge directs, order that the article and anything of a similar nature found therewith be forfeited to Her Majesty to be disposed of as the Minister or the Minister of Consumer and Corporate Affairs may direct, if the judge finds, after making such inquiry as he considers necessary, that the article is one by means of or in relation to which any of the provisions of this Act or the regulations were violated. 28 Interp

Analysis

Analysis

24. (1) An inspector may submit any article seized by him or any sample therefrom or any sample taken by him to an analyst for analysis or examination. 2

Report

(2) Where an analyst has made an analysis or examination he may issue a certificate or report setting forth the results of his examination or analysis.

Regulations

Regulations

25. (1) The Governor in Council may make regulations for carrying the purposes and provisions of this Act into effect, and, in particular, but not so as to restrict the generality of the foregoing, may make regulations 28 Interp

(a) declaring that any food or drug or class of food or drugs is adulterated if any prescribed substance or class of substances is present therein or has been added thereto or extracted or omitted therefrom;

(b) respecting

(i) the labelling and packaging and the offering, exposing and advertising for sale of food, drugs, cosmetics and devices,

(ii) the size, dimensions, fill and other specifications of packages of food, drugs, cosmetics and devices,

(iii) the sale or the condition of sale of any food, drug, cosmetic or device, and

(iv) the use of any substance as an ingredient in any food, drug, cosmetic or device,

to prevent the consumer or purchaser thereof from being deceived or misled as to its design, construction, performance, intended use, quantity, character, value, composition, merit or safety, or to prevent injury to the health of the consumer or purchaser. 1976-77, c. 28, s. 16(2).

(c) prescribing standards of composition, strength, potency, purity, quality or other property of any article of food, drug, cosmetic or device;

(d) respecting the importation of foods, drugs, cosmetics and devices in order to ensure compliance with this Act and the regulations;

(e) respecting the method of preparation, manufacture, preserving, packing, storing and testing of any food, drug, cosmetic or device in the interest of, or for the prevention of injury to, the health of the consumer or purchaser;

(f) requiring persons who sell food, drugs, cosmetics or devices to maintain such books and records as the Governor in Council considers necessary for the proper enforcement and administration of this Act and the regulations;

(g) respecting the form and manner of the Minister's indication under section 12, including the fees payable therefor, and prescribing what premises or what processes or conditions of manufacture, including qualifications of technical staff, shall or shall not be deemed to be suitable for the purposes of that section;

(h) requiring manufacturers of any drugs described in Schedule E to submit test portions of any batch of such drugs and respecting the form and manner of the Minister's indication under section 13, including the fees payable therefor;

(i) not inconsistent with this Act, respecting the powers and duties of inspectors and analysts and the taking of samples and the seizure, detention, forfeiture and disposition of articles;

(j) exempting any food, drug, cosmetic or device from all or any of the provisions of this Act and prescribing the conditions of such exemptions;

(k) prescribing forms for the purposes of this Act and the regulations;

(l) providing for the analysis of food, drugs or cosmetics other than for the purposes of this Act and prescribing a tariff of fees to be paid for such analysis;

(m) adding anything to any of the schedules, in the interest of, or for the prevention of injury to, the health of the consumer or purchaser, or deleting anything therefrom;

(n) respecting the distribution or the conditions of distribution of samples of any drug;

(o) respecting

(i) the method of preparation, manufacture, preserving, packing, labelling, storing and testing of any new drug, and

(ii) the sale or the conditions of sale of any new drug,

and defining for the purposes of this Act the expression "new drug"; and

(p) authorizing the advertising to the general public of contraceptive devices and drugs manufactured, sold or represented for use in the prevention of conception and prescribing the circumstances and conditions under which and the persons by whom such contraceptive devices and drugs may be so advertised.

Regulations respecting imported drugs

(2) Without limiting or restricting the authority conferred by any other provisions of this Act or any Part thereof for carrying into effect the purposes and provisions of this Act or any Part thereof, the Governor in Council may make such regulations governing, regulating or prohibiting

(*a*) the importation into Canada of any drug or class of drugs manufactured outside Canada, or

(*b*) the distribution or sale in Canada, or the offering, exposing or having in possession for sale in Canada, of any drug or class of drugs manufactured outside Canada,

as the Governor in Council deems necessary for the protection of the public in relation to the safety and quality of any such drug or class of drugs.

Analysts

(3) The Governor in Council may designate as an analyst any person on the staff of the Department for such time as that person is employed in the Department or for such time during the period of such employment as he may direct.

Inspectors

(4) The Governor in Council may designate as an inspector any person on the staff of the Department or the Department of Consumer and Corporate Affairs for such time as that person is employed in either the Department or the Department of Consumer and Corporate Affairs or for such time during the period of such employment as he may direct.

Penalties

Penalties

26. Every person who violates any of the provisions of this Act or the regulations is guilty of an offence and is liable

Type 'B' (D) Offence

section 27

(*a*) on summary conviction for a first offence to a fine not exceeding five hundred dollars or to imprisonment for a term not exceeding three months or to both, and for a subsequent offence to a fine not exceeding one thousand 724 740
dollars or to imprisonment for a term not exceeding six months, or to both; [4
and

(*b*) on conviction upon indictment to a fine not exceeding five thousand dollars or to imprisonment for a term not exceeding three years, or to both.

Time limit

27. A prosecution under paragraph 26(*a*) may be instituted at any time within twelve months from the time the subject-matter of the prosecution arose.

Venue

28. A prosecution for a violation of this Act or the regulations may be instituted, heard, tried or determined in the place in which the offence was committed or the subject-matter of the prosecution arose or in any place in which the accused is apprehended or happens to be.

Want of knowledge

29. (1) Subject to subsection (2), in a prosecution for the sale of any article in contravention of this Act or the regulations, if the accused proves to the satisfaction of the court or judge that

(*a*) he purchased the article from another person in packaged form and sold it in the same package and in the same condition the article was in at the time he purchased it, and

(*b*) that he could not with reasonable diligence have ascertained that the sale of the article would be in contravention of this Act or the regulations,

the accused shall be acquitted.

Notice

(2) Subsection (1) does not apply in any prosecution unless the accused, at least ten days before the day fixed for the trial, has given to the prosecutor notice 25(3) Interp
in writing that he intends to avail himself of the provisions of subsection (1) and has disclosed to the prosecutor the name and address of the person from whom he purchased the article and the date of purchase.

Evidence

Certificate of analyst

30. (1) Subject to this section, in any prosecution for an offence under section 26 or an offence mentioned in subsection 36(1) or 44(1), a certificate of an analyst stating that he has analyzed or examined an article, sample or 2
substance submitted to him and stating the results of his analysis or examination is admissible in evidence and in the absence of evidence to the contrary is proof of the statements contained in the certificate without proof of the signature or official character of the person appearing to have signed the certificate.

Attendance of analyst

(2) The party against whom a certificate of an analyst is produced pursuant to subsection (1) may, with leave of the court, require the attendance of the analyst for the purposes of cross-examination.

Notice

(3) No certificate shall be received in evidence pursuant to subsection (1) unless the party intending to produce it has, before the trial, given to the party against whom it is intended to be produced reasonable notice of such intention together with a copy of the certificate.

Name of manufacturer

31. (1) Proof that a package containing any article to which this Act or the regulations apply bore a name or address purporting to be the name or address of the person by whom it was manufactured or packaged is *prima facie* proof, in a prosecution for a violation of this Act or the regulations, that the article was manufactured or packaged, as the case may be, by the person whose name or address appeared on the package. 2

Offence by employees

(2) In a prosecution for a violation of this Act or the regulations it is sufficient proof of the offence to establish that it was committed by an employee or agent of the accused whether or not he is identified or has been prosecuted for the offence.

Copies of records

(3) In a prosecution for a violation of this Act or the regulations a copy of a record or an extract therefrom certified to be a true copy by the inspector who made it pursuant to paragraph 22(1)*(c)* is receivable in evidence and is *prima facie* proof of the contents thereof.

Possession of adulterating substances

(4) Where a person is prosecuted under this Act for having manufactured an adulterated food or drug for sale, and it is established that

(a) the food or drug has by regulation been declared to be adulterated if any prescribed substance has been added thereto, and

(b) such person had in his possession or on his premises any such prescribed substance,

the onus of proving that the food or drug was not adulterated by the addition of such substance lies on the accused.

prima facie — assumed to be proved and true unless evidence is given to disprove

Exports

Exports

32. This Act does not apply to any packaged food, drug (other than a drug or other substance defined as a controlled drug by Part III or as a restricted drug by Part IV), cosmetic or device, not manufactured for consumption in Canada and not sold for consumption in Canada, if the package is marked in distinct overprinting with the word "Export", and a certificate that the package and its contents do not contravene any known requirement of the law of the country to which it is or is about to be consigned, has been issued in respect thereof in prescribed form and manner.

PART III

CONTROLLED DRUGS

Definitions

33. In this Part

"controlled drug"

"controlled drug" means any drug or other substance included in Schedule G;

"possession"

"possession" means possession as defined in the *Criminal Code;*

Criminal Code

3. (4) For the purposes of this Act,

(a) a person has anything in possession when he has it in his personal possession or knowingly

(i) has it in the actual possession or custody of another person, or

(ii) has it in any place, whether or not that place belongs to or is occupied by him, for the use or benefit of himself or of another person; and

(b) where one of two or more persons, with the knowledge and consent of the rest, has anything in his custody or possession, it shall be deemed to be in the custody and possession of each and all of them.

"traffic"

"traffic" means to manufacture, sell, export from or import into Canada, transport or deliver, otherwise than under the authority of this Part or the regulations. 2

2. In this Act

"sell" includes sell, offer for sale, expose for sale, have in possession for sale, and distribute;

Trafficking in controlled drug

34. (1) No person shall traffic in a controlled drug or any substance represented or held out by him to be a controlled drug. 33

Possession for trafficking

(2) No person shall have in his possession any controlled drug for the purpose of trafficking. 33

Offence

Type 'B' (E) Offence

IPA offence 178.1 CCC

(3) Every person who violates subsection (1) or (2) is guilty of an offence and is liable

(a) upon summary conviction to imprisonment for eighteen months; or

(b) upon conviction on indictment, to imprisonment for ten years.

Procedure in prosecution for possession for trafficking

35. (1) In any prosecution for a violation of subsection 34(2), if the accused does not plead guilty, the trial shall proceed as if the issue to be tried is whether the accused was in possession of a controlled drug.

Idem

(2) If, pursuant to subsection (1), the court finds that the accused was not in possession of a controlled drug, he shall be acquitted, but, if the court finds that the accused was in possession of a controlled drug, he shall be given an opportunity of establishing that he was not in possession of the controlled drug for the purpose of trafficking, and thereafter the prosecutor shall be given an opportunity of adducing evidence to the contrary.

Idem

(3) If the accused establishes that he was not in possession of the controlled drug for the purpose of trafficking, he shall be acquitted of the offence as charged; and if the accused fails to so establish he shall be convicted of the offence as charged and sentenced accordingly.

Burden of proof

36. (1) No exception, exemption, excuse or qualification prescribed by law is required to be set out or negatived, as the case may be, in an information or indictment for an offence under section 34 or under section 421, 422 or 423 of the *Criminal Code* in respect of an offence under section 34.

Criminal Code

421 (Attempts and Accessories after the fact), 422 (Counselling, etc., offence which is not committed), 423 (Conspiracy).

Idem

(2) In any prosecution under this Part the burden of proving that an exception, exemption, excuse or qualification prescribed by law operates in favour of the accused is on the accused, and the prosecutor is not required, except by way of rebuttal, to prove that the exception, exemption, excuse or qualification does not operate in favour of the accused, whether or not it is set out in the information or indictment.

30. (1) Subject to this section, in any prosecution for an offence under section 26 or an offence mentioned in subsection 36(1) or 44(1), a certificate of an analyst stating that he has analyzed or examined an article, sample or substance submitted to him and stating the results of his analysis or examination is admissible in evidence and in the absence of evidence to the contrary is proof of the statements contained in the certificate without proof of the signature or official character of the person appearing to have signed the certificate.

(2) The party against whom a certificate of an analyst is produced pursuant to subsection (1) may, with leave of the court, require the attendance of the analyst for the purposes of cross-examination.

(3) No certificate shall be received in evidence pursuant to subsection (1) unless the party intending to produce it has, before the trial, given to the party against whom it is intended to be produced reasonable notice of such intention together with a copy of the certificate.

Search and seizure

37. (1) A peace officer may at any time

(*a*) without a warrant enter and search any place other than a dwelling-house, and under the authority of a writ of assistance or a warrant issued under this section, enter and search any dwelling-house in which he reasonably believes there is a controlled drug by means of or in respect of which an offence under this Part has been committed;

(*b*) search any person found in such place; and

(*c*) seize and take away any controlled drug found in such place and any other thing that may be evidence that an offence under this Part has been committed.

Warrant to search

(2) A justice who is satisfied by information upon oath that there are reasonable grounds for believing that there is a controlled drug, by means of or in respect of which an offence under this Part has been committed, in any dwelling-house may issue a warrant under his hand authorizing a peace officer named therein at any time to enter the dwelling-house and search for controlled drugs. 28 Interp

Writ of assistance

(3) A judge of the Federal Court of Canada shall, upon application by the Minister, issue a writ of assistance authorizing and empowering the person named therein, aided and assisted by such person as the person named therein may require, at any time, to enter any dwelling-house and search for controlled drugs. 2

Powers of peace officer

(4) For the purpose of exercising his authority under this section, a peace officer may, with such assistance as he deems necessary, break open any door, window, lock, fastener, floor, wall, ceiling, compartment, plumbing fixture, box, container or any other thing.

Application for restoration

(5) Where a controlled drug or other thing has been seized under this Part, any person may, within two months from the date of such seizure, upon prior notification having been given to the Crown in the manner prescribed by the regulations, apply to a magistrate within whose territorial jurisdiction the seizure was made, for an order of restoration under subsection (6).

Order of restoration

(6) Subject to subsection (8), where, upon the hearing of an application made under subsection (5), the magistrate is satisfied

(a) that the applicant is entitled to possession of the controlled drug or other thing seized, and

(b) that the thing so seized is not or will not be required as evidence in any proceedings in respect of an offence under this Part,

he shall order that the thing so seized be restored forthwith to the applicant, and where the magistrate is satisfied that the applicant is entitled to possession of the thing so seized but is not satisfied as to the matters mentioned in paragraph *(b)*, he shall order that the thing so seized be restored to the applicant

(c) upon the expiration of four months from the date of such seizure, if no proceedings in respect of an offence under this Part have been commenced before that time, or

(d) upon the final conclusion of any such proceedings, in any other case.

Where no application made

(7) Where no application has been made for the return of any controlled drug or other thing seized pursuant to this Part within two months from the date of such seizure, or an application therefor has been made but upon the hearing thereof no order of restoration is made, the thing so seized shall be delivered to the Minister who may make such disposition thereof as he see fit.

Forfeiture of controlled drug

(8) Where a person has been convicted of an offence under this Part, any controlled drug seized pursuant to this Part, by means of or in respect of which the offence was committed, and any money so seized that was used for the purchase of that controlled drug, is forfeited to Her Majesty and shall be disposed of as the Minister directs.

Sections not applicable

(9) Subsections 22(7) and (8) and section 23 are not applicable in the case of any thing seized under this Part.

Regulations

38. (1) The Governor in Council may make regulations for carrying out the purposes and provisions of this Part, and in particular but without restricting the generality of the foregoing, may make regulations, 28 Interp

(a) authorizing the manufacture, sale, importation, transportation, delivery or other dealing in controlled drugs and prescribing the circumstances and conditions under which and the persons by whom controlled drugs may be manufactured, sold, imported, transported, delivered or otherwise dealt in;

(b) providing for the issue of licences for the importation, manufacture or sale of controlled drugs;

(c) prescribing the form, duration and terms and conditions of any licence described in paragraph *(b)* and the fees payable therefor, and providing for the cancellation and suspension of such licences;

(d) requiring persons who import, manufacture, sell, administer or deal in controlled drugs to maintain such books and records as the Governor in Council considers necessary for the proper administration and enforcement of this Part and the regulations made under this Part and to make such returns and furnish such information relating to the said controlled drugs as the Governor in Council may require;

(e) authorizing the communication of any information obtained under this Part or the regulations to provincial professional licensing authorities; and

(f) prescribing a fine not exceeding five hundred dollars or a term of imprisonment not exceeding six months, or both, to be imposed upon summary conviction as a penalty for the violation of any regulation.

Amendment of Schedule

(2) The Governor in Council may, from time to time, amend Schedule G by adding thereto or deleting therefrom any substance, the inclusion or exclusion of which, as the case may be, is deemed necessary by him in the public interest.

Sections 26, 29 and 31 not applicable

39. Sections 26, 29 and 31 are not applicable in any proceedings in respect of an offence under this Part or the regulations made under this Part.

Criminal Code

3. (4) For the purposes of this Act,

(a) a person has anything in possession when he has it in his personal possession or knowingly

(i) has it in the actual possession or custody of another person, or

(ii) has it in any place, whether or not that place belongs to or is occupied by him, for the use or benefit of himself or of another person; and

(b) where one of two or more persons, with the knowledge and consent of the rest, has anything in his custody or possession, it shall be deemed to be in the custody and possession of each and all of them.

Interpretation Act

28. In every enactment

"Governor in Council", or "Governor General in Council" means the Governor General of Canada, or person administering the Government of Canada for the time being, acting by and with the advice of, or by and with the advice and consent of, or in conjunction with the Queen's Privy Council for Canada;

PART IV

RESTRICTED DRUGS

Definitions

40. In this Part

"possession" — "possession" means possession as defined in the *Criminal Code;* 3(4) CCC

"regulations" — "regulations" means regulations made as provided for by or under section 45;

"restricted drug" — "restricted drug" means any drug or other substance included in Schedule H;

"traffic" — "traffic" means to manufacture, sell, export from or import into Canada, transport or deliver, otherwise than under the authority of this Part or the regulations. 2

2. In this Act

"sell" includes sell, offer for sale, expose for sale, have in possession for sale, and distribute;

Possession of restricted drug

41. (1) Except as authorized by this Part or the regulations, no person shall have a restricted drug in his possession.

Type 'B' (D) Offence

(2) Every person who violates subsection (1) is guilty of an offence and is liable

(*a*) upon summary conviction for a first offence, to a fine of one thousand dollars or to imprisonment for six months, or to both, and for a subsequent offence, to a fine of two thousand dollars or to imprisonment for one year, or to both; or 724 740

(*b*) upon conviction on indictment, to a fine of five thousand dollars or to imprisonment for three years, or to both.

Trafficking in restricted drug

42. (1) No person shall traffic in a restricted drug or any substance represented or held out by him to be a restricted drug. 40

Possession for the purpose of trafficking

(2) No person shall have in his possession any restricted drug for the purpose of trafficking. 40 3(4) CCC

Type 'B' (E) Offence

IPA offence 178.1 CCC

(3) Every person who violates subsection (1) or (2) is guilty of an offence and is liable

(*a*) upon summary conviction, to imprisonment for eighteen months; or

(*b*) upon conviction on indictment, to imprisonment for ten years.

Procedure in prosecution for possession for trafficking

43. (1) In any prosecution for a violation of subsection 42(2), if the accused does not plead guilty, the trial shall proceed as if the issue to be tried is whether the accused was in possession of a restricted drug contrary to subsection 41(1).

Idem

(2) If, pursuant to subsection (1), the court finds that the accused was not in possession of a restricted drug contrary to subsection 41(1), he shall be acquitted, but, if the court finds that the accused was in possession of a restricted drug contrary to subsection 41(1), he shall be given an opportunity of establishing that he was not in possession of the restricted drug for the purpose of trafficking and thereafter the prosecutor shall be given an opportunity of adducing evidence to the contrary.

Idem

(3) If, pursuant to subsection (2), the accused

(*a*) establishes that he was not in possession of the restricted drug for the purpose of trafficking, he shall be acquitted of the offence as charged but he shall be convicted of an offence under subsection 41(1) and sentenced accordingly; or

(*b*) fails to establish that he was not in possession of the restricted drug for the purpose of trafficking, he shall be convicted of the offence as charged and sentenced accordingly.

724. (2) No information in respect of an offence for which, by reason of previous convictions, a greater punishment may be imposed shall contain any reference to previous convictions.

740. (1) Where a defendant is convicted of an offence for which a greater punishment may be imposed by reason of previous convictions, no greater punishment shall be imposed upon him by reason thereof unless the prosecutor satisfies the summary conviction court that the defendant, before making his plea, was notified that a greater punishment would be sought by reason thereof.

(2) Where a defendant is convicted of an offence for which a greater punishment may be imposed by reason of previous convictions, the summary conviction court shall, upon application by the prosecutor, and upon being satisfied that the defendant was notified in accordance with subsection (1), ask the defendant whether he was previously convicted, and if he does not admit that he was previously convicted, evidence of previous convictions may be adduced.

(3) A summary conviction court that holds a trial pursuant to subsection 738(3) may, if it convicts the defendant, make inquiries with respect to previous convictions, whether or not the defendant was notified that a greater punishment would be sought by reason thereof.

(4) For the purposes of this section, a previous conviction may be proved in the manner prescribed by section 594. 1953-54, c. 51, s. 712.

594. (1) In any proceedings,

(a) a certificate setting out with reasonable particularity the conviction or the conviction and sentence in Canada of a person for an indictable offence, signed by

(i) the person who made the conviction,

(ii) the clerk of the court in which the conviction was made, or

(iii) a fingerprint examiner,

is, upon proof that the accused is the person referred to in the certificate, evidence that the accused was so convicted or so convicted and sentenced without proof of the signature or the official character of the person appearing to have signed the certificate;

(b) evidence that the fingerprints of the accused are the same as the fingerprints of the person whose fingerprints are reproduced in a certificate issued under subparagraph *(a)*(iii) is, in the absence of any evidence to the contrary, proof that the accused is the person referred to in that certificate;

(c) a certificate of a fingerprint examiner stating that he has compared the fingerprints attached to that certificate with the fingerprints reproduced in a certificate issued under subparagraph *(a)*(iii) and that they are those of the same person is evidence of the statements contained in the certificate without proof of the signature or the official character of the person appearing to have signed the certificate; and

(d) a certificate under subparagraph *(a)*(iii) may be in Form 42, and a certificate under paragraph *(c)* may be in Form 43.

(2) In any proceedings, a copy of the summary conviction in Canada of an accused, signed by the person who made the conviction or by the clerk of the court in which the conviction was made, is, upon proof of the identity of the accused, evidence of the conviction of the accused without proof of the signature or the official character of the person appearing to have signed it.

(3) An accused against whom a certificate issued under subparagraph (1)*(a)*(iii) or paragraph (1)*(c)* is produced may, with leave of the court, require the attendance of the person who signed the certificate for the purposes of cross-examination.

(3.1) No certificate issued under subparagraph (1)*(a)*(iii) or paragraph (1)*(c)* shall be received in evidence unless the party intending to produce it has given to the accused reasonable notice of his intention together with a copy of the certificate.

(4) In this section "fingerprint examiner" means a person designated as such for the purposes of this section by the Solicitor General of Canada.

Burden of proving exception, etc.

44. (1) No exception, exemption, excuse or qualification prescribed by law is required to be set out or negatived, as the case may be, in an information or indictment for an offence under this Part or under section 421, 422 or 423 of the *Criminal Code* in respect of an offence under this Part.

Criminal Code

421 (Attempts and Accessories after the fact), 422 (Counselling, etc., offence which is not committed), 423 (Conspiracy).

Idem

(2) In any prosecution under this Part the burden of proving that an exception, exemption, excuse or qualification prescribed by law operates in favour of the accused is on the accused, and the prosecutor is not required, except by way of rebuttal, to prove that the exception, exemption, excuse or qualification does not operate in favour of the accused, whether or not it is set out in the information or indictment.

30. (1) Subject to this section, in any prosecution for an offence under section 26 or an offence mentioned in subsection 36(1) or 44(1), a certificate of an analyst stating that he has analyzed or examined an article, sample or substance submitted to him and stating the results of his analysis or examination is admissible in evidence and in the absence of evidence to the contrary is proof of the statements contained in the certificate without proof of the signature or official character of the person appearing to have signed the certificate.

(2) The party against whom a certificate of an analyst is produced pursuant to subsection (1) may, with leave of the court, require the attendance of the analyst for the purposes of cross-examination.

(3) No certificate shall be received in evidence pursuant to subsection (1) unless the party intending to produce it has, before the trial, given to the party against whom it is intended to be produced reasonable notice of such intention together with a copy of the certificate.

Application of sections 37 & 38 38

45. (1) The provisions of sections 37 and 38 apply in respect of this Part.

Idem

(2) For the purposes of subsection (1),

(a) there shall be substituted for the expression "controlled drug", wherever it appears in section 37 or 38, the expression "restricted drug"; and

(b) a reference in section 37 or 38

(i) to "Schedule G" shall be deemed to be a reference to Schedule H, and

(ii) to "this Part" shall be deemed to be a reference to Part IV.

Additional regulations

(3) In addition to the regulations provided for by subsection (1), the Governor in Council may make regulations authorizing the possession or export of restricted drugs and prescribing the circumstances and conditions under which and the persons by whom restricted drugs may be had in possession or exported.

37. (9) Subsections 22(7) and (8) and section 23 are not applicable in the case of any thing seized under this Part. *(Part III)*

Sections not applicable

46. Sections 26, 29 and 31 are not applicable in any proceedings in respect of an offence under this Part or the regulations.

SCHEDULE H

Lysergic acid diethylamide (LSD) or any salt thereof
N,N-Diethyltryptamine (DET) or any salt thereof
N,N-Dimethyltryptamine (DMT) or any salt thereof
4-Methyl-2, 5-dimethoxyamphetamine (STP (DOM)) or any salt thereof
3,4-methylenedioxyamphetamine (MDA) or any salt thereof
3-methoxy-4, 5-methylenedioxyamphetamine (MMDA) or any salt thereof
N-methyl-3-piperidyl benzilate (LBJ) or any salt thereof
2,3-dimethoxyamphetamine or any salt thereof
2,4-dimethoxyamphetamine or any salt thereof
2,5-dimethoxyamphetamine or any salt thereof
2,6-dimethoxyamphetamine or any salt thereof
3,4-dimethoxyamphetamine or any salt thereof
3,5-dimethoxyamphetamine or any salt thereof
4,9-dihydro-7-methoxy-1-methyl-3H-pyrido (3,4-b) indole (Harmaline) and any salt thereof
4,9-dihydro-1-methyl-3H-pyrido (3,4-b) indol-7-ol (Harmalol) and any salt thereof
4-methoxyamphetamine or any salt thereof
3-[2-(Dimethylamino)ethyl]-4-hydroxyindole (Psilocin) or any salt thereof
3-[2-(Dimethylamino)ethyl]-4-phosphoryloxyindole (Psilocybin) or any salt thereof
2,4,5-Trimethoxyamphetamine or any salt, isomer, or salt of isomer, thereof
3,4-methylenedioxy-N-methylamphetamine or any salt thereof.
N-(1-phenylcyclohexyl) ethylamine or any salt thereof SOR/78-425
4-bromo-2, 5-dimethoxyamphetamine or any salt thereof SOR/78-425
1-[1-(2-thienyl) cyclohexyl] piperidine and its salts SOR/78-650

SCHEDULE G

Amphetamine and its salts
Barbituric acid and its salts and derivatives
Benzphetamine and its salts
Butorphanol and its salts
Diethylpropion and its salts SOR/78-426
Methamphetamine and its salts
Methaqualone and its salts
Methylphenidate and its salts SOR/78-426
Pentazocine and its salts
Phendimetrazine and its salts
Phenmetrazine and its salts
Thiobarbituric acid and its salts and derivatives

NARCOTIC CONTROL ACT

CHAPTER N-1

An Act to provide for the control of narcotic drugs

SHORT TITLE

Short title

1. This Act may be cited as the *Narcotic Control Act.*

INTERPRETATION

Definitions

2. In this Act

"analyst"

"analyst" means a person designated as an analyst under the *Food and Drugs Act* or under this Act;

"conveyance"

"conveyance" includes any aircraft, vessel, motor vehicle or other conveyance of any description whatever;

"marihuana"

"marihuana" means *Cannabis sativa L.;*

"Minister

"Minister" means

(a) with respect to Part I, the Minister of National Health and Welfare, and

(b) with respect to Part II, the Minister of Justice;

"narcotic"

"narcotic" means any substance included in the schedule or anything that contains any substance included in the schedule;

"narcotic addict"

"narcotic addict" means a person who through the use of narcotics,

(a) has developed a desire or need to continue to take a narcotic, or

(b) has developed a psychological or physical dependence upon the effect of a narcotic;

"opium poppy"

"opium poppy" means *Papaver somniferum L.;*

"possession"

"possession" means possession as defined in the *Criminal Code;*

> Criminal Code
>
> 3. (4) For the purposes of this Act,
>
> *(a)* a person has anything in possession when he has it in his personal possession or knowingly
>
> (i) has it in the actual possession or custody of another person, or
>
> (ii) has it in any place, whether or not that place belongs to or is occupied by him, for the use or benefit of himself or of another person; and
>
> *(b)* where one of two or more persons, with the knowledge and consent of the rest, has anything in his custody or possession, it shall be deemed to be in the custody and possession of each and all of them.

"traffic"

"traffic" means

(a) to manufacture, sell, give, adminster, transport, send, deliver or distribute, or

(b) to offer to do anything mentioned in paragraph *(a)*

otherwise than under the authority of this Act or the regulations.

724. (2) No information in respect of an offence for which, by reason of previous convictions, a greater punishment may be imposed shall contain any reference to previous convictions.

740. (1) Where a defendant is convicted of an offence for which a greater punishment may be imposed by reason of previous convictions, no greater punishment shall be imposed upon him by reason thereof unless the prosecutor satisfies the summary conviction court that the defendant, before making his plea, was notified that a greater punishment would be sought by reason thereof.

(2) Where a defendant is convicted of an offence for which a greater punishment may be imposed by reason of previous convictions, the summary conviction court shall, upon application by the prosecutor, and upon being satisfied that the defendant was notified in accordance with subsection (1), ask the defendant whether he was previously convicted, and if he does not admit that he was previously convicted, evidence of previous convictions may be adduced.

(3) A summary conviction court that holds a trial pursuant to subsection 738(3) may, if it convicts the defendant, make inquiries with respect to previous convictions, whether or not the defendant was notified that a greater punishment would be sought by reason thereof.

(4) For the purposes of this section, a previous conviction may be proved in the manner prescribed by section 594.

594. (1) In any proceedings,

(a) a certificate setting out with reasonable particularity the conviction or the conviction and sentence in Canada of a person for an indictable offence, signed by

(i) the person who made the conviction,

(ii) the clerk of the court in which the conviction was made, or

(iii) a fingerprint examiner,

is, upon proof that the accused is the person referred to in the certificate, evidence that the accused was so convicted or so convicted and sentenced without proof of the signature or the official character of the person appearing to have signed the certificate;

(b) evidence that the fingerprints of the accused are the same as the fingerprints of the person whose fingerprints are reproduced in a certificate issued under subparagraph *(a)*(iii) is, in the absence of any evidence to the contrary, proof that the accused is the person referred to in that certificate;

(c) a certificate of a fingerprint examiner stating that he has compared the fingerprints attached to that certificate with the fingerprints reproduced in a certificate issued under subparagraph *(a)*(iii) and that they are those of the same person is evidence of the statements contained in the certificate without proof of the signature or the official character of the person appearing to have signed the certificate; and

(d) a certificate under subparagraph *(a)*(iii) may be in Form 42, and a certificate under paragraph *(c)* may be in Form 43.

(2) In any proceedings, a copy of the summary conviction in Canada of an accused, signed by the person who made the conviction or by the clerk of the court in which the conviction was made, is, upon proof of the identity of the accused, evidence of the conviction of the accused without proof of the signature or the official character of the person appearing to have signed it.

(3) An accused against whom a certificate issued under subparagraph (1)*(a)*(iii) or paragraph (1)*(c)* is produced may, with leave of the court, require the attendance of the person who signed the certificate for the purposes of cross-examination.

(3.1) No certificate issued under subparagraph (1)*(a)*(iii) or paragraph (1)*(c)* shall be received in evidence unless the party intending to produce it has given to the accused reasonable notice of his intention together with a copy of the certificate.

(4) In this section "fingerprint examiner" means a person designated as such for the purposes of this section by the Solicitor General of Canada.

PART I

OFFENCES AND ENFORCEMENT

Particular Offences

Possession of narcotic

3. (1) Except as authorized by this Act or the regulations, no person shall have a narcotic in his possession. 2 3(4) CCC

Criminal Code

3. (4) For the purposes of this Act,

(a) a person has anything in possession when he has it in his personal possession or knowingly

(i) has it in the actual possession or custody of another person, or

(ii) has it in any place, whether or not that place belongs to or is occupied by him, for the use or benefit of himself or of another person; and

(b) where one of two or more persons, with the knowledge and consent of the rest, has anything in his custody or possession, it shall be deemed to be in the custody and possession of each and all of them.

Type 'B' (E) Offence

(2) Every person who violates subsection (1) is guilty of an offence and is liable

(a) upon summary conviction for a first offence, to a fine of one thousand dollars or to imprisonment for six months or to both fine and imprisonment, and for a subsequent offence, to a fine of two thousand dollars or to imprisonment for one year or to both fine and imprisonment; or 724 740

(b) upon conviction on indictment, to imprisonment for seven years. 1968-69, c. 41, s. 12.

Trafficking

4. (1) No person shall traffic in a narcotic or any substance represented or held out by him to be a narcotic. 2

Possession for purpose of trafficking

(2) No person shall have in his possession any narcotic for the purpose of trafficking.

Type 'E' Offence
IPA offence 178.1

(3) Every person who violates subsection (1) or (2) is guilty of an indictable offence and is liable to imprisonment for life. 669

Importing and exporting

5. (1) Except as authorized by this Act or the regulations, no person shall import into Canada or export from Canada any narcotic.

Type 'E' Offence
IPA offence 178.1

(2) Every person who violates subsection (1) is guilty of an indictable offence and is liable to imprisonment for life but not less than seven years.

Cultivation of opium poppy or marihuana

6. (1) No person shall cultivate opium poppy or marihuana except under authority of and in accordance with a licence issued to him under the regulations. 2

Type 'E' Offence

(2) Every person who violates subsection (1) is guilty of an indictable offence and is liable to imprisonment for seven years.

Destruction of plant

(3) The Minister may cause to be destroyed any growing plant of opium poppy or marihuana cultivated otherwise than under authority of and in accordance with a licence issued under the regulations.

Prosecutions

Burden of proving exception, etc.

7. (1) No exception, exemption, excuse or qualification prescribed by law is required to be set out or negatived, as the case may be, in an information or indictment for an offence under this Act or under section 421, 422 or 423 of the *Criminal Code* in respect of an offence under this Act.

Criminal Code

421 (Attempts and Accessories after the fact). 422 (Counselling, etc., offence which is not committed), 423 (Conspiracy).

Idem

(2) In any prosecution under this Act the burden of proving that an exception, exemption, excuse or qualification prescribed by law operates in favour of the accused is on the accused, and the prosecutor is not required, except by way of rebuttal, to prove that the exception, exemption, excuse or qualification does not operate in favour of the accused, whether or not it is set out in the information or indictment.

Procedure in prosecution for trafficking

8. In any prosecution for a violation of subsection 4(2), if the accused does not plead guilty, the trial shall proceed as if it were a prosecution for an offence under section 3, and after the close of the case for the prosecution and after the accused has had an opportunity to make full answer and defence, the court shall make a finding as to whether or not the accused was in possession of the narcotic contrary to section 3; if the court finds that the accused was not in possession of the narcotic contrary to section 3, he shall be acquitted but if the court finds that the accused was in possession of the narcotic contrary to section 3, he shall be given an opportunity of establishing that he was not in possession of the narcotic for the purpose of trafficking, and thereafter the prosecutor shall be given an opportunity of adducing evidence to establish that the accused was in possession of the narcotic for the purpose of trafficking; if the accused establishes that he was not in possession of the narcotic for the purpose of trafficking, he shall be acquitted of the offence as charged but he shall be convicted of an offence under section 3 and sentenced accordingly; and if the accused fails to establish that he was not in possession of the narcotic for the purpose of trafficking, he shall be convicted of the offence as charged and sentenced accordingly.

Certificate of analyst

9. (1) Subject to this section, a certificate of an analyst stating that he 2
has analyzed or examined a substance and stating the result of his analysis or examination is admissible in evidence in any prosecution for an offence mentioned in subsection 7(1), and in the absence of evidence to the contrary is proof of the statements contained in the certificate without proof of the signature or the official character of the person appearing to have signed the certificate.

Attendance of analyst

(2) The party against whom a certificate of an analyst is produced pursuant to subsection (1) may, with leave of the court, require the attendance of the analyst for the purposes of cross-examination.

Notice

(3) No certificate shall be received in evidence pursuant to subsection (1) unless the party intending to produce it has, before the trial, given to the party against whom it is intended to be produced reasonable notice of such intention together with a copy of the certificate.

Search, Seizure and Forfeiture

Search and seizure

10. (1) A peace officer may, at any time,

(a) without a warrant enter and search any place other than a dwelling-house, and under the authority of a writ of assistance or a warrant issued under this section, enter and search any dwelling-house in which he reasonably believes there is a narcotic by means of or in respect of which an offence under this Act has been committed;

(b) search any person found in such place; and

(c) seize and take away any narcotic found in such place, any thing in such place in which he reasonably suspects a narcotic is contained or concealed, or any other thing by means of or in respect of which he reasonably believes an offence under this Act has been committed or that may be evidence of the commission of such an offence.

Warrant to search dwelling-house

(2) A justice who is satisfied by information upon oath that there are reasonable grounds for believing that there is a narcotic, by means of or in respect of which an offence under this Act has been committed, in any dwelling-house may issue a warrant under his hand authorizing a peace officer named therein at any time to enter the dwelling-house and search for narcotics.

Interpretation Act

28. In every enactment

"oath" includes a solemn affirmation or declaration, whenever the context applies to any person by whom and case in which a solemn affirmation or declaration may be made instead of an oath; and in like cases the expression "sworn" includes the expression "affirmed" or "declared";

Writ of assistance

(3) A judge of the Federal Court of Canada shall, upon application by the Minister, issue a writ of assistance authorizing and empowering the person named therein, aided and assisted by such person as the person named therein may require, at any time, to enter any dwelling-house and search for narcotics.

Powers of peace officer

(4) For the purpose of exercising his authority under this section, a peace officer may, with such assistance as he deems necessary, break open any door, window, lock, fastener, floor, wall, ceiling, compartment, plumbing fixture, box, container or any other thing.

Application for restoration

(5) Where a narcotic or other thing has been seized under subsection (1), any person may, within two months from the date of such seizure, upon prior notification having been given to the Crown in the manner prescribed by the regulations, apply to a magistrate within whose territorial jurisdiction the seizure was made for an order of restoration under subsection (6).

Order of restoration

(6) Subject to subsections (8) and (9), where upon the hearing of an application made under subsection (5) the magistrate is satisfied

(a) that the applicant is entitled to possession of the narcotic or other thing seized, and

(b) that the thing so seized is not or will not be required as evidence in any proceedings in respect of an offence under this Act,

he shall order that the thing so seized be restored forthwith to the applicant, and where the magistrate is satisfied that the applicant is entitled to possession of the thing so seized but is not satisfied as to the matters mentioned in paragraph *(b)*, he shall order that the thing so seized be restored to the applicant

(c) upon the expiration of four months from the date of the seizure, if no proceedings in respect of an offence under this Act have been commenced before that time, or

(d) upon the final conclusion of any such proceedings, in any other case.

Where no application made

(7) Where no application has been made for the return of any narcotic or other thing seized under subsection (1) within two months from the date of such seizure, or an application therefor has been made but upon the hearing thereof no order of restoration is made, the thing so seized shall be delivered to the Minister who may make such disposition thereof as he thinks fit. 2

Forfeiture of narcotic upon conviction

(8) Where a person has been convicted of an offence under section 3, 4 or 5, any narcotic seized under subsection (1), by means of or in respect of which the offence was committed, any money so seized that was used for the purchase of that narcotic and any hypodermic needle, syringe, capping machine or other apparatus so seized that was used in any manner in connection with the offence is forfeited to Her Majesty and shall be disposed of as the Minister directs.

Forfeiture of conveyance upon application

(9) Where a person has been convicted of an offence under section 4 or 5, the court may, upon application by counsel for the Crown, order that any conveyance seized under subsection (1) that has been proved to have been used 2
in any manner in connection with the offence be forfeited, and upon such order being made the conveyance is forfeited to Her Majesty and, except as provided in section 11, shall upon the expiration of thirty days from the date of such forfeiture be disposed of as the Minister directs. 1968-69, c. 41, s. 14.

Application by person claiming interest

11. (1) Where any conveyance is forfeited to Her Majesty under subsection 10(9), any person (other than a person convicted of the offence that resulted in the forfeiture or a person in whose possession the conveyance was when seized) who claims an interest therein as owner, mortgagee, lienholder or holder of any like interest may, within thirty days after such forfeiture, apply by notice in writing to a judge for an order under subsection (4).

Date of hearing

(2) The judge to whom an application is made under subsection (1) shall fix a day not less than thirty days after the date of filing of the application for the hearing thereof.

Notice

(3) The applicant shall serve a notice of the application and of the hearing upon the Minister at least fifteen days before the day fixed for the hearing.

Order by judge

(4) Where, upon the hearing of an application, it is made to appear to the satisfaction of the judge,

(a) that the applicant is innocent of any complicity in the offence that resulted in the forfeiture and of any collusion in relation to that offence with the person who was convicted thereof, and

(b) that the applicant exercised all reasonable care in respect of the person permitted to obtain possession of the conveyance to satisfy himself that it was not likely to be used in connection with the commission of an unlawful act or, in the case of a mortgagee or lienholder, that he exercised such care with respect to the mortgagor or lien-giver,

the applicant is entitled to an order declaring that his interest is not affected by such forfeiture and declaring the nature and extent of his interest.

Appeal

(5) The applicant or the Minister may appeal to the court of appeal from an order made under subsection (4) and the appeal shall be asserted, heard and decided according to the ordinary procedure governing appeals to the court of appeal from orders or judgments of a judge.

Application to Minister

(6) The Minister shall, upon application made to him by any person who has obtained a final order under this section,

(a) direct that the conveyance to which the interest of the applicant relates be returned to the applicant; or

(b) direct that an amount equal to the value of the interest of the applicant, as declared in the order, be paid to him.

Definitions

(7) In this section

"court of appeal"

"court of appeal" means, in the province in which an order under this section is made, the court of appeal for that province as defined in the definition "court of appeal" in section 2 of the *Criminal Code;*

"judge"

"judge" means

(a) in the Province of Quebec, a judge of the Superior Court for the district in which the conveyance in respect of which an application for an order under this section is made, was seized,

(b) in the Provinces of Newfoundland and Prince Edward Island, a judge of the Supreme Court thereof,

(b.1) in the Provinces of New Brunswick, Alberta and Saskatchewan, a judge of the Court of Queen's Bench thereof,
1978-79, c. 11, s. 10, I. 20.

(c) in the Yukon and Northwest Territories, a judge of the Supreme Court thereof, and

(d) in any province not referred to in paragraphs *(a)* to *(c)*, a judge of the county or district court for the county or district in which any such conveyance was seized. 1972, c. 17, s. 2; 1974-75-76, c. 48, s. 25; 1978-79. c. 11, s. 10, I. 20.

General

Regulations 12. The Governor in Council may make regulations 28 Interp

(a) providing for the issue of licences

(i) for the importation, export, sale, manufacture, production or distribution of narcotics, and

(ii) for the cultivation of opium poppy or marihuana; 2

(b) prescribing the form, duration and terms and conditions of any licence described in paragraph *(a)* and the fees payable therefor, and providing for the cancellation and suspension of such licences;

(c) authorizing the sale or possession of or other dealing in narcotics and prescribing the circumstances and conditions under which and the persons by whom narcotics may be sold, had in possession or otherwise dealt in;

(d) requiring physicians, dentists, veterinarians, pharmacists and other persons who deal in narcotics as authorized by this Act or the regulations to keep records and make returns;

(e) authorizing the communication of any information obtained under this Act or the regulations to provincial professional licensing authorities;

(f) prescribing the punishment by a fine not exceeding five hundred dollars or imprisonment for a term not exceeding six months, or both, to be imposed upon summary conviction for breach of any regulation; and

(g) generally, for carrying out the purposes and provisions of this Act.

Designation of analyst 13. The Governor in Council may designate any person as an analyst for the purpose of this Act.

Amendment of schedule 14. The Governor in Council may, from time to time, amend the schedule by adding thereto or deleting therefrom any substance, the inclusion or exclusion of which, as the case may be, is deemed necessary by him in the public interest.

Interpretation Act

28. In every enactment

"Governor in Council", or "Governor General in Council" means the Governor General of Canada, or person administering the Government of Canada for the time being, acting by and with the advice of, or by and with the advice and consent of, or in conjunction with the Queen's Privy Council for Canada;

Criminal Code

2. In this Act

"court of appeal" means

(a) in the Province of Ontario, the Court of Appeal,

(b) in the Province of Quebec, the Court of Appeal,

(c) in the Province of Nova Scotia, the Appeal Division of the Supreme Court

(d) in the Province of New Brunswick, the Court of Appeal,

(e) in the Province of British Columbia, the Court of Appeal,

(f) in the Province of Prince Edward Island, the Supreme Court,

(g) in the Province of Manitoba, the Court of Appeal,

(h) in the Province of Saskatchewan, the Court of Appeal,

(i) in the Province of Alberta, the Court of Appeal,

(j) in the Province of Newfoundland, the Court of Appeal,

(k) in the Yukon Territory, the Court of Appeal, and

(l) in the Northwest Territories, the Court of Appeal;

SCHEDULE

1. Opium poppy *(Papaver somniferum)* its preparations, derivatives, alkaloids and salts, including:

   (1) Opium,
   (2) Codeine (Methylmorphine),
   (3) Morphine,
   (4) Thebaine,

   and their preparations, derivatives and salts, including:

   (5) Acetorphine,
   (6) Acetyldihydrocodeine,
   (7) Benzylmorphine,
   (8) Codoxime,
   (9) Desomorphine (dihydrodeoxymorphine),
   (10) Diacetylmorphine (heroin),
   (11) Dihydrocodeine,
   (12) Dihydromorphine,
   (13) Ethylmorphine,
   (14) Etorphine,
   (15) Hydrocodone (dihydrocodeinone),
   (16) Hydromorphone (dihydromorphinone),
   (17) Hydromorphinol (dihydro- 14-hydroxymorphine),
   (18) Methyldesorphine (Δ^6-deoxy-6-methylmorphine),
   (19) Methyldihydromorphine (dihydro-6-methylmorphine),
   (20) Metopon (dihydromethylmorphinone),
   (21) Morphine-N-oxide (morphine-N-oxide),
   (22) Myrophine (benzylmorphine myristate),
   (23) Nalorphine (N-allylnormorphine),
   (24) Nicocodine (6-nicotinylcodeine),
   (25) Nicomorphine (dinicotinylmorphine),
   (26) Norcodeine,
   (27) Normorphine,
   (28) Oxycodone (dihydrohydroxycodeinone),
   (29) Oxymorphone (dihydrohydroxymorphinone),
   (30) Pholcodine (β-4-morpholinoethylmorphine), and
   (31) Thebacon (acetyldihydrocodeinone),

   but not including:

   (32) Apomorphine,
   (33) Cyprenorphine,
   (33.1) Naloxone,
   (34) Narcotine,
   (35) Papaverine, and
   (36) Poppy seed.

2. Coca *(Erythroxylon)*, its preparations, derivatives, alkaloids and salts, including:

   (1) Coca leaves,
   (2) Cocaine, and
   (3) Ecgonine (3-hydroxy-2-tropane carboxylic acid).

3. *Cannabis sativa*, its preparations, derivatives and similar synthetic preparations, including:

    (1) Cannabis resin,
    (2) Cannabis (marihuana),
    (3) Cannabidiol,
    (4) Cannabinol (3-n-amyl-6,6,9-trimethyl-6-dibenzopyran-1-ol),
    (5) Pyrahexyl (3-n-hexyl-6,6,9-trimethyl-7,8,9,10-tetrahydro-6-dibenzopyran-1-ol), and
    (6) Tetrahydrocannabinol.

4. Phenylpiperidines, their preparations, intermediates, derivatives and salts, including:

    (1) Allylprodine (3-allyl-1-methyl-4-phenyl-4-piperidyl propionate),
    (2) Alphameprodine (α-3-ethyl-1-methyl-4-phenyl-4-piperidyl propionate),
    (3) Alphaprodine (α-1,3-dimethyl-4-phenyl-4-piperidyl propionate),
    (4) Anileridine (ethyl 1-[2-(p-aminophenyl) ethyl]-4-phenylpiperidine-4-carboxylate),
    (5) Betameprodine (β-3-ethyl-1-methyl-4-phenyl-4-piperidyl propionate),
    (6) Betaprodine (β-1,3-dimethyl-4-phenyl-4-piperidyl propionate),
    (7) Benzethidine (ethyl 1-(2-benzyloxyethyl)-4-phenylpiperidine-4-carboxylate),
    (8) Diphenoxylate (ethyl 1-(3-cyano-3,3-diphenylpropyl)-4-phenylpiperidine-4-carboxylate),
    (9) Etoxeridine (ethyl 1-[2-(2-hydroxyethoxy) ethyl]-4-phenylpiperidine-4-carboxylate),
    (10) Fentanyl (1-phenylethyl-4-(phenylproprionylamino)-piperidine),
    (11) Furethidine (ethyl 1-(2-tetrahydrofurfuryloxyethyl)-4-phenylpiperidine-4-carboxylate),
    (12) Hydroxypethidine (ethyl 4-(m-hydroxyphenyl)-1-methyl-4-phenylpiperidine-4-carboxylate),
    (13) Ketobemidone (1-[4-(m-hydroxyphenyl)-1-methyl-4-piperidyl]-1-propanone),
    (14) Methylphenylisonipecotonitrile (4-cyano-1-methyl-4-phenylpiperidine),
    (15) Morpheridine (ethyl 1-(2-morpholinoethyl)-4-phenylpiperidine-4-carboxylate),
    (16) Norpethidine (ethyl 4-phenylpiperidine-4-carboxylate),
    (17) Pethidine (ethyl 1-methyl-4-phenylpiperidine-4-carboxylate),
    (18) Phenoperidine (ethyl 1-(3-hydroxy-3-phenylpropyl)-4-phenylpiperidine-4-carboxylate),
    (19) Piminodine (ethyl 1-[3-phenylamino)propyl]-4-phenylpiperidine-4-carboxylate),
    (20) Properidine (isopropyl 1-methyl-4-phenylpiperidine-4-carboxylate), and
    (21) Trimeperidine (1,2-5-trimethyl-4-phenyl-4-piperidyl propionate),

    but not including:

    (22) Carbamethidine (ethyl 1-(2-carbamylethyl)-4-phenylpiperidine-4-carboxylate),
    (23) Oxpheneridine (ethyl 1-(2-hydroxy-2-phenylethyl)-4-phenylpiperidine-4-carboxylate).

5. Phenazepines, their preparations, derivatives and salts, including:

   (1) Proheptazine (hexahydro-1,3-dimethyl-4-phenyl-4-azepinyl propionate),

   but not including:

   (2) Ethoheptazine (ethyl hexahydro-1-methyl-4-phenylazepine-4-carboxylate),
   (3) Metethoheptazine (ethyl hexahydro-1,3-dimethyl-4-phenylazepine-4-carboxylate), and
   (4) Metheptazine (ethyl hexahydro-1,2-dimethyl-4-phenylazepine-4-carboxylate).

6. Amidones, their preparations, intermediates, derivatives and salts, including:

   (1) Dimethylaminodiphenylbutanonitrile (4-cyano-2-dimethylamino-4,4-diphenyl butane),
   (2) Dipipanone (4,4-diphenyl-6-piperidino-3-heptanone),
   (3) Isomethadone (6-dimethylamino-5-methyl-4,4-diphenyl-3-hexanone),
   (4) Methadone (6-dimethylamino-4,4-diphenyl-3-heptanone),
   (5) Normethadone (6-dimethylamino-4,4-diphenyl-3-hexanone), and
   (6) Phenadoxone (6-morpholino-4,4-diphenyl-3-heptanone).

7. Methadols, their preparations, derivatives and salts, including:

   (1) Acetylmethadol (6-dimethylamino-4,4-diphenyl-3-heptanyl acetate),
   (2) Alphacetylmethadol (α-6-dimethylamino-4,4-diphenyl-3-heptanyl acetate),
   (3) Alphamethadol (α-6-dimethylamino-4,4-diphenyl-3-heptanol),
   (4) Betacetylmethadol (β-6-dimethylamino-4,4-diphenyl-3-heptanyl acetate),
   (5) Betamethadol (β-6-dimethylamino-4,4-diphenyl-3-heptanol),
   (6) Dimepheptanol (6-dimethylamino-4,4-diphenyl-3-heptanol), and
   (7) Noracymethadol (α-6-methylamino-4,4-diphenyl-3-heptanyl acetate).

8. Phenalkoxams, their preparations, derivatives and salts, including:

   (1) Dimenoxadol (dimethylaminoethyl 1-ethoxy-1,1-diphenylacetate),
   (2) Dioxaphetylbutyrate (ethyl 2,2-diphenyl-4-morpholino butyrate),

   but not including

   (3) Propoxyphene (4-dimethylamino-3-methyl-1,2-diphenyl-2-butyl propionate).

9. Thiambutenes, their preparations, derivatives and salts, including:

   (1) Diethylthiambutene (N,N-diethyl-1-methyl-3,3-di-2-thienylallylamine),
   (2) Dimethylthiambutene (N,N,1-trimethyl-3,3-di-2-thienylallylamine), and
   (3) Ethylmethylthiambutene (N-ethyl,1-dimethyl-3,3-di-2-thienylallylamine).

10. Moramides, their preparations, intermediates, derivatives and salts, including:
    (1) Dextromoramide (*d*-1-(3-methyl-4-morpholino-2,2-diphenylbutyryl) pyrrolidine),
    (2) Diphenylmorpholinoisovaleric acid (2-methyl-3-morpholino-1,1-diphenylpropionic acid),
    (3) Levomoramide (*l*-1-(3-methyl-4-morpholino-2,2-diphenylbutyryl) pyrrolidine), and
    (4) Racemoramide (*d,l*-1-(3-methyl-4-morpholino-2,2-diphenylbutyryl) pyrrolidine).

11. Morphinans, their preparations, derivatives and salts, including:
    (1) Levomethorphan (*l*-1,2,3,9,10,10a-hexahydro-6-methoxy-11-methyl-4H-10,4a-iminoethanophenanthrene),
    (2) Levorphanol (*l*-1,2,3,9,10,10a-hexahydro-11-methyl-4H-10,4a-iminoethanophenanthren-6-ol),
    (3) Levophenacylmorphan (*l*-1,2,3,9,10,10a-hexahydro-11-phenacyl-4H-10,4a-iminoethanophenanthren-6-ol),
    (4) Norlevorphanol (*l*-1,2,3,9,10,10a-hexahydro-4H-10,4a-iminoethanophenanthren-6-ol),
    (5) Phenomorphan (*d,l*-1,2,3,9,10,10a-hexahydro-11-phenethyl-4H-10,4a-iminoethanophenanthren-6-ol),
    (6) Racemethorphan (*d,l*-1,2,3,9,10,10a-hexahydro-6-methoxy-11-methyl-4H-10,4a-iminoethanophenanthrene), and
    (7) Racemorphan (*d,l*-1,2,3,9,10,10a-hexahydro-11-methyl-4H-10,4a-iminoethanophenanthren-6-ol),

    but not including:

    (8) Dextromethorphan (*d*-1,2,3,9,10,10a-hexahydro-6-methoxy-11-methyl-4H-10,4a-iminoethanophenanthrene),
    (9) Dextrorphan (*d*,1,2,3,9,10,10a-hexahydro-11-methyl-4H-10,4a-iminoethanophenanthren-6-ol),
    (10) Levallorphan (*l*-11-allyl-1,2,3,9,10,10a-hexanhydro-4H-10,4a-iminoethanophenanthren-6-ol), and
    (11) Levargorphan (*l*-11-propargyl-1,2,3,9,10,10a-hexahydro-4H-10,4a-iminoethanophenanthren-6-ol),
    (12) Butorphanol and its salts.

12. Benzazocines, their preparations, derivatives and salts, including:;
    (1) Phenazocine (1,2,3,4,5,6-hexahydro-6,11-dimethyl-3-phenethyl-2,6-methano-3-benzazocin-8-ol), and;
    (2) Metazocine (1,2,3,4,5,6-hexahydro-3,6,11-trimethyl-2,6-methano-3-benzazocin-8-ol),

    but not including:

    (3) Pentazozine (1,2,3,4,5,6-hexahydro-6,11-dimethyl-3-(3-methyl-2-butenyl)-2,6-methano-3-benzazocin-8-ol), and
    (4) Cyclazocine (1,2,3,4,5,6-hexahydro-6,11-dimethyl-3-(cyclopropylmethyl)-2,6-methano-3-benzazocin-8-ol).

13. Ampromides, their preparations, derivatives and salts, including:
    (1) Diampromide (N-[2-(methylphenethylamino)-propyl]-propionanilide),
    (2) Phenampromide (N-[2-(1-methyl-2-piperidyl)-ethyl]-propionanilide),
    (3) Propiram (N-(1-methyl-2-piperidinoethyl)-N-2-pyridylpropionamide).

14. Benzimidazoles, their preparations, derivatives and salts, including:

    (1) Clonitazene (2-(p-chlorobenzyl)-1-diethylaminoethyl-5-nitrobenzimidazole),
    (2) Etonitazene (2-(p-ethoxybenzyl)-1-diethylaminoethyl-5-nitrobenzimidazole).

15. Phencyclidine, its salts and derivatives.

--NOTES—

WAR MEASURES ACT

CHAPTER W-2

An Act to confer certain powers upon the Governor in Council in the event of war, invasion, or insurrection

SHORT TITLE

Short title

1. This Act may be cited as the *War Measures Act.*

EVIDENCE OF WAR

Evidence of war, etc.

2. The issue of a proclamation by Her Majesty, or under the authority of the Governor in Council shall be conclusive evidence that war, invasion, or insurrection, real or apprehended, exists and has existed for any period of time therein stated, and of its continuance, until by the issue of a further proclamation it is declared that the war, invasion or insurrection no longer exists.

Interpretation Act

28. In every enactment

"Governor in Council" or "Governor General in Council" means the Governor General of Canada, or person administering the Government of Canada for the time being, acting by and with the advice of, or by and with the advice and consent of, or in conjunction with the Queen's Privy Council for Canada;

POWERS OF THE GOVERNOR IN COUNCIL

Special powers of Governor in Council

3. (1) The Governor in Council may do and authorize such acts and things, and make from time to time such orders and regulations, as he may by reason of the existence of real or apprehended war, invasion or insurrection deem necessary or advisable for the security, defence, peace, order and welfare of Canada; and for greater certainty, but not so as to restrict the generality of the foregoing terms, it is hereby declared that the powers of the Governor in Council extend to all matters coming within the classes of subjects hereinafter enumerated, namely,

(a) censorship and the control and suppression of publications, writings, maps, plans, photographs, communications and means of communication;

(b) arrest, detention, exclusion and deportation;

(c) control of the harbours, ports and territorial waters of Canada and the movements of vessels;

(d) transportation by land, air, or water and the control of the transport of persons and things;

(e) trading, exportation, importation, production and manufacture;

(f) appropriation, control, forfeiture and disposition of property and of the use thereof.

Force of law

(2) All orders and regulations made under this section have the force of law, and shall be enforced in such manner and by such courts, officers and authorities as the Governor in Council may prescribe, and may be varied, extended or revoked by any subsequent order or regulation; but if any order or regulation is varied, extended or revoked, neither the previous operation thereof nor anything duly done thereunder, is affected thereby, nor is any right, privilege, obligation or liability acquired, accrued, accruing or incurred thereunder affected by such variation, extension or revocation.

Imposing penalties

4. The Governor in Council may prescribe the penalties that may be imposed for violations of orders and regulations made under this Act, and may also prescribe whether such penalties shall be imposed upon summary conviction or upon indictment, but no such penalty shall exceed a fine of five thousand dollars or imprisonment for any term not exceeding five years, or both. 28 Interp

No release of arrested alien

5. No person who is held for deportation under this Act or under any regulation made thereunder, or is under arrest or detention as an alien enemy, or upon suspicion that he is an alien enemy, or to prevent his departure from Canada, shall be released upon bail or otherwise discharged or tried, without the consent of the Minister of Justice.

Coming into force by proclamation

6. (1) Sections 3, 4 and 5 come into force only upon the issue of a proclamation of the Governor in Council declaring that war, invasion or insurrection, real or apprehended, exists. 28 Interp

Proclamation to be submitted to Parliament

(2) A proclamation declaring that war, invasion or insurrection, real or apprehended, exists shall be laid before Parliament forthwith after its issue, or, if Parliament is then not sitting, within the first fifteen days next thereafter that Parliament is sitting. 25 Interp

Opportunity for debate

(3) Where a proclamation has been laid before Parliament pursuant to subsection (2), a notice of motion in either House signed by ten members thereof and made in accordance with the rules of that House within ten days of the day the proclamation was laid before Parliament, praying that the proclamation be revoked, shall be debated in that House at the first convenient opportunity within the four sitting days next after the day the motion in that House was made.

Revocation of proclamation by resolution

(4) If both Houses of Parliament resolve that the proclamation be revoked, it ceases to have effect, and sections 3, 4 and 5 cease to be in force until those sections are again brought into force by a further proclamation but without prejudice to the previous operation of those sections or anything duly done or suffered thereunder or any offence committed or any penalty or forfeiture or punishment incurred.

Canadian Bill of Rights

(5) Any act or thing done or authorized or any order or regulation made under the authority of this Act, shall be deemed not to be an abrogation, abridgement or infringement of any right or freedom recognized by the *Canadian Bill of Rights.*

Interpretation Act

25. (1) Where the time limited for the doing of a thing expires or falls upon a holiday, the thing may be done on the day next following that is not a holiday.

(3) Where there is a reference to a number of days, not expressed to be clear days, between two events, in calculating the number of days there shall be excluded the day on which the first event happens and there shall be included the day on which the second event happens.

28. In every enactment

"proclamation" means a proclamation under the Great Seal;

"Great Seal" means the Great Seal of Canada;

PROCEDURE

Fixing compensation

7. Whenever any property or the use thereof has been appropriated by Her Majesty under this Act, or any order in council, order or regulation made thereunder, and compensation is to be made therefor and has not been agreed upon, the claim shall be referred by the Minister of Justice to the Federal Court of Canada, or to a superior or county court of the province within which the claim arises, or to a judge of any such court. 28 Interp

Forfeitures

8. Any ship or vessel used or moved, or any goods, wares or merchandise dealt with, contrary to any order or regulation made under this Act, may be seized and detained and shall be liable to forfeiture, at the instance of the Minister of Justice, upon proceedings in the Federal Court of Canada or in any superior court.

Rules

9. Every court mentioned in sections 7 and 8 may make rules governing the procedure upon any reference made to, or proceedings taken before, such court or a judge thereof under those sections.

Interpretation Act

28. In every enactment

"county court" in its application to the Province of Ontario includes, and in its application to the Province of Newfoundland means, "district court";

"Federal Court" means the Federal Court of Canada;

"province" means a province of Canada, and includes the Yukon Territory and the Northwest Territories;

"superior court" means

(a) in the Province of Ontario, Nova Scotia, Prince Edward Island or Newfoundland, the Supreme Court of the Province,

(b) in the Province of Quebec, the Court of Appeal and the Superior Court in and for the Province,

(c) in the Province of British Columbia, the Court of Appeal and the Supreme Court of the Province,

(d) in the Province of Manitoba, Saskatchewan, Alberta or New Brunswick, the Court of Appeal for the Province and the Court of Queen's Bench for the Province,

(e) in the Yukon Territory or the Northwest Territories, the Supreme Court thereof,

and includes the Supreme Court of Canada and the Federal Court of Canada.

—NOTES—